ASSESSING TEACHERS FOR PROFESSIONAL CERTIFICATION: THE FIRST DECADE OF THE NATIONAL BOARD FOR PROFESSIONAL TEACHING STANDARDS

ADVANCES IN PROGRAM EVALUATION

Series Editors: Robert E. Stake and Saville Kushner

ADVANCES IN PROGRAM EVALUATION   VOLUME 11

ASSESSING TEACHERS FOR PROFESSIONAL CERTIFICATION: THE FIRST DECADE OF THE NATIONAL BOARD FOR PROFESSIONAL TEACHING STANDARDS

EDITED BY

LAWRENCE INGVARSON

Australian Council for Educational Research, Camberwell, Australia

JOHN HATTIE

Department of Teaching, Learning, and Development, Faculty of Education, The University of Auckland, Auckland, New Zealand

ELSEVIER
JAI

Amsterdam – Boston – Heidelberg – London – New York – Oxford
Paris – San Diego – San Francisco – Singapore – Sydney – Tokyo

JAI Press is an imprint of Elsevier

JAI Press is an imprint of Elsevier
Linacre House, Jordan Hill, Oxford OX2 8DP, UK
Radarweg 29, PO Box 211, 1000 AE Amsterdam, The Netherlands
525 B Street, Suite 1900, San Diego, CA 92101-4495, USA

First edition 2008

British Library Cataloguing in Publication Data
A catalogue record for this book is available from the British Library

ISBN: 978-0-7623-1055-5
ISSN: 1474-7863 (Series)

For information on all JAI Press publications
visit our website at books.elsevier.com

Printed and bound in the United Kingdom

08 09 10 11 12   10 9 8 7 6 5 4 3 2 1

Working together to grow
libraries in developing countries
www.elsevier.com | www.bookaid.org | www.sabre.org

ELSEVIER   BOOK AID
International   Sabre Foundation

CONTENTS

LIST OF APPENDIX

LIST OF CONTRIBUTORS

Wanda K. Baker	Arizona State University, Scottsdale, AZ, USA
Lloyd Bond	The Carnegie Foundation for the Advancement of Teaching, Stanford, CA, USA
Hilda Borko	School of Education, University of Colorado, Boulder, CO, USA
Janet Clinton	School of Population Health, Faculty of Medical and Health Sciences, The University of Auckland, Auckland, New Zealand
Kirsten R. Daehler	Science Cases for Teacher Learning Project, WestEd, Redwood City, CA, USA
Linda Darling-Hammond	School of Education, Stanford University, Stanford, CA, USA
Alan Davis	School of Education and Human Development, University of Colorado, Denver, CO, USA
Drew Gitomer	Educational Testing Service, Rosedale Road, Princeton, NJ, USA
John Hattie	Department of Teaching, Learning, and Development, Faculty of Education, The University of Auckland, Auckland, New Zealand
Kristin Hershbell	Office of Research, Planning, and Grants, City College of San Francisco, San Francisco, CA, USA

Lawrence Ingvarson	Australian Council for Educational Research, Camberwell, Australia
Richard M. Jaeger[†]	Formerly at the Center for Educational Research and Evaluation, University of North Carolina, Greensboro, USA
Susan Moore Johnson	Harvard Graduate School of Education, Cambridge, MA, USA
Jody McCarthy	Mathematics, Science, and Technology Program, San Francisco, CA, USA
Pamela A. Moss	School of Education, University of Michigan, Ann Arbor, Michigan, USA
Mari Pearlman	Higher Education Division, Educational Testing Service, Princeton, NJ, USA
Steven A. Schneider	Program Director Mathematics, Science, and Technology, WestEd, San Francisco, CA, USA
Jerome Shaw	Department of Education, University of California Santa Cruz, Santa Cruz, CA, USA
Tracy W. Smith	Department of Curriculum and Instruction, Appalachian State University, Boone, NC, USA
Guillermo Solano-Flores	School of Education, University of Colorado, Boulder, CO, USA
Gary Sykes	College of Education, Michigan State University, East Lansing, MI, USA
Grace Taylor	School of Education and Human Development, University of Colorado, Denver, School of Education, Denver, CO, USA
Sam Wineburg	School of Education, Stanford University, Stanford, CA, USA
Kenneth Wolf	School of Education and Human Development, University of Colorado, Denver, School of Education, Denver, CO, USA

FOREWORD

I am pleased to write the Foreword as a small contribution to the essays and commentaries collected in this book by Lawrence Ingvarson (Australia) and John Hattie (New Zealand), whose years of dedication and determination made the project possible and nurtured it to completion.

In the book, assessment experts review and comment on the performance assessments developed for National Board Certification (NBC), the national (but *not* Federal) program for advanced professional teacher certification in the United States. The NBC was developed and is operated by the National Board for Professional Teaching Standards (NBPTS), a national but non-governmental organization. I had the honor of being the first President and CEO of the NBPTS, a position I held from 1987 to 1999, during its first 12 years of existence.

Looking back on this experience, it was, frankly, an amazing process, one really without precedent in education in the United States. Today, reading these expert commentaries on the assessments and how they were developed, I am reminded of how challenging the task proved to be, and how hundreds and thousands of teachers and other experts became involved in developing NBC. Every aspect of the system had to be invented "from scratch", as we say in the US, as we moved step-by-step through the many phases of developing NBC.

In this Foreword, I do not critique the essays and commentaries in the book; I leave that for the readers of the book. Instead, as the NBPTS' first president, I will offer my perspective on the professional and political contexts for its development in the US, on the process of attracting and coordinating teams of the nation's best assessment experts and psychometricians, on the politics and policies used to anchor NBC solidly as a permanent feature in the American educational system, and on the challenges still faced by the NBPTS as, in 2007, it celebrates the 20th anniversary of its founding.

THE CONTEXT IN WHICH NBPTS WAS FOUNDED

In 1987, when the NBPTS was established and began its work, there were no advanced teaching standards or performance assessments for teachers and teaching in the US, or, to the best of our knowledge at the time, in any other nation. Schools were being subjected to widespread criticism for allegedly poor academic performance, summarized famously in a government report, "A Nation at Risk", that was released by the US President Ronald Reagan with great media fanfare in 1985. State governors, CEOs of large corporations, and leaders of teacher unions led in organizing a response, focusing on new standards for what students should learn in school, and placing pressure on schools to produce better student achievement. In the decade that followed, standards for what students should be expected to learn were developed for all subject fields and grade levels. Typically, the standards in the subject-matter fields were developed in almost complete isolation from each other, and much of the work was done within individual states, so a nationally coherent system did not emerge.

Looking back at this process, the standards movement attracted enormous attention, but there was inadequate communication and coordination among groups and states. As standards were written, states began contracting with assessment organizations to develop new student tests. The lack of coordination was further evident as these tests were developed, frequently not addressing desired standards for what students should learn, and, still further, without concomitant programs of curriculum and professional development to align the schools and the capacities of teachers to the new standards. Finally, looking back on this process, government leaders and education reformers placed all their bets on attempted reforms *within* classrooms. Student testing became the principal strategy to leverage improved achievement, without reforming the traditional bureaucratic structure of schools, the curriculum, teacher education, and professional development, or, perhaps most significantly, the social and economic circumstances of families that clearly shape much of the observed variations in what children achieve in schools.

In fact, the traditional bureaucratic structure of schools in the US, operating with state and local systems, reflects little faith in the wisdom of teachers. Status and rewards accrue to those furthest, and sometimes farthest, from the classroom. The best paid do not teach; they are typically former teachers who are "promoted" and paid more money *not* to teach. Little distinction is made between the first-year and the 15th-year teacher. Typically, policy assumes that teachers need to be told what to do and how to do it, not asked to use professional judgment and expertise.

Against this backdrop, the National Board was established as a national, non-governmental organization in 1987 with a three-part mission:

1. to establish high and rigorous standards for what accomplished teachers should know and be able to do;
2. to Board-certify teachers who meet the standards; and
3. to advance related educational policies and reforms.

The composition of the NBPTS board of directors was unprecedented. The board was composed of some 63 members (restructured in 2006 to 27 members). More than half were classroom teachers in K-12 schools. Additional members included presidents of the nation's two large teacher unions, heads of teaching disciplinary and specialty organizations, academics, university presidents, state governors, corporate CEOs, and prominent citizens. Its chair was former North Carolina Governor James B. Hunt, Jr., whose dedication and leadership were vital to building the NBPTS. The vice-chair was an experienced teacher.

DEVELOPING THE STANDARDS AND ASSESSMENTS

It was decided from the beginning that the priority in developing NBC was "to do it as fast as we could do it but only as fast as we could do it right". I am proud to say that within the board and its expanding circle of friends, this became known as "Kelly's Law".

There were essentially five major parts of the development process: preparing an over-arching substantive vision of accomplished teaching, encompassing all subject fields and grade levels; designing a framework for certificate fields within which NBC would be offered; establishing policies (e.g., prerequisites for candidacy) under which NBC would be offered; developing standards for each certificate field; and last but definitely not least, developing assessments based on the standards for each certificate field.

In its first year, the NBPTS board of directors focused on one thing – preparing a substantive statement of *What Teachers Should Know and Be Able to Do*. Dozens of organizations and experts and hundreds of educators were consulted in the process of finalizing this statement. The board achieved unanimous support for this statement and it was published in 1989. It would be fair to say that few expected the Board to survive, let alone succeed, and virtually no one anticipated a board unanimous in its support for the content and even the wording of the statement. In this statement, the NBPTS posited its now famous five "propositions" describing what accomplished teachers should know and be able to do.

1. Teachers are committed to students and their learning.
2. Teachers know the subjects they teach and how to teach those subjects to students.
3. Teachers are responsible for managing and monitoring student learning.
4. Teachers think systematically about their practice and learn from experience.
5. Teachers are members of learning communities.[1]

The second step, closely following the first, was to design the Framework of Certificates. The resulting Framework emphasized knowledge at four age groupings of children and how they grow and develop, and knowledge of subject-matter content and how to teach it to all children. The Framework thus yielded some 24 fields in which NBC would be offered; an example of a field is *Early Adolescence/English Language Arts*.[2]

The NBPTS then moved to establish the initial policies under which NBC would be offered. It was decided that all persons with college degrees and three years of teaching experience would be eligible to become candidates provided that a fee sufficient to cover the costs of administering the assessments was paid by, or for, the candidate. Candidates were not required to have teacher education degrees. Every state required teacher education for a person to obtain a license to teach in public schools, but about half the states did not require a license for persons teaching in non-government or private, schools, which in the US enroll about 15% of all students. Note that the prerequisite policy was designed to permit school administrators and teacher educators who had three years of teaching experience to become candidates for NBC.

Standards were developed for each certificate field. For each field, the NBPTS appointed a committee of about 15 teachers and academic experts and assigned them the task of developing standards consistent with and based on the five propositions in *What Teachers Should Know and Be Able to Do*. This was begun with two committees, whose work constituted the first or pilot projects, and gradually expanded into other fields. The work of each committee took about a year and a half to complete.

As standards were being developed, a separate process was designed and implemented to develop assessments. For this effort, the NBPTS issued RFPs and conducted merit reviews of proposals from aspiring contractors, universities, and testing companies. The NBPTS set broad parameters within which contractors were to develop assessments; two that were historically noteworthy were that the assessments must authentically examine actual teaching performance and were not to include any multiple choice questions.[3]

Assessment development products in the first fields selected for development received intense scrutiny from NBPTS consultants and from the board itself. Lengthy board meetings were utilized to assure that teachers and others on the board were intimately familiar with assessment designs, rationales for particular designs, and strengths and weaknesses of proposed assessment items. When problems were found, the process was stopped and the problems fixed. In one case, this delayed by an entire year the scoring of the performances of the first cadre of some 200 candidates.

Soon, NBPTS created and funded an entire team of the nation's finest assessment experts and psychometricians. This collaborative group, totally independent of assessment development contractors, was known as the Technical Advisory Group or the TAG; its co-directors were Lloyd Bond and Dick Jaeger (now deceased). It included Bob Lynn, Lorrie Shepard, Dick Haertel, and several other highly regarded experts. Lee Shulman was retained separately as an independent advisor.

Through these mechanisms, the NBPTS obtained invaluable advice that was extraordinarily useful. While initial assessments were being offered to candidates seeking NBC, the assessments were modified and improved on almost an annual basis, as ongoing research by TAG and others revealed ways to make the assessments more rigorous psychometrically, more efficient and effective for candidates, and more cost-realistic for NBPTS. Indeed, the NBPTS continues to this day to offer improvements and enhanced candidate flexibility in its assessments.

THE POLITICS OF ESTABLISHING AND FUNDING NBC

The composition of the NBPTS board of directors directly suggests the unprecedented coalition assembled to develop this organization and its program. There had never been a board like this created in the United States education enterprise. Key education and teaching groups had never – never – come together to talk about what constituted accomplished teaching. Achieving consensus in such a broadly based group of leaders was achieved only through extraordinary, almost constant consultation, with dozens of constituency organizations. These consultations continued for over a decade. Virtually every NBPTS policy, and every step of the development of NBC, was vetted through collaborating organizations. Every education organization was involved. No one was excluded.

This breadth of collaboration created understanding and acceptance of the lengthy development process and why it was needed in order to "do it right". It also established a political coalition that was very useful in obtaining funding. As developmental work extended over many years, and costs mounted, funders were assured by the strength of the working coalition that the result would be a sustainable and important new feature in American education.

Initial financial support came from private foundations, notably the Carnegie Corporation of New York, and leading US corporations. Later, substantial Federal financial support was provided, through leadership from President Bill Clinton and bi-partisan leaders of the Congress. Over the first 15 years of the NBPTS, its development programs required about $100 million of Federal money and over $80 million of grants from foundations and corporations. These sums, while perhaps seeming large to educators, should be seen in the context of a public school system that during those years was spending about $400 billion *per year*. Neither the Federal government nor private funders had any control, or influence, over the content of the standards, assessments, and related policies of the NBPTS. And, at no time did NBPTS borrow money, or mortgage its future; all developmental costs were covered by grants and contributions.

All the product development work on the "supply" side would not on its own yield a politically sustainable program of NBC. Attention was also essential on the "demand" side. A major effort was undertaken in the 1990s to obtain new state-funded incentives for teachers to become candidates for NBC, and state-funded salary increases for teachers who became National Board Certified Teachers (NBCTs). By the end of that decade, more than 40 states had adopted policies to support candidates, and provided direct state-paid salary increases. In several large states and cities, the added salary payments amounted to 10%, 12%, or even 20% increases per year for NBCTs who continued to teach in the classroom. These payments were designed to be sustained during the 10-year life of a teacher's certification, after which they would have to have their certification renewed by NBPTS. The support of a large number of the nation's governors from both political parties was key to achieving these state policies.

Additional impact relevant to professional sustainability is clear from extensive adoption of NBPTS substantive principles within teacher education programs. The nation's principal agency that accredits programs of teacher education in the US, the National Council for Accreditation of Teacher Education (NCATE), adopted a critically important and, in the long run, very influential policy that accredited programs had to have standards for what their graduates should know and be able to do, a method for assessing whether graduates met those standards, and assurance that their standards and assessments were "aligned" with those of the NBPTS. Thus, the architecture of an aligned profession became possible, and is, in fact, happening.

Another policy of NBPTS that was of paramount importance in persuading teachers to "trust" the NBC process was the decision that all assessors who were judging candidate performances and other submissions within the assessment had to be current practicing classroom teachers within the certificate field of the candidates whose performances were being assessed. Thus, teachers examined the work of other teachers. Cynics predicted favoritism and lax observance of standards. Exactly the opposite occurred. Teachers who were trained and accepted as assessors demon- strated a high fidelity to the integrity of the assessment and scoring standards, and, as an added bonus, found that the process of scoring performances led to major improvements in their own teaching.

Another critically important element of the NPBTS strategy on the "demand" side of the work was to secure the support of the two major teacher unions, the National Education Association and the American Federation of Teachers. While their presidents and other officials were members of the Board, and constant effort was made to keep their governing bodies fully briefed on all developments and issues, it was teacher union members themselves – teachers – who stood up in union forums and testified that NBC was good for teachers, helped them become better teachers, and should be supported by the unions. This professional and substantive understanding was the basis for the unions to accept differential salaries for teachers who became NBCTs, the first time in US history that teacher unions accepted a measure of teaching quality as the basis for salary increases.

The result of all this collaborative work is a system that has survived for its first 20 years and is still getting stronger. There are now some 55,000 NBCTs in the US. Tens of thousands of other teachers have taken the assessments and are not yet certified. Hundreds of thousands of others use the content of NBPTS' five propositions, its standards, and its assessment methodologies, during teacher education and professional development programs. Portfolios of evidence of teaching performance and student learning are now routinely experienced in teacher education and professional development arenas. Teachers observing each others performances occur on a widespread basis now. Almost none of these activities occurred before NBC was launched.

Finally, teachers know that teachers did it – they controlled the board of directors, they wrote the standards and approved every assessment, and they score the performances of every candidate.

CHALLENGES FOR TODAY AND TOMORROW

Despite these historic innovations, the NBPTS faces challenges. One is constantly to upgrade and improve the assessments, while maintaining high fidelity to the standards and professional credibility of the assessments. Progress is being made on these agendas. Inside the NBC process, candidates now can take one or two parts of the assessment (rather than all at once) and "bank" the scores. Most administrative aspects of candidacy are now done online. NBCTs now help prospective candidates prepare for candidacy, and candidates are encouraged to consult one another as they work through the portfolio process.

A second challenge is to nurture and maintain support from teacher unions and other organizations of educators. In the past five years, union leadership energies have moved from professional quality concerns to Federal policy, as the controversial No Child Left Behind program has come to dominate Federal policymaking. Union support for NBC and NBPTS is highly desirable but perhaps not as essential as it was in the early years. Still, political support from unions and other teacher organizations is vital at state and local levels, as funding for NBCT salary increases comes up for annual review and appropriation.

A third challenge is to attract larger numbers of candidates so that the population of NBCTs grows to a more influential scale within schools and states. The NBPTS needs stronger marketing and recruiting strategies and is taking steps to establish both; both are needed.

A fourth challenge is to explain, and explain again, the substantive vision of NBC to policymakers as well as to educators. These explanations must start with the conceptions of teaching and learning embedded in the student learning sections of the assessments. Insist that critics have read the standards and are engaged substantively. Demonstrate how "working the NBC program" is a catalyst for powerful professional growth. Become a major policy voice in public dialogue and think about the goals of education reform and how accomplished teachers contribute to those goals.

Finally, leaders of NBPTS must collaborate with tens of thousands of NBCTs and other friends to think and act more imaginatively about education reforms and how teaching and learning should be central to them. The 100-year-old bureaucratic structure of schools as top-down and command-and-control organizations must be challenged, and refreshed with modern knowledge about how healthy, learning organizations of professionals can function effectively with decentralized authority and trust in the professionals deliver the main service of the organization. Teachers need to be taught how to be leaders in creating new schools, perhaps charter schools, or founding "firms" of professionals offering instructional and professional services.

In short, the professional vision of accomplished teaching is only half the agenda. It was appropriate during the NBPTS' first 20 years to focus intently on building the system of NBC. Now, NBPTS must increasingly become more directly and powerfully engaged in reforms of schooling itself, so that accomplished teaching can be found in ever-larger numbers of classrooms, and the impact of accomplished teaching felt more fully and equitably in the lives of students.

James A. Kelly

NOTES

1. An elaborated version of the NBPTS propositions can be found on its website: http://www.nbpts.org/the_standards

2. A full list of certificate fields can be found in the Introductory chapter, or on the NBPTS website http://www.nbpts.org/for_candidates/certificate_areas1

3. Chapter 6 provides a case study from Steven Schneider and colleagues at one of the first "Assessment Development Laboratories".

CHAPTER 1

INTRODUCTION

Lawrence Ingvarson and John Hattie

The National Board for Professional Teaching Standards (NBPTS) is the most ambitious attempt by any country to establish a certification system for teachers who reach high professional standards. Since it was established in 1987, international interest in the National Board has grown steadily. No other country, however, has made a similar investment in establishing a professional body with the capacity to provide a rigorous certification system that is valued by all stakeholders. As other countries place increasing importance on policies designed to attract, develop and retain effective teachers (Organization for Economic Cooperation and Development (OECD), 2005), there is growing interest in the extensive research that has underpinned the Board's certification system and guided its implementation.

The Board's mission has been driven by a simple principle: to place more value on teaching, we must learn how to evaluate teacher performance in ways that are valid, reliable and fair (NBPTS, 1989). The task to achieve this principle remains a challenge, as poorly conceived performance pay schemes and teacher incentive programs continue to be promoted in many countries (Ingvarson, Kleinhenz, & Wilkinson, 2007). It is rare to find supporting research for these schemes or validation of their procedures.

In his foreword to this volume, Jim Kelly describes the background to the Board and gives a sense of how exciting the early years were as the Board went about fulfilling its unique mission (see also Buday & Kelly, 1996). Both the editors of this volume came in contact with the NBPTS in the early days of its existence and became convinced of its relevance to their own

Assessing Teachers for Professional Certification:
The First Decade of the National Board for Professional Teaching Standards
Advances in Program Evaluation, Volume 11, 1–21
Copyright © 2008 by Elsevier Ltd.
All rights of reproduction in any form reserved
ISSN: 1474-7863/doi:10.1016/S1474-7863(07)11001-2

countries: Lawrence Ingvarson, from Australia, when he was on a sabbatical at Stanford University in 1989. There he met Lee Shulman and his team of researchers working on the Teacher Assessment Project, which provided some of the important foundations for the National Board's certification system (e.g., Bird, 1990; Collins, 1991; Shulman, 1987; Shulman & Sykes, 1986; Wilson & Wineburg, 1991; Shulman, 1991); and John Hattie, from New Zealand, who took up an appointment at the University of North Carolina at Greensboro and became part of the Technical Analysis Group (TAG), which was led by Richard Jaeger and Lloyd Bond.

Since the work of the NBPTS has become known, several other countries have been exploring the idea of national professional bodies with similar functions to those of the NBPTS (Ingvarson & Kleinhenz, 2006a, 2006b). There is growing recognition that the quality of teaching and educational reform is dependent on new career structures for teachers, *as teachers*. However, any serious move in this direction will depend on the kind of work on teaching standards and performance assessment reported in this volume that has been undertaken by the NBPTS. The National Board aimed to build a profession-wide system that would provide incentives for all teachers to attain high standards of teaching – one that would be recognized by local education authorities, for career advancement, and by state governments and licensing authorities, for license renewal and portability purposes (NBPTS, 1989).

The development of these standards, assessments, and now a growing number of National Board-Certified teachers (NBCTs) did not happen overnight – there was a long and exciting learning curve, and this book charts many of the debates, resolutions, and questions during the first 10 years of the Board's development. The main purpose of this book is to bring together some of the Board's extensive research for international as well as non-specialist audiences. One of the many reasons why the Board's work is noteworthy is the quality of research and evaluation it has put into all stages of its work. Another is the extent to which it has subjected its standards and certification process at every stage of development to critique by leading figures in educational measurement, as many chapters in this volume illustrate. As a result, the NBPTS has made a major contribution to international understanding about how to develop valid standards and reliable methods for assessing and esteeming teacher performance.

This book also aims to provide some of the many lessons the Board has learned about how to make a professional certification system for teachers manageable and affordable, which is perhaps an even greater challenge. These lessons are worth learning because, as the Board's Founding

President Jim Kelly points out in the Foreword, the Board was able, somehow, to convince funding agencies in the early years, including Federal Governments (from both sides of the political divide) to be patient – that the job was only worth doing if it was to be done well. The Board argued that it would take 20 years to fully establish a national certification scheme. It could never be established within the three-to-four-year timeline that many politicians face. As well as raising the many issues of such standard-based assessment of accomplished professionals, this book can help those who may be considering certification schemes in their own country to understand why a long-term perspective is necessary.

PROFESSIONAL CERTIFICATION

"Certification", in the context of this book, is an endorsement by a professional body that a member of that profession has attained a specified set of advanced performance standards. Application for NBPTS advanced certification is usually voluntary and available to all members of the profession (who have had to have at least three years experience in the profession). It is based on assessment of performance; it is not an academic qualification, or a record of professional development courses attended. It is portable – it belongs to the person (it is not a job or position or classification specific to a school or employer). A professional certification system is not in itself a performance pay scheme, but it does aim to provide a service to the profession, to the public and to employing authorities seeking a credible basis on which to provide incentives for professional development and recognition to teachers who reach high standards. Most important, it acknowledges that the individual who gains this certification is demonstrably teaching at the highest levels in our profession.

As an advanced certification system, the NBPTS aims to complement, not replace, the statutory responsibility of states to set entry standards and license new teachers. States retain the constitutional responsibility for entry standards and licensing teachers. As David Mandel, the first NBPTS vice-president responsible for standards development put it:

> We make a distinction. It's the employers' responsibility to set licensing (registration) standards; and it's the profession's job to set standards for advanced certification. And both parties should have a voice in the way the other carries out its responsibility.

The NBPTS has worked hard to ensure that teachers who gain Board certification also gain local support and recognition from education authorities (Barringer & Taras, 1998). As Jim Kelly points out in his Foreword, the Board recognized early that it was vital to promote the development of a market for the teachers it certified. The first NBCTs were granted certification in 1994. Since then, more than 120,000 teachers have applied and nearly 55,000 have become "National Board-Certified Teachers". Today, virtually every state in the USA, and more than 25 percent of all school districts, offer financial rewards or incentives for teachers seeking National Board Certification. There is still a long way to go in a nation of over two-and-half million teachers, but the NBPTS has already lasted much longer than most merit pay schemes with similar aims, but very different methods of assessing teacher performance.

THE ARCHITECTURE OF THE NBPTS CERTIFICATE FIELDS

The Directors of the National Board (during the first 10 years two-thirds majority were practicing teachers) decided early on that the Board's standards and certificates needed to reflect that there were many distinct fields of expertise in teaching. Primary and early childhood school teachers were just as much specialists in their field as secondary science or English teachers were in theirs. They believed one set of generic standards could not capture the specific knowledge, skills and attitudes that support accomplished practice in fields as diverse as early childhood education and high school science teaching.

Consequently, the Board developed standards and certification in 24 specialist fields (NBPTS, 2005). The fields are defined by subject areas to be taught (e.g., science, English, mathematics), and by developmental levels of students (early childhood, middle childhood, early adolescence, adolescence and young adulthood). The architecture of these certificate fields was governed by the Board's following policy position:

- There is a core of professional knowledge that all NBCTs should command.
- There are knowledge, skills and methods particular to different stages of student development that NBCTs working with such students should command.
- There are subject- and discipline-specific knowledge, skills and methods that NBCTs should command. This includes a core of subject- and discipline-specific knowledge that all NBCTs in each subject area should command.

• Each certificate will be designed to require a demonstration of depth as well as breadth of knowledge.

As a result of this policy, teachers can now apply for NBPTS certification in one or more of the following 24 certificate areas, which cover 15 subject areas and are classified into 7 student age categories:

Art
　　Early and Middle Childhood
　　Early Adolescence through Young Adulthood
Career and Technical Education
　　Early Adolescence through Young Adulthood
English as a New Language
　　Early and Middle Childhood
　　Early Adolescence through Young Adulthood
English Language Arts
　　Early Adolescence
　　Adolescence and Young Adulthood
Exceptional-Needs Specialist
　　Early Childhood through Young Adulthood
Generalist
　　Early Childhood
　　Middle Childhood
Library Media
　　Early Childhood through Young Adulthood
Literacy: Reading – Language Arts
　　Early and Middle Childhood
Mathematics
　　Early Adolescence
　　Adolescence and Young Adulthood
Music
　　Early and Middle Childhood
　　Early Adolescence through Young Adulthood
Physical Education
　　Early and Middle Childhood
　　Early Adolescence through Young Adulthood
School Counseling
　　Early Childhood through Young Adulthood
Science
　　Early Adolescence
　　Adolescence and Young Adulthood

Social Studies – History
  Early Adolescence
  Adolescence and Young Adulthood
World Languages Other than English
  Early Adolescence through Young Adulthood

WHY IS PROFESSIONAL CERTIFICATION IMPORTANT?

As the OECD (2005) report *Teachers Matter* points out, there is widespread concern across OECD countries about the attractiveness of teaching as a career. Better pay and career prospects attract better quality graduates, and poor salary ranks high among the reasons good teachers leave the profession (Chevalier, Dolton, & McIntosh, 2007). Most countries do not have effective schemes to recognize and reward quality teaching, and policy makers who want to place greater value on good teaching are seeking schemes for evaluating teaching that are valid, reliable and fair.

The 2006 edition of the OECD's report, *Education at a Glance* (OECD, 2006), indicates that the average salary at the top of the incremental scale is only 1.70 times the starting salary. (It is nearly three in Korea and Japan.) In other words, the typical salary scale for teachers does not place high value on evidence of *teacher quality* or professional development. Thus, the current salary structure may be a weak instrument for rewarding quality teaching. It does not provide incentives for professional development leading to accomplished teaching nor reward evidence of attaining high standards of performance. The NBPTS model has been driven, in part, by a desire to create a defensible (from both a measurement and a professional acceptance point of view) system to identify and esteem accomplished teaching – and thus can serve as one goal for teachers as they work through their current promotion systems. One of its major features is that it does not replace current systems, but can sit alongside them.

The NBPTS provides an example of a well-researched certification scheme for measuring teacher quality that can provide a service to governments and employers seeking a reliable indicator of teacher quality. A recent survey of public opinion about *teacher quality* in the USA found that all groups recognized the importance of *teacher quality* and strongly supported reforms that would lead to significant increases in teacher salaries, provided there were better guarantees that these increases rewarded evidence of professional development and quality teaching (Hart & Teeter, 2002).

Perhaps the most important reason for establishing a professional certification system lies, however, in its potential for strengthening teaching as a profession, as the chapters by Linda Darling-Hammond and Gary Sykes in this volume illustrate. Standards are the gateway to greater professional self-direction. A certification system is a means by which the teaching profession can build its own infrastructure for defining high-quality teaching standards, promoting development toward those standards and providing recognition to those who meet them.

One of the main reasons for establishing a certification system is to increase the effectiveness of professional development for teachers. It is primarily by engaging more teachers in more effective modes of professional learning that such a system can make a major contribution to improving student learning. Professional standards linked to advanced certification place individuals in a more active and responsible role with respect to their professional learning. Valid standards clarify what teachers should get better at over the long term if they are to play a significant part in improving their schools and the 'quality' of learning.

The NBPTS demonstrates that the teaching profession has the capacity to build a standards-guided professional learning system that will strengthen the quality of teaching and learning in schools. Responsibility for the development and application of professional standards builds commitment to those standards, whereas imposition of standards leads to mere compliance. An initiative such as the NBPTS is very much in the interest of governments and other employing authorities and therefore to be encouraged through remuneration and career paths that better reflect what a highly accomplished teacher is worth, not only to their school, but to our society and our economy.

Responsibility for the development and application of professional standards enables the profession to play a stronger role in relating research to practice. Developers of standards such as those of the NBPTS must synthesize the implications of research on effective teaching practices. Responsibility for the development and application of professional standards enables the profession to exercise more control over its professional learning. The capacity to develop advanced certification standards gives the profession the ability to play a stronger role in defining the long-term goals of their own professional learning. Responsibility for the development and application of professional standards enables the profession to play a more significant role in providing recognition to members who meet its standards and a service to employing authorities that want to encourage effective professional learning and reward evidence of its attainment.

OVERVIEW OF THE NATIONAL BOARD CERTIFICATION SYSTEM

The scale of work involved in developing a national certification system for accomplished teachers is extensive. The main components in the National Board's certification system are listed below with reference to relevant chapters in this volume, where these components are elaborated upon. These chapters convey some of the work and the people involved, however, it was impossible to do justice here to all the teachers and researchers who have made significant contributions to the development of the Board's certification system.

Standards Development is conducted in large measure by standards committees of 12–15 teachers and other educators appointed by the NBPTS. Their role is to advise its Board of Directors on the criteria for accomplished practice that should be established in each certification field. Teacher associations play a significant role here. John Hattie in Chapter 4 reviews how the Board took care to ensure the validity and legal defensibility of the procedures used to develop the standards. In Chapter 5, Sam Wineburg presents an argument accepted by the Board's Directors for embedding teaching standards in the content that students are expected to learn.

Assessment Development in the early years was conducted by testing organizations, research institutes, colleges, universities and regional laboratories working independently and in consortia that were selected through a competitive merit review process to serve as assessment development laboratories (ADLs). Their task was to design and test assessment packages for the initial certification fields. Teacher associations also worked with these organizations on policy advisory groups and steering committees. Chapter 6 by Steven Schneider and colleagues provide a case study of the work of one of the early ADLs. Mari Pearlman reviews the evolution of the NBPTS' approach to standards-based assessment of teacher knowledge and performance in Chapter 3.

Assessment Operations were conducted by The Psychological Corporation (TPC) in the initial field test of the first two certification fields during the 1993–1994 school year. TPC served as the intake point for candidate applications; managed the logistics of assessment materials production and distribution and site selection and operations; and oversaw the recruitment, selection, training, screening and functioning of assessors. It became clear that the greatest costs in a certification system were those associated with assessing candidate performances.

Since that time, the Educational Testing Service (ETS) has played a major role in developing the system for conducting the assessments of applications and this early work is comprehensively described by Mari Pearlman in Chapter 7. For Board Directors, it was important that the process of preparing evidence of their practice for certification was, in itself, a source of professional learning for applicants. Kenneth Wolf and Grace Taylor in Chapter 13 describe one of the first of many studies in this area. The NBPTS placed major importance on ensuring that teachers who were not successful in their first attempt at certification received sensitive and useful feedback. The Board commissioned research by Kenneth Wolf, Alan Davis and Hilda Borko into the feasibility of different forms of feedback, which is reported in Chapter 14.

Technical Analysis of the Board's developing assessment system was conducted by a team of experts in education measurement – the Technical Analysis Group (TAG). Their key role was to assure the professional credibility and legal defensibility of the NBPTS system. Their task was to provide independent advice to NBPTS on the nature and quality of the assessment packages through the conduct of studies of validity, reliability, bias and adverse impact reviewed by Pamela Moss in Chapter 10. They have also overseen the development and implementation of the procedures NBPTS uses to set performance standards in each field as described by Dick Jaeger in Chapter 8. The Board has continued to subject its assessment system to rigorous review, documented in annual *Technical Analysis Reports* from the ETS. Drew Gitomer describes the procedures initially used to assess the reliability of the Board's scoring system in Chapter 9 and John Hattie and Janet Clinton describe one of the first of many studies that aim to test the validity of the Board's certification system in Chapter 11. Tracy Smith, Wanda Baker, John Hattie and Lloyd Bond undertook the follow up validity study, and their findings are provided in Chapter 12.

WHAT MAKES THE NBPTS UNIQUE?

Ingvarson and Kleinhenz (2006a) recently reviewed international reforms in relation to systems designed to give recognition to teachers who reached advanced standards. These reforms usually included the creation of new career pathways to give higher status to good teaching and keep good teachers in positions where they can share their expertise and lead other teachers. The review included, for example, the "Threshold" reforms from England, the "Chartered Teacher" concept in Scotland and the "Level 3

Classroom Teacher" in Western Australia, as well as others. The NBPTS certification system stood out clearly in this review as different from other schemes for recognizing and rewarding good teaching in several significant respects.

The Extent and Rigor of Underpinning Research

As mentioned earlier, one of the unique features of the National Board was the extent to which it subjected its standards and certification process at every stage of development to scrutiny by the most respected experts in educational measurement.[1] In the early years this was the responsibility of the TAG, led by Richard Jaeger (Bond, Smith, Baker, & Hattie, 2000; Crocker, 1997; Jaeger, 1998; Lloyd, Engelhard, & Crocker, 1995; Smith et al., Chapter 12, this volume). This book documents the research conducted by the Board to ensure that the foundations for its certification system were sound. As Jim Kelly pointed out, in the early days NBPTS directors understood that the Board would live or die according to the rigor of its certification and the respect it gained.

It is notable that teacher respect for certification also depended on rigor. While Ingvarson and Kleinhenz found that the NBPTS system for identifying accomplished teachers was the most rigorous, it was also the system that had gained the most respect. Contrary to some expectations, evidence indicated it also had the strongest effect on teachers' professional learning as a consequence of its rigor as a summative assessment.

The National Board continues to encourage rigorous evaluations of every aspect of its certification system. Its openness to critique distinguishes it from many schemes with similar purposes (Ingvarson, 2002; Ingvarson et al., 2007). It uses its own funds to invite leading researchers to design and conduct studies to evaluate the validity of its certification system.

There is now a large body of research on the National Board's standards and methods for assessing performance. Several independent research studies have shown on balance that teachers who gain National Board Certification have better student outcomes than those who do not (Cavalluzo, 2004; Goldhaber & Anthony, 2004; Harris & Sass, 2007; Vandevoort, Amrein-Beardsley, & Berliner, 2004; Wilson, Darling-Hammond, & Berry, 2000). In a major study using longitudinal data covering all the North Carolina students in grades 3, 4 and 5 for the years 1995–2004, Clotfelter, Ladd and Vigdor (2007) found that licensing (registration), experience as a teacher and National Board Certification each had significant effects on mathematics achievement. However, further qualifications such as Masters Degrees obtained after five years of teaching were associated with negative effects on student achievement. This research, among other validity studies, indicates that National Board Certification would be a more direct way of rewarding performance than typical pay schedules in the USA (Odden & Wallace, 2006).

The Independence of the NBPTS

The NBPTS was the only example we could find in the teaching profession, internationally, of an independent professional body that awarded professional certification. Schemes with similar purposes in England, Scotland and Australia, for example, were each initiated by, and responsible to, government, or government agencies. In contrast, the NBPTS provides profession-wide standards and a portable professional certification. It aims to provide a service that is credible and useful to all education authorities, employers and the public, as well as the profession.

The Level of Professional Involvement and Ownership

As the chapters in this volume by Schneider and colleagues, Pearlman and Moss indicate, teachers have played, and continue to play, a decisive role in every component of the Board's certification system; including the development of standards and assessment methods, the setting of standards, the training of assessors and the operation of the scoring system. We could not find another certification system that placed as much trust in the capacity and willingness of teachers to develop and operate a certification system.

Members of other professions are often surprised by the limited extent to which governments and employing authorities entrust the teaching profession to develop its own systems for quality control and professional certification. Most merit pay schemes in the past and most current performance pay schemes are developed by governments or employing authorities, not professional bodies. The English Threshold standards, for example, were developed by a private consulting firm, not the national professional associations of teachers (Ingvarson, 2002). Consequently, such reforms gain little support from teachers and teacher organizations (Wragg, Haynes, Wragg, & Chamberlin, 2004).

The Separation Between Certification and Recognition

The NBPTS provides certification, but it relies on governments and employing authorities to provide recognition of its certification. It does not tell employing authorities how its certification should be used, however it works hard to convince them to build a market for National Board certified teachers (Barringer & Taras, 1998). It separates the system for assessing performance and certification from industrial arrangements about salaries and career structures between employers and teacher organizations within particular jurisdictions where the micro politics of school life come into play. Merit pay schemes have often foundered on the rocks of accusations of bias and cronyism and negative effects on relationships between teachers. A standards-based assessment system such as the NBPTS model minimizes these effects by separating the system of certification from the mechanisms at the local level for recognizing and rewarding accomplished teachers.

Effects on Professional Learning

There is a considerable body of research indicating that the process of preparing for NBPTS certification necessarily engages teachers in professional learning practices likely to improve their teaching. From the early days of the NBPTS, the process of assessment and certification was conceived as a powerful vehicle for engaging teachers in effective modes of professional learning (Darling-Hammond, 1992; Robinson, 1998; Snowden, 1993). A study commissioned by the Board (NBPTS, 2001) sampled the views of 10,000 NBCTs. This study found that teachers believed the certification process had:

- made them better teachers (92%),
- was an effective professional development experience (96%),
- enabled them to create better curricula (89%),
- improved their ability to evaluate student learning (89%) and
- enhanced their interaction with students (82%), parents (82%) and colleagues (80%).

Similar surveys of teachers in England showed the opposite. Few teachers believed the process of applying for the threshold had any beneficial effects on professional development and most said it had lowered teacher morale (Wragg et al., 2004).

One of the central reasons for establishing a certification system is to engage all teachers in effective modes of professional learning. Professional development programs in most school systems fall far short of this. A certification system has the capacity to create a standards-based professional learning system (Elmore, 1996; Ingvarson, 1998; Ingvarson & Kleinhenz, 2006b; Snowden, 1993). Its standards give teachers a clear idea of what their profession expects should improve with experience. And, if the certification leads to substantial forms of recognition, it provides incentives for all to reach high standards.

Teachers who have been through the process of assembling evidence about their teaching and applying for Board certification routinely rate the process as the most beneficial form of professional development they have ever had (Tracz et al., 1995). Perhaps most important, the research suggests that standards-based schemes for assessing teacher performance and providing certification that leads to increased pay do not have the negative and divisive effects that so many earlier performance pay schemes had on staff relationships (Anagnostopoulos & Sykes, 2006).

Board-certified teachers are in high demand and are often mentors and leaders in their schools. This is largely because members of the education and wider communities are confident that the Board's stringent efforts to ensure the rigor, fairness, validity and reliability of its assessments can be depended upon to provide credible guarantees of teacher quality. Board-certified teachers are thus rewarded in terms of enhanced status and expanded employment opportunities as well as financial remuneration. Many districts now integrate Board certification into collective bargaining and their salary frameworks (Odden & Wallace, 2006).

A Sound Foundation for Reforming Teacher Pay Systems

There is increasing evidence that the NBPTS certification system can provide a sounder foundation for recognizing and rewarding good teaching than most merit pay schemes (Ingvarson & Kleinhenz, 2006a, 2006b). Odden and Kelley (2002) reviewed the history of merit pay schemes. One of the main reasons why many schemes failed was the absence of research and evaluation of the kind reported in this volume. The most critical component of any performance pay scheme is the system for assessing teachers' knowledge and skill. That system must be sound in terms of educational measurement. It must be based on multiple sources of evidence that cover the full scope of what teachers are expected to know and be able to do, as defined in the standards. Performance pay schemes based only on, for example, value-added measures of student achievement, cannot provide a valid and legally defensible basis for making decisions about individual teachers. The NBPTS Board focused its standards and assessment methods directly on the quality of what students were doing, learning and experiencing as a result of the conditions for learning established by the teacher.

Value-Added Methods for Assessing Teacher Performance

Some argue that, in contrast to NBPTS certification, more economical and valid assessment of teacher performance can be obtained through value-added measures of student achievement. Millman (1997) reviewed four of these schemes in the USA, each using different kinds of student assessment. Two of them used "value-added" models for isolating and estimating school and teacher effects; the Tennessee Value-Added Assessment System (TVAAS) and the Dallas Value-Added Accountability System. Proponents of these schemes claim that they are able to separate the effects of teachers and schools from the effects of factors such as family background and class cohort characteristics.

The consensus among many who have closely examined these schemes is that they do not provide, and are unlikely to provide, a valid basis for decisions about the quality of individual teachers, such as those involved in performance-related pay schemes (Braun, 2005; Gordon, Kane, & Staiger, 2006; Kupermintz, 2002; McCaffrey, Lockwood, Koretz, & Hamilton, 2003; Raudenbush, 2004). Some regard schemes such as the TVAAS as flawed because they use national norm-referenced tests that are usually insensitive to the effects of teachers "instructional efforts" (Popham, 1997). A danger with such schemes is that they may use student assessment data for a purpose that was not initially intended. That is, they may use students' scores on a nationally standardized test to assess the performance of a teacher when the test scores have not been validated for the latter purpose. Such tests are usually designed to discriminate between students, not teachers. In a recent review of the literature on the use of value-added modeling (VAM) in estimating teacher effects, McCaffrey et al. (2003) concluded that:

> ... VAM-based rankings of teachers are highly unstable, and that only large differences in estimated impact are likely to be detectable given the effects of sampling error and other sources of uncertainty. Interpretations of differences among teachers based on VAM estimates should be made with extreme caution. (p. 113)

The reliability of value-added estimates depends on the quality of the student achievement measures that underpin them, and the margins of error in most existing measures need to be understood. While there have been significant advances in our ability to measure educational growth, we are a long way from measures with anything like the reliability of, say, measures of growth in children's weight or height. In addition, measures available so far are limited mainly to reading and numeracy in the primary years. For most subjects in the primary curriculum, and for most teachers of the secondary curriculum, there are no measures to which value-added modeling could be applied. This means that measures of student-achievement growth should only be used in conjunction with several other independent sources of evidence (and, of course, where there is a high level of confidence in their reliability).

Standards-Based Approaches to Assessing Teacher Performance

The NBPTS, in contrast, illustrates a standards-based approach to evaluating teacher performance. A major trend in reforming teacher pay systems is to define performance in terms of what teachers know and can do – the quality of the conditions they provide for learning – and evidence about what their students are doing as a direct result of their teaching, including what they are learning over time. These schemes are often referred to as knowledge- and skills-based pay systems (Odden & Kelley, 2002). Professional "standards" provide the vehicle for defining what teachers should know and be able to do in these schemes. Knowledge- and skills-based pay systems aim to provide stronger links between pay increases and evidence of capacity to meet standards of teaching. Progress in this area has been greatly facilitated by more sophisticated methods of standards-based assessment of teaching performance, such as those developed by the NBPTS.

There is general agreement among experts in teacher evaluation that a valid and reliable scheme for assessing teacher performance for high-stakes decisions must draw on several types of evidence. Such schemes need to encompass the full scope of what a teacher is expected to know and be able to do, not only to ensure their professional credibility, but increasingly, their legal defensibility.

Teaching standards are increasingly used to describe the full scope of what teachers are expected to know and be able to do. A set of standards typically includes a wide range of elements such as "creating productive learning environment", "knowledge of content", "promoting student learning" and "contribution to school and professional community", among others. Assessment of a teacher's performance against each of these standards for high-stakes decisions calls for very different types, as well as multiple forms, of evidence, such as those used by the NBPTS.

A valid and reliable scheme for assessing individual teacher performance for high-stakes decisions therefore requires multiple, independent sources of evidence and multiple, independent trained assessors of that evidence. This means that any single measure, such as measures of student achievement on standardized achievement tests cannot alone provide a reliable basis for making performance-related pay decisions about the efforts of individual teachers.

SYNOPSIS

Section 1 of this volume focuses on the key task of developing standards and assessments. *Linda Darling-Hammond* looks at the influence of professional standards and certification on teacher education and professional development. *Mari Pearlman*, as the Director of the ETS work as the General Contractor for the NBPTS, has been deeply involved in the design and architecture of NBPTS assessments and overseeing the operation and future development of new certificate fields. This chapter outlines the history of the earliest years until there was a major rethinking of the assessment models in the late 1990s. Pearlman led the team that reconsidered this new model and many major issues about assessment of complex tasks in a valid and authentic manner are raised in this reconsideration. *John Hattie* was a member of the TAG commissioned by the NBPTS to provide research and advice on the psychometric quality of the Board's work. He has done valuable work in developing and applying procedures for validating professional standards. *Sam Wineburg* has a 10-year perspective on the Board's work from the time he worked with Shulman's Teacher Assessment Project (TAP) to this paper, a version of which he first completed for the TAG. He takes up the key issue of subject-matter knowledge in standards and assessments. The early work of the ADLs, commissioned by the NBPTS, will be of interest to international readers, especially. *Steven Schneider* directed one of the Board's early ADLs and with colleagues, documents their experiences in working for the NBPTS.

Section 2 brings together papers about the conduct of performance assessments. *Mari Pearlman's* chapter describes the approaches that ETS has developed for analyzing and scoring performance assessments. *Richard Jaeger*, who directed the TAG, describes the valuable work he conducted on setting standards. *Drew Gitomer* reports on the standard procedures used to gather information about the reliability of NBPTS assessments.

Section 3 brings together three papers examining validity in relation to the NBPTS certification process. *Pamela Moss* examines validity issues in relation to analyzing and interpreting evidence from complex performance assessments. *John Hattie* and *Janet Clinton* report an independent validity study comparing the performance of teachers who had gained certification with those who had not. *Tracy Smith* and her co-authors carried out a validity study of the certification and outline their findings.

The fourth section includes two chapters examining the effects of National Board certification. *Kenneth Wolf* and *Grace Taylor* provide a report based on interviews with National Board candidates about the effects of the process on their professional development. *Kenneth Wolf, Alan Davis* and *Hilda Borko* report on their investigation of the effectiveness of various forms of feedback that candidates may receive after taking NBPTS assessments – a critical issue.

The final section widens the focus and looks at the NBPTS in the context of educational reform and as a national system for evaluating teachers. *Gary Sykes* examines the NBPTS as a strategy for educational reform in relation to other strategies, such as choice and systemic reform. *Susan Moore Johnson* brings experience with the teacher unions to examine the potential of the NBPTS to reform pay systems and career structures for teachers.

There have been several books on teacher evaluation in the last 20 years (e.g., Millman, 1997; Millman & Darling-Hammond, 1990; Stronge, 2002) but none that has concentrated on issues related to building a system of teacher evaluation for professional recognition and advanced certification for career advancement. No one yet has brought together a coherent set of research papers on the work of a national professional body attempting to establish a system of teacher evaluation for career development: for example, the process of developing teaching standards; the development of methods for gathering valid evidence for assessing performance on the standards; the setting of performance standards; and the selection and training of teachers to provide reliable assessments of the evidence that candidates submit.

This book brings together a set of research-based papers that represent the progress that was made by the NBPTS during its first decade, as well as highlighting some of the tasks that remained at the end of the first decade, in developing a standards-driven teacher-evaluation system for professional recognition and, hopefully, career advancement. The emphasis is on the first decade of development, and as Pearlman's chapter indicates, the NBPTS is now moving in different directions, although still building on the research and development outlined in this book. The book follows a simple structure, beginning with the contextualization of the establishment of the NBPTS, and then several chapters about the development of the Board's assessment system. The next three sections examine its implementation, its validity, and its effects on professional development. The final section looks backwards over the Board's achievements, and forward to the place of the Board in future educational reform.

The Board's work adds new professional dimensions to teacher evaluation. Its work on standards and assessments is likely to lead to new approaches to, and conceptions of, teacher accountability to professional standards. Standards enable the profession to define stable, long-term goals for what teachers are expected to get better at. Standards provide the necessary reference points for the work of professional learning communities. The Board's work therefore has the potential to reform the professional development system for teachers radically and shift its control into the hands of the profession.

NOTE

1. Members of the TAG included, at various stages, David Berliner, Lloyd Bond, Linda Crocker, Alan Davis, George Engelhard, Ed Haertel, Ron Hambleton, John Hattie, James Impara, Bob Linn, Brenda Lloyd, Barbara Plake, Richard Shavelson, Marnie Thompson, Ross Traub, Sam Wineburg and Ken Wolf.

REFERENCES

Anagnostopoulos, D., & Sykes, G. (2006). What difference does difference make? The meanings of Board Certification and sentiments of teaching. Paper presented at the Annual meeting of the American Educational Research Association, San Francisco, CA.

Barringer, M. D., & Taras, M. R. (1998). *Harnessing support for National Board Certification: Building alliances among employers, policy-makers and the NBPTS* (Internal discussion document). Arlington, VA: National Board for Professional Teaching Standards.

Bird, T. (1990). The school teacher's portfolio: An essay on possibilities. In: J. Millman & L. Darling-Hammond (Eds), *The new handbook of teacher evaluation: Assessing elementary and secondary school teachers* (pp. 241–256). Newbury Park, CA: Sage.

Bond, L., Smith, T., Baker, W., & Hattie, J. A. (2000). *The certification system of the National Board for Professional Teaching Standards: A construct and consequential validity study.* Greensboro, NC: Center for Educational Research and Evaluation.

Braun, H. I. (2005). *Using student progress to evaluate teachers: A primer on value-added models.* Princeton, NJ: Policy Information Centre, Educational Testing Service, Educational Testing Service.

Buday, M. C., & Kelly, J. (1996). National Board Certification and the teaching profession's commitment to quality assurance. *Phi Delta Kappan, 78,* 215–219.

Cavalluzo, L. (2004). *Is National Board certification and effective signal of teacher quality?* Washington, DC: The CNA Corporation.

Chevalier, A., Dolton, P., & McIntosh, S. (2007). Recruiting and retaining teachers in the UK: An analysis of graduate occupation choice from the 1960s to the 1990s. *Economica, 74*(293), 69–96.

Clotfelter, C. T., Ladd, H. F., & Vigdor, J. L. (2007). *How and why do teacher credentials matter for student achievement?* National Bureau of Economic Research, Working Paper No. 2828. Cambridge, MA: National Bureau of Economic Research.

Collins, A. (1991). Portfolios for biology teacher assessment. *Journal of Personnel Evaluation in Education, 5,* 147–167.

Crocker, L. (1997). Assessing the content representativeness of performance assessment exercises. *Applied Measurement in Education, 10,* 83–95.

Darling-Hammond, L. (1992). Creating standards of practice and delivery for learner-centered schools. *Stanford Law and Policy Review, 4,* 37–52.

Elmore, R. (1996). Getting to scale with successful educational practices. In: S. H. Furhman & J. O'Day (Eds), *Rewards and reform: Creating educational incentives that work* (pp. 294–329). San Francisco: Jossey-Bass.

Goldhaber, D., & Anthony, E. (2004). *Can teacher quality be effectively assessed?* Unpublished manuscript. Seattle, WA: Centre on Reinventing Public Education, University of Washington.

Gordon, R., Kane, T. J., & Staiger, D. O. (2006). *Identifying effective teachers using performance on the job* (White Paper 2006-01). Washington, DC: Brookings Institute, The Hamilton Project.

Harris, D. N., & Sass, T. R. (2007). *The effects of NBPTS-certified teachers on student achievement.* Working Paper no. 4. Washington, DC: Urban Institute and the National Centre for Analysis of Longitudinal Data in Education Research. Available online from http://www.caldercenter.org/PDF/1001060_NBPTS_Certified.pdf

Hart, P. D., & Teeter, M. (2002). *A national priority: Americans speak on teacher quality.* Princeton, NJ: Educational Testing Service.

Ingvarson, L. C. (1998). Professional development as the pursuit of professional standards: The standards-based professional development system. *Teaching and Teacher Education, 14*(1), 127–140.

Ingvarson, L.C. (2002). *Strengthening the profession: A comparison of recent reforms in the USA and the UK* (ACER Policy Briefs No. 2). Camberwell, Victoria, Australia: ACER. Available from http://www.acer.edu.au/publications/policybriefs.html

Ingvarson, L. C., & Kleinhenz, E. (2006a). *Standards for advanced teaching: A review of national and international developments.* Canberra: Teaching Australia. Retrieved on 30 May 2007 from http://www.teachingaustralia.edu.au/ta/go/home/projects/standards/pid/480

Ingvarson, L. C., & Kleinhenz, E. (2006b). *A standards-guided professional learning system*. Melbourne, VIC: Centre for Strategic Education. Available online from www.cse.edu.au

Ingvarson, L. C., Kleinhenz, E., & Wilkinson, J. (2007). Research on performance pay for teachers. Canberra: Department of Education, Science and Training. Available online from http://www.dest.gov.au/NR/rdonlyres/D477C6A5-C8EF-4074-8619-FF43059445F8/16287/ACERPerformancePaypaperMar07.pdf

Jaeger, R. M. (1998). Evaluating the psychometric qualities of the National Board of Professional Teaching Standards' assessments: A methodological accounting. *Journal of Personnel Evaluation in Education, 12*(2), 189–210.

Kupermintz, H. (2002). *Teacher effects as a measure of teacher effectiveness: Construct validity considerations in TVAAS (Tennessee Value-Added Assessment System)* CSE Technical Report #563. Los Angels, CA: National Centre for Research on Evaluation, University of California.

Lloyd, B., Engelhard, G., & Crocker, L. (1995). Achieving form to form comparability: Fundamental issues and proposed strategies for equating performance assessments of teachers. *Educational Assessment, 3*(1), 99–110.

McCaffrey, D., Lockwood, J. R., Koretz, D. M., & Hamilton, L. S. (2003). *Evaluating value-added models for teacher accountability*. Santa Monica, CA: Rand Corporation.

Millman, J. (Ed.) (1997). *Grading teachers, grading schools: Is student achievement a valid evaluation measure?* . Thousand Oaks, CA: Corwin Press.

Millman, J., & Darling-Hammond, L. (1990). *The new handbook of research on teacher evaluation*. Newbury Park, CA: Sage.

National Board for Professional Teaching Standards. (1989). *Toward high and rigorous standards for the teaching profession*. Detroit, MI: Author.

National Board for Professional Teaching Standards. (2001). *National Board Certification Candidate Survey*. Arlington, VA: Author.

National Board for Professional Teaching Standards. (2005). *Framework of National Board Standards and Certificates*. Retrieved on 23 May 2007 from www.nbpts.org/standards/stds

Odden, A., & Kelley, C. (2002). *Paying teachers for what they know and do: New and smarter compensation strategies to improve schools* (2nd ed.). Thousand Oaks, CA: Corwin Press.

Odden, A., & Wallace, M. (2006). *New directions in teacher pay*. Consortium for Policy Research in Education, University of Wisconsin-Madison, USA.

Organization for Economic Cooperation and Development. (2005). *Teachers matter: Attracting, developing and retaining effective teachers*. Paris, France: OECD.

Organization for Economic Cooperation and Development. (2006). *Education at a glance*. Paris, France: OECD.

Popham, W. J. (1997). Consequential validity: Right concern-wrong concept. *Educational Measurement: Issues and Practice, 16*, 9–13.

Raudenbush, S. W. (2004). What are value-added models estimating and what does this imply for statistical practice? *Journal of Educational and Behavioral Statistics, 29*(1), 121–129.

Robinson, S. (1998, April). Performance-based assessments and licensing: The link between standards and assessments. Paper presented at the Annual meeting of the American Educational Research Association, San Diego, CA.

Shulman, L. S. (1987). Assessment for teaching: An initiative for the profession. *Phi Delta Kappan, 69*(1), 38–44.

Shulman, L. S. (1991). *Final report of the teacher assessment project*. Palo Alto, CA: Stanford University.

Shulman, L. S., & Sykes, G. (1986). A national board for teachers? In search of a bold standard. Paper prepared for the Task force on teaching as a profession, Carnegie forum on education and the economy. New York: Carnegie Corporation.

Snowden, C. D. (1993). Preparing teachers for the demands of the 21st Century: Professional development and the NBPTS vision. Paper prepared for the National Board for Professional Teaching Standards, Oct.

Stronge, J. H. (2002). *Qualities of effective teachers*. Alexandria, VI: Association for Supervision and Curriculum Development.

Tracz, S. M., Sienty, S., Todorov, K., Snyder, J., Takashima, B., Pensabene, R., Olsen, B., Pauls, L., & Sork, J. (1995, April). Improvement in teaching skills: Perspectives from National Board for Professional Teaching Standards field test network candidates. Paper presented at the Annual meeting of the American Educational Research Association, San Francisco, CA.

Vandevoort, L. G., Amrein-Beardsley, A., & Berliner, D. (2004). National Board certified teachers and their students' achievement. *Educational Policy Analysis Archives, 12*(26). Retrieved on 23 May 2007 from http://epaa.asu.edu/epaa/v12n46/

Wilson, S. M., Darling-Hammond, L., & Berry, B. (2000). *A case of successful teaching policy: Connecticut's long-term efforts to improve teaching and learning*. Research Report No. R-01-2. Seattle, WA: Centre for the Study of Teaching and Policy, University of Washington, Seattle. Retrieved on 23 May 2007 from http://depts.washington.edu/ctpmail/Reports.html

Wilson, S., & Wineburg, S. (1991). Subject matter knowledge in the teaching of history. In: J. E. Brophy (Ed.), *Advances in research on teaching* (pp. 303–345). Greenwich, CT: JAI Press.

Wragg, E. C., Haynes, G. S., Wragg, C. M., & Chamberlin, R. P. (2004). *Performance pay for teachers: The experiences of heads and teachers*. London: Routledge.

SECTION 1:
DEVELOPING STANDARDS AND PERFORMANCE ASSESSMENTS FOR PROFESSIONAL CERTIFICATION

CHAPTER 2

RESHAPING TEACHING POLICY, PREPARATION, AND PRACTICE: INFLUENCES OF THE NATIONAL BOARD FOR PROFESSIONAL TEACHING STANDARDS

Linda Darling-Hammond

ABSTRACT

By 2006, the National Board for Professional Teaching Standards had offered advanced certification to 50,000 accomplished teachers using performance-based assessments of their teaching knowledge and practice (about 2% of the US teaching force). However, the Board has had much greater impact than the initial numbers of certified teachers suggested. As the first professional effort to define accomplished teaching, it has also had an enormous influence on standard-setting for beginning teacher licensing, teacher education programs, teacher assessment, on-the-job evaluation, and professional development for teachers throughout the United States. This chapter describes some of the results of the Board's work, evaluates its impact, and discusses issues that it raises for the future of teaching and the nature of the teaching career.

Assessing Teachers for Professional Certification:
The First Decade of the National Board for Professional Teaching Standards
Advances in Program Evaluation, Volume 11, 25–53
Copyright © 2008 by Elsevier Ltd.
ISSN: 1474-7863/doi:10.1016/S1474-7863(07)11002-4

As we have entered the 21st century, it is increasingly clear that the capacities teachers needed in order to succeed at teaching much more challenging content to a much more diverse group of learners can only be widely acquired throughout the teaching force by greater investments in teacher preparation and development. Such reforms will require comprehensive restructuring of the systems by which states and school districts license, hire, induct, support, and provide for the continual learning of teachers (Carnegie Forum on Education and the Economy (CFEE), 1986; Holmes Group, 1986, 1996; National Commission on Teaching and America's Future (NCTAF), 1996).

In the United States, new standards for teacher education accreditation and for teacher licensing, certification, and ongoing evaluation have become a prominent lever for promoting system-wide change in teaching (Darling-Hammond, Wise, & Klein, 1995). The NCTAF (NCTAF, 1996) argued that:

> Standards for teaching are the linchpin for transforming current systems of preparation, licensing, certification, and ongoing development so that they better support student learning. (Such standards) can bring clarity and focus to a set of activities that are currently poorly connected and often badly organized ... . Clearly, if students are to achieve high standards, we can expect no less from their teachers and from other educators. Of greatest priority is reaching agreement on what teachers should know and be able to do to teach to high standards. (p. 67)

The effort to define what successful teachers should know and be able to do – and the use of assessments of such knowledge and skills to make decisions about entry and continuation in teaching – gained steam with the advent of new standards for student learning promulgated by both national associations and state governments (Darling-Hammond, 1997; O'Day & Smith, 1993). These standards posited a more active, integrated, and intellectually challenging curriculum for all students, not just the most academically able. Thus, they also anticipated more diagnostic teaching providing multiple pathways to learning so that a wider range of students were enabled to succeed.

The education reforms of the 1990s also created a broader range of roles for teachers in developing curriculum and assessments of student performance; coaching and mentoring other teachers; and working more closely with families and community agencies. Finally, school-based management and shared decision-making initiatives relied for their success on the capacity of education practitioners to make knowledgeable judgments about teaching, program design, and school organization. Recognizing that teachers needed to have access to much greater knowledge in order to meet these demands, policymakers began to link efforts to raise standards for students to initiatives that would also raise standards for teachers. This spurred substantial changes in teacher preparation programs across the United States (e.g., Darling-Hammond, 2006). Approaches to initial licensing, induction, and ongoing professional development were being reconsidered, and a new National Board for Professional Teaching Standards (NBPTS or the National Board) began to offer advanced certification for highly accomplished teachers.

An analogue to the bodies that offer board certification in medicine, architecture, and accounting, the mission of the National Board is to "establish high and rigorous standards for what accomplished teachers should know and be able to do, and to develop and operate a national, voluntary system to assess and certify teachers who meet these standards" (NBPTS, 1989, p. 1). The 63-member Board, established in 1987 with a majority of practicing classroom teachers, organized its standards development around five major propositions, which were more fully elaborated in the standards for each of 30 areas defined by subject matter discipline and developmental level. These propositions address teachers' knowledge about and commitment to student learning; understanding of subject matter and of how to teach it well; ability to manage and monitor the learning process; capacity to reflect on and learn from their teaching; and willingness to participate in a professional learning community, contributing to the profession as a whole.

By 2006, the Board had certified about 50,000 teachers using performance-based assessments of their teaching knowledge and practice (about 2% of the US teaching force). However, the Board has had much greater impact than the initial numbers of certified teachers suggested. As the first professional effort to define accomplished teaching, it has also had an enormous influence on standard-setting for beginning teacher licensing, and it has begun to shape the nature of many teacher education programs. Furthermore, the work of the Board has affected teacher assessment, on-the-job evaluation, and professional development for teachers throughout the United States. In this chapter, I describe some of the results of the first decade of the Board's work, evaluate its impact, and discuss issues that its efforts raise for the future of teaching and the nature of the teaching career.

STANDARD SETTING IN TEACHING

In order to appreciate the spillover effects of the National Board's work, it is important to understand where it fits into the organization and governance of the teaching profession in the United States. At least in the U.S., professions generally set and enforce standards in three ways: (1) through professional accreditation of preparation programs; (2) through state licensing, which grants permission to practice; and (3) through certification, which is a professional recognition of high levels of competence (Darling-Hammond et al., 1995).[1] The accreditation process is meant to ensure that all preparation programs provide a reasonably common body of knowledge and structured training experiences that are comprehensive and up-to-date. Licensing examinations are meant to ensure that candidates have acquired the knowledge they need to practice responsibly. The tests generally include both surveys of specialized information and performance components that examine aspects of applied practice: Lawyers must analyze cases and, in some states, develop briefs or memoranda of law to address specific issues; doctors must diagnose patients via case histories and describe the treatments they would prescribe; engineers must demonstrate that they can apply certain principles to particular design situations. These examinations are developed by members of the profession through state Professional Standards Boards.

In addition, many professions offer additional examinations that provide national recognition for advanced levels of skill, such as certification for public accountants, board certification for doctors, and registration for architects. This recognition generally takes extra years of study and practice, often in a supervised internship and/or residency, and is based on performance tests that measure greater levels of specialized knowledge and ability. Those who have met these standards are then allowed to do certain kinds of work that other practitioners cannot. The certification standards inform the other sets of standards governing accreditation, licensing, and relicensing: They are used to ensure that professional schools incorporate new knowledge into their courses and to guide professional development and evaluation throughout the career. Thus, these advanced standards may be viewed as an engine that pulls along the knowledge base of the profession. Together, standards for accreditation, licensing, and certification comprise a "three-legged stool" (NCTAF, 1996) that supports quality assurance in the mature professions.

This stool has been quite wobbly in the quasi-profession of teaching, which has not required accreditation for schools of education and, for many years, did not have professionally developed standards or valid assessments for licensing or advanced certification. Whereas professions typically assume responsibility for defining, transmitting, and enforcing standards of practice, teachers, at least in the United States, have historically had little or no control over most of the mechanisms that determine professional standards. In professions like medicine, nursing, architecture, accounting, and law, professional standards boards composed of expert members of the profession establish standards for education and entry. Until the 1990s such boards were absent in teaching. Instead, in most states, authority for determining the nature of teacher preparation, the types and content of tests used for licensure, and the regulations that governed practice resided in governmental bodies (legislatures and school boards) and in administrative agencies (state departments of education and central offices). These authority relations tended to produce bureaucratic rather than professional controls over teaching – that is, controls aimed at standardizing procedures rather than at building knowledge that could be applied differentially depending on the demands of a particular subject, the social context in a specific community, or the needs of a given child.

There have been at least two problems with the development of a common knowledge base for teaching. First, the development of useful and usable knowledge about teaching has been a long, slow process of assembling and connecting insights across many fields, including human development and learning, motivation and behavior of individuals and groups, the nature of intelligence and performance, and the effects of curricular approaches and teaching strategies. Much has been learned in all of these areas over the last 30 or 40 years through both the experimental pursuit of theoretical knowledge and the codification of the "wisdom of practice" (Shulman, 1986), that is, the understanding of teaching developed by expert practitioners. Another problem, however, is that of knowledge diffusion. While researchers at the end of the 1990s had a greater understanding of teaching and learning than they once did (e.g., Bransford, Brown, & Cocking, 1999), there were few reliable vehicles for transmitting this knowledge to the field. In the United States, education knowledge has been disseminated largely through research journals and monographs read by other researchers, rather than clinical journals widely read by practitioners. Although there are areas of consensus among "experts" in the field who read the same journals and attend the same conferences, these are not widely shared among practitioners or policymakers.

Because education has not had common standards or well-developed, universal vehicles for accrediting professional education programs and licensing candidates, it has lacked the primary means other professions use to incorporate knowledge advances into the training of each generation of practitioners. The way in which medicine, for example, ensures that new research knowledge actually gets used is by including it on medical licensing examinations and specialty board examinations and in accreditation guidelines to which professional schools and hospitals must respond. In education, however, teacher examinations have reflected little of what might be called a knowledge base for teaching (Darling-Hammond et al., 1995; Haertel, 1991; Shulman, 1987).

Finally, in part because of the great disjunction between knowledge production and use, there have been longstanding differences in the field about the nature of imparting knowledge and the goals of practice. These disputes, often tacit, are guided by different presumptions about how students learn and what effective teachers should know and do. On the one hand, the bureaucratic management of teaching has involved a quest for instructional tools and systems that can be prescribed for teacher use. Such a quest rests on the assumption that students are sufficiently standardized that they will respond in routine and predictable ways to a common stimulus, and that teaching tasks are sufficiently routine that they can be proceduralized. On the other hand, a more professional conception starts from the assumption that, because students learn in different ways and at different rates, teaching must be responsive to their needs if it is to be effective. As a consequence, teachers must make decisions in nonroutine situations using a multifaceted knowledge base applied through highly developed judgment and skill.

In the bureaucratic conception of teaching work, there is little rationale for substantial teacher education or ongoing opportunities for learning: if teaching can be routinized, teachers need only the modest training required to apply the procedures indicated by a textbook, curriculum guide, or management technique. The professional conception, however, emphasizes the *appropriateness* of teaching decisions to the goals and contexts of instruction and the needs of students. It envisions evaluation not as a discrete annual event staged to determine whether teachers adequately administer the expected procedures, but as a constant feature of organizational life for practitioners who inquire continually into the usefulness of their actions and revise their plans in light of these inquiries. In this view, teachers construct knowledge about their students, classrooms, and subject matter in the course of practice, just as they use knowledge that has been developed by researchers and other teachers (Darling-Hammond, 1996).

A great many decisions by actors outside the classroom determine what conceptions of teaching knowledge govern teachers' opportunities to learn both before they enter teaching and throughout their careers. These decisions are reflected in the content and character of teacher education and professional development programs that either seek to educate teachers to use wide-ranging knowledge or train them to implement set routines; in the standards that govern licensing, teacher evaluation, and professional development; in the daily schedules that isolate teachers or engage them in collective learning and problem solving; and in the organizational structures that determine who will decide all the above.

Some policymakers and educators believe that one of the most important policy strategies for improving teaching and learning is the recent development of standards by teachers themselves. In the late 1980s, several major reports calling for the professionalization of teaching have argued that teachers must take hold of professional standard-setting if teaching is to make good on the promise of competence that professions make to the public (CFEE, 1986; Holmes Group, 1986). Teacher education leaders have suggested that teachers and teacher educators must take greater control over their own destiny. A powerful place where this can be done is in standards-setting. According to Imig (1992) professionals need to define high standards, they must have rigorous expectations, and then hold peers to these standards and expectations.

The NCTAF concluded that newly created standards for teacher education accreditation, initial licensing, and advanced certification of teachers "could become a powerful lever for change" (NCTAF, 1996, p. 30). The Commission report noted:

> Of greatest priority is reaching agreement on what teachers should know and be able to do in order to teach to high standards. This standard-setting task was left unaddressed for many decades, but it has recently been accomplished by the efforts of three professional bodies that have closely aligned their work to produce standards outlining a continuum of teacher development derived directly from the expectations posed by new student standards. (NCTAF, 1996, pp. 67–68)

These three bodies include the NBPTS, an independent organization established in 1987, as the first professional body to set standards for the advanced certification of veteran accomplished teachers. The Board's standards were used, in turn, to guide the work of the Interstate New Teacher Assessment and Support Consortium (INTASC), a consortium of 33 states working together on "National Board-compatible" licensing standards and assessments for beginning teachers both before they enter teaching and during their first two years on the job. This effort, in turn, has informed the work of the National Council for Accreditation of Teacher Education (NCATE), which incorporated the performance standards developed by INTASC for judging pre-service teacher education programs. NCATE then began working with universities to help them design advanced master's degree programs organized around the standards of the National Board. Thus, these sets of interlocking standards created a developmental continuum for teachers, from pre-service teacher education through licensing and induction, through advanced study and ongoing professional development that included but was not limited to advanced certification.

The standards developed by the NBPTS, INTASC, and NCATE are linked to one another and to the new student standards developed by professional associations such as the National Council of Teachers of Mathematics (NCTM). These initiatives reflect knowledge about teaching and learning that supports a view of teaching as complex, contingent on students' needs and instructional goals, and reciprocal – that is, continually shaped and re-shaped by students' responses to learning events. The standards and assessments take into explicit account the teaching challenges posed by a student body that is multicultural and multilingual, that possesses multiple intelligences, and that includes diverse approaches to learning. By incorporating new subject-matter standards for students and the demands of learner diversity, as well as the expectation that teachers must collaborate with colleagues and parents in order to succeed, the standards define teaching as a collegial, professional activity that responds to considerations of subjects and students. By examining teaching in the light of learning, they put considerations of effectiveness at the center of practice. This view contrasts with that of the technicist perspective of teacher training and evaluation, in which teaching is seen as the implementation of set routines and formulas for behavior, unresponsive to the distinctive attributes of either clients or curriculum goals.

Another important attribute of the National Board standards is that they are *performance-based*: that is, they describe what teachers should know, be like, and be able to do rather than listing courses that teachers should take in order to be awarded a license. This shift toward performance-based standard-setting is in line with the approach to licensing taken in other professions and with the changes already occurring in a number of states. This approach aims to clarify what the criteria were for a determination of competence, placing more emphasis on the abilities teachers develop than the hours they spend taking classes. Ultimately, performance-based licensing standards could enable states to permit greater innovation and diversity in how teacher education programs operate by assessing their outcomes rather than merely regulating their inputs or procedures. Well-developed assessments of candidates, if they actually measure the important attributes of teaching knowledge and skill, can open up a variety of pathways and types of preparation for entering teaching without lowering standards as current emergency licensure provisions and many alternative certification programs do.

As a result of these combined initiatives, systems of licensing and certification that directly assess what teachers know and can do are gradually replacing the traditional methods of requiring graduation from an approved program or tallying specific courses as the basis for granting program approval, a license, or credit for professional growth. Furthermore, because the three sets of standards described above are substantively connected and form a continuum of development along the career path of the teacher, they conceptualize the main dimensions along which teachers can work to improve their practice. By providing vivid descriptions of high-quality teaching in specific teaching areas, "they clarify what the profession expects its members to get better at ... . Profession-defined standards provide the basis on which the profession can lay down its agenda and expectations for professional development and accountability" (Ingvarson, 1997, p. 1).

INFLUENCES OF STANDARDS AND ASSESSMENTS ON TEACHER LEARNING

The assessments developed by the National Board and INTASC stand in contrast to first-generation approaches to teacher-testing that have relied primarily on multiple-choice tests of basic skills and subject-matter knowledge or generic observations of teaching performance. The new assessments seek to assess teaching knowledge and skill through portfolios and performances that included authentic, complex teaching tasks as well as systematic, content- and context-based analyses of on-the-job performance. Proponents argue that such strategies will not only improve the validity of teacher assessment but also support the development of teacher education programs organized more explicitly around the attainment of important teaching abilities.

The standards themselves are educative because they vividly portrayed the attributes of good teaching. This example from the standards for Early Adolescence/English Language Arts teachers provides an illustration of how the Board articulates what highly accomplished teachers need to know and be able to do in a fashion that integrates understanding of learners and learning, educational goals, teaching, pedagogy, and context. Part of the discussion of "Standard I: Knowledge of Students" states:

> Accomplished middle-grades English teachers create classrooms centered around students; in these classrooms all students take pride in their growing language facility

and in their increasingly adventurous explorations of literature and other texts... . While they believe all students can learn, accomplished teachers are keenly aware that not all students learn in the same way... . Because language acquisition builds on prior achievements and experiences, accomplished English language arts teachers make it a point to find out early in the school year who their students are as individual learners – and use this knowledge to help shape decisions in the classroom.

Practically everything about the young adolescent learner is grist for the middle grades English teacher's mill, including an awareness and appreciation of the student's cultural, linguistic and ethnic heritage, family setting, prior learning experiences, personal interests, needs and goals. In particular, knowing their students entails gaining a sense of each student's capacity to read, write, speak and listen in English and/or other languages... . The accomplished middle-grades English teacher complements his or her knowledge of individual students with a broad perspective on patterns of adolescent development and language acquisition. Such teachers know that children mature according to their own internal biological clocks and that a wide variation in students' developmental stages and life experiences within the same classroom is to be expected and accommodated. (NBPTS, 1993, p. 9)

These discussions are further elaborated with vignettes that provide vivid descriptions of teachers enacting the standards. The vignettes illustrate how teachers draw upon many kinds of knowledge – knowledge of content, of teaching strategies, of curriculum, and of their students – when they are making decisions. Such vignettes, along with actual samples of teachers' reflections, analyses, and performances on the examinations, are used as benchmarks in the scoring process and as feedback to candidates when they receive their scores. The standards and vignettes closely resemble richly described cases that incorporate context and illuminate the teacher's capacity to transform knowledge into decisions in distinctive situations. As Shulman (1992) has argued, cases are particularly suited to teaching and teacher education, because both are instances of transformation:

(T)eaching is a form of transformation in which teachers create representations of complex ideas that connect with the constructions of their students. Case methods are a particular strategy of pedagogical transformation – a strategy for transforming more propositional forms of knowledge into narratives that motivate and educate. If, however, the knowledge base and reasoning processes of teaching (or law, medicine, or other practical domain) are themselves case-based, then the use of case methods does not require a very elaborate transformation... . The field is itself a body of cases linked loosely by working principles, and case methods are the most valid way of representing that structure in teaching. (Shulman, 1992, p. 17)

The standards provide the working principles that reflect the knowledge base and reasoning processes used by accomplished teachers. The Board's assessments – a portfolio completed over several months of teaching and performance tasks completed in an assessment center – provide a means for teachers to demonstrate not only what they do but how they reason their way to each decision. Evidence of teaching includes videotapes, plans, assignments, and samples of student work, accompanied by discussions of goals, intentions, and analyses of student learning. Teachers evaluate textbooks and materials, analyze teaching events, assess student learning and needs, and defend teaching decisions based on their knowledge of learning, curriculum, students, and pedagogy.

Ken Howey (n.d.) described how the principled guidance of the standards, applied in the context of daily practice, could inform the work of teacher educators and reduce the great divide between theory and practice:

> In education generally, and in teacher education specifically, there has been great reluctance to relate practice to research and theory. Cloaked in the popular but silly notion that teaching and learning are too situated and complex for generalization, too many "teacher educators" deify a quaint and romantic view of craft knowledge and model it badly. Increasingly, support for teachers' decisions and actions should be derived both from such sources as ethical standards, personal inquiry, and guiding principles and propositions derived from theory and research ... . One's beliefs about teaching and learning and corresponding instructional decisions need to be publicly shared and defended. The NBPTS has been a major catalyst toward this as a reality. (Howey, n.d., p. 7)

The Board's approach supports inquiry into the effects of one's actions as a teacher on students and their learning. First, it takes a long view of the course of instruction, documenting how teaching and learning evolve over a number of weeks and attending to how the events occurring at a given moment in time relate to what has gone on in the previous weeks and to the particular needs of students in the class. Second, it provides a variety of ways to examine teaching in the context of students and subjects, and to examine whether teachers can recognize and address important contextual considerations. These strategies for tying commentary to specific, con-textualized teaching events provide examiners with information regarding the rationale for curricular and pedagogical decisions. Third, the portfolio, through the samples of individual student work over time, enables an examination of how student learning is influenced by teaching, how teachers' analyses of student work and progress influence teaching decisions and practices and how these in turn support, or fail to support, student progress. Because teachers are asked to select the students with diverse approaches to learning and to display their work over time in relation to teaching actions, the teacher's ability to recognize and support different learning styles and needs is also tapped.

Teachers report that the process of analyzing their own and their students' work in light of standards enhances their abilities to assess student learning and to evaluate the effects of their own actions (Athanases, 1994). Evidence suggests that the assessments may not only expand what is *measured* about teaching but also what is *learned.* In an early pilot of portfolios in the Stanford Teacher Assessment Project, which led to the National Board's work, 89% of teachers who participated felt that the portfolio process had had some effect on their teaching. Teachers reported that they improved their practice as they pushed themselves to meet specific standards that had previously had little place in their teaching (Athanases, 1994).

Most frequently mentioned were teachers' approaches to the assessment of their students. As the portfolio continually demanded evidence of how teachers planned and adapted their instruction based on individual as well as collective student needs, teachers expanded the variety of informal as well as formal assessments they used to keep track of learning, paying more attention to how individual students were doing. Teachers also found themselves adjusting their instruction more frequently in response to these assessments. The analytic process teachers undertook often expanded their overall understanding of student learning in ways that had more far-reaching implications for their teaching. For example, one teacher described how she began to better understand students' writing development in ways that strengthened her ability to support them:

> Putting together a portfolio forced me to spend a great deal of time looking over student work (student portfolios). I was able to develop an understanding of patterns in the growth of third graders in written response to literature. This knowledge has been valuable to me this year as my students work in their literature response journals. The Assessment of Students entry had given me the opportunity to look at the responses to literature of five diverse students. This year when I began literature response journals I was more quickly aware of where the students were and how I could help them to develop their responses and thereby increase their understanding of and appreciation of literature. (Athanases, 1994, p. 431)

Teachers noted that they continued to use practices they had developed to meet the portfolio requirements; that they better understood how various aspects of children's development and learning interact; that they were able to integrate skills more effectively in their planning; that they were more aware of their actions and thought harder about the rationales for all of their decisions; that they were more deliberate and self-confident in approaching their teaching decisions; and that they had gained colleagues with whom to brainstorm and solve problems.

Another study of teachers' perceptions of their teaching abilities before and after completing portfolios for the National Board found that teachers reported statistically significant increases in their performance in each area assessed (planning, designing, and delivering instruction; managing the classroom; diagnosing and evaluating student learning; using subject-matter knowledge; and participating in a learning community, Tracz, Sienty, & Mata, 1994; Tracz, Sienty, Todorov, Snyder, & Takashima, et al., 1995). They often commented that videotaping their teaching and analyzing student work made them more aware of how to organize teaching and learning tasks, how to analyze whether and how students are learning, and how to intervene and change course when necessary. More recent research that followed comparison groups of teachers over time found that teachers who undertook Board certification did indeed change their assessment practices significantly more over the course of their certification year than did teachers who did not participate in the Board certification process (Sato, Chung, Darling-Hammond, Atkin, & Dean, et al., 2006).

Teachers have repeatedly said that they learned more about teaching from their participation in the assessments than they learned from any other previous professional development experience (e.g., Haynes, 1995). Typical is the account offered by Virginia high school English teacher Rick Wormeli, who credits the National Board Certification process with changing his teaching. During the course of the assessment, his close scrutiny of his work in light of the standards caused him to integrate other subjects into his lessons, reorganize reading discussion groups, and discard the vocabulary book that taught words out of context in favor of using words from the students' work. Even after he had finished the assessment, he continued to experiment with the changes he had begun. "I can't turn it off," he noted. New Jersey teacher Shirley Bzdewka agreed. In addition to creating a group of colleagues with whom she continued to share ideas and solve problems, she believed the assessment process deepened her approach to teaching.

> I know I was a good teacher. But ... . I am a much more deliberate teacher now. I can never, ever do anything again with my kids and not ask myself, "Why? Why am I doing this? What are the effects on my kids? What are the benefits to my kids?" It's not that I didn't care about those things before, but it's on such a conscious level now. (Bradley, 1994, p. 19)

These same effects on practice were reported by beginning teachers who experienced the Board-compatible assessments created by the INTASC consortium (Bliss & Mazur, 1997; Pecheone & Stansbury, 1996). The INTASC standards articulate what entering teachers should know, be like, and be able to do in order to practice responsibly, and to develop the kinds of deeper expertise that will eventually enable highly accomplished practice. The introduction to these model standards states:

> The National Board and INTASC are united in their view that the complex art of teaching requires performance-based standards and assessment strategies that are capable of capturing teachers' reasoned judgments and that evaluate what they can actually do in authentic teaching situations. (INTASC, 1992, p. 1)

The INTASC task force developed its standards by building upon the work of the National Board, the student standards committees, new licensing standards in a number of states and efforts of performance-oriented teacher education programs. The resulting standards are articulated in the form of 10 principles, each of which is further elaborated in terms of the knowledge, dispositions, and performances it implies. These, in turn, are the basis for subject-specific standards. In summary form, the 10 principles have been listed in Table 1.

As is true of the National Board standards, the INTASC standards explicitly acknowledge that teachers' actions or performances depend on many kinds of knowledge and on dispositions to use that knowledge and to work with others to support the learning and success of all students. The more detailed description of knowledge, dispositions, and performances that explain these principles provide a basis for evaluating evidence about the achievement of the standard, thus providing guidance for both preparation and assessment.

The INTASC standards have become the basis for a staged set of examinations that evaluate subject-matter knowledge and knowledge about teaching and learning in paper and pencil tests at the end of pre-service education, and then assess applied teaching skills when the candidate is practicing under supervision during an internship or induction year through a portfolio assessment much like that of the National Board. More than 15 INTASC states banded together to construct a new Test of Teaching Knowledge as the basis for an initial teaching license. The prototypes for this test included constructed response items in response to scenarios of teaching, samples of student work, and videotapes of classroom events that seek to evaluate whether prospective teachers understand the fundamentals of child development, motivation and behavior, learning theory, the identification of common learning difficulties, principles of classroom management, and strategies for student assessment. This initiative became the basis for the Educational Testing Service's Principles of Learning and Teaching Test.

Table 1. Principles for Beginning Teacher Licensing from the Interstate New Teacher Assessment and Support Consortium (INTASC).

Number	Principle
Principle 1	The teacher understands the central concepts, tools of inquiry, and structures of the discipline(s) he/she teaches and can create learning experiences that make these aspects of subject matter meaningful for students
Principle 2	The teacher understands how children learn and develop and can provide learning opportunities that support their intellectual, social, and personal development
Principle 3	The teacher understands how students differ in their approaches to learning and creates instructional opportunities that are adapted to diverse learners
Principle 4	The teacher understands and uses a variety of instructional strategies to encourage students' development of critical thinking, problem solving, and performance skills
Principle 5	The teacher uses an understanding of individual and group motivation and behavior to create a learning environment that encourages positive social interaction, active engagement in learning, and self-motivation
Principle 6	The teacher uses knowledge of effective verbal, nonverbal, and media-communication techniques to foster active inquiry, collaboration, and supportive interaction in the classroom
Principle 7	The teacher plans instruction based upon knowledge of subject matter, students, the community, and curriculum goals
Principle 8	The teacher understands and uses formal and informal assessment strategies to evaluate and ensure the continuous intellectual and social development of the learner
Principle 9	The teacher is a reflective practitioner who continually evaluates the effects of his/her choices and actions on others (students, parents, and other professionals in the learning community) and who actively seeks out opportunities to grow professionally
Principle 10	The teacher fosters relationships with school colleagues, parents, and agencies in the larger community to support students' learning and well-being

Ten states also worked together to develop and pilot portfolio assessments for novice teachers to undertake either during student teaching or during a mentored first year of practice, scored by state-trained assessors as the basis for determining whether an initial or continuing professional license will be issued. Like the National Board portfolio, the INTASC portfolio prototypes emphasize content pedagogy along with the capacity to attend to student needs. These prototypes have provided the foundation for pre-service teacher portfolios embedded into student teaching in Wisconsin and California and for beginning teacher portfolios used during an induction period in Connecticut.

The portfolio assessments examine how teachers plan and guide instruction around new standards for student learning, evaluate student learning and adapt teaching accordingly, use a variety of curriculum material, and handle problems of practice. For example, in mathematics, one assessment task requires teachers to plan an instructional unit structured around the NCTM standards of mathematical problem solving, reasoning, communication, and connections; show how they use curriculum tools including manipulatives and technology; and reflect on and revise the instruction in practice. Other tasks require teachers to analyze student work and assess learning for purposes of planning, diagnosis, feedback, and grading.

Zeichner (1993) noted that, while focusing on outcomes, the INTASC and National Board standards differed in important ways from earlier attempts to institute competency-based teacher education (CBTE) in the 1970s. While the earlier efforts sought to breakdown teacher behaviors into tiny discrete skill bits, articulating literally hundreds of desired competencies to be individually assessed, these more recent efforts are defined at a broader level, communicating a vision about what teachers should know and be able to do, and resting on expert judgments to evaluate the ways in which they demonstrate their capacity to do it. Ingvarson (1997, p. 1) noted as well that these kinds of standards "go far deeper into the nature of what it means to teach well than the lists of criteria and competencies typical of most managerial models for teacher appraisal and evaluation."

The view of teaching articulated in the recent performance-based standards demands, as the INTASC report suggested, "that teachers integrate their knowledge of subjects, students, the community, and curriculum to create a bridge between learning goals and learner's lives." (INTASC, 1992, p. 8). Thus, rather than fragmenting and trivializing teacher knowledge and performances by specifying minute behaviors to be exhibited on demand, these efforts use research about practice to define the *kinds* of knowledge and understandings teachers should be able to use in an integrated fashion based on their analysis of their goals and students.

Tony Romano, a seventh-grade math teacher in Stamford, Connecticut who was part of the pilot group for the INTASC-based Connecticut portfolio, found this assessment process much more helpful to the development of his teaching than the generic classroom observations that were part of Connecticut's earlier induction program. Romano recalls that, after he recorded each lesson every day for 6 weeks, "I would have to reflect on what I had done and how I would change the lesson to make it better, and (answer) basic questions like: How did I meet the needs of every student?" This process posed a very different set of questions for him than a process that asked him to demonstrate specific behaviors, which focused his attention on his own performance rather than the learning of the students.

> Although I was the reflective type anyway, it made me go a step further. I would have to say, okay, this is how I'm going to do it differently. I think it made more of an impact on my teaching and was more beneficial to me than just one lesson in which you state what you're going to do ... . The process makes you think about your teaching and reflect on your teaching. And I think that's necessary to become an effective teacher.

USES AND EFFECTS OF THE STANDARDS

In a short time, the teaching standards achieved a noteworthy consensus among policymakers and members of the profession: By 1997, 10 years after the National Board was founded, 33 states belonged to INTASC, and at least 24 had formally adopted or adapted the INTASC standards for beginning teacher licensing. More than 20 states were involved in developing or piloting INTASC assessments for either the pre-service Test of Teaching Knowledge or the portfolio for beginning teachers. Twenty-six states and more than 70 school districts had established incentives for teachers to pursue National Board certification, including fee supports, professional development offerings, and stipends or advancement opportunities for those achieving certification. Seventeen states had agreed to accept National Board certification as the basis for granting a license to out-of-state entrants or as the basis for granting "recertification" to experienced teachers. Eight had agreed to offer higher salaries to teachers successful in achieving certification. School districts like Cincinnati, Ohio and Rochester, New York had incorporated the National Board standards into teacher-evaluation criteria, using it as one basis for recognition as a "lead teacher" who mentors others and as a basis for salary increments in a performance-based compensation schedule.

In addition, by 1997, 41 states had established partnerships with the NCATE – more than double the number engaged in such partnerships three years earlier. These partnerships encouraged the use of national professional standards in the construction of teacher education programs. And 14 states had established fully independent or quasi-independent professional standards boards for teaching like those that exist in other professions to set standards for licensing and preparation. New boards like those in Indiana, Georgia, and Kentucky adopted the continuum of teaching standards represented by NCATE, INTASC, and the NBPTS as a foundation for redesigning the preparation, licensing, induction, and ongoing professional development of teachers.

These actions, collectively, lay the groundwork for what Ingvarson (1997) called a standards-guided model of professional development, which includes:

1. Profession-defined *teaching standards* that provide direction and milestones for professional development over the long term of a career in teaching;
2. An *infrastructure for professional learning* whose primary purpose is to enable teachers to gain the knowledge and skill embodied in the teaching standards;
3. Staged career structures and pay systems that provide *incentives and recognition* for attaining these teaching standards; and
4. A credible system of *professional certification* based on valid assessments of whether teachers have attained the levels of performance defined by the standards.

Although a number of these components were put in place, the full impact of professional standards – widespread use for professional development, as well as for making decisions about which institutions are allowed to prepare teachers, which individuals are allowed to enter teaching, and how advancement in the field will be acknowledged – has yet to occur.

Thus far, only Connecticut has a fully functioning system of INTASC-based performance assessments, although several other states, including California, are currently bringing portfolio systems online as part of initial licensure (e.g., Pecheone & Chung, 2006). Although 50,000 teachers were National Board Certified by 2006 –a 50-fold increase from a decade earlier – the Board's intentions to have certified twice as many by then were undermined by reductions in federal funding associated with political resistance from those opposed to the professionalization of teaching (e.g., Finn & Kanstoroom, 1999). Nonetheless, while the pace of change has been somewhat slowed during an era of push-back against professional influences on practice, slower but steady progress has been made.

The standards, as they are being implemented, are exerting greater leverage on practice than program approval and licensing systems have in the past. For one thing, the standards offer a conception of teaching that was linked to student learning, and they used performance-based modes of assessment. These two features together engaged teachers in activities that helped them evaluate their effects on students and actively refine their practice, a much different outcome than that associated with the completion of multiple-choice tests. The standards envision licensing, certification, and accreditation systems that are structured to *develop* more thoughtful teaching rather than merely to *select* candidates into or out of teaching. They do this by engaging teachers in the individual and collective analysis of teaching and its effects, and in professional decision-making. They offer new roles for teachers that involve them more deeply in the processes of assessment. For example, in addition to being assessed themselves, teachers:

- sit on boards and committees, in charge of developing and reviewing the standards and assessments;
- participate in the writing, piloting, and refinement of assessment tasks;
- analyze the practice of exemplary teachers to develop standards, tasks, benchmarks, and professional development materials aimed at helping other teachers meet the standards;
- serve as assessors for the assessments; and
- act as mentors for teachers who are developing their portfolios (Darling-Hammond et al., 1995; Delandshere, 1996).

Because these activities center around authentic tasks of teaching which are examined from the perspective of standards within the contexts of subject matter and students, they create a setting in which serious discourse about teaching can occur. Because evidence of the effects of teaching on student learning is at the core of the exercises, candidates and assessors continually examine the nexus between teachers' actions and students' responses. Focusing on the outcomes of practice while making teaching public in this way creates the basis for developing shared norms of practice (Shulman, 2004).

Connecticut's process of implementing INTASC-based portfolios for beginning teacher licensing illuminates how this can occur. Connecticut's licensing system was designed as much to be a professional development system as a measurement activity, and educators were involved in every aspect of its development and implementation, so that these opportunities were widespread. Each assessment was developed with the assistance of a teacher in residence in the department of education; advisory committees of teachers, teacher educators, and administrators guided the development of standards and assessments; hundreds of educators were convened to provide feedback on drafts of the standards; and many more were involved in the assessments themselves, as cooperating teachers and school-based mentors who worked with beginning teachers on developing their practice, as assessors who were trained to score the portfolios; and as expert teachers who convened regional support seminars to help candidates learn about the standards and the portfolio development process. Individuals involved in each of these roles are engaged in preparation that is organized around the examination of cases and the development of evidence connected to the standards.

System developers Pecheone and Stansbury (1996) explain how the standards are used in professional-development settings for beginning and veteran teachers:

> The state support and assessment system must be centered around standards that apply across contexts and that embrace a variety of teaching practices. Teaching is highly contextual, however, varying with the strengths and needs of students, strengths of the teacher, and the availability of resources. The support program needs to help beginning teachers see how to apply general principles in their particular teaching contexts. The design currently being implemented in the Connecticut secondary projects begins support sessions by modeling selected principles, then having teachers discuss work they have brought (e.g., a student assignment, a videotape illustrating discourse, student work samples) in light of the principles presented.

> For experienced teachers who will become the assessors and support providers the reverse is true. They typically understand contextual teaching practices well. Although they are acquainted with the general principles at some level because they keep abreast of developments in their teaching specialty, they do not generally have extensive experience in either articulating the principles to others or in seeing their application across multiple contexts. An intensive training program for both assessors and mentors ensures similar understandings among individuals and gives them opportunities to articulate how these principles are applied in classrooms. (pp. 172–173)

These processes can have far-reaching effects. By one estimate, a majority of Connecticut's teachers have been prepared and have served as assessors, mentors, or cooperating teachers under either the earlier-beginning teacher-performance assessment or the more recently developed portfolios. By the year 2010, 80% of elementary teachers and nearly as many secondary teachers will have participated in the new assessment system as candidates, support providers, or assessors (Pecheone & Stansbury, 1996, p. 174).

Creating licensing and certification systems that are deliberately constructed so as to actively support the development of teaching knowledge, skills, and dispositions is a new undertaking. This effort places greater attention on both the validity of the assessments – that is, the extent to which they represent authentic and important tasks of teaching – and on the relationship between assessment and teacher learning. For the most part, previous testing programs were designed primarily to screen out candidates rather than to encourage better training or induce good practice. In these new systems, decisions about what is tested and how it is tested are made as much on the basis of whether test content and methods encourage useful teacher learning and teaching practice as on the ability of tasks to rank or sort candidates. This concern for consequential and systemic validity has implications for the nature of the assessments developed and for the ways in which they are used.

Delandshere (1996), for example, argues that to be valuable for teacher learning, assessments must be dynamic and principled rather than static and prescribed; that is, they must allow for the construction of knowledge and for diverse practices that are the result of principled action in different contexts, rather than presuming one set of unvarying behaviors. Further, she suggests that:

> In order for an assessment to have a continuous effect on teaching and learning, teachers must play an important role in defining and discussing their own knowledge during the assessment process. (p. 110)

Affirming the notion that explicit work on knowledge construction is an important benefit of powerful assessments, teacher-education students who complete a portfolio based on the INTASC standards during their internship year at the University of Southern Maine have found the experience transforms their approach to learning as well as teaching.

> The process prompts the interns to take a new kind of responsibility for learning to teach, what is called "authoring" their learning. No longer do interns simply present a list of courses or grades for credentialing. They now must construct and present evidence of their mastery of learning to teach – their readiness to take responsibility for a class of learners. (Lyons, 1996, p. 66)

The process of defining and discussing knowledge as it applies to an instance of teaching also occurs when standards are used in the study of cases, a strategy increasingly used by preservice teacher educators and teacher networks or study groups to help teachers think about and develop their practice. Cases and narratives about teaching illuminate the concerns and dilemmas of teaching. Yet to be educative, they need to be linked to broad principles of knowledge (Bliss & Mazur, 1997; Carter, 1993). Standards can provide the structure for making meaning of cases, while cases can provide the vitality that makes standards come alive. Together they can nurture the reflective dialogue, collective focus on student learning, de-privatization of practice, and shared norms and values that characterize professional communities (Ingvarson, 1997).

Bliss and Mazur (1997) found that using the INTASC standards as a basis for analyzing cases allowed preservice teachers to gradually integrate standards, theory, and actual classroom practice. With repeated opportunities to reflect on cases in this way, they moved from simple awareness of standards or critiques of teaching actions to an appreciation of principled decision-making and an ability to plan approaches to, or changes in, their own teaching. Other researchers who have used curriculum standards in mathematics and science as a basis for case-based professional development have found that they stimulate professional dialog, which contributes to professional knowledge-building as well as to collaborative curriculum reform (Barnett & Ramirez, 1996; Ingvarson & Marrett, 1997; Schifter & Fosnot, 1993). Assessment systems like those of the National Board and INTASC support this kind of knowledge-building as they allow teachers to construct and discuss their understandings while they continually reflect on, critique, and defend their practice.

PREPARING TEACHERS TO MEET THE STANDARDS

A critical concern regarding standards is that they represent meaningful goals for candidates and colleges to prepare for. The goal in standard-setting should not be to increase the failure rates of candidates but to improve the caliber of their preparation for the real tasks of teaching. One of the most important aspects of the new standards for teaching is that, like those of other professions, they bring clarity to the pursuit of teaching skills by focusing on performance on critical teaching tasks rather than listing courses to be taken or testing arcane knowledge in forms far distant from its actual use. The fact that candidates consistently report that they learn from the new standards and that the assessments actually help them develop and refine their skills suggests that these efforts may advance the overall capacity of the profession to do its work, rather than merely rationing slots in a more constrained labor market.

While there is reason to be enthusiastic about how the new assessments promote reflection that is satisfying to teachers, serious questions remain about how to prepare teachers for the more sophisticated practice the new standards represent. There is presently limited knowledge of what learning opportunities – in preservice settings, induction contexts, later professional development activities, and school-based work – are associated with success in meeting the new teaching standards. As Wilson and Ball (1996) noted:

New teacher assessments are for teacher educators what the new student assessments are for teachers. They represent the standards toward which teacher educators must aim ... . Reformers hope that changing the process by which new teachers are licensed will in turn effect changes in how they are prepared. Less well understood, however, are the challenges this presents for teacher educators, who must devise ways of preparing beginning teachers to succeed on these performance-based assessments. (p. 122)

This challenge is made greater by the fact that reforms of schooling expand the gap "between where prospective teachers start and where they are to end up" (p. 124). That is, what beginners know from their own schooling experience is even more likely than in the past to be dissimilar from reform visions of education, and hence to require greater learning and unlearning on their parts. In addition, the kind of teaching for critical thinking and deep understanding envisioned by the new standards is more difficult to develop because it is more indeterminate and less susceptible to prescription. When children actually think, there is no way to predict precisely what they will uncover and what paths they will pursue.

Knowledge is just beginning to accrue regarding effective strategies for preparing beginning teachers for the kind of practice that takes account of student thinking in the pursuit of challenging subject-matter goals. There is much to learn about the efficacy and trade-offs of various tactics for building thoughtful, multidimensional practice. Wilson and Ball suggest that these tactics may include the creation and use of new images of practice through school-based work with teachers who engage in such practice; through curriculum materials like written cases, videotapes of practice, and computerized databases of linked artifacts of teaching that allow inquiries into lessons, units, teacher thinking, and student work; and through modeling the pedagogy anticipated by new standards in the teacher education program itself.

The value of these strategies is that they capture the interactive nature of teaching, the fact that teaching is what teachers do, say, and think *with students, concerning knowledge*, in a particular social organization of instruction (Cohen & Ball, 2001). Teaching cannot be well-understood without taking all of these interactions into account, simultaneously, in practice. Thus, professional-development tools are particularly powerful when they allow for the study of teaching in light of these factors, not in the abstract or piece by piece.

A number of colleges of education have found that the new teaching standards and assessments support the development of such tools (e.g., Harris, Terrell, & Russell, 1997; Lyons, 1996). Colleges have found that in order to demonstrate the knowledge and skills outlined by INTASC and the National Board, candidates need many more opportunities to learn about practice *through* practice, including structured exhibitions and performances and extended clinical experiences integrated with coursework (e.g., Darling-Hammond, 2006). Representative of many was this description of changes at the University of Arkansas at Monticello, sparked by the Arkansas Teacher Licensure principles which were based on the INTASC standards and by the standards of NCATE, which became the basis for all program approval in the state:

> Specific reforms in teacher education at UAM included the development of a (year-long) internship, a completely restructured curriculum, and a performance-based assessment system involving observations, portfolios, simulations, interviews, and exams ... . Certain schools in eight school districts that have joined in a special partnership relationship with the university, designated Professional Development Schools, host the senior year interns ... . Traditional and separately identified courses (i.e., American Education, Introduction to Special Education, etc.) have been replaced by integrated content courses ... . Education professors work in teams to continually revise the curriculum, facilitate delivery of content, and provide student assessment beyond written exams. (Harris et al., 1997, pp. 16–17)

Similarly at the University of North Dakota, the creation of portfolio assessments of teaching in response to NCATE's expectations for entry and exit performance standards led not only to exciting new assessments for prospective teachers, guided by standards that reflected and went beyond the INTASC work, but also to the development of portfolios for young children in the elementary school with which the university worked most closely in a professional development school relationship. In a context that nurtured authentic assessment for children and teachers for many years, the North Dakota initiatives illustrated how six years of work with standards-based assessment in a school/university partnership could contribute to the simultaneous renewal of schools and teacher education programs (Harris & Gates, 1997). Teachers found that this work both enhanced their knowledge of children and their understanding of their own teaching.

In a similar fashion, work with the National Board standards and assessments shaped a simultaneous renewal process for schools and the college of education at George Washington University. As dean Mary Futrell (1996) noted:

> The commitment to portfolios, assessment, reflection, and active learning are core values in our emerging curriculum. Perhaps the use of these principles and strategies is nowhere reflected more than in the work the school is doing to support teachers in our area who are voluntarily seeking to become nationally certified by participating in the National Board for Professional Teaching Standards assessment and certification process. We have formed partnerships with nine school districts to support teachers, and we are using our experiences with the NBPTS certification process to help define how to prepare teachers to be more reflective in their teaching and to work in restructured school environments. (p. 46)

These wide-ranging initiatives and the models increasingly used for authentic assessment of teaching are all informed, directly or indirectly, by the Board's efforts to define and document accomplished teaching. The spillover effects do not stop at the boundaries of education schools, but find their way into the classrooms of young children as well. Efforts by NCATE and the National Board to work with schools of education to use the Board's standards as the basis for constructing advanced master's degree programs help teachers work toward accomplished teaching to produce an even wider range of possibilities.

While evidence of the power of these tools for engendering more thoughtful practice is hopeful, we still do not know what combinations of teacher development opportunities and school conditions are most likely to result in high quality teaching of the sort anticipated by the standards and, in turn, in high levels of student learning. Nor do we know which combinations of conditions will be cost-effective or whether these vary based on the context, stage of teaching career, etc. These questions must be studied in the context of teacher development efforts that seek to create such learning opportunities and then to evaluate their effects. Finally, while there is substantial testimony to the fact that teachers learned a great deal by participating in these assessments, we are just beginning to understand what kind of learning takes place, under what circumstances, and how it can be harnessed to the cause of sustained professional development and widespread improvements in teaching. The continued expansion of these efforts will rely on such research as well as on further policy development.

CONCLUSION

Professional standards for teaching hold promise for mobilizing reforms of the teaching career and helping to structure learning opportunities that reflect the complex, reciprocal nature of teaching work. Their potential value lies partly in their authenticity – their ability to capture the important interactions between teachers and students, and content and contexts that influence learning. In addition, the participatory nature of the accompanying assessment systems supports knowledge development widely throughout the profession, enhancing the establishment of shared norms by making teaching public and collegial. Finally, the connection of a continuum of teaching standards to one another and to new student standards may bring focus and coherence to a fragmented, chaotic system that earlier left teacher-learning largely to chance.

Teaching standards are not a magic bullet, however. They cannot by themselves solve the problems of dysfunctional school organizations, outmoded curricula, inequitable allocations of resources, or lack of social supports for children and youth. Standards, too, like all other reforms, hold their own dangers. Standard-setting in all professions must be vigilant against the possibility that practice can become constrained by the codification of knowledge that does not sufficiently acknowledge legitimate diversity of approaches or advances in the field; that access to practice can become overly restricted on grounds not directly related to competence; or that adequate learning opportunities for candidates to meet the standards may not emerge on an equitable basis. Although there are many dilemmas to be resolved and barriers to be overcome, the efforts thus far of educators and policymakers to confront and address these concerns leave much hope that new standards for teaching can make an important contribution to the education of educators who are prepared for the challenges of the 21st century.

NOTE

1. In US education, the term "certification" has often been used to describe states' decisions regarding admission to practice, commonly termed licensing in other professions. Until the creation of the NBPTS, teaching had had no vehicle for advanced professional certification. To avoid confusion between the actions of this professional board and those of states, I use the terms licensing and certification as they are commonly used by professions: "licensing" is the term used to describe state decisions about admission to practice and "certification" is the term used to describe the actions of the National Board in certifying accomplished practice.

REFERENCES

Athanases, S. Z. (1994). Teachers' reports of the effects of preparing portfolios of literacy instruction. *Elementary School Journal, 94*(4), 421–439.

Barnett, C., & Ramirez, A. (1996). Fostering critical analysis and reflection through mathematics case discussions. In: J. A. Colbert, P. Desberg & K. Trimble (Eds), *The case for education: Contemporary approaches for using case methods* (pp. 1–13). Boston: Allyn & Bacon.

Bliss, T., & Mazur, J. (1997, February). How INTASC standards come alive through case studies. Paper presented at the Annual meeting of the American Association of Colleges for Teacher Education. Phoenix, AZ.

Bradley, A. (1994). Pioneers in professionalism. *Education Week, 13*(30, April 20), 18–21.

Bransford, J. D., Brown, A. L., & Cocking, R. R. (1999). *How people learn: Brain, mind, experience, and school.* Washington, DC: National Academy Press. http://www.nap.edu/html/howpeople1/

Carnegie Forum on Education and the Economy (CFEE) (1986). *A nation prepared: Teachers for the 21st century.* Washington, DC: Carnegie Forum on Education and the Economy, Task Force on Teaching as a Profession.

Carter, K. (1993). The place of story in the study of teaching and teacher education. *Educational Researcher, 22*(1), 5–1218.

Cohen, D. K., & Ball, D. L. (2001). Making change: Instruction and its improvement. *Phi Delta Kappan, 83*(1), 73–77.

Darling-Hammond, L. (1996). The right to learn and the advancement of teaching: Research, policy, and practice for democratic education. *Educational Researcher, 25*(6), 5–17.

Darling-Hammond, L. (1997). *The right to learn.* San Francisco: Jossey-Bass.

Darling-Hammond, L. (2006). *Powerful teacher education: Lessons from exemplary programs.* San Francisco: Jossey-Bass.

Darling-Hammond, L., Wise, A. E., & Klein, S. (1995). *A license to teach: Building a profession for 21st century schools.* Boulder, CO: Westview Press.

Delandshere, G. (1996). From static and prescribed to dynamic and principled assessment of teaching. *The Elementary School Journal, 97*(2), 105–120.

Finn, C. E., & Kanstoroom, M. (Eds). (1999). *Better teachers, better schools.* Washington, DC: Thomas B. Fordham Foundation.

Futrell, M. (1996). Involvement in educational renewal and the Network for Innovative Colleges of Education Program. *Teacher Education Quarterly, 23*(1), 45–48.

Haertel, E. H. (1991). New forms of teacher assessment. In: G. Grant (Ed.), *Review of Research in Education* (Vol. 17, pp. 3–29). Washington, DC: American Educational Research Association.

Harris, L. B., Terrell, S. M., & Russell, P. W. (1997). Using performance-based assessment to improve teacher education. Paper presented at the 77th annual conference of the Association of Teacher Educators, University of Arkansas at Monticello (ERIC Document Reproduction Service No. ED406346).

Harris, M. M., & Gates, J. S. (1997). Standards in simultaneous renewal. *Action in Teacher Education, 19*(2), 27–37.

Haynes, D. (1995). One teacher's experience with National Board assessment. *Educational Leadership, 52*(8), 58–60.

Holmes Group. (1986). *Tomorrow's teachers: A report of the Holmes Group.* East Lansing, MI: The Holmes Group.

Holmes Group. (1996). *Tomorrow's schools of education.* East Lansing, MI: The Holmes Group.

Howey, K.R. (n.d.). *The NBPTS propositions for accomplished teachers: Implications for pre-service teacher preparation.* Columbus, OH: Ohio State University.

Imig, D. G. (1992). *The professionalization of teaching: Relying on a professional knowledge base.* St. Louis, MO: AACTE Knowledge-Base Seminar.

Ingvarson, L. (1997). *Teaching standards: Foundations for professional development reform.* Melbourne, Australia: Monash University.

Ingvarson, L., & Marrett, M. (1997). Building professional community and supporting teachers as learners: The potential of case methods. In: L. Logan & J. Sachs (Eds), *Meeting the challenge of primary schooling for the 1990s* (pp. 229–243). London: Routledge.

Interstate New Teacher Support and Assessment Consortium. (1992). *Model standards for beginning teacher licensing and development: A resource for state dialogue.* Washington, DC: Council for Chief State School Officers.

Lyons, N. P. (1996). A grassroots experiment in performance assessment. *Educational Leadership, 53*(6), 64–67.

National Board for Professional Teaching Standards. (1989). *Toward high and rigorous standards for the teaching profession.* Detroit, MI: NBPTS.

National Board for Professional Teaching Standards (1993). *Early Adolescence/English Language Arts standards.* Washington, DC: NBPTS.

National Commission on Teaching and America's Future. (1996). *What matters most: Teaching for America's future.* New York: National Commission on Teaching and America's Future, Teachers College, Columbia University.

O'Day, J. A., & Smith, M. S. (1993). Systemic reform and educational opportunity. In: S. H. Fuhrman (Ed.), *Coherent policy: Improving the system* (pp. 250–312). San Francisco: Jossey-Bass.

Pecheone, R., & Chung, R. (2006). Evidence in teacher education: The Performance Assessment for California Teachers (PACT). *Journal of Teacher Education, 57*(1), 22–26.

Pecheone, R., & Stansbury, K. (1996). Connecting teacher assessment and school reform. *Elementary School Journal, 97,* 163–177.

Sato, M., Chung, R., Darling-Hammond, L., Atkin, M., Dean, S., Greenwald, E., Hyler, M., & Vaughn, K. (2006). *Influences of National Board Certification on teachers' classroom assessment practices.* Palo Alto, CA: Stanford University, National Board Resource Center.

Schifter, D., & Fosnot, C. T. (1993). *Reconstructing mathematics education: Stories of teachers meeting the challenge of reform.* New York: Teachers College Press.

Shulman, L. S. (1986). Those who understand: Knowledge growth in teaching. *Educational Researcher, 15*(2), 4–14.

Shulman, L. S. (1987). Knowledge and teaching: Foundations of the new reform. *Harvard Educational Review, 57*(1), 1–22.

Shulman, L. S. (1992). Toward a pedagogy of cases. In: J. Shulman (Ed.), *Case methods in teacher education* (pp. 1–29). New York: Teachers College Press.

Shulman, L. S. (2004). *Teaching as community property: Essays on higher education.* San Francisco: Jossey-Bass.

Tracz, S. M., Sienty, S., & Mata, S. (1994, February). The self-reflection of teachers compiling portfolios for National Certification: Work in progress. Paper presented at the Annual meeting of the American Association of Colleges for Teacher Education, Chicago, IL.

Tracz, S. M., Sienty, S., Todorov, K., Snyder, J., Takashima, B., Pensabene, R., Olsen, B., Pauls, L., & Sork, J. (1995, April). Improvement in teaching skills: Perspectives from

National Board for Professional Teaching Standards field test network candidates. Paper presented at the Annual meeting of the American Educational Research Association, San Francisco, CA.

Wilson, S. M., & Ball, D. (1996). Helping teachers meet the standards: New challenges for teacher educators. *The Elementary School Journal, 97*(2), 121–138.

Zeichner, K. M. (1993). *Reflections on the career-long preparation of teachers in Wisconsin.* Madison, WI: University of Wisconsin.

CHAPTER 3

THE DESIGN ARCHITECTURE OF NBPTS CERTIFICATION ASSESSMENTS

Mari Pearlman

ABSTRACT

To appreciate the distance the National Board for Professional Teaching Standards (NBPTS) certification program has come, and the speed with which it has traveled that distance, a glance at its first decade from the perspective of assessment development is essential. The particulars of the history of the NBPTS's assessment strategies and designs have determined in many ways the current assessment architecture: the evolution of the assessment's design reveals the growth in our knowledge of innovative assessment strategies and formats and their uses. In this chapter, I will briefly summarize the history of the NBPTS assessment program, then describe and analyze the earliest assessment designs, some intermediate approaches, and then the current iteration (commonly referred to as the next generation certificates). I will finally detail the current assessment architecture, connecting that architecture to both the history and the lessons learned from the initial assessments.

Assessing Teachers for Professional Certification:
The First Decade of the National Board for Professional Teaching Standards
Advances in Program Evaluation, Volume 11, 55–91
Copyright © 2008 by Elsevier Ltd.
ISSN: 1474-7863/doi:10.1016/S1474-7863(07)11003-6

To examine only the current status of National Board for Professional Teaching Standards (NBPTS) development would be to ignore important and valuable lessons that contributed to the process. The initial lessons were learned in the context of the early development of the first three certificates, and those lessons were applied to development of 10 more certificates. At that point, we stepped back to take account of what had been learned and once more applied those lessons to the next generation of development, initially for 3 new certificates and then to all 16 previously developed certificates. At each stage the changes built demonstrably on previous lessons learned.

EARLY HISTORY OF NBPTS

From its beginnings in 1987, the NBPTS set out to re-imagine the culture and dynamics of teaching as a profession. One of the most powerful supports for this vision was the link the NBPTS asserted between teaching's attainment of full status as a learned profession and the existence of a rigorous assessment, both national and voluntary, that would certify the expertise of successful test takers.[1] But if teaching as a profession had been systematically under-conceptualized by all its stakeholders – teacher-educators, would-be and experienced practitioners, consumers – the state of assessment as generally practiced in, by, and for teaching was even more woefully inadequate to the task of certifying expertise. As Lee Shulman, the intellectual (and in many cases, practical) father of many of the assumptions underlying NBPTS assessment design, pointed out in a 1987 article:

> The actions of both policymakers and teacher educators in the past have been consistent with the formulation that teaching requires basic skills, content knowledge, and general pedagogical skills. Assessments of teachers in most states consist of some combination of basic-skills tests, an examination of competence in subject matter, and observations in the classroom to ensure that certain kinds of general teaching behavior are present. In this manner, I would argue, teaching is trivialized, its complexities ignored, and its demands diminished. Teachers themselves have difficulty in articulating what they know and how they know it. (Shulman, 1987b, p. 6)

In other words, the lack of sophistication in the assessment of teaching had led to an impoverished view of the profession. An assessment worthy of the complexities of teaching, Shulman argued, would be based on standards that fulfill the following imperatives:

> ... [the standards] must be closely tied to the findings of scholarship in the academic disciplines that form the curriculum (such as English, physics, and history) as well as those that serve as foundations for the process of education (such as psychology,

sociology, or philosophy); they must possess intuitive credibility (or "face validity") in the opinions of the professional community in whose interests they have been designed; and they must relate to the appropriate normative conceptions of teaching and teacher education. (Shulman, 1987b, p. 5)

Thus, one of the NBPTS's most critical initial accomplishments was the publication of a document that was once the statement of a vision and the specification of a domain of assessment, *Toward High and Rigorous Standards: What Teachers Should Know and Be Able To Do* (NBPTS, 1991). However, even though a common vocabulary and an articulated domain of assessment are critical first steps in assessment design, the NBPTS vision was far more ambitious. The NBPTS rejected the traditional approach to the assessment of education (and many other) professionals. In the traditional approach, the domain is specified largely by more or less thorough job-analysis techniques that reveal what its practitioners actually do on the job and what is important to their success in the job. The NBPTS chose to take a bolder approach to definition of the specific nature of the domain for each of the 33 fields for which it envisioned separate certification assessments. It impaneled groups of luminaries (teachers and teacher-educators, with teachers forming the majority on every panel) from each of the fields and asked them to articulate a vision, rising from the bedrock of *Toward High and Rigorous Standards*, of what teachers in each field *ought* to know and be able to do. Categorically rejecting the current overall state of the art in teaching as precisely the problem they wished to solve (hence the avoidance of the traditional job analysis), the NBPTS began the assessment project by insisting that a definition of accomplished practice by accomplished practitioners should constitute the domain of the certification assessments.

The literary critic Edward Said echoed the Talmud in *Beginnings: Intention and Method* (1975) by reminding his readers that all beginnings are hard. The early stages of the NBPTS certification assessments were no exception. Armed with only a broad sense of what format *not* to utilize – for example, it was clear that traditional multiple-choice tests, the anathema of the education enterprise in the eyes of the reform movement, would not do – the NBPTS and its early advisers began with the conviction that no matter what efforts would be needed to make it so, the certification assessment worthy of the high aims of the NBPTS must be as visionary and daring as its sponsoring Board. Much of the conventional wisdom cherished by professional test developers and psychometricians was viewed with great suspicion by the NBPTS in these early days. Such characteristics as the notorious unreliability and hence indefensibility for high-stakes purposes of complex performance-assessment tasks, the enormous costs associated with evaluating complex tasks, and the concomitant and seemingly inescapable vagaries of human judgment were known to the initial decision makers on the NBPTS and quite deliberately taken as challenges to "think outside the box."

The most important of these "unboxed" thinkers was Lee Shulman, whose charge from the Carnegie Task Force on Teaching (which was the parent of the NBPTS) was to conduct a program of research directed at the answers to three questions:

> What do teachers need to know and know how to do? How can that knowledge and skill be assessed? And how can a program of assessments be designed that will be adequate to the complexities of teaching while remaining equitable for all candidates who might apply? (Shulman, 1987a, p. 42)

From this call a research program was developed, intended to provide "working models" for the NBPTS's assessment developers. This work on prototypes was part of a larger conception of what the NBPTS's certification program might look like:

> The ideal teaching assessment is unlikely to take the form of a single examination for which a candidate "sits" during a designated period, as is the case with the NTE and its state-level equivalents. Instead, it is more prudent to imagine teacher assessment as an ongoing set of at least the following procedures: written assessments, assessment center exercises, documentation of performance during supervised field experiences, and direct observation of practice by trained observers. These procedures can be aggregated into a coherent body of evidence – kept in a portfolio or some sort of cumulative record – that documents the teaching capacities of each candidate. This portfolio would be submitted for review to the representatives of the National Board of Professional Teaching Standards at some time after the candidate had successfully completed the residency requirements. (Shulman, 1987a, p. 39)

The work of the Stanford Teacher Assessment Project (TAP) focused, then, on the construction of tasks that were intended to serve in the assessment-center portion of the certification assessment. (The progress of this work is recorded in a series of technical reports published by the Stanford TAP between 1988 and 1992.) This research by Shulman and his students into teaching began from an entirely different premise from almost all the previous research in this area. Teachers themselves were consulted about their work, their ideas, their analyses of their own practices, and their sense of what worked and what did not. This early reliance on, and recognition of the importance of, teachers' voices was and continues to be of critical importance in all NBPTS development work. From these searching conversations with accomplished practitioners (the "wisdom-of-practice studies"), Shulman and his students fashioned tasks (the "assessment prototypes") designed primarily for discovery of teachers' ways of knowing, and for their revelatory power in the ongoing search for a definition of expertise in this most dynamic and unpredictable and yet least analyzed of the learned professions. Many seminal articles in the field of performance assessment for teachers grew out of this work and its technical report series, and a number of the nation's current leading education researchers have worked with or directly on this project (Edward Haertel and Samuel Wineburg, to name just two).

THE EARLY DAYS

The NBPTS awarded its initial assessment development contracts in 1990, to two different university-based development groups, the Performance Assessment Laboratory at the University of Georgia (Early Adolescence/ Generalist or EA/G) and the University of Pittsburgh/Connecticut State Department of Education collaborative (Early Adolescence/English Language Arts or EA/ELA). When these developers were funded and began their work on assessment development, much of the foundation conventionally thought of as an essential basis for assessment design was not yet finished. The standards for the certification fields on which the development groups were working were in the initial stages of composition, thus making the domain of assessment a moving target. In addition, assessment developers did not talk to Standards Committee members in these early days, lest the Standards Committee members feel limited by assessment practicalities and thus refrain from articulating important parts of the domain. Furthermore, early assessment developers were urged, through the medium of NBPTS Request for Proposals (RFPs) for assessment development, to consider multi-modal assessment strategies, by which was meant a smorgasbord of techniques that borrowed from realms as disparate as writing and art assessment (the portfolio) and corporate training and staff development (the assessment center).[2] Many parts of Shulman's early model for a new kind of assessment were still being bandied about, including the notion of classroom observation by trained observers, elaborate written assessments, samples of teaching practice, and the kind of elaborated simulation that Shulman's Stanford TAP was at work to define.

   The perceived deficits of conventional multiple-choice testing for the assessment of writing (the inability to directly assess the construct, the focus merely on certain aspects that lend themselves to a five-option item) and the solution that was offered by the use of portfolios (i.e., direct samples of writing) is analogous to the issues surrounding the assessment of teachers' classroom practice. The writing portfolio offered a way to see into what has come to be understood as the real complexities of learning to write well: writing for different purposes and to different audiences, developing robust and useful strategies and processes for writing, and becoming aware of one's own methodologies as a writer. The portfolio itself is designedly a voyage of discovery for its maker, and part of its purpose is the revelation that occurs through the process of collecting and reflecting on the work. Indeed, in many writing assessment portfolios examination of such learning by the learner was part of the task of making the portfolio (Camp, 1993).

In a similar fashion, the teacher portfolio tasks designed by the Stanford TAP researchers were constructed to discover how teachers thought, how they employed their past experience in coping with the present challenges, what heuristics they invented to process the mountain of information they dealt with each day, how they combined knowledge of their subjects with knowledge of students and teaching methods, how issues of classroom management and planning were interwoven with issues of conceptual and process goals for student learning. Many of the TAP tasks explored the responses of teachers to situations (a simulated class made up of role-playing child ringers) or pedagogical problems (a box full of disparate material given to mathematics teachers as the stimulus for a lesson-planning prompt) that researchers believed might reveal on the fly, as it were, the very combination of creativity, ingenuity, and developed knowledge and skill on which accomplished teaching seemed to depend. But the Stanford researchers had never intended to "score" the conversations about teaching they structured with practitioners in the "wisdom-of-practice" studies. And even in the simulations they built as prototypes, they had chosen only five individuals' responses to "score" after their field test. Moreover, they were under no constraints about making and defending summative judgments.

That the tasks might pose problems for replication for many different test takers, that they required the careful attention of highly skilled adminis-trators, watchers, auditors, and interactors, that they yielded extremely interesting results that no one had any idea how to really "score" (though some were clearly much better than others) was, quite properly, not the focus of the researchers' attention. But such issues lie at the very heart of high-stakes assessment, since demonstrable equity and fairness in the delivery and scoring of a valid assessment is what is meant by "legal defensibility." And not being able to deliver the same prompt under the same conditions to *every* candidate, combined with not being able to articulate clear and credible criteria for classifying various performances undermines the utility and fundamental validity of any assessment.

Through these first forays by the Stanford TAP researchers in development, the essential nature of a portfolio, whatever that might mean, as a medium for the measurement of a complex, ill-structured domain like teaching came to be an assumption of all NBPTS assessment strategy. The assessment was to focus on best practice, rather than typical practice; that is, there would be no attempts to generalize about what a teacher's daily practice was like from the assessment data. Rather, the certification would be based on the teacher's demonstration of capability, the achievement of accomplished practice in the instances captured through the assessment. Determined to break with the usual kind of standardized assessment common in education, which samples a domain of knowledge, skills, or abilities by selecting what may seem to test-takers randomly chosen and quite isolated and decontextualized pieces of the domain and then, through the conventions of classical test theory, hypothesizes about the test-taker's knowledge of the overall domain, the NBPTS set out from the beginning to participate in "authentic" assessment. Since the goal was to make the assessment as true as possible to the "real" world of teaching, some kind of performance assessment was mandated.[3] But what, exactly, that performance assessment should look like was not as clear. The burgeoning interest in portfolio assessment for students around the United States coincided with the beginning of the NBPTS's work. Portfolio assessment seemed at that time to offer a very attractive counter to many deficits critics cited in more traditional assessments. Furthermore, in these early stages, a portfolio seemed an almost infinitely flexible strategy for assessment that could, in itself, encompass multiple assessment modalities and occasions.

Proponents argued that portfolio assessment privileges individual judgment and personal choice: it depends, after all, on the selections of the person being assessed for its substance. In addition, portfolios accommodate complexity and individual differences. The portfolio-maker can explain his/her meaning at leisure, there is no timed and straight-jacketed response mode, each portfolio maker is *assumed* to be different from the other. Portfolios also seemed to accommodate, indeed welcome, a very broad range of types of evidence of accomplishment and achievement. In many ways, the portfolio, a collection of artifacts and samples of work, seemed an ideal medium for the representation of a teacher's practice. It could be assembled over time, it could be shaped by the details of a teacher's own context, it could reflect much more closely the actual complexities and dynamic surprises of a teacher's working life. Finally, portfolios for teachers, like student portfolios, could themselves be what Dennie Wolf calls critically important "episodes of learning" (Wolf, 1993) that would, by engaging teachers in the assessment tasks, develop the analytical and reflective skills so necessary to the reformation of the teaching profession.

The second part of the assessment, a two-day "assessment center," was designed to bring teachers together and allow them to engage in a professional dialogue (very similar to the "wisdom of practice" studies at Stanford), as well as respond to simulation-based exercises. Particular focus on a teacher's content knowledge and what Shulman called "pedagogical content knowledge" (Shulman, 1987b, p. 8) was to be the purpose of the assessment center. Techniques long used in industrial and organization psychology, but little known to education – in-basket exercises, role-playing simulations, leaderless group discussions – were specified for this assessment-center portion of the assessment.

Still influenced by the suspicion that attended any assessment of teachers that did not involve live observation by knowledgeable viewers, the early NBPTS RFPs also specified that classroom observation should be explored by developers, in addition to the portfolio and assessment center components. (This requirement was later dropped as being impractical given difficulties of both finding and training a sufficient number of assessors who would be able to travel to candidates' classrooms, and of maintaining adequate levels of training and comparability among these assessors.) At the same time, the NBPTS funded a groundbreaking study of videotape as a medium for representing teaching (Frederiksen & Wolfe, 1992) that demonstrated with little ambiguity just how powerful videotape could be as a medium for information about teachers' practice. Equal in importance, however, according to Frederiksen and Wolfe's study, was the power of videotape to help teachers learn to engage in professional discussions with each other, to break down the traditional barriers of isolation still the norm in most school settings, and to focus analytical attention on teaching episodes that could be revisited rather than merely remembered.

At around the same time that the initial developers were at work on the first assessment designs, serious scholarly consideration of the conceptual underpinnings of performance assessment was growing. In 1989, for example, Grant Wiggins (1989) (who seems to have been the originator of the catch phrase "authentic assessment") and J. R. Frederiksen and A. Collins published influential articles that emphasized the consequential aspects of the validity of such assessments, i.e., their effects on teaching strategies and student learning, as well as the qualities by which the validity of such assessments should be judged. In 1991, Linn, Baker, and Dunbar published a seminal article that asserted the need to "rethink the criteria by which the quality of educational assessments are judged" and suggested a set of such criteria. In 1992, Messick addressed the National Council on Measurement in Education on just these validity criteria and others, and illustrated how each of them were contained within the general validity standards for construct validity (American Educational Research Association, American Psychological Association, and the National Council for Measurement in Education (AERA, APA, & NCME), 1985; Messick, 1989) – a speech later revised and published in 1994.

In each of these articles, important conceptual and analytical criteria – most importantly, the twin dangers of construct under representation and construct irrelevant variance – were articulated in the context of performance assessments. These criteria would eventually make their way explicitly into design decisions we made for the NBPTS assessments. The discoveries developers made by trial and error, described in the following section, confirmed again and again the centrality of the validity issues these theoreticians raised – and the cost of initially ignoring them.

THE INITIAL ASSESSMENT DESIGNS

The early NBPTS assessments enthusiastically embraced the promises of "authentic" assessment. Throughout these early explorations of assessment possibilities, the emphasis on exploration of innovative and often untried assessment modalities led to stringent avoidance of the conventional, usually highly analytical and hence – it was believed – reductive methodologies. Indeed, the notion that this assessment was more than a means to the certification decision was a crucial NBPTS assumption about the assessment program, which aimed to model and reform by its very existence, in addition to the exemplary teachers it would certify and send forth as reforming agents. This reform-through-assessment approach is aligned with what Frederiksen and Collins (1989, p. 27) called systemically valid assessment that "induces in the educational system curricular and instructional changes that foster the development of cognitive skills that the test is designed to measure."

Portfolio tasks in the 1993–1994 edition of the EA/ELA assessment, for example, were first cousins of Stanford TAP tasks. The portfolio consisted of three very complex tasks: one focused on the teaching of writing, one on the teaching of literature, and one on a teacher's command of planning instruction and interconnecting the strands of English Language Arts over an entire instructional unit. The requirements were formidable for each task. For example, in the Planning and Teaching Exercise, which focused on a three-week unit of teaching, teachers were asked to submit the following artifacts: a 45-minute videotape, a detailed three-week lesson plan (with daily entries showing what the teacher will do, the students will do, and the times allotted), instructional artifacts relevant to the videotape, and a detailed analytical commentary with no page limit specified, but at least 10 pages recommended. In each task, no matter what the teacher's context or teaching circumstances, candidates were required to focus on issues of multicultural education and its challenges in their classrooms. Later this focus was recognized to be an unnatural imposition for some teachers and an overemphasis on the importance of this theme in the EA/ELA Standards.

In a similar fashion, one of the three initial pilot entries from the Adolescence and Young Adulthood/Mathematics (AYA/M) assessment asked teachers to design a unit that was built around project-based learning, put their students into groups during this unit, design a rubric with the students to evaluate the final projects, videotape at least two student groups presenting their project results to the class, submit the rubrics as the class used them, and write a 10-page analytical commentary. Eager to match the freedom and creativity of the classroom-based portion of the assessment in the assessment center portion of the assessment, the initial NBPTS assessments given at these centers lasted for no less than two days. Candidates were required to travel to the center closest to them and there to undergo a series of exercises. The actual exercises took more than eight hours each day to administer. In the case of the EA/G assessment, one of the days lasted almost 11 hours. The exercises were very elaborate, involving structured interviews, a unit planned around a piece of commercial software that had been sent out to candidates beforehand, leaderless group discussions that were videotaped, and extensive written exercises. Many of these exercises recalled assessment prototypes developed by Stanford TAP participants, and part of the design was the inclusion of time and encouragement for teacher candidates to engage with each other in "professional dialogue."

For the assessment center portion of the English Language Arts assessment in particular, the kinds of tasks explored by the researchers at Stanford were fundamental influences. The blend of Shulman's "wisdom-of-practice" research with the assessment prototypes led to interesting development approaches in this case. For example, teachers were asked to read a group of age-appropriate novels prior to coming to the assessment center. When they arrived, they were grouped with a varying number of other teachers, usually unknown to them, and videotaped participating in a leaderless group discussion. The premise of the discussion was that they were a curriculum committee whose charge was to choose novels from the given group (and defend that choice) for an urban school district with students from multiple ethnic and cultural backgrounds. The design assumed that such a discussion would benefit the teachers and allow them an opportunity to talk to other professionals, advantages that were quite separate from the function of the exercise as a measurement tool. In another exercise from the same assessment, teachers were given a group of student papers to read and then interviewed about their insights into these students' writing.

While it is true that all of the early assessment tasks were innovative and unlike anything else ever offered as a possible assessment for teachers,[4] attempts to score these tasks led to the realization that the romance of task design, and not a disciplined approach to matching evidence with standards-based decisions about teachers had dominated the NBPTS development scene through the development of the first two assessments. Throughout this initial design phase, which lasted about three years (1991–1994), the focus was almost entirely on articulating an assessment methodology that would be commensurate with the tremendous complexity of real teaching. The line was blurred between what kinds of tasks and requirements would be appropriate and useful for high-stakes, summative assessment (which certification assessment attached to financial rewards for those who achieve it most assuredly is), and what kinds of tasks and requirements would allow teachers to learn and explore important and under-emphasized aspects of their practice. In fact, that such a distinction might exist was not really a topic of discussion. What was much less effectively discussed than the differences between good assessment and good professional development was how the richness and complexity built into the portfolio and assessment-center tasks might be fairly evaluated, and what structures might shape such evaluative activities.[5]

CRITIQUE AND ANALYSIS

From the perspective of a national assessment program that must be standardized – i.e., be able to offer to all candidates who qualify the same opportunity to perform regardless of any variables that are not directly related to the constructs being measured – it appears, in retrospect, that the tremendous creative vitality and powerful revelations unleashed by Shulman and his students and by the growing sophistication of writing assessment through portfolios had curious effects on the early assessment designs. Perhaps the most succinct way to characterize these effects would be to say that the purposes and structures appropriate for research were confused with the purposes and structures necessary for sound assessment. As mentioned earlier, the desire to provide candidates with rich professional development opportunities sometimes overlooked, or at least blurred, summative assessment needs. Furthermore, in the push to be innovative, creative, and unfettered by conventional practice, developers forgot to think about what value wisdom of practice as assessment developers might add to the final assessment design. We eventually learned that we needed to approach the development process with construct measurement at the forefront, without losing sight of the importance of task design. We needed to pay more attention to specific ways in which construct irrelevant variance might be designed into our structures, we needed to engage with the difficult issues of depth of measurement versus breadth of coverage of the domain, and we needed to consider with some rigor the meaning of freedom and constraint *for assessment* purposes.

The legacy of the early NBPTS design efforts can be summed up in three critical lessons: detailed articulation of scoring criteria must be part of initial task design, complex domains are not *necessarily* best measured by operationally complex assessments, and not everything in the standards was equally critical to measure in order to make the certification decision. In the process of recognizing these three critical lessons, we also learned that professional development and high-stakes assessment are not always compatible.

How assessment developers should judge the success of their efforts was clear from the outset. The NBPTS had developed, in addition to the rather specific directions about assessment modalities mentioned above, the criteria by which assessment developers' ideas and products should be evaluated. These were the APPLE criteria, and they remain the highest and most rigorous of standards by which NBPTS assessment developers can be judged: *Administratively* feasible, *Professionally* acceptable, *Publicly* credible, *Legally* defensible, *Economically* affordable.[6] While a great deal of care and attention was being paid to professional acceptability and public credibility, less attention was directed to the issue of economic affordability or feasibility of administration.

It is consideration of the APPLE criteria, and perhaps more importantly, of their interactive effects, that shaped the changes in assessment design during the next five years, following the initial appearance of the first NBPTS certification assessments as field tests (and, indeed, continues to shape the latest design innovations). It is interesting to note the overlap of these five evaluation criteria with the essential validity criteria discussed in Messick's (1994) article.

Lesson one – know precisely how a task will be scored BEFORE you ask people to respond to its demands – was the (searing) lesson of the initial field tests of EA/G and EA/ELA. It was the experience of the first field-test scoring sessions that proved to be the catalyst for new ways of thinking about assessment design for NBPTS assessments. The EA/G portfolio included one task that took assessors between four and five hours to *single score* and the field-test version of the EA/ELA assessment could not, in fact, be scored at all using the originally proposed scoring approach because it was so labor-intensive – training alone took about two weeks, *for each portfolio task*. And *one* of the assessor training tools was a 900-page manual.

The costs associated with the early scoring needs of these behemoth entries were prohibitive, far exceeding any fee charged by even the most expensive certification assessments in the United States, many of which are designed for professionals whose incomes far exceed those of teachers. But even without the consideration of economic affordability the scoring systems were unworkable from a strictly practical point of view: getting the assessors trained, keeping the evaluations they made consistent and credible, moving the material around. And from the most basic of validity criteria, the reliability of the scores, it was clear that a design that relied on very few, very large tasks about which reliable assessor judgments could not be made, had to be overhauled.

A new discipline had to be applied to the development process. In conjunction with the teacher development teams, we had to begin to ask ourselves at every step "Why do we require this piece of evidence?" We began to see the value in creating the rubrics as part of the task to help us address this very question. A cyclical process was set up – as we clarified what we would privilege in the rubric, we were able to refine what the task directions told candidates to do and as we further understood the scope (and oftentimes also limitations) of the task we were able to further clarify the rubric. This evolutionary process for task development continued through the teacher members of the development teams trying out various iterations in their classrooms and the wider national pilot-testing process. Each cycle provided an opportunity to ensure that the Standards, the task directions, and the rubrics were converging. It also made sense that this knowledge of what the task required should be shared with candidates rather than being kept a secret. Thus, in the next edition of certificates that were developed candidates were not scored on any aspect of their performance that they had not been explicitly asked to demonstrate and discuss.

In the initial foray into scoring for high-stakes, summative purposes, the NBPTS began to see that complex portfolio-based assessments used for certification purposes posed challenges that no assessment program had ever faced, much less resolved. How to keep the richness and complexity of the tasks and also to satisfy the imperative of replicability, equity in delivery, and scorability was a formidable problem. And it appeared that, of all the APPLE criteria, administrative feasibility might be the most important in shaping design decisions. Administrative feasibility – the operations side of assessment – always sounds pedestrian. The conventional view is that after all of the conceptual and developmental work – the intellectual part of assessment development – is complete, then someone else figures out how much to ship, how to get the boxes out, which computers to use, and how to package and convey materials and all the myriad other details of assessment delivery.

Whatever the veracity of this view for more conventional assessments, in complex performance assessment like the NBPTS assessments, administrative feasibility is a fundamental validity issue. For example, in the EA/ELA assessment center exercises described above, the difficulty of training interviewers to a consistent standard, as well as replication of one of the difficulties the TAP researchers had much earlier identified with their own interviews – the difficulty of when to probe and when to move on – undermined the validity of performances on the videotaped interview (Haertel, 1990, p. 285). It was impossible to group candidates into same-size groups for discussions. Issues of control and dominance rather than content and pedagogical knowledge shaped the leaderless group discussion performances. And in much the same way several portfolio tasks stumbled against the issue of administrative feasibility in one of two ways: first, some tasks assumed such a narrow view of accomplished teaching that it became impossible for teachers to comply with task directions without significant changes and disruptions to their practice; and second, some tasks asked for such extensive documentation that the responses created were so voluminous as to be impossible to deal with. As the next section will demonstrate, the current tasks give space for candidates to select appropriate teaching and learning approaches for their particular students' needs in a particular time.

In short, these early designs, for all their flair and innovative surfaces, were nearly impossible to administer outside a laboratory. The initial engagement with the difficulties of scoring assessments that were designed with such fidelity to state-of-the-art research and reform ideals required a return to some fundamental validity questions that are, or should be, part of every developer's wisdom of practice. These questions in turn led to a careful reconsideration of such issues as domain specification, the effects on design of an assessment based on standards, the use of portfolio methodology, and, finally, the shaping power of operational concerns.

The critical questions that we ask ourselves in order to determine whether or not an assessment can offer supports of various kinds for validity claims are always difficult to answer with any certainty. They include all of the following: Does the assessment measure what it purports to measure? How do we know? Is what it measures worth knowing about? Is the information the assessment yields relevant to the kinds of decisions it engenders? Does performance on the assessment vary based on variance in test takers' mastery of the test's targeted content? Does performance vary based on other unintended sources of variance in test takers' or testing conditions? What are the consequences for the test taker of taking the test? Did we intend for those to be the consequences?

These are vexing questions when the domain of assessment can be precisely stated and the mode of assessment rigidly controlled by the test maker, as in a multiple-choice test of, say, basic chemistry. When the domain of assessment is loosely structured and dynamic, like teaching, and further obscured by an absence of agreement – or even a common vocabulary – among teaching professionals about the basic structure or taxonomy of the domain and what constitutes evidence of accomplishment in it, these questions become very difficult indeed to answer. And even the definition of "validity" itself is broadened and transformed by the sheer size, length, and complexity of performance assessments of the magnitude of the NBPTS certification assessments. What we learned through the early years of trial and error tends to confirm the notion that validity for such assessments is most appropriately seen as a function of the interplay of many parts of the assessment system: the design decisions, the task directions and their mode of presentation, the operational details that attend the delivery of the assessment, and the scoring criteria and their application and implementation.

As I mentioned above, in the beginning it seemed that as assessment developers we could hardly do less than meet the NBPTS Standards on their own high ground. An assessment worthy of those standards, we thought, would need to demonstrate our comprehension of the standards' richness and our own knowledge of the teaching profession. We needed to embody the values of those standards in assessment specifications by creating tasks as rich and multifarious as the teaching practice they were designed to capture. Furthermore, eager to alter the narrow focus of assessment and demonstrate that it could itself be an instrument of reform, the designers of the earliest NBPTS portfolios designed tasks to initiate practitioners into the most important aspects of the reform movement's embrace of reflective practice, to operate as catalysts for change in classrooms, rather than as structures that might capture what teachers were actually doing in those classrooms.

By trying to match the complexity of the tasks to the complexity of the standards, and trying to create tasks that also led to deep learning, we made a fundamental error in judging possible answers to some of those basic validity questions I mentioned above. What we created on our first pass was an assessment with tremendous face validity. However, the design left no space for evidence from the very people we aspired to evaluate. We had filled most of the social space in the assessment with our own demonstrations of what we thought, what we knew, what we hoped, what we wished for about teaching and student learning, and how we wished to alter teachers in the process of assessing them. And when the time came to score these tasks, we learned that we had not thought much at all about the teachers who were so gamely responding to our directions. We did not really know with any precision what it was we were measuring, and, of course, we could not really tell when we measured it. And the difficulties with scoring criteria and methods also led us to consider more critically task design for richness and complexity – was the *appearance* of complexity actually interfering with good assessment?

In addition, the type of design mandated by the NBPTS for its certification assessments – multi-media portfolios assembled over time and elaborate timed simulations to which teachers responded on demand – placed this ambitious new certification assessment squarely in the camp of "authentic" assessment. In choosing this label, we acted on an assumption so widely held that it is often treated as axiomatic, and that is that authentic assessments mirror in their design the constructs they measure. Thus, if one aims to measure a complex and dynamic domain, the assessment used would itself be complex and dynamic. And, of course, by contrast, assessments that look rather simple and whose design characteristics and limitations we understand, like multiple choice, are *ipso facto* appropriate only for rather simple domains. And to the extent that multiple-choice tests attempt the assessment of more complex domains, they are recognizable as inauthentic by their methodology alone. That there might be some virtuous reasons for these limits imposed on assessment designs, other than the craven ones like cost and efficiency, did not occur to us until later, after some suffering and the acquisition of renewed respect for examinations of cost and efficiency. Indeed, we learned that such examinations may themselves be part of an examination of larger validity issues in performance assessment.[7]

What we learned we had to create was an assessment design that demanded that teachers demonstrate what *they* knew, thought, hoped, and wished for, and that helped them to make that demonstration as clear and cogent as possible to assessors who, though skilled practitioners themselves, had no personal knowledge of that teacher's teaching context or philosophy. We learned to respect the voice of the teacher by allowing candidates to articulate their teaching context, their pedagogical decisions, and their analysis of those decisions so that the response could be judged in the light of the particular context.

The first lesson – know first what constitutes evidence, and evidence of what if you want to be able to score performance tasks – emerged forcibly from the initial attempts to score field test responses. The second – maybe we had over-constructed these performance tasks and confused both ourselves and the teacher candidates – emerged as a possible driver of our scoring dilemmas. In rethinking the assessment design and how we might get out of the way of the teachers themselves, a third critical lesson emerged: we had designed the initial assessments with insufficient analysis and understanding of the domain.

I have alluded above to the simultaneous development of assessments and Standards in the initial NBPTS assessment development efforts. This could lead to misfits between domain specifications and assessments in any field, but when the NBPTS Standards themselves were breaking new ground and articulating the vocabulary that could begin to define accomplished practice, the problem grew much more daunting. Both the NBPTS Standards – in articulating the values and criteria – and the Stanford TAP – in articulating actual habits of mind, behaviors, judgments, and actions – were constructing a vocabulary that carved out a domain where one had not existed before. The sheer size and complexity of the domain of accomplished teaching was overwhelming. It seemed that teaching resembled no other professional work, except possibly emergency room medicine, in the volatility of the working environment, the practitioner's lack of control over the conditions and even the substance of the work he/she was required to perform, and the constant and unremitting demands for physical, intellectual, moral, and psychological alertness that the work demanded. Given the complexity and extent of the domain, it seemed that any sample of relevant occasions on which to base an inference about accomplishment (which is, after all, what assessment is supposed to be doing) was much less firmly grounded than assessment design decisions usually are. So even the initial assessment design work of construct definition and articulation was beset with confusion.

The NBPTS Standards (now complete), gradually caught up with the development effort and, by 1999 were in final draft form when assessment development began. Each Standards document became the official domain of each of the assessments. And they expressed a very clear set of values about teaching and learning, one in which student learning is primary, all students are valued, multiple talents and ways of learning are cherished, and teachers are expected to command the content they teach as well as the full range of pedagogical expertise required to make all of these values a reality each day in the classroom. The articulation of the domain through the NBPTS Standards in each certification area was itself such a tremendous accomplishment, and the Standards were (and are) a profound contribution to the body of professional knowledge that informs teaching at every level.

However, the Standards are not themselves assessment specifications, nor can the domain articulated through these Standards be assessed in a way that matches tasks directly, Standard by Standard, to the domain. Our early attempts to design an assessment that could measure the NBPTS Standards were based on a critical mistaken assumption: to measure accomplishment in a domain articulated by standards, the assessment had to encompass those standards, to include them. What we learned is that not everything in those standards is assessable by current measures. We did not always recognize this lack of knowledge either, because it is not as self-evident as it may sound. Furthermore, we learned that while the standards must divide up the relevant parts of the domain in order to allow for full articulation of the nuances of accomplished teaching, the assessment could not avoid simultaneously assessing multiple standards by its tasks. Getting at standards in isolation from other standards led directly to "inauthentic" tasks and an impoverished vision of the teacher's work.

Furthermore, development of the assessment tasks became harder when we considered the nature of the domain specification in the NBPTS Standards. The Standards articulate quite specifically the nature of accomplished teaching in particular fields and at particular developmental levels. What they do not do is discriminate among all the qualities and characteristics they articulate: everything is important, nothing is either less or more important. The assessment design must choose from among all of these qualities and characteristics, for several reasons. Some of them we had (and have) no idea how to assess. This is a reflection on the state of our art, not a judgment of the Standards. And, as our encounter with scoring and task richness so clearly demonstrated, we could not ask for everything because we would end by being able to do very little with it. We had to make choices and be selective, not only because the candidates have a day job, but also because we could not follow through on our part of the transaction and equitably evaluate the candidates' work if we did not set some limits. So the topography of the assessment represented an interpretation of the Standards document, rather than a reflection of it.

Recognizing that not everything in the Standards could be assessed led to the next set of validity concerns we discovered as we grappled with the design of complex performance assessments. Simply put, the issues became

- What should we ask for?
- What will we do with it when we get it?

This was the area in which we discovered most painfully our inability to sample just anything, or to purport to measure certain parts of the domain of accomplished teaching, at least directly. We created assessment tasks like those described above that, in their concern for getting teachers to demonstrate student learning over time, asked for a rich array of student work. When that arrived, it turned out to be as much as 100–150 pages of material *for a single teacher*. In addition, we asked for videotape of students reporting the results of group investigations to the whole class. Not only were these extremely taxing for an assessor to watch attentively, they told us virtually nothing at all about the teacher's practice, except perhaps his/her good fortune in having articulate and poised children to videotape, or the contrary. Furthermore, we discovered the importance of conscious and deliberate sampling demands on the part of the developer – complete freedom to choose sounded much more "authentic" when we began. It became clear as we reaped the whirlwind that we had done the candidates no favors and we had dealt the validity of the assessment as a whole a body blow by this rather laissez-faire approach to rigorous requirements. What we needed to do was to consider the domain as articulated in the Standards, and from the constructs in that domain extrapolate to the kinds of evidence we might require that would bear on measurement of those constructs.[8]

From asking for evidence we had no idea how to use, evaluate, compare, or store, we learned that in performance assessment every design decision is an operational decision. And since all performance artifacts must be evaluated by human beings – themselves professional practitioners in the field being evaluated – who are intensively trained to do just that in the same way for every candidate, what artifacts one asks for and the physical and cognitive demands they place on the evaluator is a critical validity issue.

We started out with the sense that we were researchers whose primary focus was how to reform teaching, until our painful encounter with field-test scoring made us realize that we were research-based assessment developers whose primary interest was how to assess teaching and whose primary responsibility was a summative assessment, though the means to that assessment might well yield (and has yielded) a treasure trove of evidence for researchers, as well as providing candidates with a profoundly important professional development experience. Recognizing that we were assessment developers more than researchers forced us to see that we needed to focus on issues of evidence and inference, and on the imperatives imposed by Standards-based assessment. We could not measure directly how a teacher thinks, how she combines what she knows about a subject with what she knows about teaching methods, the particular – and usually both rapid and complicated – inferences about children and their learning she makes all day every day, and a whole host of other important qualities and characteristics. We had to design tasks to capture evidence that will allow us to make strong inferences – and inferences as close as possible to the thing being measured – about a teacher's practice.

Furthermore, these tasks were obliged to offer every teacher, regardless of the very uneven distribution of resources, assistance, support, and challenge across classrooms in the United States, an equal opportunity to display excellence in the context of his/her own teaching setting. Score variance could not be due to the readiness of a teacher's students to learn, to the teacher's access to sophisticated equipment and a rich array of instructional resources, to the teacher's affinity for a particular style of instruction regardless of the students she teaches. And, of course, the task had to allow us to compare all candidates and simultaneously leave sufficient room for all candidates to demonstrate what they were really doing.

An inevitable inference from all of these lessons was also that we could not privilege teachers' professional development equally with a valid classification assessment that led to real life-changing consequences for the teacher participants. In many cases, what we needed to do to create a good assessment meant a less rich and rewarding professional development task for participants.

What we learned from our struggles with the consequences of our earliest designs – candidate responses and the difficulty of scoring them – were some important distinctions among sources of evidence, and some critical connections among elements of the assessment design. Finally, the issue of task directions – what to say, how much to explain, and how to keep it simple – emerged as a crucial element in the validity of the entire assessment. The following section outlines how the lessons learned were then applied to the development of the next wave of 10 certificates over three years.

DESIGN ARCHITECTURE FROM 1996 TO 1999

In the portfolio portion of the assessment it became clear that the two most powerful sources of direct evidence of a teacher's practice were examples of student work and videotape of classroom interaction that involved discourse among students and the teacher. These had been among the sources of evidence solicited from candidates from the earliest drafts of NBPTS assessments. However, it was only after the experience with the initial field-test scorings that the full implications and influence of "choice" in an assessment portfolio emerged as a critical factor in assessment design. Which student work samples teachers chose, what particular occasions in the classroom were selected for videotape excerpts – these decisions essentially determined the course of a teacher's response to an assessment task. And, because the notions of the portfolio as a voyage of discovery and the teacher as learner/researcher were fundamental assumptions in the early portfolio designs, virtually no guidance about making such choices for this particular occasion and purpose had been given to candidates.

Indeed, given the influence of using portfolios in writing situations, the commentary was only minimally structured for candidates, since portfolios are chosen as a methodology in order to accommodate individual differences. To structure the discourse within a portfolio, it was believed, was to undermine this basic respect for the candidate's autonomy. As a result, the commentary received from the candidate was in many cases only loosely connected to these artifacts of direct evidence. As a result of placing the burden of choice and structure on the candidate, the assessment unintentionally measured a candidate's sophistication with portfolio assessment methodology. Teachers who were canny about choosing evidence – which is likely not the same thing as being an accomplished practitioner, and may not even be highly correlated with accomplished practice – and good at structuring a narrative about their teaching, though not necessarily a narrative that explicated and reflected on the evidence submitted, looked much more accomplished.

Re-examination of the domain articulated in the Standards and of our task directions in light of these considerations led to some refocusing of what tasks should be asked of teacher candidates and what should be included in a set of task directions.[9] First, it was clear that the developers' beliefs, thoughts, and understandings in relation to the NBPTS vision were irrelevant to the work at hand. Thinking, then, of the intended audience – the teacher candidates – and about the primacy of equity concerns, we refashioned our approach. It was crucial that every candidate be required to meet the same task requirements – there could be no "optional" evidence. Nor could the requirements be such that access to resources of any kind beyond the media most essential to the assessment (a video camera, student work samples, a typewriter, or word processor for the analytical commentaries) would make a difference in a candidate's chances to perform well. Furthermore, it was our responsibility to level the performance field as much as possible. We needed to remove as sources of variance differential access to certain kinds of information.

Thus, in the portfolio task directions, we provided detailed advice on making good choices based on the actual candidate samples we had seen. In addition, we thoroughly structured the analytical commentary so that ability to organize complex prose about a very complicated professional job would not be part of the domain of measurement.[10] And we required that the analysis be focused very directly on the samples of evidence the teacher had chosen and that the teacher extrapolate from these samples to the larger world of his or her teaching in general. Finally, the domain basis of each task, quoted directly from the Standards document for the particular assessment, appeared as the opening section of each set of task directions, and the scoring rubric (also Standards-based) appeared as a section of task directions. In other words, the match between the evidence a candidate was asked to provide and the evidence that the rubric would privilege was seamless – if it was important, we asked for it. There was no hidden agenda (see Appendix A for the full text of the directions for an EA/ELA portfolio task from this period).

Second, we reconsidered the entire scope of the assessment as a whole, with particular attention to validity concerns. The early designs had prized an approach to task construction that never repeated anything. However, if we were to take even a small step toward one critical underpinning of assessment validity, generalizability, we needed to quite deliberately design overlapping samples of evidence. In the earliest assessment designs, a teacher could respond to all portfolio entries using a very limited selection of students and classes. In the restructured portfolio we mandated the sampling of classroom-based evidence so that multiple students as well as multiple occasions over time were included in the evidence. In the assessment center portion of the assessment, early designs encouraged (in fact, required) teachers to respond to prompts in terms of what they would do in their own classrooms, based on their experience with the simulation situation. If they had no experience with the simulation situation – which in some cases would be quite likely, since it suggested things as an urban, multi-ethnic student context for the prompt – it was too bad for the candidate. It was extremely hard to figure out what to do with a candidate's sincere and earnest account of what he or she would do under certain circumstances. It seemed much more probing and productive of evidence we might trust to pose a structured problem that all teachers of a particular subject at a particular level might be expected to know how to handle. For example, when teachers of EA/ELA are given, in advance of the assessment center, a series of articles on second-language learning to read and consider, and then asked to evaluate examples of oral and written languages from an English language learner in terms of the student's language status, additional information needed to plan instruction, and suggested strategies for instruction and assessment, all teachers at this level should be able to respond (see Appendix B for the full specifications of the EA/ELA assessment center from this period).

All the changes in design approach led us to consider whether *looking* authentic, i.e., privileging open choice and discovery and avoiding structured response protocols, might be rather different from *being* authentic. Surely the latter would mean that we created an assessment architecture that allowed accomplished practice to shine through, whether or not the practitioner had any experience at all with portfolio assessment or simulations. And surely also authenticity would entail intense scrutiny of the evidence closest to the work itself, with the fewest possible distractions or excursions into abstractions about teaching in general (not *these* students at *this* time in *this* place, or the characteristics of this particular work sample or stimulus) or beliefs and feelings about Education writ large.

What came to characterize our approach both to task design, and to scoring, was a focus on the difference between the surface features of teaching and the underlying substantive structure of a teacher's command of the essential elements of professional knowledge and practice as they are defined in the NBPTS standards. Defining the difference between surface and substance, and assisting candidates in focusing on substance through their analytical and reflective writing became the most important task for assessment developers. We articulated a deceptively simple structure for the

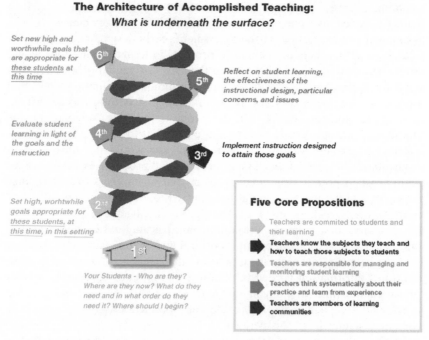

Fig. 1.   Architecture of Accomplished Teaching.

analysis of responses, as well as the analysis of the task directions to candidates, shown in Fig. 1.

This diagram, which is still used in both assessment design and scoring as the central graphical representation of the NBPTS definition of accomplished teaching, shows that an accomplished practitioner always has the same intellectual framework for her teaching, no matter what the surface features of her teaching context. And the order of the analytical work that supports accomplished teaching is also invariant, though doubtless far more subtle and rapid in actual practice. As the diagram suggests (at the bottom), an accomplished teacher begins with an assessment of who these learners are, what they know and are able to do, and where she intends to lead their learning. Planning instruction for each student and each class is based on this knowledge of the particular students in the particular context. And every instructional effort is accompanied by assessment of what the students learned. The reflection is an opportunity for the teacher to question whether the students met the learning goals, whether some did not, what the next steps in the learning sequence should be, and in this reflection the accomplished teacher links what actually happened with what was designed to happen. The results of that reflection feed directly back into knowing the students and their learning, new instructional design, further reflection and so on.

The diagram deliberately uses a double helix to illustrate this cycle in order to indicate the complexity of this process because the accomplished teacher is conducting the process at multiple levels: for the class, for particular individuals, for the lesson, for the unit, and for the entire year. The critical elements of accomplished practice, then, had nothing to do with resources, particular teaching styles, and the use of one textbook or curriculum over another. Accomplished practice was about thinking about learners and learning, and making conscious and deliberate choices that fostered learning for particular students.

By means of this analytical tool, we began to define the differences between what things "looked like" in any particular classroom – which was, of course, very divergent in any group of candidates – and the ways in which accomplished practice, regardless of its "look" shared common underlying architectural features.

The architecture of all NBPTS assessments built on the strengths of portfolio as an assessment methodology as well as on the power of simulation-based, structured prompts in the assessment center. The portfolio originally consisted of six separate tasks, four of which were classroom-based and contextualized by the candidate's own teaching situation. The other two addressed constructs fundamental to the Standards-based definition of accomplished practice: a teacher's work with families and the whole school community in the service of student learning and a teacher's accomplishments in the teaching profession as it is connected to student learning (termed "Documented Accomplishments" entries) (see Appendix C for the overall assessment design for the EA/ELA assessment from this period).

The candidate was constrained by the task directions and overall selection rules in ways that served two purposes. The first was to provide extensive scaffolding for the teacher's deliberative and analytical commentary on his/her work, so that inexperience with analysis and reflection did not prevent the thoughtful and accomplished practitioner from demonstrating his/her abilities. Second, the selection rules assured some breadth in the selection of classroom-based evidence, even for the teacher in a self-contained classroom. The requirement that student work samples and videotaped classroom interactions be taken from separate units and separate students, and, when teachers teach multiple classes, from different classes, provided a kind of minimum coverage of some of the teacher's instructional terrain. The portfolio tasks always asked for evidence from two sources – direct evidence in the form of student work and videotaped classroom interaction, artifacts of instruction, documents and verifications of accomplishment – and the teacher's own analysis of these materials. It was in the nexus formed by the direct evidence and the teacher's comments on the meaning and significance of that evidence that the heart of the assessment lay.

The assessment center, originally two full days built around teachers' conversations and interactions with each other – clearly privileging professional development – became a single day of computer-delivered written assessment, designed to assess content and pedagogical content knowledge. The prompts were always based on a stimulus that simulated a problem or situation central to a teacher's practice in the subject area and at the developmental level being assessed. The prompts were deliberately kept as consistent and invariant as possible (with an eye to comparability and replicability), while the stimulus was changed from administration to administration. Common stimulus materials included student work samples, instructional resource packages, professional articles, and content-specific artifacts like reproductions of art works (for the Early Adolescence and Young Adulthood Art (EAYA/A) assessment) or complex multi-step problems in which process, not result, is critical (for the Adolescence and Young Adulthood Mathematics (AYA/M) assessment).

The shift in the focus of the assessment center signaled our belief that we could not provide teacher candidates with both a meaningful opportunity to interact with their professional colleagues and a valid and reliable set of assessment center exercises in the context of economically affordable assessment. In addition, the design of the assessment center valued both content knowledge *and* pedagogical content knowledge. No assessment-center design consisted entirely of content knowledge assessment with no link to the candidate's classroom practice or pedagogical knowledge (see Appendix B).

THE NEXT GENERATION OF NBPTS ASSESSMENTS

For three years, development proceeded at an impressive pace and the NBPTS expanded the areas covered to 16 certificates with the result that by 1999 82% of US teachers had access to an NBPTS certificate in their field (Harman, 2002, personal communication).[11] Development was about to begin on the elementary Art certificate and two certificates for Physical

Education when ETS was given permission to begin work on the Next Generation of National Board assessments, using these three new certificates as the test-bed. The Next Generation assessments provided an opportunity to reflect on the lessons learned in the previous three years, to respond to candidates' comments and concerns, to apply psychometric lessons learned, and to respond to criticisms of the NBPTS that its assessment was insufficiently focused on content knowledge. The following paragraphs outline how and why the next generation of NBPTS certificates differed from what had been previously developed.

In an effort to better understand the contribution that individual portfolio tasks made to the overall reliability of the assessment and the certification decision, a small study was carried out to investigate the effects of removing one or more entries/exercises on the overall reliability of the assessment. Data from the 1997–1998 cohorts of the EA/G and MC/G certificates were used. Two measures of reliability[12] were calculated after excluding score data from one classroom-based entry (either student work or video-based), one documented accomplishments entry, and one assessment center exercise. As expected, reliability did drop but not to unacceptable levels, as shown in Table 1.

In fact, while this study provided some reassurance that all 10 exercises were not necessary to ensure high reliability, the Next Generation of assessments still has 10 components.

Development work began with the portfolio entries and two significant changes occurred. First, the total number of portfolio entries changed from six to four by combining the two documented accomplishment entries into one and having one less classroom-based entry. Second, the format of each entry was modified. These changes were driven in part by a greater understanding of how much information was truly sufficient to make a

Table 1. Contribution that Individual Portfolio Tasks to Overall Reliability of the Assessment and the Certification Decision.

	Exercise Reliability			Assessor Reliability		
	All 10 entries/ exercises	1AC, 1 DAE 1 SW removed	1AC, 1 DAE 1 video removed	All 10 entries/ exercises	1AC, 1 DAE 1 SW removed	1AC, 1 DAE 1 video removed
EC/G	0.80	0.74	0.72	0.91	0.89	0.88
MC/G	0.76	0.67	0.69	0.90	0.88	0.88

reliable dichotomous decision of certified or not certified. An additional factor was feedback that we had received from both candidate groups and development teams across certificates. This feedback consistently indicated that we said too much in the entry directions. In an attempt to scaffold the directions for candidates, we were often redundant in explanations. Furthermore, the NBPTS Standards documents were undergoing revision, since some of them had been published for over 10 years. The Standards were being updated to reflect changes specific to the particular fields they represented, along with a more uniform focus on technology and on teaching diverse learners. Redesigning the assessment provided an additional opportunity to ensure that the assessment remained congruent with the Standards.

The following section explains in more detail the Next Generation structure of entry directions. The principles of assessing the underlying nature of accomplished teaching rather than making judgments based on surface features did not change as we revised the portfolio. However, we were able to refine our understanding of the answer to the question "how much information is enough?"

The decision to combine the two documented accomplishment tasks – one of which focused on how the candidate worked with students' families and caregivers while the other focused on how the candidate worked within their profession – came about as a result of the newer Standards documents. These tended to have a single standard devoted to both types of "work outside the classroom," and from scoring thousands of documented accomplishments tasks by 1999, we saw evidence that often candidates were not sure where best to place evidence of this kind of work, as it often overlapped. The new style single Documented Accomplishments task placed emphasis still on the areas addressed by the original two tasks, but obviated the need for a candidate to decide where best to place evidence. Additionally, the single task emphasized more clearly that the candidate should select evidence that is clearly linked to student learning in some way.

Development then proceeded to the assessment center exercises and again a number of significant changes were made. First, the number of exercises and duration of testing time changed from four 90-minute tasks to six 30-minute tasks. This reduction in testing time, however, was accompanied by a sharper focus on the purpose of the assessment center testing. In the early development days, when portfolio assessment was much more of an unknown entity in the arena of high-stakes testing, the assessment center was almost envisioned as a support to the measurement quality of the portfolio, or even a check on the authenticity of the portfolio entries (a role that could never be operationalized). This approach was seen in the way that exercises were designed – stimulus materials were most commonly classroom scenarios, student work, or student profiles/descriptions that candidates were asked to use to demonstrate their mastery of assessment of student work, lesson plan design, management of classroom discussions and interactions. Content knowledge was addressed by the subject matter embedded within these "real-life" scenarios. Some of the NBPTS's detractors based their criticisms of the entire certification enterprise on the limited assessment of content knowledge. As it became clear that the design of existing NBPTS assessments had levels of reliability that matched or exceeded any other performance assessment, and with the realization of the redundant and somewhat inefficient nature of the assessment center approach, a new method was employed: evidence-centered design.

Evidence-centered design (ECD)[13] provides a task-development framework that requires developers to engage in a painstaking process of deciding what claims they want to be able to make about candidates' content knowledge, what evidence they would require to support those claims, and therefore, what type of task would best provide that evidence. In addition to the redesign efforts, NBPTS development was also facing the need to be able to produce multiple comparable forms of the assessment center exercises, given the increases in candidate volume. The ECD approach provided a structure that could produce disciplined measurement claims as well as clear specifications for task designs that were replicable over time. The "shell" that results from the use of evidence-centered design methodologies articulates with precision both the claims and the evidence structure that underlie the task. What is constant and what is variable within a task is also articulated, so that variance – and particularly irrelevant variance – is controlled or eliminated.

During 2000–2001, the new structure of three classroom-based entries, one consolidated documented accomplishments entry and six content-focused assessment center exercises was then applied to the existing certificates in a large development effort.

Appendix D presents the overview of portfolio requirements and the assessment center specifications for one of the newly developed Next Generation NBPTS assessments, the EA/ELA assessment. A matrix of the EA/ELA Standards assessed by each exercise is included in this appendix. Appendix E presents an example of one of the portfolio tasks for that same NBPTS certification assessment. This single example of portfolio task directions is paradigmatic, since one of our most important accomplishments to date is the creation of a common approach to these directions. In every certification assessment, the directions are presented in the same order, with the same specificity, and according to the same design considerations. This has obvious fairness and equity consequences, but it also allows us to focus much more closely on fundamental validity issues, most particularly construct irrelevant variance and construct representativeness.

STRUCTURE OF THE PORTFOLIO ENTRY DIRECTIONS

As detailed in the previous section, the structure of the next generation of NBPTS portfolio entries was revised based on comments from candidates, development team members and assessors regarding their structure. The fundamental principles of leaving room for candidates to show evidence of *their* context and *their* practice remained the same – however, it was an opportunity to streamline, reduce the repetition, and add more graphics to provide for alternate learning strategies. This new structure placed greater importance on providing the critical information up front, with supplementary material, while important, placed later in the directions.

Much earlier in this chapter, I enumerated the characteristics commonly understood to be the strengths of portfolio assessment: their ability to accommodate complexity, reality, and individual differences, the opportunities they provide for the candidate to provide details of his or her own context and to collect evidence over time; the emphasis they place on personal choice, to name a few. Each of these characteristics are strengths, but the problem is that none of them is true unless prior to releasing the instructions to the portfolio-maker the developer of the tasks has made very deliberate and thoughtful design decisions, chief among them are decisions about how to evaluate what will be returned by the portfolio-maker and what to value in what is returned. This underlying – and inviolable – condition imposes a certain discipline on the designer of portfolio assessments.

Maybe the most important fact for a developer to realize is that portfolios shift much of the burden of assessment from the developer of the assessment to the person taking or completing the assessment. Most assessments, whether multiple-choice or constructed response, or even a performance assessment (like diving, or figure skating, or life-saving tests), have some things in common. The test maker or giver decides the content of the test, the timing of the test, the format of the response and the like. In portfolio assessment, much more decision making on the content, the format, and the presentation and the timing of the response is shared with the person assessed.

A portfolio assessment, at least theoretically, also reduces the effects of another limitation of all tests and assessments, that they are merely samples of one kind of a person's behavior – often not the behavior about which we seek to make a statement – and thus we have to make big inferences from the sample to the thing we really want to know, which is the person's ability in a particular area on a day-to-day, ongoing basis. In portfolios, the emphasis is on the selection of direct evidence of relevant behavior – a much more extensive collection of evidence that is selected from behaviors very close, if not identical, to the behaviors about which we seek to generalize – and it is selected over a longer period of time. The theoretical result is a much fuller picture of the real abilities of the person being assessed. In addition, of course, a portfolio could give the reader a window into a person's development over time, which might be the most revealing feature of portfolio assessment.

All of this rich possibility gives rise to what we might call the paradox of performance assessment design: it is critical to leave enough room in the assessment task for the test taker to fully represent his/her command of the particular task. At the same time, in order to convey what we value and how we will express those values through our evaluation process, we must give the test taker lots of information. I described before what we did in our first attempt to create performance tasks that answered the demands of interpretation of the standards through task specification and an expression of our values. What we forgot to do was leave room for the actual practice of the person responding to the task. On the other hand, if the task is too open-ended, it will be impossible to compare one response to another – a necessity in scored assessments – and to fairly evaluate all responses according to the same set of criteria – also a necessity in a well-regulated high-stakes assessment.

The sample instructions in the appendices show some of the ways we have structured the NBPTS portfolio tasks to resolve this paradox. Since teachers will be responding to these tasks using whatever particular class and students this year's fateful hand has dealt them, the task needs to be open to almost any school situation that falls within the particular domain being assessed. (This excludes, thus, special kinds of classes and individual instruction and the like.) This particular requirement is one of the many reasons that we worked with as diverse a teacher development team as possible so as to have representation from as many situations as possible. Pilot testing widened this pool even further. Furthermore, all **NBPTS** standards prize certain qualities in practitioners, regardless of their subject area, personal style, or the individual context of their teaching and these qualities must be prized by the evaluative criteria, and critically, demonstrable in the task posed for the candidate. In other words, it would be unfair for the rubric to value a characteristic such as feedback to students and yet for the candidate not to be given directions to demonstrate it. In addition, there are behaviors thought to be characteristic of accomplished teachers – a sense of self-efficacy, a continuous ability to monitor and adjust to classroom conditions on the fly – that are difficult to sample consistently in a performance-based assessment that focuses on actual practice and demands the use of student work products.

And in addition to all these assessment-related concerns, there is another that is even more important. Teachers have no experience of performance assessment for themselves and often not for students either. Most teachers have never been asked to take themselves seriously as professionals and to talk about their planning, decision-making, and analysis as they work. Thus, even the terms of the assessment may be foreign to them – they may quite literally not know what we mean.

As a consequence, these directions need to provide a level playing field for all teachers – the sophisticated performance assessment veteran as well as the complete novice. This is an equity concern, but it is also a validity concern. We cannot be measuring what we think we are measuring if our measurement target (the candidate) remains largely ignorant of the terms and conditions that govern the sampling strategy we are using. In other words, lack of evidence of a particular characteristic should support the inference that the candidate was not accomplished in that area, rather than that the candidate did not understand that he or she was to demonstrate that characteristic, which in fact they possessed in abundance. This is, the reason for the carefully articulated structure of these instructions.

Task instructions begin with a statement of the domain for this task, and this statement comes directly from the relevant standards. Immediately following this italicized opening, this Standards-based statement is "translated" into the practical world of the teacher's work in the section entitled "What do I need to do?" which provides a brief explanation in specific terms of the focus of the entry, in addition to a graphic display and bulleted list of the major components which must be submitted in order to complete the entry. References to sections that include more specific requirements for these components is provided in this section, but not given in detail, to eliminate overwhelming candidates at the beginning of the process.

What follows the initial outline of the focus of the entry is the "How will my response be scored?" section which articulates the scoring criteria. The candidate is provided with the rubric for the top-level response. Cross-referencing this section with the opening italicized section, as well as the Written Commentary questions, illustrates how the same words and phrases repeated in each section. In other words, once a candidate knows what to do, he/she is immediately presented with what will be valued in a high scoring response. One of the changes made in the Next Generation development cycle was to move this section from the end to much closer to the front so that candidates could see the connections more clearly.

What appears next is the part of the task directions that explain to the candidate what he/she must write about practice, the Written Commentary questions. This part of the candidate's response is critical to the assessor's ability to evaluate the connection between *what* is going on in the classroom and *why* the teacher has chosen to do things in that way. As the architecture diagram makes clear (see Fig. 1), the *why* is the driver in evaluation of the *what*. In general, teachers are inexperienced in analysis of practice. Furthermore, they have few opportunities to write formal presentations about their work. To reduce the construct irrelevant variance associated with writing ability, as well as to ensure that all candidates considered the same critical elements, the instructions here are very specific. The Commentary questions are essentially the outline of an analysis, so that the task of structuring all that one might say about evidence of a particular instance of teaching practice is not part of the challenge of these tasks. There are requirements for labeling the response parts and page limits. In every portfolio task, as I noted above, there is more than one source of evidence of practice. There is always evidence in the teacher's own voice – this is the Written Commentary. But in addition, there is confirmatory evidence from student work, instructional artifacts, and/or videotape. And the Written Commentary always requires the teacher to explicitly explain, analyze, and contextualize these other sources of evidence. Thus, the ideal of connected practice is embodied in these directions and teachers are helped to accomplish this goal through the structure of the assessment.

The following section, "Making Good Choices," is an important section of the directions, and it represents a critical design innovation. It is here that we share what we have learned from scoring about successful choices in portfolio assessment. Each of these sections is tailored to the particular entry, and each is deliberately and tightly connected to the scoring rubric.

It is in this section of the task directions that we try to undercut the notion of assessment as mystery, which is the way most candidates (indeed most test takers of any kind) think of it. This is the guide to "test-wiseness," and it appears as an integral part of the directions to candidates. The final section deals with various formatting and practical issues.

The critical validity issue for the NBPTS assessment is, of course, does the assessment really discriminate between accomplished teachers and those who are truly less accomplished? This is the principal concern of the NBPTS's Assessment and Certification Advisory Panel, but one critical underpinning for this claim to validity is the connections we make between the standards, the tasks, and the standards once again. This set of instructions demonstrates how we have attempted to use the standards to specify the focus of the assessment task, the means of completing the task successfully, and the ways such success will be determined when the response is scored (see Chapter 7, this volume, on scoring for an account of the evolution of a scoring system for these assessments).

In the first decade of its existence, the NBPTS assessment system moved from multiple, deliberately experimental approaches through initial standardization to the current format – a remarkable journey of design, development, and response to empirical evidence from practice and use. At the time of this writing, more than 50,000 teachers across some 23 fields of teaching hold National Board Certification. The vocabulary that describes accomplished teaching, the involvement of state governments in fundamental shifts in resource allocation for teachers, the ways in which evidence of such accomplishment might be gathered and evaluated, and the connection of National Board Certification with salary increases and other incentives have permanently altered the landscape of educational policy, assessment practice, and discussions about career paths for teachers. Changes in education policy in the first decade of the 21st century, technology advances, and the accumulation of psychometric data about these assessments makes further change and enhancement in the design of the NBPTS assessments both inevitable and exciting.

NOTES

1. The 1986 report of the Carnegie Task Force on Teaching as a Profession, *A Nation Prepared*, which called for the creation of an NBPTSs, asserted as its mission "to establish standards for high levels of competence in the teaching profession, to assess the qualifications of those seeking Board certification, and to grant certificates

to those who meeting the standards" (Carnegie Task Force on Teaching as a Profession, 1986, p. 62).

2. See an early account of the Stanford TAP use of these techniques in Haertel (1990).

3. Gitomer (1993) discusses the dimensions of performance assessment as they contrast with those of more traditional tests. These are articulated as the time span covered by the assessment task, the specificity of the assessment information, the closeness to educational objectives, which he defines as "proximity of assessment goals to the ultimate objectives of an educational institutions, which can be expressed in behaviors, results, and educational effectiveness. A longer time span, more general information (i.e., assessment of command of a particular algorithmic formula in mathematics is specific; an assessment of understanding of which formula to choose in a particular situation and why it is appropriate would be more general), and closer alignment of the assessment goals to ultimate goals of education are characteristic of performance assessments.

4. The philosophical and intellectual underpinnings of this assessment design have been thoroughly discussed in articles by two of the principal investigators, Ginette Delandshere and Anthony Petrosky, one of whose central interests has been the complex interactions – and to some extent, inherent conflicts – in performance assessments like these between the nature of knowledge and performance and its evaluation in some summative fashion for the purposes of certification (Delandshere & Petrosky, 1994, 1998).

5. In fact Haertel (1990, p. 291) suggested as early as 1990 that potential threats to validity in design and in scoring models were a matter of concern and should be carefully monitored, but at that time there was no data to elucidate what such threats might look like, and hence no real direction to follow in preventing such threats.

6. The APPLE criteria approach to encapsulating the NBPTS's critical assessment values was the brainchild of Joan Snowden, the NBPTS Vice President of assessment development through 1994.

7. Messick (1994, p. 14) articulates this problem very clearly: "The portrayal of performance assessments as *authentic* and *direct* has all the earmarks of a validity claim but with little or no evidential grounding." That is, if authenticity is important to consider when evaluating the consequences of assessment for student achievement, it constitutes a tacit validity standard, as does the closely related concept of directness of assessment. "We need to address what the labels authentic and direct might mean in validity terms. We also need to determine what kinds of evidence might legitimize both their use as validity standards and the nefarious implication that other forms of assessment are not only indirect, but inauthentic."

8. As Messick (1994, p. 14) points out, two conventional tenets that underlie construct validity, construct under representation and construct irrelevant variance, directly jeopardize authenticity and directness, respectively. He goes on to name "key distinctions that must be taken into account in conceptualizing the nature of performance assessments. These include contrasts between performances and products, between the assessment of performance per se and performance assessment of competence or other constructs, between structured and unstructured problems and response modes, and between breadth and depth of domain coverage. This last topic highlights a central tension in performance assessment, which is the degree of generalizability that is empirically sustainable for performance scores."

9. The final form of the portfolio task directions owes a great debt to the Early Childhood Generalist Assessment Development Laboratory at Education Development Center in Boston, which was led by Joanne Brady.

10. It is instructive to imagine one's own difficulties if faced with the task of representing professional performance by selection of particular artifacts of that work accompanied by an analytical commentary that contextualized and explained their significance. Even with the assistance of carefully structured directions, this kind of choice is a formidable challenge.

11. Currently, with 24 certificates available, 95% of US teachers have access to National Board Certification.

12. For more details on how reliability estimates are calculated for NBPTS assessments, see Chapter 9 (this volume) by Gitomer.

13. Messick (1994) describes a construct-centered approach to performance assessment in which the developer "would begin by asking what complex of knowledge, skills, or other attributes should be assessed, presumably because they are tied to explicit or implicit objectives of instruction or are otherwise valued by society [in this case valued in NBPTS Standards]. Next [the developer would consider] what behaviors or performances should reveal those constructs, and what tasks or situations should elicit those behaviors." Messick notes that an advantage of this approach is that "focusing on constructs also alerts one to the possibility of construct-irrelevant variance that might distort the task performance, its scoring, or both." This construct-centered approach forms the heart of evidence-centered design: a focus on the construct as described in the Standards leads to the identification of claims that the developer would want to be able to make and therefore leads to the solicitation of evidence to support those claims. The theoretical foundation of this approach has been extensively documented in the work of Mislevy, Steinberg, and Almond (1999, 2002, 2003).

ACKNOWLEDGMENTS

This chapter could not have been completed without the assistance of Dr. Caroline Wylie, ETS Research & Development.

REFERENCES

American Educational Research Association, American Psychological Association, and National Council on Measurement in Education. (1985). *Standards for educational and psychological testing.* Washington, DC: APA, AERA, & NCME.

Camp, R. (1993). The place of portfolios in our changing views of writing assessment. In: R. E. Bennet & W. C. Ward (Eds), *Construction versus choice in cognitive measurement: Issues in constructed response, performance testing, and portfolio assessment* (pp. 183–212). Hillsdale, NJ: Lawrence Erlbaum Associates.

Carnegie Task Force on Teaching as a Profession. (1986). *A nation prepared: Teachers for the 21st century.* Hyattsville, MD: Carnegie Forum on Education and the Economy.

Delandshere, G., & Petrosky, A. (1994). Capturing teachers' knowledge: Performance assessment a) and post-structuralist epistemology, b) from a post-structuralist perspective, c) and post-structuralism, d) none of the above. *Educational Researcher, 23*(5), 11–18.

Delandshere, G., & Petrosky, A. (1998). Assessment of complex performances: Limitations of key measurement assumptions. *Educational Researcher, 27*(2), 14–23.

Frederiksen, J. R., & Collins, A. (1989). A systems approach to educational testing. *Educational Researcher, 18*(9), 27–32.

Frederiksen, J. R., & Wolfe, E. W. (1992). *A report from the video portfolio project: Standards of the NBPTS that are amenable to video portfolio assessment.* Unpublished research report. Princeton, NJ: Educational Testing Service.

Gitomer, D. H. (1993). Performance assessment and educational measurement. In: R. E. Bennet & W. C. Ward (Eds), *Construction versus choice in cognitive measurement: Issues in constructed response, performance testing, and portfolio assessment* (pp. 241–263). Hillsdale, NJ: Lawrence Erlbaum Associates.

Haertel, E. (1990). Performance tests, simulations, and other methods. In: J. Millman & L. Darling-Hammond (Eds), *The new handbook on teacher evaluation: Assessing elementary and secondary school teachers* (pp. 278–294). Newbury Park, CA: Sage.

Linn, R. L., Baker, E. L., & Dunbar, S. B. (1991). Complex, performance-based assessment: Expectations and validation criteria. *Educational Researcher, 20*(8), 15–21.

Messick, S. (1989). Meaning and values in test validation: The science and ethics of assessment. *Educational Researcher, 18*(2), 5–11.

Messick, S. (1994). The interplay of evidence and consequences in the validation of performance assessments. *Educational Researcher, 23*(2), 13–23.

Mislevy, R. J., Steinberg, L. S., & Almond, R. G. (1999). *On the roles of task model variables in assessment design.* Reports – Descriptive Speeches/Meeting Papers no. CSE-TR-500: National Center for Research on Evaluation, Standards, and Student Testing, Los Angeles, CA.

Mislevy, R. J., Steinberg, L. S., & Almond, R. G. (2002). Design and analysis in task-based language assessment. *Language Testing, 19*(4), 477–496.

Mislevy, R. J., Steinberg, L. S., & Almond, R. G. (2003). *On the structure of educational assessments.* Reports – Descriptive no. CSE-TR-597. Center for the Study of Evaluation, National Center for Research on Evaluation, Standards, and Student Testing, Los Angeles, CA.

National Board for Professional Teaching Standards. (1991). *Toward high and rigorous standards: What teachers should know and be able to do.* Washington, DC: Author.

Said, E. (1975). *Beginnings: Intention and method.* New York: Basic Books.

Shulman, L. S. (1987a). Assessment for teaching: An initiative for the profession. *Phi Delta Kappan, 69,* 38–44.

Shulman, L. S. (1987b). Knowledge and teaching: Foundations of the new reform. *Harvard Educational Review, 57,* 1–22.

Wiggins, G. (1989). A true test: Toward more authentic and equitable assessment. *Phi Delta Kappan, 79,* 703–713.

Wolf, D. P. (1993). Assessment as an episode of learning. In: R. E. Bennet & W. C. Ward (Eds), *Construction versus choice in cognitive measurement: Issues in constructed response, performance testing, and portfolio assessment* (pp. 213–240). Hillsdale, NJ: Lawrence Erlbaum Associates.

CHAPTER 4

VALIDATING THE SPECIFICATION OF STANDARDS FOR TEACHING: APPLICATIONS TO THE NATIONAL BOARD FOR PROFESSIONAL TEACHING STANDARDS' ASSESSMENTS [☆]

John Hattie

ABSTRACT

This chapter outlines and applies criteria for evaluating the validity of the process for establishing standards that identify what accomplished teachers in a given field should know and do. The argument defended in this chapter is that when individuals use tests and assessments for various purposes, they need to be concerned not only with the distributive validity issues relating to the adequacy of content or consequences of the assessment. They also need to evaluate the validity of the procedures used

[☆]The material contained herein is based on work supported by the National Board for Professional Teaching Standards. Any opinions, findings, conclusions, and recommendations expressed herein are those of the author and do not necessarily reflect the views of the NBPTS.

Assessing Teachers for Professional Certification:
The First Decade of the National Board for Professional Teaching Standards
Advances in Program Evaluation, Volume 11, 93–111

ISSN: 1474-7863/doi:10.1016/S1474-7863(07)11004-8

to specify the content domains that lead ultimately to decisions recommended as part of the test instrument. The procedural and the distributive fairness of tests both need to be considered when deciding on the validity of tests and assessments.

The National Board for Profession Teaching Standards (NBPTS) undertook a major project to certify accomplished teachers in a number of fields. The Board has devised such standards for over 30 areas of teacher work – elementary and secondary, language arts, and physical education, etc. This chapter outlines and applies criteria for evaluating the validity of the *process* for establishing the standards that identify what accomplished teachers in a given field should know and do. It is important to note that this chapter concerns only the *process* by which the NBPTS content standards were developed. Not considered here, but equally important, is the content of the standards (e.g., relevance, representativeness, criticality, frequency), the translation of the content standards into performance standards, and the performance of other tasks using subject-matter experts (see Chapters 5 and 6, by Sam Wineburg and Steven Schneider et al., respectively). The process by which the standards were developed is a critical factor in determining the validity of the subsequent operationalizations of the NBPTS procedure for identifying and rewarding accomplished teachers.

Most of the discussions and procedures addressing validity are concerned with the outcomes or consequences of the assessment procedure. Procedures to assess validity arguments like multi-trait multi-method, contrasting groups, and factor analysis are more concerned with distributive issues; i.e., the outcomes of the relationships between tests and decisions. These procedures are dealt with at great length in most texts on validity, including Messick's (1989) reconceptualization of the notions of validity. This traditional methodology of determining content validity relates to the degree to which assessment tasks map the construct of interest. A further consideration is the procedural attributes of measurement; i.e., the validity of the procedures or processes used to arrive at the final test or set of standards that ultimately dictate the instrumentation and consequential score interpretations.

The argument defended in this chapter is that when individuals use tests and assessments for various purposes, they need to be concerned not only with the distributive validity issues relating to the adequacy of content or consequences of the assessment. They also need to evaluate the validity of the procedures used to specify the content domain that lead ultimately to decisions recommended as part of the test instrument. The procedural and the distributive fairness of tests both need to be considered when deciding on the validity of tests and assessments.

CONTENT VALIDITY

While there are many pronouncements from professional psychometric bodies as to appropriate standards for specifying the content domain, there are few guidelines that inform the process of establishing standards for highly accomplished professionals – particularly when it is far from established that any members are identified before the completion of this task (see Linn, Baker, & Dunbar, 1991). The usual content validity methods typically relate to the relevance of the test to the applied purpose and the utility of the test in the applied setting. Messick (1995) argued that such relevance can come from a number of sources, including professional judgments about the relevance and representativeness of test content to the content of the applied domain; evidence that the test validity reflects processes and constructs are deemed important in domain functioning; or from significant test correlations with criterion measures of domain performance.

The following six criteria have been used by the NBPTS (1991) to assess the validity of the procedures used to specify the standards for teaching from which a test is developed. These criteria are:

1. That the integrity of certification requires that the certifying board be administratively independent of any other professional organization.
2. That the certifying board be solely responsible for constructing the standards.
3. That the certifying board be composed primarily of those who are already highly accomplished practitioners.
4. That the universe of competencies be clearly defined.
5. That the process of defining the complex content domain be developed on a sound scientific basis.
   That formal instructions be provided to the Standards Committee delineating their roles and responsibilities in setting the standards and demarcating the boundaries of the universe of content.
   That the process of developing the standards be formally documented.
   That after the standards are formally approved, Committee members have confidence in the process.

6. That the process involves defining critical aspects of practice that are the distinguishing characteristics of highly accomplished teachers.

   • That a process be followed that ensures high standards are set that recognize the variety of contexts in which teachers practice and that do not prescribe a single model.

   • That various disciplinary groups, the states, National Council for Accreditation of Teacher Education (NCATE), other Standards Committees, and others should have opportunities to respond to the standards.

   • That the Standards Committee serves as the sounding board for the development of the assessment measures and assists in designing fair and trustworthy processes.

   • That a wide sampling of agreement be sought for the standards from the major professional groups regarding the appropriateness and level of standards.

These standards could be considered generic to many professional certification bodies, although in the present case they have been applied to the development of teaching related standards (particularly for Early Adolescence/Generalist and Early Adolescence/English Language Arts Teachers, EA/G and EA/ELA, respectively; Hattie, 1994, 1996; Hattie & Sackett, 1995). A justification for each of these criteria will now be presented.

Criterion 1. That the integrity of certification requires that the certifying board be administratively independent of any other professional organization.

This guideline is taken from the National Commission for Certifying Agencies (NCCA, 1991) procedures, which state that: "Administrative independence signifies that all policy decisions relating to certification matters are the sole decision of the certifying body and not subject to approval by any other body" (NCCA, 1991, Standard 2c).

Such independence is necessary to ensure that all critical concerns are addressed without undue influence, that many views are encouraged and considered, that problems relating to test development do not override the specification of the content domain, and that the resulting standards are clearly referent to the National Board's vision of a highly accomplished teacher in the particular content domain and age level. There has been a similar entreaty to foster independence as a precursor to integrity within the evaluation area (Scriven, 1994). This criterion is not meant to imply that certifying boards, such as the NBPTS, cannot seek advice, but that it takes responsibility for the consequent standards. It can set up committees to advise on the standards, although the final authority for their acceptance rests with the certifying board. In the case of the NBPTS, it established Standards Working Groups, which had priority over the test development and other psychometric phases, and ultimately reported their recommendations for approval by the National Board. This onus of responsibility is reflected in the various statements that defined the task for each Standards Committee, such as:

> The certifying body, in this case the National Board, however is free to appoint committees, and these have included: the Certification Standards Working Group (CSWG), Staff and Board Liaison to the Standards Committee, Assessment Development Laboratories (ADL), Technical Analysis Group (TAG), field test network, and the Education committees. Although the Board encourages cross-fertilization of ideas and collaboration, it has established the priority of the Standards Committee over the ADLs and has established the Committee as an autonomous advisory body: The National Board makes all final decisions.

Criterion 2. That the certifying board be solely responsible for constructing the standards.

This criterion derives from Standard 2c-3 from the NCCA guidelines, which states that "The certifying board shall be solely responsible for examination content and construction, item-writing, and test administration, and for the establishment of all individual qualifications for certification such as academic requirements" (NCCA, 1991, Standard 2c-3).

The 1991 version of the NCCA Standards presumes that a professional organization will be responsible for certification. NCCA's predecessor, the National Commission for Health Certifying Agencies stated that there are two key models by which private national agencies certify health occupations: (1) creation of a free-standing, public interest body, which is not part of any other organization, and (2) a model where certification is carried out by a division or accompaniment of a professional association. They suggested that first model was the ideal certification model.

The first model is "ideal" because there are fewer opportunities for undue influence in the setting of the standards. In the present case, a variant of the first model was used. The NBPTS is a free-standing, public interest body that is not part of any other organization. The certifying board may be administratively independent of any professional organization, but it also important for the validity of the process that the certifying board also be solely responsible for constructing the standards. This does not mean that ONLY the certifying board is involved, as there can be an extensive network of advisors who can make submissions to the board and comment on drafts of the standards. This National Board, for example, set up Standards Committees across the certification fields consisting of members who are NOT members of the National Board. Evidence of sole responsibility on the part of the NBPTS can be provided by an investigation of the deliberations of the certifying board. For example, in the Standards Committee for the ELA, debates about a number of contentious issues and the manner in which they were resolved are indications of the independence of the Committee.

Examples of these debates follow:

- Are some subjects (e.g., Great Books exploration) more conducive to successful achievement than other subjects?
- Should the Standards Committee attempt a definition of the ELA?
- Ought the focus of classrooms of outstanding practitioners in middle grades ELA be principally on content, on skills, on pupils?
- Is there "core knowledge" in ELA that all candidates for Board certification must be expected to possess in some depth?
- Is it necessary for teachers to be able to talk about theory or is it sufficient to show knowledge through classroom practice?
- From what sources should instructional knowledge be derived? What weight should theory and teaching experience and subject experience be given?
- Is there a "sacred body" of literature that the highly accomplished teacher should have a close knowledge of?
- What is unique about ELA for early adolescents?

An evaluation of the Committee's deliberations on these questions provides a rich source of information about whether the criterion of "sole responsibility" was met. For example, on February 11, 1991, five members of the Standards Committee were given an assignment relating to the standard, *Knowledge of Subject* in respect of ELA. All rejected the idea that the National Board defined any consistent, identifiable body of literature appropriate to all young adolescents. They argued instead that teachers demonstrate that they know how to evaluate and select appropriate literature, are familiar with the range and diversity of literature which will engage adolescents as readers and thinkers; command appropriate literature that reflects the cultures of the student population; choose readings which are accessible and inviting to adolescents; and comprehend that how learning takes place as these are more important to successful teaching than any specific curricular content.

At the third meeting of the EA/ELA Standards Committee (Pittsburgh, May 12–14, 1991), many of these major issues were resolved. They decided that at the heart of the ELA curriculum was the creation and interpretation of texts for the purpose of making personal meaning of the world and imagining alternative perspectives. They decided to write vignettes to anchor theory in practice, illustrate the standards, and reassure candidate that there can be many and various models of exemplary practice.

This standard is met by the National Board in that, while it devolves major responsibility to writing the standards to the various Committees it establishes, the National Board finally debates then accepts, rejects, or requests modifications of the standards.

Criterion 3. That the certifying board be composed primarily of those who are already highly accomplished teachers.

It is critical that those with most knowledge of the content domain form the majority of the group devising the content domain. This majority needs to be informed, via practising the teaching position, of the nuances of the tasks, the multi-facets of daily interactions, and possess a deep knowledge of the teaching task. Of course, knowledgeable experts from other domains can assist in this process. The closest precedent for this criterion is found in the Standards for Educational and Psychological Testing (American Psychological Association, American Educational Research Association, & National Council for Measurement in Education, APA, AERA, NCME, 1985), which states that:

> When subject-matter experts have been asked to judge whether items are an appropriate sample of a universe ... the relevant training, experience, and qualifications of the experts should be described (Standard 1.7).

A first source of evidence for meeting this standard can be derived from investigating the manner in which the National Board selected members of its Standards Committees. The National Board's policy states that the majority of the members of the Standards Committee must be "highly regarded teachers who are regularly engaged in teaching elementary, middle, and/or high school students". The notion of a "regularly engaged" teacher is now formally defined by Board policy statement as a person who spends at least half of their time teaching children.

The Standards Committee is appointed by the Chair of the National Board, acting on the recommendation of the President and subject to the approval of the Board of Directors. The actual process for identifying the members of this "certifying body" is extensive. For each standard committee, approximately 100 or more persons were identified as possible members. Nominations for membership were then solicited from and circulated among leaders of major professional groups (disciplinary organizations, unions, and others), the Board's own members, the Board's staff, and by personal contact. Many organizations were asked for comments on appropriate members, curriculum vitae were requested, and the staff (usually the teacher-in-residence) interviewed the most promising nominees. The final list aimed to balance various factors such as region, ethnicity, gender, and expertise in different subject areas. References were also sought from these nominees and from independent sources. A list of the most promising nominees was shared with the pertinent disciplinary and specialty organizations and with various Board members to gain further insight. A final slate was then prepared for the President to recommend to the Chair, who was the appointing authority.

The final panel was then further evaluated with respect to the range of qualifications, gender, current position, involvement in regional and national organizations, visibility within their professions (e.g., held or holding offices in professional organizations, collaborated on higher education projects, received awards from national organizations or otherwise achieved prominence), and experience with standards-setting activities in their field. For example, there were 17 members who served on the EA/ELA Standards Committee: 10 were female, 10 White, 3 African-American, 2 Hispanic, 1 Asian, they came from 16 States, and 9 were currently teaching in schools.

Criterion 4. That the universe of competencies be clearly defined.

The universe of competencies refers to the more generic competencies from which the subject-specific standards were derived. The standards that evolve needed to be based on a clearly defined universe of competencies, in the case of the National Board, competencies as to what the accomplished teacher knew and was able to do. This does not mean that a narrow dictionary definition of the competencies need be specified, but rather a considered, well-articulated web of arguments and open sentences. Each of the National Board's Standards Committees, given this universe of competencies, had the task of converting them into particular standards.

The Standards for Educational and Psychological Testing are not so forthcoming on what it means by a "sound scientific basis" for determining the content of the standards, although they repeatedly emphasized that the domain of knowledge or skills being assessed should be clearly stated. The

Standards for Educational and Psychological Testing (APA, AERA, & NCME, 1985) state that:

> The specifications used in constructing items or selecting observations and in designing the test instrument as a whole should be stated clearly. The definition of a universe or domain that is used for constructing or selecting items should be described (Standard 3.2).

> When content-related evidence serves as a significant demonstration of validity for a particular use, a clear definition of the universe represented, its relevance to the proposed test use, and the procedures followed in generating test content to represent that universe should be described (Standard 1.6).

> When content-related evidence of validity is presented, the rationale for defining and describing a specific job content domain in a particular way (e.g., in terms of tasks to be performed or knowledge, skills, abilities, or other personal characteristics) should be clearly stated clearly. That rationale should establish that the knowledge, skills, abilities said to define the domain are the major determinants of proficiency in that domain (Standard 10.6).

> Any construct interpretations of tests used for licensure and certification should be explicit, and the evidence and logical analyses supporting these interpretations should be reported (Standard 11.2).

All these Standards refer to an explication of the universe. The manual claims that the methods to establish content-related validity:

> often rely on expert judgments to assess the relationship between parts of the test and the defined universe .... The first task for test developers is to specify adequately the universe of content that a test is intended to represent, given the proposed uses of the test .... Expert professional judgment should play an integral part in developing the definition of what is to be measured, such as describing the universe of content. (APA, AERA, NCME, 1985, pp. 10–11)

Although it is critical to note that no tests are actually being created, these remarks point to criteria for judging the process used by the National Board to develop its standards. Evidence relevant to this process includes:

a. As a consequence of reading the Board's vision, multiple readers should derive similar conceptions of highly accomplished teachers. Over 100 teachers, academics, superintendents, subject experts were sent copies of the standards during their development and their views were requested as to the clarity of the standards. The responses of these respondents were analyzed to evaluate whether there was agreement about the clarity of the standards.

b. Seeking advice from multiple sources of "expert professional judgment". As a consequence of this expert advice, the standards were modified.

There are over 100 major revisions of the standards in the files of the National Board, and many more minor modifications to words, phrases and style.

For all the Standards created by the National Board in the first decade of its existence, these criteria were met. In some subsequent evolvements of the Standards, there were more efforts to develop a common rubric from which to develop the Standards.

Criterion 5. That the process of defining the complex content domain be developed on a sound scientific basis.

This set of criteria refers to the more specific process of developing the subject-specific standards, from the more generic National Board standards. There was little guidance in the test validity literature as to what this process should be. It was recommended that this process involve delineating the roles and responsibilities of the Standards Committee members involved in developing the standards, demarcating the boundaries of the universe of content, fully documenting the process, and creating a process in which the National Board and the communities it serves had confidence.

Criterion 5a. That formal instructions should be provided to the Standards Committee by the National Board delineating their roles and responsibilities in setting the standards and demarcating the boundaries of the universe of content.

Evidence can be obtained via correspondence from the National Board asking the Standards Committee to write the standards. In his April 1990 letter of appointment to the committee, Board President James Kelly defined the Standards Committee's task as:

> to translate the Board's policy statement on "What teachers should know and be able to do" into operational standards for the field of Early Adolescence/English Language Arts, and to work collaboratively with the Assessment Development Laboratory that we will be supporting for this certification field. The ADL's role and responsibility is to build an administratively feasible, professionally acceptable, publicly credible, legally defensible and economically affordable assessment package around these standards – not just another test." (Kelly, 1990, personal communication)

Included in Kelly's correspondence were various documents; the most relevant to the process of setting standards were described in the EA/G report. They included: Towards High and Rigorous Standards for the Teaching Profession; A Plan to Set Standards; The Handbook for NBPTS

Standards Committees; Criteria for Writing NBPTS Standards: Guidance paper.

Criterion 5b. That the process of developing the standards be formally documented.

It is imperative for the validation of the standard setting process that the process itself be formally documented, and evidence for meeting this standard includes a synopsis of the extensive documentation usually required to set standards. Such documentation can highlight a number of critical incidents or issues such as whether the process as outlined by the Board was followed, whether draft standards were sent to relevant stake holders, the extent to which public comment was sought, the frequency and nature of the revisions to the standards, and the interactions with the ADL (commissioned independently to devise tests relative to the standards).

In the case of the EA/ELA Standards setting process, there is extensive documentation kept in the Board's Washington Office. An extensive table in the final report of the validation process (Hattie & Sackett, 1995) indicated the comprehensiveness of these files. Moreover, approximately 100 major revisions of the Standards document have been retained in the files.

This documentation also indicates the degree to which the Standards Committee took control of the process. It is possible to set up an independent Standards Committee and have powerful individuals from, for example, the Governing Board, or subject-expert organizations, reducing the independence of the Standards Committee. Thus, the documentation can be used to assess whether these "significant others" took a facilitating or liaison role rather than a directing role. Similarly, it is informative to note the tone of the memos from the Board staff to the members.

Further, the documentation can be used to demonstrate how the Committee resolved the majority of the issues. For example, during the development of the Early Adolescence/Generalist (EA/G) standards, there was a major issue relating to circumscribing the role of a "generalists" versus a subject specialist. The issue was: Should a generalist have specialist knowledge in all the subjects they taught and how to teach them, or should there be some reduced requirement? This topic was the "toughest territory we had to navigate" (January 15, 1992). A synopsis of how this issue was resolved illustrates the manner in which the Standards Committee remained independent in its mission, how it sought advice from other professionals and other Standards Committees, and how the Board's Liaison staff prompted the committee to seek a clear stance and responded to their requests. A range of processes were used including: assignments for the next meeting ("write a memorandum on what content knowledge (and of what kind) highly accomplished generalists need to know, what they need to know about engaging students with that knowledge, and what kinds of developmental understandings should inform their choice of content and pedagogy" (December 10, 1990); a synopsis of these replies was circulated asking for members to concentrate on this issue as it was to be discussed at the next meeting; after a further Standards Committee meeting, a new draft was circulated ("Of critical importance was the decision to require the generalist to have broad knowledge in the core disciplines and the arts, to have in-depth knowledge in at least one discipline, and most significantly, to approach all teaching in a holistic, integrative manner"; April 25, 1991).

Members also were asked to create vignettes to exemplify their beliefs on this issue; a synopsis of two models that were supported by the members was circulated for comment (the teacher who actively teaches all or nearly all subjects, and the specialist teacher who has mastered the art of working with other specialists to provide an integrated education to students). The suggested compromise was to accept both models and allow candidates to choose an assessment exercise more related to one model than the other; a new draft encompassing these viewpoints was attached and the Standards Committee was asked to comment and vote on this matter.

The point of this elaboration is to demonstrate the deferment by other professionals and other Standards Committees to Standards Committee members, even when the most contentious issue led to extended debate and little resolution.

Criterion 5c. That after the standards are formally approved, Committee members have confidence in the process.

There are two major sources of evidence suggested for this criterion. First, the tone of the comments from members of the Standards Committee could be assessed from reading all the minutes of meetings, memos, letters, and replies.

There were no memos from any member indicating that the Board or staff person was misguided (or problematic). Typically, comments from Committee members were to the contrary. This is not to imply that the Committee was engaged in a series of compromises whereby particular views were excluded. The deliberations clearly indicate that contrary views were evident, lengthy discussions and debates were the norm, and on some issues there was major division of opinion. It seemed that on all occasions no vote was ever taken, as most differences were resolved after lengthy debate (Hattie, 1996).

A second source of evidence comes from a survey of Standards committee members after they had completed their task. The first two questions asked if the respondents felt that their Standards Committee was knowledgeable about what it takes to be a highly accomplished teacher and represented the major points of view in the field. In the case of the English Language Arts Standards Committee, for example, all agreed that their Committee was composed of extremely able members. Some noted a skew toward more contemporary views of good teaching or toward "those holding the Board's view", which is not surprising, given that one of the criteria of selection was that the teachers saw a possibility of shared vision with the Board's ideals.

Criterion 6. That the process involves defining critical aspects of practice that are the distinguishing characteristics of highly accomplished teachers.

Criterion 6a. That a process be followed that ensures that high standards are set that recognize the variety of contexts in which teachers practice and that do not prescribe a single model.

It is important to recall that these validity criteria do not address the correctness or stringency of the standards, but rather address the issue whether a suitable process was implemented to ensure that the process of delineating the complex content domain was valid or defensible. The major sources of information to address this "process" are twofold.

First, a survey of practicing teachers was undertaken by the Standards Committee. These teachers were asked to rate each standard with respect to three statements using a 5-point scale ranging from "strongly agree" to "strongly disagree". The statements were: "This standard describes a critical aspect of highly accomplished teaching practice within this field", "I feel confident that I could meet this standard", and "This standard is easily understood". Only the first and third questions are important from a content validity perspective.

There were 393 forms returned relating to the EA/ELA standards. Of all the respondents, 78% were from teachers, 13% from administrators, and 9% classified as others (e.g., university). The responses came from 40 states. When asked if they would consider seeking Board Certification, 83% said "yes". Seventy-one percent of the males and 85% of the females said "yes", and of the teachers 91% of the non-white respondents, 88% of the urban teachers, and 95% of the rural teachers said "yes". Ninety-eight point five percent of the teachers and 90% of the non-teachers responded "strongly agree or agree" that each of the 14 standards described a critical aspect of highly accomplished teaching practice within this field. Similarly, 87% of the teachers and 82% of the non-teachers claimed that the standards were easily understood. In general, the teachers more than non-teachers both understood the standards and agreed that they described a critical aspect of highly accomplished teaching practice.

Second, a survey was conducted of a self-selected group ($N = 51$) for ELA who wrote letters to the Standards Committee or Board. They were asked whether they considered the standards too low or too demanding.

Criterion 6b. That various disciplinary groups, the states, NCATE, other Standards Committees, and others should have opportunities to react to the standards.

Evidence relating to this criterion can be derived from an inspection of the minutes and other documentation. Such evidence includes:

- The amount and nature of input from disciplinary groups, the states, NCATE, and others.
- Key interest groups were invited to send liaison people to the EA/ELA Standards Committee meetings (although such observers had no voting or decision-making powers within the Standards Committees).
- Opportunities for these others to hear the current thinking of the Standards Committee, and comment on the standards. Opportunities included presentations at various conferences, to State Departments of Education, and similar organizations.
- Documentation of the replies received from an extensive search for public comment to the Standards was undertaken.
- Whether revisions were made, and the nature of the revisions, as a consequence of this input.
- The frequency and nature of feedback from teachers in the field.

All these opportunities were provided in the development of the National Board's subject standards.

Criterion 6c. That the Standards Committee serve as the sounding board for the development of the assessment measures and assist in designing fair and trustworthy processes.

The National Board stated "each Standards Committee will confirm that the assessment package developed in response to its standards accurately reflects its vision of accomplished teaching" (NBPTS, n.d., p. 5). This was achieved by: having representatives of the ADLs in attendance at Standards Committee meetings; ensuring that the committees receive regular reports from the ADLs on their work in progress; commenting on the prototype assessment products as they are developed; and participating regularly in the review of draft ADL assessment instruments, protocols and scoring guides, in exercise development, and in pilot or field tests.

A major research project mapping the standards onto the assessment tasks was also conducted for each of the Standards (e.g., Crocker, 1994).

Criterion 6d. That a wide sampling of opinion be sought for the standards from the major professional groups regarding the appropriateness and level of the resulting standards.

The most frequently occurring sequence for developing content standards across many professions begins with the identification of the job elements. Licensed practitioners often are asked to place the elements in priority order. Finally, the knowledge and skills needed to perform the job tasks safely and effectively are inferred and become the content standards that guide the item and test development. As such analyses are not possible when there are no presently credentialed workers; an alternative procedure involves seeking advice from the major professional groups with a stake in determining "highly accomplished teachers". If the field is a new one, then professionals who are likely to be so certified perform the review. In the present case, particularly given the difficulties of agreeing who were "highly accomplished teachers", it was not possible to independently identify such teachers before the establishment of the standards that would serve as the basis for such selection.

Smith, Greenberg, and Muenzen (1993) reviewed procedures employed by various licensure and certification agencies in defining content standards, and concluded that "there is no single correct process for developing content specifications. Combinations of approaches may be appropriate depending on the purpose, scope, and financial and personal resources available to the credentialing organization" (p. 11). The agencies they reviewed implemented one of two overall strategies. "The first approach emphasizes the contribution of a relatively small, but select group of subject-matter experts who are responsible for the development of the content specifications. The composition of the expert panel typically includes academics and practitioners" (p. 12). The second approach supplemented the work of the subject-matter experts by a survey of credentialed practitioners as a verification check on the accuracy and completeness of the initial delineation. "Clearly, the second approach is the most common among the credentialing agencies we reviewed" (p. 13).

Evidence regarding this standard can be obtained from three major sources:

a. Seeking the views of professional organizations, state bodies, teachers, and academics. The NBPTS process for establishing standards included two major reviews: one seeking the views of professional organizations, state bodies, teachers, and academics; and the other seeking the views of teachers (described under Standard 6a). This seemed to meet the criteria that are normal among other professional credentialing groups, and perhaps even went beyond previous practice as identified in Smith et al.'s (1993) review.

An examination of responses from many organizations indicated the extensiveness of the respondents, and provided evidence as to the clarity and appropriateness of the standards.

Reviews and critiques of the draft EA/G from teachers, scholars, field representatives of national associations, state departments of education, and the Field Test Network were largely positive, expressing praise for the Committee's comprehensiveness and encouragement for the National Board as it pursued its task ... . A small portion of the reviewers were concerned that the standards may be too broad and general for a teacher to adequately self-assess where they were in relation to the standards. Recommendations to address this concern included the addition of supportive explanations and vignettes. Many respondents praised the cross-referencing of various standards. They felt this emphasized the holistic nature of teaching. There was also general agreement that these standards would be useful as a framework for the professional development of teachers in the field (Hattie, 1996).

b. Soliciting the views of these interest groups as to the clarity, appropriateness, relevance, and usefulness of the standards. Many of the organizations that made submissions were surveyed and asked for their general comments and then specifically asked to address four questions:
   • If you were a candidate for National Board Certification, would you have a clear understanding of NBPTS's expectations?
   • Are these standards too demanding or too lax?
   • Are the important aspects of highly accomplished practice in this field given enough emphasis?
   • How useful would these standards be as a framework for the professional development of teachers in this field?
c. Seeking the views of teachers (described under Standard 6a).

CONCLUSIONS

The methodology used by the NBPTS to develop the high and rigorous standards continues to be improved. As early as 1992, there was a discussion by the National Board about a new format for the Standards. This new format:

> might present highly accomplished teaching in a more narrative fashion that includes vignettes and rubrics that clearly show the distinction between highly accomplished and less accomplished practice ... . We might also want to consider a form that lends itself to narration, active language and description of specific teacher actions and ideas. Such an approach might allow more opportunity than the current form provides for depicting the numerous interactions that occur when exemplary teaching takes place. Working from the current form with its delineated and isolated Propositions and Standards, several overlapping and interrelated teacher actions, stages and steps can be combined to form the nucleus of new standards that lend themselves to narration. (p. 8)

The process for setting the NBPTS standards was not as systematic as may be implied in this chapter. After the first Standards were written for EA/ELA, it was acknowledged by the National Board that the process for setting standards "has been fluid as NBPTS has attempted to invent and reinvent the process as it proceeded and to respond to constructive criticism and opportunities to improve the end product as they have emerged" (p. 1). The major lessons that were learned from the experience related to:

- ensuring more coordination between standards committees, such as developing standards within a single discipline concurrently and then later deciding to appoint a single committee for each new disciplinary cluster.
- clarifying the relationship between the standards development and assessment development work. As was demonstrated from the experiences of the EA/G there was almost parallel development of the standards and the assessment procedures. This, at least, ensured that there would be operational assessment available quickly, and a fuller appreciation of why the committees came to the decisions they did. However, this also meant that the ADLs had to attempt to anticipate, as best as they could, where the committees were headed and this anticipation was not always accurate – which lead to increased costs in terms of time, energy, and loss of some momentum. The NBPTS decided not to commence the assessment development work until, at a minimum; there was a set of draft standards accepted by the Certification Standards Working Group.
- involving the various discipline and specialty groups of interest in the deliberations of the Standards Committee. Initially, representatives from

such groups were not permitted to attend the various meetings, whereas to ensure a greater flow of discussion particularly in the earlier stages, the NBPTS came to allow all interested groups to name representatives to serve as observers to the appropriate committees. Some organizations have chosen to exercise this option while others, believing their interests were already well represented, have chosen not to.

• recasting the standards from centering around the five propositions towards "structuring standards that focus on critical and observable teacher actions which, at the same time, resolves the tension between describing the seamless character of exemplary practice and the need to pull practice apart into its several critical aspects" (p. 5). This move toward writing standards more in terms of observable teacher actions or end results allowed more focus on key teacher actions, created more holistic portraits of accomplished practice, and provided the ADL with crisper frameworks to guide their work.

Throughout this evolution of the Board's approach to developing standards, it can be seen that there were major initiatives by the NBPTS to ensure that a valid process for establishing standards had taken place to encourage input, criticism, and reactions from the expert judgment of practitioners in the field. There were few guidelines in the literature to assist in this process. For all the test standards that were generated by professional groups, few directly addressed the process of defining the domain to be tested. General admonitions such as sound practice and good documentation were made, but specific requirements concerning the process appear to be lacking. The six criteria outlined in this chapter evolved out of the processes adopted by the National Board, and they could subsequently serve to procedurally validate future Standards.

REFERENCES

AERA, APA, NCME. (1985). *Standards for educational and psychological testing*. Washington, DC: American Psychological Association.

Crocker, L. (1994). *A methodology for content validation of assessment packages developed by the National Board for Professional Teaching Standards* (final report). Greensboro: University of North Carolina, Center for Educational Research.

Hattie, J. (1996, September). *A description and evaluation of the process used to establish NBPTS Early Adolescence through Young Adulthood/Art Certification Standards*. Greensboro, NC: National Board for Professional Teaching Standards, Technical Analysis Group, Center for Educational Research and Evaluation, University of North Carolina-Greensboro.

Hattie, J. A. (1994). *A validation study of the NBPTS English Language Arts assessment procedure.* Technical Advisory Group, National Board for Professional Teachers.

Hattie, J. A., & Sackett, P. (1995). A description and evaluation of the NBPTS' initial process for establishing teacher certification standards. Paper commissioned by the National Board for Professional Teacher Development. National Board for Professional Teaching Standards, Technical Analysis Group, Center for Educational Research and Evaluation, University of North Carolina-Greensboro, Greensboro NO.

Linn, R. L., Baker, E. L., & Dunbar, S. B. (1991). Complex, performance-based assessment: Expectations and validation criteria. *Educational Researcher, 20,* 15–23.

Messick, S. (1989). Validity. In: R. L. Linn (Ed.), *Educational measurement* (3rd ed., pp. 13–103). New York: Macmillan.

Messick, S. (1995). Validity of psychological assessment: Validation of inferences from persons' responses and performances as scientific inquiry into score meaning. *American Psychologist, 50*(9), 741–749.

National Board for Professional Teaching Standards. (n.d.). *Handbook for NBPTS standards committees.* Detroit, MI: NBPTS.

National Board for Professional Teaching Standards. (1991). *Criteria for writing NBPTS standards: Guidance paper.* Detroit, MI: NBPTS.

National Commission for Certifying Agencies. (1991). *NCCA Standards for accreditation of national certification organizations.* Washington, DC: National Commission for Certifying Agencies of the National Organization for Competency Assurance.

Scriven, M. (1994). The final synthesis. *Evaluation Practice, 15,* 367–382.

Smith, I. L., Greenberg, S., & Muenzen, P. M. (1993). *Procedures employed by selected licensure and certification agencies in defining content standards: A report to the technical advisory group.* Detroit, MI: NBPTS.

CHAPTER 5

THE ROLE OF SUBJECT-MATTER KNOWLEDGE IN TEACHER ASSESSMENT

Sam Wineburg

ABSTRACT

This chapter outlines some of the challenges in assessing teachers' subject-matter knowledge. After reviewing traditional ways of mapping a domain, such as job analysis and "wisdom of practice," the author alights on the two constructs, depth and breadth, that have come to define how teachers' subject-matter knowledge is conceptualized. He argues that these two constructs constitute an impoverished vocabulary that misrepresents the complexity of the subject-matter knowledge teachers most need for effective instruction. He proposes an expanded set of constructs – differentiation and elaboration, qualification, integration, generativity, and epistemological knowledge – that better approximate the complexity of a subject-matter domain and serve as a better guide for creating an assessment system.

Assessing Teachers for Professional Certification:
The First Decade of the National Board for Professional Teaching Standards
Advances in Program Evaluation, Volume 11, 113–138
Copyright © 2008 by Elsevier Ltd.
ISSN: 1474-7863/doi:10.1016/S1474-7863(07)11005-X

INTRODUCTION

Educational reforms come and go. But among reform initiatives, the National Board for Professional Teaching Standards (NBPTS)[1] has been unique in placing teachers' subject-matter knowledge at the center of teaching excellence. Teachers need to know more than content – how to manage kids, how to deal with parents, and so on – but without deep subject-matter knowledge these other things are trifling. Contrary to popular (and anti-intellectual) notions that a "good teacher can teach anything," the Board took a clear position: excellent teachers are rooted in the subject matter that they teach – they know it deeply and broadly, and their knowledge is flexible and generative.

Such descriptions often elicit nods and assent. We all want liberally educated teachers, masters of their subject matter. Where this work gets hard, of course, is when we try to translate slogans into assessment schemes. Too often, notions of deep knowledge turn into numbers of correct answers on multiple-choice tests. When we turn to psychometricians for counsel, it turns out that they offer us little help to solve the knowledge question. Yes, they have numerous techniques in their armamentarium – Rasch models, Item Response Theories, and other techniques that dazzle and awe. But many of these techniques rest on notions of knowledge that fit cozily with behaviorism and stand strikingly out of step with current notions of knowledge informed by cognitive scientists and disciplinary specialists. At no time in this century has the gap been greater between psychologists who develop tests and measurements and those who develop cognitively based theories of learning.

It was precisely this breach that I fell into when I was named to the Technical Assistance Group (TAG) of the National Board. Composed of some of the premier measurement specialists of our time, the TAG offered the Board advice on issues of measurement and assessment. Although trained at Stanford, under Lee Shulman, and a part of the original research group that designed the prototype assessments for the Board, I did not consider myself an "assessment person." Rather, I was a cognitively oriented educational psychologist, rooted in the discipline of history. I was bilingual. I could follow arcane statistical discussions – and even ask an informed question – but my chief role on the TAG was to ask questions about content, to think about the "goodness of fit" between technical psychometric issues and the contours and integrity of the disciplines.

And so it was that I was asked to address the question at the heart of the Board's entire enterprise: "How should the domain of subject-matter content knowledge that can reasonably be expected of candidates for National Board Certification in a particular field be defined?" In accepting the Board's commission, I was asked to consider the following questions:

> *How should the Board specify the depth and breadth of subject-matter knowledge that should be expected of highly accomplished teachers?*

> *With what degree of specificity and in what form should the Board characterize the domain of subject-matter knowledge required for National Board Certification of teachers in the field for which it is developing certification standards?*

> *What criteria should be used for judging whether the specifications for subject-matter knowledge in each field are adequate?*

I undertook this assignment with the understanding that I would use a single domain of knowledge – history/social studies – as my point of reference. I did so for two simple reasons. First, the question of "What constitutes an adequate definition of subject-matter knowledge?" The first question put to me, could easily turn into a life's work if I were to embrace all domains of knowledge. Second, my own knowledge begins to fray the moment I venture beyond my familiar turf. Historical understanding has a shape and texture different from mathematical or artistic understanding; the Board has recognized as much by underscoring in its standards knowledge of content-specific pedagogy. I explicitly left to those with expertise in other domains to search for points of contact. In what follows, I lay out in abbreviated form my responses to the Board's charge. In the first part of this chapter, I focus on the nature of subject-matter knowledge for assessment. In the second part, I turn briefly to the kinds of assessments we should employ to examine this knowledge. I end by considering the implications of the Board's work for other efforts aimed at the reform of teaching.

BACKGROUND

The question of what subject-matter knowledge teachers need to know fits into the category of queries that supplicants, as a last resort, submit to the sphinx. The answer, they find, is like a dense ball of yarn with a mind of its own; no matter how steady the hands, they cannot prevent the yarn from unraveling. The tendency in such situations is to abandon the effort in frustration. But before we let the yarn unravel, let us consider some of the traditional means that have been used to address the above questions.

Job Analysis

One method that has been used to determine what teachers need to know has been job analysis, a strategy whereby teachers are surveyed about the knowledge relevant to their work. On the basis of these surveys, lists of competencies are drawn up and new inductees to the field are evaluated on the basis of their ability to demonstrate these competencies. Variations on job analysis are many (often observations are employed), but all derive from a common principle: if we want to know what members of a given profession ought to know (or do), then we must study what existing members already know and do.

The problem with job analysis is that it is a profoundly conservative strategy. At a time when there is general agreement that education is in need of an overhaul, job analysis looks to the status quo for images of the future. The images of teaching that can be gleaned by randomly sampling existing classrooms lead to the dismal conclusion that what is must be. It is a conclusion bereft of imaginativeness and creativity.

The Strategy of "Wisdom of Practice"

Another way to go about determining the subject-matter knowledge that "can be reasonably expected" of accomplished teachers is to look only at accomplished teachers. This was the strategy employed by the Stanford Teacher Assessment Project (TAP).

TAP's Wisdom of Practice research (Shulman, 1986, 1987a) was predicated on the notion that there are many things about good teaching that remain in the heads of wise practitioners that never find their way into the research literature. Wisdom of Practice research was an attempt to codify this knowledge by intensively studying a few non-representative teachers, carefully selected by a process of peer-nomination, supervisor recommendation, and word of mouth. By looking at what united these teachers, the knowledge they shared, and the perspectives they held in common, we hoped to build a general framework of what good history teachers know. In other words, our standards for what good teachers ought to know were to be derived from what they did know.

In actuality, the process we used was much less tidy than the above description suggests. Many of the names in our Wisdom of Practice pool came, initially, from recommendations by members of a professional organization dedicated to developing intellectually rigorous curricula with rich subject-matter content, a perspective that aligned neatly with the view of teaching embraced by the TAP. Moreover, not all 11 of our Wisdom of Practice teachers received equal attention. The two history teachers who received the most attention were, in many respects, living embodiments of a theoretical model of teaching: their classrooms pivoted on each teachers' pedagogical content knowledge, their curriculum was organized on the basis of students' prior knowledge and preconceptions, and their own teaching was informed by a deep understanding of the substantive and syntactic structures of the subject matter (Schwab, 1978). In other words, those teachers who received the most intense scrutiny were those most in alignment with the model of teaching that guided the work of this project.

So, at first glance, what appeared to be an empirical process of generating nominations and looking for overlap turned out to be a deeply theory-laden process that used empirical observations to develop and further refine theory. Put differently, a normative model of good teaching (cf. Shulman, 1986, 1987a, 1987b) led us, if not to select, then certainly to focus on a small number of good teachers. What these teachers did and what they knew then helped us to elaborate our conceptions of teacher knowledge.

The problem with this position, of course, is that a different group of researchers with a different set of conceptions about good teaching would doubtless select a different group of Wisdom of Practice teachers. As a research strategy Wisdom of Practice does not speak to the question of where the criteria to define "wisdom" come from in the first place.

Statements of Professional Organizations

A third avenue of possible guidance is the statements and reports made by professional teacher organizations in the different content areas. Indeed, this is the strategy taken by the National Board's standards committee in mathematics, which drew heavily from the report of the National Council for the Teaching of Mathematics (National Council of Teachers of Mathematics [NCTM], 1989) in determining the aspects of mathematical knowledge that teachers ought to possess. But as several authors note (cf. Gerhke, Knapp, & Sirotnik, 1992; Sykes & Plastrik, 1993), the discipline of mathematics may be the exception rather than the rule.

In history/social studies, a more confusing picture emerges. In the United States, one can look to the National Council for History Education or the more established National Council for the Social Studies (NCSS) and the animosity between the two runs deep. Even if we were to choose, arbitrarily, the largest of these, the NCSS, the guidance offered by their written documents is a far cry from the specificity of the NCTM Standards. Consider this recent NCSS definition of what constitutes the social studies:

> Social studies provides coordinated, systematic study drawing upon such disciplines as anthropology, archeology, economics, geography, history, law, philosophy, political science, psychology, religion, and sociology, as well as appropriate content from the humanities, mathematics, and natural sciences. (cited in McBride, 1993, p. 281)

As McBride (1993) has argued, based on this definition, there is little that social studies do not embrace. In his words:

> The [NCSS] definition ... permit[s] just about anyone who wants a career change to argue that they are prepared to teach courses in social studies. Our field could become the catch basin for the most ill-equipped generation of teachers we have seen in a long time, and just when the country needs the most qualified people in the classroom. (p. 282)

In order to provide guidance in defining subject-matter knowledge, definitions from professional organizations must exclude as well as include, must de-emphasize as well as highlight. When statements do not do so, they provide little guidance in delineating the subject-matter knowledge teachers most need to know.

Summary

The above options suggest that questions of subject-matter knowledge definition cannot be answered by empirical means. This is a normative enterprise that rests on deliberation and judgment. One could reasonably claim that such a process is highly subjective. Like the Wisdom of Practice approach, the results of the standards committees are dependent on the views of its members; standards committees made up of different members would likely come to different conclusions. This is obviously true, but there still remains a fundamental difference between the Wisdom of Practice approach and the approach taken by the various "Standards Committees" of the NBPTS. Wisdom of Practice creates the illusion that its results are empirically based when, in fact, the most important decision in this form of research is the selection of the sample, a process that is normative in its essence. But with Standards Committees no such confusion is possible. The establishment of standards is a process of determining "what should be" rather than "what is." It is a process that must draw on judgment and deliberation, and call forth values and norms. To the charge that others would erect different standards, this approach answers, "Yes. Others may do it differently. But we feel that these standards reflect our considered judgment and we are willing to defend them."

THE QUESTION OF SPECIFICITY

If there is no other reasonable way to define standards for subject-matter knowledge than by making people sit down at a table and engaging them in a deliberative process, we must still address the question of specificity. How general and how specific should the guidelines be for teachers' subject-matter knowledge? The reports of the various NBPTS standards committees varied widely on this issue. For purposes of illustration, I compare two of these reports, the standards for teaching mathematics in Adolescence and Young Adulthood (AYA/M), and standards of the Early Adolescent/Generalist (EA/G) Standards Committee.

In the Mathematics Standards Report (NBPTS, 1994), the section on subject-matter knowledge (Knowledge of Mathematics) occupies five double-spaced pages. It begins with some overarching statements about the nature of mathematics as a domain of knowledge, but by the third paragraph starts to enumerate specific mathematical concepts teachers should know. In describing mathematics as the science and art of patterns, the report specifies, in particular, that teachers should be fluent in pattern features such as "symmetry, randomness, stability, similarity, continuity, periodicity, and linearity" (p. 17). When the document states that accomplished teachers use "functions as a powerful, unifying idea" and are conversant in linear, trigonometric, exponential, and logarithmic functions, one assumes that the nature of this understanding is at a level beyond that of an advanced high school math student.

The final two pages of the subject-matter section acknowledge a debt to the standards documents of the National Council of Teachers of Mathematics (1989) and the Mathematical Association of America. Six spheres of mathematics are laid out, including "number systems and number theory," "algebra and linear algebra," "geometry," "statistics and probability," "calculus," and "discrete mathematics." While the document still leaves room for varying interpretations, it provides many ideas to an assessment developer, prospective candidate, or interested parent about the nature of accomplished subject-matter knowledge in mathematics.

The EA/G Standards Document provides a description of subject-matter knowledge in six different areas: English language arts, mathematics, history and social studies, science, the arts, and health. The section on mathematics occupies about two and a half pages, about half the size of the section in the AYA/M document. Highly accomplished generalists "are knowledgeable about the foundations of mathematics, including algebra, geometry, statistics, probability, functions, and the study of patterns and number sense" according to the first sentence of this section (p. 22). But beyond this one sentence, the rest of the selection offers little guidance for what mathematical content is most important to know.

Quite a different problem surfaces in the section on history/social science. Here, the problem is less one of determining what content the teacher should know, but what content lies beyond the scope of teacher knowledge. The accomplished generalist not only knows "world and United States history and geography" (whatever "knowing world and United States history" means) but has a "foundation of knowledge in the social sciences including geography, political science, and economics" (p. 20). Such teachers know "how history is written," and the nature of argument in history and the social sciences. In light of the above description, it is fair to ask, is there anything the accomplished teacher does not know about history and the social sciences?

The above definition of content knowledge may offer flexibility and inclusiveness but it offers little guidance. To state that accomplished teachers "know world and United States history" without providing a clear sense of what they know about them is to offer a statement hollow of meaning. Should the teacher be familiar with ancient Greece but not ancient Ghana? Keynesian economics but not rational choice theory? The Sykes-Picot Pact but not Article 10 of the League of Nations Agreement? And what, exactly, should teachers know about "how history is written," the ability to recognize different historical genres, or the ability to engage in and succeed at an exercise in historiography? What level of knowledge should a teacher possess with respect to history and the social sciences? Should such knowledge go substantially beyond the content of high school history/social studies courses? In sum, standards that remain at such a high level of generality provide no bounds to the types of inferences that can be drawn on their basis.

WHAT CONSTITUTES AN ADEQUATE DEFINITION OF SUBJECT MATTER?

Let us start by acknowledging the poverty of our vocabulary. When discussing issues of subject-matter knowledge, we become boxed in by binary oppositions – breadth/depth, content/process, and declarative/procedural – as if knowledge only comes packaged in a form more complex than an either/or. Despite concerns about "teachers knowing their subject," our thinking about the subject matter that teachers need to know has remained embarrassingly underdeveloped.

This under-conceptualization is the historical legacy of twentieth-century psychology. North American psychology has a penchant for the universal, seeking to establish general laws of learning, homothetic theories, and culture-free constructs of mind. In the early part of this century, two schools of educational psychology, one stressing the generic nature of knowledge, the other focusing on what was unique about different domains, competed for adherents. Chicago's Charles Judd, who stressed the distinctive "psychologies" of the different subjects in the curriculum (see Wineburg, 1994, 1996), could not muster the appeal of the all-embracing stimulus–response behaviorism of Columbia's E. L. Thorndike. The battle raged for many years, but as the historian of education Ellen Condliffe Lagemann (2000) succinctly put it, Thorndike won.

Behaviorism comes bundled with an epistemology. It views knowledge as the aggregation of independent units, or "bonds," between a stimulus and a response. Given this assumption, knowledge could be broken down in minute parts and tested bit by bit. To see how this assumption played out in practice, it is instructive to go back to the early years of testing. One of the first large-scale history tests in the United States was created by Bell and McCollum (1917), who tested 1,500 Texas students on a list of names, dates, and events believed by teachers to be important things all students should know. In this and many subsequent tests, history was carved into thousands of minute pieces, and sorted according to the dualism of breadth and depth. Breadth indicated the chronological range of a student's knowledge, i.e., the ability to answer questions that spanned the period from the *Mayflower* to the contemporary era. Depth indicated how much a student knew about any one topic or period. The task of sampling the historical domain could be easily dispensed-with by doing two things: first, creating a timeline of American history, using each presidential administration as the organizing unit on the timeline. Second, listing subsidiary events, people, or dates that corresponded to the chronological unit. Once the domain was charted, one could sample horizontally and vertically in creating a test.

The above description is admittedly a simplification, but it does illustrate how breadth and depth, as assessment constructs, fit cozily with behaviorist notions of knowledge as isolated bits and pieces. One could think about a knowledge domain similar to the way one thought about prospecting for oil: How expansive a territory to search (breadth) and how far down to drill (depth). The only problem with this analogy is that knowledge domains are not flat surfaces.

BEYOND "BREADTH AND DEPTH"

The dimensions of breadth and depth view the problem of knowledge as one of amount rather than kind. Built into the way these terms are used is the assumption that there is an equivalence of all parts, that knowledge of one segment of the timeline is as good as knowledge of another. History, however, is about connection, integration, motivation, and significance. History without high points and low points is no longer history but chronicle. Consider this attempt, by historian William Cronon (1992), to provide an account of the American West shorn of markers of significance and causal connections:

> Five centuries ago, people traveled west across the Atlantic Ocean. So did some plants and animals. One of these – the horse – appeared on the Plains. Native peoples used horses to hunt bison. Human migrants from across the Atlantic eventually appeared on the Plains as well. People fought a lot. The bison herds disappeared. Native peoples moved to reservations. The new immigrants built homes for themselves. Herds of cattle increased. Railroads moved people and other things into and out of the regions. Crops sometimes failed for lack of rain. During the 1930s, there was a particularly bad drought. ... Then the drought ended. (Cronon, 1992, p. 1351)

Cronon uses the above illustration, which sounds eerily like many school textbooks, as an example of "chronicle" as opposed to history. Each event or sentence carries equal weight. Each stands on its own. No plot, no sense of story, no connection to bind disparate events together.

Most striking, there are no high points. The two linear dimensions of breadth and depth cannot account for high points in a domain, places to stand that allow one to view the domain better than if one stood elsewhere. Domains, in this sense, are less the plains of Iowa than the terrain of Northern California, where valley and mountain, flatland and rolling hill combine into one. In the middle of an Iowa cornfield it does not matter where you stand, the same scenery rolls on for miles. But if one wants to see far in a landscape marked by peaks and valleys, it is better to perch on a peak.

Depth

What, then, is meant by the notion of depth of subject-matter knowledge? What does it mean to possess in-depth knowledge of the American Revolution, the Civil War, the Depression or any one of a number of topics? If depth meant the ability to identify myriad numbers of discrete facts about the Revolution or the Civil War, then the person who could do so might be well-positioned to teach either of those topics, but as Cronon's tongue-in-cheek "history" suggests, this is not the case. Someone who possesses in-depth knowledge about these topics can separate the peripheral from the central, can see the forest for the trees, and possesses knowledge organized in interconnecting networks of meaning and significance.

One of the most extended treatments of the concept of depth is provided by Suzanne Wilson (1988). Wilson studied a group of experienced history teachers, novice history teachers, experienced teachers of English, and graduate students in history in an attempt to understand the interaction between subject-matter knowledge and pedagogical reasoning. She used four categories to explore the notion of depth of knowledge: differentiation, elaboration, qualification, and integration. Differentiation referred to an individual's understanding of multiple facets of a concept or an event; elaboration addressed knowledge of detail about these events or concepts; qualification located this knowledge within an epistemological framework, speaking to issues of historical context, and the uncertain and tentative nature of historical knowledge; integration addressed causal and thematic linkages. As an example of Wilson's categories, consider the responses of two teachers, Clea, an experienced English teacher, and Bryan, an experienced history teacher, on the question of the Tennessee Valley Authority (TVA, see Table 1).

Differentiation and Elaboration

Clearly Bryan's response is longer than Clea's, but length does not necessarily mean depth, since we all know people who can speak volubly but say little. But in this instance, length is not a function of puffery but of a response that contains more "stuff." Bryan's definition of the TVA is more differentiated than Clea's; he sees the TVA's purpose as going beyond the provision of electricity to spur land development, to provide a means of flood control, to lead to the restoration of fisheries and the creation of recreational sites, and so on. The response bears aspects of elaboration as well as the type of detail that separates history from chronicle and provides texture to accounts. The location of an atomic plant at Oakridge is not a

Table 1. Tennessee Valley Association Task (from Wilson, 1988).

	Definitions of the TVA
Clea	It was the first of the rural electrification programs. It provided, not free, but very cheap electricity to the Tennessee Valley.
Bryan	The TVA was an attempt to come to grips with the problems of the entire region. The Tennessee Valley was perhaps the single most afflicted area in the United States. It had once been a very beautiful region but it had been exploited by over-forestation, over-farming, by a river that frequently ran rampant, because of the ruination of the environment. So the Authority, set up during the New Deal, sought to resuscitate an entire valley. But not just with the building of dams, dams, which could prevent floods, that would enable flood control, that would generate power, power generated by these dams. Which, in the meantime, would create not just flood control, but also enable means of navigation, the restoration of fisheries, and the creation of recreational facilities. It was the creation of power for sale to resuscitate the entire region. The success of it, I suppose, can be demonstrated when, at the beginning of World War II, it was seen as a reliable source of power to allow the installation of atomic facilities in the TVA's area at Oakridge, TN. The only other place was in the Washington state area, which was near two of our other greatest dams, Bonneville and, more importantly, Grand Coulee. And regardless of what we happen to feel about atomic power and the bomb, the point of the matter was that demonstrates the success of the generating capacity of the area. The Tennessee Valley was transformed by the TVA and all its many works from one of the most poverty-stricken areas of the United States into one of the most diverse and prosperous areas in the United States. It is also important that many people alluded to it as an exercise in socialism and, in many ways, it was the most radical of the New Deal proposals. It put the government into business, particularly in the power business. And it was in direct competition with other power companies. Indeed, a lawyer for the power companies in the cases that tested the constitutionality of the TVA-gained fame in his own right and ended up as Roosevelt's opponent in the presidential election of 1940. Wendell Wilkie was that man.

- This metaphor, as well as the larger discussion it hinges on, comes from conversations with Lee Shulman (see in particular Shulman, 1987a, and 1987b).
- Obviously, knowledge of the Great Depression would be multi-dimensional, including the elements of the five dimensions laid out above. This knowledge would also reflect an understanding of the epistemological basis of historical understanding.
- Much of what I argue here applies to portfolio entries as well. Because I take up the issue of portfolio assessments in a previous paper for the TAG, I focus here on assessment center exercises.

detail for detail's sake but a metric to gauge the success of the entire reclamation effort. Wendell Wilkie is not an isolated bit of knowledge under the category of "political candidates," but part of a grand narrative about a president who moved government into the private sector versus forces that saw government's duty as staying out of the world of business.

Qualification

Wilson's third dimension of subject-matter depth is qualification. There are many ways historical knowledge can be qualified but Wilson focused on two: the act of placing statements about the past in historical context and the recognition of indeterminateness and uncertainty about historical-knowledge claims.

Integration

Integration is the fourth aspect of subject-matter depth in Wilson's scheme. The integration of subject-matter knowledge speaks to the ability to see patterns in historical knowledge, to know how such knowledge fits into a larger scheme of historical significance. The claim to "know history" is a statement that one knows why an event is important, how it links to other events, what its antecedents were, and how it affected future events. Knowing any one of these aspects in isolation misses the point.

Generativity

Alongside Wilson's four aspects of differentiation, elaboration, qualification, and integration, I believe we must add a fifth dimension, generativity. Generativity would be used to characterize subject-matter knowledge that reflects cutting-edge scholarship of those ideas, conceptions, interpretations, and findings that have created major shifts in disciplinary understanding. The generativity of subject-matter knowledge indicates, to some extent, an individual's understanding of the growth points in a discipline, those areas of scholarship that generate excitement and which have the potential for changing our understanding.

Generativity of subject-matter knowledge is crucial for teachers for several reasons. Without generative knowledge teachers are at the behest of textbook accounts, for without this form of knowledge teachers possess neither the resources nor the awareness to update textbooks, supplement their narratives, or offer a different perspective. Second, the possession of generative knowledge testifies to the fact that a teacher has remained a student of his/her discipline. We would expect this from accomplished teachers. Professionals, no matter the field, "keep up" and take pride in staying abreast of new knowledge in their fields.

These five aspects of subject-matter knowledge add complexity to the unitary notion of "depth" with which we began. In place of two perpendicular lines, one representing breadth, the other depth, we have loops between ideas, boldfaced labels that mark importance and significance, dotted lines that indicate uncertainty and qualification, vectors reaching outward toward new knowledge. But still other dimensions of subject-matter knowledge figure centrally in any conception of mature disciplinary understanding. These dimensions are considered next.

Epistemological Knowledge

So far I have focused on what Joseph Schwab (1978) called "substantive knowledge," or knowledge of the major facts, concepts, events, growth points, and interpretative schools that lend shape to disciplinary understanding. But subject-matter knowledge goes well beyond this. Someone who knows history knows more than what history books, even good ones, say. Such an individual knows how the books know, knows how historical claims are introduced, evaluated, warranted, and judged by members of a disciplinary community. This individual knows how new knowledge in the discipline comes about and how historical claims are introduced, evaluated, and disputed. Moreover, to use Ryle's distinction between "knowing that" and "knowing how," this person's knowledge extends beyond knowing that historians consider the perspective of the author when weighing the trustworthiness of historical claims. Such a person knows how to determine and weigh an author's perspective when evaluating a piece of history (cf. Wilson & Wineburg, 1993). Such knowledge is at the core of what we call disciplinary knowledge, for "discipline" refers not only to an organized body of knowledge but to the fact that knowledge comes about by using a disciplined and systematic set of criteria and procedures (Wineburg & Wilson, 1991).

A person who possesses epistemological knowledge "thinks" like a historian, asking questions about context, showing caution at the pronouncement of a unilateral causal statement, corroborating evidence, and so on (cf. Wineburg, 1991). To know how to construct a historical argument, to know how to evaluate and question sources, to know when analogies to other events are appropriate and when they are misleading is not a generic "thinking skill," a "process," or a disembodied system of "metaknowledge." It is content knowledge in the richest sense.

Summary

Given the above image of subject-matter knowledge, how should a group that seeks to specify teaching standards think about defining subject-matter knowledge? The following guideposts are offered: At a minimum, such a group needs to specify the actual topics, concepts, the interpretative schools and approaches that feature prominently in a domain. For example, in the domain of history/social studies, to suggest that someone should "know US and world history" is not productive. The Board should aim for a middle-range designation that lies between the individual fact ("The Olive Branch Petition," "The Quebec Act") and the macrodescriptor ("modern America" or the "methods of the social science"). A middle-range designation for both of the above macrodescriptors might be "The Great Depression" or "the notion of control in sociology and psychology."

The topics, schemes, concepts, and perspectives that are identified for assessment should be selected because they offer a strategic view on the domain, both in a topical and an epistemological sense.

In making choices about content, a standards committee must offer a rationale for why a particular selection has been made. Specifying that the "European Encounter" is a topic that accomplished teachers must know should be accompanied by a statement that outlines why this topic merits attention and how it connects to other key topics in the domain.

Not all features of subject matter are areas of growth and excitement. A standards committee must specify growth points in a domain so that the generativity of teachers' knowledge will be among the aspects of subject-matter knowledge that are assessed.

HOW SHOULD SUBJECT-MATTER KNOWLEDGE BE ASSESSED?

Part of the NBPTS's motivation in asking for this paper was the perception by some NBPTS members that subject-matter knowledge was receiving short shrift in the early versions of assessment exercises. Some have suggested that, rather than embedding the assessment of subject-matter knowledge in portfolio and performance assessments, it be separated out and assessed directly using traditional paper-and-pencil tests. I begin this section by addressing this suggestion. I focus specifically on multiple-choice tests for two reasons: (a) they are the most common form of paper-and-pencil tests and (b) because there are already a number of well-known multiple-choice tests for testing advanced subject-matter knowledge.

The advantages of multiple-choice tests (MCTs) are well known. They are cheap and easy to score compared to newer forms of assessment. Unlike portfolios and performance-based assessments, the psychometric properties of MCTs are well-known. Although many believe that MCTs cannot tap depth of subject-matter knowledge, such tests are often recommended for wide sampling of the domain, a measure (at least from the perspective of adherents of MCTs) of one's "breadth" of domain knowledge.

MCTs also provide flexibility. The format of the item, a stem with four choices, is an empty vessel and as knowledge changes, new content can be put into this vessel without the extensive time and development that is necessary when creating other forms of assessment. And while items that measure such hybrids as "pedagogical content knowledge" may offer new challenges, some researchers believe that hurdles can be overcome and this integrative aspect of teaching can also be assessed in an objective form (Carlson, 1990). Given these attributes, and the fact that off-the-shelf measures for subject-matter knowledge (e.g., the GRE Subject-Matter Tests) exist, considerable attention needs to be paid to MCTs.

An Alternative View

Do multiple-choice tests "cover the domain"? Obviously, the answer to this question depends on one's definition of the domain. If we were to define the domain of history as facts of all important people, events, and dates from the landing at Plymouth Rock to the landing of American troops on Kuwaiti soil, then a long MCT would go far in "covering the domain." We could designate long lists of topics, not unlike those that guided the composition of the NAEP exam in history (Finn & Ravitch, 1988), and sample from them in creating a subject-matter examination for teachers.

But as I argued in the previous section, this image of the domain leaves out as much as it includes. Whole spheres of historical knowledge are never addressed in such a depiction. Attempts to capture an understanding of how historical knowledge is created are trivialized by items that ask if historians use corroboration to (a) confirm hypotheses, (b) establish facts, (c) create theories, or (d) all of the above, when what we are interested in is not whether teachers can recognize the keyed answer, but whether they can apply their knowledge of historiography in a situation that bears on teaching.

The same argument applies to the attempt to create multiple-choice items to assess "pedagogical content knowledge." Shulman (1987b) defines this form of knowledge as

> that special amalgam of content and pedagogy that is uniquely the province of teachers, their own special form of professional understanding. ... It represents the blending of content and pedagogy into an understanding of how particular topics, problems, or issues are organized, presented and adapted to the diverse interests and abilities of learners, and presented for instruction. (p. 8)

Carlson (1990), who worked on item development for the Connecticut Elementary Education Certification Examination, claimed that, with concerted effort, items measuring pedagogical content knowledge could be developed:

> ... we attempted to create test items that require the application of pedagogical knowledge to specific content areas. For example, it is a general pedagogical principle that concrete experiences should precede abstract experiences. A test item in mathematics that requires examinees to choose the most appropriate sequence in which to present three measurement activities to students requires not only knowledge of the general principle but also mathematical knowledge about measurement. The examinee will have to use the mathematical knowledge to analyze each measurement activity in light of the general pedagogical principle of concrete before abstract. In other words, the examinee will have to have knowledge of mathematics in order to recognize the correct application of the pedagogical principle. This type taps pedagogical content knowledge. (Carlson, 1990, p. 160)

It is instructive to look carefully at the type of item Carlson proposes. We must assume that it represents his most developed thinking since it is the most extensive example offered. First, let us consider the "general pedagogical principle" that "concrete experiences should precede abstract experiences." Carlson assumes that the "principle" is general, i.e., that it obtains across subject-matter domains as well as across topics within mathematics. But is this the case? For example, Lampert, widely cited for her work in teaching mathematics, began a lesson on graphing with a highly abstract problem. In light of Carlson's principle, Lampert was in error.

Carlson fundamentally misunderstands Shulman's concept of pedagogical content knowledge. The above item is "nowhere near what I mean by pedagogical content knowledge" (Lee Shulman, personal communication, August 7, 1994). Carlson has construed pedagogical content knowledge as a kind of algorithmic process by which a general (and in this case, highly dubious) pedagogical principle is applied to a specific content area. But pedagogical content knowledge is the integration of knowledge of subject matter and how best to teach it given (a) the specific nature of the subject matter, (b) a particular group of students, (c) the context in which one teaches, (d) what has already come before in the curriculum and what will come after, (e) the prior knowledge students bring to instruction, and (f) the community in which one dwells (cf. Wilson, 1995). If Carlson believed that it was "not easy to write" multiple-choice items given his misunderstanding of pedagogical content knowledge, it is fair to assume that, with a fuller understanding, he would find the process next to impossible.

Part of the problem with using multiple-choice items to tap pedagogical reasoning is that teaching, in its accomplished forms, is the quintessential "ill-structured" problem. Ill-structured problems are those "without definite criteria for determining when the problem is solved" (Frederiksen, 1984, p. 199); they are characterized by complexity and their ability to dodge any single answer. By its very nature, the multiple-choice item requires knowledge to be disembedded from the context of practice and a "right" or "best" answer to be erected. Adopting a "right answer approach" to teaching jeopardizes the claim to professionalism, for professionals are characterized not by their ability to select right answers but by their ability to offer reasoned judgments about their choices and actions (cf. Darling-Hammond, 1986).

There is some consensus that MCTs are useful in ascertaining whether individuals possess entry-level knowledge. Such tests may play a role in initial licensure examinations. But National Board certification has been conceptualized as a confirmation that one is an "accomplished teacher." Accomplished teachers do not merely possess bits of knowledge but know how to apply knowledge thoughtfully and provide a warranted explanation for their application. MCTs are not well suited for assessing this capacity.

Performance Assessments
In this section, I consider the benefits and drawbacks of performance assessments and what they might tell us about teachers' subject-matter knowledge. Conventional wisdom dictates that the virtues of performance assessment contain their vices as well. By providing an in-depth look at knowledge use, these assessments dig deeply into a particular area but necessarily neglect other important areas of a person's knowledge base. In gaining a glimpse of depth of subject-matter knowledge, we must, perforce, sacrifice breadth.

This position is widely held. In the section that follows, I will argue that part of it is true, part of it false, and part of it (probably the biggest part) still unknown. In developing this argument, I will draw liberally on an analysis of three performance exercises from the TAP's History assessment

(Wilson & Wineburg, 1993). A consideration of what performance assessments can and cannot do without referring to particular assessments and particular responses would require a level of abstraction that is neither useful nor particularly accurate.

The Move to Performance Assessment

One way to view performance assessments is to see them as devices that allow us to do what we have always done, but better. This view allows us, for example, to leave unchanged our broader beliefs about teaching, about knowledge, and about knowledge-for-teaching as we move from a National Teachers Examination (NTE) style teacher assessment to the latest generation of performance assessments.

But there is another way to interpret the move toward performance assessment. Here, performance assessments are not technical advances that allow us to do something we have always done – a washing machine instead of a washbasin – but symbols of a paradigm shift in how we conceptualize the work of teaching and learning. In this view, as Linda Darling-Hammond (1986) has written, performance assessments would symbolize a shift from a bureaucratic to a professional view of teaching. In the former, teachers are seen as little more than functionaries who execute the mandates of higher-ups. They do not question these mandates, overrule them, or alter them in light of their own experience or circumstance. The emphasis here is not how teachers think or reason, but whether they know what to do, know what rule to apply, and conform to a preset image of "effective teaching."

In contrast, the professional view of teaching depicts teachers as skilled individuals who engage in thoughtful analyses about the needs of children, taking into account issues of subject matter, pedagogy, and child development. In making decisions, they draw on a rich knowledge base similar to the knowledge bases of professionals in other fields. The essential quality sought in such individuals is not whether they know a fact or principle in isolation but whether, faced with the day-to-day imperatives of teaching, they can use what they know to promote children's growth and development. The focus in assessment becomes the quality of teachers' professional reasoning: is it warranted, does it draw on multiple sources of information, does it reflect "best practice" in the professional community, is it flexible, creative, thoughtful?

In what follows, I limit myself to the two main concerns that have been expressed regarding performance assessments and subject-matter knowledge: first, the "narrow sampling" problem, or the notion that performance assessments go deep but do not "cover much of the water"; and second, the notion that performance assessments are "process fixated," that tests without a firm command of subject-matter knowledge can "talk a good game" and still get by. In taking up these concerns, I train my lens on a single example of a performance assessment developed by the TAP. A more thorough accounting of this exercise, as well as detailed analyses of other performance assessments, can be found in Wilson and Wineburg (1993).

Textbook Evaluation Exercise

TAP's Textbook Evaluation exercise was a three-hour open-ended exercise (Wineburg & Kerdeman, 1989). Unlike assessments in the battery that had interactive interview components, this exercise had an open-ended response format and was completely self-administered. This exercise thrust teachers into the realm of professional judgment by asking them to critique a textbook selection on the basis of the "soundness of the history offered," the degree to which the book reflected "recent scholarship in history," its effectiveness in "addressing the historical misconceptions many students possess," its usefulness as a tool for promoting social studies skills, and so on. Questions darted among aspects of subject matter, pedagogy, and content-specific pedagogy.

Candidates were given a 27-page selection from a leading U.S. history textbook (Todd and Curti's [1982] *Rise of the American Nation*, a chapter on the antecedents to the American Revolution) along with 14 pages of supplementary material drawn from the teacher's manual and student workbook. A special response form was provided in which candidates could write their responses to both broad questions (e.g., "How does the text measure up with regard to recent scholarship in history?") that allowed for a flexibility of topics and approaches, and specific questions that focused on a particular paragraph or statement in the text ("Evaluate the explanation of foreign aid to the rebels on pp. 126–127"). Even though candidates were free to focus on any feature in 27 pages of text, and the response form provided the flexibility to do so, we directed candidates' attention to three particular subtopics: (a) the issue of taxation and representation, (b) the role of women and minorities, and (c) the Boston Massacre.

What kind of performance would candidates need in order to perform well on this exercise? For the dimension of subject-matter knowledge, candidates producing commendable or exemplary work would not only display factual, theoretical, and conceptual knowledge about the main topic and subtopics covered by the text selection, they would also be able to discuss critically other topics not explicitly mentioned in the book. Candidates would also exhibit familiarity with the historiography of the period (major interpretations and schools of thought). Finally, outstanding candidates would demonstrate familiarity with recent scholarship in the discipline of history, as it pertained to the main topic of the American Revolution and the three subtopics.

In the area of content-specific pedagogy, candidates performing on a commendable or exemplary level would display pedagogic savvy and sophistication. They would exhibit keen awareness of the range of possibilities that exist for using high school history texts. In addition, exemplary candidates would address how students of different reading levels and motivations might react to this text selection. They would show insight into how students' misconceptions about specific historical events or persons, or the discipline of history itself, might be influenced, strengthened, or dismantled by this book. Finally, outstanding candidates would provide evidence that, if required to use the text in the classroom, they would possess the knowledge and skill to improve it as a tool of instruction.

Given this description, how do we think about the issue of sampling? Was there "adequate and representative sampling" of the domain in creating this exercise?

If we define our domain as American history, then, clearly, there were huge chunks left out. It would be entirely possible for a candidate to have extensive knowledge about this period but know little about other periods. Nor can we make the claim that knowledge of the issues and concerns of the American Revolution are somehow parallel to or representative of the particular issues and concerns of America's entrance into World War II. So, in one sense, knowledge of one topical period in American history cannot be "representative" of another.

Within history, at least, the decision to focus on one topic and not another spawns sets of questions. But the issue of sampling can be asked differently. What aspects of epistemological knowledge were sampled by this exercise? There were several, but let me focus on just one: the candidates' ability to identify the interpretive stance of the text. One example will have to suffice.

In one of the focused questions, we asked candidates to evaluate the following explanation of Pontiac's Rebellion. The text passage read:

> Under the able leadership of Pontiac, an Ottawa chief, the Indians joined forces to prevent any further invasion of their lands. For nearly a year, the Indians and whites were locked in a desperate struggle. The Indians destroyed most of the British forts west of Niagara. Death and destruction raged along the length of the western frontier.

Finally, British and colonial troops recaptured the forts. The Indians accepted generous peace terms. Pontiac declared, "We shall reject everything that tends to evil, and strive with each other to see who shall be of the most service in keeping up that friendship that is so happily established between us." (Todd & Curti, 1982, pp. 88–89)

We expected that even candidates without extensive knowledge of the time period would be able to recognize the position of the text in characterizing peace terms as "generous." One of the most in-depth responses we received put the issue like this:

The book never mentions why Pontiac had to sue for peace. With the French gone there was no one to supply them with powder and shot they needed to sustain a protracted war. "Generous" was hardly the way the Indians felt about the ever-increasing land encroachments by the colonists, acts that were in flagrant violation of the Proclamation of 1763. The book makes it seem that warm friendship prevailed among the whites and Indians after this event. Pontiac's Rebellion was inspired by an attempt to save Indian culture from rum, Christianity, and the other ways of the white man. The treaty was a short break in the inevitable march toward Indian defeat.

In contrast to this, consider the response of Ed, an experienced teacher who called this passage "clear, accurate, and grade appropriate." Based on this one question, it would be wrong to draw any conclusions about Ed's knowledge. But when juxtaposed with his comment in another section of the exercise that he knows of "no recent scholarship which is neglected ... concerning the three subtopics," combined with difficulties he experienced in identifying the perspective of documents in the documentary history exercise, a pattern begins to emerge. Even though this man possessed extensive factual knowledge of the textbook history (correcting a student who had written that "a lot of tea" was thrown overboard in the Boston Tea Party with the precise number, "342 chests"), he seemed less knowledgeable about and less able to identify the interpretive frameworks historians use to bring meaning to the past.

Is this exercise "representative" of the ways in which teachers interact with textbooks? Clearly not, but we knew that before we began. Is it "representative" of the way that teachers ought to interact with textbooks? This question makes no sense, for it mixes a concept drawn from the world of experience representativeness with a normative conception of how teachers should regard curricular materials. Rather than thinking in terms of representativeness, we might better ask the question in terms of importance. Is it important for teachers to be able to identify the perspective of a textbook, to compare its treatment of key events with their knowledge base of new developments in the discipline? Should teachers know how to identify the weaknesses in suggested classroom activities and show that they can use their knowledge of students and subject matter to improve them? Our answer was yes.

But none of this responds to the claim that a candidate might have extensive knowledge of a period that we did not select, or might have extensive knowledge only of the period we did select. How can we make inferences based on sampling from a restricted topical range? The only way to sample from all periods – short of having candidates check into the assessment center for a month – would be through multiple-choice or short answer tests. But we should recognize that the depth/breadth question is also a question about the unit of scale. If our domain is "history," world and U.S., then how many items would we need before we could make any kind of reasonable judgment? If we restricted our domain to American history, the range is still expansive. Even by restricting our focus to the American Revolution, there were still limitless possibilities for showing one's knowledge. The open-endedness of our response form was intended to give candidates the full opportunity to use whatever knowledge they had about the period. Finally, our assessment differed from an Advanced Placement (AP) test or a Graduate Record Examination (GRE) subject-matter test in one important way. Rather than expecting candidates to be prepared to respond to questions on the full range of American history, we announced to them months before our mock assessment the particular topic and subtopics of the assessment.

If such a strategy were pursued, wouldn't candidates cram for such an assessment? While there is always this possibility (indeed probability) that "cram-course" study guides would be developed on "Recent Developments in Historiography: American Revolution," there are few ways to learn (in a 2-day workshop) how to use knowledge to detect and critique the underlying perspective of a text. These kinds of cognitive activities require the orchestration of diverse forms of knowledge, and nothing in the literature would suggest that such deep forms of understanding can be taught in an intensive one-week seminar, no matter how intensive it is.

Feasibility performance assessments are not better mousetraps but devices that, in tapping teachers' thought processes and knowledge use, reflect an image of teaching that has undergone a profound social transformation. But symbols, no matter how progressive, have a cost, and in the case of performance assessments the costs are high. Compared to traditional forms of assessment, the costs of performance assessments are astronomical. The bulk of performance assessments developed by the TAP required interactive interviews, the completion of open-ended and unstandardized responses, and, sometimes, samples of actual teaching. All of this might be easier to swallow if we had unambiguous evidence that there is a clear relationship between teachers' scores on performance assessments and their actual teaching practice, but even this is lacking. Nor is this lack due to the fact that in the rush to develop performance assessments, aspects central to basic research and development were cast to the wind. What kind of study would "validate" performance assessments that are based on an image of teaching that is far from universally held? For there to be a shred of logic in the typical criterion-based validation study (correlations between scores on performance assessments and either supervisors' ratings and/or students' gain scores), we would have to insure that supervisors shared the same conception of teaching as that embedded in the performance exercises, and that the tests for students did so as well. There are few places where such luxurious conditions prevail.

CONCLUSION

It is useful to place the work of the NBPTS in the context of the many standards movements that swept across the United States in the 1980s and 1990s. The common theme in these diverse movements was the aspiration to teacher excellence: standards should be rigorous and should allow policy makers to draw distinctions between what is mediocre and what is exemplary.

In preparing to write this commissioned paper for the NBPTS, I conducted phone interviews with selected Board members. I remember one conversation with the late Albert Shanker, who spoke passionately about the laxity of teaching standards in the U.S. compared to the rigorous standards in many European countries. In the U.S. we want teachers to know everything except content, Shanker lamented. His role on the Board, he told me, was to insure that this trend was turned around.

There was something to Shanker's complaint. A decade or so of "process-product" educational research had turned up only modest correlations between subject-matter knowledge and ratings of teaching effectiveness. Some commentators, in a cynical and anti-intellectual twist, even wondered whether teachers could possess "too much knowledge," going on to posit an inverted "U" relationship between teachers' knowledge and student achievement! However, careful research on the nature and texture of teachers' subject-matter knowledge was virtually nonexistent in the research literature. In fact, research on teachers' subject-matter knowledge was called "the missing paradigm" by Shulman (1986) in his review of the field.

When subject-matter knowledge is operationalized as the number of courses on a transcript or number of correct items on a multiple-choice test, correlations between "knowledge" and teaching performance are modest. All this proves is that deep and flexible knowledge cannot be captured by bean-counting. The knotty questions of "What kind of knowledge does a teacher possess?" and "What can the teacher do with this knowledge?" must be considered. If we care about these questions, we must think hard about how to address them.

The NBPTS put such questions at the heart of its enterprise. To be sure, teachers need to know many things – how kids develop, how to organize the classroom for cooperative groups, how to set a tone for classroom management – but all of these things must be understood in the context of content. Teaching history to 16-year-olds is not the same as teaching fractions to 7-year-olds. In an age still intoxicated by educational fads, the enduring legacy of the NBPTS is its clarity about where to begin the discussion of teacher excellence. The first thing to find out is what teachers know about the subjects they teach.

NOTE

1. Also referred to as the National Board, or the Board.

REFERENCES

Bell, J. C., & McCollum, D. F. (1917). A study of the attainments of pupils in United States history. *Journal of Educational Psychology, 8,* 257–274.

Carlson, R. E. (1990). Assessing teachers' pedagogical content knowledge: Item development issues. *Journal of Personnel Evaluation in Education, 4,* 157–173.

Cronon, W. (1992). A place for stories: Nature, history, and narrative. *Journal of American History, 78,* 1347–1376.

Darling-Hammond, L. (1986). A proposal for evaluation in the teaching profession. *Elementary School Journal, 86,* 533–551.

Finn, C., & Ravitch, D. (1988). No trivial pursuit. *Phi Delta Kappan, 69*(April), 559–564.

Frederiksen, N. (1984). The real test bias. *American Psychologist, 39,* 193–202.

Gerhke, N., Knapp, M., & Sirotnik, K. (1992). In search of the school curriculum. *Review of Research in Education, 18,* 51–110.

Lagemann, E. C. (2000). *An elusive science: The troubling history of education research.* Chicago: The University of Chicago Press.

McBride, L. W. (1993). Point of view. *Social Education, 39,* 282–283.

National Board for Professional Teaching Standards. (1994). *Mathematics standards.* Washington, DC: Author.

National Council of Teachers of Mathematics. (1989). *Curriculum and evaluation standards for school mathematics.* Reston, VA: Authors.

Schwab, J. J. (1978). Education and the structure of the disciplines. In: I. Westbury & N. J. Wilkof (Eds), *Science, curriculum, and liberal education* (pp. 229–272). Chicago: University of Chicago Press.

Shulman, L. S. (1986). Those who understand teach: Knowledge growth in teaching. *Educational Researcher, 15*(2), 4–14.

Shulman, L. S. (1987a). Assessment for teaching: An initiative for the profession. *Phi Delta Kappan, 69,* 38–44.

Shulman, L. S. (1987b). Knowledge and teaching: Foundations of the new reform. *Harvard Educational Review, 57*(1), 1–22.

Sykes, G., & Plastrik, P. (1993). *Standard setting as educational reform.* Trends and Issues Paper no. 8. ERIC Clearinghouse on Teacher Education and American Association of Colleges for Teacher Education, Washington, DC.

Todd, L. P., & Curti, M. (1982). *Rise of the American nation.* New York: Harcourt Brace Jovanovich.

Wilson, S. M. (1988). *Understanding historical understanding: Subject-matter knowledge and the teaching of U.S. history.* Unpublished doctoral dissertation, Stanford University.

Wilson, S. M. (1995). Performance-based assessment of teachers. In: S. W. Soled (Ed.), *Assessment, testing and evaluation in teacher education* (pp. 189–219). Norwood, NJ: Ablex.

Wilson, S. M., & Wineburg, S. S. (1993). Wrinkles in time: Using performance assessments to understand the knowledge of history teachers. *American Educational Research Journal, 30,* 729–769.

Wineburg, S. S. (1991). Historical problem solving: A study of the cognitive processes used in the evaluation of documentary and pictorial evidence. *Journal of Educational Psychology, 83,* 73–85.

Wineburg, S. S. (1994). The cognitive representation of historical text. In: G. Leinhardt, I. L. Beck, & C. Stainton (Eds), *Teaching and learning in history* (pp. 85–135). Hillsdale, NJ: Lawrence Erlbaum Associates, Inc.

Wineburg, S. S. (1996). The psychology of learning and teaching history. In: D. C. Berliner & R. C. Calfee (Eds), *Handbook of educational psychology* (pp. 423–437). New York: Simon & Schuster Macmillan.

Wineburg, S. S., & Kerdeman, D. (1989). *Exercise prototype: The analysis of textbooks in history.* Technical Report no. H-7. Stanford University, Teacher Assessment Project, Stanford, CA.

Wineburg, S. S., & Wilson, S. M. (1991). Subject-matter knowledge in the teaching of history. In: J. E. Brophy (Ed.), *Advances in research on teaching* (pp. 305–347). Greenwich, CT: JAI.

CHAPTER 6

DEVELOPING A NATIONAL SCIENCE ASSESSMENT FOR TEACHER CERTIFICATION: PRACTICAL LESSONS LEARNED

Steven A. Schneider, Kirsten R. Daehler, Kristin Hershbell, Jody McCarthy, Jerome Shaw and Guillermo Solano-Flores

ABSTRACT

Creating something entirely new, something important, something for which there is no agreed upon "right way," set model, or solid precedence is exciting – and, at times, frustrating. Developing the Adolescence and Young Adulthood assessment for science teachers (AYA/S) of students aged 14 to 18+ for the National Board for Professional Teaching Standards (NBPTS) is a case in point. This chapter describes our experiences as an Assessment Development Laboratory (ADL) and looks at some of the challenges inherent in developing a large-scale assessment that is complex, strives to be innovative, and must be closely aligned with a given set of standards. Some of the external challenges we faced included shifting and unclear expectations, the conflicting needs of multiple stakeholders and a deadline that was dramatically shortened

Assessing Teachers for Professional Certification:
The First Decade of the National Board for Professional Teaching Standards
Advances in Program Evaluation, Volume 11, 139–174
Copyright © 2008 by Elsevier Ltd.
ISSN: 1474-7863/doi:10.1016/S1474-7863(07)11006-1

midway through the process. Within the assessment development process itself we also needed to consider how best to involve teachers, address issues of equity and standardize the process to maximize efficiency. We share some stories to illustrate not only the challenges but also the insights gained and lessons learned during the early years if the project with the hope that they provide a useful historical perspective relevant for other large-scale assessment development projects.

THE WESTED ASSESSMENT DEVELOPMENT LABORATORY

The Assessment Development Laboratory (ADL) team at WestEd[1] was formed in the spring of 1994 when the NBPTS awarded WestEd a two-year contract to develop the Adolescent and Young Adult/Science (AYA/S) assessment aligned with the *Adolescence and Young Adulthood/Science Standards for National Board Certification* (hereafter referred to as "*AYA/S Standards*"). This type of standards-driven assessment for teachers was a natural spin-off from the national trend in standards-driven reform for students, itself an outgrowth of systemic reform in the 1980s (Smith & O'Day, 1991). The NBPTS' competitive bid asked ADLs to develop a two-part assessment system consisting of a portfolio and a series of assessment center exercises. In doing so, ADLs of all content areas were required to undertake the tasks outlined in Table 1.

To meet this challenge, WestEd assembled a diverse team of respected, high caliber teachers, measurement experts, and leading science educators. Steven Schneider, the director of WestEd's science and mathematics program, served as co-Principal Investigator along with Mary Budd Rowe, professor of Science Education at Stanford University. Mary Budd Rowe, an original member of the NBPTS, provided an important link between the WestEd team and the NBPTS. She brought the history of the NBPTS to WestEd and offered wisdom in a familiar face to the NBPTS.

Other core team members and key advisors included past presidents of the National Science Teachers Association, teachers who were also members of the NBPTS' AYA/S Standards Committee, and representatives from internationally recognized informal science education organizations, including Lawrence Hall of Science and the Exploratorium. Being geographically close and well connected to Stanford University allowed the team to call on the expertise of the NBPTS' visionaries, such as Lee Shulman, and

Table 1.   Tasks Required of ADLs in Developing NBPTS Assessments.

- Work with a NBPTS-appointed Standards Committee in the certificate field as it complete[d] its definition of the domain of knowledge, skills, and abilities that reflect highly accomplished teaching in that field; and engage the Standards Committee in the planning, design, and review of performance assessment exercises that are consistent with the definition of highly accomplished teaching specified by the Committee.
- Develop exercises and scoring procedures that assess the construct of accomplished teaching defined by the Standards Committee in the certificate field, and integrate the assessment exercises into complete assessment packages.
- Work with other ADLs, the Technical Analysis Group (TAG),[a] the Field Test Network (FTN), and the National Board Certification (NBC) delivery system contractor in meeting the overall research and development objectives of the NBPTS.
- Conduct a field test of all assessment exercise packages and scoring procedures developed by the ADL, in cooperation with the NBPTS' FTN and TAG, including the training of administrators and assessors for the field test. This evolved over time to include a three-part pilot test – both local and national in scope – in place of a formal field test.
- Produce on schedule supporting resources and materials that are essential to the operational administration and scoring of complete assessment packages, including comprehensive informational materials for certification candidates, training materials for those who administer, and score the assessments and feedback to candidates on their performances.
- Work collaboratively with NBPTS staff to discuss and review on a regular basis the plans for and progress of the assessment development and related efforts.

[a]The TAG was a group of advisors whose task was to oversee the psychometric soundness of the entire assessment process.

other leading science educators and psychometricians. Most importantly, our team was composed almost entirely of past and present teachers. This made us better able to listen carefully to other teachers, thereby maintaining connections, credibility, and an allegiance to what science teachers valued. While the high caliber of WestEd's team members and our close connections to many important stakeholders helped us to work in a highly politicized environment, we were not completely buffered from difficult circumstances and internal tensions.

Assessment Development: Starting Up and Skidding to an Abrupt Halt

When we began our work with the NBPTS in the spring of 1994, it was with a healthy sense of idealism and in a climate supportive of innovation. Helping to fuel our enthusiasm was the knowledge that we were part of a larger effort. After all, a handful of other new ADLs had also just received funding from the NBPTS to develop assessments in different content areas, and several university-based ADLs, Georgia and Pittsburgh, were already a year or more into the development and pilot testing of the assessments for Early Adolescence/Generalist (EA/G) and Early Adolescence/English Language Arts (EA/ELA) certificates, respectively. While the Georgia and Pittsburgh ADLs had already made significant progress in their own assessment development efforts, the NBPTS' Technical Advisory Group (TAG) and the NBPTS itself were still cautiously encouraging experimentation, putting few if any constraints on how the "new" ADLs should go about finding solutions to the inherent challenges of such a complex assessment system.

WestEd's Science ADL received passing words of advice and caution, such as, "Don't make portfolio entries too large or cumbersome," "We can't afford to take half a day to score a single entry," "Videotapes are very telling pieces of evidence and should be central to the portfolio," and "Interviews don't work as assessment center exercises." At this time, there seemed to be many more questions than solutions. In general, there was a tone of "Do your best, share what you know with other ADLs, but keep in mind that this is a high-profile, nationally important project."

In this climate, we began simultaneously developing the portfolio entries and assessment center exercises. The portfolio entries would focus on a teacher's practice in the classroom, while the assessment center would focus on teacher's content knowledge. We had a fairly well-defined structure for developing the portfolio aspect of the assessment, yet parameters for developing the assessment center exercises were less clearly defined.

Based on our literature review and dozens of conversations with science teachers, we created a conceptual framework to guide our work, which addressed important questions such as: How can we be sure to address what is at the heart of science teaching? How can we design the assessment to allow teachers to demonstrate their accomplishments in different, yet equally valid ways? What are the best ways to gather second-hand evidence about a teacher's practice? And most importantly: How can we ensure balanced and thorough coverage of the AYA/S Standards?

In developing the assessment center exercises we struggled with the fact that the NBPTS' AYA/S Standards, still only in draft form, did not clearly specify the content knowledge domain, focusing more on instruction and classroom environment instead. We were required to address content knowledge across four scientific disciplines (i.e., biology, chemistry, Earth and space science, and physics), but the depth and breadth were not specified. What the AYA/S Standards did make clear was that hands-on investigations, problem solving, and inquiry are at the heart of teaching all science, regardless of the specific discipline.

Given these guidelines, we needed to determine the implications for the assessment center exercises. In particular, we considered whether it was feasible to have teachers manipulate tools and equipment at an assessment center. Could a computer simulation satisfactorily replicate the kind of thinking that occurs in a laboratory setting? In these early months, we explored several different computer-based simulations, developed prototype exercises, and made substantial progress in defining the domain of content knowledge required.

Then, within eight months of our having begun development, the NBPTS halted development efforts across all the ADLs because its resource development efforts had not kept up with the costs. We no longer had funding to continue our work.

While our development process was interrupted, it was not completely halted, and in general we followed the steps outlined in Fig. 1. This figure provides an overview of the entire assessment development process and participants.[2]

Assessment Development: Take Two

Eager to resume our work, in 1995 we co-authored with the NBPTS a proposal to the National Science Foundation (NSF) and successfully obtained funding to continue development. In the interim period, the NBPTS had restructured its entire development process, opting to replace the ADLs with one general contractor to develop, revise, and administer the assessments for all certificates. By the time we received our NSF funding, we found ourselves the only remaining ADL, with the Educational Testing Service (ETS) now responsible for all the other certificates.

Thus, this second stage of development brought with it a changed context. The NBPTS now placed greater emphasis on the timely development of new assessments based on a standard structure and did not encourage experimentation. An emphasis on standardization emerged as a way to ensure efficiency in both development and administration, theoretically allowing the NBPTS to develop and offer a broad range of certificates more quickly. The NBPTS believed its new standardized structure for assessment development struck a balance between addressing technical concerns and keeping administration costs reasonable (e.g., reducing scoring time).

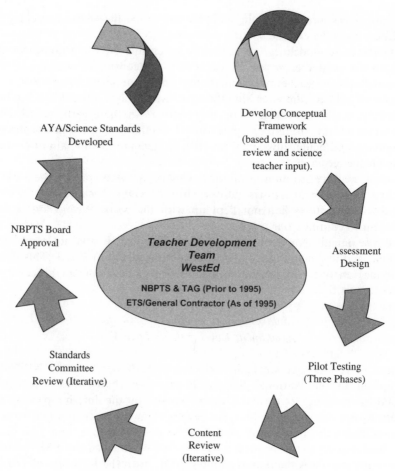

AYA/Science Standards
Developed

Develop Conceptual
Framework
(based on literature)
review and science
teacher input).

NBPTS Board
Approval

*Teacher Development
Team
WestEd*

NBPTS & TAG (Prior to 1995)
ETS/General Contractor (As of 1995)

Assessment
Design

Standards
Committee
Review (Iterative)

Pilot Testing
(Three Phases)

Content
Review
(Iterative)

Fig. 1. The Assessment Development Process.

By late 1995, the AYA/S Standards had also been finalized, and the TAG
had been phased out. In addition, the NBPTS had found that significantly
fewer minority candidates were becoming NBPTS certified in those
certificate areas already offered. This "adverse impact" became a development concern, and we had the additional charge of ensuring that the
assessment neither discouraged nor unfairly disadvantaged any group of
candidates. To complicate the situation further, a nine-month delay in
actually receiving the NSF funding,[3] combined with pressures to make the

AYA/S certificate available as soon as possible, necessitated greatly compressing the remaining development cycle. Our original development timeline of 18 months for the portfolio was now reduced to 12 months. At about the same time, with great sadness, we experienced the death of Mary Budd Rowe, whose vision and style had guided much of our work.

As we moved ahead in this changed context, we struggled most with identifying those areas of the proposed assessment system that were now defined by the NBPTS and those areas that were still open to our innovation. Recognizing that the NBPTS had now made some decisions about the general development and standardization of the certification system, we were uncertain as to which elements, if any, we could continue to shape. For example, regarding the portfolio, we were told by the NBPTS to follow a template with five portfolio entries, including two entries based on student work and written commentary as evidence, two other entries based on video segments and written commentary as evidence and one entry focusing on teachers' documented accomplishments outside of the classroom. However, we wondered how much latitude, if any, remained for including different response formats in the portfolio. Also, were the format and sequence of the entry directions fixed? Could lessons learned from the pilot that might deviate from the standard template be incorporated into the final portfolio?

We all had gone into this project hoping that we could develop an innovative, state-of-the-art assessment that then could be standardized in its implementation. Many of us had been attracted to this project because of the opportunity to innovate. This sudden shift in the NBPTS' expectations seemed to fall back on old paradigms. Could we resign ourselves to maintaining these old paradigms?

With respect to the assessment center exercises, many of the NBPTS' new development parameters also differed from our earlier work in 1994. For example, the NBPTS had determined that all assessment center tasks should be completed over six hours in one day, something we had originally proposed and that was later supported by the NBPTS' experience. Another change was that the assessment center exercises would be delivered via computer, on site at a Sylvan Technology Center (of which there are more than 200 across the United States). As with the portfolio development, we found ourselves wondering if the drive for standardization left any opportunity for innovation and, if so, where, and to what degree. While the NBPTS was moving toward having the assessment center element of each certificate be composed of four 90 min, written essay exercise blocks, we were hoping that one of these blocks could contain computer simulations to serve as a substitute for hands-on investigations. Would there be any place for lab simulations? How would teachers respond to the heavy emphasis on writing? How would teachers respond to having to take the entire assessment on a computer given the likelihood of their having different levels of computer experience?

This, then, was the shifting context in which we carried out the work of developing the AYA/S assessment. Each of the following three sections contains several illustrations of some specific lessons learned in developing the portfolio entries, the assessment center exercises and the scoring system, respectively.

STORIES OF DEVELOPMENT: THE PORTFOLIO

The five stories in this section describe: (1) how we strove to obtain balanced and thorough coverage of the AYA/S Standards as the portfolio entries collectively changed over time; (2) how the use of a development "shell" contributed to consistency, efficiency, and user-friendliness; (3) how the use of alternative response formats (e.g., audiotape) solved some problems and created others; (4) how the need for creating fair assessments may result in greater prescription and less teacher choice; and (5) how best to assure face validity with science teachers in the field, while addressing the technical considerations of assessment.

Portfolio Creation and Evolution

As we look back over the development of the AYA/S portfolio, we jokingly call it the "incredible expanding-shrinking portfolio." That is, the portfolio's size has changed substantially over time in response to changes in current wisdom, a changing political climate, competing demands of the APPLE[4] criteria, and, ultimately, which stakeholder(s) had final say. Despite this tug-of-war, our bottom line was to ensure balanced and thorough coverage of the 13 separate AYA/S Standards.

In the early months of the first year of development (Spring of 1994), we reviewed the work done by others, convened conversations with dozens of leading educational researchers, and consulted research findings to create an internal document or "conceptual framework" that provided theoretical guidance for the portfolio development. This conceptual framework provided working definitions of our tasks, spelled out different approaches used in assessment development, explored research findings about the differences between expert and novice teachers, and helped us to clarify the skills and types of teacher knowledge we wanted to target in the assessment.

On a theoretical level, we thought about the development of the portfolio in terms of three components: one or more *tasks* that required teachers to demonstrate what they know and can do in teaching science; the *response format* in which science teachers provide evidence of their competencies; and the *scoring system* by which candidates' performances are judged (Ruiz-Primo & Shavelson, 1996; Solano-Flores & Shavelson, 1997). We intended the portfolio to provide a rich picture of a teacher's abilities in the context of his or her own classroom, and here we took guidance from Shulman (1998, p. 34), who described a school-site portfolio as a "structured history of a carefully selected set of coached or mentored accomplishments substantiated by samples of student work and fully realized only through reflective writing, deliberation, and serious conversation."

One of the first most important things we did was to bring together a team of science teachers, including teachers from the AYA/S Standards Committee and the WestEd development team to breathe life into the science portfolio. We began by trying to answer questions such as: What is essential to good science teaching? What is unique to teaching science? How can the AYA/S Standards guide our choices?

Weeks later, when our list of ideas, shared experiences and visions covered chart paper on several walls, we divided into smaller groups and worked on consolidating these ideas into the titles and content of actual portfolio entries. After much conversation and some compromise, the groups came to an agreement on the essence of five portfolio entries. Specifically, at that time, we determined that the entries would focus on the following: (1) teaching major ideas in science; (2) assessing student work; (3) hands-on scientific inquiry; (4) professional commitment; and (5) portfolio reflections and science teaching philosophy (Table 2). The 13 AYA/S Standards were distributed across these five entries in a way that to some extent allowed for multiple coverage of each standard. This provided teachers with the opportunity to illustrate how they met the standards in more than one way and more than one teaching situation.

Several months later, things changed – yet again. In October 1994, the half-dozen ADLs were invited to Washington, DC to share lessons learned, discuss development challenges, and hear TAG members present their findings from earlier development work. At this meeting, the ADLs were asked to increase the number of entries in each portfolio to between nine and 12, with the expectation that doing so would increase the dependability

Table 2. Comparison of the Evolving Portfolio Entries and Standards Coverage.

The *Original 5* Portfolio Entries	The *Interim 9* Portfolio Entries	The *Final 6* Portfolio Entries
1. Teaching toward the development of major ideas in science (Standards: I-Understanding Students, III-Instructional Resources, VI-Equitable Participation, VIII-Conceptual Understanding, IX-Contexts of Science)	1. Major ideas (Standards: II-Knowledge of Science, VI-Equitable Participation, VIII-Conceptual Understanding, IX-Contexts of Science)	1. Teaching major ideas over time (Standards: I-Understanding Students, II-Knowledge of Science, III-Instructional Resources, VI-Equitable Participation, VIII-Conceptual Understanding, IX-Contexts of Science, XIII-Reflection)
2. Assessing my student's work (Standards: II-Understanding Students, IV-Engagement, X-Assessment)	2. Assessing my class (Standards: I-Understanding Students, IV-Engagement, X-Assessment)	2. Assessing student work (Standards: I-Understanding Students, II-Knowledge of Science, VI-Equitable Participation, X-Assessment, XIII-Reflection)
3. Science inquiry (Standards: I-Understanding Students, V-Learning Environment, VII-Science Inquiry)	3. Assessing individual students (Standards: I-Understanding Students, IV-Engagement, X-Assessment)	3. Hands-on scientific inquiry (Standards: II-Knowledge of Science, III-Instructional Resources, IV-Engagement, V-Learning Environment, VI-Equitable Participation, VII-Science Inquiry, VIII-Conceptual Understandings, XIII-Reflection)
4. Professional Commitment (Standards: XI-Family and Community Outreach, XII-Collegiality and Leadership, XIII-Reflection)	4. Hands-on investigation (Standards: III-Instructional Resources, IV-Engagement, V-Learning Environment, VII-Science Inquiry)	4. Discussions about science (Standards: II-Knowledge of Science, IV-Engagement, V-Learning Environment, VI-Equitable Participation, VII-Science Inquiry, VIII-Conceptual Understanding,
5. Portfolio reflections and teaching philosophy (Standard: XIII-Reflection)	5. Inquiry through discourse (Standards: IV-Engagement, V-Learning Environment, VII-Science Inquiry)	
	6. Real world connections (Standards: IV-Engagement, V-Learning Environment, VII-Science Inquiry, IX-Contexts of Science)	
	7. Beyond the classroom (Standard: XI-Family and Community Outreach)	
	8. Professional commitment (Standard: XII-Collegiality and Leadership)	

Table 2. (*Continued*)

The *Original 5* Portfolio Entries	The *Interim 9* Portfolio Entries	The *Final 6* Portfolio Entries
	9. Portfolio cover letter (Standard: XIII-Reflection)	IX-Contexts of Science, XIII-Reflection)
		5. Documented accomplishments I (Standard: XII-Collegiality and Leadership)
		6. Documented accomplishments II (Standard: XI-Family and Community Outreach)

of the assessment scores. From a practical perspective, this was encouraging because the scoring time for each entry would be greatly reduced, and in theory, the overall scoring time would also be reduced.

For our ADL, this was nearly double the number of entries we had been developing. Along with the other ADLs, we went back to the drawing board with our teacher developers, asking ourselves, which of our existing entries were relatively large? Were there natural divisions in these existing entries? Did we need to develop new entries to fill holes in our sampling of the AYA/S Standards? The answers to these questions led us to develop an expanded set of nine portfolio entries (see the second column of Table 2). And, in fact, our teachers, by and large, felt that these slimmer and more tightly focused entries were more manageable to assemble.

Yet one year later (1995), after the NBPTS had hired ETS to replace the other ADLs, a still newer set of portfolio development guidelines was adopted. In the intervening year, the costs associated with developing, delivering, and scoring its assessment package had emerged as a major concern for the Board. A cost analysis had indicated that the time involved in scoring assessments was the major expenditure. To keep costs down and to reduce the workload for teachers, the NBPTS now recommended that the number of portfolio entries be reduced to six. In addition, both the Board and ETS wanted standardization across certificates. Moreover, the new structure prescribed two student work-based entries and two videotape-based entries, all of which focused on the particular content of the certificate, and two additional entries that were identical for candidates irrespective of their content specialty. Our challenge was now to pare down to six the nine portfolio entries we had already developed while simultaneously ensuring coverage of the AYA/S Standards.

To do this, we rebuilt the matrices to look at the content coverage and distribution of the AYA/S Standards across the different entries. It was easy to fall into the trap of looking for every standard in every piece of evidence a teacher provided; however, to better guide teachers in selecting their most compelling evidence, we needed to focus each entry narrowly around a manageable number of standards. But what constitutes a manageable number of standards to be addressed in each entry? What evidence are teachers being asked to collect in each entry? What type of artifacts provides the best evidence for each standard?

Each re-conceptualization of the portfolio required that we carefully map back the entries onto the AYA/S Standards to ensure internal consistency among the focus of the entry, the description of the nature of the entry, the standards being addressed, the questions teachers would respond to in the written commentary, the explanation and advice with respect to how responses would be scored, and the scoring system (e.g., rubric). Table 2 provides a comparison of the portfolio entries and AYA/S Standards coverage as the entries evolved throughout development. Table 3 provides a summary of the final AYA/S portfolio entries.

We had begun developing the portfolio with the idealistic notion that it would be an assessment written by science teachers for science teachers that aimed to cover the standards. However, coverage of the standards proved to be only a small, albeit important, consideration in the development process. In reality, during quarterly review sessions, the development of the portfolio was influenced by select members of the NBPTS staff, a couple of staff members representing the general contractor (ETS), and several NBPTS Board members – each bringing his or her own perspective about criteria and priorities. Much later, our work was also reviewed by the AYA/S Standards Committee and approved by the NBPTS Board of Directors. We inevitably had to balance multiple needs, multiple opinions, and often competing components of the APPLE criteria. To name but a few, these concerns included teachers' needs, the need for standardization to lower scoring costs, and making the assessment equitable. To balance these various influences and to be most efficient in a climate of continuous change, we found that we had to be flexible, patient, and resilient. This meant being willing to go back to the drawing board repeatedly, focusing on the exciting intellectual challenges rather than the mundane frustrations.

Table 3.   Narrative Overview of the Portfolio Entries.

The Portfolio Entries

The five entries in the AYA/S portfolio can be grouped in three categories based on the primary source of evidence: those based on student work, videotape clips, or your work outside the classroom. Descriptions of each entry are provided below based on this categorization.

Entries based primarily on *student work samples*
The first essential source of evidence about your practice is student work: what do you ask your students to do, how do you interpret student responses, and what do you do with this information. There are many kinds of student work; these portfolio entries attempt to sample types that are important for science teachers of adolescents and young adults. In the Written Commentary for each entry, you will be asked to analyze each of the students' work samples and explain this work in the context of your teaching.
1. Teaching major ideas over time
   In this entry you will demonstrate how you weave instructional activities together to promote students' understanding of one major idea in science. You will need to submit an *Overview of Instruction*, three *Activity Descriptions*, each accompanied by two *Student Work Samples*, and a *Written Commentary* that collectively describe and illustrate your approach to teaching a major idea in science over time.
2. *Assessing student work*
   In this entry you will demonstrate how you assess the progress of your students during a period of instruction. You will need to submit three Assessment Descriptions, each accompanied by two Student Work Samples, and a Written Commentary that collectively describe and illustrate your approach to assessment.

   You must feature different classes in each of these two entries based on student work. In addition, you must select a different lesson or unit for each of the four classroom-based entries. For further guidance, refer to the Entry Tracking Form.

Entries based primarily on *videotape clips*
There is no better evidence of what a teacher does than actual classroom practice. For this reason, video clips of practice in varying situations and circumstances are essential evidence for the accomplishments of teachers. These portfolio entries sample a teacher's classroom practice across different classes and across different content during the year. In addition, these video clips are designed to sample different kinds of instruction and classroom interactions. In the Written Commentary for each entry, you will be asked to analyze each of the video clips and explain the featured interactions in the context of your teaching.
3. *Hands-on scientific inquiry*
   In this entry you will demonstrate your skill in engaging your students in hands-on scientific investigations that foster independent thinking. You will need to submit a *Written Commentary* and a *Videotape* that describe and illustrate your approach to engaging students in hands-on science to investigate a scientific concept. You will also submit *Instructional Artifacts* that clarify what is happening in the videotape.
4. *Discussions about science*
   In this entry you will show how you engage students in discussions that increase their understanding of science and make those discussions interesting, accessible, and relevant. You will need to submit a *Written Commentary* and a *Videotape* that describe and illustrate

Table 3. (*Continued*)

how you engage students in discussing scientific concepts and solving problems in a scientific way. You will also submit *Instructional Artifacts* that clarify what is happening in the videotape.

You must feature different classes in each of these two entries based on videotape clips. In addition, you must select a different lesson or unit for each of the four classroom-based entries.

Each videotape entry must be accompanied by a photocopy of a government-issued photo ID such as a driver's license or school district ID. The photo ID should be enlarged to double its actual size, so that both your photo and your name are clearly visible. A sample of a photocopied government-issued photo ID appears at the end of this section.

Entry based primarily on *work outside the classroom*
The third essential source of evidence about a teacher's practice reflects those aspects of teaching that do not occur in the classroom with students, but in a teacher's interactions with students' families, with the school and local communities, and with colleagues.

5. *Documented accomplishments*
In this entry you will provide evidence of some of your professional work outside of the classroom. You will need to submit descriptions and documentation of those activities and accomplishments that illustrate your commitment to the families and communities of your students along with your contributions to the teaching profession.

Source: Reprinted with permission from the National Board for Professional Teaching Standards. www.nbpts.org. All rights reserved.

"Shells" for Standardization and Simplification

In developing the AYA/S assessment, we were aware of the importance – and challenge – of coming up with cost-efficient procedures for developing the portfolio entries. We intended to honor the "E" (economic affordability) of the APPLE criteria. Being cost-efficient meant finding ways to simplify and standardize the development process to create consistent portfolio entries.

To meet this challenge, we drew on experience we had gained on other projects using "shells" to develop multiple constructed-response assessments (Solano-Flores & Shavelson, 1997). In the context of alternative assessment, shells serve as blueprints, or templates, for efficiently generating assessments in a short period of time by providing step-by-step guidelines for assessment developers (Solano-Flores, Jovanovic, Shavelson, & Bachman, 1999). In this particular context, a shell served as a development tool that outlined the separate sections of each portfolio entry and described what type of information should be provided, where that information should be provided, and in what format. This would allow for consistency in the content, sequence, and format of information across all portfolio entries

Table 4. Shell for AYA/S Portfolio.

(a) Excerpts from the Development Shell for the AYA/S Portfolio	(b) Excerpts from the AYA/S Portfolio Entry I
3. Instructions	What do I need to do?
3.1 Write the subheading, *what do I need to do?*	Submit three **Activity Descriptions**, each accompanied by two **Student Work Samples** (see illustration below); an **Overview of Instruction**; and a **Written Commentary** that collectively describe and illustrate your approach to teaching a major idea in science over time. **You must submit all of these products in order for your response to be scorable.**
3.2 In a short paragraph describe what the candidate needs to submit. The last sentence should read in bold, *You must submit all of these products in order for your response to be scorable.*	
3.3 Write the paragraph, *In the table on the next page, you will find a checklist of what you need to do to complete this entry. Following the table is a detailed description of how to make good choices as you plan and prepare your response. Specific requirements for each product are described in later sections.*	In the table on the next page, you will find a checklist of what you need to do to complete this entry. Following the table is a detailed description of how to make good choices as you plan and prepare your response. Specific requirements for each product are described in later sections.
3.4 Provide a graphic that illustrates the products.	
_____page break_____	
3.5 Provide a 3-column table with a checklist describing what the candidate needs to do to complete the entry. The columns should read, *BEFORE the period of instruction, DURING the period of instruction* and *AFTER the period of instruction*.	

(see Table 4 for an example of a shell that served as an evolving document throughout development of the AYA/S portfolio).

The use of a shell in the AYA/S assessment simplified the development of the complex portfolio entries that involved a variety of products (e.g., narratives, videotape footage, samples of student work). Moreover, to ensure standardization across a wide range of teacher candidates with different backgrounds who taught in very different contexts, and to eliminate adverse impact, the directions to the teacher candidates needed to be long, precise, and exhaustive. For every entry, these directions had to specify what actions the teacher candidates should take to submit their responses and the format criteria that the candidates should adhere to (e.g., page limits, font size, specifications for videotape footage). The directions even had to anticipate possible misunderstandings from the candidate and provided directions on what not to do (e.g., "Do not submit more than five pages; assessors will not read more than the text length specified").

The shell we developed consisted of a set of directions specifying the sections that every entry should contain and the sequence in which those sections should appear. As with other forms of alternative assessment, the portfolio entries underwent pilot testing through an iterative process of try-out, review, and revision (Solano-Flores & Shavelson, 1997). In this process, the content and format of the shell also evolved and became more detailed, to the extent that it even specified where page breaks should be inserted.

This approach of updating the shell, based on our experience of trying out and revising the entries, had two unanticipated benefits. First, the shell became a document that formalized our thinking at each stage of development about the portfolio and the nature of knowledge and skills we intended to address. Second, in revising the entries for every new pilot test, we frequently found ourselves using the shell as a frame of reference; it became a succinct description that summarized how we wanted to format and sequence the portfolio. Thus, although the shell could not tell us much about the content of the entries, it certainly helped to make our discussions more systematic. This allowed us to think carefully about the content of the portfolio without having to re-conceptualize how to present that information over and over each time we tackled a new entry.

Due to time constraints, we wanted to develop the portfolio entries simultaneously, assigning each entry to a different team member for development and revisions. But we knew the potential problems. In reviewing other portfolios over time, we had noticed that entries within a particular portfolio might vary considerably in format and even style, which could, in turn, make it difficult for a teacher candidate to understand how one entry differed from another in terms of content and focus. Using a shell ensured that we could develop entries simultaneously *and* have continuity across all entries, eliminating any potential confusion for teachers once the assessment became operational. A common structure across entries, then, not only facilitated the process of portfolio development but also ensured assessment fairness. Candidates could navigate through the separate portfolio entries more easily when they only had to become familiar with one user-friendly format and one sequence of instructions.

The use of a shell thus became a critical tool for the development process – for both the portfolio and the assessment center activities as that work progressed. Its role was especially important given the magnitude of the project, the great number of developers, and the changing expectations.

Exploring Alternative Response Formats

Developing the first portfolio entry (Entry 1: Teaching Major Ideas Over Time) was especially interesting because it raised a number of complex development questions, which in turn provided us with important lessons. This was due in part to the nature of Entry 1 and in part to the fact that it was the first to be fully developed. To understand some of these questions and challenges, we provide next an overview of Entry 1, and we then describe the development considerations we faced.

Table 5 is an excerpt from Entry 1 that describes the nature of the entry and provides teachers with a summary of what they must submit. We developed this entry to reflect the important notion of teaching a major conceptual unit in science and to provide a holistic look at teaching by focusing on an extended instructional period (i.e., a minimum of three weeks). Entry 1 was designed to complement the videotape-based entries that show more discrete pieces (e.g., 20-min teaching moments). Other portfolios had not addressed this "over time" aspect; yet, the art of weaving instructional activities together to develop students' understanding of science concepts is essential to good science teaching.

In addition, our intent was for Entry 1 to capture teachers' reflective thoughts throughout an extended period of instruction, thereby allowing

Table 5. Description of Portfolio Entry 1: Teaching Major Ideas Over Time[a].

What is the nature of this entry?
In this entry you will demonstrate how you weave instructional activities together to promote students' understanding of one major idea in science. Through an overview of a period of instruction, selected activities, samples of student work, and a written commentary, you will provide evidence of how you teach over a period of time. This includes how you sequence and plan instructional activities, support your teaching with instructional resources, and illustrate the relevance of science to all of your students. This entry also asks that you reflect on your instruction and describe, analyze, and evaluate how you promote student learning over a period of time.

---

[a]All examples from the AYA/S assessment reflect the final version as developed by WestEd. Further, revisions were implemented by the general contractor after delivery of the assessment to the NBPTS.

assessors to gain an understanding of how accomplished teachers monitor and adjust their instruction to better address students' needs. Capturing teachers' thoughts as they teach and not merely their reflections weeks later was an important objective, but not easy to accomplish. The AYA/S Standards place high value on teacher reflection; Standard XIII: Reflection states, "Accomplished science teachers constantly analyze, evaluate and strengthen their practice in order to improve the quality of their students' learning experiences." Thus, each portfolio entry required teachers to reflect on their practice. Moreover, current educational research indicated that the degree to which instructional decisions were based on deliberate rationale or intuition is a continuum, with accomplished teachers generally on the higher end and novice teachers on the lower end (see, for example, Berliner & Gage, 1989).

Teachers reflect informally about their teaching all of the time. Yet given the great importance of reflection, we felt we needed to formalize the reflective processes. Thus, each entry contains questions that probe teachers' reflective practice. In our first attempt to capture teachers' reflective thoughts during the period of instruction, we asked them to keep a daily log of class activities along with their thoughts about successes, failures and next steps. From this log, they would select several examples to submit with their portfolios. Although this idea was conceived by teachers from the development team, other practicing teachers who reviewed the entries in focus groups were generally not receptive to the idea. They made comments such as, "I do this kind of reflection all of the time, but I never write it down. When would I find the time during the day?," "I'm sure some people like keeping journals, but I'm not one of them," and "I'm a science teacher, not an English teacher."

We were getting a clear message that, although a written log might be a solution for teachers of English or Language Arts, many science teachers were resistant. In fact, as science teachers looked at the portfolio as a whole, they were overwhelmed by the writing demands. Interestingly, other teams who were developing assessments in different content areas found similar concerns. Although most teachers and development teams agreed that accomplished teachers should also be competent writers, they were concerned that the assessment might more directly measure their written communication skills rather than their skill in teaching. In particular, science teachers questioned whether they would be able to adequately represent in writing what they were able to accomplish in the classroom.

These concerns pushed our team to ask: What alternative response formats would serve the same assessment purpose and allow teachers to utilize different modes of communication? We considered a novel substitute – allowing teachers to use an audiotape to record their reflections. The assessment could provide guiding questions that teachers responded to via tape recorder. These questions would capture their expectations prior to the period of instruction, along with their mid-course thoughts and end-of-unit reflections. But, while lessening the writing demand on teachers, the use of audiotape also raised as many questions as it addressed. Would classroom teachers like it? Would talking into a tape recorder be foreign or uncomfortable? What technological challenges and additional burden would audiotapes present? What were the scoring implications? Would it be necessary to transcribe candidates' responses? Would scoring be more time consuming and more costly, and outweigh the benefits gained? Would alternative biases be introduced? Could the use of an audiotape offer a means to address issues of adverse impact documented among specific teacher groups? Would honoring teaching as an oral profession lend greater professional acceptability? Would the use of an audiotape support teachers' own assessment efforts to address their students' multiple intelligences? Would audiotaping actually reduce the amount of writing or would teachers write their responses and then read what they wrote into the tape recorder?

Audiotaping clearly introduced unknown variables, but it also promised solutions to some important issues. Could videotape – a better-known entity because it was already required in other portfolio entries – be used to record teachers' reflections? With videotape, teachers could both "show" and "tell" their responses. What were the assessment implications? How is using video to capture teachers' reflective thoughts different from taping a class while the teacher is teaching? Although little research existed around the use of videotaping or audiotaping for this purpose, we were interested in exploring the possibility.

In agreement with the NBPTS and the general contractor, we pilot tested Entry 1 in all three response formats – a subgroup of teachers responded to questions in writing, another group audiotaped their reflections, and a third group responded on videotape. Although this pilot test did not have the design of a formal study, it yielded exploratory information as to the feasibility of these modes, both with classroom teachers and with the assessors during a pilot scoring session.

Careful review of a small pilot test sample of teachers' portfolio entries, along with their responses to questionnaires and interviews, showed that teachers were willing and able to record their reflections using tape recorders and video cameras. Several of the teachers reported being somewhat uncomfortable talking into a tape recorder, while others liked the idea.

However, talking "to" a video camera seemed artificial and left some teachers more uncomfortable than being videotaped while teaching their classes. Although teachers were prompted to provide "show-and-tell" videotaped responses (e.g., by showing three-dimensional student products or visual teaching props), we found that all of the teachers who used videotape gave a "talking-heads" response (e.g., each teacher sat and talked squarely into the camera), thereby providing little or no additional information from that given on an audiotape.

There were many similarities between scoring an audiotape and a videotape. Due to scoring time constraints and logistics, assessors would not be able to rewind a tape and view or listen to any section more than once. Assessors would need to make use of a note-taking sheet to keep careful record of evidence presented in the tapes. While audiotapes would allow assessors to refer to other pieces of evidence (e.g., student work samples) while listening to the teachers' explanations, videotapes required continuous viewing. Many questions were raised about the use of audiotapes and assessor bias. However, our experience in training assessors to view a videotape and make a fair evaluation gave us confidence that it would also be possible to address issues of bias (e.g., regional accents) introduced by an audiotape (see the section entitled, "The Power of Videotape Footage in Bias Training").

Again, because this was merely an exploratory, not a formal, comparative study, we could not conclusively answer many of our initial questions. For example, we had no information as to whether or not audio- or videotape might address the concerns of adverse impact or significantly reduce the writing demands for teachers. Although scoring times were comparable between the audiotape versions and the written responses, we could not guarantee that it would not take longer to score the audiotapes, especially if producing a written transcript were deemed necessary.

These unknowns, along with possible cost increases, pressure to have operable assessments in the shortest possible time, and the concerns of working under a compressed development timeline tilted the scales. The NBPTS chose to use a well-established response format (i.e., written responses) until someone could conduct further research on alternative response formats (e.g., audiotapes). Although we could not disagree with this decision, we regretted that the short timeline and economic restrictions prevented us from further investigating the possibilities and limitations of this form of assessing teachers. In this instance and others, we were continually reminded that innovation requires sufficient time and resources.

As we also discovered in developing this entry, the development process often involves a series of trade-offs. As with any task, portfolios will favor some teachers over others depending on their ability to articulate in writing versus other response formats (whether graphic or oral, for example). Both in our interaction with the NBPTS and within our team, there was always a tension between creativity and methodological soundness. Certain solutions may create other problems, and often there is no single right answer.

The Tension between Individual Creativity and Measurement Necessity

Our development of the AYA/S assessment confirmed that measurement concerns sometimes outweigh allowances for individual difference and creativity. We experienced a constant tension between wanting to develop open-ended portfolio entries that allowed for a greater latitude of responses and the need to restrict both the content and the format of teachers' responses with highly specific and prescriptive prompts.

Creative, inspired, and accomplished science teachers are likely to come up with very different responses to an open-ended assessment. In high stakes instances such as NBPTS certification, this is not always a good thing. An assessment must balance competing objectives such as soliciting concrete evidence that is readily comparable across candidates while at the same time allowing appropriate leeway for individuals to respond in a manner that accurately portrays their best teaching. Below we describe the evolution of the portfolio entry directions for the "Instructional Context" section of the written commentary as a small example of this tension between open-endedness and specificity.

All portfolio entries required a written commentary. It was perhaps *the* key opportunity for candidates to supply evidence that they were meeting the standards addressed by a particular entry. This commentary was where the candidate could explain connections among disparate pieces of evidence (e.g., student work samples or videotape footage), communicate insights, and share pertinent information found nowhere else in the NBPTS assessment (e.g., student background data).

A crucial part of the written commentary was the segment in which candidates were asked to supply background information that would help assessors understand arguments and justifications made by the candidate later on in the commentary. This segment, which was called the "Instructional Context," had an initial prompt that was fairly uniform across all entries. An examination of this prompt in early and late versions

Table 6.   Evolution of "Instructional Context" Prompts.

Early Version	Late Version
Provide information about the context of this class that is *relevant* to this entry. Remember that this response is intended to give information about the particular students in this particular entry. This might include such information as the subject matter of the class, the grouping of the students in the class, and individual details about the particular students who appear in the video. You might wish to add details about the "personality" of the particular class, or any other information that could help an assessor "see" your class.	What are the features of your teaching setting that are relevant to this entry? It is important that you help an assessor "see" your students and your class to understand better how it functions. In your description, include: the title, subject matter, and size of the class; a description of your students' skills, knowledge, and previous experiences that relate to the science you teach; the particular challenges this group of students represents; and any other realities of the social and physical teaching context (e.g., available resources, heterogeneity of the class, and ethnic and linguistic diversity) that are relevant to this entry.

of the portfolio entries illustrates how we had to "close the box" by prescribing the information that candidates had to include in their Instructional Context response so that the performance of all candidates would be assessed on an equal basis (see Table 6).

The early version of the Instructional Context prompt was suggestive and inclusive. Phrases such as "This might include," and "You might wish to add" lent, superficially at least, a degree of open-endedness to what the candidate was being asked to do. One could argue that, in a high stakes environment, any "suggestion" should rightly be interpreted as a "directive."

In pilot tests of early versions, some teachers appeared to take the "hidden directive" approach. They supplied certain "might wish to" information that others did not and subsequently fared better in scoring than those who interpreted the prompt more literally. Accordingly, we attempted to level the playing field by revising later versions of the prompt to specifically request that *all* candidates include certain information such as title, subject matter, and size of the class. These particular details, while seemingly obvious and mundane, were important in understanding the student work or teacher's choices; nevertheless they were absent or not readily discernible in some teachers' responses.

We retained a certain degree of open-endedness in the prompt by wording the final portion to read, "and any other realities of the social and physical teaching context ... that are relevant to this entry." Although some guidance was given in the form of possible "realities" (e.g., available resources, ethnic, and linguistic diversity), candidates were free to choose those that fit their own particular situation. We, as assessors, could not know all the contextual details that should be included. Because of this, the box needed to remain "open" and candidates had to carefully choose what information to include.

As this example shows, the "open" versus "closed" box posed an unavoidable and significant dilemma for developers. When designing any assessment, developers must consider the limits of candidate choice. We chose to temper our decisions in this regard by using a measurement-oriented fairness rule: if candidates' responses were likely to be scored more accurately if they were specifically requested to do something, then they should be asked to do it. Some may recognize this rule as a variant of the "TTWYW" or "Tell Them What You Want" admonition. The importance of this axiom should not be underestimated, especially in instances of high stakes assessment.

This was an important lesson, all the more so because we found it counterintuitive. We had thought that allowing teachers to respond more openly to a prompt would allow for greater fairness in their expressions of accomplishment and, ultimately, in scoring. However, this openness actually led to greater interpretation on the part of the candidates and, thereby, induced greater inequity.

Involvement of Science Teachers in Assessment Development

We knew that the substantial involvement of practicing science teachers was key to successful assessment development. Yet, we wondered how best to involve teachers in a substantial, rather than superficial, way. We did not want to squander classroom teachers' efforts on the time-consuming stages of writing, "wordsmithing," and polishing the assessment, or on addressing issues of consistency, adherence to policy, and technical assessment considerations.

Practicing teachers were particularly valuable given their keen knowledge of the audience, their advice for making the assessment relevant, and their subsequent advocacy on behalf of a project they believed in. For example, Mary Budd Rowe was concerned that the assessment should immediately excite and engage science teachers. In developing the assessment, we imagined what it would be like to be a science teacher receiving this

Table 7. Excerpt from Portfolio Entry 1 of the AYA/S Assessment.

Accomplished science teachers focus their curriculum to develop an in-depth understanding of the major ideas in science. This curriculum embodies accurate and coherent relationships between concepts, as well as connections to other scientific disciplines, students' personal experiences, "real life" applications, the larger social context, and the history of how scientific ideas and discoveries have evolved and matured. New ideas take on meaning when they are relevant, placed in larger contexts, and connected to previous experiences and knowledge ...

assessment package in the mail. What would a teacher read first? How would each portfolio entry be introduced?

It was easy for our team of teacher developers to understand the experience of teacher candidates, and, consequently, they had dozens of ideas for how best to begin each entry so as to be inviting to teachers. We experimented with inspirational quotes and teacher-written, personal vignettes, but in the end the NBPTS' standardized format prescribed a digested summary of what is expected of accomplished teachers (see Table 7).

We attempted to make choices and employ a process that balanced science teachers' values, voices, and needs with the technical considerations of the assessment. We found that teacher developers on our team greatly assisted us in assuring the appeal and face validity of the portfolio to classroom teachers. We found that the best way to maintain an allegiance to teachers was to ensure that they were central to the process of development. This meant providing the time and resources to ensure that teachers were present and heard at all stages of development.

This does not imply that even the most accomplished classroom teacher has the experience, skills, or time to be involved in every aspect of development. However, on our development team, teachers were invaluable in generating ideas, reviewing materials, pilot testing the assessment, and participating in scoring. Teachers on the development team were also excellent liaisons between assessment experts and other teachers. They became excellent ambassadors for the NBPTS, and contributed to the professional acceptability of the assessment. Development team teachers facilitated focus group discussions and, as teachers themselves, could readily hear what would resonate with other teachers. It was valuable that our core leadership team was composed almost entirely of past and present science teachers who worked alongside a diverse group of top-notch practicing teachers.

STORIES OF DEVELOPMENT: THE ASSESSMENT CENTER

The two stories in this section highlight issues relating to the development of the assessment center exercises. The first describes how we defined the content knowledge that an accomplished high school science teacher should possess. The second describes how we designed the assessment center activities to capture a teacher's depth and breadth of knowledge within a vast content domain. It is important in reading the following section to remember that the NBPTS had determined that the total time for administering the assessment center exercises should not exceed six hours.

Defining Content Knowledge

In developing the assessment center component of the science assessment, we faced interesting challenges in defining the vast and complex knowledge domain – the "Knowledge of Science." As noted before, although the AYA/S Standards placed importance on teachers' subject matter knowledge, they did not specifically define the content knowledge science teachers should possess (see Table 8 for excerpts from Standard II: Knowledge of Science). Further complicating this issue, the science certificate issued by the NBPTS was the same for all science teachers, regardless of their specialty area (biology, chemistry, Earth and space science, and physics).

Exploring how best to define the domain of science content caused us to question what grain size of knowledge was appropriate – at what level of depth and breadth should teachers understand content within each of the four specialty areas?

To address the first challenge in developing the model for the assessment center – the limited specificity about content knowledge in the AYA/S Standards – we turned to nationally recognized documents that described content standards for *students*, such as the *National Science Education Standards* (National Research Council, 1996), *Benchmarks for Science Literacy* (American Association for the Advancement of Science, 1993), and the *Science Framework for California Public Schools K-12* (California Department of Education, 1990). At the time of our work, no documents existed that outlined content standards for science *teachers* (other than the AYA/S Standards). Therefore, we created a document that combined the AYA/S Standards and the other national standards documents that served

Table 8.   Excerpts from the AYA/S Standards.

Standard II: Knowledge of Science

Accomplished science teachers have a broad and current knowledge of science and science
   education, along with an in-depth knowledge of one of the subfields of science, which they use
   to set important learning goals ...

(2) Fundamental Ideas of Science

Accomplished science teachers also possess a broad grasp of the fundamental laws, principles,
   theories, facts, and ideas that constitute the body of scientific knowledge and of their
   associated vocabulary and terminology. Science is a collaborative social enterprise that builds
   on the achievements of previous generations. Exemplary teachers are conversant with the
   major conceptual paradigms that researchers have developed over the years in the core
   science disciplines and use that knowledge to inform their practice. The breadth of their
   knowledge base, organized by discipline, includes a firm understanding of the following
   aspects of science:

Physical Sciences

The basic properties of matter and principles governing its interactions; the forms energy takes,
   its transformation from one form to another, and its relationship to matter; motion and the
   principles that explain it; the nature of atoms and molecules, and the way in which atoms and
   molecules can be transformed into different arrangements of matter; and the forces that exist
   between and within objects and atoms ...

Source: Reprinted with permission from the National Board for Professional Teaching
Standards. www.nbpts.org. All rights reserved.

as a framework for outlining the content and organization of assessment
center exercises.

To address the second challenge, the complexity of having multiple
disciplines within the science knowledge domain, we synthesized the various
national and local standards documents for grades 9–12 and organized their
content into the areas that are typically taught in the United States –
biology, chemistry, Earth and space science, and physics. The result of this
synthesis was a set of five domains (the four mentioned previously and an
additional, cross-disciplinary domain referred to as Common Aspects of
Science) subdivided into core concepts (see Table 9 for an outline of these
core concepts; these core concepts include a number of subtopics, which we
have not included here).

While perhaps obvious, it is worth highlighting the importance of
knowing what you want to assess before trying to develop exercises that
measure achievement of that knowledge or skill. In determining what we
needed to assess, we found that we had to be resourceful by tapping into
other standards documents and synthesizing those documents to delineate
the domain of knowledge a candidate should possess.

Table 9. Science Knowledge Domains.

Physics
Motions and forces
Conservation of energy and increase in disorder
Interactions of energy and matter

Chemistry
Structure of atoms
Structure and properties of matter
Chemical reactions

Earth and Space
Energy in the earth system
Geochemical cycles
Origin and evolution of the earth system
Origin and evolution of the universe

Biology
The cell
The molecular basis of heredity
Biological evolution
The interdependence of organisms
Matter, energy, and organization in living systems
The behavior of organisms
The human organism

Common Aspects of Science
I. Basic ideas in science
   Systems, order, and organization
   Evidence, models, and explanation
   Change, constancy, and measurement
   Evolution and equilibrium
   Form and function
II. Societal issues of science
   IIa. Technology
      Abilities of technological design
      Understandings about science and technology
      Science and technology in local, national, and global challenges
   IIb. Environment and society
      Personal and community health
      Population growth
      Natural resources
      Environmental quality
      Natural and human-induced hazards
      Science as a human endeavor
      Historical perspectives
III. Investigation skills
   Abilities necessary to do scientific inquiry
   Understandings about scientific inquiry
   Nature of scientific knowledge

Assessment Center Design

Our next task was to design exercises that would allow us to assess the scope and level of content knowledge that a candidate possessed. With science, in particular, we faced the challenge of designing an assessment that authentically captured the skills and knowledge central to science – namely, scientific inquiry in the lab. The assessment center was designed to assess a candidate's *depth* of knowledge with exercises that addressed an area of emphasis that a candidate could choose (e.g., biology, chemistry, Earth and space science, or physics) along with Common Aspects of Science[5] (e.g., the methodological, philosophical, and social dimensions critical to all scientific disciplines). We assumed a minimum of first-year, college-level knowledge for all the exercises we developed.

In addition, a candidate's *breadth* of knowledge was to be assessed by exercises that focused on the three complementary comprehensive areas outside the candidate's chosen area of emphasis. Thus, for example, a candidate whose chosen emphasis was physics would be assessed in depth in physics and Common Aspects of Science, whereas the breadth of their knowledge was assessed in the remaining three comprehensive areas (biology, chemistry, and Earth and space science; see Table 10).

In collaboration with NBPTS and ETS, we also introduced the notion of "depth-breadth of knowledge" to address the knowledge that is related to establishing connections across content areas around basic (universal) ideas in science. More specifically, depth-breadth of knowledge referred to a teacher's capability to understand how a basic idea such as the relationship between form and function – whose principles are the same regardless of

Table 10.   Depth (D) and Breadth (B) of the Knowledge Assessed by Emphasis Area.

Teacher's Chosen Area of Emphasis	Domains				
	Physics	Chemistry	Earth and Space	Biology	Common Aspects of Science
Physics	D	B	B	B	*D*
Chemistry	B	*D*	B	B	D
Earth and space	B	B	*D*	B	D
Biology	B	B	B	*D*	D

content area – applied to the candidate's area of emphasis and how that idea could be identified in phenomena that belonged to complementary content areas.

In addition to addressing the design challenges related to defining content domain, we recognized that different methods for measuring knowledge tap into different aspects of academic achievement (Baxter & Shavelson, 1994; Dalton, Morocco, Tivnan, & Rawson, 1994; Ruiz-Primo & Shavelson, 1996). Therefore, to achieve dependable scores, following the suggestion made by Resnick and Resnick (1992), among others, we combined different types of exercises, from short answer exercises to constructed-response exercises – such as essay items or performance tasks.

Given all this, we formalized an assessment center structure that was consistent with the four 90-min blocks prescribed by the NBPTS (see Table 11). A candidate's depth of knowledge was assessed in two 90-min blocks of exercises that addressed both content and pedagogical content knowledge, including essay exercises intended to elicit inquiry-and-analysis skills, student work analyses, and laboratory investigations intended to elicit science process skills. The breadth of knowledge exercise block consisted of brief essays. Exercises that addressed depth-breadth of knowledge consisted of three 30-min essay exercises that required the teacher to establish connections across content areas using a given basic idea in science.

Common Aspects of Science were assessed in the context of a teacher's area of emphasis. For example, a physics teacher might be asked to discuss the implications of the invention of the laser with respect to science, technology, and society. This ensured that reasoning about societal issues of science (technology and environment) and investigation skills were assessed within a context that was most relevant to the teacher.

One of the bigger challenges we faced was how best to assess science process skills in the absence of authentic, hands-on laboratory investigations. Originally, we designed investigations that were carried out with computer simulations of processes in science that candidates could manipulate. We believed that, although computer simulations were not perfect surrogates for authentic hands-on tasks (nor are paper-and-pencil investigations), the administration of computer simulations would be less expensive and logistically simpler than hands-on tasks. In addition, computer simulations could bring more validity to the tasks included in the assessment and elicit a kind of knowledge highly valued by science teachers.

We used Science Explorer 3.0 (LOGAL™, 1996), a personal computer software package to develop the original investigations. This software provided a series of interactive, inquiry-oriented explorations in science.

Table 11. Final Assessment Center Structure.

Block of Exercises	Activities	Type of Exercise	Completion Time (Minutes)
1. Core concept I from major content area	Problem solving: data interpretation		30
(Depth)	Design an instructional strategy to teach a concept	Essay	30
	Analyze student work based on science misconceptions		30
2. Facts and concepts in non-major areas	Answer three exercises in non-major content area I		30
(Breadth)	Answer three exercises in non-major content area II	Brief essay	30
	Answer three exercises in non-major content area III		30
3. Integrated knowledge in major and non-major areas	Draw on knowledge from a non-major content area		30
(Depth–Breadth)	Discuss topic in major content area and relate to non-major content area	Essay	30
	Content/context connections		30
4. Core concept II from major content area	Problem solving: use of procedures		30
(Depth)	Real-world connections in science	Essay	30
	Issues of current relevance		30

With these simulations, we developed performance tasks in which candidates investigated phenomena by manipulating variables and observing the results of their actions. Due to their innovative nature, we attempted to ensure that these simulations would not privilege candidates who had experience with computers or certain problem-solving styles.

Despite, and in part *due to*, the innovative nature of these exercises, the NBPTS decided not to include these simulations in the assessment. That determination may have been driven in part by the decision to deliver the assessment center exercises through the Sylvan Technology Center computer operating system because it could have been difficult to align the architecture of the simulations with ETS' existing proprietary operating system. We did, however, transform these simulations into paper-and-pencil prompts, building on the knowledge we gained in developing the actual, "hands-on" simulations.

In the end, we were reminded of the lesson learned when developing portfolio entries – innovation requires a significant commitment of time and resources, and in the period of innovative uncertainty where new questions emerge, difficult decisions had to be made. While the use of cutting-edge technology may have provided a solution for assessing depth of teacher's knowledge and science process skills, technology also amplified uncertainty, risk, and resources needed for assessment development.

STORIES OF DEVELOPMENT: SCORING

Our charge in developing the AYA/S assessment included developing a scoring system. Because of the documented "adverse impact" that appeared to affect certain groups of candidates, we believed that the scoring system should include a bias training component to help reduce the impact of potential assessor bias. The story in this section highlights how powerful bias training can be with the aid of videotape footage and dyad discussions around that footage.

The Power of Bias Training for Scorers

Bring a group of teachers together from all over the country and everyone will have a different opinion about how best to teach a class of students. Teachers hold passionately to their ideas and argue vehemently about the merits of how and what should be taught. During scoring sessions that we facilitated to assess the usability and appropriateness of the scoring rubrics, we encouraged the 15 or so participating teachers to draw on their professional knowledge to make informed scoring decisions, while simultaneously recognizing bias that emerges as a result of differences in each of our teaching experiences and contexts.

To address the potential problem of bias, we brought this issue to the scorers' attention, talked about the ways in which strong emotional reactions could be an indicator of bias, and emphasized the need to consider only the rubric criteria (rules for scoring) when making scoring decisions. We also used diverse performances for training scorers, hoping that, through discussions about these performances, we would flush out many of the biases that could result in an adverse impact on any particular group of teachers.

Despite these efforts, we witnessed multiple instances of bias on the part of mainstream scorers when looking at performances by non-mainstream teachers in non-mainstream school environments. For example, one scorer said, "You can't expect much from kids in that setting anyway," as many other scorers nodded in agreement. Obviously, such lowered expectations of students resulted in a distorted view of many successful classrooms. Similarly, in response to a videotape of an African-American teacher from New York City, many scorers described his performance as "ranting and raving." Others defended his communicative style, saying that he was "preaching" to his students in a way that is appreciated and understood within African-American culture. This videotape seemed like a clear example of "culturally informed practice" that was not viewed equitably by mainstream scorers.

Overall, in these early pilots of national teacher assessments, we witnessed many instances of miscommunication among scorers as teachers tried to interpret what was happening in school environments different from their own. Even though the leaders at these scoring sessions were themselves a diverse group, they did not have the tools to educate people about these differences or to help the teacher scorers become more cognizant of their own culturally informed point of view (Ladson-Billings, 1995) and the bias that resulted from assuming that one's own communicative style is, as Lisa Delpit says in her book *Other People's Children* (Delpit, 1995), "simply 'the way it is.'"

Through these early experiences, we came to several realizations: (1) telling mainstream scorers to be aware of bias was not enough; (2) mainstream teachers were in many cases unfamiliar with non-mainstream learning environments and the communicative styles and patterns within these environments; and (3) videotapes of teachers' performances have the power to evoke bias in scorers when they encounter unfamiliar environments. Knowing that bias had to be revealed before it could be transformed, we decided to use videotapes of teachers in diverse settings to evoke bias, discuss reactions, then provide information that could inform scorers so they might more fairly and effectively interpret other teachers' performances.

In our final pilot, we carefully selected short (e.g., 4–6 min) segments of videotape showing six teacher performances from widely different contexts, both mainstream and non-mainstream. As a rule, each of the selected performances had to have been scored highly (i.e., at level 3 or 4 in the 4-point rubric) in an earlier pilot. While viewing each videotape segment, scorers wrote down their reactions to the teachers' and students' actions, the students' demeanor, and the interactions between students and teacher. After viewing the videotape segment, each scorer evaluated his or her response to the performance, discussing his or her feelings about the style of interaction and his or her analysis of the effectiveness of the interactions.

Scorers then paired up to discuss their responses with another scorer, using a strategy called a dyad. In a dyad, one person speaks uninterrupted for a short period of time (e.g., two minutes); then the other person speaks uninterrupted for the same length of time. The dyad rules also require that you listen closely, always maintain confidentiality, never interrupt, and never judge what is being said (Weissglass, 1995). Through this dyad process, at least two things were accomplished: (1) scorers verbalized their own reactions to another person, thereby giving those reactions more conscious reality, and (2) scorers heard a second perspective, often one that differed from their own. This second perspective in many cases surprised people and had the effect of making them aware that their own interpretation could be highly "uninformed" or was only one interpretation among other equally valid interpretations.

Scorers went through this process six times with the six different videotapes. Afterwards, we met as a large group to discuss reactions to the videotapes and the process. Many noted how comfortable they felt with teachers who mirrored their own style of interaction and how uncomfortable they felt when asked to interpret something that differed in terms of style. At this time, an expert on cultural patterns of communication and the leader of our sensitivity review team, Sharon Nelson-Barber, answered questions and discussed some of the features of these different performances in terms of use of authority, use of language, emphasis in instruction, and other qualities that differ across cultural settings.

Though this videotape sequence was only one of the four parts of the bias awareness training, many scorers said it was the most powerful and transformative part for them. In fact, many felt that it opened a new door, and they wanted to see even more videotapes of different teaching contexts and to gain even more information about different patterns of communicative style.

Mainstream teachers may not know what is outside of their experience and may have difficulty interpreting different cultural contexts. Yet, since teachers in general are communicators and observers of interaction, and as most pride themselves on this skill and knowledge, they all found the videotapes to be a highly valued resource. They also found the overall experience to be transformative, not only in their role as scorers but also in their roles within their classrooms and communities.

Thus, we confirmed that bias training in general, and videotape footage in particular, provided powerful experiences for scorers. Although it was time consuming, it would, in large part, contribute toward making an assessment more equitable.

CONCLUSION

Learning from others can save valuable time and money. As one would imagine, we gained valuable insights from our own development work and that of other ADLs. The stories we have shared highlight some of the issues that arose for us, and, in conclusion, we have presented some of the more global issues here for the benefit of others.

The assessment development process must be mainly concerned with technical aspects such as content coverage, equity, and psychometric issues, yet the process was shaped by many more forces than just methodological and content considerations. It was a complex social process in which developers had to consider and balance the multiple and sometimes conflicting interests, needs, and priorities of all stakeholders. At times, trade-offs were essential. One way to smooth this process was to involve all stakeholders from the beginning and throughout development.

In assessment development as in many other efforts, innovation requires substantial time and resources. One must consider these issues up front in order to appropriately address them when budgeting and setting timelines.

Perhaps most fundamentally, we found it valuable to draw on existing research. Our hope was that our experiences would also shed light on the assessment development process and contribute to the knowledge base.

NOTES

1. WestEd, formerly Far West Laboratory for Educational Research and Development, is one of the original regional educational laboratories created by the United States Congress in 1966. WestEd is a not-for-profit agency committed to improving education through research, development, and service.

2. Note that several of the major players who were involved prior to 1995 were no longer involved after the NBPTS' reorganization, and new players subsequently emerged.

3. The U.S. Government was "shut down" due to a budget dispute in the U.S. Congress. This resulted in nine months of funding delays from the National Science Foundation.

4. NBPTS identifies five criteria for assessment development abbreviated with the acronym "APPLE," which stands for Administrative feasibility, Professional acceptability, Public credibility, Legal defensibility, and Economic affordability. These were the criteria that all ADLs were instructed to use to develop assessments.

5. The AYA/S Standards Committee determined that it is possible for a candidate to submit a portfolio in one teaching area of emphasis but sign up for the Assessment Center in another area of emphasis.

REFERENCES

American Association for the Advancement of Science. (1993). *Benchmarks for science literacy.* New York: Oxford University Press.

Baxter, G. P., & Shavelson, R. J. (1994). Science performance assessments: Benchmarks and surrogates. *International Journal of Educational Research, 21,* 279–298.

Berliner, D., & Gage, N. L. (1989). Nurturing the critical, practical, and artistic thinking of teachers. *Phi Delta Kappan, 71*(3), 212–214.

California Department of Education. (1990). *Science framework for California public schools: Kindergarten through grade twelve.* Sacramento, CA: California Department of Education.

Dalton, B., Morocco, C. C., Tivnan, T., & Rawson, P. (1994). Effect of format on learning disabled and non-learning disabled students' performance on a hands-on science assessment. *International Journal of Educational Research, 21,* 299–316.

Delpit, L. (1995). *Other people's children: Cultural conflict in the classroom.* New York: W.W. Norton & Company.

Ladson-Billings, G. (1995). Multicultural teacher education: Research, practice, and policy. In: J. Banks & C. Banks (Eds), *Handbook of research on multicultural education* (pp. 747–749). New York: Macmillan.

LOGAL™. (1996). *Science explorer 3.0 [Software].* Cambridge, MA: LOGAL Software, Inc.

National Research Council. (1996). *National science education standards.* Washington, DC: National Academy of Sciences.

Resnick, L. B., & Resnick, D. P. (1992). Assessing the thinking curriculum: New tools for educational reform. In: B. G. Gifford & M. C. O'Conner (Eds), *Changing assessments: Alternative views of aptitude, achievement and instruction* (pp. 37–75). Boston: Kluwer Academic Publishers.

Ruiz-Primo, M. A., & Shavelson, R. J. (1996). Rhetoric and reality in science performance assessments: An update. *Journal of Research in Science Teaching, 33*(10), 1045–1063.

Shulman, L. (1998). Teacher portfolios: A theoretical activity. In: N. Lyons (Ed.), *With portfolio in hand: Validating new teacher professionalism* (pp. 23–38). New York: Teachers College Press.

Smith, M. S., & O'Day, J. (1991). *Putting the pieces together: Systemic school reform. CPRE Policy Briefs.* New Brunswick, NJ: Consortium for Policy Research in Education.

Solano-Flores, G., Jovanovic, J., Shavelson, R. J., & Bachman, M. (1999). On the development and evaluation of a shell for generating science performance assessments. *International Journal of Science Education, 21*(3), 293–315.

Solano-Flores, G., & Shavelson, R. J. (1997). Development of performance assessments in science: Conceptual, practical and logistical issues. *Educational Measurement: Issues and Practice, 16*(3), 16–25.

Weissglass, J. (1995). It will take more than good will: Avoiding lip service and promoting equity in education. *Multicultural Education* (Summer), *2*(4), 17–20.

SECTION 2:
ASSESSING TEACHER
PERFORMANCE

CHAPTER 7

THE EVOLUTION OF THE SCORING SYSTEM FOR NBPTS ASSESSMENTS

Mari Pearlman

ABSTRACT

The scoring system for the National Board for Professional Teaching Standards (NBPTS) assessments was a groundbreaking undertaking that brought with it a host of unanticipated challenges. These, in turn, generated a complete revision of the approach to scoring and the design underwent a number of changes during the first decade. Beginning with an analytical model which was so ambitious that it was entirely too cumbersome and complex to be undertaken within a reasonable timeframe, assessment developers had to systematically redesign a scoring system that would be at once reliable, valid, and operationally feasible.

The current scoring system used for all National Board for Professional Teaching Standards (NBPTS) assessments rests on several important assumptions, some of which have been constant from the very beginning of the assessment development. The first is perhaps the most important and far-reaching in its consequences, both operationally and from a validity perspective: the only people allowed to serve as assessors for NBPTS certification assessments are teachers currently teaching in the field and at

Assessing Teachers for Professional Certification:
The First Decade of the National Board for Professional Teaching Standards
Advances in Program Evaluation, Volume 11, 177–209
Copyright © 2008 by Elsevier Ltd.
ISSN: 1474-7863/doi:10.1016/S1474-7863(07)11007-3

the developmental level of the teachers whose responses they evaluate. (National Board Certified Teachers (NBCTs) are also allowed to train/score even though they are no longer in the classroom. They can score only in their area of certification.) This means that the scoring system is truly founded on the principle of judgment by expert peers. The second assumption has also been constant from the outset, and that is that any scoring system would be grounded in the use of benchmarks and samples of performance for training assessors, and that these performances would be used to define the qualitative terms of any scoring criteria contained in scoring rubrics. Further, a constant assumption has been that the NBPTS standards for the given certificate area are the only source of evaluative criteria for candidate responses.

Finally, with one very early exception, discussed below, the NBPTS scoring scale has always been a four-point scale (1-low, 4-high). The reasons for this decision are largely ones driven by validity considerations: since this is a certification decision, we are essentially engaged in making a dichotomous classification at the end of all the scoring. However, because the final decision rests on a complicated combination of averaged individual task scores that are differentially weighted, and because each separate portfolio task generates a large and complicated array of evidence, it would be an oversimplification as well as a probable source of error in judgment, to classify each task response dichotomously. Indeed, the rubrics for all NBPTS performances define the level '3' response as accomplished teaching, the level at which certification is awarded. The critical distinction in the score scale is, thus, between the level '2' and level '3' performance. The experiences recounted below have taught us, however, that accurate evaluation of candidate responses requires a more extended scale to accommodate the true range of performances assessors see and evaluate. What follows is a detailed account of how we came to fashion and use the current scoring system. The discussion culminates in a detailed description of the current system, with examples of its apparatus and its outcomes.

THE HISTORICAL BACKGROUND

When the NBPTS first began the assessment development process, the issues associated with scoring and assessor training for complicated and lengthy performance assessments were not much discussed. A much greater preoccupation was ensuring that the actual design of the assessment itself be sufficiently bold and ambitious, regardless of the challenges such a design might pose for scoring (see Chapter 3). The focus on the challenges of task design was understandable, since the vision and mission of the NBPTS demanded assessments that would break the mold of traditional tests, particularly tests for teachers. As I discuss at some length in Chapter 3, attention from serious and credible researchers into teachers' "wisdom of practice" and their expert professional knowledge was one of the driving forces behind the NBPTS mission and vision. This research focus on teacher expertise fueled the concentration on visionary assessment methodologies.

During these early design stages, the NBPTS had the advantage of advice from what was probably the most stellar group of psychometric luminaries ever assembled as an advisory panel to any assessment program (the Technical Advisory Group or TAG, headed by Richard Jaeger).[1] The TAG was very interested in issues of scoring and consequent reliability and validity indices. However, like the assessment developers described in Chapter 3, the psychometricians were also on a journey into the unknown, and the focus on task design was the most critical first order of business. Almost all of the psychometric theory that grounds analyses of assessment data is founded on kinds of assessment in which the developers take care of their end and the psychometricians analyze the resulting numbers at their end. Many of the assumptions on which classical test theory depends – test–retest reliability, split-half reliability, order effects, occasion effects, and the like – turned out to be, at best, an uncomfortable fit with an assessment that was at once this big and complicated, and this short, or "item-poor" in psychometric analytical terms.

And the initial cohort (1990–1991) of NBPTS assessment developers' firsthand knowledge of scoring anything this complicated was also, necessarily, limited. While the developers of one of the two initial certificates, the Early Adolescence/English Language Arts (EA/ELA), had relatively more experience with complex assessment than any one else working on the NBPTS assessments (because of the ambitious program of the Connecticut State Department of Education in teacher licensing), no one had actually tried to score more than a handful of complex performances.[2] And the developers, responding to their charge from NBPTS to boldly go where no one had ever gone before, and for very high stakes to the people who would be their subjects, were preoccupied with how to measure what had only recently been articulated about teaching practice. However, even in these early stages, some participating psychometricians were well aware of the possible pitfalls in complex performance-assessment design and scoring.[3]

Two things were clear to everyone involved: this was a high-stakes assessment whose classification decisions must be legally defensible, and the means to those classification decisions, or the assessment tasks themselves, could resemble nothing that had ever been used before to measure what teachers know and are able to do. These two imperatives, in combination with the NPBTS's aspiration to use assessment to reform teaching, led to the struggle to find an operationally feasible, legally defensible, economically affordable, and professionally credible scoring system.

FIRST EFFORTS

It was not at all clear initially that the scoring system should produce individual task scores. Indeed, there was a strong sense among both the teams producing the initial assessments (the Performance Assessment Laboratory at the University of Georgia for Early Adolescence/Generalist (EA/G) and the University of Pittsburgh/Connecticut State Department of Education collaborative for Early Adolescence/English Language Arts (EA/ELA)) that the most valid approach to evaluating these performances might well be dimensional scoring. The dimensions would be the Standards, and the scores produced would be cross-cutting, using the various assessment tasks as lenses into some underlying substructure of teaching as defined by the Standards document.

The initial design of the Performance Assessment Laboratory at the University of Georgia for Early Adolescence/Generalist (EA/G) assessment paid meticulous attention to the challenges of scoring. Mindful of the call to legal defensibility for these assessments, the developers designed an assessment that used a highly analytical scoring scheme that yielded multiple data points for each task. The initial scoring design used a seven-point scale. Each of the assessment tasks was scored on three or more of the EA/G Standards, with a separate rubric for each standard. Standard scores across several tasks were then aggregated to form a final score on that standard, not on the task itself.

The design of assessment tasks that led to this kind of analytical scoring scheme – tasks in which evidence was fragmented and categorized by the candidate so that the scoring could be clearly linked to a standard – was categorically rejected by the NBPTS Board at its first review. As a consequence, the entire architecture of the assessment was reconceived, resulting in a structure that went to the opposite extreme and required very complicated and highly abstract holistic scoring criteria, in a methodology that required the assessors to use multiple layers of evaluative criteria, writing, and rewriting versions of evidence notes before making the final holistic decision.

The developers in the University of Pittsburgh/University of Connecticut collaborative thought a great deal about what scoring should be like, elaborating parallels between this kind of complex assessment scoring and adjudication protocols as disparate as those used in Olympic competition and the United States justice system (private communication from Anthony Petrosky to Miles Myers, the then Executive Director of the National Council of Teachers of English, 1995). These developers also believed that what they called, after Foucault, the "discourse community" that had created the EA/ELA Standards would wholly define and delimit the universe of meaning for scoring (Delandshere & Petrosky, 1994).

In addition, this development team designed a scoring system that put the professional development of the teacher-assessors at the forefront of the methodology: teachers' experience of and learning from the application of the scoring system was a priority in its design, and, it was thought, a critical contribution to the work of reformation of teaching practice. No one had really tried to implement these scoring schemes in large-scale, high-stakes assessment, and no one had any experience of the effects of very large amounts of complicated evidence on an assessor's ability to evaluate candidate responses. Nor had anyone engaged the issue of what challenges might arise in the encounter between summative, high-stakes scoring imperatives and portfolio and assessment center tasks that had been designed as much to capture the ongoing growth of the candidate as to measure achieved skills and abilities. And certainly no one had thought about what might be the differences between training for the purposes of learning and development, and training for the purposes of legally defensible, operationally feasible scoring.

It was the experiences that attended the first NBPTS field-tests' scorings that suddenly focused a bright light on the dilemmas associated with scoring assessments that were breaking new ground and that no one had ever had to evaluate before. In 1993–1994, the NBPTS recruited teachers all over the United States as participants in the first two field tests of the initial EA/G and EA/ELA assessments. Teachers paid no fee and were promised the possibility of certification if they attained the standard established by the NBPTS after the scoring of these field tests. Approximately 500 teachers completed the entire assessment, portfolio and two-day assessment center, for one or the other of the two assessments. The NBPTS was publicly committed to announcing the results of the scoring of these field tests sometime before the end of the 1994–1995 school year, the earlier the better.

What happened in each case changed the course of assessment design for the NBPTS, and also focused intense scrutiny on issues associated with training, judgment, bias, and the definition of "enough." Furthermore, for the first time it became very clear that operational feasibility was a validity issue in complex performance assessment like this. Such issues as the difficulty of providing a demonstrable link between the performance itself and the final score, the difficulties of moving responses this large from one assessor to another, the sheer cognitive load on assessors, the elapsed time to score a performance and the fatigue engendered in assessors by such big performances, the challenge presented by the necessity for showing that everything a candidate had submitted had been considered and that all parts were kept together and logged and handled with precision – the "custody of the evidence" – proved to be formidable.

In the case of the EA/G assessment, the developers were able to launch a scoring system and score the field test candidates' responses with sufficient technical quality to report and defend certification decisions. However, what it took to accomplish this goal was staggering. The responses to the tasks developed in the second round of design (after the initial, highly analytical model was rejected) were overwhelming in their amplitude. One of the three portfolio tasks required four to five hours to *single score.* And every task was double-scored. The assessor training required four to five full days, and in that time assessors could practice score only about four benchmark examples of performance prior to beginning "live" scoring. Furthermore, the diffuse nature of the task directions, and the extremely open-ended nature of the requirements made the apparatus required for scoring formidable: assessors were trained to take notes using one fully elaborated set of criteria, then summarize those notes using another set of criteria, and finally arrive at a score decision using a third set of criteria. The reference materials used by assessors were bound in books of several hundred pages each.

The dangers of exceeding the cognitive limits of any human being by sheer volume of information and instruction were not inconsiderable throughout all of this process, as assessors' own accounts of fatigue and frustration made clear. The final monetary cost of this scoring far exceeded any fee that could possibly be charged for an assessment and doomed an ongoing assessment program to an exponentially increasing deficit. But as discouraging as the monetary cost was the human cost, since it was clear that to replicate such scoring and training would require Herculean efforts. Trainers who could themselves master the sheer volume of detail would be hard to find, the openness of the task directions made each new response an adventure in uncharted territory that required the constant task of judgment, and teachers – who said this was a profoundly important but fundamentally exhausting experience – might well not wish to serve as assessors more than one time, particularly since their honorarium for such work was extremely modest. In addition, this system would require a huge number of assessors in any large-scale application such as that the NBPTS envisioned. It was not clear that there were enough qualified teachers available and willing in the entire United States to staff the scoring system, even without thinking about costs.

The case of the EA/ELA field-test scoring was more complicated. Results of the pilot test scoring for this certificate indicated, in the view of the NBPTS, that the scoring scheme devised by the developers was problematic. Even more time-consuming and elaborate than that eventually launched by the EA/G developers, this scoring approach required almost two weeks of intensive training prior to beginning the scoring of "live" cases. It also seemed to be based as much on a commitment to the professional development of the assessors as on the defensible scoring of the field-test candidates, and required the development and use by assessors of materials that exceeded the bounds of cognitive possibility (one of several such materials was a 900-page training manual). The original system gave "professional dialogue" among the assessors a prominent role in the scoring process. Two assessors worked together on a candidate's materials to arrive at a single score, and then together wrote extensive summaries explaining the bases for their decisions. This dialogue was considered to be one of the highlights of the scoring system's claims to validity and professional development potential. This kind of professional dialogue approach, though modified, continued as a part of the NBPTS scoring system past the initial field-test year, until it was clear that no amount of training or monitoring we could invent could overcome the influence of interactive variables, like control and dominance among the assessors. And these, of course, were defined as quite certain sources of error in the decisions.

In addition, the scoring system was not clearly connected to the EA/ELA Standards, a fundamental validity issue. Instead, the scoring system was based on a five-dimension system that the Pittsburgh/Connecticut colla-borative had used as the basis for development of the assessment tasks in the period before the EA/ELA Standards were completed, but after the contract for assessment development had begun. The scoring system, like that initially used by the University of Georgia, was founded on a belief that dimensions underlying performance were the critical focus of scoring. Unlike the University of Georgia, however, the Pittsburgh/Connecticut approach to dimensional scoring was always holistic, and it used not the Standards, but the original five dimensions the developers had used. After the EA/ELA Standards were adopted, the developers submitted "mappings" to show that the five dimensions mapped onto the Standards, but these mappings appeared to be idiosyncratic and open to multiple conceptual challenges.

Concerned about the feasibility and validity of this approach, the NBPTS commissioned the Educational Testing Service (ETS) to devise an alternative scoring scheme that would be EA/ELA Standards-based, efficient to use, and clearly defensible. A pilot test of the Pittsburgh/ Connecticut and the ETS scoring schemes using the same 100 cases from the field test sample resulted in the NBPTS's rejection of both scoring approaches, and their decision to postpone the EA/ELA scoring for a full year while a satisfactory scoring scheme was devised. The NBPTS chose ETS as its contractor for this task, and ETS engaged as expert consultants the members of the review panel that had rejected both the initial scoring schemes.

It was this difficult circumstance of being charged with the invention of a scoring system for an assessment in whose development we had played no role whatsoever that taught us some of our most important lessons about complex performance assessment. Both design and scoring strategies were fundamentally altered as a result of the struggle with the construction of a scoring scheme for the EA/ELA assessment that would honor the responses candidates had made to the tasks as written, and yet also honor the Standards as they were written. Further, such a scoring scheme had to be workable in real time, using the services of EA/ELA teachers who would be encouraged to participate in this activity more than once. And the apparatus for the scoring system, as well as the exact details for training assessors had to be replicable and portable, so that they could be used over and over and seen to be consistent over changes in time, place, and personnel.

Some of the most important lessons about the impact of design on scoring learned from the year (1994–1995) we spent working with the panel of external experts on the EA/ELA scoring system[4] now seem so simple as to go without saying. However, no one had said any of them in time to save our initial draft of the Adolescence and Young Adulthood/Mathematics (AYA/M) assessment – created contemporaneously with the creation of the overhauled EA/ELA scoring system – from many of the same problems inherent in the design of the field-test version of the EA/ELA assessment. (Our struggles with design are more fully recounted in Chapter 3.) The first and most important rule is what we might call the "consciousness" rule:

when developers create task directions, they *must* know what it is they value in a response to those directions. That is, the scoring rules must be explicit in the task directions. Performance assessment should aspire to the condition of the explicit scoring rules for multiple-choice assessment: "Choose the single best answer and fill in the oval that corresponds to the letter of that option."

But equally important is a considered long-term projection of the consequences of what we think we want candidates to give us. Not only do developers need to think about what kind of evidence candidates should submit, they also need to think about what they – the parties responsible for evaluation – will do with this evidence when they get it. Simple questions need to be asked early: If we ask for 'x,' will we know what to make of it? Will we be able to see it? Will we be able to move it around from one assessor to another? How long will it take us to look at it? What equipment will we need to look at it?

Allied to these seemingly mundane considerations is the much more serious question of how much evidence is enough for assessors to be able to make a valid decision with reasonably low levels of inference. Early NBPTS tasks asked for lavish amounts of evidence, evincing a tacit assumption that more evidence must be more valid. What the initial ETS tussle with scoring revealed was that more was often less, since the more precise the teacher-candidate's analysis of either student work or videotape, the better our sense of the teacher's skills and abilities. But precise analysis is virtually impossible if we ask for lots of student work samples, or a 45-minute videotape. The sheer volume of information tended to blur the picture of the teacher's practice. The importance of *choice*, both by the developers creating the assessment structure itself and candidates responding to it, as a feature of successful portfolio assessment had never been more evident.

Furthermore, it became clear that assessors themselves, teachers, were overwhelmed by the sheer volume of evidence and displayed a less certain grasp of the criteria for evaluation as the amount of paper or length of the videotape increased. What seemed to happen was that assessors began to invent their own individual heuristics as the volume of evidence mounted, ignoring the carefully constructed apparatus designed to guide their scoring decisions. These heuristics often involved the assessors' latching onto the first clear bits of evidence that they found in a massive response, and these first impressions then drove their entire interpretation of the response.

A larger framework of assumption was revealed by our efforts to design a scoring system after the fact, a system that could equitably evaluate the approximately 250 candidates who were waiting patiently – and, in the end, waited for over a year – for their scores. In Chapter 3, I discussed at some length the effects of designing tasks that attempt to capture important aspects of the domain of measurement without thinking carefully about how much space has been given in the task for the teacher's own practice to emerge. Throughout the assessment, it became clear that the uncomfortable fit between the original five dimensions used for task development and the EA/ELA Standards had created a number of requirements in the tasks that were not fully scorable using the EA/ELA Standards as the basis for evaluation.

Furthermore, none of the tasks in the assessment told candidates straightforwardly what the criteria for evaluation would be. No scoring criteria or advice about how to "do your best" were included in any task directions. And while the teacher's ability to analyze his/her practice, reflect on its significance for further instructional planning, and use each experience to deepen professional knowledge was highly prized (as it still is in these assessments), teachers were given little guidance in this complex and unfamiliar task. Repeatedly, the panel designing the EA/ELA scoring system asked themselves "Is this fair?" when considering elements of the task responses that were clearly important through the lens of the EA/ELA Standards, but which had not been stressed or clearly stated in the task directions. In the final scoring system, a parsimonious approach to what could be considered for scoring was taken for each of the nine EA/ELA tasks: only if candidates could clearly have known they needed to include such material and/or analysis was the element used in the scoring system.

Perhaps the greatest advantage (for future design and scoring decisions) of our enforced engagement with the problem of designing a scoring system for an already completed assessment was our exposure to multiple samples of candidate performances. It was this immersion in the actual stuff of responses that made obvious our underconceptualization of the difficulties of evaluating complex, multimedia portfolios along with elaborate simulations in the assessment center. The sheer variety of candidates' contexts and teaching circumstances, in combination with the voluminous and unpredictable nature of the evidentiary artifacts, made it clear that we could not possibly be fair to each candidate if we did not impose some rather rigid structure on the evaluative activities necessary to arrive at final scores. On the other hand, the whole of a candidate's response, when all parts of the response to a task were considered together, was often different in kind from the individual parts. And we often did not have some essential pieces of information that would help to make sense of candidate responses because the assessment task had not asked for that information. Thus, both task design and scoring design were affected by our exposure to candidate responses.

For scoring, the volume and variety of responses made some effective middle ground that combined elements of analytical scoring with the best features of holistic judgments seem imperative. Furthermore, the hundreds of cases we examined made it obvious that there was a wonderful variety of accomplished practice in the living, busy world of teaching in the United States. No one style or model of excellence sufficed to encompass all of the Standards-based practice we were seeing in these samples. These two qualities – the amplitude of the evidence and the variety of its presentation modes – made the training of assessors a formidable challenge. We knew this because in our small working group prior to any assessor training, particular surface characteristics of different responses evoked passionate responses in members of the panel, even though analysis according to the Standards revealed that responses some panelists really disliked were, indeed, accomplished. And others, equally passionately championed because of their look or feel, were not so accomplished.

It was at this point that the four-point score scale, in use by all NBPTS developers since the revision of the earliest EA/G design and scoring system, was modified to include pluses and minuses on the ordinal numbers. These pluses and minuses, we learned, were important to assessors' abilities to classify performances in the ordinal number categories, which the rubrics define as very clearly different from each other. Like all assessments, of course, each score point yields a range of performances – candidates produce responses that are "almost" the next category, either above or below the ordinal number category. And assessors were much better able to make the ordinal distinctions when allowed to "shade" their judgments up or down according to the evidence they found. The score scale that resulted are presented in Table 1.

The numerical distinctions between the score "families" allowed us to teach assessors to classify the performance as a whole according to its family, and then tailor their judgment according to the particulars of the evidence they evaluated in an individual performance. The assessor training, detailed below, focused on the differences between the ordinal categories, so that assessors felt confident about the judgment.

Table 1. Score Scale.

0.75	1	1.25	1.75	2	2.25	2.75	3	3.25	3.75	4	4.25
1−	1	1+	2−	2	2+	3−	3	3+	4−	4	4+

The panel's experience of the importance of an analytical approach to candidate responses – though not necessarily an analytic scoring scheme – and the demonstrated effectiveness of a more elaborated score scale forced us to examine and articulate in a far more structured fashion what, exactly, it was that the NBPTS Standards valued in teachers' practice. This analysis led both to design decisions discussed in Chapter 3, as well as to the fully developed assessor training program described below. What we did in response to the exigencies of the moment in the case of the EA/ELA field test, and have continued to refine in our further NBPTS assessment development and scoring, was to impose on ourselves the methods of well-conducted essay scoring. Given the difference in the sheer size of responses in a conventional essay assessment and the NBPTS certification assessments, this approach held us to a very high standard. Modifications of these methods and sometimes inventions of new methods were necessary in the evolution of scoring, particularly in light of the criterion-referenced nature of the NBPTS assessments.

Briefly put, essay scoring depends on the interconnection of several important elements: the prompt itself, the rubric (or articulated scoring rules), multiple samples of responses for each level of the scoring rubric, and a training plan, with qualification guidelines for assessors. We incorporated all these standard essay scoring elements into the NBPTS scoring system, though because of the complexity and amplitude of candidate responses, the elements were often more complex in themselves and in their interrelationships. Indeed, the multiple sources of evidence for each assessment task, and the variation in media (student work, videotape, teacher commentary) made the logistics of scoring itself a major operational and validity challenge.

This essay scoring model was a challenging strategy to employ well when responses were brief (two to four pages) and very consistent, constrained within the limitations imposed by the prompt. And for the NBPTS assessment center tasks, this approach worked well even though the responses were longer than any traditional essay assessment currently in use. In the NBPTS portfolio task scoring, however, this strategy presented formidable challenges because the size and nature of the portfolio responses pitted thorough training of assessors against the limits of time and attention possible for ordinary human beings to marshal in service of intellectual activity.

Two broad areas of endeavor emerged as critical parts of NBPTS scoring's attempt to meet the high and rigorous standards established by essay scoring such as the College Board's Advanced Placement program. The first was the area of assessor training. What was an effective approach to preparing assessors to evaluate such big and unpredictable responses?

How could we create the functional equivalents of multiple samples in responses that take 45 min to single score? And the second area was scoring materials: what should assessors be given to help guide them through the process of evaluation of very large and very complicated portfolio tasks?

ASSESSOR TRAINING

There were a number of challenges that attended the training of NBPTS assessors. First was the unfamiliarity of the structure of the assessment itself. Few teachers had experience with portfolio assessment, and fewer still with the challenges of presenting their own professional work through such a sampling mechanism. In addition, the NBPTS assessments used media – video recording, student work, and analytical writing – in ways that were new to teachers. Videotape in particular demanded careful attention in training, since it appeared to be The Truth, as opposed to "a truth" about a teacher's practice. That is, the visual representation of teaching in a videotape seemed, at first glance, to be absolutely credible as a record of what "really is happening." Only when the effects of such visual details as the noise level, the classroom furnishings and ambiance, the arrangement of students and desks, the kinds of equipment and resources on view were considered did the role of interpretation of the "picture" become clear. Furthermore, without careful training, viewers of videotape, especially teachers viewing teaching (which they believed they *knew* how to interpret), could not readily separate what they saw from a value-laden interpretation of what it meant and signified. And the interpretations teachers made of what they saw were dependent on their own range of experience and their own methods of practice.

We discovered this scoring challenge early on, when one group of expert scorers roundly denounced a teacher's commentary on the videotape they viewed as "untruthful." Since the teacher was describing the school and classroom context of the video, something she presumably knew more about than anyone else, we found this curious. When we probed for reasons for this passionate disagreement with the teacher about her own classroom, we found that the *appearance* of the classroom – organized and rather conventional – struck the viewers as not at all the way a classroom in a low-income school serving at risk students would look. What were they expecting? They reported that they expected to see visible signs of neglect in the school building and equipment and visible signs that the students were "poor." It turned out, of course, that none of the viewers of this particular videotape had ever taught in a school setting like the one reflected in the commentary and on the videotape.

Student work also evoked passionate responses in teachers who had to be carefully instructed to always consider the context for the work before judging its appropriateness and efficacy. The highly detailed analytical commentary candidates were (and still are) required to write made demands that were unfamiliar to teachers, since candidates were required to look at their decisions and provide rationales for them, to examine videotape and student work from their teaching and reflect on its significance. And an overarching challenge was how to balance the final evaluation among sources of evidence in a portfolio task, since the final scoring decision is a holistic judgment that considers all evidence, taken together.

Second, there was the primary labor of any assessor training session, which was to figure out how to present to all assessors the scoring apparatus and samples in a way that would ensure consistent application of the scoring rules and *at the same time* encourage the use of professional expertise in the evaluation of each response. In the case of the NBPTS assessments this was particularly difficult, since both the scoring apparatus and the sample responses were voluminous. As I said above, one of the most important aspects of NBPTS assessor training became the management and presentation of very large volumes of information in a way that made sense to teachers and could be deployed by them throughout the scoring session.

Third, a whole new focus for assessor training emerged through the scoring of NBPTS assessments, partly because of the nature of the evidence media. By NBPTS policy, only teachers currently engaged at least half the time in teaching can serve as assessors. Retired trainers/assessors can work for three years as long as they worked for five previous years – and they must have teaching experience in the field and at the developmental level they score. The exclusive use of expert judges, rather narrowly defined, gives the NBPTS scoring enormous professional credibility and face validity. However, it created a concomitant cluster of training challenges. We referred to these challenges, rather loosely, as issues of "bias." In reality, however, the issues we engaged in developing this training were likely more complicated than that word suggests.

At the center of bias-awareness training was the individual teacher-assessor's own practice and often strongly held (and strongly defended) notions about the society in which they lived and operated and what constituted acceptable teaching practice (and, of course, less-accomplished teaching practice). The NBPTS assessment owes its existence in part to the recognition that teachers' expertise and wisdom of practice had never been codified into a body of professional knowledge similar to that owned by other learned professions like law and medicine. The certification program was an attempt to redress that balance and in the process to contribute to that body of knowledge. But highly analytical self-awareness and the habit of reflection on one's professional decisions and actions and the rationales that led to them are limited even among the best practitioners to their own contexts and experiences. There has been no more generalized framework within which one might reflect on teaching practice.

As a consequence, most teacher-assessors began the scoring session with convictions about teaching they had never examined, and beliefs about their own practices and those of others that they had never analyzed. And these convictions and beliefs were, in most cases, teachers' ideas of "truth" about teaching practice. This was the framework which, without the intervention of training, teacher-assessors would use to define the qualitative words in the scoring rubric, words like "consistent," "thorough," "strong," "uneven," "limited." And this was also the framework that teachers believed constituted their professional expertise and judgment. Thus the bias-reduction training went hand-in-hand with the training on the appropriate use and application of the rubrics. The first aspect of training helped assessors minimize the impact of peripheral surface features of a candidate's performance, while the second grounded the assessors in features that they had to attend to when making a scoring decision. Simply telling assessors that they should not make biased judgments was not sufficient. Assessors needed much more help in uncovering their own biases and preferences. Over time, the NPBTS scoring system came to include a series of specifically focused tasks that led the assessors to consider both personal preferences and societal biases that might interfere with their ability to award a valid and fair score to a candidate.

PERSONAL PREFERENCE VERSUS PROFESSIONAL EXPERTISE: BIAS-REDUCTION TRAINING

One of the most important and most innovative aspects of the NBPTS assessor training program was the inclusion of an extensive set of tasks for assessors that were designed to guide assessors to an in-depth examination of their assumptions, biases and preferences, and training in how to disarm them during scoring. During the training, we described this process as a way of becoming aware of personal preference and its possible interference with professional expertise, which was what we wanted to liberate.

Following the introduction, assessors participated in the first of several bias-reduction tasks that were woven into the training sequence. The bias tasks were somewhat different for portfolio and assessment center training, because the nature of the tasks created different opportunities for biases to emerge in scoring. But both sets of bias-reduction tasks were designed to provide assessors with opportunities to gain insight into their own value systems and biases and then give them tools for disarming their biases in scoring. Both sets of tasks involved individual writing and reflection followed by group discussion. In both portfolio and assessment center scoring, the bias-reduction training began with an introduction that explained the importance of identifying and eliminating the effects of personal bias on scoring. Assessors were assured that each and every one of them had biases, preferences, and assumptions that were a part (and often a necessary part) of the way they negotiated reality. It was explained that these biases, assumptions, and preferences might constitute an individual set of scoring criteria that had no place in fair assessment. A set of ground rules to build a safe environment for exploring personal biases was then established. These ground rules were intended to promote personal honesty and respect for the difficulty of the work that lay ahead. The bias-reduction tasks are summarized below and then discussed individually in more detail.

The first task, "Competence/Incompetence" focused on assessors' personal preferences by asking them to consider what signaled, for each of them, competence and incompetence when they met people for the first time. The goal was for assessors to recognize personal triggers that may make them favor or disadvantage a candidate based on information that was not pertinent to the scoring decision. This task helped bring subconscious preferences to a conscious level. The second task was called "Self-Awareness" and focused on personal preferences in teaching style. In the third task assessors were presented with brief vignettes that described teaching scenarios. They were asked to "score" these individually. The goal of this task was to further assessors' understanding of how making false inferences about someone else's teaching could impact scores. The fourth task, "Awareness of societal bias," was conducted later in training after assessors were more comfortable with one another, and directly addressed societal biases such as racism, sexism, and classism – and, importantly, the potential impact of these on scoring. The aim of the fifth task, "Awareness of writing biases," was for assessors to identify their own writing style preferences and consider how these preferences could impact judgments.

At the beginning of the training, assessors established a personal record of very specific triggers that might make them score a candidate higher or lower than deserved. This was crucial, since awareness of how biases affect judgments was not sufficient; this awareness must translate into behavioral differences in the actual scoring. At the end of each bias task, assessors added to their lists, and as they watched videotapes and discovered other triggers, they were asked to note those as well. Assessors kept their trigger lists throughout scoring and were expected to refer to them often.

A final aspect of training that contributed to bias-reduction was the selection of benchmark cases. Low-scoring minority teachers were used as benchmark examples only if they were balanced with high-scoring minority teachers, for example. A consistent and deliberate effort was made to select benchmark cases that reflected multiple school contexts as well – diversity in academic achievement, SES of students, size and type of school settings, and the like was critical in representing the range of practice assessors would have to evaluate. Benchmark cases were also selected with common personal preferences in mind that were typically discussed in the first bias-reduction task. Even though the trainer had already pointed out that these constituted personal preferences that were not in the scoring rubrics and therefore should not form the basis for making judgments, assessors may not have been in complete agreement. Examples were sought in the benchmarks that challenged stereotypes and personal preferences.

All the bias-awareness tasks were woven into assessor training, alternating between examining scoring materials or candidate responses and the bias-reduction tasks. The first two bias-awareness tasks for portfolio scoring were entitled "Competence–Incompetence" and "Self-Awareness." These tasks focused on teachers' notions of accomplishment and competence, initially in the world at large, and then in the realm of teaching. It also tapped into teachers' "pet peeves" and notions of incompetence. The first task used in the assessment center was called "Connection of Accomplished/ Not Accomplished to Content Area" and focused on the content knowledge one could expect to see in a 30-min task.

THE METHOD

Individual Writing

Assessors responded in writing to the following four questions:

1. When you are in a supermarket, library, gym, a state office, etc., what characteristics of an employee do you look for to signify competence?

Think about non-verbal cues such as body language, demeanor, pitch of voice, and dress, as well as verbal signals.

2. In those or similar settings, what signals do you look for to signify incompetence? Again, think about non-verbal cues, such as body language, demeanor, pitch of voice, and dress, as well as verbal signals.
3. What do I do particularly well as a teacher? What about my practice marks me as an accomplished teacher?
4. What are teaching practices that I dislike?

Assessors wrote individually in response to these questions, and then shared their responses with the full group, as the trainer charted the responses. Throughout the sharing and discussion, the trainer took pains to help assessors see the distinction between individual values and biases and the criteria in the scoring system. For example, it was not uncommon for assessors to name "appears well-organized" or "has a neat appearance" as signs of competence. In fact, organization and appearance in themselves did not appear in any NBPTS standards document, and the trainer would point this out. One early childhood teacher named "classroom is too neat" as a sign of incompetent teaching. While this may have been a helpful signal to her in her work as a mentor to early childhood teachers, it was not part of the NBPTS evaluation system. Another common sign of competence may be "has a good sense of humor." Interesting discussions arose from comments such as this as trainers sought to help assessors understand that their sense of humor may not be the same as another person's and that care needed to be taken to judge the appropriateness of a teacher's humor, using students' reactions as one indicator. These were the sorts of biases, assumptions, and preferences that arose in response to this task. The discussion was serious but had lighthearted moments, as assessors began to see the complexity of tacit assumptions they were carrying.

In the assessment center version of this, task trainers had to ensure that assessors not only understood the distinction between signs of competence/incompetence as articulated in the Standards, but that they also understood the limitations of the assessment center tasks as vehicles for demonstrating those characteristics – or while most portfolio entries addressed at least half the Standards, assessment center tasks typically only addressed one or two.

In the third bias task, assessors were presented with a series of vignettes which were brief descriptions of a classroom or teaching scenario. Assessors independently rated each vignette as either an accomplished or not accomplished excerpt. They then worked in pairs to take one vignette and extrapolate to what might happen next, based on how they had initially rated it. As a whole group, the various "stories" were shared. What became apparent from this task was how different assessors could have different interpretations of the same vignette based on personal experiences or knowledge. This task helped assessors understand the danger in either making too large an inference based on limited evidence or of reading too much between the lines, a practice called "story telling."

The fourth task, "Awareness of societal bias," was conducted later in training after assessors were more comfortable with one another, and directly addressed societal biases such as racism, sexism, and classism. This task did not attempt to correct "misinformation" about particular groups of people per se; instead, it sought to demonstrate how assessors have internalized many of the stereotypes that are prevalent in society. First, assessors individually wrote word-associations in response to stimulus phrases such as, "Hispanic woman," "urban," "youthful," etc. Next, assessors wrote a brief reflection on any patterns that they noticed in their responses, and considered what might have caused those patterns. The trainer then led the group in a discussion, reassuring assessors that they did not need to share personal information. Common themes that arose included shock or distaste at what they wrote, realizing that it was not "politically correct" or that the information was largely based on societal stereotypes, and surprise that they reverted to these societal stereotypes when they had no other information to base their associations on. A strong emphasis of this task was that everyone had a reaction at some level to circumstances different than their own, and that often those reactions were influenced by stereotypes. Becoming aware of how these stereotypes had been internalized and being willing to confront them were important outcomes for assessors during this task.

The fifth and final bias-awareness task for portfolio and assessment center training was the writing bias task. In this task, assessors reviewed short excerpts of candidates' writing, extrapolated to what they thought the rest of the response might be like, and on the basis of the excerpt assigned a score to the samples. The excerpts were selected to exemplify a range of writing styles. After discussion of these excerpts, the trainer informed the assessors that all of the excerpts came from high-scoring NBPTS performances. The aim of this task was for assessors to identify their own writing style preferences and consider how these preferences could impact judgments. Trainers led assessors in an in-depth discussion about the potential impact on scoring that different forms of writing, different stylistic approaches, or issues of grammar/vocabulary might have.

As assessors proceeded through the bias-reduction tasks, they created a personal bias "Trigger List," which became an integral part of the assessor's scoring "tool-kit." Assessors created a list of their biases about teaching, students, or competence in general. They also noted the direction that their biases tended to run in once they were triggered, as this could differ from assessor to assessor. For example, some assessors may have initially responded to classrooms in poorly resourced schools in an overly sympathetic manner, while others might not have been able to appropriately value the constraints limited resources might place on the teacher.

Bias issues for assessment center assessors tended to be much more focused, just as the prompts themselves were much more focused than the portfolio tasks. The first task connected the content knowledge of the certificate area to accomplishment, and assessors also completed the assessment center version of the writing task.

Individual Writing

- What content knowledge should you expect to see in the responses to the assessment center tasks?

Trainer Questions that followed:

1. Which items are addressed in the standards?
2. How much content can be addressed in a 30-min, on-demand task?

CONSTRUCTING UNDERSTANDING: TRAINING MATERIALS

Essay scoring typically depends on a plethora of examples of responses at each score point to establish in assessors' minds the essential nature of a score point – "twoness" or "threeness" – regardless of the individual characteristics of a particular person's response. When responses are, at most, two to three pages long, this is a very sensible approach to training. In fact, many essay-scoring sessions begin by requiring the assessors to respond themselves to the prompt they will be scoring, so that they experience firsthand the challenges and possible variations in responses. The NBPTS assessment center prompts were scored in precisely this fashion. The NBPTS portfolio required a much more complicated approach to assessor training. Prior to seeing any candidate responses, the assessors needed to be fully aware of the nature of this assessment, to understand the Standards, to comprehend the extremely complicated task directions, to become familiar with the scoring apparatus, and to explore and analyze the geography of their own biases. All of this required a much more elaborate set of training materials than a set of candidate responses, though that set was formidable enough.

The assessor training program, which took three full days for NBPTS portfolio tasks, began with orientation to standards-based assessment. Learning the content and the use of each of the documents described below in the "Scoring Materials" section was one of the central tasks of assessor training. Early in training, assessors were presented with all the elements of the scoring system and guided through a close examination of them. For portfolio training, this presentation included the following elements (see Appendix F for a full list of the portfolio assessor training materials):

1. the *Five Core Propositions*, which undergirded all NBPTS Standards;
2. the *Standards*, with special attention to the standards addressed by the task being scored;
3. the Architecture of Accomplished Teaching which connected the Propositions and Standards to the Task Directions (see Fig. 1 on page 78);
4. the *Task Directions*, with special attention to the links between the five core propositions, the standards and the directions, as well as a careful noting of the exact requirements of the task;
5. the *Rubric*, with special attention to the links between the rubric and the task directions and the standards, as well as a careful examination of the structure and content of the rubric.
6. *Aspects of Teaching Addressed in the Rubric*, with opportunities given to match the aspects to the exact language of the rubric at the four levels of performance;
7. the *Score Scale*, with attention to the clustering of scores in the score "families" and the proper use of plus and minus scores;
8. the *Note-Taking Guide*, with attention to the connection between the guiding questions and the rubric and the process of locating, recording, and evaluating evidence;
9. the *Score Path*, with attention to the standardization of procedures and required checks against bias;

10. the *Entry Scoring Records* (ESRs), with attention to their purpose and
    general note-taking approaches. More detailed instruction on note
    taking was provided later in the training.

For assessment center scoring, the scoring system was somewhat less
complex, although the elements were essentially the same. The five core
propositions played a much less prominent role, and assessment center tasks
tended to only focus on a limited number of Standards. The List of Essential
Features (rather than aspects) was presented following the rubric, and its
relationship to the rubric was made clear.

Following this initial segment of the training, assessors were introduced to
their first candidate responses. What evolved since the initial invention of a
scoring system for the EA/ELA field test was an adaptation of the
procedures common in essay scoring that allowed for the length and
complexity of the responses, and was further shaped by the criterion-
referenced nature of the NBPTS assessment.

The scoring approach used for the NBPTS assessments has been
described as "multi-aspect holistic scoring" (private communication with
Marnie Thompson) in order to convey how evidence was identified in the
candidate's response against the aspects particular to that task – the multi-
aspect part – and then holistically evaluated in order to decide on a single
score, whose rubric description best matched the overall performance – the
holistic part. The following excerpt in the assessor-training manual
elaborates on why both parts of the scoring approach were essential:

> Your job as an assessor is to reach an appropriate balance between analytic scoring and
> holistic scoring. If you err too far on the side of analytic scoring, you won't be able to see
> the actual teaching before you. Instead you'll see a forest of little bits that doesn't
> accurately represent teaching – teaching is a complex art or science that cannot be
> properly understood as the sum of its parts. But if you err too far on the side of pure
> holistic scoring, you are likely to miss essential components of the performance, simply
> because teaching is such a complex activity. That is why we have combined holistic and
> analytic elements into our scoring system. (NBPTS, 2002, pp. 46–47)

For each portfolio task in the NBPTS assessments, a set of 20 sample
responses or "cases" were chosen as the training set. Six of these were
benchmarks; the remaining 14 were training and qualifying samples. The
NBPTS score scale had four ordinal numbers and also included the use of
"plus" and "minus" on each ordinal number (see scale illustration in Table
1 above). The level defined in the rubrics as "accomplished," which means
that the teaching under review met the criteria established in the NBPTS
Standards for accomplished practice in the certificate field, was the level 3 on

the score scale. Thus, one of the most critical training issues was the clear definition of the distinction between the *top* of the level 2 performances (the 2+) and the *bottom* of the level 3 performances (the 3−). For this reason, the benchmark set included two examples of performances at the 2nd and 3rd levels. Furthermore, to instantiate from the outset the basic premise of the NBPTS assessments, that accomplished teaching is a matter of underlying architecture rather than surface detail, each benchmark at a particular score point was deliberately chosen to look quite different in its surface details from its counterpart(s).

Attention was paid to ensure that the benchmarks and training samples differed in terms of the content featured in the task, in teacher and student demographics, class size, student ability, and teaching styles. For example, it was important that all high-scoring performances not be sampled from small advanced classes in suburban schools. The architectural similarities of the training samples, in contrast to the differences in their surface details, were a principle subject of discussion during the training session. Just as in essay scoring, the benchmark performances were chosen for their clarity in demonstrating the salient characteristics of performance at the particular score point, as such characteristics were articulated in the scoring rubric. A scaffolded learning approach was used for assessor training – for the first set of examples the trainer *told* the assessors what the score was and helped them understand why, and see the connections to the rubric. For later examples, the assessors scored the responses on their own first and then discussed the actual benchmarked score, with the trainer guiding assessors to connect evidence in the response to the score.

In addition to the performances themselves, benchmarks were accompanied by a record of evidence ESR that had been completed by the teacher who would serve as the assessor trainer for that portfolio task. The trainer also created a marginal annotation of the written commentary text of each benchmark response, tying the candidate's written analysis to the rubric, and helping assessors see the evidence cited in the ESR. The benchmarks were presented to assessors in a spiral-bound book, which was used throughout the scoring session as a reference tool. Assessors were told which score point each benchmark represented as it was presented, and a benchmark 3 performance was the first sample response assessors saw. The first example was followed by the benchmark 2, the benchmark 1, the benchmark 4, and a second 2 and a second 3. Assessors were encouraged to discuss the benchmarks as they were presented, but classification of each response as an exemplar of a particular score point was pre-established.

Rubric-defined links among responses that were classified similarly were emphasized in this initial portion of the training.

After the benchmarks were presented, assessors were given training samples to classify. They were not told in advance of their own consideration of these samples what the score ought to be, nor were they given records of evidence to look at in advance of their evaluations. For each training sample, the trainer's record of evidence was circulated after assessors had reached their own decisions so that assessors could compare their record of evidence and evaluation of that evidence to that of the trainer's. Once again, links among samples within the same score "family" (1, 2, 3, 4) were emphasized. Training samples had been carefully chosen to amplify the assessors' understanding of the range of possible responses. The critical distinction between a level 2 and a level 3 performance was emphasized in the training samples just as it was in the benchmarks, but trainers had more freedom in the use of training samples than they did in the presentation of benchmarks. Some groups of assessors may have had more difficulty grasping certain elements of the rubric; training samples had been carefully chosen to demonstrate a variety of scoring challenges.

During this portion of the training, each assessor independently scored each training sample, one at a time or in paired sets. Before the discussion of a training sample began, the trainer collected the scores assigned by each assessor. Then, the trainer announced the validated score of the training sample, and led a discussion that focused on the reasons for the score. In the discussion, the focus was on the validated score and the reasons for it, and not on the reasons for alternative scores. Assessors who scored the response correctly cited the evidence and link it to the rubric. Assessors who gave other scores had an opportunity to cite their reasons for scoring the case the way they did, so that the trainer could understand the misconceptions that assessors may have been harboring, but the trainer took pains to keep the score from becoming the subject of debate. In the early stages of training, assessors may have had difficulty locating evidence within the voluminous and sometimes oddly written responses. This was often the reason for lower scores being assigned. When appropriate, the trainer may have directed assessors to consider bias or personal preferences as another possible source of their misconceptions.

As the group worked through the training samples, the trainer carefully monitored the work of each assessor, keeping a log of their scores and reviewing their records of evidence. Trainers conferred privately with each assessor at least once during this portion of training. The purpose of this conference was to provide encouragement and targeted guidance and answer questions assessors may have had.

Trainers began this portion of training with samples that illustrated the 3–2 distinction. From that point on, they followed a predetermined order of case presentation. They knew which samples presented certain challenges or illustrated certain scoring issues. The collected training samples represented both clear-cut and more ambiguous scoring decisions, as well as providing examples of scores at all levels of the score scale.

The final stage of the training process was the qualification round. In this qualification round, assessors independently scored five or six pre-selected cases. These cases were deliberately selected to represent the score scale and were generally clear-cut in their presentation of the evidence. The goal was to determine whether assessors could apply the scoring criteria properly to typical responses. Assessors who did not demonstrate competence in this round were not asked to continue to live scoring. For assessment center scoring, the decision to move assessors forward to live scoring was made on the basis of their performance on the training sample set alone, as the assessment center responses were more straightforward and not as difficult to score reliably. Infrequently, an assessor did not qualify and was not invited to participate in the actual scoring. Occasionally, an assessor was deemed to be almost ready, merely in need of additional training and practice. Such training was provided to move them into readiness. These assessors were monitored very closely in live scoring, with trainers "reading behind" them to ensure the validity of their scores.

BLAZING A TRAIL: SCORING MATERIALS

Holding ourselves to the principles of a well-managed essay scoring committed us to the use of a rubric and samples of performance that would operationalize or demonstrate the meaning of all of the qualitative words and judgments in that rubric. But the NBPTS assessment represented an unfamiliar assessment methodology. This was a criterion-referenced assessment based on a very clearly articulated domain. Both the criterion and the domain appeared in the NBPTS Standards for each certificate, and it was critical that assessors understood the parts of this document that were germane to the particular task they were scoring. In addition, this was a portfolio assessment, and the directions for each task were lengthy, complicated, and inextricably connected to the scoring criteria. Furthermore, the size and engaging messiness of the portfolio responses revealed to us from the outset that the rubric/samples apparatus could not alone ensure an equitable evaluation of all parts of each candidate's response. It became clear that we needed to create much more elaborate structures to guide assessors in making judgments.

Though each assessor assigned only a single score to each task response, the scoring system was not a simple holistic one in which assessors reached a holistic judgment about the response based on their impressions. Instead, the scoring system was highly analytic even as it was holistic, and it was supported by a set of documents that directed assessors to examine multiple aspects of the performance and then evaluate the evidence against a rubric that addressed the way these aspects, considered collectively, served to characterize a performance that could be judged in holistic terms. For portfolio tasks, these documents included a list of the aspects of teaching addressed by the rubric, and a note-taking guide which assessors had to use in the process of noting and recording evidence. In the scoring process prior to the Next Generation redesign (see Chapter 3), these documents also included a scoring path document that systematically moved assessors through the same series of steps for every performance they scored. In the redesign of the training which accompanied the Next Generation redesign of the assessments, this method of assuring assessor consistency was incorporated into the training itself, and this document eliminated.[5]

Ensuring that all parts of the evidence candidates were required to submit, received careful and equal attention from assessors required the creation of a note-taking guide and an accompanying record of evidence. Because the rubrics themselves were lengthy and complicated – each score point (there are four ordinal numbers from 1 (low) to 4 (high)) required half a page to describe – we learned that further assistance in considering the contribution to the whole made by a particular source of evidence was necessary. And while early versions of NBPTS scoring systems required extremely labor-intensive records of evidence from the assessors, which we wanted to avoid, we learned that to jettison all note-taking by assessors was dangerous. In the 35–45 min it took to evaluate a portfolio task, what one noticed at the beginning was often lost or completely transformed by the end of the reading period. The analytical process that the note-taking guide directs assessors to follow in the creation of their accompanying record of evidence required a thorough review of everything the candidate had submitted, with each piece considered in light of the relevant part of the rubric. Assessors must note evidence or absence of evidence on each relevant aspect in the "Aspects of Teaching Addressed in the Rubric," and then evaluate the quality of the noted evidence as they proceeded choosing from the list of "Evaluation Words – for example, Goals evidence –"curriculum goals stated "Evaluation: Global but tied to state curriculum and particular lesson."

The final questions in every note-taking guide required assessors to review the record of evidence thus far, and consider all of the evidence holistically. Only after these final questions had been considered did assessors decide on the numerical score for the response.[6] These final questions helped assessors to see the forest, as it were, having previously been noting evidence about the trees.

MORE ABOUT RUBRICS

Rubrics are designed to recognize qualities of teaching consistent with the Standards. However, rubrics are not designed to privilege particular behaviors or teaching methods. Each set of Standards and corresponding set of rubrics were designed to recognize that teachers could demonstrate accomplished practice in varying teacher contexts and using different teaching approaches and styles. Irrespective of the certificate, all teachers needed to consistently demonstrate that they understood the needs of their students, that they had a firm grasp of content and how to teach that content, that they established a productive and effective learning environment, that they could assess their students with insight, and that they could reflect on their practice. Though these requirements were non-negotiable, the assessment system recognized that there was no prescribed way of demonstrating accomplishment. The rubric's levels were tied to the quality of the evidence in the performance, as opposed to being personalized to the candidate himself/herself. The qualifiers, "clear, consistent, and convincing," "clear," "limited," and "little or no" described the evidence as the rubric descended from level 4 to level 1. Careful reading of the levels of the rubric shows that a level 3 performance was keyed to a level of performance that might be considered "accomplished" on the task. A level 2 performance may occasionally show hints of accomplishment, but overall falls short. This was true for all NBPTS rubrics, both assessment center and portfolio.

As the example below shows, portfolio rubrics contained highly structured and detailed descriptions of complex performance qualities of teaching. Each level of the rubric began with a similarly worded "holistic focus statement" which was closely tied to the focus of the task, as described in the "What is the nature of this task?" section of the task directions. Following the holistic description was a more detailed narrative description of the likely performance qualities of a teacher at that level, covering the aspects of teaching addressed in the task. Assessors were trained to decide where the "preponderance of evidence" placed the performance on the score scale. It was understood that all candidates who scored a "3" might not have the same profile of performance on all the aspects addressed in the rubric, yet the preponderance of evidence placed the response in the "3rd" category.

The narrative format was deliberately adopted to encourage assessors to attend to the whole response, even as they were considering aspects of the performance. The aspects were closely tied to the Standards assessed by the task, but were not necessarily mapped to distinct or whole Standards. Instead, they were the manifestations of the Standards in the context of a specific task that was common in teaching in the field under assessment. In the example below, the aspects of teaching addressed are: *knowledge of students as individuals and as learners; goals, and connection between goals and instruction; understanding of the reading and writing process; encouragement of and response to student responses to reading and writing; use of instructional resources, use of assessment; communication with students about their writing; and reflection.* Assessors used the aspects and their descriptors as a guide for organizing their analysis of each performance, but they did not assign aspect-level scores. Each aspect was addressed at each level of the rubric, if only to note its absence, which sometimes occurred in the lower levels of performance. See Appendix G for a sample rubric; this rubric was part of the scoring packet for the task presented as an example of a Next Generation EA/ELA portfolio task in the Appendix D (discussed in Chapter 3, Design).

ASSESSMENT CENTER TASK RUBRICS

For assessment center tasks, the underpinnings of the scoring system were not quite as extensive. Assessors worked with the rubric and, usually, a "List of Essential Features" that augments the rubric and is keyed to the specific stimulus for that administration of the task. Assessment center rubrics are written to be broad enough to cover different stimulus materials that may have accompanied the prompt and changed over time. The List of Essential Features was a highly specific treatment of the requirements to achieve a score of 4 that was couched within the particulars of a given set of stimulus materials. The rubrics were structured similarly to the portfolio rubrics, using an opening holistic statement, followed by more detailed descriptors, though the rubrics tended to be much briefer and highly focused, due to the more focused nature of the prompts. Again, the rubric's levels were tied to the quality of the evidence in the performance, and the same qualifiers – "clear, consistent, and convincing," "clear," "limited," and "little or no" were used. See Appendix H for a sample assessment center task and its rubric.

CHALLENGES TO THE MODEL

The decision to adapt essay scoring strategies and scoring rules for NBPTS scoring provided a strong frame for scoring of complex performances, but it also created some challenges. This approach to scoring was sample-intensive, and a sufficiently broad range of samples is critical to the validity of the scoring system, since qualitative levels in the rubric were operationally defined by performance samples. In addition, in NBPTS scoring it was critical to demonstrate the difference between surface features and substantive, Standards-related architecture in examples of teaching. The only way to do this was to choose multiple different-looking examples of teaching. However, the NBPTS's vision of the teaching profession was built on a definition of teaching by both content area and developmental level of the students being taught, and the Board decided very early in its existence that some 26 different fields would be targeted for certification assessment development. Some of these fields, like Early Childhood Generalist, Middle Childhood Generalist, Adolescence and Young Adulthood English Language Arts, Exceptional Needs, had very large numbers of teachers. Others, like Early Adolescence through Young Adulthood English as a New Language, World Languages other than English – had much smaller total teaching populations. The issue of dealing with low volume certificates posed a particular challenge in a scoring model that was dependant on candidate performances to define and operationalize the rubrics. However, modifications to the benchmarking process that included multiple readings of each selected response and greater discussion about the distinction between each score family allowed even low volume certificates to be scored.

SCORING OUTCOMES

The first iteration of the training program and the use of and controls on the scoring process described above was implemented for the first time in the summer of 1997 in the scoring of the 6 NBPTS assessments in operation during 1996–1997. Subsequently it was applied to 7 assessments in 1997–1998, 12 in 1998–1999, 16 in 1999–2000, 19 in 2000–2001, 24 assessments in 2001–2002, and all the subsequent years through 2007. In each year, the scoring system was systematically reviewed after the summer scoring sessions ended, and changes and refinements to the scoring and training materials were implemented. In addition, the methods used to train assessor trainers, select and validate benchmark and sample cases, and manage the enormous and ever-increasing volume of candidate response materials (in 2001–2002, there were over 200,000 separately scored tasks to monitor and manage) were refined each year. The results of the scoring indicate that the training program and the scoring system yielded satisfactory results.

Reliability of scores, however that term is defined, has been a weakness for complex performance assessments. Very early in the NBPTS's history, Stanford TAP researchers, scoring the initial field-test responses to their simulation-based task prototypes, achieved "good-to-excellent agreement, but that was after the separate raters had discussed the tasks at length, and collaborated in developing scoring rules." (Haertel, 1990, p. 291). Haertel went on to say that "[a] more stringent test of reliability would depend on scoring by persons less intimately involved in task and scoring development." The results of the 2001 NBPTS scoring spoke to this more stringent test, and they were impressive.

The reliability of scores on these assessments was estimated in a number of different ways. When we estimated reliability based on error variance that could be attributed only to assessors, we obtained an upper bound reliability coefficients for the entire assessment (Method 1). When we estimated reliability based on error variance that could be attributed to both assessors and to tasks, we obtained a lower bound on the reliability coefficients for the entire assessment (Method 2). Table 2 below reports these results for the 2000–2001 cycle with data for 19 certificates.

We have some empirical evidence that the attention lavished on process control and training made a significant difference in the technical quality of the data for this assessment. The single assessment carried substantially unchanged from 1995–1996 to 1996–1997, except for the tightening of task directions and the implementation of the new scoring system, was the EC/G assessment. An analysis of the reliability of the scores generated by assessors for the tasks in this assessment revealed a substantial gain in task reliability from 1995–1996 to 1996–1997. Indeed, the gains were equal to those that could be realized for the assessment only by adding 8 new tasks to the 10 already part of the assessment (Wolfe, Gitomer, & Carter, 1998).

While technical measurement quality was a critical element in the legal defensibility and, ultimately, the validity of the assessment and of the decisions it supported, one of the most important other outcomes of the scoring was the effect participation in the process had on the assessors, who almost universally reported that such participation was the single most

Table 2. Reliability of Scores for the 2000–2001 Cycle.

	Reliability Based on Error Variance Assessors Only		Reliability Based on Error Variance Assessors + Tasks	
	REL	SEM	REL	SEM
EC/generalist	0.85	15.34	0.75	19.98
MC/generalist	0.85	15.64	0.74	20.22
EA/generalist	0.85	15.57	0.73	21.15
EAYA/art	0.82	17.10	0.70	21.78
EA/English Language Arts	0.86	15.22	0.77	19.59
AYA/math	0.91	14.45	0.75	24.66
AYA/science	0.91	14.79	0.76	23.98
AYA/English Language Arts	0.87	15.98	0.75	22.69
EA/mathematics	0.91	14.65	0.81	21.69
EA/science	0.88	14.26	0.72	21.72
EA/social studies	0.85	16.66	0.74	22.01
AYA/social studies	0.91	13.95	0.77	21.99
EMC/ENL	0.91	12.84	0.80	19.70
EAYA/ENL	0.94	11.88	0.83	20.10
ECYA/ENS	0.87	16.28	0.75	23.01
EAYA/CTE	0.86	15.59	0.70	22.45
EMC/PE	0.93	12.98	0.78	22.88
EAYA/PE	0.92	13.20	0.72	24.55
EMC/art	0.87	13.38	0.69	20.76

profound professional development experience in their careers. The rigor and intellectual challenge of the training and scoring period were a new experience for most teachers. To be regarded as intellectuals, and as professional experts, was, sad to say, almost unique in their experience, and they thrived on such a definition of their roles. What made the experience so valuable was that the rigorous framework of shared vocabulary and values necessary to the scoring training programs created a community of intellectual peers. This, in combination with the accountability measures that were part of the scoring system, led participants to achieve a new level of intellectual and personal engagement with the profession of teaching. Indeed, the kinds of professional dialogue that occurred during any scoring session, at breaks, at lunch, after the day was over, convinced us that the University of Pittsburgh/Connecticut DOE collaborative was absolutely correct in their intuition that scoring and training could be a critical element in the reformation of teaching. While we enforced a rigorous separation among assessors when they were making their judgments in order to ensure independent professional judgments for all candidates, what they saw, thought, and learned during the scoring sessions was impressive. They reported that their practice was forever changed, as was their vision of what teaching was and could be (Howell & Gitomer, 2000).

NOTES

1. The membership of the NBPTS's TAG included, at various times, the following eminent researchers, theorists, and teachers: David Berliner, Linda Crocker, George Engelhard, Ronald Hambleton, Edward Haertel, Robert Linn, Brenda Loyd, Jason Millman, Barbara Plake, Paul Sackett, Hari Swaminathan, Ross Traub, and many other eminent scholars.

2. Indeed, as Shulman (1988) noted, everything to do with scoring was fluid. The TAP developers had "decided that group members should suggest some general arrangements for scoring tasks, but should not get bogged down in the difficult details of scoring criteria and procedures." (p. 19). This proved to be a fateful decision, as this chapter illustrates. In the event, when the field test responses were complete, the TAP researchers decided to "start small ... (and) selected three tasks and five candidates from each field test" to score (p. 37).

3. Haertel (1990) discussed the problems inherent in the trade off between administrative feasibility and introduction of construct irrelevant variables, the dangers of limited contextualization of performance tasks, the challenges inherent in gaining adequate interrater reliabilities, the criticality of clarity in task demands and the like.

4. The chair of that panel was James Marshall of the University of Iowa, who had been the chair of the original review panel the NBPTS had initially engaged to review the two scoring systems. Other panel members were Isabel Aguirre, a teacher at a bilingual primary school in Los Angeles Unified School District; Sheridan Blau from the University of California, Santa Barbara, a noted researcher and writer on teaching; Estelle Brown, a teacher of teachers at Bethune Cookman College in Florida; Patricia Fitzsimmons-Hunter, an EA/ELA teacher from Springfield, Massachusetts; Peg Graham, an experienced teacher and new teacher-educator from the University of Georgia; Rhoda Moses, an EA/ELA teacher from Somerset, New Jersey; Peter Smagorinsky, a teacher-educator from the University of Oklahoma; Janet Smith, an EA/ELA teacher from Iowa; Karen Smith, the assistant to the executive director of the NCTE; Susan Stires, a teacher from Maine, and Michele Surat, an EA/ELA teacher from Fairfax, Virginia.

5. The "Scoring Path" legislated the order in which assessors considered parts of the evidence. This emerged as critically important, given the emphasis in the assessment as a whole on the shaping power of a teacher-candidate's particular teaching context on his/her practice. Only when the contextual framework of the practice is known can a judgment of the efficacy and professional expertise of the goals, instructional strategies, and reflective analyses evinced in the response be made. Thus, the teacher-candidate's voice, through the medium of the written commentary, has to be heard *first* in the assessor's encounter with a response. Second, some forms of evidence – videotape in particular – are so immediately engaging and powerfully persuasive that careful controls on the "weight" of evidence sources in the overall judgment need to be imposed. The scoring path document also

provided a way to remind assessors to consider for *every* candidate the same criteria for evaluation.

6. Haertel (1990) saw this very early in the Stanford TAP experience, which suggested "that scoring methods for teacher performance tasks should be neither too holistic nor too fragmentary. Global judgments of the quality of performance are likely to be inconsistent from one judge to another, and difficult to defend. On the other hand, checklists of very small elements of behavior may be unduly sensitive to the total amount of writing or talking by an examinee and are likely to be inflexible, favoring one approach to a task over other equally valid approaches. An intermediate course assumes that scorers are seasoned practitioners, and relies on their knowledge and judgment, but provides substantial guidance about the dimensions according to which performances are to be evaluated, the procedures to be followed in scoring, and the level of performance to be judged acceptable" (pp. 287–288).

ACKNOWLEDGMENTS

This chapter could not have been written without the conceptual and practical support and contributions of Marnie Thompson, who has served the NBPTS for many years, first as an assistant to the original TAG at the University of North Carolina, Greensboro, then as a consultant to the Educational Testing Service on NBPTS scoring, and a former member of the ETS Research and Statistics Division staff.

REFERENCES

Delandshere, G., & Petrosky, A. (1994). Capturing teachers' knowledge: Performance assessment a) and post-structuralist epistemology, b) from a post-structuralist perspective, c) and post-structuralism, d) none of the above. *Educational Researcher*, *23*(5), 11–18.

Haertel, E. (1990). Performance tests, simulations, and other methods. In: J. Millman & L. Darling-Hammond (Eds), *The new handbook on teacher evaluation: Assessing elementary and secondary school teachers* (pp. 278–294). Newbury Park, CA: Sage.

Howell, P., & Gitomer, D. H. (2000). What is the perceived impact of National Board scoring on assessors? Paper presented at the Annual meeting of the American Educational Research Association, April. New Orleans, LA.

National Board for Professional Teaching Stnadards. (2002). *Assessor training manual*. Arlington, VA: Author.

Shulman, L. S. (1988). The paradox of teacher assessment. In: J. Pfleiderer (Ed.), *New directions for teacher assessment: Proceedings of the 1988 ETS Invitational Conference* (pp. 13–27). Princeton, NJ: Educational Testing Service.

Wolfe, E. W., Gitomer, D. H., & Carter, R. (1998). The influence of changes in assessment design on the psychometric qualities of scores. Paper presented at the Annual meeting of the American Educational Research Association, April. San Diego, CA.

CHAPTER 8

SETTING PERFORMANCE STANDARDS FOR NATIONAL BOARD ASSESSMENTS: A REPRISE ON RESEARCH AND DEVELOPMENT

Richard M. Jaeger[†]

ABSTRACT

This chapter details the standard-setting methods used in the development of the NBPTS assessments. The dominant Profile Judgment Method was originally applied only to the NBPTSs Early Adolescence/English Language Arts assessment (EA/ELA). Although extremely flexible, it proved to be too complex, and increased the likelihood of false-negative errors in candidate classification. The Direct Judgment Method was found to be combatively economical; however, it was the Judgmental Policy Capturing (JPC) approach that was used since its approach was more akin to the everyday judgments we all make. The two-stage process of the JPC method will be describe in detail, using the standard-setting process used with the Early Adolescent through Young Adult/Art (EAYA/A) Assessments as an example.

[†]Deceased

Assessing Teachers for Professional Certification:
The First Decade of the National Board for Professional Teaching Standards
Advances in Program Evaluation, Volume 11, 211–229
ISSN: 1474-7863/doi:10.1016/S1474-7863(07)11008-5

When the National Board for Professional Teaching Standards (to be referred to as the NBPTS, the Board, or the National Board interchangeably) began its teacher certification program, existing methods for determining appropriate standards of performance (e.g., Angoff, 1971; Ebel, 1972; Jaeger, 1982; Nedelsky, 1954) could not be applied to the Board's assessments. Most of the standard-setting methods in use at the time applied solely to tests composed of traditionally scored, selected-response items. Indeed, the method formulated by Nedelsky (1954) can only be used with tests composed of multiple-choice items. These methods are inapplicable to the kinds of performance standards used by the NBPTS for several reasons: they assume unidimensional, summative scoring of tests; they apply solely to dichotomously-scored test items; implicitly, and they rely on the unbiasedness property of the Central Limit Theorem to average the judgment errors associated with individual test items. Once again, new measurement methodology had to be developed.

Beginning in 1991, the NBPTS sponsored an intensive program of research on the development of standard-setting methods appropriate to its complex performance assessments. The progress achieved through the National Board's research on standard-setting was reported regularly at meetings of the American Educational Research Association and the National Council on Measurement in Education and through the journal literature (Jaeger, 1994a, 1995a, b; Jaeger, Hambleton, & Plake, 1995; Plake, Hambleton, & Jaeger, 1997; Putnam, Pence, & Jaeger, 1995).

Three alternative standard-setting procedures were used with the NBPTS assessments since 1991. The Dominant Profile Judgment Method, described in Plake et al. (1997), was originally developed by Jaeger and later refined by Hambleton and Plake. The method was applied only to the NBPTSs EA/ELA assessment, one of the initial two assessments developed by the Board. It required panels of standard-setting judges to specify the lowest profile of performance on the exercises that composed an NBPTS assessment that should result in candidates receiving National Board Certification. All candidates with profiles of performance that dominated the specified minimum (in the sense of having score values equal to or greater than the minimum) also would be certified.

The Dominant Profile Judgment Method resulted in the specification of a complex, multi-component performance standard. For example, to be certified a candidate had to achieve a given total score across all exercises in an assessment, *and* achieve at least a specified minimum score on a subset of exercises considered by panelists to be most critical, *and* achieve a score greater than one on each of the exercises in the assessment. Although many standard-setting panelists appreciated the flexibility afforded by the Dominant Profile Judgment Method, this approach to standard-setting was abandoned when it became clear that the complex performance standards it produced substantially reduced measurement reliability and, in particular, dramatically increased the probability that false-negative errors of candidate classification would occur.

The principal weakness of the performance standards produced by the Dominant Profile Judgment Method was their partially conjunctive nature. Whenever certification of candidates depends in part on their performance on a single assessment exercise, as with a standard that prohibits earning a score below some threshold on any given exercise, resulting reliability will be low. Regardless of the method used to derive them, conjunctive standard-setting rules – that is, rules that invoke multiple hurdles to achieve certification – should be avoided for this reason.

The standard-setting procedure applied most frequently to the National Board's assessments was termed Judgmental Policy Capturing (JPC). The method is described in a number of papers by Jaeger (1994b, 1995a, b) and Jaeger et al. (1995), its principal architect. When the NBPTS assessments were expanded to include ten assessment exercises, the JPC procedure had to be modified so as to present a judgment task that imposed reasonable cognitive demands on standard-setting panelist. A two-stage procedure was used for this purpose. A description of the modified procedure and an illustration of its application follows.

Standard-setting procedures are, at base, methods for eliciting the reasoned judgments of qualified experts on test scores or levels of assessment performance that warrant some valued classification of examinees. Performance-standard-setting methods vary in the size and composition of the panels of experts used, in the training of panelists and the stimuli used to elicit panelists' judgments, in the decision aids used to inform panelists' judgments, and in the procedures used to compute performance standards from the judgments elicited. These aspects of the two-stage JPC procedure will be described in turn.

THE STANDARD-SETTING PANEL

The National Board for Professional Teaching Standards used panels composed of 15 National Board Certified teachers to develop performance standards for consideration by its Board of Directors. Larger panels were used in the Board's earlier standard-setting studies, but post-hoc analyses revealed that classifications of candidates for National Board Certification differed very little, if at all, across randomly sampled panels of size 15.

In an initial study of the two-stage JPC methodology, the method was applied to the NBPTS Middle Childhood/Generalist (MC/G) assessment. For that investigation of the new standard-setting method, five National Board Certified teachers composed the standard-setting panel. Each panelist had participated in an earlier, operational standard-setting study for a National Board assessment and was thus familiar with the single-stage JPC procedure that had been used with the National Board's assessments in the past.

THE STRUCTURE OF THE STANDARD-SETTING WORKSHOP

Panelists first studied the exercises that composed the National Board's MC/G assessment and were instructed on the meaning of each possible score on each exercise. They then received instruction on the standard-setting method, and finally, applied the method over a seven-day period. Although panelists were familiar with the National Board's fundamental approach to standard-setting, they were not familiar with the MC/G assessment nor with the two-stage JPC procedure they were to apply. These knowledge deficits were remedied during the first activity of the workshop, in which an overview of the structure and composition of the MC/G assessment was provided, followed by a description of the two-stage JPC procedure.

When setting a performance standard, panelists first considered the 13 MC/G assessment exercises within each of the four groups:

Group 1: Content and Curriculum Exercises.
 This group contained five exercises that focused on components of the MC/G curriculum.
Group 2: Professional Accomplishments and Family Engagement.
 This group contained three exercises that focused on candidates' professional development (PD), professional service records, and work with students' families.
Group 3: Student Work and Curricular Decisions.
 This group contained four exercises that focused on judgments grounded in samples of student work and decisions concerning appropriate curriculum based on those judgments.

Group 4: The Teaching and Learning Exercise.
This one exercise was considered by itself because of its breadth, complexity, and demand on candidates.

Panelists were asked to imagine that candidates for MC/G certification had been assessed using only the exercises in the group they were considering. The same standard-setting procedure was applied to the exercises within each group: Panelists were first instructed on the demands imposed by each exercise in the group and the meaning of each score a candidate could receive on each exercise. Panelists read and discussed benchmark responses to each exercise that had received scores central to each score family (exercises in the NBPTS assessments are scored on a scale composed of four families, with "1—" the lowest possible score and "4+" the highest possible score). Panelists learned how each exercise scoring rubric was applied to each response, and why each response was an exemplar of performance for a given score family. The nature of weak and strong responses within each score family was then discussed.

Following this training, panelists applied the JPC procedure (described later description). They then received the results of statistical analyses of their initial judgments, reviewed and discussed the feedback they had received, and then applied the JPC procedure a second time.

To apply the JPC procedure, panelists need to understand the meaning of each score level for each exercise. The complexity of the National Board's assessment exercises and the extensiveness of candidates' responses to these exercises necessitated a full day of training on the exercises in each group, and an additional day of training on the meaning of each score level for the Teaching and Learning Exercise.

The Judgmental Policy Capturing Procedure – Stage 1

Panelists were shown 200 profiles of scores that hypothetical candidates for certification as MC/Gs might have earned on the five exercises in Group 1 (Content and Curriculum) of the MC/G assessment. They were told to consider each profile of scores as though it (1) represented the score profile of an actual candidate and (2) was the *sole* basis for judging the level of accomplishment of the candidate as an MC/G teacher. It should be noted that the use of hypothetical profiles of performance was unique to this study of the two-stage JPC procedure. When the procedure was applied operationally, panelists are shown actual profiles of performance of candidates for certification. This had been the practice in earlier NBPTS standard-setting workshops.

Panelists were asked to work silently and independently as they classified each profile of scores on the Group 1 exercises into one of the following categories:

(4) teaching that *exceeds* the National Board's standards for MC/G certification,

(3) teaching that *satisfies* the National Board's standards for MC/G certification,

(2) teaching that incorporates *some of* the National Board's standards for certification MC/G, or

(1) teaching that incorporates *few if any* of the National Board's standards for MC/G certification.

Prior to the panel's classification of any profiles of performance, these scale points were clearly defined in terms of the National Board's description of an "Accomplished" teacher – the level of performance that the Board had designated as requisite to National Board Certification.

After panelists had completed their classifications of the 200 profiles of scores for Group 1 exercises, ordinary-least-squares multiple regression analysis was used to fit a compensatory model (Coombs, 1964) to each panelist's judgments. The hypothetical candidates' scores on the five Group 1 exercises were treated as independent variables, and panelists' classifications of profiles (on the 1-to-4 scale described above) were used as a dependent variable. This analytic model was used to "capture" the judgment policy for each of the five panelists who classified candidates' profiles of performance.

JPC provides a consistent mapping function that uses judgment data to develop a monotone relationship between a multidimensional profile of scores on individual exercises and a holistic judgment scale. When analyzed, the mapping function reveals two essential elements of the relationship. First, the leniency or severity of the judge in classifying an entire profile of scores (e.g., What scores on the five exercises in Group 1 must be earned in order to be classified at Level 3 on the holistic judgment scale?). Second, the process reveals the relative weights a judge accords each of the scores in a profile when classifications on the holistic judgment scale are made.

After panelists' judgments had been analyzed, panelists were provided with several forms of feedback on the results of their first round of JPC, together with instruction on how to interpret the feedback. They were given a graph composed of five side-by-side box-and-whisker charts that illustrated the distribution of relative weights members of the panel had assigned to each of the five exercises in Group 1. Superimposed on these box-and-whisker charts was a line graph that showed the relative weights that they (an individual panelist) had assigned to each of the five exercises in Group 1. This graph permitted each panelist to learn about the relative value they had attached to each of the exercises in Group 1, when they classified candidates' profiles of performance and to contextualize their weightings in those applied by their fellow panelists.

The second form of feedback provided to panelists was an extensive table that showed for each of the 200 profiles of performance they had classified, the category in which they had placed the profile, the "score" attached to the profile by their JPC model, and the "score" attached to the profile by a JPC model that represented the entire panel. Additional columns of the table highlighted any differences between these three scores and indicated whether or not the panelist's model and the entire panel's model would have resulted in the candidate receiving or being denied National Board Certification. It should be noted here that a compensatory model for the entire panel was formed by computing a weighted average of the intercepts of the panelists' individual models and weighted averages of corresponding unstandardized regression coefficients of the panelists' individual models. The weights used were the inverses of the estimated variances of the coefficients of panelists' models. Thus, the model of a panelist whose judgments led to more-reliable estimation of regression coefficients received greater weight when a model for the entire panel was formed.

This table permitted panelists to examine and understand the severity or leniency of their classifications of profiles and, particularly, the overall levels of profiles that led them to distinguish between candidates whose performances on the Group 1 exercises warranted National Board Certification and candidates whose performances did not warrant National Board Certification.

Once they had examined this feedback, panelists engaged in an extensive discussion of the characteristics of the five Group 1 exercises and the benchmark performances that characterized various scores on those exercises. They discussed their relative weightings of the exercises in Group 1 and their judgments concerning the appropriate classification of profiles they judged to be close to the points of division between categories.

Following this discussion, panelists once again worked independently to classify each of the 200 profiles into the four categories described earlier. Panelists' classification of profiles during the second round of JPC reflected their knowledge of the decisions they had made during the first round (which was provided as part of the stimulus material used during the second round), their understanding of the relative weights they and their fellow panelists had applied to each exercise, the reasoning underlying those weights, and their knowledge of the consequences of their first-round decisions (in terms of the percentage of candidates who would have received National Board Certification, had the Board adopted their first-round model as its standard-setting strategy).

The entire sequence of activities that occurred for the exercises in Group 1 – training on the exercises and the meaning of each possible score level, an initial round of JPC, analysis of judgments and provision of feedback, panelists' discussion of feedback, a second round of JPC – was repeated for the three exercises in Group 2 (Professional Accomplishments), and for the four exercises in Group 3 (Student Work and Curricular Decisions). This sequence of activities for the three groups that contained more than one exercise constituted the first stage of the two-stage JPC procedure.

The Judgmental Policy Capturing Procedure – Stage 2

The basic structure of Stage 2 of the JPC procedure was quite similar to that of Stage 1. Panelists received training on the task they were to perform and on the meaning of elements in the score profiles they were to classify. They then completed three rounds of JPC. Panelists were given analytic feedback and engaged in extensive discussion between each pair of rounds.

The principal difference between Stage 1 and Stage 2 of the JPC procedure was in the composition and meaning of the profiles that panelists were asked to classify. In Stage 1, profiles were composed of candidates' scores on individual exercises. Panelists were asked to treat a profile of scores on exercises in a given group as though they provided the only evidence of teaching accomplishment for each candidate.

During Stage 2, panelists were shown 200 profiles composed of four elements. The first three elements in each profile represented the values produced by the panel's JPC models for a given candidate, based on Stage 1 JPC results for Group 1, Group 2, and Group 3, respectively. The fourth element in a candidate's profile was her or his score on the Teaching and Learning Exercise. To elaborate, the first element of a candidate's profile was a score on the holistic judgment scale that ranged from (4) teaching that *exceeds* the National Board's standards for MC/G certification, to (1) teaching that incorporates *few if any* of the National Board's standards for MC/G certification, based on a weighted average of panelists' Round 2, Stage 1 JPC models for Group 1 exercises. The second and third elements represented scores on the same scale, based on similar models for Group 2 and Group 3 exercises, respectively. The fourth element of a candidate's Stage 2 profile was the candidate's score on the Teaching and Learning Exercise. During Stage 2 of JPC, panelists classified these four-element profiles for each candidate into the four categories on the holistic judgment scale used during Stage 1.

The judgment task presented to panelists during Stage 2 of JPC was more complex than that posed during Stage 1 in several respects. First, the four elements of the profiles panelists were shown were not on a conceptually common scale. The first three elements represented scores on a holistic judgment scale that was a continuum between 0.75 (1−) and 4.25 (4+), but the last element represented a score on a single exercise that referred to the 12-point scale associated with the scoring rubric for that exercise. This difference required panelists to translate the score for the Teaching and Learning Exercise to the holistic judgment scale by asking themselves the question "Suppose I were to classify the level of accomplishment of this candidate solely on the basis of her or his performance on the Teaching and Learning Exercise, what would my judgment be?" Second, each element of the profile represented a candidate's performances on a different number of exercises, and on exercises that differed in fundamental focus and demand; for example, the exercises in Group 1 assessed candidates' subject-matter knowledge and ability to specify appropriate curriculum elements, whereas the exercises in Group 2 assessed the significance of candidates' PD activities; the importance of their professional contributions to their students, their school, and their field; and the significance of their involvement of their students' families in the academic growth of their students. Panelists also had to keep in mind the relative weights the panel's policies had assigned to the individual exercises within each group – information to which they could refer during Stage 2.

COMPUTING AN INTEGRATED STANDARD-SETTING POLICY

One JPC outcome for Stage 1 was a set of regression models for the entire panel that were of the form:

$$\hat{Y}_{jk} = a_j + \sum_{i=1}^{nj} b_{ij} X_{ijk} \quad \text{for } j = 1, 2, 3$$

$$\hat{Y}_{jk} = a_j + \sum_{i=1}^{nj} bX$$

where, $\hat{Y}_{jk}$ denotes the score resulting from application of the standard-setting panel's Round 2 JPC policy to the scores of Candidate k for exercises in Group j; a_j denotes the intercept of the panel's Round 2 JPC model for exercises in Group j; b_{ij} denotes the unstandardized regression coefficient of exercise i in Group j in the panel's Round 2 JPC model for exercises in Group j; n_j denotes the number of exercises in Group j; and X_{ijk} denotes the score of Candidate k on exercise i in Group j.

Once these models had been fit to the judgment data collected during Round 2 for each group of exercises, the predicted scores produced by each equation were subjected to a linear transformation that compensated for regression to the mean. This was necessary because the points on the scale of the dependent variable in these analyses had defined meaning (i.e., a score of 3 denotes a holistic judgment that a candidate has exhibited performance on a profile of exercises that warrants National Board Certification). The linear transformation used ensured that a candidate who earned a score of 4 on every exercise in a group (during Stage 1 of the standard-setting process) would receive a score of 4 on the holistic judgment scale for that group of exercises and that a candidate who earned a score of 1 on every exercise in a group would receive a score of 1 on the holistic judgment scale, regardless of the coefficient of determination associated with the panel's regression model for that group. Were the predicted scores not transformed in this way, candidates' opportunities to gain National Board Certification would be an artifact of the goodness of fit of the JPC regression model.

Stage 1 of the JPC procedure also produced for the panel's JPC models, a set of relative weights associated with the exercises in each group. These relative weights represented the proportion of the coefficient of determination of the regression model that was associated with each of the exercises in a group. Relative weights, RW_{ij} are given by:

$$RW_{ij} = b_{ij}r_{ij}/R_j^2$$

where, b_{ij} denotes the standardized regression coefficient of exercise i in Group j; r_{ij} denotes the correlation between scores on exercise i in Group j and the predicted scores for Group j resulting from the panel's JPC model for Group j; and R_j^2 denotes the coefficient of multiple determination associated with the panel's JPC model for Group j.

Stage 2 of the standard-setting procedure produced parallel results. Among them was a compensatory JPC model for the entire panel that was of the form:

$$\hat{Y}_k = a + \sum_{j=1}^{3} b_{ij} \hat{Y}_{jk} = b_{T\&L} X_{T\&Lk} \quad k = 1, 2, 3$$

where, $\hat{Y}_k$ denotes the score resulting from application of the standard-setting panel's Round 3, Stage 2 JPC procedure to the transformed holistic judgment scale scores of Candidate k for exercise Groups 1, 2, and 3 resulting from Round 2, Stage 1 of the JPC procedure and to the score of Candidate k on the Teaching and Learning Exercise; a denotes the intercept of the panel's Round 3, Stage 2 JPC model; b_j denotes the unstandardized regression coefficient of the linearly transformed holistic judgment scale scores resulting from Round 2, Stage 1 of the JPC procedure for exercises in Group j; $b_{T\&L}$ denotes the unstandardized regression coefficient of candidates' scores on the Teaching and Learning Exercise; and $X_{T\&Lk}$ denotes the score of Candidate k on the Teaching and Learning Exercise.

Relative weights associated with the four elements of the Stage 2 profile also were computed, using a formula that paralleled the one given above for the Stage 1 analysis.

Analytic results for Stages 1 and 2 of the JPC analysis were combined by nesting each of the panel's Round 2, Stage 1 regression models within the panel's Round 3, Stage 2 regression model. This produced an integrated model for all 13 exercises in the MC/G assessment that was of the form:

$$\hat{Y}_k = \left(a + \sum_{j=1}^{3} a_j b_j \right) + \sum_{j=1}^{3} b_j \sum_{i=1}^{n_j} b_{ij} X_{ijk} + b_{T\&L} X_{T\&Lk}$$

where, $\hat{Y}_k$ denotes the predicted score of Candidate k on the overall holistic judgment scale, and all other terms have been defined earlier.

A linear transformation parallel to that used with predicted scores resulting from Round 2 of Stage 1 was applied to the predicted scores produced by this equation, thus placing candidates' predicted holistic judgment scores on a scale that produced a predicted score of 4 when a candidate earned scores of 4 on all 13 exercises and a predicted score of 1 when a candidate earned scores of 1 on all 13 exercises. Again, this linear transformation compensated for statistical regression effects.

Using the definitions of scale values associated with the holistic judgment scale, a score of 2.75 corresponded to the lower limit of an interval associated with accomplished teaching that warranted National Board Certification. This scale value thus became the NBPTS performance standard for its MC/G assessment. The JPC procedure enabled panelists to identify profiles of performance on the 13 exercises of the MC/G assessment that warranted, and did not warrant National Board Certification, because they produced holistic judgment scale scores that were, respectively, above or below 2.75.

STANDARD-SETTING RESULTS FOR THE MC/G ASSESSMENT

Since the profiles of candidate performance used in this study were fictitious, the results of applying the two-stage JPC procedure to the exercises of the National Board's MC/G assessment were merely illustrative. Nonetheless, it is important to note that panelists made discriminations in their judgments concerning the relative importance of the 13 exercises in the MC/G assessment, and that the assessment procedure produced judgments that would have resulted in a modest percentage of the fictitious candidates receiving National Board Certification. This latter result is of some interest because the distributions of exercise scores used in the fictitious profiles were based on the actual distributions associated with the National Board's Early Adolescence/English Language Arts (EA/ELA) assessment.

Fig. 1 contains a line graph that shows the relative weights associated with each of the 13 exercises in the MC/G assessment, as produced by the panel's final Round 2, Stage 1 and Round 3, Stage 2 policies. Three of the 13 exercises – Teaching and Learning (T&L), Reflecting on Student Work-2 (RSW-2), and PD – received markedly higher weights than did the other 10 exercises. The ratio of the largest relative weight to the smallest is almost three-to-one, indicating that panelists did not regard the 13 exercises as equally important in identifying candidates whose performances warranted National Board Certification. The panel's final standard-setting policy would have resulted in 29 percent of the fictitious candidates receiving National Board Certification, had their scores on the 13 exercises of the MC/G assessment been based on actual responses.

As shown in Fig. 2, the individual standard-setting policies of the five panelists produced quite homogeneous percentages of candidates who would have been certified by NBPTS (had the National Board adopted each

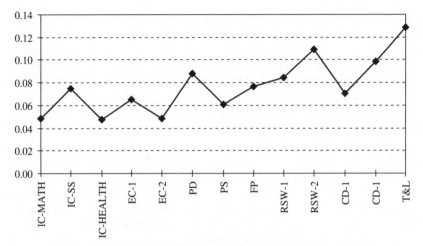

Fig. 1. Distribution of Final Relative Weights Assigned by Panelists to the 13 Exercises of the National Board for Professional Teaching Standards' MC/G Assessment.

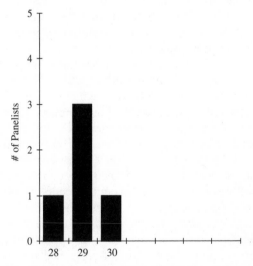

Fig. 2. Distribution of Percent of Candidates for National Board Certification as MC/Gs Who Would be Certified, Were the National Board for Professional Teaching Standards to Adopt Individual Panelists' Final Standard-Setting Policies.

panelist's standard-setting policy), thus indicating substantial agreement among the panelists on an appropriate policy. Three of the five panelists produced a policy that would have resulted in 29 percent of candidates receiving National Board Certification, and the policies of the other two panelists would have resulted in National Board Certification for 28 percent of candidates and 30 percent of candidates, respectively.

Setting performance standards is a process of eliciting reasoned judgments from experts who are knowledgeable about the demands of the test or assessment for which a standard is to be set, who understand the meaning of scores at various levels on the scale or scales used to summarize examinees' performances, and who fully comprehend the definitions of ability associated with the performance standard or standards they have been asked to establish. As assessments and their scoring become increasingly complex and multidimensional, the task of setting a reasoned performance standard becomes ever more difficult and demanding.

As noted elsewhere (Jaeger, 1995b), those who serve on standard-setting panels rarely come to the task with well-formed conceptions of appropriate performance standards. Often, panelists must be educated about the issues and information that must form the basis of a reasoned performance standard despite their general expertise in the subject area for which a standard is to be set. In addition, panelists must be provided with opportunities to absorb, examine, apply, and reconsider their often-newly-gained knowledge about the test or assessment, its scoring, and the meaning of a defined performance standard.

Setting performance standards is an example of a larger class of problems identified in the psychological literature as judgment or decision-making tasks (Pitz & Sachs, 1984). A judgment or decision-making task (JDM) is characterized by uncertainty of information or outcome, or by an outcome dependent on personal preferences, or both. If panelists are to provide reasoned recommendations on an appropriate performance standard, the process through which they consider alternatives and come to judgment must help to resolve their uncertainties. Jaeger (1994a) has argued that resolution of uncertainty occurs through an iterative process that incorporates initial judgment, information on the conse-quences of initial judgments, the opportunity to learn about the rationales underlying fellow panelists' judgments, and opportunities to reconsider initial judgments in light of the information gained from these sources. If this is so, iterative JPC should result in panelists having increasing levels of comfort with their recommended performance standards as they gain information.

PANELISTS' COMFORT WITH THEIR RECOMMENDATIONS

Trustworthy data on panelists' levels of comfort with the performance standards they recommended were collected for both rounds of JPC for exercises in Groups 2 and 3 of Stage 1 and for all three rounds of Stage 2. Panelists indicated their level of comfort on a 10-point scale, with 10 designating "Totally Comfortable." Mean levels of comfort increased from 6.5 to 8.0 from Round 1 to Round 2 of Stage 1 JPC for Group 2 exercises (with minimum comfort levels of 4 and 7, respectively); from 6.2 to 7.4 from Round 1 to Round 2 of Stage 1 JPC for Group 3 exercises (with minimum comfort levels of 6 and 7, respectively); and ranged from 7.2 to 6.5 to 8.3 for Rounds 1, 2, and 3 of Stage 2 JPC (with minimum comfort levels of 6, 6, and 8, respectively). All final-round maxima on the one-to-ten comfort scale equaled 9.

These results suggest that the features of iterative JPC result in a desired reduction of uncertainty among standard-setting panelists, and in performance standards that panelists can endorse for operational use without hesitation. They also suggest that two-stage JPC can be used with performance assessments containing as many as 13 exercises as long as adequate and appropriate training of standard-setting panelists is provided.

THE NATIONAL BOARD'S MORE-RECENT STANDARD-SETTING PROCEDURES

The major operational disadvantages of JPC are its complexity, length, and cost. When used operationally, panels of 15 teachers who applied JPC spent five to seven days in standard-setting workshops. It is not surprising, then, that a more efficient alternative to JPC was desired by the National Board. Such an alternative was developed in 1996 and was used to develop performance standards for the NBPTS assessments during that year.

The newer standard-setting procedure, termed the Direct Judgment Method (DJM), was designed to elicit two kinds of judgments: (1) the relative weights that should be assigned to the assessment center exercises and portfolio entries that composed a National Board assessment when overall performance scores were computed for candidates, and (2) the lowest overall performance score on an assessment that should result in a candidate receiving National Board Certification. Separate panels of expert teachers engaged in procedures designed to elicit these judgments.

The procedure was designed to secure judgments concerning the relative weights that should be assigned to the exercises and entries that composed a National Board assessment was an adaptation of multidimensional judgment procedures developed during the late 1970s (Edwards, 1977; Edwards & Newman, 1982). It is perhaps best illustrated through the detailed instructions given to the panel of teacher developers who provided such recommendations for the National Board's Early Adolescence through Young Adult Art (EA/AYA/A) assessment. Those instructions are in Appendix A.

PROCEDURE FOR DETERMINING A CUT SCORE

Once the weights associated with each of the portfolio entries and assessment center exercises in a National Board assessment had been determined, it was possible to calculate an overall performance score for each candidate for certification. That score was merely the weighted sum of the products of the candidate's score on each entry and exercise and the weight associated with that entry or exercise. However, there still remained the question: "What overall performance score must a candidate earn in order to gain National Board Certification?"

To answer this question, the judgments of panels of 15 expert teachers elicited through a process that posed the question quite explicitly. Members of these panels received several days of training on the nature of the exercises and entries that composed the National Board assessment for which they were to recommend a performance standard, and on the meaning of each possible score a candidate could earn on each exercise. Benchmark performances of candidates were reviewed in detail by panelists to the point that they understood the criteria and performance levels associated with each possible score level.

Following this training, panelists were shown the profiles of scores actually earned by each candidate who had completed the assessment. These profiles were rank ordered, from highest to lowest, by overall performance score. Panelists were then asked to work independently to identify the lowest overall performance score that, in their professional judgment, should result in a candidate receiving National Board Certification.

Once each panelist had indicated her or his judgment concerning the lowest overall performance score associated with National Board Certification, a distribution of such recommendations was compiled and presented to all panelists in graphical form. Panelists could therefore determine the leniency or severity of their own recommendation in the context of those provided by their fellow panelists. Each panelist also was asked to provide a brief oral rationale for the recommendation that she or he provided.

After reviewing the distribution of recommended performance standards, hearing their fellow panelists explain their recommendations, and having an opportunity to explain their own recommendation, panelists were again asked to provide independent recommendations concerning lowest overall performance score that, in their professional judgment, should result in a candidate receiving National Board Certification. The distribution of these recommendations was compiled and graphed, and the median of the distribution was computed. The median of the panel's distribution of recommended performance standards was used as the Technical Analysis Group's recommended performance standard in its report to the NBPTS Board of Directors.

SOME CONTRASTS AND CONCLUSIONS

This DJM of eliciting recommended weights for the exercises and entries of a National Board assessment, and for eliciting recommended performance standards, contrasts conceptually with the implicit judgment modeling that characterizes JPC. Since there was no "true" performance standard against which one could "validate" any recommendation, it was not possible to conclude that either method resulted in a more appropriate performance standard.

The DJM had the advantage of comparative economy. The procedure required less time than JPC to secure judgments on appropriate weights for the entries and exercises that composed a National Board assessment.

In favor of the JPC approach, one could argue that the kinds of judgments it required are more consistent with common, everyday experience. We frequently make overall judgments of value or worth on the basis of our complex analyses of the elements that compose the object of judgment. When selecting everything from automobiles to theater tickets to houses, we consider multidimensional attributes and come to reasoned judgments on the basis of complex, mental integration of our perceptions of quality, aesthetic appeal, safety, economy, efficiency, etc. We are not typically asked to attach specific weights to the attributes of objects we decide to select or reject. Thus one could argue that the DJM is inconsistent with everyday experience, whereas the JPC procedure seeks integrated judgments that are commonplace in human decision-making. Whether this advantage produces higher levels of validity when performance standards are set is an open question that invites further research. To examine the question, one would first have to specify what it means to set a "valid" performance standard – an important issue that falls well beyond the scope of this chapter.

In summary, then, the National Board sponsored substantial research on the methodology of setting standards on performance assessments. The research has produced an abundance of professional literature and at least three standard-setting procedures that the National Board has used at various times in the development and operation of its assessment program. As Pearlman (1997) noted, a totally satisfying standard-setting method for performance assessments has yet to be developed, and the National Board continues to sponsor research on this important methodological issue.

ACKNOWLEDGMENTS

This paper was completed while the author was a Fellow at the Center for Advanced Study in the Behavioral Sciences at Stanford University. I am grateful for financial support provided by The Spencer Foundation under Grant Number 199400132.

REFERENCES

Angoff, W. H. (1971). Scales, norms, and equivalent scores. In: R. L. Thorndike (Ed.), *Educational measurement* (2nd ed., pp. 508–600). Washington, DC: American Council on Education.
Coombs, C. (1964). *A theory of data.* New York: Wiley.
Ebel, R. L. (1972). *Essentials of educational measurement.* Englewood Cliffs, NJ: Prentice-Hall.
Edwards, W. (1977). How to use multiattribute utility measurement for social decision making. *IEEE Transactions on Systems, Man and Cybernetics, 7,* 326–340.
Edwards, W., & Newman, J. R. (1982). *Multiattribute evaluation.* Beverly Hills, CA: Sage.
Jaeger, R. M. (1982). An iterative structured judgment process for establishing standards on competency tests: Theory and application. *Educational Evaluation and Policy Analysis, 4,* 461–475.
Jaeger, R. M. (1994a). Setting standards for complex performances: An iterative judgmental policy capturing strategy. Presented at the Annual meeting of the American Psychological Society, Washington, DC.

Jaeger, R. M. (1994b). On the cognitive construction of standard-setting judgments: The case of configural scoring. Presented before the NCES/NAGB Conference on Standard-Setting Methodology, Washington, DC.

Jaeger, R. M. (1995a). Setting performance standards through two-stage judgmental policy capturing. *Applied Measurement in Education, 8,* 15–40.

Jaeger, R. M. (1995b). Setting standards for complex performances: An iterative, judgmental policy-capturing strategy. *Educational Measurement: Issues and Practice, 14*(4), 16–20.

Jaeger, R. M., Hambleton, R. L., & Plake, B. S. (1995). Eliciting configural performance standards through a sequenced application of complementary methods. Presented at the Annual meeting of the American Educational Research Association, San Francisco.

Nedelsky, L. (1954). Absolute grading standards for objective tests. *Educational and Psychological Measurement, 14,* 3–19.

Pearlman, M. A. (1997). What technology cannot offer for setting standards on complex performance examinations. Presented at the Annual meeting of the American Educational Research Association, Chicago, IL.

Pitz, G. F., & Sachs, N. J. (1984). Judgment and decision: Theory and application. *Annual Review of Psychology, 35,* 139–163.

Plake, B. S., Hambleton, R. K., & Jaeger, R. M. (1997). A new standard-setting method for performance assessments: The dominant profile judgment method and some field-test results. *Educational and Psychological Measurement, 57,* 400–411.

Putnam, S. E., Pence, P., & Jaeger, R. M. (1995). A multi-stage dominant profile method for setting standards on complex performance assessments. *Applied Measurement in Education, 8,* 57–83.

CHAPTER 9

RELIABILITY AND NBPTS ASSESSMENTS

Drew Gitomer

ABSTRACT

This chapter discusses the reliability of the NBPTS assessments. In order to meet the challenge of ensuring reliability of a complex performance assessment, particular attention was given to the design of the assessment and scoring processes. Several models for considering and determining the reliability of the assessment are also introduced. Results from two assessment cohorts are presented. These results demonstrate that the design features of the NBPTS system support a relatively reliable set of assessments without compromising the complexity of the teaching performance it was designed to assess.

When a teacher applies for National Board Certification, they are committing themselves to undertaking a significant task, one that has personal, professional, and often, economic consequences. In an ideal world, after an individual completes the entire assessment, we should "know," unequivocally, whether or not that individual is an accomplished teacher. Unfortunately, no assessment can be so precise. Maybe the candidate sent in an unusually strong portfolio entry, one that is not at all representative of any other lesson that the teacher could provide. Possibly,

Assessing Teachers for Professional Certification:
The First Decade of the National Board for Professional Teaching Standards
Advances in Program Evaluation, Volume 11, 231–253
Copyright © 2008 by Elsevier Ltd.
ISSN: 1474-7863/doi:10.1016/S1474-7863(07)11009-7

the candidate did not feel well during the assessment center activities. It is also possible, that one or more assessors did not score a performance consistent with the rubric for an entry. These, and other factors, are all potential contributors to measurement error. All assessments contain some degree of measurement error, and the NBPTS assessments are no different. Error refers to unsystematic, or random, variation that contributes to how someone performs on an assessment (cf. Feldt & Brennan, 1989). Error is a given in measurement – it does not imply any sense of "mistake."

Establishing the reliability of complex performance assessments in earlier years was a particular challenge, especially because such assessments typically included far fewer discrete items than traditional multiple-choice assessments (Koretz, Stecher, Klein, & McCaffrey, 1984; Shavelson, Baxter, & Gao, 1993). Increasing the number of items generally increases the reliability of any assessment. However, the design of the National Board for Professional Teaching Standards (NBPTS) assessments only yielded ten scores, making it that much more challenging to develop an assessment that could provide reliable estimates of an individual's level of teaching accomplishment.

Because of the high stakes associated with the NBPTS assessments and because of the psychometric challenges such an assessment presented, it was necessary to pay significant attention to the reliability of these assessments. This chapter focuses on the reliability of NBPTS assessments from two distinct, but complementary perspectives. One perspective examines reliability from the viewpoint of assessment design, and discusses initiatives to improve the reliability of these assessments through refinements in assessment task design and scoring processes. Methods used for assessment development and scoring are designed to minimize the effect of irrelevant factors as much as possible. A second perspective examines methods for characterizing and monitoring the reliability of the NBPTS assessments. This discussion also presents data relevant to the reliability of the NBPTS assessments from two years (1996–1997 and 1997–1998).

POTENTIAL SOURCES OF MEASUREMENT ERROR IN THE NBPTS ASSESSMENT SYSTEM

There are a number of candidate sources of measurement error in the NBPTS assessment design. However, it is important to recognize that although potential sources of error can be identified, it is not always possible to estimate that error. The following sections describe four potential sources of measurement error in the National Board assessments: *assessment occasions; school setting; exercise sampling;* and *assessors.*

Assessment Occasions

One important source of measurement error is the occasion of the assessment. Would candidates perform similarly if they took the assessment on another occasion? Would we draw the same conclusions about the candidate if they submitted their portfolio in each of the two successive years? This is an important question, for we would hope that the assessment reflects teaching performance that does not depend greatly on when the candidate completed the assessment. However, to investigate this source of unreliability, candidates would need to take the assessment on two separate occasions. We did not have this kind of data available and did not anticipate having it in the foreseeable future. The assessment was simply too demanding to ask individuals to retake an assessment as one might for a 2-hour test. Furthermore, the experience of completing an NBPTS assessment is likely to cause candidates to improve in exactly those proficiencies and practices the assessment is intended to measure – in fact, it would be both surprising and disappointing if candidates did not benefit from working through the assessment. Thus, although stability of performance across occasions of teaching, in the absence of any real changes in proficiency, is a concept that makes sense theoretically, there is no practical way to measure it.

School Setting

A second potential source of measurement error is the particular school setting in which the candidates taught. It would be desirable to dismiss the possibility that accomplished teaching is site-specific or a function of where the candidates taught. However, to investigate this source of measurement error, candidates would need the opportunity to provide evidence of accomplished teaching practices in multiple school settings. Because the portfolio is developed using evidence from the candidate's own classroom, and showcases long-term engagement with the teacher's own students, it is extremely difficult to imagine how a teacher, except under unique conditions, could demonstrate their practice in multiple school settings. Thus, it is also not feasible to collect this type of information.

Exercise Sampling

A third source of measurement error is the selection of particular exercises for a given assessment. If the exercises of the various NBPTS certificates are considered to be a sample from a larger domain, or pool, of possible exercises all measuring accomplished teaching, then it is reasonable to ask: Would candidates perform similarly on a different set (sample) of exercises? Most educational assessments estimate reliability using some kind of *alternate forms* approach, the logic being that any set of specific items on a test is simply a random sample of potential items that can all be used to address the relevant assessment construct(s).

Whether the reliability of an assessment built to NBPTS specifications is appropriately estimated by alternate forms in a traditional measurement sense is debatable. While all NBPTS analyses have assumed an alternate forms approach to reliability, it is not unequivocally clear that such an assumption is warranted. It is possible to argue that the items in the assessment are not random samples from a large pool at all, but rather are *fixed*. To be fixed suggests that a specific entry cannot be replaced randomly from a pool. Rather, its design means that this item, and no other item, is particularly well suited to assess a specific aspect, or aspects, of teaching. It is possible to argue that the exercises were but one possible sample from a larger domain of accomplished teaching or alternatively, the exercises, for all intents and purposes, comprised a fixed assessment of accomplished teaching.

Assessors

A fourth source of measurement error is attributable to the assessors who score the candidates' performances. The evidence candidates submit attesting to their accomplished teaching practices should be viewed and interpreted comparably by different sets of equally trained and qualified assessors. The key question is whether a candidate, given a different set of assessors, would fare similarly on the assessment. Assessor reliability can be examined with respect to candidate performance on each exercise, each component of the assessment, and on the assessment as a whole.

Given these circumstances, we estimated measurement error due to exercise sampling and assessors only. The details of these estimation procedures and assessment results for two particular administration years are provided in a later section. However, we first turn our attention aspects of design that can influence the reliability of a complex performance assessment.

DESIGNING RELIABLE NBPTS ASSESSMENTS

In order to enhance reliability, an assessment needs to be focused only on aspects of performance relevant to the objective of the assessment. A challenge was to reduce the likelihood that performance on an assessment was subject to aspects that were irrelevant to the objective, and unaccounted for in assessment design. An aspect is unaccounted for if it is not intended to be relevant to the assessment, yet turns out to influence how well an individual performs. For example, suppose that an assessment is designed to measure writing skill of college freshmen by developing a short essay. Assume that some proportion choose to compose by hand, while most chose to use a word processing program. In scoring these essays, we might find that some of those who write by hand have handwriting that, while decipherable, is less than elegant. If these essays are scored lower, then we have a situation in which an unaccounted for factor, handwriting legibility, is influencing assessment performance. Further, handwriting is obviously irrelevant to the assessment objective, or all students would have been asked to write by hand.

The NBPTS assessments are designed to assess the highly complex act of teaching. The challenge is to focus the assessment while, at the same time, ensuring that the assessment is not simplified, or even trivialized, to satisfy psychometric reliability concerns. It is always possible to improve reliability by narrowing the focus of assessment to aspects that require little human judgment and that are consistent characteristics of any individual teacher. For example, we could assess questioning in a classroom discussion by counting the number of times a teacher asked a "Why" question. While agreement among assessors would be high, and it is likely that a teacher would consistently employ such a strategy, such a measure does not begin to evaluate the effectiveness of questioning strategies that a teacher can use. Does the teacher pursue the first answer with follow-up questions that deepen and broaden a discussion, for example? While the counting of why questions is not unrelated to the assessment objective, it is a constrained measure that only scratches the surface of the nature of effective questioning. Less mechanistic and more interpretive assessment frameworks are required. Yet, adopting such frameworks makes it more challenging to develop a reliable assessment. In this section, we describe how we developed and implemented assessment frameworks that both honored the complexity of teaching and had sound measurement characteristics.

An assessment will be more reliable to the extent that the individual items or exercises are measuring related knowledge and skills. In such a case, each exercise provides a different window into measuring the target construct, in this case accomplished teaching. While each of the NBPTS exercises was designed to measure a different slice of teaching, they are linked by an overarching model of teaching that is captured in the *Architecture of Accomplished Teaching* (shown in Fig. 1, Chapter 3 by Pearlman, this volume). This framework, described in more detail by Pearlman (Chapter 7, this volume), guided both the development and scoring of all exercises. While no specific teaching methods or strategies are defined, there are essential qualities that characterize accomplished teaching, regardless of context, and that define the construct we are attempting to assess. The centrality of this framework in guiding design and scoring helped to make the ten exercises that comprise the assessment more than a random set of interesting teacher activities.

Candidates for NBPTS assessment are attempting to provide evidence about their accomplishment as teachers, making their best cases possible. The assessment, particularly the portfolio, does not attempt to sample representative practice, but asked teachers to present their teaching as best they could. Candidates are encouraged to select classroom-based evidence from the better part of a school year. Assessors need to be as sure as possible that if a candidate provides evidence of teaching that is less than accomplished, that it is not because the candidate had misunderstood the requirements and expectations for an assessment exercise.

In performance assessment, a significant challenge is to reduce the number of assumptions and inferential leaps that an assessor must make in rendering a judgment about a performance. Judgments should be made on evidence presented by the candidate, no more and no less. Assessors should not be forced into assuming that a candidate could have shown some ability "if they had only been asked" or that "they probably could have done it had they picked a different class to show."

This is not to say, however, that assessors do not make any inferences. In fact, assessors are accomplished teachers themselves and they do make inferences based on their expertise as teachers. However, these inferences are based only on the evidence presented, not on evidence that they assume might have been presented. For example, if a teacher were to see a classroom that had students asking questions of each other in a respectful manner, an assessor might make a reasoned judgment, based on professional experience, that the teacher had spent significant effort establishing a learning climate in which such interchange was valued and modeled. This is a different inference than one, for example, in which the assessor assumes that a discussion would have occurred had the candidate not misunderstood the exercise directions.

Pearlman (Chapter 7, this issue) describes the characteristics of NBPTS assessments and how each feature was designed to support candidates to structure their entries and provide evidence relevant to the intended purpose of the respective entries. Pearlman also describes how the training of assessors and the processes of scoring are intended to discipline judgments so that assessors are attending only to aspects of performance relevant to the purpose of an entry, and doing so in a consistent manner. We highlight several assessment features that were designed to improve the measurement quality, including the reliability of these assessments. These features were implemented in the assessments to increase the likelihood that what candidates are asked to present and what assessors expected to see are aligned.

To begin with, we tried to reduce the guessing – candidates should not have to guess what assessors want to see and assessors should not have to guess what candidates might have said. We tried to reject the notion sometimes present in testing contexts that "the good ones will know what we're after." The clearest statement of what is expected in a response appears in the section of the candidate instructions entitled "How Will My Response Be Scored?" (see Appendix A). This section is actually an approximation of the 4-level (highest level) of the rubric for the exercise. This section tells candidates exactly what is valued by assessors when their response is scored.

It is critical to note that the language in this section, and the corresponding rubric, refers to qualities that are sought in the response, rather than specific behaviors. This assessment attempted not to be prescriptive in terms of particular ways in which a teacher could be accomplished, but instead tries to recognize that accomplished teaching could be realized with a variety of approaches. While judgments about the absence or presence of specific behaviors rather than qualities might made for a more reliable assessment, such a mechanistic view of teaching would be antithetical to the holistic nature of teaching espoused by the respective standards.

Another clarification of expectations in the portfolio is intended by the "Making Good Choices" (see Appendix A) section, written to help candidates make decisions that were likely to help them (and correspondingly protect them from making poor decisions) as they craft their entry. This section does not deal with the logistics of the entry, but rather with making and avoiding decisions that supports or hurts their entry, respectively. Suggestions are included for the selection of classes to videotape or students to follow, and for selecting instructional units and activities. For example, while most teachers of elementary students would include some type of drill and practice in their instruction, such activities are probably not the best opportunity to showcase classroom discussion. This is not to say that it could not happen, but that in reviewing the work of previous candidates, such a choice is not seen as a frequent path to a high score.

Another design feature that we included to improve the likelihood that candidates responded as best they can was to add more structure to the questions in their commentary for each entry. Earlier NBPTS assessments tended to have fewer questions with less guidance about how to structure the response and allocate relative emphasis to different sections. In a sense, candidates were given a broad set of questions and asked to structure an essay addressing those questions. Responses to these entries suggested that candidates might not have been giving sufficient attention to some issues while overly attending to others. They might have organized their response in ways that made it more difficult for an assessor to locate evidence as well. In order to reduce candidates having to make assumptions about how much to attend to each issue, the commentary was broken down into specific questions, with guidelines for page limits given as well. While still conducive to an integrated essay, the questions and questioning structure were designed to cue the candidate in how to organize the essay and how to attend to different issues with appropriate emphasis.

As Pearlman (Chapter 7, this volume) notes, scoring issues and processes were as much a part of assessment design as were task directions. She describes the design of the NBPTS scoring architecture, certainly as complex and thorough a performance assessment scoring model as existed in educational measurement at the time.

Here, we highlight some of the key features of scoring that have been implemented. All are designed to discipline the reading and interpreting of the evidence, ensuring that judgments remained governed by the rubric and standards only and are grounded in the evidence presented. Training is designed to reduce, if not eliminate, the tendency for idiosyncratic considerations to be brought to bear on the judging of evidence, and to discourage assessors from going beyond the evidence and making judgments that require unsupported inferences.

Relative to earlier NBPTS efforts, and also relative to other complex performance initiatives, we expose assessors to a large number of benchmark and training samples during training. This is done to hone their judgments and to learn the different ways in which scores at different levels could be achieved. This results in a more elaborated and lengthier training process. Such time is not made available in the typical performance assessment scoring session, usually because the economics of the situation preclude extensive training.

Attention to potential biases is a significant part of assessor training, designed to enhance the likelihood of sound judgments grounded in the rubric and the reduction of judgments irrelevant to the rubric. As Thompson (1998) noted, bias training is interleaved between the processing of training and benchmark samples, also adding time to the training process. Bias could surface, for example, when a candidate is judged adversely because the style of teaching deviates from an assessor's own practice, even when the candidate's performance is accomplished by definition of the rubric and respective standards.

Guiding and bridging questions that serve to structure the way in which assessors consider the evidence produced by candidates are provided. These questions are designed to keep assessors focused on the judgments they are required to make and reduce the possibility of assessors focusing on the less relevant or obscure aspects of a candidate's response. Note too, the changes in the scoring path. Whereas, the scoring path for the previous year had been primarily procedural, the subsequent year's document focused assessors much more on the analysis of evidence produced in the response.

Finally, the rubrics themselves have undergone significant change in focus and structure. Prior years tended to be more analytic, highlighting specific behaviors that might be observed at a score point. As discussed in the context of the "How my Response will be Scored" section, the more recent rubrics consciously avoid noting the presence or absence of specific behaviors at any score point. The problem with including specific behaviors in a holistic rubric is that an assessor may be at sea when the weight of evidence suggests one point on the scale, but an expected behavior for that score point is not observed (or vice versa). In such cases, assessors often invent rules to deal with this conflicting information. Under the present scheme assessors only weigh the preponderance of evidence regarding observed qualities of performance – they do not have to account for the presence or absence of specific acts. In addition, the weighting schemes for deriving composite scores have been changed.

ESTIMATING THE RELIABILITY OF NBPTS ASSESSMENTS

There is no single correct way to estimate reliability of an assessment. Instead, our approach is to use multiple indices to estimate and communicate different sources of measurement error. The most definable source of measurement error in a performance assessment such as the NBPTS assessment is that which is attributable to assessors. Estimates of this error source indicate the extent to which candidates would be judged differently had their performances been scored by different assessors. We were able to estimate this error because, in almost all cases, at least two assessors judged each performance. For the 1996–1997 administration, all exercises were scored by at least two assessors for the four certificates that were scored using standard procedures: Early Childhood/Generalist (EA/G); Middle Childhood/Generalist (MC/G); Early Adolescence/English Language Arts (EA/ELA) and; Adolescence through Young Adulthood/ Mathematics (AYA/M). For the remaining two certificates, Early Adolescence/Generalist (EA/G) and Early Adolescence through Young Adulthood/Art (EAYA/A), the number of candidates in 1996–1997 was relatively small, necessitating an alternative, small-sample scoring model. For these two certificates, four assessors used a quasi-consensus process to yield a single score per exercise per candidate. Initial individual assessor judgments were not part of the data record for candidates. For the 1997–1998 administration, a seventh certificate was added (Adolescence through Young Adulthood/Science, AYA/S), and all were scored using the standard double-scoring model. The only exception was that for the six established certificates, a significant proportion of the two Documented Accomplishment Exercises (DAE) were scored by only one assessor.[1]

One way to examine assessor consistency is to consider the absolute levels of agreement between pairs of assessors. One important measure we used was the proportion of cases for which there was substantial disagreement in assessors' scores (i.e., greater than 1.25). Differences in excess of 1.25 necessitated a third read by the lead assessor/trainer for a given exercise. The proportion of assessors' scores differences which met this threshold are presented, summed over exercises, for each certificate for two NBPTS administrations is presented in Table 1. In addition to mean proportions across exercises, the range of differences exceeding 1.25 across exercises is also given. Assessor differences meeting, or exceeding this threshold were relatively infrequent, but did exhibit variation both within and between certificates. Whether these variations were due to the nature of the exercise

Table 1. Proportion of Cases for Which Initial Scores Differed by More than 1.25.

Certificate	Proportion of Cases 1996–1997	Range Across Exercises	Proportion of Cases 1997–1998	Range Across Exercises
Early Adolescence/ Generalist	–	–	0.06	0.00–0.09
Early Childhood/ Generalist	0.05	0.01–0.09	0.04	0.01–0.10
Middle Childhood/ Generalist	0.06	0.02–0.14	0.04	0.01–0.07
Early Adolescence through Young Adulthood/Art	–	–	0.03	0.00–0.12
Early Adolescence/ English Language Arts	0.05	0.00–0.10	0.04	0.02–0.06
Adolescence and Young Adulthood/ Mathematics	0.03	0.00–0.08	0.04	0.00–0.08
Adolescence and Young Adulthood/Science	–	–	0.07	0.03–0.12

being scored, or the qualities of particular assessors making the judgments is not clear.

The proportion of cases requiring adjudication was relatively low. Table 2 presents a closer examination of assessor agreement. The table presents, across all exercises for each certificate, the cumulative proportion of assessor differences for each certificate, showing that there was a high level of agreement between assessors. Perfect agreement would result in a difference of zero. These data also suggest that assessors were fairly consistent in assigning scores to candidates' performances. Approximately 90% of all paired ratings are within 1 point across all certificates and for both years of administration.

These descriptions of assessor agreement do not provide an overall estimation of the potential effect of any inconsistencies on the performance of a candidate across the ten exercises, which made up the assessment. If we assume that assessor error is randomly distributed, then errors tend to balance each other out as the number of exercises increases. An estimate of assessor reliability that accounted for inconsistencies across all ten exercises was computed as the proportion of score variance due to the covariance in assessors' scores. To the extent that assessors did not systematically agree

Table 2.   Cumulative Proportion of Scores by Amount of Disagreement
between Assessors.

	0.0	0.25	0.50	0.75	1.0	1.25
Certificate (1996–1997)						
Early Adolescence/Generalist	–	–	–	–	–	–
Early Childhood/Generalist	0.24	0.47	0.61	0.77	0.90	0.96
Middle Childhood/Generalist	0.20	0.43	0.56	0.72	0.86	0.93
Early Adolescence through Young Adulthood/Art	–	–	–	–	–	–
Early Adolescence/English Language Arts	0.23	0.49	0.63	0.73	0.88	0.95
Adolescence and Young Adulthood/Mathematics	0.39	0.58	0.72	0.86	0.93	0.97
Adolescence and Young Adulthood/Science	–	–	–	–	–	–
Certificate (1997–1998)						
Early Adolescence/Generalist	0.23	0.47	0.58	0.72	0.88	0.94
Early Childhood/Generalist	0.21	0.47	0.61	0.77	0.91	0.96
Middle Childhood/Generalist	0.22	0.47	0.62	0.77	0.91	0.96
Early Adolescence through Young Adulthood/Art	0.21	0.42	0.58	0.75	0.90	0.97
Early Adolescence/English Language Arts	0.21	0.45	0.60	0.77	0.91	0.96
Adolescence and Young Adulthood/Mathematics	0.33	0.48	0.62	0.82	0.91	0.96
Adolescence and Young Adulthood/Science	0.21	0.42	0.59	0.76	0.88	0.93

with each other, the estimate of reliability would decrease. We also estimated assessor reliability for each exercise and for each major section of the ten exercises (classroom portfolio, documented accomplishment, and assessment center). For the interested reader, Appendix J presents a mathematical explanation of the procedure.

Table 3 presents the reliability estimates for the total assessment and for each of the three components of the assessment (in-class portfolio, documented accomplishments, and assessment center). These reliabilities also allowed us to estimate the standard error of measurement of candidate's total assessment scores. Across all certificates, reliability of assessors was very high, particularly when all exercises were included. Based on these findings, it does not appear that candidate's scores were significantly influenced by their luck in drawing particular assessors. Nevertheless, scores were not so precise that candidates might not have been misclassified. The impact of measurement error on the certification decision is discussed subsequently.

It is worth noting, that reliabilities could be relatively high even when some assessors disagreed with each other. This would occur when there was systematic variation in how assessors judged performances. For

Table 3. Reliability Estimates Based on Assessor Consistency (Standard Error of Measurement in Parentheses).

	Overall		In-Class Portfolio		DAE Portfolio		Assessment Center	
Certificate (1996–1997)								
Early Adolescence/Generalist	—		—		—		—	
Early Childhood/Generalist	0.94	(13.0)	0.88	(9.9)	0.96	(1.6)	0.90	(7.3)
Middle Childhood/Generalist	0.91	(13.0)	0.88	(9.0)	0.93	(2.0)	0.82	(9.0)
Early Adolescence through Young Adulthood/Art	—		—		—		—	
Early Adolescence/English Language Arts	0.94	(12.2)	0.87	(10.3)	0.96	(1.7)	0.92	(7.4)
Adolescence and Young Adulthood/Mathematics	0.98	(9.0)	0.92	(8.4)	0.98	(1.5)	0.97	(6.4)
Adolescence and Young Adulthood/Science	—		—		—		—	
Certificate (1997–1998)								
Early Adolescence/Generalist	0.90	(11.7)	0.86	(8.5)	0.94	(1.9)	0.81	(7.7)
Early Childhood/Generalist	0.92	(11.7)	0.86	(8.1)	0.91	(2.5)	0.86	(7.3)
Middle Childhood/Generalist	0.92	(11.4)	0.87	(7.8)	0.90	(2.0)	0.83	(7.4)
Early Adolescence through Young Adulthood/Art	0.92	(12.3)	0.87	(10.5)	0.43	(3.4)	0.89	(5.4)
Early Adolescence/English Language Arts	0.91	(12.1)	0.86	(8.3)	0.55	(5.3)	0.87	(7.1)
Adolescence and Young Adulthood/Mathematics	0.96	(11.8)	0.91	(8.1)	0.92	(2.4)	0.94	(8.0)
Adolescence and Young Adulthood/Science	0.94	(10.8)	0.91	(7.2)	0.53	(5.6)	0.87	(5.9)

example, one assessor might always score performances 0.5 lower than would another assessor. Their judgment of the relative merit of different performances, however, was highly consistent. In these cases, assessors might differ in "harshness," though they were highly reliable in that knowing the score assigned by one assessor was highly predictive of the score assigned by a second assessor. Myford and Engelhard (2002) used the FACETS model (Linacre, 1989) to study the consistency of judgments across assessors. They concluded that despite some relatively small variation in assessor harshness, the 12-point scale was applied in a consistent manner. Further, they determined that the likelihood was very low that, individual candidates' final scores were determined by the particular assessors who judged their work.

Though we had the most direct information about assessor error, we were aware that there were other sources of measurement error that could not be estimated, such as error attributable to occasions or settings. Would a candidate do similarly from year-to-year? Would a candidate perform similarly if their teaching situations changed? The particular circumstances of the NBPTS assessments made it impossible to estimate these sources of error. In fact, given the explicit professional development goals associated with NBPTS participation, there would be disappointment if candidates did not improve their performance year-to-year. Given other sources of error, even if they could not be estimated, we could be certain that estimates of reliability that only account for assessor inconsistency were likely to be an upper bound of a reliability estimate.

Most often, reliability estimates in educational measurement are based on assumptions of exercise or item sampling. In these cases, an assumption is made that there is a population of potential test items from which the items appearing on a test form are a random sample, and that a given individual would perform similarly no matter which set of items are selected. Assuming that multiple equivalent forms could be created, the *alternate forms* reliability is estimated by examining the relationship among items within an assessment.

Though it is common to estimate such error, in the case of NBPTS assessments, it is debatable whether the assumption of the exchangeability of exercises is appropriate. Certainly, for the portfolio exercises, it is difficult to conceive of different exercises that would be equivalent in terms of what evidence they elicit about teaching accomplishment. Portfolio tasks are fixed in that we expect candidates to respond to a predetermined set of exercises, and not other exercises that might be thought of as measures of teacher accomplishment. Even for the assessment center, exercises could be considered fixed in the sense that there is a structure that defined each exercise. Though there are multiple forms of a given exercise, the overall assessment center design remains constant and the exercise structures are invariant.

Nevertheless, some measurement experts argue that we should estimate measurement error based on exercise sampling for several reasons. First, there is a pragmatic argument claiming that since there remains measurement error unaccounted for, and since the only error that can be estimated is that which might be attributable to exercises, then this estimate, while not wholly satisfactory in terms of assessment design, represents a lower bound estimate for measurement error. To make this argument more acceptable, one could also argue that portions of the exercises are exchangeable in that all measured common attributes of teaching shown in Fig. 1 of Pearlman's chapter (Chapter 3, this volume) as the architecture of teaching.

Thus, we adopted a strategy to report a second reliability, that which is due to exercise variability. Reliabilities for exercises, sections, and the total assessment are estimated using an alternate forms approach consistent with the procedures established by Ross Traub and Richard Jaeger early in the history of NBPTS assessment development. This method is described in Appendix K.

Table 4 presents the overall reliability estimates for each of the certificates for both administration years, and also the reliability of the three component parts of the each certificate (classroom-based portfolio entries, documented accomplishment portfolio entries, and assessment center exercises). These estimates, although representing a lower bound of reliability, indicated that the ten exercises, taken together, are measuring common aspects of accomplished teaching.

ESTIMATING DECISION ACCURACY

Ultimately, the most important reliability issue for a certification assessment has to do with the consistency of the certification decision. Imagine that we could "know with certainty" whether or not an individual was truly accomplished. What is the likelihood that the results of the assessment would mirror this "truth" when we account for measurement error? What is the probability that certification decisions are accurate given measurement error due to either assessors or exercises? Two factors will affect the accuracy of a classification decision. First, the more reliable the assessment,

Table 4. Reliability Estimates Based on Exercise Sampling (Standard Error of Measurement in Parentheses).

	Overall		In-Class Portfolio		DAE Portfolio		Assessment Center	
Certificate (1996–1997)								
Early Adolescence/Generalist	0.72	(19.0)	0.49	(15.2)	0.32	(5.2)	0.68	(11.0)
Early Childhood/Generalist	0.85	(19.7)	0.73	(15.1)	0.56	(5.4)	0.70	(12.6)
Middle Childhood/Generalist	0.78	(20.2)	0.68	(14.9)	0.48	(5.4)	0.62	(13.1)
Early Adolescence through Young Adulthood/Art	0.84	(19.2)	0.71	(17.0)	0.53	(3.5)	0.72	(8.9)
Early Adolescence/English Language Arts	0.81	(22.1)	0.64	(16.8)	0.33	(6.7)	0.71	(13.8)
Adolescence and Young Adulthood/Mathematics	0.87	(22.8)	0.76	(14.6)	0.23	(8.8)	0.80	(16.7)
Certificate (1997–1998)								
Early Adolescence/Generalist	0.74	(20.8)	0.55	(15.8)	0.44	(6.2)	0.59	(12.8)
Early Childhood/Generalist	0.80	(18.1)	0.65	(13.1)	0.41	(6.2)	0.64	(11.7)
Middle Childhood/Generalist	0.76	(18.0)	0.63	(12.9)	0.27	(5.3)	0.55	(12.0)
Early Adolescence through Young Adulthood/Art	0.79	(20.8)	0.70	(17.5)	0.09	(4.5)	0.56	(11.8)
Early Adolescence/English Language Arts	0.80	(18.5)	0.65	(13.0)	0.42	(6.3)	0.63	(12.5)
Adolescence and Young Adulthood/Mathematics	0.85	(21.6)	0.72	(14.0)	0.52	(5.8)	0.76	(15.0)
Adolescence and Young Adulthood/Science	0.79	(22.5)	0.64	(15.5)	0.33	(5.6)	0.68	(16.2)
Adolescence and Young Adulthood/Science	—		—		—		—	

the more accurate the certification decision. Second, the closer an individual's score is to the performance standard,[2] the more likely there would be a classification error.

For the National Board assessment, only candidates whose weighted-total scores are equal to or greater than 275 points are certified. The assessment should be designed and implemented to minimize the misclassification of candidates. The results could be in error by certifying candidates who should not be certified or by denying certification to candidates who should be certified. These errors in classification are known as false-positive errors and false-negative errors, respectively. The probability of committing a classification error was estimated for each assessment (Subkoviak, 1976). Decision accuracy is estimated in two ways, based on the two different reliability estimates, and are presented in Table 5. Note that it is not possible to identify specific candidates who are falsely classified, but only the likelihood that particular numbers of candidates are falsely classified. The statistical procedures for estimating decision accuracy are presented in Appendix L.

The false-positive and false-negative estimates were smaller when calculations are based on assessor consistency, because reliability estimates were higher for assessor consistency than for exercise sampling. Nevertheless, we do know that at least some small proportion of candidates was incorrectly classified. For some candidates, those who were in the false-positive group, error worked in their favor. For other candidates, measurement error worked against their interests. Though we cannot change the proportion of classification errors, it is possible to make policy decisions that would influence the relative proportion of false-positive and false-negative errors. For example, the NBPTS system is designed so that a score of 275 represented the "true" passing score. That is, if we could know with certainty, that an individual was truly a "275," then we would set the performance standard at 275. However, because any score contains measurement error, a person who scored 275 may have had a "true" performance level some number of points below or above 275. If we were to set the performance standard at 290, then we would be fairly certain that very few individuals with true scores below 275 were awarded certification. Unfortunately, we would increase the likelihood that individuals with true scores above 275 were denied certification (high false-negative rate). Similarly, if we set the passing score at 260, we would be fairly certain that individuals with true performance levels above 275 would be granted certification, but we would grant certification to many individuals who had true performance levels lower than 275 (high false-positive rate). Depending

Table 5. Decision Accuracy Estimates Based on Two Methods of
Reliability Estimation.

	Exercise Sampling		Assessor Consistency	
	Probability of false-negative decisions	Probability of false-positive decisions	Probability of false-negative decisions	Probability of false-positive decisions
Certificate (1996–1997)				
Early Adolescence/ Generalist	0.07	0.09	–	–
Early Childhood/ Generalist	0.05	0.06	0.04	0.04
Middle Childhood/ Generalist	0.07	0.08	0.04	0.05
Early Adolescence through Young Adulthood/Art	0.06	0.07	–	–
Early Adolescence/ English Language Arts	0.07	0.06	0.04	0.03
Adolescence and Young Adulthood/ Mathematics	0.06	0.06	0.02	0.02
Adolescence and Young Adulthood/ Science	–	–	–	–
Certificate (1997–1998)				
Early Adolescence/ Generalist	0.08	0.09	0.05	0.05
Early Childhood/ Generalist	0.07	0.08	0.04	0.05
Middle Childhood/ Generalist	0.08	0.08	0.05	0.05
Early Adolescence through Young Adulthood/Art	0.06	0.08	0.04	0.04
Early Adolescence/ English Language Arts	0.08	0.07	0.05	0.05
Adolescence and Young Adulthood/ Mathematics	0.06	0.05	0.04	0.03
Adolescence and Young Adulthood/ Science	0.08	0.07	0.04	0.04

on the goals of the assessment system, policy-makers may choose to increase the proportional likelihood of one error or another. As just one example, for highly elite positions with large numbers of candidates, such as astronauts, policies are likely to opt for increasing the number of false-negative decisions, since there is grave consequence for selecting anyone who may not have "the right stuff."

Graphically, we can illustrate the likelihood of a misclassification of any individual given their assessment score. Obviously, the closer one's score is to the performance standard, the higher the likelihood of a classification error. Also, the more scores within the assessment sample that fall close to the performance standard, the greater the likelihood of classification errors. We are more certain about individuals who score 375 than those who score 275. For each certificate, a set of two "gull-wing curves" is produced; each one based on one of the reliability estimation procedures.

Figs. 1 and 2 represent the gull-wing curves for the MC/G 1996–1997 assessment. Several patterns are evident and consistent across all certificates. First, the likelihood of false-positive and false-negative misclassifications was approximately equal. Second, the likelihood of misclassification was greatest at the performance standard (275) and dropped rapidly as scores differed from the standard, in either direction. Finally, misclassifications due to assessor inconsistency were less likely than that due to that attributable when we assume exercise sampling error.

THE RELATIONSHIP OF ASSESSMENT DESIGN TO MEASUREMENT QUALITY

By traditional standards, the NBPTS assessments included a relatively small number of exercises, raising the challenge of developing a reliable assessment in a high-stakes environment. Our approach was to increase the quality of measurement for every component of the assessment through careful attention to design characteristics of the exercises and to scoring processes. A study by Wolfe and Gitomer (2001) provides evidence that these design considerations did, in fact, enhance the measurement quality of the NBPTS assessments.

Wolfe and Gitomer compared changes in the reliability of the EC/G assessment between the 1995–1996 and 1996–1997 administrations. While the general structure of the exercises did not change, a number of significant design changes described earlier in the chapter, were

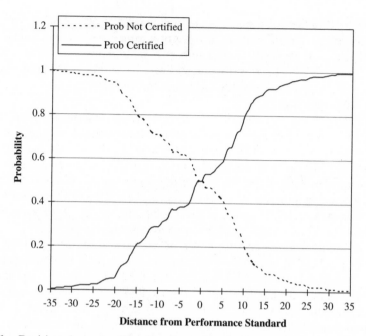

Fig. 1. Decision Accuracy Plot Based on Assessor Consistency for the Middle
Childhood/Generalist Certificate.

implemented between these two administrations. When the authors
examined changes in reliability of the assessment, they found first,
that assessor agreement increased significantly between the two administrations. The number of cases that required resolution by a third assessor
was approximately halved, with corresponding increases in reliability
estimates. When examining the reliability attributable to exercises,
Wolfe and Gitomer (2001) found that the increases due to design changes
was equal to the impact of adding eight new exercises. Thus, attention
to design features for an assessment has important practical implications for performance assessment. Without significant additional scoring
or administration costs, the measurement quality of performance assessments can be enhanced through attention to the design and scoring
processes described in Chapters 3 and 7 of this volume, written by
Mari Pearlman.

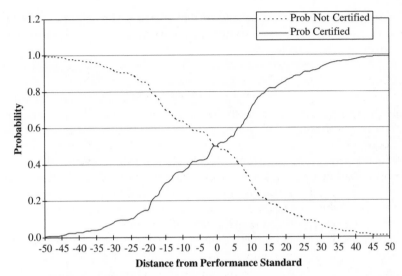

Fig. 2. Decision Accuracy Plot Based on Exercise Sampling for the Middle Childhood/Generalist Certificate.

CONCLUDING REMARKS

Using relatively standard estimation procedures, NBPTS assessments are relatively reliable instruments, particularly when compared with recent forays into educational performance assessment. Certainly, careful attention to design features of the exercises and of scoring processes enhances the consistency of measurement. In fact, the need to enhance reliability without resorting to large numbers of exercises requiring shorter responses necessitated a principled approach to assessment design that was not commonplace. In traditional multiple-choice assessment, for example, reliable assessments could be realized through the inclusion of many items. This had the unfortunate consequence, in most cases, of producing assessments that had only limited principles guiding their construction.

These increases in reliability were not achieved at the cost of overly constraining the assessment. Portfolio entries still allowed for individuals to present their own contextualized practice and there were many ways to respond to most assessment center prompts. Scoring still required the interpretive judgment of expert assessors. In the arena of performance assessment, it was critical to realize that increases in reliability were not necessarily associated with strategies that reduced the interpretive characteristics of the assessment.

Finally, we noted that estimating reliability in a complex performance assessment such as NBPTS remains a significant challenge. As noted at the outset, it is not at all clear that exercises are random samples from a universe of items, most especially for the portfolio items. Thus, we adopted estimation procedures that are not wholly consistent with the assumptions undergirding the assessment design. And yet, the field had not conceptualized sufficiently the kinds of models that would appropriately model measurement error in an assessment context such as that of the National Board. As we pursued alternative ways of thinking about measurement issues for complex and heavily contextualized assessments, we struck a compromise by reporting a range of reliability estimates, each having known weaknesses. Nevertheless, these data did provide a baseline against which we could make annual comparisons of measurement quality as characteristics of the assessment and testing population underwent change.

NOTES

1. A number of details about the NBPTS assessments have changed during the ensuing years. In addition to some 24 certificates being offered, the structure of the assessment has changed. The ten exercises of the current assessment are comprised of six assessment center exercises and four portfolio exercises, of which three are classroom-based and one documents other accomplishment. The system now double scores only about 25% of all cases. Double scoring, and reliability analyses are conducted early in the scoring session to ensure that assessors are scoring reliably. Despite these changes, the basic approaches to ensuring and monitoring reliability described in this chapter have not changed.

2. In other educational assessment contexts, the performance standard is often referred to as a *cut score*. That terminology has not been used by NBPTS, and thus, it is referred here as a *performance standard.*

ACKNOWLEDGMENTS

I owe a debt of gratitude to many individuals who helped to provide the intellectual basis for this chapter. Skip Livingston conceptualized and implemented the reliability models. Mari Pearlman and Marnie Thompson were the primary drivers of the assessment design and scoring protocols. Rick Tannenbaum and Caroline Wylie provided substantial support in implementing our analytic methods. The Measurement Research Advisory Panel (MRAP) for NBPTS provided outstanding feedback and input over the years we developed our models. Of course, the author is fully responsible for any errors in the chapter.

REFERENCES

Feldt, L. S., & Brennan, R. L. (1989). Reliability. In: R. L. Linn (Ed.), *Educational measurement* (3rd ed., pp. 105–146). New York: American Council on Education/MacMillan Publishing Company.

Koretz, D. M., Stecher, B., Klein, S., & McCaffrey, D. (1984). The Vermont portfolio assessment program: Findings and implications. *Educational Measurement: Issues and Practice, 13*(3), 5–16.

Linacre, J. M. (1989). *Many-faceted Rasch measurement.* Chicago: Mesa Press.

Myford, C. M., & Engelhard, G. (2002). Evaluating the psychometric quality of the National Board for Professional Teaching Standards Early Childhood/Generalist Assessment System. *Journal of Personnel Evaluation in Education, 15*(4), 253–285.

Shavelson, R. J., Baxter, G. P., & Gao, X. (1993). Sampling variability of performance assessments. *Journal of Educational Measurement, 30,* 215–232.

Subkoviak, M. J. (1976). Estimating reliability from a single administration of a criterion-referenced test. *Journal of Educational Measurement, 13,* 265–276.

Thompson, M. (1998). Data quality as a function of different scoring models. Paper presented at the Annual meeting of the American Educational Research Association, San Diego, CA.

Wolfe, E. W., & Gitomer, D. H. (2001). The influence of changes in assessment design on the psychometric quality of scores. *Applied Measurement in Education, 14*(1), 91–107.

SECTION 3:
VALIDITY ISSUES RELATED TO NBPTS CERTIFICATION

CHAPTER 10

A CRITICAL REVIEW OF THE VALIDITY RESEARCH AGENDA OF THE NATIONAL BOARD FOR PROFESSIONAL TEACHING STANDARDS AT THE END OF ITS FIRST DECADE ☆

Pamela A. Moss

ABSTRACT

This chapter, completed in 1999, provides an overview and critical analysis of the validity research agenda undertaken by the National Board for Professional Teaching Standards (NBPTS) for its assessment to

☆This chapter focuses on the National Board's validity research agenda as it existed at the end of its first decade. The chapter was completed and sent to the original editor in 1999. The set of National Board for Professional Teaching Standards (NBPTS) studies reviewed, the validity theory and other literature cited, and the descriptions of the various activities, working groups, etc. of the NBPTS, reflect only what was available and current at the time the manuscript was written. The original article appears, with minor edits, in the pages that follow. Current information about the National Board for Professional Teaching Standards can be found on their website (www.nbpts.org).

Assessing Teachers for Professional Certification:
The First Decade of the National Board for Professional Teaching Standards
Advances in Program Evaluation, Volume 11, 257–312
Copyright © 2008 by Elsevier Ltd.
All rights of reproduction in any form reserved
ISSN: 1474-7863/doi:10.1016/S1474-7863(07)11010-3

certify accomplished teachers at the end of its first decade of assessment development and implementation. The review is presented in three major sections: (a) an overview of the validity criteria underlying the review; (b) a description of the National Board's research agenda presented in its own terms, focusing first on the studies that were routinely carried out for each certificate and second on the "special studies" that were not part of the routine agenda; and (c) a series of six critical observations and explanations based on the validity issues described in the first section.

INTRODUCTION

In this chapter, I provide a critical review of the National Board's validity research agenda at the end of its first decade as it can be reconstructed from publications and other available documents. In developing the review I tried, first, to represent the research agenda as comprehensively and fairly as possible, reprising the arguments that explained the choices about what was done (and left undone) in the validity research undertaken, and leaving aside my evaluation of the work until a subsequent section. Following that overview, the chapter moves to a critical analysis of this work. There, I draw on two overlapping conceptualizations of validity that I used as touchstones to evaluate the National Board's validity research agenda. These include the conceptualizations of validity reflected in (a) the then current *Standards for Educational and Psychological Testing* [American Educational Research Association, American Psychological Association and the National Council for Measurement and Evaluation (AERA, APA, NCME, 1985)], which refer to the extent to which the available evidence supports the intended interpretation, and (b) what Cronbach (1988, 1989) called a "strong" program of validity research, which shares with Messick's (1989a, 1996) conceptualization of validity an emphasis on seeking challenges to the proposed meaning and use of test scores. My emphasis in both sections is on the architecture of the validity research agenda and the design of the studies it encompassed rather than on the results or conclusions of particular studies. The overarching question is the extent to which the evidence provided enabled sound professional judgment about the validity of the interpretations and uses of these assessments for the certification of accomplished teachers.

A comprehensive examination of the validity of the National Board for Professional Teaching Standards (NBPTS) certification decisions should begin with the documentation and evaluation of the process through which the five core propositions and the certification standards within each subject area and level were developed. Given space and time constraints, I chose to limit my review to the processes of assessment development and evaluation following the creation of the standards in which the assessments are based. (Hattie, in Chapter 4 of this volume, describes the process through which the content standards were developed and the means through which that process was documented and evaluated.)

Furthermore, since the studies undertaken by the National Board during the first 10 years (of which I was aware) focused on what might be called the interpretive rather than the consequential aspect of validity – emphasizing the interpretation of scores in light of their intended use – this paper addresses only that part of what might be considered a more comprehensive validity research agenda. This comment is in no way intended as a criticism. Since the National Board was still heavily engaged in assessment development, the studies appropriately emphasized the information necessary initially to support the operational use of the assessment.

VALIDITY TOUCHSTONES

This section provides a brief overview of the sources that guided me in evaluating the Board's validity research agenda: the 1985 *Standards for Educational and Psychological Testing* (AERA, APA, NCME, 1985) to which the National Board's researcher's held themselves accountable, and the conceptualization of validity reflected in the work of Cronbach (1988, 1989) and Messick (1989a, 1996), which emphasize the importance of seeking challenges to the intended meaning and use of test scores.

The *Standards for Educational and Psychological Testing* (AERA, APA, NCME, 1985) were the major source of the criteria to which the National Board's assessment developers held themselves accountable: "All NBPTS assessments are developed to comport with the technical requirements for certifications assessments described in the Standards" (Educational Testing Service, ETS, 1998, p. 5). In essence, the Standards provided an overview of issues that should be addressed and the kinds of evidence that should be provided to enable professional judgment about the validity of a given interpretation and use of test scores. As described in the introduction to the 1985 Standards, the "the purpose of publishing the Standards is to provide criteria for the evaluation of tests, testing practices, and the effects of test use. Although the evaluation of the appropriateness of a test or application should depend heavily on professional judgment, the Standards can provide a frame of reference to assure that relevant issues are addressed" (AERA, APA, NCME, 1985, p. 2).

In the validity chapter of the Standards, validity was described as referring to "the degree to which ... evidence supports the inferences that are made from test scores" (AERA, APA, NCME, 1985, p. 9). Readers were told, "Evidence of validity should be presented for the major types of inferences from which the use of a test is recommended" and that "a rationale should be provided to support the particular mix of evidence presented for the intended uses" (p. 13). Although construct-, content-, and criterion-related evidence were described as possible types of evidence, and "an ideal validation includes several types of evidence which span all three of the traditional categories" (p. 9), "the quality of evidence is of primary importance, and a single line of solid evidence is preferable to numerous lines of evidence of questionable quality. Professional judgment should guide the decisions regarding the forms of evidence that are most necessary and feasible in light of the intended uses of the test and any likely alternatives to testing" (p. 9). In addition to the validity chapter, many other chapters in the Standards were relevant to the work, and I refer to these chapters, from time to time, in my critique.

Cronbach (1988), arguing for what he called a "strong" program of validity research was critical of the "confirmationist bias [that] ... colored the *Standards*" (p. 152). He raised the concern that from this perspective "validation consists not so much in questioning the proposed interpretation as in accumulating results consistent with it" (p. 152). In contrast, a "strong" program of "calls for making one's theoretical ideas as explicit as possible, and then devising deliberate challenges" (Cronbach, 1988, p. 13). From this perspective, "[v]alidation gives a construction a hard time by searching out conditions under which it breaks down and by looking into plausible alternative interpretations" (Cronbach, 1989, p. 153); it looks "for circumstances that can render the test interpretation or the construction invalid" (Cronbach, 1989, p. 165).

Messick thematized major rival hypotheses or threats to construct validity as "construct underrepresentation" and "construct-irrelevant variance" (Messick, 1989b, 1994). "Construct underrepresentation" refers to a test that is too narrow in that it fails to capture important aspects of the construct. "Construct-irrelevant variance" refers to a test that is too broad in that it requires capabilities irrelevant or extraneous to the proposed construct.

Although validity research is always designed in light of the intended interpretation and use of the test, both Cronbach and Messick suggested general categories of evidence to consider in any testing situation – categories that revised and extended the construct-, content-, and criterion-related evidence categories that appeared in the 1985 testing Standards. Messick (1989b), for instance, suggested we can:

- appraise the relevance and representativeness of the test content in relation to the content of the domain about which inferences are to be drawn, ...
- examine relationships among responses to the tasks, items, or parts of the test – that is, the internal structure of test responses, ...
- survey relationships of the test scores with other measures and background variables – that is, the test's external structure, ...
- directly probe the ways in which individuals cope with the items or tasks, in an effort to illuminate the processes underlying item response and task performance, ...
- investigate uniformities and differences in these test processes and structures over time or across groups and settings – that is the generalizability of test interpretation and use, ...
- see if the test scores display appropriate variations as a function of instructional and other interventions, ... [and]
- appraise the value implications and social consequences of interpreting and using the test scores (Messick, 1989b, p. 6; bullets and paragraphing inserted to highlight categories).

Cronbach (1989) noted that validation cannot proceed along all lines at once and suggested that:

The priority assigned to a line of inquiry depends on four features:

- Prior uncertainty. Is the issue genuinely in doubt?
- Information yield. How much uncertainty will remain at the end of a feasible study?
- Cost. How expensive is the investigation, in time and dollars?
- Leverage. How critical is the information for achieving consensus in the relevant audience? (Consensus regarding the appropriate use of the test, or consensus that it should not be used.) (Cronbach, 1989, p. 165).

An extension of the practice of seeking challenges to favored theories that Cronbach and Messick championed was reflected in Messick's (1989b) "Singerian" approach to inquiry which seeks challenges from beyond the primary professional discourse community. In this approach, one inquiring system or theory is evaluated in terms of another in order "to illuminate the scientific and value assumptions of constructs and theories so that they may

be subjected to either empirical grounding or policy debate, or both."
(Messick, 1989b, p. 63). "It is precisely such mutual confrontation of
theoretical systems, especially in attempting to account for the same data,
that opens their underlying scientific and value assumptions to public
scrutiny and critique" (Messick, 1989b, pp. 61–62). He argued that "the
recognition and systematic application of multiple perspectives is beneficial
in a variety of ways, because it tends to broaden the range of values, criteria,
and standards deemed worthy of consideration" (Messick, 1989b, p. 88).

The only one of these perspectives on validity that was in any sense a
professional imprimatur was the 1985 *Standards for Educational and
Psychological Testing*. Cronbach himself suggested that the validity research
underlying most tests, including good tests, is confirmatory in nature:
"Despite many statements calling for focus on rival hypotheses, most of
those who undertake CV have remained confirmationist. Falsification,
obviously, is something we prefer to do unto the construction of others"
(Cronbach, 1989, p. 153; note CV in original refers to construct validity).

And Messick's Singerian mode of inquiry is rarely practiced within the
measurement profession; albeit, it is a theme that resonates across multiple
philosophies of social science. And so, when I draw on these criteria to
critique the work of the National Board, I am holding them to higher
standards than professional consensus would require, and, in so doing, am
raising questions about conventional practice of validity research more
generally.

At this point, I turn to a description of the validity research agenda
undertaken by the National Board in its first decade and invite readers to
consider with me the application of these criteria of validity to the National
Board's work. Following that description, I use these criteria to provide a
critical analysis of the Board's work.

OVERVIEW OF NBPTS VALIDITY
RESEARCH AGENDA

Preliminary Considerations

Roles and Responsibilities of Validity Researchers
Responsibility for carrying out the validity research agenda resided
primarily with two working groups: the Technical Analysis Group (TAG),
a panel comprised primarily of leading researchers in psychometrics,
co-directed by Richard Jaeger and Lloyd Bond from the University of

North Carolina at Greensboro (1991–1996), and the Educational Testing Service (ETS), Division of Teaching and Learning (1996 to present), which worked under contract to the Board with specific direction from senior National Board staff. Ultimately, the National Board itself was responsible for policy decisions that guided the assessment. The TAG developed and implemented the research agenda that led to the set of studies and documentation routinely undertaken by ETS for each of the Board's certificates (which I refer to as "Routine Documentation and Research"). In addition, ETS, TAG, and members of the National Board staff carried out studies that were designed to address particular validity questions (which I refer to the "Special Studies"). To advise ETS, the Board formed a new technical advisory group, the Measurement Research Advisory Panel (MRAP), which included many members of the original TAG. Unlike TAG, whose members carried out the research agenda for the Board, the responsibility of MRAP was primarily advisory. I was not a member of the original TAG, although I attended two meetings; I was a member of MRAP. However, except where explicitly cited, the ideas in this paper are my own and are not intended to represent the views of MRAP, ETS, TAG, or the National Board.

Sources of Information Consulted
Constructing a comprehensive picture of the National Board's validity research agenda was a complicated task. While members of the ETS and National Board staff were generous in providing copies of reports I requested, there was no single document available from the National Board or in the published literature that comprehensively covered the research undertaken as of 1998. Comprehensive overviews of the technical documentation and studies routinely undertaken for each certificate were available in the Technical Analysis Report (TAR) prepared by ETS (1998), in retrospective synopses prepared by Jaeger (1997, 1998), and in the Assessment Analysis Reports (AAR) compiled each year for each certificate. There was no such document that comprehensively characterized special studies undertaken. Annotated bibliographies available from the National Board (www.nbpts.org) listed work undertaken or in progress at the time they were written, although various personal communications suggested that not all of these studies were completed. Some of the studies listed in the 1994 and 1995 bibliographies served as precursors to the studies that came to be routinely undertaken for each certificate and, for these areas, I chose to focus on the then current work rather than on its antecedents. (Chapters 3 and 7 by Pearlman, and Chapter 8 by Jaeger refer to some of this earlier work.)

Later completed papers and plans for individual studies were provided to me by colleagues at the National Board or ETS in 1998. From these collections of papers and annotated bibliographies, I tried to reconstruct the architecture of the validity research agenda undertaken by the National Board including both the routine documentation and research studies and the special studies and I shared drafts of this chapter with colleagues at the National Board and ETS to make sure I had not overlooked reports they considered essential to understanding their work.

The Recruitment of Teachers for Research and Development Work
The composition of research and development panels was an important part of the validity argument. Before proceeding with the description of the individual routine and special studies, I describe the practices typically undertaken by the Board at the time in recruiting diverse panels of experienced teachers. In the interests of space, I will not repeat this description for each study unless there were exceptions.

Whenever the Board's contractors recruited a panel of teachers to participate in the development or research agenda for a given certificate, they recruited experienced teachers who taught the subject and level appropriate to the certificate. References and credentials were checked and frequently an interview or an observation would precede the selection of a panel member. They also attempted to assemble panels that were diverse in terms of race/ethnicity, school context, and gender. In the reports of this work, they consistently described the breakdown of each panel in terms of gender and race/ethnicity. Most panels were drawn from the geographic area where the activity was occurring, although certain activities involved attention to geographic diversity as well.

ROUTINE DOCUMENTATION AND STUDIES

In this section, I refer to the documentation practices and research studies that were routinely carried out for each new certificate or administration. It is on this evidence that the validity argument for a given certificate primarily rested. Jaeger (1997, 1998) characterized the major sets of studies carried out by the National Board's TAG during its six years of operation (1991–1996) as falling into four principal areas "(1) validating the Board's assessments, (2) characterizing the reliability of the Board's assessments, (3) establishing standards of performance ... and (4) investigation of the presence and degree of adverse impact and bias in the Board's assessment"

(Jaeger, 1998, p. 189). The category, entitled "validating the Board's assessments", comprised content-related evidence of validity and a "scoring validation" study, which I treat separately. I have organized my review of the routine documentation and studies in terms of these five broad categories plus a preliminary category that describes the evidence available from the process of assessment development and scoring (see Table 1 for a summary of the routine studies and documentation).

Development and Architecture of the Assessment

The process through which the National Board's assessments were developed and their architecture, along with the rationale for these choices, were crucial pieces of validity evidence. Here I cover validity evidence relevant to the development, tryout, and revision of the assessment tasks, the development of the scoring rubrics and the selection of benchmarks to illustrate the scoring rubrics, and the training and certification of assessors. Since Pearlman (Chapters 3 and 7, this volume) provides an extensive description of the rationale and procedures through which the assessment tasks and scoring practices were developed, I will not repeat that information here. In the context of this chapter, I will focus on the then available documentation of these processes, the uses to which it was put, and on any review or evaluation activities that supported the initial development.

Initial Development of Assessment Tasks and Rubrics
As described in the TAR, "The process underlying development of each assessment is viewed as being a central contributor to its validity" (ETS, 1998, p. 9). The members of the Teacher Assessment Development Team (TADT), approximately eight experienced teachers, "critique draft exercises, report back on trials, revise exercises, and confirm their authenticity" (ETS, 1998, p. 9). The scoring rubrics were developed simultaneously "to ensure that the exercises focus only on the Standards, ... that inferences based on candidate submissions will be tied directly to the rubrics, ... [and] that evidence sought from candidates is consistent with evidence that will be considered in the rubric" (pp. 9–10). The rubrics were based on an ascending four-point scale with 3 indicating a "passing" score. "During the development period each teacher on the TADT pilot tests two to three of the initial drafts of the portfolio exercises, ... recruits other teachers as pilot participants and supports them through the pilot-test, using support

Table 1. Routine Documentation and Studies.

Validity Issue	Frequency of Study	Brief Description	Sources Consulted
Assessment development			
Initial development of tasks and scoring rubrics	Each certificate	Approximately eight teachers develop and try out exercises, recruit and support other teachers to try out exercises, examine responses, and develop scoring rubrics. A multi-state pilot test, with 10–20 additional teachers follows initial development. Documentation to guide process provided.	ETS (1998; TAR), Jaeger (1997, 1998) and Pearlman (Chapter 7, this volume)
Selecting benchmarks	Each certificate	For each exercise, 2–3 benchmarks to illustrate each score level, training papers, and qualifying papers are selected (and annotated) by team of two teachers and reviewed by one teacher. Floating personnel assist. Extensive documentation to guide process is provided. (Note exceptions for small sample scoring.)	
Training/certifying assessors and scoring	Each administration	Assessors for each certificate are trained with benchmarks and training papers that illustrate scoring issues. They are tested on qualifying papers before being allowed to score. Extensive documentation to guide process is provided. (Note exceptions for small sample scoring.) Each exercise is scored by two assessors; adjudication is required if assessors' scores differ by more than a certain amount.	

Reporting scores	Each administration	Candidates receive a letter announcing results, their raw scores on each exercise, the exercise weights, their composite score, and the score needed to pass. (Samples available.)	ETS (1998; TAR), Jaeger (1997, 1998), and (e.g., Benson & Impara, 1996; ETS, 1998; AAR)
Content-related evidence of validity	Each certificate	Panels of 9–19 teachers independently rate (a) extent to which each of standards describes a critical aspect of highly accomplished teaching, and (b) the importance and relevance of each exercise and rubric to each standard and to the overall domain of accomplished teaching.	
Scoring validation	Each administration	Panels of 6–8 teachers rank randomly selected pairs of exercise responses from adjacent score points and ranking is compared to scores. Each pair of cases is rated by two panelists who consider four pairs of cases for a total of 26–32 judgments per certificate. Panelists also rate the extent to which the assessors' notes are relevant to and cover all the appropriate standards for that exercise.	ETS (1998; TAR), Jaeger (1997, 1998), and (e.g., ETS, 1998; AAR)
Reliability			
Error associated with assessors	Each administration	Each exercise is scored by two assessors. Estimates of assessor reliabilities and standard error of measurement are provided for total score, for each component part (classroom-based portfolio, documented accomplishment, and assessment center exercises), and for each exercise. Estimates include	ETS (1998; TAR), and (e.g., ETS, 1998; AAR)

Table 1. (*Continued*)

Validity Issue	Frequency of Study	Brief Description	Sources Consulted
Error associated with exercises	Each administration	proportion of cases for each exercise on which assessors' scores differ by a certain amount, including proportion of cases requiring adjudication. Estimates of exercise reliabilities and standard errors of measurement are provided for total score, for component parts, and for each exercise based on the ten different exercises contained in the assessment. No alternative forms estimates are available	
Overall decision consistency	Each administration	Misclassification estimates – estimates of proportion of candidates incorrectly passing and failing – are calculated separately for variation due to assessors and exercises.	
Weighting and standard setting Early standard setting and weighting studies and justification of uniform standard	Multiple strategies tried (1993–1996)	Four different approaches were tried to set exercise weights and determine a passing score. The first three approaches all involved some strategy for having panelists examine and categorize profiles of scores across exercises as passing or not. The fourth had panelists independently (a) rank exercises by weight and estimate percentage increase (or decrease) in weight each exercise should be given	ETS (1998; TAR), Jaeger (1997, 1998), and Chapter 8 (this volume)

		and (b) review composite scores and accompanying exercise profiles to draw lines to indicate passing scores.	
Justification of a uniform standard and limited options for weighting	1997	On the basis of empirical evidence from early studies, logical argument, and consideration of impact, all available for review, Board set uniform standard and a set of four possible weighting strategies.	ETS (1998; TAR)
Current weighting studies	Each certificate	Panels of 6–8 teachers choose from among four possible weighting schemes after reviewing 15 hypothetical profiles of exercise scores that represent different patters of performance.	
Current standard confirmation studies	Each certificate	Panels of approximately nine teachers independently review actual candidate profiles for all candidates whose scores fall within range of the predetermined passing score, rank ordered by total score, and draw lines to indicate passing score recommendation.	
Disparate impact and bias Estimating disparate impact	Each certificate, if feasible	Certification rates reported by gender, ethnicity (African–American, Hispanic, Asian, Native American, and White, where sample sizes permit), and school context (urban, rural, suburban).	ETS (1998; TAR), (e.g., ETS, 1998; AAR), and Bond (1997, 1998)
Investigating influence of race/ethnicity of assessor on score differences between African-American and White (non-Hispanic) candidates	Each certificate, if feasible	Examined all exercise scores in each certificate where one assessor was black and one was white (non-Hispanic) to see if (a) whether African-American and White assessors scored candidates	Bond (1997, 1998)

Table 1. (*Continued*)

Validity Issue	Frequency of Study	Brief Description	Sources Consulted
		differently, regardless of candidate race and (b) if there was an interaction between race of assessor and race of candidate.	
Investigating influence of writing demand of exercise on scores differences between African-American and White (non-Hispanic) candidates	Each certificate, if feasible	Examined interactions of candidate race and exercise type (classified by amount of writing demanded) to see if writing demand was related to differences in scores between African-American and White (non-Hispanic) candidates.	ETS (1998; TAR), and Bond (1997, 1998)

Note: This is the evidence that is routinely provided for each certificate and administration and on which the validity argument for a given assessment rests.

material provided by ETS, [provides and discusses] feedback on the support material ... examines the copies of pilot responses, applies preliminary scoring criteria to the responses, and recommends modification to the scoring criteria" (ETS, 1998, p. 10).

In addition to the review provided by the TADT, there was an external review that provided "independent verification of the appropriateness and relevance of the exercises" (ETS, 1998, p. 10) and reviews by the relevant Standards committee "to insure that the intent of the Standards is preserved" (ETS, 1998, p. 11). Following initial development and try out, a multi-state pilot-test, involving 10–20 teachers, was also carried out for each exercise.

Selecting Benchmarks and Training and Certifying Assessors
During the first operational year of each assessment, after the responses had been returned, a benchmarking session was held when benchmarks, training samples, and qualifying cases were selected. "Benchmarks are typical, clear-cut performances that exemplify the characteristics of each score level" (ETS, 1998, p. 58). "Training samples are cases that raise interesting issues and are not as clearly assigned to a category as benchmarks" (ETS, 1998, p. 58). Qualifying cases were used to certify readers.

As the authors of the TAR noted, "Benchmarks 'anchor' the score scale and rubric for the assessors – the language of the rubric is made 'real' and pegged to a level of accomplishment through concrete examples" (ETS, 1998, p. 58). As such, the process through which they were selected was a crucial part of the validity research agenda.

"For both portfolio and assessment center exercises, a total of nine benchmarks are selected, two at each whole number score point, and a third benchmark at the 3-level. Multiple benchmarks at each level are used to help assessors understand that responses with different surface features may attain the same score. That is, there is not one teaching approach, type of class, or content that signals accomplishment" (ETS, 1998, p. 58).

"Benchmarking is done by assessor trainers and other qualified teaching experts who are extensively trained before beginning the work of selecting cases ... Each exercise has at least two expert educators dedicated to picking samples for that exercise. One of these will be the lead trainer, the person responsible for training and supervising assessors, for the exercise. In addition, there are numerous 'floating' personnel who assist each bench-marking pair in making their selections. These individuals may be assessment professionals, Standards committee members, or National Board members" (ETS, 1998, p. 58). Those selecting the benchmarks were told to "Choose the pairs (and the triplet at the 3-level) so that assessors see that there were different ways to achieve a score – vary the class size, type, and content and the teacher's style" (ETS, 1998, Appendix 1, p. 23). Assessment developers encouraged benchmarkers, who also served as assessor trainers to "search for samples for which scoring is likely to be sensitive to potential assumptions and biases on the part of assessors" (p. 60) and to compile a list of such issues for assessor training:

> Benchmarkers are provided a list of illustrative contrasts that disconnect construction irrelevant characteristics from score level, such as responses that demonstrate excellent writing ability in overall weaker performances, and poor writing ability in stronger performances, teacher-directed approaches in strong and weak performances, student centered approaches in strong and weak performances, strong content knowledge with weaker pedagogical strategies and strong pedagogical strategies with weaker content knowledge. Benchmarkers are also carefully guided to make wise use of minority candidate responses. (ETS, 1998, p. 60)

After the benchmarks, training samples, and qualifying cases were selected, validation began. "Validation is carried out by one or more reviewers who were not part of the original team who selected responses. Validators read individual performances and sets of performances, [score them,] and discuss what they find with the benchmarkers" (p. 60). "For vertical validation, four responses representing each score point are read in top-down order to ensure that the differences between the levels are clear, match differences in the rubric, and are more or less 'evenly spaced'." (p. 60). For 'horizontal validation,' the validators were asked to read all or that majority of the responses at a single score level to see if they matched the rubric descriptor for that level and shared the same core qualities. "At the end of the selection and validation process, each selected case has had at least three independent scores assigned to it" (p. 60). "Once scores on selected cases have been validated, benchmarkers annotate a copy of each of the nine benchmarks [and complete] an exercise scoring record ... that helps assessors see the basis for the score and provides examples of how to take down evidence" (pp. 60–61).

"Training [of assessors] is followed by a qualifying round, in which assessors must demonstrate adequate agreement with validated trainers' scores on five to six pre-selected cases ... In assessment center training sessions, trainers closely monitor performance on the training samples to determine which assessors are competent to be released into live scoring" (p. 61). "Assessors are reminded that if they encounter a case that is so anomalous or weird that they cannot score it, they should ask for help from the trainer" (p. 67).

The procedures described above refer to "large sample" scoring that was used when the number of available cases was at least 80. Eighty "is the minimum number required to guarantee a reasonable sampling range from which to draw benchmarks and other training samples to anchor the scoring system" (ETS, 1998, p. 40). For small sample scoring, there were no formal benchmarks. Rather, "fourteen cases that seem to represent the range of cases in the entire sample are pre-selected by the trainers" (p. 40) and "all the assessors ... come to consensus on the scores of those cases" (p. 40). "The set of consensus cases then serves as a common reference point for further scoring to ensure consistency." "To ... compensate for the absence of benchmarks, each case is scored by four or five assessors, thus increasing the reliability of the final exercises score" (p. 40).

Reporting Scores
When candidates were informed of the results of the test, they received a letter announcing the results, a sheet that listed their raw scores on each exercise and their composite score. They were given the weights of each exercise and the score needed to achieve certification. Candidates who failed the exam were told about banking and retake options. A handbook on interpreting the scores was provided to candidates with a summary of the rubrics (descriptions of the four performance levels) for each exercise.

Content Related Evidence of Validity
As Jaeger (1997, 1998) noted "the current assessment structure is grounded in substantial research on the reliability and content validity of the Board's early assessments" (1997, p. 5). Jaeger located the Board's choice to emphasize content-related evidence of validity in the 1985 *Standards for Educational and Psychological Testing* (AERA, APA, NCME, 1985) and in the 1978 *Uniform Guidelines on Employee Selection Procedures* (Equal Employment Opportunity Coordinating Council, EEOC, 1978). He noted first that although these sources recognize multiple types of validity evidence, content-related evidence of validity "is often most readily available for certification of licensure tests" (p. 10). He further explained why a conventional job analysis, typically seen as crucial to validity, was not appropriate for National Board assessments: Unlike most certification tests, the National Board assessments were (a) voluntary (rather than manda-tory), (b) focused on an advanced (rather than minimal) level of accomplishment, and (c) "grounded in a well articulated vision of teaching that is forward-thinking" (p. 11), which emphasized what teachers "*should* know and be able to do" (rather than what they routinely know and do).

It is because of this last point that a conventional job analysis, which would probably consist of an "examination of the tasks performed by a random sample of teachers on any given day," was not appropriate for this assessment.

Content-related studies of validity were carried out "to monitor whether the Standards were a good representation of accomplished practice, whether the exercises mapped onto the Standards, and whether the scoring rubrics were appropriate" (ETS, 1998, p. 119). For each certificate, independent panels of teachers were selected who teach that subject at the appropriate level. Panels in 1996–1997 ranged in sizes from 9 to 19 (ETS, 1998, p. 11). Following training to familiarize them with the materials, panelists were asked to respond to a set of questionnaires, each containing mostly Likert-type items that asked them to rate (a) the extent to which each of the standards described a critical aspect of highly accomplished teaching practice, (b) the relevance and the importance of each exercise in the portfolio and assessment center to each standard and to the overall domain, (c) the relevance and importance of the descriptions in the scoring guide to each standard and to the overall domain (see, e.g., Benson & Impara, 1996). Exercise ratings also included questions about the extent to which each was necessary, realistic, and frequently practiced. Scoring guide ratings included questions about whether the descriptions were necessary, distinguished highly accomplished teaching, matched the exercise for which they were designed, and included factors irrelevant to the domain. All rating forms contained some space for comments. As the technical manual stated: "The results of the studies suggested a strong pattern supporting the content validity of each certificate" (ETS, 1998, p. 120).

Scoring Validation

Another routine study that was referred to in the technical manual as "scoring validation" occurred after the scoring of the exercises for a given certificate had been completed. A panel of six (Jaeger, 1997) to eight (ETS, 1998) teachers with appropriate content expertize, not previously trained in the NBPTS scoring, were asked to examine pairs of responses randomly selected to represent adjacent score points for a given exercise along with the records of evidence kept by the assessors of those responses (but not the scores themselves). After being exposed to the relevant standards, the instructions given to the candidate, and the scoring rubric, the members of the panel provided three kinds of ratings: (a) a rank ordering of the responses from the two candidates, (b) a rating of "withitness" – the extent to which the original assessors' written evaluations addressed *only* the criteria contained in the relevant standards (i.e., avoided irrelevant criteria), and (c) a rating of "representativeness" – the extent to which the assessors' written evaluations addressed *all* the criteria contained in the relevant standards. Each pair of cases was rated by two panelists; each panelist considered four pairs of cases, two from the portfolio and two from the assessment center; and all exercises except the documented accomplishments were included in the pool. The authors of the technical manual concluded that "Overall, the work of the panelists supported the claims to validity made by the scoring system and the judgments of performances it records" (ETS, 1998, p. 122).

Reliability
To understand the nature of the estimates of reliability and error of measurement provided, it is necessary to understand how the exercises were scored and the overall composite score produced. The assessment was comprised of 10 exercises each scored independently by two assessors (experienced teachers who taught in the same subject area and level as the candidates). For the portfolio exercises, there was only one form; for the assessment center exercise, the instructions and questions remained the same but the supporting materials (professional articles, students' work, possible instructional materials) varied *from year to year*. The 12-point score scale was divided into four score "families" anchored by the whole numbers 1, 2, 3, and 4. A family consisted of the whole number, the whole number minus .25, and the whole number plus .25. So, for instance, the 'one' family consisted of 0.75, 1.00, and 1.25, the 'two family consisted of 1.75, 2.00, 2.25, and so on, up through the top score of 4.25 (as describe by Pearlman, Chapter 7, this volume). For a given exercise, if the two assessors' scores differed by 1.25 or less then the scores were averaged; if the scores differed by more than 1.25 then a third, more experienced, reader was brought in to adjudicate the scores. [This approach to combining assessors' scores was used for "large sample" scoring, when the number of cases exceeded 80 (four of the six certificates administered in 1996–1997); for assessments with smaller sample sizes, a consensus system was used – see Pearlman, Chapter 7, this volume]. The resulting scores for each exercise were weighted and aggregated to form an overall composite score for each candidate. The total composite score could vary from 75 to 425. This composite was then compared to a predetermined passing score (which will be described in the following section).

Three general approaches to estimating reliability and/or errors of measurement were taken. First, they considered *error associated with assessors*. "The key question is whether a candidate, given a different set of assessors, would fare similarly, on the assessment" (ETS, 1998, p. 109). Here, they estimated assessor reliability in two different ways. The TAR reported the proportion of cases, across all exercises, on which assessors' scores differed by given amounts (ranging from 0 to greater than 1.25). The policy adopted required adjudication for scores that differed by more than 1.25. The TAR also provided an estimate of assessor reliabilities and standard errors of measurement for the total assessment and for each of the component parts. The authors of the TAR concluded that "these data support the conclusion that assessors had a high level of agreement in their scoring of candidate performances" (ETS, 1998, p. 112).

Second, they considered *error associated with exercise sampling*. The key question was "Would candidates perform similarly on a different set (sample) of exercises?" (ETS, 1998, p. 109). Following a procedure suggested by Traub and Jaeger (1995), the authors of the technical manual reported exercise reliability and standard errors of measurement for the entire assessment, for the set of in-class portfolio exercises, for the set of documented accomplishment portfolio exercises, and for the set of assessment center exercises. Estimates for individual exercise scores were reported in the relevant AAR. The authors of the TAR raised cautions about interpreting such alternative forms estimates of reliability:

> Whether an assessment with the current design can be considered to allow for alternative forms in a traditional measurement sense is debatable. It is possible to argue that the exercises are but one possible sample from a larger domain of accomplished teaching or that the exercises, for all intents and purposes, comprise a fixed assessment of accomplished teaching. (ETS, 1998, pp. 107–108)

Third, *estimates of decision consistency* for the assessments were provided by estimating the probabilities of a false negative (failing when one should have passed) and of a false positive (passing when one should have failed). These misclassification estimates were calculated separately based first on reliability due to exercise sampling and second on reliability due to assessor consistency. As the TAR pointed out, "it is important to note while the likely number of misclassified candidates can be approximated, it is not possible to identify these candidates" (ETS, 1998, p. 113).[1] The TAR also provided graphs that plotted the conditional probability of being certified at different possible "true" scores: "the probability of candidates meeting or not meeting the performance standards who had 'true' performance levels at various distances above and below the performance standard of 275 points" (ETS, 1998, p. 115), again separately for estimates based on exercise sampling and assessors. As they noted in the EA/ELA AAR, "decisions will be more consistent for those individuals further from the performance standard, in either direction" (ETS, 1998, p. 25).

Weighting and Standard Setting

The National Board adopted a uniform structure for the assessment (four in-class portfolio exercises, two documented accomplishment portfolio exercises, and four assessment center exercises), a limited pool of possible weighting schemes, and a uniform performance standard. In this section, I review briefly the Board's rationale for these choices and describe the studies then routinely undertaken to "confirm" the performance standard and to select from among the four possible weighting strategies. Jaeger (1997, and Chapter 8, this volume) and the TAR described the research agenda and rationale that led to these choices.

Earlier Research on Weighting and Standard Setting

Part of the evidence in support of the Uniform Performance Standard and the small subset of possible weighting strategies was based on earlier judgmental standard setting and weighting procedures used by TAG. As Jaeger described (1997, 1998, this volume, Chapter 8), three different approaches to standard setting were initially tried out by TAG: (a) the Dominant Profile Judgment method, (b) Judgmental Policy Capturing method, and (c) Two-Stage Judgmental Policy Capturing method. All these procedures involved some strategy for having panelists examine and categorize profiles of scores across exercises. For each certificate, this judgmental procedure resulted first in weights for each exercise and second in a recommended passing score. The Dominant Profile Judgment method asked panelists "to specify the lowest profile of performance on the exercises." It was rejected because it resulted in a partially conjunctive model, which the exercise level reliabilities did not support. For instance, a candidate might fail the exam for receiving a score below the threshold on a single exercise that was insufficiently reliable for that determination. The single-stage Judgmental Policy Capturing method, which asked panelists to classify many profiles of scores, was revised to the two-stage method because as the number of exercises increased, so did the cognitive demand on the panelists who had to consider simultaneously the meaning of all the scores as they judged a profile. The two-stage Judgmental Policy Capturing method asked panelists to first consider profiles from subsets of exercises within categories, subset by subset, and then to consider profiles of scores across the subsets. Jaeger (1997) described an initial try-out of the two-stage Judgmental Policy Capturing model. None of these procedures were used for operational decisions.

A fourth strategy was developed by TAG because of concerns about the time and cost of the previous strategies, although Jaeger (1997) argued the Judgmental Policy Capturing method required judgments that were "more consistent with common, everyday experience" (p. 91). This "Direct Judgment method" (Jaeger, 1997) was used for the 1995–1996 operational decisions.[2] During the weighting phase, (described in Baker, Huff, Price, McKenzie, & Jaeger, 1996), panelists went through a multi-stage procedure to produce exercise weights by ranking and assigning importance weights through a complex, iterative process that involved comparing an exercise to all those above (or below) it in rank and considering what percentage increase (or decrease) in weight should be given. For the standard setting phase, the exercise weights were used to create a composite score and panelists then examined a table of candidates' profiles (exercise and composite scores) rank ordered by composite score. They were asked to draw a line between profiles that represented (1) the lowest-scoring candidate who should ... receive ... certification ... and (2) the highest scoring candidate who should not ... receive ... certification. The median of the panel's distribution of recommended performance standards became the recommendation to the Board.

Rationale for Uniform Performance Standard and a Limited Number of Possible Exercise Weights
The performance standards that were recommended through these studies provided empirical evidence that informed the decision to use a uniform performance standard across all certificates. [See the 1998 Technical Analysis Report for detailed arguments.] The authors of the TAR and TAG reports were careful to note that the results from any standard setting study were simply recommendations to the Board. As Harman described:

> We have been consistently advised by legal counsel and the TAG that the recommendation of the panels is only one piece of information the Board may legitimately use in establishing a performance standard. Other valid considerations include the adverse impact that a performance standard has on minority groups within

the candidate population, the absolute numbers of minority candidates certified, and the relative importance the national Board places on avoiding false negative and false positive errors when awarding National Board Certification. (Harman, 1997, in ETS, 1998, p. 85)

The performance standard for all certificates was set at 263 on a composite score scale that ranged from 75 to 475, which was "one half of a standard error of measurement below the objective cut score of 275 that is designed into the assessment through the rubrics" (ETS, 1998, p. 90). When scores were reported to candidates, 12 points were added to each overall score so that the passing standard was described as 275, which was equivalent to obtaining the lowest score in the 3 family – that is the lowest 'passing' score – on each exercise (ETS, 1998, p. 98). Since the scores were weighted and averaged, this allowed higher scores on some exercises to compensate for lower scores on others.

In their report to the board, ETS argued that "A uniform standard of 263 contributes to the equivalence of different assessments, and minimizes the proportion of false negative decisions, while at the same time preserving standards of performance that are consistent with the NBPTS vision" (ETS, 1998, p. 87). The TAR noted that having a uniform standard allowed candidates to know "in advance of committing their energies to the assessment, what it requires to achieve certification," (p. 89) and it avoided having the standard of certification be cohort dependent.

Four possible distributions of weight (each totaling 100 across the 10 exercises) were selected. After a review of the judgmental procedures used by TAG and other high stakes assessments, the ETS team concluded "that judgmental weighting procedures often result in somewhat arbitrary and minute differences in weights assigned to exercises, with no clear basis for the resulting differences in weight" (ETS, 1998, p. 72). And so, the selected patterns differed in terms of the relative weights given to the exercises in different categories (classroom-based portfolio, documented accomplishment, and assessment center); they were identical in holding all weights within a category constant (so that, for instance, all of the exercises in the assessment center received the same weights). The TAR noted "Within these broad categories, there exists no empirical evidence that the differences among exercises are great enough to warrant differential weights. Across the categories, however, there are significant differences that might give rise to differential weights" (ETS, 1998, p. 72).

The options for weighting schemes, each of which summed to 100 across the 10 exercises were (a) equal weights across sections (10 each for four classroom-based portfolio exercises, 10 each for two documented accomplishment exercise, and 10 each for four assessment center exercises, designated 10-10-10), (b) two patterns that weighted classroom-based portfolio exercises more heavily than assessment center exercises with documented accomplishments weighted least (12-6-10 or 15-4-8), and one pattern that privileged the assessment center exercises (8-4-15).

Weighting Studies

To determine exercise weights for a given certificate, a panel of 6–8 teachers was asked to select a weighting scheme from among the four weighting schemes described in the previous section. Before selecting weights, panelists participated in "extensive review and discussion of the content addressed the demand on candidates and the types of evidence sought in each exercise" (ETS, 1998, p. 72). To help them in choosing amongst the weighting schemes, panelists were given 15 hypothetical profiles of scores that represented different patterns of performance along with the total scores that would be computed under each of the four possible weighting schemes. They were also told that an overall score of 275 represented accomplished practice. Following discussion, panelists independently selected a weighting scheme and the results were tallied and presented to the group. Following another round of discussion, individuals were given an opportunity to revise their choices independently. The final selection for the weighting strategy to be used in the assessment was based on the strategy the majority of teachers chose. For all but one of the 1996–1997 certificates, the set of weights selected was 12-6-10, for classroom-based portfolio, documented accomplishment, and assessment center exercises, respectively; for Early Adolescence Through Young Adult Art (EAYA/A), the sets of weights selected was 15-4-8.

Standard Confirming Studies

Following the Board's decision to use a uniform performance standard, ETS conducted the first "Performance Standard Confirmation Study" (ETS, 1998, p. 91) for the Adolescent and Young Adult/Mathematics (AYA/M) certification, which was the only certificate administered in 1996–1997 that had not been previously administered operationally. A panel of nine AYA/M teachers reviewed each exercise in the assessment package along with the rubrics, the guiding questions used by the exercise assessors, and representative examples of performance for each exercise for score point levels 2 and 3. They were also reminded of some "facts" about NBPTS scores: (a) that there were no prior assumptions about the proportion of candidates who would pass or fail the exam; (b) "the '3' level performance (3– to 3+) [or 2.75–3.25] is the performance that "meets the Standards" and, thus, candidates whose scores reflect that level of accomplishment overall warrant certification" (ETS, 1998, p. 91); (c) that exercises were weighted differently and that the weights were already fixed; and (d) that the scoring system was fully compensatory and that "there is NO minimum certification qualifying score on any part of the assessment" (p. 91). To confirm the passing standard, panelists then went through the following process. Panelists received "actual candidate score profiles for all ... candidates whose weighted total scores fell between 240 and 300" (ETS, 1998, p. 92) along with their weighted total score. Profiles were presented in rank order by weighted total score. (All weighted total scores included the uniform constant of 12.) Panelists were then asked to draw two lines: "one that represented the point at which they were certain candidates should NOT be certified and another that representing the point at which they were certain candidates should be certified" (ETS, 1998, p. 92). They were then asked to draw a third line that represented the certify/do not certify standard. For each line, they were asked to articulate a rationale. On the basis of one study, ETS concluded that "the certification standards chosen confirm the NBPTS certification standard of 275 (263 plus 12 point constant)" (p. 93).

Bias and Disparate Impact
The TAG and ETS routinely undertook analyses with each administration to inform questions of bias and adverse impact. The authors of the research reports were careful to point out the distinction between bias and adverse impact. Adverse impact occurs when there is a substantial difference in the certification rates of two groups "An assessment is said to exhibit disparate impact with respect to a specified subgroup of the population (the focal group) if the rate at which candidates in that subgroup are assigned a given classification (pass or accept) is substantially below the rate of some normative reference group" (Bond, 1998, p. 211). "Determining whether adverse impact, to the extent that it exists, results from genuine differences between the performances of groups or is an artifact of deficiencies in the assessment system requires additional study and investigation" (Jaeger, 1997, p. 93). Bond further noted that "although some information is available on potential *external causes* of disparate impact, such as number of advanced degrees and level of candidate support in preparing assessment portfolios, the central focus of these studies is potential sources of disparate

impact that are traceable to the *assessment system itself*" (Bond, 1998, pp. 211–212). "An assessment is said to exhibit bias if significant, systematic differences in performance among subgroups in the examinee population can be ascribed to actual flaws or deficiencies in one or more aspects of the assessment system itself that have the effect of disadvantaging members of a specific group" (Jaeger, 1997, pp. 93–94).

With respect to adverse impact, the National Board routinely reported certification rates by gender, ethnicity, teaching setting (urban, suburban, rural, e.g., ETS, 1998) along with the distribution of candidates broken down by group membership; they also reported average scores by exercise broken down by gender and ethnicity (where sample sizes permit). As ETS described,

> In the case of the 1996–97 certificates, the certification rate for African-American candidates was approximately 40% of the certification rate for White (non-Hispanic) candidates. This indicates the existence of adverse impact for African-American candidates. There were insufficient numbers of other racial/ethnic minority candidates to allow us to draw conclusions that would be considered statistically meaningful. Similarly, though not so extreme, the certificate rate for male candidates was approximately 76% of the certification rate for female candidates, indicating the existence of adverse impact for male candidates. (ETS, 1998, p. 106)

Bond (1998) cautioned that because National Board certification is voluntary, the group of teachers that attempted certification was in no way a random sample and that "the rates of certification observed so far may or may not be close to what would be found if we had a random sample" (p. 213).

As the TAR pointed out:

> The National Board is committed to ensuring equity throughout every aspect of its work. Toward this end, the National Board has established a variety of policies and procedures designed to ensure diversity and fair representation of minority teachers throughout all facets of its administration and assessment operations. (ETS, 1998, p. 106)

It is important to note, as well, the extensive and carefully consistent training of assessors (particularly with respect to illuminating their personal biases) were important aspects of the routine validity argument with respect to issues of bias.

As part of their routine investigation of bias, the National Board examined scores by race/ethnicity of the assessor where assessors from different groups evaluated the same exercise responses. "An important question of fairness is whether assessors of different backgrounds might differentially value performances by candidates from different back-grounds" (p. 122). To this end "all performances in each certificate for which one assessor was African-American and one was White (non-Hispanic) were examined ... Two questions were asked. Firstly, whether African-American and White (non-Hispanic) assessors scored candidates, regardless of race, similarly, and secondly, whether there was an interaction between the race of candidates and the race of assessors – that is, did assessors of each race consider candidates of both races similarly." (p. 122). ETS (1998) cautioned

> that the numbers reported do not represent the number of candidates who had exercises scored by both an African-American and a White assessor, but the number of instances within a particular certificate of exercises being scored by both an African-American and a White assessor. For example, if an African-American candidate had three exercises scored by an African-American and a White assessor, that would count as three cases in the analysis for that certificate. (ETS, 1998, p. 122)

For the three certificates where sample size was sufficient to support the analysis and for the overall analysis, "the race of the assessor was not a statistically significant factor in the scores candidates received, nor was there an interaction between race of candidates and the race of assessors" (p. 123). In other words, there were no significant differences in the average scores given by African-American and White assessors and this was true for both African-American and White candidates.

In addition, Bond (1997, 1998) reported the Board had routinely examined interactions of candidate race and exercise type, as potential internal sources of disparate impact (although this was not described in the TAR). The focus of these studies was on writing ability as a potential source of construct irrelevant variance – in other words, as a potential cause of differences between groups of candidates that was not directly relevant to the construct of accomplished teaching.

Bond reported the design and results of the 1993–1994 Early Adolescence/Generalist (EA/G) certificate as "typical." To investigate impact of writing demand on disparate impact, they compared differences in the performance of African-American and White candidates on the exercise with highest writing demand versus (a) the exercise with the lowest writing demand and (b) the average of all other exercises. Bond reported that while there were significant main effects – significantly lower scores on both types of exercises by African-American candidates and significantly lower scores on high writing demand exercises by all candidates, there was no significant interaction. In other words, the difference in performance between

African-American and White candidates was not significantly related to the writing demand of the exercise. He did note a non-significant trend, however, for relatively higher scores by White candidates on the writing-intense exercise.

ETS (1998) noted that there were many potential sources of bias in addition to those that could be routinely investigated, and the National Board mounted an extensive research agenda that addressed these issues and which is described under special studies below.

SPECIAL STUDIES

In this section, I briefly describe those special studies that were not routinely carried out for each certificate, but that were relevant to the National Board's validity work. I have grouped the studies into four categories: (a) evidence regarding disparate impact and bias, (b) evidence based on candidates' perspectives, (c) evidence based on information about accomplished teaching that was external to the assessment, and (d) evidence based on alternative approaches to scoring and standard setting. These included studies that were planned and in progress at the time, as well as those completed.

Evidence Regarding Disparate Impact and Bias

Bond classified the Board research into sources of disparate impact as focusing on external and internal sources. He noted that the Board was "understandably more concerned about identifying and removing any internal components of the assessment itself that may unfairly disadvantage" (Bond, 1998, p. 215). Here I describe special studies undertaken, which supplemented the routine studies described above. These special studies focused on the disparate impact on African-American candidates.

Completed Studies
The Board examined three potential *external* sources of disparate impact on African-American candidates when compared with White non-Hispanic candidates: "years of teaching experience, number of advanced degrees, and level of support received during portfolio preparation" (Bond, 1998, p. 214). Bond (1997, 1998, based on what appears to be the results from the two certificates administered in 1995–1996) said "62 per cent of all White

candidates and 54 percent of all African-American candidates have degrees beyond the baccalaureate. Fifty-eight percent of all White candidates and 62 per cent of all African-American candidates have ten or more years of teaching experience" (p. 215). He concluded that these were not "fruitful sources of disparate impact" (p. 215).

To investigate the possibility of differing levels of support during the process of portfolio evaluation, the TAG conducted in-depth phone interviews with candidates from the field tests for the first two certificates (EA/G and EA/ELA, respectively). They "interviewed 37 of 40 African-American field test candidates ... who submitted complete scorable performances and 60 White candidates matched as closely as possible on available information such as school location and years of teaching experience" (p. 216). Candidates were asked to describe "in detail the exact nature of the support they received" (p. 216). Bond reported "In virtually all categories of collegial, administrative, and technical support, White and African-American candidates received comparable support. In those few instances where the level and quality differed, they tended to favor African-American candidates" (p. 216). He concluded "the level and quality of support was not a major factor in the disparate impact" (p. 216).

Studies of *internal sources of disparate impact* – (a) interaction of candidate and assessor race and (b) interaction of candidate race and exercise type – completed (as of 1998) are described above under routine studies.

Studies Underway and/or Planned (in 1998)
Bond described five additional studies into the sources of disparate impact, funded by the Spencer Foundation, that were either underway or planned. These studies all focused on the EA/ELA certificates. *Study 1* was intended to address the question of whether the assessment system inappropriately privileged "constructivist, student-centered, and permissive approaches to instruction over didactic, teacher-centered and more authoritarian instructional styles" (Bond, 1998, p. 218). The focus of this study was the ELA assessment. Here, a panel of curriculum specialists, university-based researchers, and ELA teachers examined the standards, scoring rubrics and procedures, and their application to candidates' performances, reading across the entire set of evidence available on a candidate. In *Study 2*, surveys and interviews of targeted and random samples of African-American teachers addressed the question: "What elements and aspects of teaching practice do African-American teachers consider important in outstanding teaching?" (Bond, 1998, p. 219). *Study 3* extended the routine investigation

of the potential interaction between race of assessor and race of candidate and examined as well the potential interaction of teaching contexts and experience of assessors and candidates. For instance, did "assessors whose teaching contexts and experiences are similar to some of the candidates they assess appreciate and honor aspects of their performance that other assessors are insensitive to?" (Bond, 1998, p. 219). With *Study 4*, Bond and his colleagues were actively seeking nominations of African-American teachers known, through other means, to be outstanding and asking them to complete the assessment. Their "relative performance and rate of certification will be compared to other candidates" (Bond, 1998, p. 219). *Study 5* asked whether there were patterns of performance that were different for African-American teachers than for White teachers who received the same evaluation on the exercises, in general, and the video exercises, in particular. The panel working on Study 1 also compared performances of African-American and White candidates "matched as nearly as possible on total assessment score, teaching location (urban, suburban, rural), and selected demographic characteristics" (Bond, 1998, p. 220).

Evidence Based on Candidates' Perspectives
Feedback from 1993 to 1994 Field Test Candidates (Jaeger & Thompson, 1994; Noble, Chavez, & Haag, 1994). This study elicited feedback from a sample of candidates who completed the 1993–1994 field tests in EA/ELA and EA/G certificates. Candidates participated in 30 minute face-to-face interviews, a 1.5-hour focus group, and hour-long writing tasks where they responded to questions about their motivations to participate in the field test, the support they had received as they completed the school site portfolio, and the "efficiency and effectiveness of the National Board's operation" (p. 2). In each subject area, six teachers from each of three assessment center sites were invited to participate; of the 72 candidates invited, 34 agreed to participate in the study.

Qualitative analysis of the results indicated that the predominant reasons teachers chose to participate were for professional development, to achieve national certification, and for the financial benefits (a promised stipend and/ or the possibility of avoiding a registration fee when the system became operational). Seventy-seven percent of those interviewed had considered dropping out of the process at some point because of time constraints, unclear instructions for completing the portfolio, and/or personal factors. Avenues of support available to candidates included support from the National Board (written materials and a free calling number), and district, local, and personal support, although not all candidates reported using support services. Prominent among candidates' recommendations for support were the importance of providing "a multi-dimensional support system", including more technical support, more frequent communication on an informal basis, support group meetings or other regular contact with local representatives, and access to other candidates. A number of specific recommendations were made to improve the operation of the system.

"A Study on Feedback to Candidates for Certification with the National Board for Professional Teaching Standards" (Davis, Wolf, & Borko, 1999; Davis et al., 1995; Wolf & Taylor, Chapter 13, this volume). This study investigated three different forms of feedback to candidates, using materials created from the first fully operational year of the EA/G exam. The authors considered the appropriateness of the feedback to candidates for two purposes: interpreting "how well they did" (summative feedback) and enabling "useful inferences regarding ways they could improve their practice" (formative feedback). The researchers considered teachers' preferences, what teachers said they had learned from the feedback (based on interviews following their review of it), and comparisons between what teachers said they had learned and the National Board assessors' evaluation of the performance. Three types of feedback were tried out, based on two different exercises. "Cases" provided "3–4 page edited examples of representative candidates' actual performances along with the corresponding comments of a scorer" (Davis et al., 1999, p. 104), with 2 cases for the 4-level performance and 2 for the candidate's level of performance. "Performance syntheses" provided 2–3 page descriptions of the general characteristics of each performance level plus examples, organized by scoring criteria (with one description at the 4-level and one for the candidate's own score). "Illustrative summaries" provided 1 page evaluative descriptions of actual candidates' responses for each of the four possible score levels. Twenty-nine candidates, representing five different centers, 15 of whom passed the exam, agreed to participate.

The authors reported that many of the candidates said they would have preferred personalized feedback (which was not one of the options considered). Of the three options, teachers clearly preferred the extended, contextualized examples of candidate performance of the cases option, with performance syntheses second. The authors reported "After candidates read either performance syntheses or cases, most were able to identify several additional ways in which their practice could be improved and learning from both the cases and the performance syntheses closely matched the scoring criteria. (They noted that since candidates were sent the illustrative summaries in advance, it was not possible to assess their learning with respect to this form of feedback.)[3]

Evidence Based on Alternative Approaches to Scoring and Standard Setting "*The Influence of Changes in Assessment Design on the Psychometric Quality of Scores*" *Comparing Scoring Practices over Time (Wolfe & Gitomer, 2001).* In this set of analyses, Wolfe and Gitomer drew results from the 1996 and 1997 years of the EA/G examination to evaluate the impact of changes in the assessment system on various indices of reliability. The changes they cited between 1996 and 1997 included (a) providing more explicit direction to candidates so they did "not have to guess" at what was expected; (b) "increasing the number of benchmark and training samples that assessors see during training"; (c) initiating a process that encourages raters to examine and control their own biases about teaching; (d) providing more explicit "guiding and bridge questions that served to structure the way in which assessors considered the evidence produced by candidates" (Wolfe & Gitomer, 2001, pp. 97–98); and (e) eliminating any requirement for specific behaviors in the scoring rubrics so that assessors could "weigh the preponderance of evidence rather than accounting for the presence of absence of specific acts." Comparing the two years of the assessment, they reported "substantial increases" in reliability (using various indices) with "minimal increases in cost" (Wolfe & Gitomer, 2001, p. 99). They also estimated that to obtain 1997 level reliabilities with 1996 practices, they would need to triple the number of raters and double the number of items that would have substantially increased the cost. "Overall [they concluded], the evidence provided here suggests that considerable increases in assessment quality can be obtained through revisions of assessment materials and improvements in assessor training procedures" (Wolfe & Gitomer, 2001, p. 106).

"*An Experiment in Standard Setting*" *(Lewis & Pearlman, 1997).* This study explored the feasibility of a standard setting procedure that asked panelists to read across exercises from a single candidate. Lewis and Pearlman wanted standard setters to make their decisions based on their own examination of the full set of performance data rather than being based on the scores generated by other people's examination of the performance data in isolation from each other.

The study had three goals: (a) to determine if it was feasible in real time for teachers to read across a candidate's materials to make a certification decision; (b) to examine the degree of agreement among the teachers on the standard setting panel; and (c) to explore what kinds of training were necessary to support this process. It was conducted with 40 sets of candidates' materials from the EA/ELA assessment. Ten panel members were asked to read over materials for each of eight candidates, beginning with the three highest weighted exercises. They were told that they could stop reviewing materials [after the first three exercises] at any point at which they believed no evidence, positive or negative would change their decisions. All cases were reviewed by two panelists. The training, which took candidates through the elements of the assessment design and scoring, lasted only 90 min. In 34 of the 80 decisions, judges stopped reading after the third exercise and for only two decisions did judges read all exercises. On the basis of the results of these decisions, Lewis and Pearlman were able to estimate a cut score of 2.66 (on the original exercise scale) with a small standard error based on between judge information.

Evidence Based on Information External to the Assessment

"Identifying 'Highly Accomplished Teachers': A Validation Study" (Hattie & Clinton, Chapter 12, this volume; Hattie, Clinton, Thompson, & Schmidt-Davis, 1995). As Hattie and colleagues described it, the aims of this study were to (a) "present a methodology" to identify how teachers certified by NBPTS perform in the classroom compared to teachers not certified; and (b) to understand how "highly accomplished teachers manifest their expertise in classroom practice" and how "they impact on students." On the basis of a review of the literature, they identified five major dimensions "that discriminate between experienced [teachers] and experienced *expert* teachers" (Hattie et al., 1995, p. 2) that they used to guide their data collection and analysis: knowledge, insight, efficiency-management, affect, and learning outcomes. Each dimension was further subdivided into 2–4 categories. Six EA/G candidates who completed the 1993–1994 field tests were invited to participate: three whose scores were about one standard error above the cut score of 275 and three whose scores were about one standard error below the cut score. Because teachers had already received their results and were anxious to talk about them, it was impossible to keep researchers blind to candidates' status on the exam. Information was obtained from five sources: observations (verbatim transcripts recorded on a portable computer plus coded features) for one day by at least two observers; interviews; documents such as students' work and lesson plans; a video of an exemplary lesson; and commentaries on the artifacts. Some of the information – artifacts and commentaries – was taken from the portfolio that had been submitted. Two judges, who had also been observers, then

scored the collected information, piece by piece, on a scale of 1–10 for each of 29 attributes (with a high level of inter-judge reliability).

Hattie et al. (1995) reported that:

> Cluster analysis was used to assess the degree to which highly accomplished teachers have a 'family resemblance,' and the degree to which non-highly accomplished teachers have a different family resemblance. Based on this analysis, the teachers clustered into three groups (described here in terms of their certification status): (a) two failing teachers, (b) two passing teachers and one failing teacher, (c) one passing teacher who was "clearly the outstanding teacher among all six (p. 56).

Regarding the one failing teacher who resembled the two passing teachers, Hattie and colleagues recommend that the Board "consider whether the [assessment's] instructions tend to negate this excellent type of buzzing classroom activities" (Hattie et al., 1995, p. 58). The five remaining teachers, the researchers noted, had "a meaningful pattern of differences on 20 of the 29 attributes." In their recommendations, the researchers suggested a number of modifications in the design including a larger and more representative sample, data collection before release of the assessment results to researchers and teachers, not using data from the portfolio, and taking steps to offset the "halo-effect" of having the observers also serve as raters.

"The Relationship of Teaching, Student Learning, and NBPTS Certification Status" (Gitomer, personal communication; Wylie, Thomson, Siegel, & Gitomer, 2000). As Gitomer (personal communication) described this study-in-progress, its purpose was to marshal evidence regarding the following validity issues: "to establish that the characterization of a teacher's accomplishment based on [the National Board's] assessment generalizes to teaching accomplishment in the classroom and that students benefit from teaching designated as accomplished" (p. 1). During spring 1998, 40 4th and 5th grade classrooms from the 1997–1998 Middle Childhood/Generalist (MC/G) candidates were observed. The observation consisted of detailed notes from two observers of one lesson selected by the teacher; brief, structured interviews with each of four randomly selected children from the class following the observation; and debriefing interviews with the teacher. Two important questions were addressed in this study. First, was there a relationship between what students take from a lesson and independent indicators of the quality of the lesson? Second, were lesson quality and student understanding of the lesson related to performance on the NBPTS assessments? Accomplished teachers asked more questions of

individual students, asked more deep questions, and received more deep answers. Students of certified teachers exhibited greater understanding of the lesson than the students of teachers who were not certified (Wylie et al., 2000).

CRITICAL ANALYSIS OF NBPTS VALIDITY RESEARCH AGENDA

In the previous section, my intent was to describe the National Board's validity work as comprehensively and fairly as possible – to present it in its strongest possible light. In this section, I offer a more critical analysis of their work, drawing on the two overlapping conceptions of validity described in the introduction: the 1985 Standards emphasized the extent to which the available evidence *supports* the intended interpretation, and the program of validity research reflected in the work of Cronbach (1988, 1989) and Messick (1989a, 1989b, 1994) and others (e.g., Shepard, 1993), which highlighted the value of pursuing challenges to the intended interpretation and use of an assessment.

My criticism is organized in terms of a series of critical observations that focus on what I have called the routine documentation and studies – those studies that were undertaken for each certificate and/or administration – using the special studies, as appropriate, to qualify the general observations. It was the routine documentation and studies on which the validity argument for a given certificate primarily rested. As I indicated in the introduction, my focus was on the overall architecture of the Board's research agenda – the extent to which the evidence provided was sufficient to enable professional judgments of the validity of the interpretations and uses of the assessment – and not on the design or results of individual studies. By professional judgment, I refer both to the professions of educational measurement and of teaching and teacher education. Further, my emphasis, consistent with the Board's attention to assessment development, was on the interpretive, rather than the consequential aspect of validity.

It is important to note that the National Board was in the early stages of its assessment development work during the first decade, and that a number of the comments I make below about work not yet undertaken should be interpreted as suggestions for next steps rather than criticisms of a completed research agenda. Given limited time and resources, it is not possible to do everything at once. While I will raise questions about the way particular issues were empirically addressed, or about why resources were allocated to mount some studies over others, there is no question that each of the issues addressed by the Board in its routine research agenda needed to be addressed. My criticism and suggestions for next steps were offered in the spirit of collaboration in furthering the Board's mission of improving learning by improving teaching.

Observation 1

As the authors of the technical manual concluded, "Based on these analyses of the technical measurement quality of the six certificates administered in 1996– 1997, the assessments fully meet the requirements of the Standards for Educational and Psychological Testing (AERA, APA, NCME, 1985) for validity, reliability and freedom from bias" (ETS, 1998, p. 125).

Viewed from the perspective of the 'Standards', I would concur that the evidence provided in the various technical reports is adequate to support professional judgment about the operational use of the assessment. Of course, it is not the opinion of a single individual or even of a team of assessment developers that is sufficient to support this observation (a point which the authors of the 1985 Standards assert); rather it is the consensus of multiple members of the measurement profession who reviewed this work. To that end, however, the work of the assessment developers not only drew on the talents of multiple professionals, it was reviewed by members of the TAG, and subsequently MRAP, and the National Board itself, all of whom supported the readiness of the assessment for operational use.

As Jaeger (1998) noted, the emphasis in the routine studies was largely on what the Standards would characterize as content-related evidence of validity and reliability and not, at the time, on other kinds of validity evidence described in the Standards. However, as I suggested in the introduction, the validity chapter in the 1985 Standards does not require a particular kind of validity evidence: "professional judgment should guide the decisions regarding the forms of evidence that are most necessary and feasible in light of the intended uses of the test and any likely alternatives to testing" (AERA, APA, NCME, 1985, p. 9). In fact, the background text for the chapter on "professional and occupation licensure and certification," which was intended to provide specific guidance for such tests in addition to that provided in the general technical standards, acknowledged that "primary reliance must usually be placed on content evidence that is supplemented by evidence of the appropriateness of the construct being measured" (AERA, APA, NCME, 1985, p. 63) and that criterion-related evidence of validity is often unfeasible. (I will have more to say about this under Observation 4.)

More specifically, the standards in the chapter on professional and occupational licensure and certification highlighted the importance of the following types of validity evidence: clearly defining the content domain, "explaining the importance of the content for competent performance" (AERA, APA, NCME, 1985, p. 64), and not requiring abilities that are outside or beyond what is necessary for competent performance. The use of "qualified experts" to help "define the job, identify the knowledge and skills required for competent performance, and determine the appropriate level of complexity at which these knowledge and skills should be assessed" (AERA, APA, NCME, 1985, p. 65) was given as an example of one kind of evidence that complied with the standards. They also highlighted the importance providing estimates of reliability of the certification decision, telling test takers who failed what their score was, as well as the minimum score required to pass, and reporting the procedures used to combine scores to test takers "preferably" before the test was administered (AERA, APA, NCME, 1985, p. 65). Clearly, the National Board's technical reports presented evidence relevant to all of these issues.

With respect to the evidence of reliability presented – which covered sources of error due to assessors and exercise sampling, and presented estimates of decision consistency taking these sources of error into account – there are a couple of questions that might be raised about the estimates of reliability across exercises. First, the authors of the TAR themselves questioned the meaningfulness of reliability estimates that considered error associated with exercise sampling. Elsewhere, ETS researchers Lewis and Pearlman (1997) argued:

> It is important to think about how much credence we want to give traditional measures of generalizability across these entries and exercises. Since we deliberately and by design attempt to sample a multi-dimensional domain by focusing on different parts of the domain with different parts of the assessment, we might have some reason to be concerned if the various parts of the assessment were *too* highly correlated, since that might indicate that we had not succeeded in measuring a different part of the domain, but rather had sampled the same part in a different way. (p. 1)

Here, if the evidence could have been obtained, it might have been useful, to ask candidates to complete an exercise twice, focusing on a different class or unit of instruction. Of course, as the TAR (ETS, 1998) noted, differences in performance across the two exercises could not be interpreted exclusively within a reliability framework. Such a difference encompassed sources of error due to occasion and classroom context, but it was also influenced by factors such as the candidates' learning from past experience. Still it would be informative to know if the score would have been the same if candidates had submitted a response from a different classroom context on a different occasion. Second, while the overall assessment did not provide alternate forms, per se, there did appear to be alternate forms of the assessment center exercises, where the questions remained the same but the materials about which they were asked (articles, samples of student work, etc.) changed. I was surprised to find no study undertaken or planned that would allow direct reliability estimates for these alternative forms. I was also surprised not to see any discussion or estimate of error on the score report sent to candidates (as illustrated in the TAR). Although this was not explicitly required by the 1985 Standards, it is often and appropriately included in score reports.

The use of the phrase "freedom from bias" in the TAR's conclusion, while consistent with the evidence gathered to date, may have been be premature. While studies undertaken have not shown evidence that any observed adverse impact could be attributed to bias in the assessment, they were limited in scope. Furthermore, sample sizes were not large enough to estimate adverse impact for a number of focal groups. In a sense, like questions of validity, freedom from bias is always an open question as new evidence is brought to bear. And, the Board was appropriately and aggressively seeking evidence to inform professional judgment on this issue.

Observation 2

The documentation of the processes through which judges were prepared to select benchmarks and score exercises appeared thorough and replicable across certificates and administrations. It showed evidence of careful attention to illuminating and controlling individual biases of judges and to encouraging representation of a range of teaching practices consistent with the relevant standards.

The documentation provided in the appendices to the TAR and the complete set of materials available from ETS, including scripts for facilitators, provided as thorough and thoughtful a description of the scoring development and training processes as any I have seen. In my judgment, it provided an exemplary model for those engaged in similar approaches to assessment, where criteria and processes for making judgments about complex performance are expected to be standardized across assessors.

Observation 3

With the exception of the studies on bias and adverse impact, the routine studies were primarily confirmatory in nature.

For the most part, the routine studies appear to be designed to confirm that the intentions of the assessment developers were met rather than to challenge the interpretation of scores, as Cronbach and Messick would advise. In some cases, they appeared to yield very little new information. Consider, for instance, the studies providing content-related evidence of validity, where somewhere between 9 and 19 panel members independently matched various parts of the assessment to one another and to the standards. Not surprisingly, there was a strong pattern supporting the content validity of each certificate. This is not surprising because the assessments, were, in fact, carefully designed to relate to the standards. It would be at least as informative if the assessment developers were to provide, for review and audit, the logical analysis that mapped the various parts of the assessment on to one another and back to the standards, illuminating those aspects of the standards that were *not* assessed, as well as those that were.

Similarly, with the study used to confirm the Board's uniform standard of 263 plus 12 for each certificate, it is not surprising that the recommendation was consistent with the predetermined standard. The nine panelists were told before beginning the task that "the '3' level performance (−3 to +3) is the performance that 'meets' the Standards" and, thus, candidates whose scores reflected that level of accomplishment overall warranted certification. While individual panelists proposed somewhat different passing standards and dutifully provided a substantive rationale for their choices, it is hard to imagine how the predesignated passing score could be *dis*confirmed, unless the readers choose to disregard their instructions about a 3-level performance. The TAR indicated that ETS in fact recommended a different study to the Board staff, one that had panels of teachers in the certificate area examine total candidate performances – all portfolio entries and all assessment center exercises – and confirm or disconfirm the accuracy of the passing standard of 263 (ETS, 1998). This was a study that was, in my judgment, far more likely to yield useful information that could productively challenge the assumptions of the assessment developers. [The idea was partially explored by Lewis & Pearlman (1997).]

In Cronbach's (1988) terms, it is useful to ask whether the cost of these studies justifies the information yield. While confirmatory studies do protect the assessment developers from unanticipated anomalies, it is worthwhile considering whether such large panels were needed, given the extremely limited information produced, and what other studies might have been undertaken or enhanced with the additional resources.

One routine activity that might profitably have been enhanced was the validation of the benchmark performances that illustrated different performance levels on each exercise. The assessment developers appropriately described the "crucial role" (ETS, 1998, p. 58) of benchmarks, along with training and qualifying papers, in illustrating the score points and in preparing and calibrating assessors. And yet, as the TAR described it, as few as three teachers might be involved in the selection of a set of benchmarks – two to select and one to validate. If I were setting the priorities, following Cronbach's advice, I would, for instance, put far more resources and involve more teachers in benchmark validation than in the studies whose results were highly predictable. Beyond confirming the appropriateness of the selection, benchmark validation studies might have been designed to raise challenging questions about whether the benchmarks were a source of construct under-representation: Did the performances in the selected benchmarks collectively imply a narrower vision of accomplished teaching than what was reflected in the standards and the scoring rubric? Were some kinds of performances inappropriately privileged over others? (Observation 5 pursues the potential role of benchmarks.)

One routine study that might have offered more of an opportunity to challenge the intended interpretation of scores was the scoring validation study – where panelists rank ordered paired exercise responses that were then compared to the NBPTS scores for those responses. However, the fact that this study used readers who were partially (and only partially) trained in the scoring practices placed it in an ambiguous middle ground – between being simply a confirmatory study with different, cursorily trained, assessors and being a study that might have mounted a challenge to the intended interpretation by encouraging assessors to draw on their own visions of accomplished teaching to evaluate the paired cases. Also, the special study (Gitomer, personal communication; Wylie et al., 2000) that involved classroom observations and interviews with students may have been a fruitful source of challenges to score meaning based on alternative sources of evidence.

The studies of bias, which appeared to be replicated across certificates, were the most significant exception to this generalization about the confirmatory nature of the routine validity work. While the studies that drew on existing information had a number of unavoidable design problems that limited the conclusions that could be drawn, they were at least guided by explicit consideration of rival hypotheses that explored alternative, possibly construct-irrelevant explanations for differences in scores (differences in writing ability, differing ethnicities and experiences of assessor and candidate pairs, differing educational backgrounds among candidates, and so on). In addition, the brief description of the special studies planned to help understand the disparate impact on African-American candidates appear to be guided by respectful consideration of alternative perspectives.

The categories of evidence quoted from Messick (1989a) in the introduction suggested a number of additional sources for challenges to the intended interpretation and use. For instance, studies that might have examined concretely the processes candidates went through as they prepared their portfolios, including the nature of the support they received, would have been fruitful sources of challenges to score meaning. As Cronbach argued, "A performance is not explained until someone identifies the processes that generated it" (Cronbach, 1989, p. 155). Other suggestions for studies that would have raised challenges to the intended meaning and use of scores are described in subsequent sections. It is important to note that the point of such challenges is not to undermine the assessment, but to make it stronger: to the extent that it can survive rigorous attempts to challenge its interpretation and use, validity is greatly enhanced.

Observation 4

None of the routine studies involve evidence about accomplished teaching external to the assessment itself.

Viewed from the lens of the standards, there is no requirement that the Board present empirical evidence external to the assessment itself based on other ways of assessing accomplished performance. However, viewed from the lens of Cronbach's and Messick's work, that is one of the primary means through which rigorous challenges can be mounted and score meaning better understood.

The absence of such evidence is particularly salient in light of Pearlman's acknowledgment that these assessments represented only one possible interpretation of the standards: "The assessment design must choose from among all of these qualities and characteristics [reflected in the relevant content standards] ... not only because the candidates have a day job, but also because we cannot follow through on our part of the transaction and equitably evaluate the candidates' work if we do not set some limits. So the topography of the assessment represents an interpretation of the Standards document, rather than a reflection of it" (Pearlman, Chapter 7, this volume). But, if these assessment choices represent one possible instantiation of the standards, what are some other possibilities? What might the assessment look like under those conditions? Would the interpretation of candidates' capabilities differ or the decision regarding accomplishment differ? If yes, how and why? Would different candidates be considered accomplished under different instantiations? These are all important questions to answer and they require evidence that is external to the assessment itself.

While this kind of evidence has been often unfeasible in testing for licensure and certification, because candidates who fail are not permitted to practice, that is not the case with National Board certification. Candidates are all experienced teachers who continue to practice, regardless of whether they become certified teachers or not. Reviews of available validity guidance and/or of typical validity practices in assessment of teaching (e.g., Haertel, 1991; Madaus, 1990; Mehrens, 1990; Porter, Youngs, & Odden, 2001) endorsed the value of evidence external to the test. Haertel (1991) and Madaus (1990) both raised serious concerns about the over-reliance on content-related evidence of validity that, they argued, the courts have promoted. As Haertel (1991) noted, "once a validation has survived legal scrutiny, it is likely to be copied elsewhere" (p. 22). And Madaus (1990) argued "it's my contention that the precondition of 'legal defensibility' drives applied validation efforts to the detriment of a careful consideration of the evidence needed to sustain the inferences and decisions made from test scores" (p. 226). "A single line of evidence based exclusively on opinions is, I submit, insufficient to sustain the types of inferences just described" (Madaus, 1990, p. 243). Haertel (1991) continued:

> The fact that present teacher tests have survived legal challenge despite the virtual absence of criterion-related validity evidence by no means obviates the requirement for a responsible validation of new assessments. The difficulty in criterion-related validation, of course, is to formulate reliable and valid criterion measures. (p. 24)

It could be argued that there is no criterion – no better understood or accepted measure of teaching accomplishment – against which scores on the National Board assessments can be compared. However, it is important to remember the point of looking at external evidence is not so much approximating the quixotic ideal of a criterion, but rather of comparing different ways of looking at the same phenomena and trying to understand and explain the differences observed. If two measures are consistent in identifying accomplished teachers, then both are strengthened; if they differ, then understanding the reason for the difference provides an important and illuminating empirical puzzle to solve.

Of the special studies I obtained that were completed, only the classroom observation study by Hattie et al. (1995) addressed this issue. However, flaws in the design that the authors noted – for instance, that the researchers knew the scores of candidates and that some of the evidence on which they based their judgment was taken from the portfolio itself – raise questions about the interpretability of these results. The study undertaken by ETS (Gitomer, personal communication), that involved classroom observations and interviews with students, may provide a promising source of evidence external to the assessment. Similarly, Bond's (1998) planned Study 4, which identifies outstanding African-American teachers through other means and then asks them to sit for the Board's assessment appears promising as well.

Observation 5

The routine studies provided no evidence that concrete examples of teaching practice, evaluated by the assessment developers, had also been reviewed by outside professionals not carefully prepared to apply the Board's perspective on accomplished teaching.

While the standards themselves had been widely reviewed, there was no evidence in the materials I obtained of the review of concrete examples of practice by outside professionals except in the set of special studies undertaken with African-American ELA candidates. By concrete examples, I mean benchmarks, specific descriptions of individual cases, or any other illustration of actual teaching practices. The language of the standards and of the scoring rubrics on which they were based was intentionally general so as to encompass a wide and unspecified range of teaching perspectives and practices. As Jaeger (1997, 1998), ETS (1998), and Pearlman (Chapter 7, this volume) all pointed out, the meaning of the scores for a given exercise depended upon the careful selection of benchmarks. "Benchmarks 'anchor' the score scale and rubric for the assessors – the language of the rubric is made 'real' and pegged to a level of accomplishment through concrete examples" (ETS, 1998, p. 58). And, benchmarks, along with the training and qualifying papers, played an important role in helping the assessors develop their understanding of accomplished teaching. As I suggested above, considering the relationship between these concrete examples and the more abstract descriptions contained in the rubrics raises important validity questions, for instance, about construct under-representation – that the meaning of scores implicit in these collected illustrations may be narrower than the consensus underlying the standards would support.

To understand the importance of benchmarks and other concrete examples to the validity of the judgments of accomplished teaching and the seriousness of my concern about them not being reviewed outside the circle of assessment developers, consider, for instance, the description of the 4 level performance from the rubric for the EA/ELA writing assessment (quoted in the TAR, ETS, 1998).

The 4 level performance offers clear, consistent, and convincing evidence that the teacher is able to use **thoughtful analysis and assessment of students' writing** to support students' growth as writers.

The 4 level response shows clear, consistent, and convincing evidence of the teacher's **thorough knowledge of individual students as writers** through the descriptions of their backgrounds and skills and through **thoughtful analyses of student texts to understand their growth and development as writers**. There is clear, convincing, and consistent evidence that the teacher sets **attainable and worthwhile goals for student learning** and makes instructional decisions that enable student writers to achieve those goals. The 4 level response provides clear, consistent, and convincing evidence that the teacher understands the complex, recursive, individual nature of the writing process and provides a context for writing that encourages students' active exploration of their own writing process. The teacher responds to student writing thoughtfully, recognizes student progress, and offers ways for students to build on that progress. There is clear, consistent, and convincing evidence that the teacher employs varied, rich and appropriate instructional resources to support students' growth as writers. The 4 level response offers clear, consistent, and convincing evidence that the teacher **uses appropriate assessments methods** (formal and/or informal) on an ongoing basis to monitor student progress encourage student self-assessment, and plan future instruction. There is effective communication with students about their work. There is clear, consistent, and convincing evidence of the teacher's ability to accurately describe his/her practice and reflect on its appropriateness and effectiveness in meeting the challenges of teaching writing to these students (ETS, 1998, p. 46).

In understanding and applying this rubric, it is crucial to ask: What constitutes "thorough knowledge of individual students as writers," "thoughtful analyses of student texts," "attainable and worthwhile goals for student learning," "appropriate assessment methods," and so on? How will we know these practices when we see them? What kinds of performances are included and excluded from these descriptions? To continue with this example, if one were to compare the 3 level rubric to the 4 level rubric (as quoted in the TAR, ETS, 1998), one would find the relatively small differences in wording: (a) "clear, consistent, and convincing evidence" is always changed to "clear evidence", (b) the words/phrases "thorough," and "thoughtful" and "encourage self assessment" are dropped, and (c) a number of qualifying phrases are added such as "may not be as deeply articulated," "may not be as insightful," or "may show imbalance in the analysis." Again, it is important to ground the meaning of these subtle additions and deletions in concrete examples of the practices that are deemed less insightful, less clear and convincing, and so on.

My point is not to criticize the rubrics per se – clearly the scoring process has worked well in that readers completed their work efficiently, consistently agreed on scores, and wrote notes that were independently judged to be consistent with the rubric. My point is to show how crucial the benchmarks are to understanding what is meant by these descriptions and to addressing questions of construct under-representation. If all that is made available to external reviewers are the standards, tasks, and rubrics themselves, then they have insufficient evidence to evaluate the meaningfulness of the scores as an instantiation of the content standards.

I went looking elsewhere for concrete examples of practice to help me understand the meaning of a rubric and how it was applied. I read over examples of the portfolio handbooks. I turned to the examples that had of the standards themselves and of the feedback booklets that were given to candidates to help them in interpreting their scores. In none of these documents could I find descriptions of individual cases of teaching practice. Only two of the special studies I reviewed provided such descriptions: one in presenting results of classroom observations and interviews (Hattie et al., 1995) and the other in providing alternative sets of feedback materials for candidates to review (Davis et al., 1995; Davis, Wolf, & Borko, Chapter 14, this volume). I asked my contacts at the Board and ETS if any such documents existed. Pearlman (personal communication) told me that the only thing ever made available that was close was the 'case book' that comprised the feedback materials sent to ELA candidates in 1994 and 1995. She explained that this model of feedback was not pursued because "candidates indicated [in informal surveys] that it was no more helpful to them ... than the earlier, far less complicated feedback" and because is was "labor intensive."

There is, of course, no question that such examples existed and were used in assessor training. Moreover, the careful description of the process through which they were selected suggests that, to the extent possible, they represented different teaching contexts and approaches to teaching. However, as I noted above, benchmarks might have been carefully reviewed by as few as three people before they were used to train and certify assessors. And, in the routine studies, there does not appear to have been much opportunity for the National Board to benefit from having experienced teachers, outside the circle of those carefully trained to apply the Board's perspective, knowledgeably challenge the meaning of scores. [In the conclusion, I will have more to say about the implication of this observation for the Board's long-range goal of "communicat[ing] what accomplished teaching looks like" (www.nbpts.org).]

Observation 6

None of the routine studies involved integrative judgments based on comprehensive reviews of complete cases containing all the evidence provided by candidates.

Nowhere in the routine studies did anyone comprehensively consider the entire body of evidence about a candidate – reading across the 10 exercises that comprised the portfolio and the assessment center responses – to reach a judgment about that candidate's accomplishments. Rather, all of the decisions that were made about scoring, about standard setting, and about the meaningfulness of overall scores were based upon judgments of individual exercises, scoring rubrics, and/or profiles of scores across exercises.

In raising this concern, as I have elsewhere (Moss, 1994, 1996), I am not suggesting that the Board should have moved to an integrative approach to scoring that examined entire cases. That would have required substantially more training time for assessors and reduced the number of assessors who responded to a candidate's work. I was suggesting however, that it would have been extremely useful to compare evaluations that involved integrative judgments of entire cases with those based on individual exercises and profiles of scores. If the two approaches agreed, then the validity of each is strengthened; if they led to different evaluations, then it would have been crucial to understand the reason for the difference and to consider its implications for assessment design.

This observation relates as well to questions about the meaningfulness of the tasks in which teachers were asked to engage during the assessment development process. For instance, in informal observations of the existing approaches to standard setting developed by TAG, ETS researchers Lewis and Pearlman (1997) observed that there was considerable difficulty in translating profiles of scores on individual entries and exercises into a real picture of a candidate's performance among the teachers who served as standard setting panelists. Echoing an earlier argument raised by Delandshere and Petrosky (1994), they argued that the numbers that resulted from scoring were not the most critical data to consider for standard setting and noted that any other teacher's assessment might have given panelists a different conception of that teacher's accomplishment in light of the standards on which the assessment and its evaluation were based. These informal observations suggest the importance of two kinds of empirical evidence to the validity research agenda: (a) systematically documenting the actual processes in which standard setters, benchmarkers, and assessors engaged and the understandings they brought to bear as they completed their tasks, and (b) comparing alternative means of enabling teachers to make thoughtful judgments.

In its recommendation to the Board regarding standard setting, ETS proposed such a study which would have "panels of teachers in the certificate area examine total candidate performances – all portfolio entries and all assessment center exercises – and confirm or disconfirm the accuracy of the passing standard of 263." (ETS, 1998, p. 90). The small feasibility study undertaken by Lewis and Pearlman (1997) moved in this direction by asking standard setters to consider responses to multiple exercises, although it allowed them to stop short of reviewing the entire corpus of evidence. The only place where such comprehensive reviews had been planned and begun, to my knowledge, were the studies that looked across the portfolios of African-American candidates as part of the research agenda into disparate impact.

Such integrative studies might have been profitably and routinely undertaken by insiders, as ETS suggested for its standard setting work, or by outside professionals who might draw on their own criteria. In another project with which I was involved, which focused on assessment of beginning teachers (Interstate New Teacher Assessment and Support Consortium, INTASC, 1996; Moss, Schutz, & Collins, 1998), we were actively seeking outside readers who represented different perspectives within the relevant discipline and we sent them entire cases for independent review. We asked them to draw on whatever criteria they considered relevant in evaluating the cases. Our purposes were to illuminate potential problems in the benchmarks we selected (in our case, entire portfolios, since the scoring process was itself integrative) and potential biases in the standards themselves. As I argued above, the perspective of outsiders, not socialized into the National Board's standards, could go a long way towards illuminating differences in perspective that the general language of the standards glosses over, so that they could become available for professional debate.

CONCLUSION

The National Board's work in assessment development in the first decade of its operation represented an impressive accomplishment. It served as proof that complex portfolio and performance-based assessments could be mounted on a large scale and could meet professional standards of technical quality. All of us who care about such assessments have much to learn from their example. While some of my observations raise what I hope are productive critical questions about the Board's initial validity research, none of these criticisms should be taken to undermine the soundness of validity judgments when viewed from the perspective of the 1985 Testing Standards (AERA, APA, NCME, 1985). Viewed, however, from the perspective of Cronbach's "strong" program of validity research, from Messick's Singerian approach to inquiry, or perhaps from the National Board's own standards of professionally acceptable and publicly credible assessments (Pearlman, Chapter 3, this volume), there are, I believe, productive questions to raise and pursue – both about enhancing the understanding of the meaning of scores and furthering the Board's mission of improving learning by improving teaching.

There are two overlapping but distinct concerns to address in this conclusion. One concern is about what was available, privately, to the assessment developers, and the other professionals charged with reviewing their work that might challenge and elaborate the interpretation of accomplished teaching. The other concern is about what was available, more broadly, to enable widespread professional review, dialogue, and learning. There is ultimately a third concern that overshadows the other two: what was available to challenge, elaborate, or revise, as needed, the consensus reflected in the content standards themselves? How do these standards remain vital in light of evolving perspectives on accomplished teaching?

The validity argument for National Board certification was based primarily on the extent to which the assessments were consistent with the definition of accomplished teaching in the National Board's principles and the associated content standards, the extent to which the assessments could be reliably scored, and the extent to which they were free from bias. What we had publicly made available was evidence that a professionally sanctioned process (of development and confirmation) was followed that allowed us to conclude that the assessments represent *an* instantiation of the content standards. What we did not know, publicly at least, was what range of practices were included and excluded from the definition of accomplished teaching and what the meanings of scores implicit in those decisions were. What kinds of performances were considered "appropriate," "thoughtful," and "insightful" and which were not? What kinds of evidence were considered "clear, consistent, and convincing" and which were not? Of course, the assessment developers had made available the multiple examples of practice at the exercise level in the benchmarks, the training papers, and the qualifying papers, which allowed assessors to concretize and reliably apply the more abstract standards reflected in the rubric. However, in the studies routinely carried out for each certificate, there was little evidence that the assessment developers challenged these interpretations, either by encouraging independent reviews of candidates' responses by outside professionals not socialized into the Board's vision, by comparing alternative means of evaluating the existing evidence, or by comparing alternative sources of evidence about candidates for certification. And so, there was little opportunity here – either through studies controlled by the assessment developers or through public review – to knowledgeably challenge the meaning of scores as distinguishing accomplished teachers. Gitomer et al.'s in progress class-room observation study (which was later published as Wylie et al., 2000, per Waayer, personal communication) classroom observation study with EA/G candidates, Lewis and Pearlman's (1997) exploration of the feasibility of a more integrative approach to standard setting, and Bond's (1998) diverse panel's critical review of performances by EA/ELA African-American and White candidates represented important and promising steps in this direction. But these studies were not part of the routine research agenda and hence, peripheral to the validity argument associated with a given certificate. These were the kinds of studies that could productively have challenged the interpretation and use of scores and that should have, in my judgment, been routinely implemented.

The National Board states that its goal is "to improve student learning by strengthening teaching" (www.nbpts.org) and that, in service of that goal, it "reliably identifies teachers who meet high and rigorous standards and communicates what accomplished teaching looks like." The complex problem that the Board faces in furthering this goal is highlighted in the juxtaposition of the following two statements from one of its senior assessment developers, which calls for reliable scores to represent a field that is nevertheless marked by diversity of perspectives. "Clearly, a certification assessment program that cannot operationalize a reliable means to making the classification decision for which the assessment was supposedly designed cannot hope to reform teaching in the United States from within" (Pearlman, 1998, unpublished earlier draft of chapter 7, p. 9). "When the domain of assessment is loosely structured and dynamic, like teaching, and further obscured by an absence of agreement – or even a common vocabulary – among teaching professionals about the basic structure or taxonomy of the domain and what constitutes evidence of accomplishment in it, these questions [about validity] become very difficult indeed to answer" (Pearlman, Chapter 3, this volume, p. 69).

While it is possible to achieve adequately reliable scores under the conditions described in Pearlman's second quote, this was accomplished partly by acknowledging, as any assessment developer must, that the assessment represents *an* interpretation of the Standards document (Pearlman, this volume, Chapter 3) and then by pursuing a path that privileges some perspectives over others. It is the role of a strong program of validity research to understand what the consequences are of developing *this* instantiation of the standards rather than some other. Beyond that, however, it is fair to ask what is the nature and authority of the consensus that underlies these scores when the field they represent is as loosely structured, dynamic, and heterogeneous as Pearlman describes. While the dialogue surrounding the development of the core principles and content standards has moved the field forward to an articulated and widely reviewed consensus statement, this statement is (necessarily) general – to encompass a wide range of teaching practices – as are the scoring rubrics that represent it. And, even though agreement can be reached at this relatively abstract level, the decisions about accomplishment were applied to individual cases of teachers who were either included or (at least temporarily) excluded from the designated community of accomplished teachers. The abstract descriptions contained in the standards and the scoring rubric may, in fact, have glossed over real differences of perspective among developers and reviewers that only concrete examples could illuminate. And so, it seems crucial to both of the Board's goals – fairly identifying accomplished teachers and illustrating accomplished teaching – to encourage a dialogue that addresses the application of the standards to concrete examples.[4,5]

There is another set of questions that might be raised in light of the Board's commitment to grounding its vision of accomplished teaching in the judgment of experienced teachers and to illustrating what accomplished teaching looks like. While it is true that panels of teachers were involved at all the important junctures of the assessment, the scope of their involvement is limited by the specific task the assessment developers set for them – rating standards, matching rubrics and exercises to standards, reviewing performances at the exercise level, reviewing profiles of scores, and so on. Given the National Board's valuing of assessments that are "professionally acceptable" and "publicly credible," it seems crucial that the judgments are made in a way that is most meaningful to the teachers who are charged with making them. If it were widely known that nowhere in the routine assessment development process, including the process of standard setting, was anyone asked to examine the entire body of evidence from a candidate, or that concrete cases of practice were not routinely available for review outside the small community of assessment developers, how many teachers would (or should) find that credible – except perhaps in the ersatz sense that if the best psychometricians in the country say it is credible, then it must be credible?

The point of this admittedly harsh and provocative question is to highlight some of the practices that we, as measurement professionals, may take for granted about the way things are done, and to provide an opportunity for explicit critical reflection about them. There is, of course, no question that the National Board is deeply committed to involving teachers in its assessment development work and in privileging their judgments about accomplished teaching. The question I am raising – which was an unanswered empirical question as I wrote – is whether the means through which these judgments are elicited are as meaningful to those involved as other, perhaps more integrative and contextualized, approaches might be. There is much to be gained from a collaborative dialogue across professional boundaries to which all participants contribute coequally – a dialogue in which all partners try to understand the perspectives of the others framed *in their own terms* (through the particular habits of mind and practice that ground the professional community's work) and are willing to risk their own preconceptions about what things mean and how things should be done (Gadamer, 1997). This is precisely the point of Messick's Singerian approach to inquiry: "the recognition and systematic application of multiple perspectives is beneficial in a variety of ways, because it tends to broaden the range of values, criteria, and standards deemed worthy of consideration" (Messick, 1989b, p. 88).

There are risks involved in pursuing the path I have suggested – of challenging the intended interpretation of scores and making the meaning of the standards explicit through publicly available concrete examples. It is possible that the availability of this kind of evidence would give the Board's more polemical opponents an advantage, and would thereby undermine the Board's considerable political resources to use its assessments to further its goals. However, as Cronbach (1988) argued, "concentrating on plausible rival hypotheses is especially important in validation because persons unfriendly to a test interpretation are likely to use a rival hypothesis as ammunition. Proponents' prior checks on the rival hypothesis provide a potent defensive weapon – or warn them to pick a line of retreat" (Cronbach, 1988, p. 14). In addition, I would argue that the availability of this kind of evidence would greatly enhance the quality of discourse about teaching.

Even if it were shown that there was more dissensus about accomplished teaching than the abstract standards and the reliably obtained scores indicate, the professional dialogue around examples of concrete practice – and the opportunity it provides for individuals to rethink and revise their own practice in light of alternatives – would be another powerful means through which the Board can accomplish its goals of improving teaching and learning (perhaps more powerful than the means of reliably identifying accomplished teachers). [See Moss and Schutz (1999) for an extended argument.]

There is a tremendous opportunity here that has been only partially realized. If the National Board wanted to push the field forward in terms of encouraging practices consistent with its vision of accomplished teaching, then the most powerful means of accomplishing that is to get teachers to talk with one another about concrete examples of practice in light of the Board's working standards. This happened informally as candidates collaborated with their colleagues in preparing their portfolios and more formally as panels of teachers were brought in to look at small samples of candidates' work as they participated in whatever specific aspect of the assessment they were hired to address. I understand from the Board staff I talk to that these were wonderful professional development experiences for the teachers involved. What the National Board had not yet accomplished (as of 1998), through its assessment development efforts, at least, was the promotion of a more public dialogue about its standards and the practices to which they pointed. It is the dialogues around these concrete illustrations of practice from which prospective candidates might learn, as assessors do, what the Board means by accomplished teaching and through which the community of teachers, teacher educators, and others concerned with education can critically review the meaning, limitations, and possibilities of practice consistent with the standards.

It could well be that the outcome of such dialogues involves a rethinking of the criteria and values of the NBPTS standards themselves. Evolving (and revolving) perspectives on curriculum and pedagogy over the past few decades and current debates among thoughtful proponents of alternative perspectives make it clear that there is no absolute ideal on what constitutes sound teaching that can be more and more closely approximated by better and better assessment practices. There are only contexts, more or less encompassing, that allow values and the theories and practices in which they are implied to coalesce for a given time. The standards will need to be regularly reconsidered in light of new perspectives and supporting evidence about what constitutes sound teaching practice. A vital assessment system, it seems, is one that accepts this circumstance and orients itself to reflect critically on its experience. We may never reach a full national consensus about the features of accomplished teaching – in fact such an ideal has its own risks, not the least of which is the absence of diverse perspectives to challenge the favored perspective so that its proponents remain critically reflexive – but at least it will enable us to better understand our differences. And, in working to understand our differences, proponents of different perspectives come to a better, more critical, understanding of their own practice, so that it can evolve in productive ways.

NOTES

1. For decision consistency based on exercise sampling, the probability of a false negative ranges from 5% to 7% across the six certificates administered in 1996–1997; and the probability of a false positive ranges from 6% to 9%. For decision consistency based on assessor reliability, the probability of a false negative ranges from 2% to 4% across the four certificates using large sample scoring; and the probability of a false positive ranges from 2% to 5%.

2. The following description is based on Jaeger (1997), the "Conclusions on the Technical Measurement Quality" reports prepared by the TAG for the 1995–1996 administrations of the assessment, with additional details from Baker et al. (1996), a detailed report on the process for the MC/G assessment, and the historical overview of standard setting provided in the TAR (ETS, 1998).

3. Pearlman (personal communication) reports that informal feedback from candidates who had received this kind of labor-intensive feedback on the earliest

administrations of the EA/ELA (when such a feedback booklet was tried out) certificate "indicated that it was no more helpful to them than the earlier, far less complete feedback had been".

4. I recognize that there are ethical problems associated with releasing examples of poor performance. While the full range of performances might be reviewed in controlled studies, diverse examples of *accomplished* practices could certainly be made publicly available.

5. Examining the specific issues discussed by panels developing standards as they try to achieve a consensus statement is a fruitful source of rival hypotheses to consider as part of the validity research agenda. See Moss and Schutz (1999) for a critical analysis of a moment of standards development in a different context.

REFERENCES

American Educational Research Association, American Psychological Association, and the National Council on Measurement in Education (1985). *Standards for educational and psychological testing.* Washington, DC: American Psychological Association.

Baker, W., Huff, K., Price, M., McKenzie, C., & Jaeger, R. (1996). *An analysis of the degree of adverse impact in the national board for professional teaching standards' 1994–95 early childhood generalist assessment.* Greensboro, NC: National Board for Professional Teaching Standards, Technical Analysis Group, Center for Educational Research and Evaluation, University of North Carolina-Greensboro.

Benson, J., & Impara, J. (1996). *Content validation of the national board for professional teaching standards' early adolescence through young adult art assessment-field test version.* Greensboro, NC: National Board for Professional Teaching Standards, Technical Analysis Group, Center for Educational Research and Evaluation, University of North Carolina-Greensboro.

Bond, L. (1997). Adverse impact and teacher certification. Paper presented at the annual meeting of the American Educational Research Association, Chicago, IL.

Bond, L. (1998). Disparate impact and teacher certification. *Journal of Personnel Evaluation, 12*(2), 211–220.

Cronbach, L. J. (1988). Five perspectives on validity argument. In: H. Wainer & H. I. Braun (Eds), *Test validity* (pp. 3–17). Hillsdale, NJ: Lawrence Erlbaum Associates.

Cronbach, L. J. (1989). Construct validation after thirty years. In: R. L. Linn (Ed.), *Intelligence: Measurement, theory, and public policy. Proceedings of a symposium in honor of Lloyd G. Humphreys* (pp. 147–171). Chicago: University of Illinois Press.

Davis, A., Wolf, K., & Borko, H. (1999). Examinees' perceptions of feedback in applied performance testing: The case of the National Board for Professional Teaching Standards. *Educational Assessment, 6*(2), 97–128.

Davis, A., Wolf, K., Borko, H., Arenson, J., Davinroy, K., & LaRussa, A. (1995). *A study on feedback to candidates for certification with the national board for professional teaching standards.* Greensboro, NC: National Board for Professional Teaching Standards, Technical Analysis Group, Center for Educational Research and Evaluation, University of North Carolina-Greensboro.

Delandshere, G., & Petrosky, A. R. (1994). Capturing teachers' knowledge. *Educational Researcher, 23*(5), 11–18.

Educational Testing Service (ETS). (1998). *NBPTS technical analysis report, 1996–97 administration.* Southfield, MI: NBPTS.

Equal Employment Opportunity Coordinating Council. (1978). Uniform guidelines on employee selection procedures. *Federal Register, 43*(166), 38290–38315.

Gadamer, H.-G. (1997). Reflections on my philosophical journey. In: L. E. Hahn (Ed.), *The philosophy of Hans-Georg Gadamer* (pp. 3–63). Chicago: Open Court.

Haertel, E. H. (1991). New forms of teacher assessment. *Review of Research in Education, 17,* 3–29.

Hattie, J., Clinton, J., Thompson, M., & Schmidt-Davis, H. (1995). *Identifying "Highly Accomplished Teachers": A validation study.* Greensboro, NC: National Board for Professional Teaching Standards, Technical Analysis Group, Center for Educational Research and Evaluation, University of North Carolina-Greensboro.

Interstate New Teacher Assessment and Support Consortium. (1996). *The INTASC performance assessment development project.* Washington, DC: Council of Chief State School Officers.

Jaeger, R. M. (1997). Evaluating the psychometric qualities of the National Board for Professional Teacher Standards' assessments: A history of five years of research and development. A paper presented at a conference on Assessing Teachers' Knowledge and Skills, and Implications for Incentives and Compensation, Wisconsin Centre for Educational Research, University of Wisconsin, Madison.

Jaeger, R. M. (1998). Evaluating the psychometric qualities of the National Board for Professional Teaching Standards' assessments: A methodological accounting. *Journal of Personnel Evaluation in Education, 12,* 189–210.

Jaeger, R., & Thompson, M. (1994). Evaluation of the National Board for Professional Teaching standards 1993–94 field test of the Early Adolescence Generalist And Early Adolescence English/Language Arts Assessments – A summary of responses of candidates for National Board certification to questions posed during face-to-face interviews, focus group discussions, and hour-long evaluative writing tasks. Greensboro, NC: National Board for Professional Teaching Standards, Technical Analysis Group, Center for Educational Research and Evaluation, University of North Carolina-Greensboro.

Lewis, C., & Pearlman, M. (1997). An experiment in standard setting. Paper presented at the annual meeting of the American Educational Research Association, Chicago, IL.

Madaus, G. F. (1990). Legal and professional issues in teacher certification testing: A psychometric snark hunt. In: J. V. Mitchell, Jr., S. L. Wise & B. S. Plake (Eds), *Assessment of teaching* (pp. 209–261). Hillsdale, NJ: Lawrence Erlbaum Associates.

Mehrens, W. (1990). Combining evaluation data from multiple sources. In: J. Millman & L. Darling-Hammond (Eds), *The new handbook of teacher evaluation: Assessing elementary and secondary school teachers* (pp. 322–334). Newbury Park, CA: Sage.

Messick, S. (1989a). Meaning and values in test validation: The science and ethics of assessment. *Educational Researcher, 18*(2), 5–11.

Messick, S. (1989b). Validity. In: R. L. Linn (Ed.), *Educational measurement* (3rd edn., pp. 13–103). Washington, DC: The American Council on Education and the National Council on Measurement in Education.

Messick, S. (1994). The interplay of evidence and consequences in the validation of performance assessments. *Educational Researcher, 23*(2), 13–23.

Messick, S. (1996). Validity in performance assessments. In: G. W. Phillips (Ed.), *Technical issues in large-scale performance assessment* (pp. 1–18). Washington DC: National Center for Education Statistics (NCES 96–802).

Moss, P. A. (1994). Can there be validity without reliability? *Educational Researcher, 23*(2), 5–12.

Moss, P. A. (1996). Enlarging the dialogue in educational measurement: Voices from interpretive research traditions. *Educational Researcher, 25*(1), 20–2843.

Moss, P. A., & Schutz, A. (1999). Risking frankness in educational assessment. *Phi Delta Kappan, 80*(9), 680–687.

Moss, P. A., Schutz, A. M., & Collins, K. M. (1998). An integrative approach to portfolio evaluation for teacher licensure. *Journal of Personnel Evaluation in Education, 12*(2), 139–161.

Noble, A. J., Chavez, S., & Haag, S. (1994). *National Board for Professional Teaching Standards Teacher Candidates' Evaluation of the 1993–94 Field Tests.* (Technical report #94–0005). Southwest Educational Policy Studies, Arizona.

Porter, A. C., Youngs, P., & Odden, A. (2001). Advances in teacher assessment and their uses. In: V. Richardson (Ed.), *Handbook of research on teaching* (4th edn., pp. 259–297). Washington, DC: American Educational Research Association.

Shepard, L. A. (1993). Evaluating test validity. *Review of Research in Education, 19*, 405–450.

Traub, R., & Jaeger, R. (1995). *Estimates of the reliability of the National Board for Professional Teaching Standards' Early Adolescence Generalist Assessment, based on data from the 1993–94 field test of the assessment.* Greensboro, NC: National Board for Professional Teaching Standards, Technical Analysis Group, Center for Educational Research and Evaluation, University of North Carolina-Greensboro.

Wolfe, E. W., & Gitomer, D. H. (2001). The influence of changes in assessment design on the psychometric quality of scores. *Applied Measurement in Education, 14*(1), 91–107.

Wylie, E. C., Thompson, M., Sigel, I. E., & Gitomer, D. H. (2000). The relationship of teaching, student learning, and NBPTS certification status. Paper presented at the annual meeting of the American Educational Research Association, New Orleans, LA.

CHAPTER 11

IDENTIFYING ACCOMPLISHED TEACHERS: A VALIDATION STUDY

John Hattie and Janet Clinton

ABSTRACT

This chapter aims to present a methodology to address the construct validity of the NBPTS standards, exercises, and decisions to identify accomplished teachers, by asking whether National Board Certified Teachers (NBCTs) teach differently in their classrooms such that they have a greater positive and worthwhile impact on their students. The critical attributes of expert teachers are identified via a synthesis of meta-analyses and a more traditional review of the literature on expert teachers. These attributes of expert teachers then form the basis of the study to identify the characteristics that discriminate between NBCTs and non-NBCTs.

INTRODUCTION

The ultimate question as to the construct validity of the National Board of Professional Teaching Standards (NBPTS) standards, exercises, and decisions to identify accomplished teachers relates to whether National

Assessing Teachers for Professional Certification:
The First Decade of the National Board for Professional Teaching Standards
Advances in Program Evaluation, Volume 11, 313–344
Copyright © 2008 by Elsevier Ltd.
ISSN: 1474-7863/doi:10.1016/S1474-7863(07)11011-5

Board Certified Teachers (NBCTs) teach differently in their classrooms such that they have a greater positive and worthwhile impact on their students. The aim of this chapter is to present a methodology to address this question and to outline results from a preliminary investigation into the practices and effects of NBCTs compared with those teachers who participated in the assessments but did not attain NBCT status. Evidence was sought that those whose performances warranted National Board certification, typically exhibited teaching practices that were consistent with established models and theories of effective teaching and had higher quality of work produced by their students on classroom assignments.

The research on established models and theories of effective teaching will be addressed in two ways. First, the research on what works in the classroom via a synthesis of meta-analyses assists to identify the major influences on student learning, and it is expected that NBCTs are more likely to use or foster these influences. Second, a more traditional review of the literature on expert teachers, and on expertise in other domains, can identify the salient features that distinguish experts from their colleagues. From these two review methods we identify the attributes of expert teachers that form the basis of our study to identify the characteristics that discriminate between NBCTs and non-NBCTs.

A SYNTHESIS OF META-ANALYSES

We have conducted a series of studies to identify the salient effects on student learning and attitudes (both for regular and special students). These studies commenced by asking, "What is the typical effect of schooling?" and in light of the answer to this question, "What are the salient features of schooling that affect student outcomes?" (Hattie, 1987, 1992a, 1992b, 1993a, 1993b; Hattie & Jaeger, 1998). Briefly, a unidimensional continuum can be devised on which the various effects of schooling can be placed. This continuum, calibrated in effect-sizes or standard deviation units, provides the measurement basis to address the question of the effects of schooling. It is possible to statistically synthesize the results of a large number of studies, ascertain the typical effects of schooling, and identify the innovations or changes that improve achievement in a systematically positive manner. Altogether, over 30,000 effects derived from 303 meta-analyses based on 165,258 studies were computed, representing approximately 20–30 million students, and covering almost all methods of innovation.

The typical effect on student achievement, across these many studies is 0.40 (Table 1). Most innovations that are introduced in schools improved achievement by about 0.4 of a standard deviation. This is the benchmark figure and provides a "standard" from which to judge effects, and it is a comparison based on typical, real-world effects rather than based on the strongest cause possible, or with the weakest cause imaginable. At minimum, this continuum provides a method for measuring the most salient effects of schooling.

The most obvious and critical finding from this synthesis is that the most salient features related to student learning (other than what the student brings to the classroom) are in the control of the teacher. Of course, not every teacher-related innovation makes a difference, but it is those innovations that are teacher-related that are most likely to influence student learning. There are three major attributes of expert teachers identified from this synthesis:

a. *Feedback.* Expert teachers use much feedback to enhance student learning.
b. *Challenge.* Expert teachers involve students in challenging tasks – challenging relative to the students' present achievement.
c. *Management.* Expert teachers efficiently manage and structure classroom activities to allow an increased probability of feedback occurring, and engage all students in challenging tasks (that is, they do not merely implement the structures that allow this, such as introduce peer tutoring, but they introduce peer tutoring to maximize challenge and feedback).

A Synthesis of Literature Relating to Expert Teachers

In the field of education "expertise" has been extensively explored, and it is clear that expert teachers differ from other teachers in qualitative ways, typically in their meta-cognitive processing. We have much to learn from the expert-novice contrast, but this learning is more informative to the *development* of expertise, and not as informative for *identifying* expert teachers. The more appropriate contrast, and contrast of interest in the present study, is between the *experienced expert* and the *experienced non-expert* teachers.

Two procedures were used to identify the prototypic attributes of experienced expert teachers. First, an analysis of the literature across various domains of expert teachers, such as mathematics (Leinhardt, 1989; Ropo, 1987), physics (Chi, Feltovich, & Glaser, 1981), social science

Table 1. Summary of Relationships of Various Innovations to
Achievement.

Domain	Variable	No. of Studies	Effect-Size
School		**5171**	**0.25**
	Physical attributes	1850	−0.05
	Finances	658	0.12
	Aims and policy	542	0.24
	Parent involvement	339	0.46
	Class environment	921	0.56
	Retention	861	−0.15
Social		**1124**	**0.39**
	Mass media	274	−0.12
	Peer	122	0.38
	Home	728	0.67
Instructor		**5009**	**0.44**
	Style	1075	0.42
	In-service education	3912	0.49
	Background	22	0.60
Instruction		**5770**	**0.47**
	Quantity	80	0.84
	Quality	22	1.00
	Methods within various subjects	5668	0.36
Pupil		**3776**	**0.47**
Physical		**1344**	**0.21**
	Affective	355	0.24
	Disposition to learn	93	0.61
	Cognitive	896	1.04
Methods of instruction		**21382**	**0.29**
	Team teaching	41	0.06
	Individualization	630	0.14
	Audio-visual aids	6060	0.16
	Programmed instruction	220	0.18
	Ability grouping	3385	0.18
	Learning hierarchies	24	0.19
	Calculators	231	0.24
	Instructional media	4421	0.30
	Testing	1817	0.30
	Computer-assisted instruction	566	0.31
	Simulation and games	111	0.34
	Questioning	134	0.41
	Homework	110	0.43
	Tutoring	125	0.50
	Mastery learning	104	0.50
	Bilingual programs	285	0.51
	Goals	2703	0.52

Table 1. (*Continued*)

Domain	Variable	No. of Studies	Effect-Size
	Acceleration	162	0.72
	Direct instruction	253	0.82
Learning strategies		**783**	**0.61**
	Behavioral objectives	111	0.12
	Advance organizers	387	0.37
	Remediation/feedback	146	0.65
	Reinforcement	139	1.13
Grand total or mean		**44359**	**0.40**

Source: From Hattie, 1992a.

(Gudmundsdottir & Shulman, 1987), physical education (van der Mars, Vogler, Darst, & Cusimano, 1995), classroom management (Clarridge, 1989; Sabers, Cushing, & Berliner, 1991), and teacher training (Floden & Klizing, 1990). Second, the research relating to expertise in other vocations, such as the pioneering work on experts by Chase and Simon (1973) and deGroot (1965) with chess experts and more recently in medicine (Einhorn, 1974), language arts (Krabbe, 1989), business (Yekovich, Thompson, & Walker, 1991), genetic science (Kinnear & Simmons, 1990), and environmental issues (Tudor, 1992). From an extensive survey of this expert literature, and modifying a summary of this research by Berlach (1996), Table 2 summarizes the typical contrasts between experts and novices.

There maybe debates about the bi-polarity of these 18 attributes, but they do summarize the typical distinctions made between experts and novices. We acknowledge also that there are many such "lists" of attributes of experts. Some researchers have compiled their own lists after many years of research. Berliner (1986), for example, concluded that expert teachers "seem to have a different schemata than novice teachers for students," (p. 10) and these differences relate primarily to qualitative differences in meta-cognitive processing. Experts are superior in assessing students' readiness levels, presenting new skills, providing effective feedback, and providing for the individual needs of students while effectively managing the cognitive decision making of larger classes.

We propose that an expert is someone capable of doing the right thing at the right time, can succeed in adapting to the inherent constraints of the task, is involved in a cycle of processing information that converges on a series of actions that best satisfy the constraints of students and classrooms,

Table 2.   Characteristics of Expert and Novice Problem Solving Approaches.

	Expert	Novice
1.	Persistent and highly motivated to succeed	Tend to give up if the task seems too daunting
2.	Possess procedure knowledge: knowing 'that,' more process oriented strategies	Possess declarative knowledge: knowing 'how,' knowing facts, familiar with established
3.	Excellent at pattern identification and recognition	Tend often to miss patterns which are present
4.	Operate in the area of intuition, knowledge is tacit and implicit – a 'feeling'	Tend not to rely so much on intuition as on fact, knowledge is more explicit
5.	Are superior in problem solving situations calling for combinatorial reasoning	Usually favor trial-and-error as a problem-solving technique
6.	Are able to initiate short-cut approaches	Tend to solve systematically from step-to-step
7.	Analytical skills are more highly developed	Tend to assess work purely in terms of correct or incorrect
8.	Work from a highly integrated set of principles	Each new situation is often seen as a new problem
9.	Teaching routines have become automatic	Routines are rarely integrated as an understanding of the whole
10.	Have a philosophy which encompasses the goals and purposes of education	Concerned more with pragmatics than with philosophies or ideals
11.	Know their learners and their characteristics	Are more preoccupied with content than learners
12.	Are more time effective in the classroom	Takes longer to attend to organizational aspects
13.	Effective control is maintained throughout the session	Periodic lapses in control often lead to unnecessary disruption
14.	Are able to anticipate potential problems	Powers of anticipation are limited
15.	Seem to benefit and gain insight from experience	Experiences do not produce expert-like qualities
16.	Are more opportunistic planners	Tend not to make the most of forward planning opportunities
17.	Suspicious of information provided by other teachers about students and value of routines	More affected by others' opinions of students and more ready to adopt routines established by predecessor
18.	An "oughtness" exists about how things are done and are not done	If any "oughtness" does exist, it has easy malleable edges
19.	More quickly perceive the consequences of a certain action	Less ready to see consequences as results of actions

Source: Adapted from Berlach, 1996.

has diverse problem-solving strategies, and modifies behavior via an incremental revision of weights based on internally or external generated feedback concerning the past performance (Holyoak, 1990). Thus, the major differences between experts and novices relate to differing strategies for solving problems (Chi et al., 1981; Larkin, McDermott, Simon, & Simon, 1980). Expert teachers are more selective in their use of information during planning and interactive teaching, and make greater use of information and management routines (Berliner, 1986, 1987, 1988). They are more selective, however, for a particular reason: to heighten the opportunities for providing feedback to students about their progress, and informing them of appropriate challenging tasks to be undertaken in future work. It is critical to note that having more knowledge, insight, and efficiency are only means to an end. The automaticity, the encoding, etc., are powerful as *they allow more resources for the teacher to devote to other tasks – particularly in structuring challenging tasks with much feedback*. Being highly competent in the subject matter, for example, allows the teacher to devote more resources to other purposes.

There are many teachers who would satisfy most of the identified criteria for expert teachers who have smooth, organized classrooms. The difference between these (often very experienced teachers) and expert teachers, is that the former do not use the extra resources to be constantly vigilant and are often impassioned when dealing with student learning. These "floaters" or "moss-rocks" as opposed to the experts, emphasize organization and flow rather than student learning. Learning is *not* an organized, flowing experience. It is more a staccato of trial and error, a process of accommodation and assimilation, a refocusing of beliefs and under-standings, and often a process of learning, re-learning, and over-learning. The expert teacher attends to student learning by providing challenging tasks appropriate to the student, and provides much feedback relating to the tasks in a manner that ensures that this feedback is assimilated by the student. These are the processes that the expert teacher, with the extra resources, can attend to, and that which makes the difference to enhancing student learning.

Student Learning Outcomes

An obvious and simple method would be to investigate the effects of passing and failing NBPTS teachers on student test scores. Despite the simplicity of this notion, we do not support this approach. As Haertel (1986) has argued, student test scores depend on multiple factors, many of which are out of the control of the teacher. The standardized tests that are usually administered often do not reflect the classroom curriculum and learning objectives of the teachers at a particular time; tests only measure a subset of important learning objectives; and instruction of unmeasured objectives may be slighted (see also Elliott & Hall, 1985; Millman, 1981; Quinto & McKenna, 1977). As Haertel argued, if test scores are to be used in teacher effectiveness studies, it is important to recognize that:

a. student achievement must be related to a particular teacher instruction, as students can achieve as a consequence of many other forms of instruction (e.g., via homework, television, reading books at home, interacting with parents and peers, lessons from other teachers);
b. a teacher can impart much information that may be unrelated to the curriculum;
c. students are likely to differ in their initial levels of knowledge and skills, and the prescribed curricula may be better matched to the needs of some than others;
d. differential achievement may be related to varying levels of out-of-school support for learning;
e. teachers can be provided with different levels and types of instructional support, teaching loads, quality of materials, school climates, and peer cultures;
f. instructional support from other teachers can take a variety of forms (particularly in middle and high schools where students constantly move between teachers); and
g. teaching artifacts, such as the match of test content to prescribed curricula, levels of student motivation, and testwiseness can distort the effects of teacher effects.

Such a list is daunting and makes the task of relating teaching effectiveness to student outcomes most difficult. The present study does not, therefore, use student test scores to assess the impact of the NBCTs on student learning. Instead, we have identified a series of possible classroom-related effects that accomplished teachers would be expected to impact on their students. In particular, we have used a well-grounded approach to assess the *depth* of learning that teachers allow, demand of, and attain in their students. That is, if NBCTs are having a desirable impact on their students, this impact should be evident via the allowance of depth in the teachers' actual teaching in the classroom, and on the consequential student work from that teaching encounter.

Although many have emphasized the importance of "knowledge" when differentiating experts from novices, knowledge that is useful for experts may hold little meaning for novices (deGroot, 1965; Egan & Schwartz, 1979). Of more importance are the differences in the way knowledge is used in teaching situations. As Chi et al. (1981) noted with physicists, experts are more sensitive to the deep structures of the problems, whereas novices are sensitive to surface structures. This theme of deep versus surface is a major issue in our study. This contrast comes from two streams of work.

First, Marton and colleagues have analyzed conceptions of learning, and formulated two major levels of learning: surface and deep (Marton, Dall'Alba, & Beaty, 1993; Marton & Saljo, 1984). A surface approach involves minimum engagement with the task, typically a focus on memorization or applying procedures that do not involve reflection, usually aiming to gain a passing grade. The contrasting deep approach involves an intention to understand and impose meaning. The student focuses on relations between various aspects of the content, formulates hypotheses or beliefs about the structure of the problem, and relates more to obtaining an intrinsic interest in learning and understanding. High-quality learning outcomes are associated with deep approaches, whereas low-quality outcomes are associated with surface ones (see Biggs, 1987; Entwistle, 1988; Harper & Kember, 1989; Marton & Saljo, 1984). There is much evidence that teachers can also adopt a surface or a deep approach to teaching, and this has consequential effects on what and how students learn (Boulton-Lewis, 1995; Boulton-Lewis, Dart, & Brownlee, 1995; Boulton-Lewis, Wilss, & Mutch, 1996).

Second, Biggs and Collis (1982) have devised a model of learning based on the *SOLO* taxonomy (*S*tructure *O*f *L*earning *O*bjectives).There are four stages in the SOLO taxonomy, shown in Table 3.

Table 3. Levels from the Biggs and Collis SOLO Taxonomy.

Depth	Level	Description of Level
Surface	Unistructural	One aspect of a task is picked up serially and there is no relationship of facts or ideas
	Multistructural	Two or more aspects of a task are picked up serially, but are not interrelated
Deep	Relational	Several aspects are integrated into a coherent whole
	Extended abstract	That coherent whole is generalized to a higher level of abstraction

The first two levels correspond to surface learning, and the latter two to deep learning. Expert teachers are more likely to lead students to deep rather than surface learning, as these teachers will structure lessons to allow the opportunity for deep processing, set tasks that encourage the development of deep processing, and provide feedback and challenge for students to attain deep processing (Hattie, Biggs, & Purdie, 1996; Hattie & Purdie, 1998). In the present study, only the two levels of surface and deep are used, although the student work was classified into the four levels prior to this dichotomous scoring. For example, the following student essay (from a student in one of the classes observed for this study) would be classified as surface, as it only contains a series of unrelated ideas:

> If I could be any tree I would be a Redwood. A Redwood tree can live 4000 years. They are very strong and tall. They even name a forest after me. I think a Redwood is a good tree to be. I would be the state tree of my state. I would be known all the way across the state. When somebody cut me down I would fall down real hard on the ground.

The following student essay would be classified as deep, as it contains a series of related ideas that demonstrate a degree of integration and higher levels of abstraction:

> I think I would be a willow tree, because I go with the flow like a willow limbs in the wind. Like a willow in a storm, only the hardest things can get me down. I'm calm and easy going, part of nature, and cannot be missed.

THE ATTRIBUTES OF EXPERT TEACHERS

Thus, from the synthesis of literature, the meta-analyses, and this overriding premise of deep versus surface, we view an expert as someone who:

a. is capable of doing the right thing at the right time,
b. can succeed in adapting to the inherent constraints of the task,
c. is involved in a cycle of processing information and problem-solving strategies that converges on a series of actions that best satisfy the constraints,
d. is more selective in using information,
e. is attentive to affective features such as high motivation, self-efficacy, and respect for themselves and for their students,
f. optimizes opportunities and occurrence of feedback,

g. uses classroom strategies that maximize the probability of developing deep learning, and

h. has appropriately challenging student expectations and outcomes.

Three major domains of expertise can thus be identified from the traditional literature review that differentiate "expert" from "experienced but not expert" teachers (Table 4). These domains relate to explicit and implicit knowledge, insight and problem solving, and efficient management. Further, we argue that expert teachers use this knowledge, insight, strategies, and affect for a particular reason: *to heighten the opportunities for providing feedback to students about their progress, and informing them of appropriate challenging tasks to be undertaken in future work that leads to deeper learning.*

Table 4. The Major Dimensions that Discriminate between Experienced and Experienced Expert Teachers.

A. Knowledge: They have better strategies for solving problems
  1. Content knowledge
  2. Pedagogical knowledge
  3. Teaching non-specific knowledge
  4. Practical knowledge
B. Insight: They are more selective in using information during planning and teaching
  5. Selective encoding
  6. Representation of problems
  7. Multidimensional perception of class situation
  8. Pattern recognition
  9. Insight: Diversity in problem solving
C. Efficiency-Management: They make greater use of information and management routines
  10. Automaticity
  11. Planning
  12. Monitoring
  13. Class control
  14. Feedback
D. Affect: They emphasis mastery rather than performance, have high self-efficacy, and respect their students
  15. Motivation
  16. Self-efficacy
  17. Respect for students
E. Learning Outcomes: They emphasis challenging tasks that lead to deep learning
  18. Challenge of objectives
  19. Outcomes – deep learning

A. Knowledge

"Knowledge" encompasses the type and depth of knowledge required to teach a particular subject from teaching skill to knowledge of subject. An expert teacher is more adept at bringing both explicit and implicit knowledge to bear in solving problems. The "prototype expert teacher is knowledgeable. He or she has extensive, accessible knowledge that is organized for use in teaching. In addition to knowledge of subject matter and of teaching per se, the prototype expert has knowledge of the political and social context in which teaching occurs. This knowledge allows the prototype expert to adapt to practical constraints in the field of teaching – including the need to become recognized and supported as an expert teacher" (Sternberg & Horvath, 1995, p. 12). There are four specific attributes of "knowledge": content, pedagogical, teaching non-specific, and practical knowledge.

1. *Content knowledge.* The expert teacher understands the content of the subject being taught and has a deep understanding of this material. Experts and novices are not expected to differ in the amount of knowledge they have about curriculum matters or about teaching strategies. They are expected, however, to differ in how they organize and use this content knowledge. Experts possess knowledge that is more integrated, that is: combining new subject matter content knowledge with prior knowledge; relating current lesson content to other subjects in the curriculum using curriculum guidelines as a foundation for building lessons; and making them uniquely their own by changing, combining, and adding to them according to their students' needs and their own goals.
2. *Pedagogical knowledge.* The expert understands the skills necessary to teach the subject. Expert teachers are more adept at transforming subject matter knowledge into "forms that are pedagogically powerful and yet adaptive to the variations in ability and background presented by the students" (Shulman, 1987, p. 15). Pedagogical content knowledge consists of the "blending of content and pedagogy into an understanding of how particular topics, problems, or issues are organized and adapted to the diverse interests and abilities of learners for instruction" (Shulman, 1987, p. 8).
3. *Teaching non-specific knowledge.* The expert understands general teaching skills such as the use of open-ended and deep teacher-questioning

techniques, using questions for control, management, and learning, use of the classroom experiences, knowledge of developmental level of students, use quality interactions with students, and understand the most effective principles of education and student learning.

4. *Practical knowledge.* Expert teachers have "scripts" (knowledge structures that summarize information about familiar, everyday experiences) for common teaching activities such as checking homework, presenting new information providing guided practice and conducting class discussions. These scripts are usually elaborate, more complex, and more interconnected, and more easily accessible than those of novices. As a consequence of having these scripts, expert teachers often are improvisers. They can draw upon an extensive repertoire of routines or patterns of action while playing out a scene, incorporating them into a performance that is continually responsive to the audience and to new situations or events" (Borko & Livingstone, 1990, p. 475). This requires much implicit knowledge, general principles for classroom planning – all designed to be responsive to the unpredictability of classroom events. As expert teachers have well-developed systems of cognitive schemata to reduce the complexities of interactive teaching, they attend to and process information only when they believe it is relevant to following or modifying their agendas (Carter, Sabers, Cushing, Pinnegar, & Berliner, 1987).

B. Insight

Insight relates to problem solving and the use of knowledge and techniques to solve problems. "Experts don't simply solve the problem at hand; they often redefine the problem and thereby reach ingenious and insightful solutions that somehow do not occur to others" (Sternberg & Horvath, 1995, p. 14). There are five specific attributes of insight.

5. *Selective encoding.* Experts can detect a content problem and they can filter relevant from irrelevant information (such as pursuing discussion that is pertinent to the topic only). Berliner (1987) claimed that experts are able to monitor, understand, and interpret events in more detail and with more insight than either novices or advanced beginners. Expert teachers can distinguish between those lines of class discussion that are likely to further instructional goals and those that are merely diverting for students.

6. *Representation of problems.* Berliner (1987) found that experts represent problems in qualitatively different ways than do novices. Experts seem to understand problems at a deeper level than do novices; they apply concepts and principles that are more relevant to the problem to be solved (Chi, Glaser, & Farr, 1988).
7. *Multidimensional perception of class situation.* Experts are perceptive of the situation in the classroom and the relevance of the situation to learning and teaching the topic at hand.
8. *Pattern recognition.* Experts can recognize a sequence of events that occur in classrooms that in some way affects the learning and teaching of a topic. Berliner (1987) found that experts have fast and accurate pattern recognition capabilities, whereas novices cannot always make sense of what they experience. Experts are more inferring whereas novices are more literal. Experts concentrate more on information that had instructional significance, perceive more meaningful patterns, and make more meaning from the events because of their superior pattern recognition skills, in part because they organize information better.
9. *Insight: diversity in problem solving.* Experts use a variety of problem-solving techniques.

C. Efficiency-Management

10. *Automaticity.* Not only do experts perform better than novices, they also seem to do so with less effort. They achieve this because many types of cognitive skills become automatic with extensive practice and expertise. They can automate well-learned routines, can produce think-aloud protocols that are richer and more interpretative, and because of their more extensive "knowledge or scripts" have more cognitive resources to devote to other aspects of the classroom. Automaticity is insufficient by itself; experts develop automaticity so as to free working memory to deal with other more complex characteristics of the situation. That is, they use the increased opportunities to seek and give feedback.
11. *Planning.* Experts can anticipate problems. They tend to spend a greater proportion of their solution time trying to understand the problem to be solved as opposed to trying out different solutions (Lesgold, 1984). Experts are more likely to monitor their ongoing solution

attempts, checking for accuracy, and updating or elaborating problem representations as new constraints emerge (Larkin, 1983; Voss & Post, 1988).

12. *Monitoring.* Experts can detect when students are not understanding, and loose interest. Experts can ensure students are on-task.

13. *Class control.* Expert teachers have excellent classroom control. The teacher engages all students both in the tasks and in the feedback cycle, and the major topic of the classroom is related to learning.

14. *Feedback.* From our synthesis of meta-analyses, we have demonstrated that the most powerful single moderator that enhances achievement is feedback (see Table 1). The most fundamental component of teaching is imparting information to students, assessing and evaluating the students' understanding of this information, and then matching the next teaching act to the present understandings of the student. This is not feedback in the behavioral sense of input/output models, but the understanding of the constructions that student have made from the information. (Feedback is the information component whereas reinforcement is the evaluative component relating to information *and* motivation.) It is important to note that not all forms of feedback are effective, for example, the effect-sizes for extrinsic rewards is 0.37, immediate versus delayed 0.28, and punishment 0.20.

D. Affect

15. *Motivation.* The degree to which the teachers impart that students should learn so as to master the material rather than perform to get the task completed (see Dweck, 1992).

16. *Self-efficacy.* Expert teachers not only have high "teacher self-efficacy" but they are also attentive to the self-efficacy and self-concepts of their students. They spend resources ensuring that students are trained to receive feedback to verify rather than enhance their sense of efficacy of achievement; and teachers use reinforcement to help verify rather than enhance students' sense of efficacy (see Hansford & Hattie, 1982; Hattie, 1992c).

17. *Respect for students.* Respect for students relates to the manner in which the teacher treats the students, respects them as learners and people, demonstrates care for, and commitment to the students, recognizes possible barriers to learning, and seeks ways to overcome these barriers.

E. Learning Outcomes

18. *Challenge of objectives.* Expert teachers are more likely to set challenging rather than "do your best" goals relative to the students' present competencies. Perhaps one of the easiest strategies for the experienced, but not expert teacher, is to provide work to students that are time consuming but not challenging; or to provide work that may be challenging for some students and thus inappropriate for challenging other students. By setting challenging goals, teachers inform individuals:

> as to what type or level of performance is to be attained so that they can direct and evaluate their actions and efforts accordingly. Feedback allows them to set reasonable goals and to track their performance in relation to their goals so that adjustments in effort, direction, and even strategy can be made as needed. (Locke & Latham, 1992, p. X)

The scenario is that expert teachers set challenging goals and then structure situations so that students can reach these goals (see Hattie, Marsh, Neill, & Richards, 1997). If teachers can encourage students to share commitment to these challenging goals, and if they provide much feedback, then goals are more likely to be attained.

19. *Outcomes of lessons.* The degree to which the teacher plans, teaches, and requires depth of outcomes as evidenced in student outcomes. Expert teachers aim for, and achieve more deep as well as surface outcomes.

IDENTIFYING EXPERT TEACHERS

Teachers of Early Adolescence/English Language Arts (EA/ELA) were chosen for this study as this was the only assessment fully operationalized at the time of this study. EA/ELA teachers' work with 11–15-year olds "exemplify a high level of professionalism, constantly seeking to improve their practice, exercising sound, disciplined and principled judgment, and acting in the best interest of their students" (ELA Standards, NBPTS, 1993, p. 6). Three teachers who scored about one standard error above the cut-score (275) and three teachers who scored about one standard error below the cut-score were asked to participate in the study. While it would have been desirable to collect the information without knowing the final scores and status of the teacher, this was not possible as all teachers were most keen to talk with us about their experiences. Other measures, detailed below, were used to minimize the effects of knowing the final status of these teachers.

The teachers and their students were assured of anonymity, thus the teachers are called: alpha, beta, gamma for the three who passed NBPTS assessments, and chi, psi, and omega for the three who did not pass NBPTS assessments (further, all student names are fictitious). The six teachers all taught in semi-rural schools in one region of the USA. Table 5 presents the scores of these teachers on the NBPTS assessments.

The information used in this study, came from five sources:

1. *Observation of the teachers for one full day.* At least two people observed one full day of teaching. In negotiation with each teacher, a day was chosen that involved a full day of teaching unencumbered by sports, field trips, snow, etc. There were two major roles for the observers: to write a full transcript of the day's lessons and to code various features using pre-formatted coding sheets. The observers alternated tasks to avoid fatigue.
2. *Interviews with the teacher.* A structured interview asked about: reactions to specific incidents we observed; think aloud about lesson planning and intentions for learning for the lessons we observed; reactions to pre-planned scenarios; explanations of particular student behaviors; self review, "What worked for you?", "What would you do differently?"; and comments on "How you facilitate learning with reference to what we observed?".

Table 5. Scores on Each of the NBPTS Assessment Tasks for the 3 Passing (NBCTs) and 3 Failing Teachers (non-NBCTs).

	Passed (NBCT)			Failed (Non-NBCT)		
	Alpha	Beta	Gamma	Chi	Omega	Psi
Teaching and Learning	2.25	2.00	2.25	1.88	1.25	0.88
Student Learning	3.67	3.13	3.88	2.00	2.00	1.88
Post-reading interpretation	4.00	3.00	2.88	1.88	2.88	2.25
Instructional analysis	4.00	3.88	2.88	2.88	2.00	3.00
Content knowledge: text selection	3.13	2.00	4.00	3.00	2.88	3.88
Content knowledge: theory of response to literature	4.00	2.25	3.88	3.88	3.13	3.13
Content knowledge: language variation	3.88	4.00	3.88	2.00	3.00	2.67
Total	349	283	330	234	235	234

3. *Documents acquired from the teacher.* We asked for examples of student work, as much as possible from the lessons we observed. We also asked all teachers for copies of their lesson plans, although in most cases there were no such documents.

4. *A video* was made by the teacher to demonstrate an exemplary lesson. This video was based on an entire class session, in a sequence of at least three lessons, served as an example of the classroom in action.

5. *Commentaries and artifacts.* Where necessary, other parts of the NBPTS assessments were used (listed in Table 5). The use of these artifacts was minimized and the scoring was developed specifically for this study.

Upon recording all information, the information was presented in random order with names removed to two judges. Where appropriate they were asked to score each piece of evidence for each attribute on a scale of 1–10. For some attributes, alternative scoring procedures were used, as explained below. All information was transcribed and two coders independently rated the appropriate information. These coders did not know the final status of pass/not pass of these teachers and thus halo effects were minimized.

Procedures

The data collection method is provided for each attribute. Space restrictions preclude a detailed presentation of information, thus a brief example is given only when the evidence is less obvious. (The numbers correspond to the attributes cited above and in Table 4.)

A. Knowledge

1. The depth of *knowledge being taught* to the students classified using the SOLO taxonomy. In thefollowing extract, there appears to be no extension of knowledge or questions, and no evidence of knowledge being imparted. Instead, there are many surface level questions, and no depth.

   Teacher psi [Rater 1- 1/10; Rater 2–2/10]
   T: Can I have a volunteer to read their summary of the story? Noise in 8th grade section. T: Mitch, shakes head to quiet down Mitch. S begins reading story but no one can possibly hear her. T quiets another S. It's a little quieter. There are 2 boys swatting at each other in pod 4. In pod 5, a boy is making goofy faces. After S has read

story, T summarizes. Now, one thing Mary mentioned was the family kept asking for money. George, what are some things they asked for? Blaine answers.

T: What are some of the names they called him, Fred? Fred isn't sure where they are. Page 265, Fred. Colin?

T: Fred, do you see the list? Look on start of column of 265. Fred is having a hard time here, and T is making him read items off this list.

2a. Information from a narrative about "Teaching and Learning" will be scored as to depth of teacher pedagogical content. The information provided from a narrative prepared by the teachers that describes and illustrates their work with a class as they and their students explore topics, issues, or questions. The teachers were asked to attend to the learner-centered nature of their practice, the integrated approach they take to curriculum and learning, the students' learning community, and the reflective nature of their practice. This narrative was scored on a deep to surface scale.

2b. Reaction to the following scenario, adapted from Berliner (1987). As noted by Berliner, the following attributes help identify expert teachers: the necessity to take time to prepare the material; the requirement to know their students to provide insight for determining the level at which to teach; the necessity to know their students personally, so they do not need to rely on formal mechanisms of control while teaching; the concern to know the history of the students so as to know what variations are needed.

It is five weeks into the school year, and you have just been assigned a new middle school class. The previous teacher left abruptly and you have been assigned her class. The previous teacher left a grade book with grades and attendance recorded, student information cards containing demographic information on one side and teacher comments about the student on the other, corrected tests and homework assignments, and the textbook.

QUESTION: Imagine that you have no more than 4–5 min before you meet the class for the first time, what would you plan to do in the first lesson?

2c. What are the major principles underlying your teaching? The Post-reading Interpretative Discussion paper was coded to ascertain depth and appropriateness of principles of teaching. The teachers were requested to provide an interpretative discussion of a videotape they had recorded as part of their regular daily teaching. This videotape was coded using the SOLO taxonomy for presence and depth of teaching principles.

3a. Student interactions/Teacher questions. The interactions asked by students and teacher questions within a lesson will be monitored, as will the degree to which the teacher can relate the student questions to lesson objectives. For example, for teacher alpha, 24 of the teacher initiated questions or interactions were directed at the entire class (see Table 6), and 0 were asked by the teacher to groups, and 9 were directed at individuals; all 29 teacher talk to student related to content; 14 of the teacher initiated talk related to content, 14 to management and 3 to control; throughout the day, 22 instances of teacher questioning were observed and 11 were to individuals, 5 to the group, and 6 to the class; 20 of the coded questions were open and 4 were closed; 8 surface and 12 deep; and 5 were content, 6 management, and 3 control interactions or questions.

3b. The quality of teacher questions. From a transcript of the day's lessons, the quality of the questions between the teacher and student were coded using the SOLO taxonomy.

3c. The nature and quality of student questions. The interactions were coded via a 5-min observation schedule, and were coded for content or informative questions, depth of question, on- or off-task, and deep or surface responses by the teacher, as shown in Table 7.

3d. Knowledge of teaching skills. Interview: What the teacher believes is appropriate teaching. The teacher watched a pre-prepared video involving a sample English Language Arts lesson and a commentary by the teacher on the video describing her instruction. The candidates were asked to review these materials and analyze the teacher's teaching "in terms of your understanding of young adolescents and how they learn, cultural awareness, and the dynamics of discussion".

3e. Interview: How do students learn and how do you best facilitate their learning?

4a. Reaction to the following scenario, adapted from Berliner (1987).

Table 6. Scores for Each of the Six Teachers on Interactions and Questions.

	Teacher			Is their Talk			Questions			Open/Closed		Surf/Deep		Type			
	Class	Group	Individual	Content	Management	Control	Individual	Group	Class	Open	Closed	Surface	Deep	Content	Management	Control	Score
Alpha	24	0	9	14	14	3	11	5	6	20	4	8	12	5	6	3	10
Beta	22	9	24	10	24	1	17	2	16	18	24	38	5	34	7	3	4
Gamma	46	14	16	46	24	3	17	2	16	3	4	9	11	4	0	0	8
Chi	29	5	21	31	21	1	8	0	6	5	5	10	2	12	1	0	3
Omega	16	0	5	9	8	0	17	0	0	17	0	11	5	13	2	2	4
Psi	8	9	17	5	9	30	16	0	0	15	1	16	1	16	0	0	1

Table 7.   Scores on the Content, Information, SOLO, On-/Off-Task and
              Answers from the Observation Schedule.

					Task		Answers		
	Content	Information	Deep	Surface	On	Off	Deep	Surface	Score
Alpha	10	0	7	3	9	1	6	3	6
Beta	19	1	0	20	20	0	1	19	3
Gamma	15	5	0	20	20	0	2	16	3
Chi	8	5	3	10	11	4	4	11	4
Omega	13	6	7	12	18	1	1	18	1
Psi	6	0	0	6	6	0	0	6	1

Chris is a very active 12-year old who is in the sixth grade at your middle school. Academically, Chris particularly likes mathematics, reading stories about adventure, humor, and history. In addition, working on the computer and doing science experiments have a special intrigue for Chris. An accurate assessment of Chris' academic performance is affected by bilateral severe to profound hearing loss. However, on the Performance Scale of the Wechsler Intelligence Scale for Children, Chris scored in the superior range. This was also supported by performance on the Arthur Adaptation of the Leiter Scale.

Chris's inquisitiveness helps in the cultivation of interests in drawing pictures and designing buildings and models. Such curiosity is not only observed at school, but also at home where Chris pursues interests in tennis, cooking, and photography.

What would you recommend?

4b. Semi-structured interview focusing on instructional planning: questions relating to the nature of the lesson to be observed, how they planned for the lesson, what they thought about as they planned, and what factors influenced their plans.

B. Insight

5a. The level of selective encoding, and degree to which questions were used for either skill, control, or management in the classroom.

5b. Use the above scenario about Chris, and code the use of higher-order systems of categorization to analyze the problem, as opposed to merely devising ways to help Chris. Coding reflected the proficiency to filter irrelevant information, and detect the main issues in the problem situation.

6. In the post-interview, pick a situation observed during the day and ask how the teacher represented the problem, and their reactions to the situation.

7. Use overall judgments of the day, and assess whether the teachers were multidimensional or linear in their approach.

8. Provide an incident from the class day and ask their views on what was happening. Ask, "What was going on today, what worked, what did not work, and what would you do differently". Assess the degree to which they made instructional sense out of "chaos".

9. Choose a student who presented a challenge in the class. Ask the teacher to explain what was going on with the student and why they did or did not respond to that student.

C. Efficiency-Management

10. Overall judgment by observers via transcripts, structured observations, and reflections of the day as to whether: the teacher used student interactions, teaching questioning, and feedback to accomplish more than one task; management was integrated within instruction; the teacher built to a climax and a closing; and whether the class flowed among these activities.

11. The teachers were asked how they engaged students in discussion to help them build interpretations of a piece of literature and develop their discussion abilities.

12. Within five 10-min segments, code the number and percentage of on- and off-task behaviors (see Table 8).

13a. From the observation schedule in Table 9, note the type of control information and feedback provided it relates to content more than control.

Table 8. Number of On- and Off-Task Events for the Six Teachers from the Observation Schedule.

Name	On-Task	Off-Task	Score
Alpha	9	1	6
Beta	20	0	10
Gamma	20	0	10
Chi	11	4	5
Omega	18	1	9
Psi	6	0	5

Table 9. Type of Interactions from the Six Teachers.

Name	Verbal	Non-Verbal	Remove Target	Positive	Content (%)	Score
Alpha	15	4	0	1	Most	10
Beta	2	3	0	2	Half	3
Gamma	7	0	0	0	Half	5
Chi	8	0	0	0	Half	5
Omega	7	3	0	1	Little	3
Psi	16	3	2	1	Control	2

13b. Monitor how the teacher uses her position to ensure all are involved. A map of the classroom was drawn, and every 5 min the position and interaction activity of the teacher was noted.

14. From the observation schedule, note the amount and type of feedback recorded during lessons. For teacher alpha, as an example, there were 45 instances of feedback (see Table 10). Of these, 21 were positive non-verbal, 2 negative non-verbal (stern looks), 32 positive verbal, and 2 negative verbal. The majority 33/34 was content related, and 1 was classroom management.

D. Affect

15. From the class transcript, rate incidents as to how students remain enthusiastic for mastery even when the material becomes difficult.

16a. Ask in interview about a specific class: How did the lesson go? What were your first impressions?

16b. At the end of the day: How would you rate yourself today?

17. Focus on a small set of students, and ask teacher about various incidents that occurred that lead to the teacher interacting in ways that illuminate respect situations.

E. *Learning Outcomes*

18. Teachers wrote a narrative that described and illustrated their work with a class as they and their students explored topics, issues, or questions. The degree of the challenge of the content taught to the students was coded, as was the degree to which the teacher communicated the challenge, and the degree of challenge exhibited in the student work.
19. Number of student artifacts from the lessons we observed that are coded as surface or deep (see Table 11).

Table 10. Nature of Questions and Interactions from the Six Teachers.

Name	No	Non-verbal		Verbal		Content	Class	Score
		+	−	+	−			
Alpha	45	21	2	32	2	33	1	10
Beta	47	10	2	22	8	39	9	9
Gamma	23	6	2	19	2	19	4	7
Chi	15	3	2	5	2	7	4	4
Omega	16	2	0	9	7	11	4	4
Psi	17	1	6	3	7	8	8	5

Table 11. The Surface and Deep Artifacts from the Students' Work for Each of the Six Teachers.

	No. of Artifacts		Deep (%)	Score
	Surface	Deep		
Alpha	43	42	49	7
Beta	81	64	44	7
Gamma	84	17	18	2
Chi	38	21	36	5
Omega	42	40	49	7
Psi	28	10	26	3

Interpretative Comments on the Results

Table 12 presents the attribute web of the evidence for each teacher for each of the above tasks. Where there were two ratings of an attribute, the scores were averaged and rounded up to the nearest integer. A generalizability coefficient for the consistency of raters was very high (0.92).

The 29 scores from the 6 teachers were clustered to assess the degree to which the teachers have "family resemblances" (Fig. 1). There are three distinct major clusters. The two teachers who did NOT pass NBPTS assessment (psi and omega) clustered in one group. Two NBCTs and one non-NBCT clustered into the second group. Teacher alpha, was clearly the outstanding teacher among all six, clustered alone, but was grouped most like the second group of mostly "passing" teachers.

It was clear to the raters and observers that teacher chi (a non-NBCT) was more like beta and gamma (NBCTs), than like the other non-NBCTs (psi and omega). Chi, however, was less obviously "organized" in her classroom activities. Her classes were often abuzz with activity, in a frenzy with excitement, and the teacher seemingly oblivious to the organized chaos. The teacher, however, was in command of the situation. For example, during one class the teacher worked with a small group of two to three students for the entire period. Around her, other students were involved, to varying degrees of intensity, with their own work; students came and went from the classroom to other sites such as the library or the art room; and the noise levels rose. The teacher often turned to another group and made a comment, gave advice, prompted activity, returned the noise level to a buzz, and reprimanded students off-task. All this, still seated with the small group and intensively involved with them. It seemed to the observers that teacher chi may have difficulty organizing these activities in a linear manner. When we observed the video of her class, she had structured a "normal" linear class with a beginning, middle and end, and what we observed on the video had little correspondence with what we saw in her class throughout the day.

Teachers psi and omega, who failed the NBPTS assessment and who were grouped together in the present study, were placed in one group for further analysis. Teachers beta, gamma, and alpha, who passed the NBPTS assessment and who were grouped together in the present study were placed in a second group. Teacher chi is probably best omitted in the subsequent analyses, as although she failed NBPTS assessments, she probably is most appropriately classified as an accomplished teacher alongside, at least, teachers gamma and beta. Note also, that teacher

Table 12. Scores and Means for the Two Failing, Three Passing (and Teacher Gamma) and Recommended Direction of Differences.

		Low			High			Mean		
	Psi	Omega	Chi	Beta	Gamma	Alpha	Low	High	Direction
A. Attribute									
1. Content knowledge	2	3	6	3	7	9	2.5	6.3	Y
2. *Pedagogical knowledge*									
a. Narrative	2	4	8	6	3	10	3.0	6.3	Y
b. Knowing students	2	3	6	7	7	6	2.5	6.7	Y
c. Teaching principles	5	4	5	6	6	8	4.5	6.7	N
3. *Teaching non-specific knowledge*									
a. Student interactions	1	4	3	4	8	10	2.5	7.3	→Y
b. Teacher–student questions	1	3	5	5	3	9	2.5	6.7	Y
c. Student questions	1	1	4	3	3	6	1.0	4.0	→N
d. Knowledge of teaching skills	6	4	4	7	5	8	5.0	6.7	N
e. How students learn	2	3	7	8	6	9	2.5	7.7	Y
4. *Practical knowledge*									
a. Practical knowledge	7	2	7	8	3	8	4.5	6.3	N
b. Instructional planning	3	4	6	5	5	7	3.5	4.3	N
B. Insight									
5. *Selective encoding*									
a. Selective encoding	6	3	5	10	5	7	4.5	5.7	N
b. Higher-order thinking	5	2	6	4	5	4	3.5	4.3	N
6. *Representation of problems*	4	5	7	3	5	9	4.5	5.7	N
7. *Multidimensional perception*	1	2	9	8	4	10	1.5	7.3	Y
8. *Pattern recognition*	6	4	6	3	7	8	5.0	6.0	N
9. *Diversity in problem solving*	3	3	5	6	6	8	3.0	6.7	Y
C. Efficiency-management									
10. *Automaticity*	1	2	7	6	4	10	1.5	6.7	Y
11. *Planning*	1	1	5	6	5	8	1.0	6.3	Y
12. *Monitoring*	5	9	5	10	10	6	7.0	8.7	N
13. *Class control*									
a. Class control	2	3	5	3	5	10	2.5	6.0	Y
b. Involvement	5	4	4	9	7	10	4.5	8.7	Y
14. *Feedback*	5	4	4	9	7	10	4.5	8.7	Y
D. Affect									
15. *Motivation*	2	3	7	5	5	10	2.5	6.7	Y
16. Self-efficacy									
a. Self-efficacy	3	6	3	7	9	10	4.5	8.7	Y
b. Overall	3	5	7	6	7	10	4.0	7.7	Y
17. *Respect for students*	1	5	8	5	6	10	3.0	7.0	Y
E. Learning outcomes									
18. *Challenge of objectives*	1	3	7	4	5	10	2.0	6.3	Y
19. *Outcomes of lessons*	2	3	5	7	7	7	2.5	7.0	Y

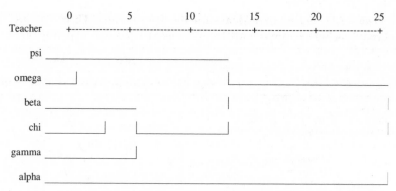

Fig. 1. Overall Scores for Each of the Six Teachers.

chi scored lower than the NBCTs on many of the efficiency-management tasks.

The means of the two low group teachers and the mean of the three high group teachers are presented in Table 5. In the final column, a judgment is made as to whether there appears to be a difference between the low and high teachers. Both the differences in the mean and, more importantly, the pattern of scores are considered in the judgment that there is No difference, that Yes, there is a difference, or that there is a tendency towards a difference or not.

Thus, we found *no* differences for student questions, knowledge of teaching skills, practical knowledge, instructional planning, selective encoding, higher-order thinking, representation of problems, problem recognition, and monitoring. These attributes primarily relate to insight or the selectivity in using information during planning and teaching and to the preparation of material/lessons.

It is important to note that these findings of no differences need to be tempered by two considerations. First, the power of the study was limited and this affects the probability of finding differences. Second, because there are no differences does not necessarily mean that these attributes are unimportant for teachers. Although there are no differences between NBCTs and non-NBCTs, say on instructional planning, this may be because both types of teachers require a similarly high level of instructional planning.

There was a meaningful pattern of differences in 19 of the 29 attributes. The following categories indicated differences between the NBPTS three passing and two failing teachers: content knowledge, pedagogical knowledge as evidenced in classroom presentation, student teacher interactions, knowledge of student learning, ability to deal with the multiplicity of information that is present in classrooms, diversity in problem solving, greater use of information and management routines (such as automaticity, planning, class control, involvement, and feedback), an emphasis on mastery rather than performance, high self-efficacy, and respect for students, and more challenge and depth in learning outcomes.

CONCLUSIONS

The major aim of this study was to demonstrate a methodology that can be used in a more systematic manner to assess the construct validity of the NBPTS system of identifying accomplished teachers. The methodology uses a variety of procedures based on actual classroom experiences, teacher thinking based on observed classroom experiences, scenarios aimed at eliciting classroom behaviors and experiences, and investigating the depth of student learning outcomes.

The teachers in this study who were National Board Certified differed from those not certified in content and pedagogical knowledge, beliefs about student learning, in problem solving, efficiency and management, affect, and learning outcomes. There were no differences on questioning, knowledge about principles of learning, insight, and classroom monitoring. Of course, much caution is needed before these results can be generalized and it is reiterated that the major impact of this study was to demonstrate a methodology to address the construct validation of the NBPTS certifications. It is comforting, however, that there were noticeable differences even with this small sample.

ACKNOWLEDGMENTS

Although they must remain anonymous, the authors are indebted to the six teachers and their students who made this report possible. Thank you. Thanks also to Holly Schmidt-Davis and Marnie Thompson for their contributions to this study.

REFERENCES

Berlach, R. G. (1996). *Self-concept integration processes in expert and novice student teachers.* Unpublished doctoral dissertation. University of Western Australia, Perth, WA, Australia.

Berliner, D. C. (1986). The place of process-product research in developing the agenda for research on teacher thinking. Paper presented at the Third Conference on Teacher Thinking and Professional Action, International Study Association on Teacher Thinking, Leuven, Belgium.

Berliner, D. C. (1987). Expert and novice interpretations of classroom data. Paper presented at the Annual meeting of the American Educational Research Association, Washington, DC.

Berliner, D. C. (1988). The development of expertise in pedagogy. Paper presented at the Annual meeting of the American Association of Colleges for Teacher Education, New Orleans, LA. (ED 298 122).

Biggs, J. B. (1987). *The Study Process Questionnaire (SPQ) users' manual.* Hawthorn, Victoria: ACER.

Biggs, J. B., & Collis, K. F. (1982). *Evaluating the quality of learning: The SOLO taxonomy.* New York: Academic Press.

Borko, H., & Livingstone, C. (1990). Cognition and improvisation: Differences in mathematics instruction by expert and novice teachers. *American Educational Research Journal, 26,* 473–498.

Boulton-Lewis, G. (1995). The SOLO taxonomy as a means of shaping and assessing learning in higher education. *Higher Education Research and Development, 14,* 143–154.

Boulton-Lewis, G., Wilss, L., & Mutch, S. (1996). Teachers as adult learners: Their knowledge of their own learning and implications for teaching. *Higher Education, 32*(1), 89–106.

Boulton-Lewis, G. M., Dart, B., & Brownlee, J. (1995). Student teachers' integration of formal and informal knowledge of learning and teaching. *Research and Development in Higher Education, 18,* 136–142.

Carter, K., Sabers, D., Cushing, K., Pinnegar, S., & Berliner, D. (1987). Processing and using information about students: A study of expert, novice, and postulant teachers. *Teaching and Teacher Education, 3,* 147–157.

Chase, W. G., & Simon, H. A. (1973). The mind's eye in chess. In: W. G. Chase (Ed.), *Visual information processing* (pp. 215–281). New York: Academic Press.

Chi, M., Feltovich, P., & Glaser, R. (1981). Categorization and representation of physics problems by experts and novices. *Cognitive Science, 5,* 121–152.

Chi, M., Glaser, R., & Farr, M. (1988). *The nature of expertise.* Hillsdale, NJ: Lawrence Erlbaum Associates.

Clarridge, P. (1989). Alternative perspectives for analyzing expertise in teaching. Paper presented at the Annual meeting of the American Educational Research Association, San Francisco, CA.

deGroot, A. D. (1965). *Thought and choice in chess.* The Hague, The Netherlands: Mouton.

Dweck, C. (1992). Motivational processes affecting learning. *American Psychologist, 41,* 1040–1048.

Egan, D. E., & Schwartz, B. J. (1979). Chunking in recall of symbolic drawings. *Memory and Cognition, 7,* 149–158.

Einhorn, H. J. (1974). Expert judgment: Some necessary conditions and an example. *Journal of Applied Psychology, 59*, 562–571.

Elliott, E. J., & Hall, R. (1985). Indicators of performance: Measuring the educators. *Educational Measurement: Issues and Practice, 4*(2), 6–9.

Entwistle, N. (1988). Motivational factors in students' approaches to learning. In: R. R. Schmeck (Ed.), *Learning strategies and learning styles* (pp. 21–51). New York: Plenum.

Floden, R. E., & Klizing, H. G. (1990). What can research on teacher thinking contribute to teacher preparation? A second opinion. *Educational Researcher, 19*(4), 15–20.

Gudmundsdottir, S., & Shulman, L. (1987). Pedagogical content knowledge in social science. *Scandinavian Journal of Educational Research, 31*(2), 59–70.

Haertel, E. (1986). The valid use of student performance measures for teacher evaluation. *Educational Evaluation and Policy Analysis, 8*, 45–60.

Hansford, B. C., & Hattie, J. A. (1982). The relationship between self and achievement/ performance measures. *Review of Educational Research, 52*, 123–142.

Harper, G., & Kember, D. (1989). Interpretation of factor analyses from the approaches to studying inventory. *British Journal of Educational Psychology, 59*, 66–74.

Hattie, J. A. (1987). Identifying the salient facets of a model of student learning: A synthesis of meta-analyses. *International Journal of Educational Research, 11*, 187–212.

Hattie, J. A. (1992a). Towards a model of schooling: A synthesis of meta-analyses. *Australian Journal of Education, 36*, 5–13.

Hattie, J. A. (1992b). *Unraveling the threads of learning in special education*. Des English Memorial Lecture, Australian Association of Special Education National Conference.

Hattie, J. A. (1992c). *Self-concept*. Hillsdale, NJ: Lawrence Erlbaum Associates.

Hattie, J. A. (1993a). Measuring the effects of schooling. *SET, 2*, 1–4.

Hattie, J. A. (1993b). What works: A model of the teaching-learning interaction. Paper presented at the Annual Conference of the Australian Teacher Education Association, Fremantle.

Hattie, J. A., Biggs, J., & Purdie, N. (1996). Effects of learning skills intervention on student learning: A meta-analysis. *Review of Educational Research, 66*(2), 99–136.

Hattie, J. A., & Jaeger, R. M. (1998). Assessment and classroom learning: A deductive approach. *Assessment in Education, 5*(1), 111–122.

Hattie, J. A., Marsh, H. W., Neill, J., & Richards, G. (1997). Adventure education and Outward Bound: Out-of-class experiences that make a lasting difference. *Review of Educational Research, 67*, 43–87.

Hattie, J. A., & Purdie, N. (1998). The SOLO model: Addressing fundamental measurement issues. In: B. Dart & G. Boulton-Lewis (Eds), *Teaching and learning in higher education* (pp. 145–176). Melbourne: ACER Press.

Holyoak, K. F. (1990). *Problem solving*. Cambridge, MA: MIT Press.

Kinnear, J. F., & Simmons, P. E. (1990). "Expert" and "novice" subjects' approaches to genetic problem solving in a computer-based setting. *Research in Science Education, 22*, 171–180.

Krabbe, M. A. (1989). A comparison of experienced and novice teachers' routines and procedures during set and discussion instructional activity segments. Paper presented at the annual meeting of the American Educational Research Association, San Francisco, CA.

Larkin, J. H. (1983). The role of problem representation in physics. In: D. Gentner & A. L. Stevens (Eds), *Mental models* (pp. 75–97). Hillsdale, NJ: Lawrence Erlbaum Associates.

Larkin, J. H., McDermott, J., Simon, D. P., & Simon, H. A. (1980). Expert and novice performance in solving physics problems. *Science, 208,* 1335–1342.

Leinhardt, G. (1989). Math lessons: A contrast of novice and expert competence. *Journal for Research in Mathematics Education, 20*(1), 52–75.

Lesgold, A. M. (1984). Acquiring expertise. In: J. R. Anderson & S. M. Kosslyn (Eds), *Tutorials in learning and memory* (pp. 31–60). New York: Freeman.

Locke, E. A., & Latham, G. P. (1992). *A theory of goal setting and task performance.* Englewood Cliffs, NJ: Prentice Hall.

Marton, F., Dall'Alba, G., & Beaty, E. (1993). Conceptions of learning. *International Journal of Educational Research, 19*(3), 277–300.

Marton, F., & Saljo, R. (1984). Approaches to learning. In: F. Marton, D. Hounsell & D. N. Entwistle (Eds), *The experiences of learning* (pp. 36–55). Edinburgh: Scottish Academic Press.

Millman, J. (1981). Student achievement as a measure of teacher competence. In: J. Millman (Ed.), *Handbook of teacher evaluation* (pp. 146–166). Beverly Hills, CA: Sage.

National Board for Professional Teaching Standards. (1993). *Early Adolescence/English Language Arts Standards for National Board Certification.* .

Quinto, F., & McKenna, B. (1977). *Alternative to standardized testing.* Washington, DC: National Education Association.

Ropo, E. (1987). Teachers' conceptions of teaching and teaching behavior: Some differences between expert and novice teachers. Paper presented at the Annual Meeting of the American Educational Research Association, Washington, DC. (ERIC Document Reproduction Service No. 287 824).

Sabers, D. S., Cushing, K. S., & Berliner, D. C. (1991). Differences among teachers in a task characterized by simultaneity, multidimensionality, and immediacy. *American Educational Research Journal, 28*(1), 63–88.

Shulman, L. S. (1987). Knowledge and teaching: Foundations of the new reform. *Harvard Educational Review, 19*(2), 4–14.

Sternberg, R. J., & Horvath, J. A. (1995). A prototype of expert teaching. *Educational Researcher, 24*(6), 9–17.

Tudor, M. (1992). Expert and novice differences in strategies to problem solve an environmental issue. *Contemporary Educational Psychology, 17,* 329–339.

van der Mars, H., Vogler, E. W., Darst, P., & Cusimano, B. E. (1995). Novice and expert physical education teachers: Maybe they think and decide differently ... . But do they behave differently? *Journal of Teaching in Physical Education, 14,* 340–347.

Voss, J. F., & Post, T. A. (1988). On the solving of ill-structure problems. In: M. T. H. Chi, R. Glaser & M. J. Farr (Eds), *The nature of expertise* (pp. 261–285). Hillsdale, NJ: Lawrence Erlbaum Associates.

Yekovich, F., Thompson, M., & Walker, C. (1991). Generation and verification of inferences by expert and trained nonexperts. *American Educational Research Journal, 28*(1), 189–209.

CHAPTER 12

A VALIDITY STUDY OF THE CERTIFICATION SYSTEM OF THE NATIONAL BOARD FOR PROFESSIONAL TEACHING STANDARDS

Tracy W. Smith, Wanda K. Baker, John Hattie and Lloyd Bond

ABSTRACT

This article describes a construct validation study of the National Board for Professional Teaching Standards' system of advanced certification. The evidence analyzed in the study included teachers' instructional objectives and lesson plans for a given instructional unit, data collected during visits to all 65 teachers' classrooms, and transcripts of scripted interviews of the teachers and their students. Two validity questions were examined in this comparative study: (a) To what extent is the National Board's vision of accomplished practice, as laid down in its Standards documents and as instantiated in its assessments, consonant with the characteristics of teaching expertise that have emerged from the research and scholarly literature?, and (b) Can National Board Certified teachers

Assessing Teachers for Professional Certification:
The First Decade of the National Board for Professional Teaching Standards
Advances in Program Evaluation, Volume 11, 345–378
Copyright © 2008 by Elsevier Ltd.
ISSN: 1474-7863/doi:10.1016/S1474-7863(07)11012-7

(NBCTs) and their noncertified counterparts (non-NBCTs) be distinguished on the basis of the quality of work produced by their students? In every comparison between NBCTs and non-NBCTs on the dimensions of teaching excellence, NBCTs obtained higher mean scores. In 11 of the 13 comparisons, the differences were highly statistically significant.

In 1996, the National Commission on Teaching and America's Future (NCTAF) asserted that the most significant factor in meeting the nation's educational goals was the level of expertise among those who teach. NCTAF challenged the nation to provide every child with his or her educational birthright: "access to competent, caring, qualified teaching" (NCTAF, 1996, p. 21). The Commission called for this objective to be met by 2006. In a more recent report, NCTAF claimed that the nation had reached a consensus that well-prepared teachers are the most valuable resource a community can provide to its young people (NCTAF, 2003). This report further stated

> The bipartisan passage of the *No Child Left Behind Act* of 2001 was a clear expression of national will. Recognizing that every American family deserves public schools that work, *No Child Left Behind* (NCLB) pledges highly qualified teachers in every classroom by the 2005–06 school year. (NCTAF, 2003, p. 4)

Although it may be clear that the nation has reached a consensus that high quality teaching is the most valuable resource a community can provide to its young people, what is not clear or agreed upon is how to define high quality teaching. While we cannot examine the many aspects of the teaching quality debate here, we will provide findings from the first comprehensive construct and consequential validity study of the assessments of the National Board for Professional Teaching Standards (NBPTS). The NBPTS is rooted in the belief that the single most important action this country can take to improve schools and student learning is to strengthen teaching (NBPTS, 2003; see also http://www.nbpts.org/about/index.cfm). A brief history of the evolvement of the NBPTS is provided in Vandevoort, Amrein-Beardsley, and Berliner (2004).

According to the organization's own description, National Board Certification measures a teacher's practice against high and rigorous standards. The process is an extensive series of performance-based assessments that includes teaching portfolios, student work samples, videotapes and thorough analyses of the candidates' classroom teaching and of their students' learning. Teachers also complete a series of written exercises that probe the depth of their subject-matter knowledge, as well as their understanding of how to teach those subjects to their students. Teachers who have participated in National Board Certification have overwhelmingly stated it is the most powerful professional development experience of their careers (Bond, Smith, Baker, & Hattie, 2000). They said the experience changed them as professionals and that through the process they deepened their content knowledge and developed, mastered, and reflected on new approaches to working with their students (http://www. nbpts.org/about/index.cfm).

As of March 2003, legislative and policy action creating incentives and recognition for National Board Certification had been enacted in 49 US states and in approximately 476 local school districts (http://www. nbpts.org/about/state.cfm). However, some states, such as South Carolina were considering cutting these incentives in order to redirect funds to meet the demands of budget shortfalls (Holland, 2003). Some policymakers were anxious to see research that National Board Certification was worth funding before they continued to support NBPTS incentive programs. In South Carolina alone the cost of incentives in 2003–2004 was $36.8 million, and the House budget had $500 million less to spend that year than a year before (Holland, 2003). The need for evidence that National Board Certified teachers (NBCTs) are qualitatively different is clear and compelling.

A PROMISING MODEL OF TEACHING EXPERTISE

Despite agreement about the need for expert teachers, there is no consensus about the characteristics of such teachers. Researchers such as Sternberg and Horvath (1995) contend that there is no "model with which to inform our performance standards – to distinguish those teachers who are expert at teaching students from those who are merely experienced at teaching students" (p. 9). Such comments posit the need for a model of teaching expertise. One model has been developed by the Board, but it was a model based on a consensus of best practice and had not been empirically tested.

The NBPTS' system of advanced, voluntary certification for K-12 teachers is based on a complex and ambitious process of performance assessment. The site-based portfolio and on-demand assessment center exercises constituted a comprehensive assessment of teaching that required candidates to present, discuss, and analyze student work (see www.nbpts.org for more detail). A persistent criticism of the NBPTS assessments had been that student achievement and the quality of student products, per se, were not a part of the assessment (Archer, 2002; Holland, 2002; Poliakoff, 2001; Schalock, Schalock, & Myton, 1998). Moreover, although candidate teachers were required to submit two videotapes (and associated commentary) featuring their instructional expertise in whole-class and small-group settings, the NBPTS assessments did not require classroom visitation and observation by trained observers. Some critics of the NBPTS assessments also questioned the validity of data submitted only by the candidates themselves (Holland, 2002; Moss & Schutz, 1999).

Others found that NBCTs were more likely to take responsibility for the educational outcomes of their students rather than blaming external factors (Whitman, 2002), to assume leadership activities (Ralph, 2003), to believe that the certification process made them more effective teachers and increased the number of professional opportunities available to them (Ralph, 2003), to have a stronger sense of confidence in their teaching (Iovacchini, 1998), to consider teaching to be a more integral part of their lives (Petty, 2002), to have attained higher degrees and read more professional journals (O'Connor, 2003), and to be considered by principals to be among the best teachers ever supervised primarily because they were knowledgeable in curriculum and instruction, collaborative, organized, dedicated, determined, and leaders (Vandevoort et al., 2004).

There is some evidence, however, that the NBPTS process may identify more than the usual numbers of false negatives and false positives (Vandevoort et al., 2004), there may be marked differences between assessments of teachers in situ compared to what they write about their teaching (Burroughs, Schwartz, & Hendricks-Lee, 2000; Van Driel, Beijaard, & Verloop, 2001), and there have been many other criticisms of the NBPTS process (Burroughs et al., 2000; Podgursky, 2001; Pool, Ellett, Schiavone, & Carey-Lewis, 2000).

The purpose of this study was to use various student outcome measures and observation data to compare the instructional practices and outcomes of teacher candidates who had been certified by NBPTS with teacher candidates who were not certified. More specifically, the present study evaluated whether students who had been taught by NBCTs produced deeper responses than students of teachers who attempted National Board Certification but were not certified. Thus, this was a consequential validity study of the NBPTS assessment methods and procedures.

NBPTS aims to identify expert teaching using a content-specific, standards-based approach. The tripartite mission of NBPTS is to establish high and rigorous standards for what expert teachers should know and be able to do, to develop and operate a national voluntary system to assess and certify teachers who meet these standards, and to advance related education reforms for the purpose of improving student learning in American schools. Starting from its policy statement, *What Teachers Should Know and Be Able to Do*, NBPTS developed certification standards in more than 20 certificate fields. The major tenets of the NBPTS model of expert teachers have been developed largely through extensive professional consensus. The philosophical foundation of all NBPTS content-area standards is expressed in five core propositions:

1. teachers are committed to students and their learning;
2. teachers know the subjects they teach and how to teach those subjects to students;
3. teachers are responsible for managing and monitoring student learning;
4. teachers think systematically about their practice and learn from experience; and
5. teachers are members of learning communities.

Prior to designing and conducting the validation study, a model of teacher expertise was developed independent of that developed by NBPTS. This model is more fully outlined in Hattie and Jaeger (1996).

The Study of Expertise

In the past 25 years psychologists have begun to study expertise as a cognitive phenomenon that is acquired and honed over time, an idea that holds out the possibility of deliberate fostering and intervention. Maslow (1971), for example, argued:

> If we want to know how fast a human being can run, then it is no use to average out the speed of a 'good sample' of the population; it is far better to collect Olympic gold medal winners and see how well they can do. If we want to know the possibilities for spiritual growth, value growth, or moral development in a human being, then I maintain that we can learn most by studying our moral, ethical, or saintly people .... Even when 'good specimens,' the saints and sages and great leaders of history, have been available for study, the temptation too often has been to consider them not human but supernaturally endowed. (p. 7).

In the mid-1980s, research related to expertise in teaching began to emerge. Unlike other domains of expertise that have been studied (i.e., chess, typewriting, piano playing), on any given day, teaching involves interaction with numerous people, including students, administrators, colleagues, and parents. Teaching requires much more social interaction expertise than the domains typically studied. An operational definition of expertise in teaching, however, has been difficult to devise, and expertise in teaching has therefore been difficult to assess. As recently as 1987, Shulman lamented that in teaching "richly developed portrayals of expertise are rare" (p. 1). He proposed a model of teaching expertise grounded in teacher knowledge, including general pedagogical knowledge with special reference to those broad principles and strategies of classroom management and organization that appear to transcend subject matter; curriculum knowledge, with particular grasp of the materials and programs that serve as "tools of the trade" for teachers; pedagogical content knowledge – that special amalgam of content and pedagogy that is uniquely the province of teachers, their own special form of professional understanding; knowledge of educational contexts, ranging from the workings of the group or classroom, the governance and financing of school districts, to the character of communities and cultures; and knowledge of educational ends, purposes, and values, and their philosophical and historical grounds.

Shulman proposed and explicated a model of pedagogical reasoning and action that involves a cycle of comprehension, transformation, instruction, evaluation, reflection, and new comprehensions: "The key to distinguishing the knowledge base of teaching lies at the intersection of content and pedagogy, in the capacity of a teacher to transform the content knowledge he or she possesses into forms that are pedagogically powerful and yet adaptive to the variations in ability and background presented by students" (Shulman, 1987, p. 15). Shulman's model represents an effort to capture the complex nature of expertise in teaching. In some ways, he suggests that many systems of teacher evaluation and assessment are insufficient because they focus on teacher behaviors and performance without reference to the content being taught.

Hattie and Jaeger (1996) proposed a model of teacher expertise based on an extensive review of the literature on expertise in general (across many domains), a review of expertise of teachers and teaching, and a synthesis of over 500 meta-analyses concerning the relative effects of various influences on student outcomes. They identified five major dimensions that discriminate between expert and experienced teachers: (a) expert teachers identify essential representations of their subject; (b) expert teachers guide learning through classroom interactions; (c) expert teachers monitor learning and provide feedback; (d) expert teachers attend to affective attributes; and (e) expert teachers influence student outcomes. Expert teachers influenced student outcomes by promoting conditions for their students to be motivated to achieve, and they had high self-efficacy about the effects of their teaching, set challenging tasks, had high achievement expectations of their students, and processed information at both a surface and a deep level. Table 1 summarizes the major dimensions.

Although each dimension was identified, defined, and described separately, expert teaching could not be accurately characterized by a set of simple, discreet behaviors. Teaching is a complex, seamless activity; therefore, the attributes cannot be used as a checklist to evaluate expert teaching. The key distinction lies in the concept of "transformation"; expert teachers compared to their merely experienced counterparts were much more adept at transforming the content and providing appropriate conditions for learning and understanding this content and this leads to more qualitatively deeper student outcomes.

This notion of transformation is supported by many studies of teacher expertise. For example, Cushing, Sabers, and Berliner (1992), on the basis of a series of experimental tasks, suggested three propositions that could be used to contrast novices, advanced beginners, and experts. First, *they differ in their perceptions and understanding of classroom events.* While novices recall random events in the classroom, experts describe classrooms in terms of what is happening instructionally and therefore are more able to make sense of and interpret classroom phenomena. Second, *they differ in the role they assume in classroom instruction.* Experts see monitoring instruction as one of their most important roles. When talking about classroom instruction, experts talk more about their own behavior than the behavior of the students, more about the method of instruction than the materials used in instruction, and are more interested in developing personal feeling for students than in remembering facts about them. Finally, *they differ in their notion of "typicality" within the classroom environment.* Experts assessed classroom and student information to determine if the situation was typical to their own experience. If they perceived the teaching situation as typical, they were, in a sense, already familiar with the management and instructional issues because of their rich experiential backgrounds. This notion of typicality influences the way expert teachers perceive and understand information and the way they see and make sense of classroom events and instruction. These three propositions involve a transforming of information, situations, roles, and events. However, similar to much of the current research, the studies were more related to distinguishing novices from experienced teachers, whereas our interest is comparing experienced teachers to expert teachers.

Table 1.   Five Major Dimensions of Expert Teachers (Adapted from Hattie & Jaeger, 1996).

Dimension	Description
(a) Expert teachers identify essential representations of their subject	Deeper representation of their teaching and learning, more integrated, connected to prior and future learning, adopt a problem-solving stance, high levels of anticipation and improvisation, more adept at identifying and using the most relevant information, anticipate difficulties students may experience.
(b) Expert teachers guide learning through classroom interactions	Ensure students understand and follow their management procedures, anticipate and prevent disruptions, aware of events that occur simultaneously, "read" verbal and nonverbal cues more efficiently, sensitive to the task demands and social situations of the classroom and needs of students, rely on their understanding of context to guide choices regarding management and instruction.
(c) Expert teachers monitor learning and provide feedback	More able to examine their own and students' responses to instruction, offer students information about their understanding that guides them to higher levels of comprehension, prioritize and reprioritize possibilities based on their teaching experience and on student responses, test hypotheses both while they are teaching and as they examine their choices while reflecting on lessons taught, and use this information to guide the next round of decisions they make regarding instruction.
(d) Expert teachers attend to affective attributes	Readily communicate their belief in students' power to overcome barriers and help them find ways to do so, less likely to indulge in blaming behaviors, display passion that is closely linked to their sense of responsibility and love of the subjects they are teaching, show more emotionality about successes and failures in their work.
(e) Expert teachers influence student outcomes	Motivate students towards more challenging goals, enhance self-efficacy, emphasize students' responsibility for their own learning, reinforce students' beliefs in themselves as learners, find ways to challenge all students to "stretch" their understanding of ideas, promote academic achievement, especially deeper approaches.

Expert Teachers as Content Experts

There are four major components to how expert teachers represent their subject: (a) how they represent their teaching and learning; (b) their adoption of a problem-solving stance; (c) their anticipation of planning and improvisation; and (d) their decision-making skills. While both experienced and expert teachers have extensive knowledge, experts differ in how they organize and use knowledge. Experts' knowledge is more integrated in that they connect new information with their own prior knowledge and that of their students. They relate current topics to other topics in the curriculum, connect the subject to other subjects, create generalizations, and teach thematic understandings. In doing so, they use the concepts and language of their subject matter to guide students toward deeper levels of understanding. Experts use the depth of their knowledge to provide content feedback to students to correct misconceptions, advance student understanding, and provide directions for new learning. Such deeper pedagogical knowledge involves the process of transforming subject matter knowledge into "forms that are pedagogically powerful and yet adaptive to the variations in ability and background presented by the students" (Shulman, 1987, p. 15). The present study examined four major transformations: identifying essential representations, setting goals for diverse learners, guiding learners through classroom interactions, and monitoring learning and providing feedback.

Identifying Essential Representations

Expert teachers have deep representations about teaching and learning (Berliner, 1987, 1988; Chi, Glaser, & Farr, 1988; Dorner & Schaub, 1994; Swanson, O'Connor, & Cooney, 1990; Westerman, 1991). They recognize patterns of student responses and use these patterns to interpret events and plan instruction. While experienced teachers draw upon their mental resources to make good instructional decisions, experts go further to construct and reconstruct curricula to meet the needs of students. Experts adapt instruction for students with varied backgrounds and abilities. While experienced teachers may solve problems based on classroom evidence, experts often respond to problems by seeking further information and formulating wider ranges of solutions. Expert teachers spend more time trying to understand the problem to be solved rather than trying out different solutions.

Setting Goals for Diverse Learners

Expert teachers adapt and modify their instruction during the flow of lessons (Shulman, 1987). While experienced teachers may make adjustments to their plans, experts are more likely to assess the impact of their instruction on an ongoing basis and make changes on the spot. Experts draw upon an extensive repertoire of patterns of action while teaching, incorporating them into instruction that is continually responsive to students. They understand the hows and whys of student success and make sound, informed decisions based on this understanding. While experienced teachers may use as much information in making decisions as experts do, experts are more adept at identifying and using the most relevant information. Experts diagnose students' needs and envision difficulties students may experience. By anticipating varied student responses, experts plan lessons that are more flexible and adaptive. They achieve a better balance between content- and student-centered instruction than other teachers achieve (Livingston & Borko, 1990).

Effectively Guiding Learning through Classroom Interactions

Expert teachers can transform the climate of classrooms. While experienced teachers may be good classroom managers, experts link management with instruction to promote deeper levels of learning. Experts develop management procedures to accomplish their goals and make sure that students understand and follow these procedures (Clarridge, 1989). Simultaneously, experts interpret students' verbal and nonverbal behavior to anticipate and prevent disruptions. Experts are adept at detecting students' loss of interest or lack of understanding so that they can prevent disengagement or disruptions (Westerman, 1991).

Expert teachers display a high level of "withitness." That is, they show that they are aware of events that occur simultaneously (Clarridge & Berliner, 1991; Kounin, 1970). While experienced teachers may be adept at interpreting student behavior, experts "read" verbal and nonverbal cues more efficiently. They filter relevant information from that which is less relevant, identifying priorities for action. They respond to the information they gather in ways that address their instructional goals and encourage academic engagement. In a similar manner, they are sensitive to the task demands and social situations of the classroom as well as the needs of students. While experienced teachers may understand the uniqueness of particular students, classes or situations, experts "read" these contextual features more intensely. Experts rely on their understanding of context to guide the choices they make regarding management and instruction. They can articulate the essential characteristics of students and classes that guide their decisions, identifying ways that particular students and particular classes need particular types of instruction.

Monitoring Learning and Providing Feedback

Expert teachers monitor students' learning by examining their own and students' responses to instruction to assess their current levels of understanding. On the basis of this monitoring, experts offer students information about their understanding that guides them to higher levels of comprehension. Such feedback, in this dimension of expertise, is more than positive reinforcement. It is information about the task, about the processes to accomplish the task, and/or about the efficacy, goals or regulation aspects relating to performing the task (Hattie & Jaeger, 1996). While experienced teachers interpret student responses, experts can detect when students do not understand and can diagnose students' interpretations and tailor the feedback they give to correct students' misunderstandings or to help them create new learning connections (Cellier, Eyrolle, & Marine, 1997; Clarridge & Berliner, 1991).

While experienced teachers may generate working hypotheses to guide their instruction, experts prioritize and reprioritize possibilities based on their teaching experience and on student responses (Berliner, 1987; Leinhardt & Greeno, 1986). Experts test hypotheses both while they are teaching and as they examine their choices while reflecting on lessons taught, and use this information to guide the next round of decisions they make regarding instruction.

Expert Teachers attend to Affective Attributes

While experienced teachers display high regard for students, experts differ in their level of commitment to students' learning. While experts recognize and acknowledge barriers to students' learning, they readily communicate their belief in students' power to overcome those barriers and help them find ways to do so. They are less likely to indulge in blaming behaviors. They also display passion that is closely linked to their sense of responsibility and love of the subjects they are teaching (Berliner, 1988). While experienced teachers may also demonstrate enthusiasm, experts differ in the extent to which they are emotionally committed to student success. Experts show more emotionality about successes and failures in their work. Experts inspire students to become more excited about learning.

Expert Teachers Influence Student Outcomes

Student outcomes include more than test scores, as expert teachers can motivate students towards more challenging goals, enhance self-efficacy, and have effects on the quality and nature of what is learned. Expert teachers encourage content mastery motivated by students' personal, intrinsic sense of satisfaction rather than just the completion of assignments (Dweck, 1992). While experienced teachers can "motivate" students to do assignments, experts emphasize students' responsibility for their own learning. Students take responsibility for what they learn as a result of being provided with opportunities to discover that their efforts affect outcomes. Expert teachers connect this sense of responsibility with students' self-efficacy, reinforcing students' beliefs in themselves as learners as well as their sense of confidence. Experts not only set challenging goals, but also structure situations so that students can reach them. While experienced teachers may challenge some students some of the time, experts find ways to challenge all students to "stretch" their understanding of ideas. Students perceive assignments and activities as thought provoking as well as engaging.

Expert teachers encourage all students to achieve and to understand content at increasingly complex levels. While experienced teachers promote academic achievement, experts do so in ways that also emphasize personal accomplishment and intellectual engagement. High quality learning outcomes are associated with deeper approaches. That is, attempts by the teacher to involve students in understanding information at greater levels of complexity. With deep approaches, students focus on relationships between various aspects of the content, formulate hypotheses or beliefs about the structure of the problem, and relate more to obtaining interest and understanding.

Concluding Comments to this Review of Attributes
of Expert Teachers

These major dimensions are aimed at distinguishing the transformational effects that experienced *expert* teachers have on classes of students compared to teachers who are merely experienced. Again, it is critical to note that these dimensions are not meant as another checklist, but as factors of a higher order notion of expertise. The complexity and elegance of teaching is to be emphasized. The questions as to relative importance and how these dimensions relate to each are more empirical questions, and thus the focus of the present study. The question of interest is whether teachers who satisfied the standards to be awarded National Board certification are different on these factors of expertise from those teachers who sat but did not achieve certification in terms of their classroom practices, classroom climates, and outcome effects on students.

METHOD

To ensure that dependable differences between NBCTs and non-NBCTs were detected, if they existed, the teaching practices and outcomes of four groups of teachers were examined and compared. Membership in the groups was determined by participants' scores on the NBPTS assessments based on the following guidelines: (a) candidates for National Board certification whose total scores on an assessment were at least one and one-fourth standard deviations below the certification score ($N = 16$); (b) candidates for National Board certification whose total scores on an assessment were between one-fourth, and three-fourths of a standard deviation below the certification score ($N = 15$); (c) candidates for National Board certification whose total scores on an assessment were between one-fourth, and three-fourths of a standard deviation above the certification score ($N = 17$); and (d) candidates for National Board certification whose total scores on an assessment were at least one and one-fourth standard deviations above the certification score ($N = 17$). The sample included teachers who sought National Board certification in two different fields – Middle Childhood/ Generalist (MC/G; $N = 34$), and Early Adolescence/English Language Arts (EA/ELA; $N = 31$). These subjects were chosen as one is a generalist and the other a subject-specific domain, there were many teachers who had passed and failed available to the research team, and the research team had conducted a mini-study to investigate the best methods for this study in these two areas (Hattie, Clinton, Thompson, & Schmidt-Davis, 1996). Sixty-five teachers were included in the sample for this component of the study. The teachers were recruited from North Carolina and Ohio, and the Washington, D.C. area. The teacher sample was divided approximately equally between the two certification areas and among the four score groups. White non-Hispanic ($N = 53$) and African American ($N = 12$) teachers were recruited proportional to their representation in the candidate population for the two certificate areas of interest. "Re-takers," candidates who had banked scores and had retaken an assessment, were excluded from the sample (Hattie et al., 1996).

Participants were recruited by telephone for participation in the study. Members of the research team read potential participants a structured protocol designed to inform them of the nature and purpose of the study, to determine whether they were currently teaching in a classroom setting appropriate for the study, and also to determine whether they were interested in participating. The research team mailed interested teachers a follow-up packet containing a letter summarizing the information they had been provided during the telephone conversation, various information and agreement forms, and a request for a class roll. The roll was used to identify two random student samples: four students for whom the teacher would save samples of classroom work, and three students who would be interviewed by the observation team.

Once an observation was arranged, a pair of trained observers was assigned to visit the classroom on the scheduled date. Information provided to the observers was limited to the teacher's name, location, teaching context (i.e., grade and subject matter), and description of the lesson to be observed. At no time were the observers given any information that might reveal the participant's certification status. To ensure a reasonable level of reliability, the two observers took turns to write the script of the classroom lessons, and these were independently coded by other trained raters (see below).

Data Collection Procedures

Prior to the data collection phase of this investigation, careful attention was given to ensuring that the design allowed for collecting evidence related to each of the dimensions of expertise described in this study. Table 2 shows

Table 2. Dimensions of Expertise in Teaching and Measures for each Dimension.

Dimension	Lesson Transcript and Observation Coding	Teacher Interview	Student Interviews	Pre-Observation Questions	Assignment Log	Student Questionnaires	Student Work Samples	Writing Sample
Use of knowledge	✓	✓						
Deep representations		✓						
Problem solving	✓	✓		✓				
Improvisation		✓	✓	✓				
Challenge of objectives		✓		✓				
Classroom climate	✓					✓		
Multidimensional perception	✓					✓		
Sensitivity to context	✓	✓						
Monitoring learning and providing feedback	✓	✓						
Test hypotheses				✓				
Respect for students	✓	✓				✓		
Passion for teaching and learning	✓	✓						
Motivation and self-efficacy						✓		
Outcomes of lessons: surface and deep			✓		✓	✓	✓	
Outcomes of lessons: achievement							✓	✓

the matrix that was used to determine and later monitor our data collection efforts.

Observations were conducted during the months of March through May in 1999 and 2000. For each observation, the observers arrived in the classroom approximately 30 min prior to the scheduled observation time. As one observer set up and tested recording equipment, the other made a classroom map and seating chart to ensure consistent identification of students during coding, and collected from the teacher a completed, open-ended preobservation questionnaire describing how the teacher had planned for the lesson to be observed. The tape recorder and extension microphones were positioned so as to capture as much classroom interaction as possible. The entire lesson, which lasted from 1 to 3 h, was tape-recorded. During the observation, Observer One completed the Narrative Running Record, a semi-structured form for recording, at 5 min intervals of as much classroom activity and interaction as possible. Observer One focused on the teacher: what the teacher said or did, how the teacher responded to the students, and how the teacher made decisions during the lesson. The observer also described body language, movement around the room, and vocal inflection that might help scorers interpret teacher–student interactions. The observer was not to provide any evaluative comment about the nature of classroom activity or interaction – only to capture the activity or interaction for scoring at a later date.

Observer Two completed the Observation Protocol, a structured coding form for recording specific types of classroom interactions at 2 min intervals throughout the observation. The observer watched and listened for 1 min of the lesson, then spent the second minute recording what occurred during the first minute. The Observation Protocol was used to capture the most important event related to feedback or classroom management that occurred during the first minute and to record any off-task behaviors that were observed. Observer Two noted the type of off-task behavior and the student engaged in the behavior. The observer would briefly describe, on the observation form, the predominant event from the minute observed, and then classify feedback, management, and off-task behaviors that were observed.

As soon as possible following the observation, the observers conducted tape-recorded interviews of three randomly selected students for approximately 10 min each. The purpose of the student interviews was to collect evidence of the students' understanding of the lesson observed. After the observation and student interviews, the observers conducted a tape-recorded interview of the teacher for approximately 1 h. The purpose of the teacher interview was to collect additional data related to the dimensions of teaching expertise. After the teacher interview, the observers gave the teacher a packet of post-observation materials to be completed and returned at a later time and concluded their visit.

The post-observation packet left by the observation team contained student questionnaires and writing prompts to be completed later as well as instructions for returning the student work samples that were collected and the completed questionnaires and writing responses. The student questionnaires included sub-scales of the Patterns of Adaptive Learning Survey (PALS; Midgley et al., 1996) to assess student goal orientation and classroom goal structure as well as student academic efficacy; a classroom climate instrument adapted by Hattie, Jaeger, Strahan, and Baker (1998) from Fraser's classroom environment scales (Fraser & Walberg, 1991); modified scales from the National Writing Project student questionnaires (Freedman, 1987); and scales developed by the research team to measure the teacher's respect for students, passion for teaching and learning, and ability to attend to multiple stimuli simultaneously. The scales are described in Table 3.

Following the observations, transcripts of the tape-recorded lessons, student interviews, and teacher interviews were prepared. Members of the research team who would not be scoring the observation and interview data reviewed the transcripts, the completed preobservation questionnaire, the observation protocol coding forms, and narrative record forms for information that might identify the teacher, the students, the school, or the observers. The reviewers deleted any such information by marking over it with a black marker and added an ID number to the top of each page of data. These artifacts of the observation were assembled as a casebook.

The Scoring System
The research team developed a separate detailed scoring rubric for each of the dimensions of teaching expertise. The rubrics were based on a four-point scale. Levels 1 and 2 described performances that were not characteristic of expert teachers for that dimension, and Levels 3 and 4 described performances that were characteristic of expert teachers. These rubrics were used to identify benchmark performances at each score level for each dimension. Table 4 presents an example of one of these rubrics, for Challenge.

Experienced classroom teachers were recruited to score the casebooks containing observation and interview data. All scorers were required to complete a rigorous training workshop before they were permitted to score

Table 3. Direction of Mean Scores on Student Questionnaire
Components for NBCTs and Non-NBCTs.

Dimension	Description	Direction
Ability goal orientation	Student purpose or goal is to demonstrate competence. The student seeks to gain favorable judgments.	+
Extrinsic goal orientation*	Student purpose or goal is external to the act of learning. The student seeks to get right answers (avoid mistakes), and to gain approval (avoid disapproval) from adults	+
Task goal orientation	Student purpose or goal is to develop competence, and extend mastery and understanding. Learning is seen as both interesting and enjoyable – an end in itself.	+
Academic efficacy	Student judgments of their ability to do their schoolwork.	–
Classroom climate	Student perceptions of cohesiveness and interpersonal relationships of the class.	–
Classroom management	Student perceptions of the clarity of rules in the class and the consistency with which those rules are enforced.	–
Friction*	Student perceptions that students engage in acting-out behavior in class or that some students in the class are fearful of other students.	–
Task goal structure	Students perceive that the purpose of academic work is to understand new material and to develop new skills.	+
Ability goal structure*	Students perceive that the purpose of academic work is to demonstrate ability and to perform better than others.	–
Extrinsic goal structure*	Students perceive that the purpose of academic work is to get good grades (avoid bad grades) and to avoid the disapproval of adults.	–
Teacher affect	Student perceptions that the teacher respects students and is passionate about teaching and learning.	+
Multidimensional perception	Student perceptions that the teacher can respond simultaneously and efficiently to multiple stimuli within the classroom, without disrupting the flow of the lesson.	+
Number of feedback	Student reports of the frequency of various forms of teacher feedback about student writing.	+

Note: Those components marked with an asterisk are associated with maladaptive patterns of learning and classroom environment.

Table 4. Scoring Rubric for Challenge.

LEVELS OF CHALLENGE			
Level 4	Level 3	Level 2	Level 1
A teacher at this level:	A teacher at this level:	A teacher at this level:	A teacher at this level:
• systematically and consistently challenges students to think • regularly promotes varied and appropriate assignments that are demanding and engaging for everyone • structures activities and lessons to assure that students can meet these challenges	• often challenges students to think but does so inconsistently • promotes some assignments as interesting, or as interesting to some students • offers general support to students who attempt to meet challenges	• only occasionally challenges students to think, some more than others • promotes a perception of assignments as necessary, if not interesting • offers little support to students to help them meet challenges	• rarely challenges students to think • promotes a perception of assignments as time-consuming and tedious • promotes a "sink or swim" mentality

Note: Expert teachers set demanding goals rather than "do your best" goals on the basis of students' present competencies. Experts not only set challenging goals, but also structure situations so that students can reach them. While expert teachers may challenge some students some of the time, experts find ways to challenge all students to "stretch" their understanding of ideas. Students perceive assignments and activities as thought provoking as well as engaging.

cases. Initial training included information about the design of the study, the observation instruments and coding procedures, and general scoring procedures. For the second phase of training, the scorers were divided into two teams of four or five members, led by members of the training team. During this phase each team was trained on a specific dimension, specifically the rubric for that dimension, examples of the kinds of data related to that dimension that were obtained from the observations and interviews, and benchmark performances on that dimension.

Scorers who successfully completed training were assigned cases to be scored only on the dimension for which they had received training. Each scoring team was divided into pairs of raters. Every possible combination of raters within a team were paired to form the maximum number of rater pairs for that team. Each case was randomly assigned to a pair of raters, neither of whom had observed that teacher. The order of cases was randomized to avoid raters receiving cases in the same order each time. Scorers were given copies of the rubric for the dimension they were scoring and a supply of scoring forms and casebooks for the cases they were to score. Actual scoring occurred off-site, typically at the scorer's residence.

Scorers reviewed each casebook in its entirety, considering all the evidence that related to the dimension being scored. Since this component of the study was related to Comparative Teaching Practices, scorers had been instructed to focus on the practice and behaviors of the teacher in weighing evidence, rather than on student behaviors. Scorers made extensive notes about the relationship between the evidence and the scoring rubric, and arrived at a judgment about whether the performance was characteristic of an expert teacher for that dimension. The scorers then completed a scoring form and initially assigned a dichotomous score for the case. Without reviewing the evidence again, each scorer next recorded his/her best judgment about which of the four score levels was most consistent with the case just scored. The scorers read and completed a scoring form for each case without consulting other team members. A website was established that contained an on-line version of the scoring form. After completing a paper scoring form, scorers visited the website and submitted their scores electronically.

The scoring manager monitored scores as they were submitted for rater agreement. If dichotomous scores for a given case did not agree, the scoring manager reviewed the scoring rubric and evidence in the case with each scorer to determine whether there was any misunderstanding about the rubric or misinterpretation of the evidence. The scoring manager was careful not to sway the judgments of the scorers, but only to monitor and clarify their understanding of the rubric for that dimension and how to interpret the evidence they found. This procedure usually resolved any disagreement between scorers, but if resolution did not occur, a third member of the team was assigned to read the case and submit a third scoring form. After team members had submitted scores for the first several cases on a dimension and the scoring manager determined that the level of rater calibration was satisfactory, the scoring manager continued to monitor scores for rater agreement, but did not further contact rater pairs who disagreed. Any further disagreements were assigned to a third rater who submitted another scoring form.

All scores were submitted within one week. After scoring for a dimension had been completed, team members came together again and were assigned to new teams for training on another set of dimensions. During this next round of training, the scorers again discussed issues of bias and calibration and received complete training on a new dimension. Each teacher received a final dichotomous score as well as a final scale (1–4) score on each dimension. The final dichotomous score was the dichotomous score assigned by the two raters if they agreed – either expert or nonexpert – on this dimension. For cases that required a third score, the final dichotomous score was the score assigned by the third reader. The final scale score was calculated by averaging the scale score assigned by the two scorers who agreed. That is, the scale scores from Scorer 1 and Scorer 2 were averaged if those two scorers provided the same dichotomous score. If they disagreed on the dichotomous score, the scale score of Scorer 3 was averaged with the original scorer who provided a dichotomous score that matched that of Scorer 3.

Of all the issues surrounding the conceptualization and assessment of accomplished practice as a teacher, none is more controversial, nor more difficult to gauge unambiguously, than the relationship between good teaching and student learning. To even pose the question whether good teaching produces better learning and higher achievement seems fatuous. In truth, the relationship between teaching and learning has proven to be one of the most intractable to establish in all of educational research. To begin with, what index shall we use for student achievement? Policy makers, public officials, and the public generally seem to have opted for measures of convenience, namely, standardized multiple-choice tests produced by major commercial publishers, or paper and pencil measures developed under state auspices to reflect the state curriculum. The limitations of such measures are well-known: an undue concentration on drill and practice; the temptation to "teach to the test" and thereby narrow and distort what is actually taught in classrooms; an emphasis by both teachers and students on quick recall and use of algorithms and isolated facts; and perhaps most disturbingly, the temptation to simply cheat. The rise of performance assessment notwithstanding, the performance of students on standardized paper and pencil, multiple-choice tests remains the standard by which teachers, principals, and schools are held accountable.

There are a number and variety of uncontrolled influences on what students learn, how much they learn, and how well they learn (both in and out of the classroom). This makes it difficult to ascribe specific student learning to a particular teacher's influence. A teacher, for example, has a given student in his or her class for only a fraction of the student's 12 years of formal public education, and within a single day a student may be influenced by a number of teachers. As a consequence, we did not use student scores on standardized achievement tests in this study, but appreciate that this then begs for further study of NBCT and non-NBCT teacher effects on student achievement.

One dimension, Outcomes of Lessons: Surface and Deep, was not scored by an analysis of the casebooks. Rather this dimension was scored by an analysis of the student work samples collected from a sample of students in each class. A separate scoring rubric and scoring form based on the SOLO taxonomy (Biggs & Collis, 1982; Hattie & Purdie, 1998) was developed to assess the depth of student responses to the assignments given by their teachers. When scoring the student work of a teacher on this dimension, the scorers reviewed each of the student artifacts submitted and provided one overall score about the depth of response from the students. As with the previous dimensions, scorers on this dimension provided a dichotomous judgment about whether the overall quality of student responses demonstrated a surface or deep level of understanding. Then scorers provided their best judgment about whether the overall depth was Unistructural, Multistructural, Relational, or Extended Abstract (or one idea, many ideas, relationships among ideas, extending the idea). The scoring manager monitored scores and contacted rater pairs about disagreements. Any disagreements were resolved by a conference during which the raters discussed the evidence that supported their judgments and reached a final determination through consensus. The final dichotomous score on this dimension was the dichotomous score agreed upon by the two raters. The final scale score was the average of the two scale scores provided by the scorers.

Three major sets of analyses are used to identify the key differences between the expert and experienced groups. The first set of analyses is more descriptive, using mean differences, and effect-sizes (ES), and this provides an overview of the findings. To then assess differences over all dimensions, discriminant function analysis (DFA) is used to ascertain the linear combination across the entire set of variables in such a way as to maximally distinguish between groups of interest. DFA takes into account the covariation among the discriminating variables and, more important, it allows an examination of the pattern of characteristics that distinguish one group from the other. An attractive derivative feature of DFA is that the pattern so identified may then be used to classify individuals into appropriate categories. To the extent that individuals are correctly classified, the inference that the groups differ on the dimensions taken as a whole is supported. Finally, a stepwise DFA was used to ascertain which of the variables most discriminate between the two groups. This stepwise procedure selects smaller subsets of the 13 discriminating variables and employs a prespecified stopping criterion when the addition of additional dimensions to the set does not result in a statistically significant improvement in the discrimination.

RESULTS

This section is divided into two major parts. In the first section, the relationship between National Board certification and the dimensions of teaching practice that have emerged from the scholarly literature is analyzed. The next section discusses the relationship between certification status and student outcomes.

Comparative Teaching Practices

To what extent is the National Board's vision of accomplished practice, as laid down in the Standards documents and as instantiated in its assessments, consonant with the characteristics of teaching expertise that have emerged from the research and scholarly literature? To answer this question, several analyses were performed. First, information relating to 13 of the 15 dimensions of comparative teaching practices and outcomes was analyzed. The set of scores assigned independently by the scorers to each of the 65 teacher casebooks provided the basis for the following analyses. Table 5 presents the inter-rater agreement indices for the 13 dimensions. As can be seen, these ranged from a low of 0.37 to a high of 0.95, with mean inter-rater reliability of 0.79. The information pertaining to Testing Hypotheses needs to be considered with much caution.

The mean scores for each dimension, by teacher certification status, along with other relevant descriptive information, are depicted graphically in Fig. 1. All but 2 of the 13 comparisons had statistically significant differences at the 0.01 level or less: monitoring and feedback, and multidimensional perceptions of classrooms were not significantly different. Eleven of the 13 ES were 0.58 or greater and only one was less than 0.40, suggesting that the observed differences between NBCTs and non-NBCTs along these teaching dimensions are distinctly different.

The DFA seeks to linearly combine the information contained in the entire set of variables under study in such a way as to maximally distinguish between groups of interest. The 13 dimensions were linearly

Table 5. Inter-rater Agreement Indices for 13 Dimensions.

Dimension	Inter-rater Agreement
Challenge	0.87
Classroom climate	0.88
Deep representations	0.79
Deep understanding and accomplishment	0.84
Improvisation	0.95
Monitor learning and provide feedback	0.87
Multidimensional perception	0.88
Passion	0.90
Problem solving	0.83
Respect	0.81
Sensitivity to context	0.62
Test hypotheses	0.37
Use of knowledge	0.72

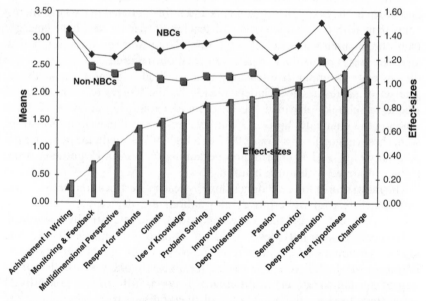

Fig. 1. Means and ES for the NBCTs and non-NBCTs Across the Teaching Dimensions.

combined into a new, single variable (the discriminant function) such that differences between NBCTs and non-NBCTs on the function are highlighted. Wilk's lambda, the statistical test for the degree of separation of the two groups, equals 0.443; χ^2 (12) = 44.47; $p < 0.0001$. The function separates NBCTs and non-NBCTs into groups with little overlap. This was seen more easily in the classification analysis, which showed that 84% of the teachers in the sample were correctly classified using discriminant function scores (85% correctly classified as non-NBCTs, and 83% correctly classified as NBCTs).

The stepwise DFA indicated that use of three of the dimensions (Challenge, Deep Representation, and Monitoring and Feedback) were sufficient to distinguish between NBCTs and non-NBCTs. More specifically, of all possible subsets, these three most effectively separate NBCTs from non-NBCTs. The addition of other dimensions into the analyses would improve the classification of candidates, but not to a statistically significant degree. The important substantive point to note, and one we will return to in the discussion, was that the relative status of teachers on these three teaching dimensions alone was sufficient to properly classify 80% of the teachers.

A more stringent test of whether NBCTs could be distinguished from non-NBCTs on the basis of teaching dimensions from the research literature was possible. This involves a comparison of Groups Two and Three, that is, teachers who were within one-fourth of a standard deviation on either side of the certification score. These were especially critical analyses inasmuch as certification errors are more likely the closer a teacher candidate is to the certification score. Using all 13 dimensions, 91% of the teachers in score Groups Two and Three were correctly classified. The stepwise analysis again resulted in the selection of only two teaching dimensions, Challenge, and Monitoring and Providing Feedback. Use of these two dimensions alone correctly classified 75% of the teachers.

Comparative Teaching Outcomes: Quality of Learning

The second investigation attempted to assess the relative extent to which NBCTs and non-NBCTs affected the quality of the student learning. We accomplished this evaluation in three stages. In stage one, work samples from four randomly chosen students in each class were independently evaluated by two assessors who made an initial dichotomous decision regarding the depth of student understanding (deep vs. surface). The small number of disagreements that occurred were resolved through discussion and conferencing between the two raters so that each work sample received a single, consensus classification. In stage two, scorers refined the initial classification into either Unistructural vs. Multistructural or Relational vs. Extended Abstract. It is noted in passing, that the inter-rater agreement for the stage two evaluation was 0.91. Stage three consisted of a consensus evaluation combining all student samples for a given teacher into a single score on the 4-point SOLO taxonomy.

The cross-tabulation of teacher certification status and the student depth of understanding according to the SOLO taxonomy is presented in Fig. 2. Seventy-four percent of student work samples in the classes of NBCTs were judged to reflect a level of deeper understanding, that is Relational or Extended Abstract, and 26% reflected a more surface understanding. This compares with 29% of the work samples of non-NBCTs so classified as deep and 71% as surface. Predictably, the difference in the level of understanding of students taught by Group 1 vs. Group 4 teachers was statistically discernible (χ^2 (1) = 7.05; $p < 0.01$).

These results were similar to the tentative conclusions reached by Hattie et al. (1998) in an ethnographic study of a much smaller sample of students

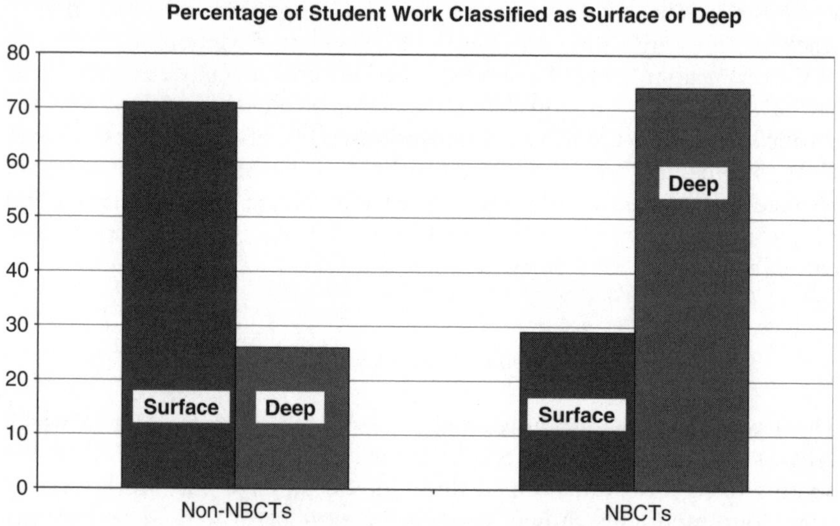

Fig. 2. Percentage of Student Work Assigned Surface or Deep for the NBCTs and non-NBCTs.

in the classes of six teachers (three NBCTs and three non-NBCTs). This finding is potentially of great importance to the teaching profession. If confirmed with additional, even larger samples, the results suggest that NBPTS, through its series of comprehensive performance assessments of teaching proficiency, is identifying and certifying teachers who are producing students differing in profound and important ways from those taught by noncertified teachers. These students appear to exhibit an understanding of the concepts targeted in instruction that is more integrated, more coherent, and at a higher level of abstraction than the understanding achieved by other students.

Comparative Teaching Outcomes:
Student Motivation and Self-Efficacy

Information related to student motivation and self-efficacy was obtained from student questionnaires administered after the end of the classroom visit. The differences in mean component scores between students of NBCTs and non-NBCTs were, on the whole, negligibly small. Table 3 shows the direction of the differences in mean scores on the components for students of NBCTs and non-NBCTs. Scores were reversed for components initially scored in the maladaptive direction. A plus sign indicates that students of NBCTs obtained higher mean scores than those of non-NBCTs; a minus sign indicates the opposite. Students of NBCTs had more favorable scores on seven out of thirteen components. A simple sign test supports the conclusion that substantive differences on these components are not present. However, a more striking difference in the mean scores for the National Writing Project Study Feedback Component was observed and may warrant further attention.

DISCUSSION AND CONCLUSIONS

This study has demonstrated that teachers certified as "accomplished" by the NBPTS assessment process are demonstrably different in their classrooms practices, and there are differences in the depth of learning achieved by their students, when compared to noncertified but otherwise experienced teachers. Non-NBCTs differed on all 13 dimensions of expertise, and the best discriminating dimensions were the level of challenge, the depth of representation, and the quality of monitoring and feedback. Most important, the majority of the student work was considered deep rather than surface learning – the opposite profile of the experienced but not-certified teachers.

Some words of caution regarding limitations are in order. First, it should be emphasized that the certified teachers who agreed to participate in this investigation were not randomly sampled from the ever-growing population of NBCTs. In a similar manner, the teachers who graciously agreed to participate in the study and who attempted certification but were unsuccessful were not a random sample of unsuccessful candidates. It follows that generalization to the larger populations of which these teachers are members should be approached with caution. The authors are of the belief that if the present investigation were replicated (with perhaps improvements discussed below), results more or less similar to those described herein would be obtained. That, however, to use a rather overworked expression, is an empirical question.

Second, in the course of this investigation we have learned what we did well, what we should have done but did not do, and perhaps most painfully, what we should not have done at all. Among the former, we believe the training materials and protocols, the training and observation leaders, and the observers and scorers were exceptional. It is easy to defend the quality of the data obtained. That said, there is also considerable room for improving and refining many of the measures in the study. Regarding the second category, the sheer number of ways the study could be improved is uncomfortably large. Given the number of factors studied, a much larger sample of teachers would have been desirable. Appropriate and reliable measures of entering achievement, as well as other adjustments for possible differences in resources, would have added to our confidence in the conclusions.

Goldhaber and Anthony (2004) used a sample of 32,399 teachers (serving 609,160 students) to estimate student-level value-added models between NBCT and non-NBCT teachers and elementary level student achievement over a 3 year period. The applicants were more effective than nonapplicants in the year that they applied in reading and math. This led Goldhaber and Anthony to conclude that the NBPTS process was "successfully identifying the more effective teachers among applicants" (p. 5). They reported a meaningful increase in the test scores (ES = 0.20) in reading and math for the NBCTs compared to the non-NBCTs, and these are even higher when the NBCTs were teaching disadvantaged students, and for the younger students. They concluded that NBCTs were more effectively producing student learning gains on state-wide assessment tests. This, complemented by the findings of the current study, suggests that NBCTs have marked effects on the quality and quantity of learning for their students.

Vandevoort et al. (2004) examined student achievement gains between 35 EC/G or MC/G NBCTs and all other teachers across 14 school districts in Arizona over a 5 year period. They used an ANCOVA design, with gain scores as the dependent variable, certification status (NBCT or non-NBCT) as the fixed factor, and pretest score of each of the SAT09 subject areas as the covariate. They also calculated ES. Students of NBCTs outperformed students of non-NBCTs on 73% of the measures over the 5 year comparisons, and the ES averaged across curriculum areas was 0.12. Vandevoort et al. (2004) claimed that this 0.12 represented a gain of "one-month advantage in achievement in comparison to the students taught by non-NBCTs" (p. 34), or students in classes taught by NBCTs were able to get in about the equivalent of 25 days more days of instruction in a typical academic year. This argument is based on the claim that an ES of 1.0 is approximately equivalent to one academic year's growth on a typical standardized test, but it is probably more important to compare the gain of 0.12 with many other innovations in education. Hattie (1999) documented the typical ES from over 500 meta-analyses and the average effect size is 0.40, so 0.12 would be considered a very small effect compared to many other influences on student achievement. It is likely, as noted in the current study, that the effects of NBCTs are more likely to be on the classroom behaviors and most important on the quality of what is being learnt by students of NBCTs compared to students of non-NBCTs.

Finally, it should be noted that there were factors that may have militated against the likelihood of finding positive results in the current study. First, the non-NBCTs in this study took the very demanding assessment of the National Board. Almost to a person, teachers who have undergone this year-long, rigorous assessment, including those who were not certified, testify to the power of that experience as a professional development activity (Bond et al., 2000). Most reported that it fundamentally changed the way they thought about and approached teaching, and that they became better teachers for the experience. Second, many of the non-NBCTs in the study enthusiastically agreed to participate because they felt that they had "something to prove." This is, of course, the well-known "John Henry" effect, the exertion of unusual effort by subjects in a study who are aware of their status as members of a control or comparison group.

There are also limitations to the current study. We had no way of ensuring that the students in these various classes were equivalent in ability and previous achievement. Given that many of these teachers had been working in the same school over previous years, had recently heard of their certification status, there was less likelihood that the NBCTs had different class assignments due to their new status. Furthermore, while the classroom observations provided rich description, the current study did not use these observations in a more qualitative analysis of classrooms. This is a further study to be conducted. Similarly, this study does not illuminate how the standards set by the National Board were enacted in the classrooms or how the standards were understood by the teachers who participated in this study.

This study was intended as a construct validation of the National Board's vision of accomplished teaching, the instantiation of that vision in assessments, and ultimately the certification decisions resulting from that assessment. In so doing, this study sought to determine the extent to which actual teachers who had achieved certification exhibited, to a measurably greater degree than their noncertified counterparts, the attributes of expert teaching as these have emerged from the research literature. We sought evidence of teaching by examining teachers' instructional planning and artifacts, by observing them in actual classrooms, by structured interviews of the teachers and their students, by examining student products and student writing, and by collecting information on the nature and variety of professional activities they engaged in. In every single comparison on the dimensions of teaching excellence between NBCTs and non-NBCTs, NBCTs obtained higher mean scores. In 11 of the 13 comparisons, the differences were statistically significant.

The conclusion seems clear: the NBCTs in this sample possessed, to a considerably greater degree than non-NBCTs, those attributes of expert teaching that have emerged from the ever-expanding body of research on teaching and learning. They possessed pedagogical content knowledge that was more flexibly and innovatively employed in instruction; they were more able to improvise and to alter instruction in response to contextual features of the classroom situation; they understood at a deeper level the reasons for individual student success and failure on any given academic task; their understanding of students was such that they were more able to provide developmentally appropriate learning tasks that engaged, challenged, and even intrigued students, without boring or overwhelming them; they were more able to anticipate and plan for difficulties students were likely to encounter with new concepts; they could more easily improvise when things did not run smoothly; they were more able to generate accurate hypotheses about the causes of student success and failure; and they brought a distinct passion to their work.

The results regarding comparative teaching outcomes may well represent the most important single finding in this investigation. The data collected on the depth of students' understanding strongly suggest that expert teachers, as exemplified by the NBCTs in this sample, were demonstrably more proficient at fostering in their students a level of understanding that was richer, more elaborated, and more meaningfully interconnected with related concepts. This finding was not restricted to a particular grade level or to a particular subject matter. It appears to be a skill of expert teachers at grade levels from middle childhood to high school. The variety of content and ability objectives in the 65 instructional units in the study spanned the spectrum: from understanding literary works, to historical and social movements; from the complexities of interdependent ecosystems, to fundamental concepts in argumentative writing.

To the extent that the NBCTs in this sample were representative of the larger population of NBCTs, the evidence from this investigation seems clear: NBCTs possess, to a considerably greater degree than non-NBCTs, those attributes of expert teaching that have emerged from a large body of research on teaching and learning. Further study of these key dimensions of difference may lead to more focused professional development to assist those experienced teachers become the experts, at least as assessed through the certification process.

We conclude this investigation with one additional caveat. The system of advanced certification developed by the NBPTS is not a minimum competency assessment; it is a certification of teaching excellence. It was not designed as a means to distinguish bad teachers from good teachers; it was designed to distinguish expert teachers from experienced ones. That the "construct" of accomplished practice as envisioned by the National Board was impressively supported by this series of investigations should not be taken to mean that the not-yet expert teachers who participated in this ambitious project are not serving their students and, indeed, the general public well.

REFERENCES

Archer, J. (2002). National Board is pressed to prove certified teachers make difference. *Education Week, 21*(20), 1–3.

Berliner, D. (1987). Expert and novice interpretations of classroom data. Paper presented at the annual meeting of the American Educational Research Association, Washington, D.C.

Berliner, D. C. (1988). The development of expertise in pedagogy. Charles W. Hunt Memorial Lecture presented at the Annual Meeting of the American Association of Colleges for Teacher Education (New Orleans, LA, February 17–20,). (ERIC Document Reproduction Service ED298122).

Biggs, J. B., & Collis, K. F. (1982). *Evaluating the quality of student learning: The SOLO taxonomy.* New York: Academic Press.

Bond, L., Smith, T., Baker, W. K., & Hattie, J. A. (2000). *The certification system of the National Board for Professional Teaching Standards: A construct validity study.* Greensboro, NC: Center for Educational Research and Evaluation, The University of North Carolina at Greensboro.

Burroughs, R., Schwartz, T. A., & Hendricks-Lee, M. (2000). Communities of practice and discourse communities: Negotiating boundaries in NBPTS certification. *Teachers College Record, 102*(2), 344–374.

Cellier, F., Eyrolle, C., & Marine, C. (1997). Expertise in dynamic environments: Results of comparison between novice and expert operators in supervision of dynamic environments. *Ergonomics, 40*(1), 28–50.

Chi, M. T. H., Glaser, R., & Farr, M. J. (Eds). (1988). *The nature of expertise.* Hillsdale, NJ: Lawrence Erlbaum Associates.

Clarridge, P. (1989). Alternative perspectives for analyzing expertise in teaching. Paper presented at the annual meeting of the American Educational Research Association, San Francisco, CA.

Clarridge, P., & Berliner, D. (1991). Perceptions of student behavior as a function of expertise. *Journal of Classroom Interaction, 26,* 1–7.

Cushing, K. S., Sabers, D. S., & Berliner, D. C. (1992). Olympic gold: Investigations of expertise in teaching. *Educational Horizons, 70*(3), 108–114.

Dorner, D., & Schaub, H. (1994). Errors in planning and decision making and the nature of human information processing. *Applied Psychology: An Interview Review, 43*(4), 433–453.

Dweck, C. (1992). Motivational processes affecting learning. *American Psychologist, 41,* 1040–1048.

Fraser, B. J., & Walberg, H. J. (1991). *Educational environments.* New York: Pergamon Press.

Freedman, S. W. (1987). *Response to student writing.* NCTE Research Report No. 23. National Council of Teachers of English, Urbana, IL. .

Goldhaber, D., & Anthony, E. (2004). *Can teacher quality be effectively assessed ?* Seattle, WA: Center on Reinventing Public Education, University of Washington.

Hattie, J. A. (1999). Influences on student learning. Inaugural Professorial Address, University of Auckland. Retrieved on 22 September 2005 from http://www.education.auckland. ac.nz/staff/j.hattie

Hattie, J. A., Clinton, J. C., Thompson, M., & Schmidt-Davis, H. (1996, February). *Identifying expert teachers.* Greensboro, NC: National Board for Professional Teaching Standards, Technical Analysis Group, Center for Educational Research and Evaluation, University of North Carolina-Greensboro.

Hattie, J. A., & Jaeger, R. M. (1996). *A model of expert versus experienced teachers.* Unpublished manuscript. University of North Carolina, Greensboro.

Hattie, J., Jaeger, R., Strahan, D., & Baker, W. (1998). *Report on the development of the assessment/data collection instruments and protocols.* Unpublished manuscript, Center for Educational Research at Evaluation, University of North Carolina at Greensboro.

Hattie, J., & Purdie, N. (1998). The SOLO model: Addressing fundamental measurement issues. In: B. Dart & G. Boulton-Lewis (Eds), *Teaching and learning in higher education* (pp. 145–176). Melbourne, Australia: ACER Press.

Holland, J. (2003). Leaders question value of teacher certification. *The Charlotte Observer*, 6B.

Holland, R. (2002). National teacher certification: Advancing quality or perpetuating mediocrity? Retrieved March 13, 2003, from http://www.lexingtoninstitute.org/education/pdf/HollandNatlTeachCert.pdf

Iovacchini, L. C. (1998). *National Board for Professional Teaching Standards: What teachers are learning?* Unpublished doctoral dissertation, College of Education, University of South Carolina, Columbia.

Kounin, J. (1970). *Discipline and group management in classrooms.* Cambridge, MA: International Thomson Publishing.

Leinhardt, G., & Greeno, J. (1986). The cognitive skill of teaching. *Journal of Educational Psychology, 78*, 75–95.

Livingston, C., & Borko, H. (1990). High school mathematics review lessons: Expert–novice distinctions. *Journal for Research in Mathematics Education, 21*(5), 372–387.

Maslow, A. H. (1971). *The farther reaches of human nature.* New York: Viking.

Midgley, C., Martin, M., Hicks, L., Roeser, R., Urdan, T., Anderman, E., & Kaplan, A. (1996). *Patterns of adaptive learning survey.* Ann Arbor, MI: School of Education, University of Michigan.

Moss, P. A., & Schutz, A. (1999). Risking frankness in educational assessment. *Phi Delta Kappan, 80*(9), 680–687.

National Board for Professional Teaching Standards (NBPTS). (2003). About NBPTS: State & local support and incentives. Retrieved April 21, 2003, from http://www.nbpts.org/about/state.cfm

National Commission on Teaching and America's Future (NCTAF). (1996, September). *What matters most: Teaching for America's future.* New York: National Commission on Teaching and America's Future.

National Commission on Teaching and America's Future (NCTAF). (2003, January). *No dream denied: A pledge to America's children.* Washington, DC: National Commission on Teaching and America's Future.

O'Connor, K. A. (2003). *Identifying the wants and needs of North Carolina upper elementary (Grades 3–5) National Board and non-National Board teachers for job success and satisfaction.* Ann Arbor, MI: ProQuest Information and Learning Company.

Petty, T. M. (2002). *Identifying the wants and needs of North Carolina high school mathematics teachers for job success and satisfaction.* Ann Arbor, MI: ProQuest Information and Learning Company.

Podgursky, M. (2001). Defrocking the National Board. *Education Next, 1*(20), 9–82.

Poliakoff, M. (2001). Mastering the basics: Foundations and the feds love national teacher certification. So why aren't "master teachers" producing results? Retrieved March 26, 2007, from http://www.philanthropyroundtable.org/article.asp?article=892&paper=1&cat=147

Pool, J. E., Ellett, C. E., Schiavone, S., & Carey-Lewis, C. (2000). How valid are the National Board for Professional Teaching Standards assessments for predicting the quality of actual classroom teaching and learning? Results of six mini case studies. *Journal of Personnel Evaluation in Education, 15*(1), 31–48.

Ralph, D. E. (2003). *National Board Certified Teachers' views of the certification process and its effect on the professional school culture.* Ann Arbor, MI: ProQuest Information and Learning Company.

Schalock, D., Schalock, M., & Myton, D. (1998). Effectiveness – along with quality – should be the focus. *Phi Delta Kappan, 79*(6), 648–670.

Shulman, L. (1987). Knowledge and teaching: Foundations of the new reform. *Harvard Educational Review, 57,* 1–22.

Sternberg, R. J., & Horvath, J. A. (1995). A prototype view of expert teaching. *Educational Researcher, 24*(6), 9–17.

Swanson, H. L., O'Connor, J. E., & Cooney, J. B. (1990). An information processing analysis of expert and novice teachers' problem solving. *American Educational Research Journal, 27,* 533–556.

Van Driel, J. H., Beijaard, D., & Verloop, N. (2001). Professional development and reform in science teaching: The role of teachers' practical knowledge. *Journal of Research on Science Teaching, 38*(2), 137–155.

Vandevoort, L. G., Amrein-Beardsley, A., & Berliner, D. C. (2004). National board certified teachers and their students' achievement. *Education Policy Analysis, 12*(46), September. Retrieved September 22 from http://epaa.asu.edu/epaa/v12n46/

Westerman, D. A. (1991). Expert and novice teacher decision making. *Journal of Teacher Education, 42*(4), 292–305.

Whitman, B. A. (2002). *Professional teachers for quality education: Characteristics of teachers certified by the Board for Professional Teaching Standards.* New Brunswick, NJ: Rutgers, The State University of New Jersey.

SECTION 4:
EFFECTS OF NBPTS
CERTIFICATION

CHAPTER 13

EFFECTS OF THE NATIONAL BOARD FOR PROFESSIONAL TEACHING STANDARDS CERTIFICATION PROCESS ON TEACHERS' PERSPECTIVES AND PRACTICES

Kenneth Wolf and Grace Taylor

ABSTRACT

Teachers are central to the learning of their students, and teacher learning is integral to teaching quality. In this study, six teachers who had recently completed the National Board assessment in the Middle Childhood/ Generalist certificate area were interviewed over a six-month period about the effects of the certification process on their views and practices. Overall, the six teachers described changes in their practices for each of the eleven standards, with nearly all of the teachers describing changes in three areas in particular – reflection, assessment, and family involvement. In addition, most of them reported that the certification experience increased their confidence as teachers in part because it validated their current practice and in part because others treated them with more

Assessing Teachers for Professional Certification:
The First Decade of the National Board for Professional Teaching Standards
Advances in Program Evaluation, Volume 11, 381–412
Copyright © 2008 by Elsevier Ltd.
All rights of reproduction in any form reserved
ISSN: 1474-7863/doi:10.1016/S1474-7863(07)11013-9

respect. Overall, four of the six teachers described their experience as having had a significant positive effect on their practice, with one teacher characterizing the effect as modest, while another reported little change. The teacher who reported few changes did so because she believed that her practices were already consistent with the National Board vision. A number of features of the National Board certification process appeared to contribute to the professional development of these teachers, including the standards themselves, the portfolio process (but not the assessment center exercises), writing structured commentaries, and collaborating with colleagues.

INTRODUCTION

From *A Nation Prepared* (Carnegie Forum on Education and the Economy, 1986) to *What Matters Most* (NCTAF, 1996), the message has been the same: Teachers are central to the learning of their students and teacher learning is integral to teaching quality. The National Board for Professional Teaching Standards (NBPTS), for example, asserts that "the single most important action the nation can take to improve schools is to strengthen teaching" (NBPTS, 1996, p. 1).

While the agenda of the NBPTS is to set high standards for teachers and certify those who meet these standards, the NBPTS contends that, "certification is more than a system for recognizing and rewarding accomplished teachers. It represents ... an opportunity to rethink the way the profession organizes itself for the continuing growth and development of its members" (NBPTS, 1996, p. 1).

It is with this backdrop that this study of the effects of the National Board certification process on teacher learning was conducted. A central claim of the NBPTS is that the Board certification experience promotes the professional development of teachers. Earlier studies supported the professional development value of the National Board experience (Athanases, 1994; Tracz, Sienty, & Mata, 1994; Tracz et al., 1995), but further studies that investigate the ways in which the Board certification experience impacts teachers' views and practices are needed.

BACKGROUND

This section provides information about the NBPTS and the Colorado Goals 2000 project, a statewide program that provided financial and professional support for the teachers in this study to participate in the National Board certification process.

The National Board for Professional Teaching Standards

The NBPTS is a non-profit organization that was created from a recommendation of the Carnegie Foundation for the Advancement of Teaching in its landmark report, *A Nation Prepared: Teachers for the 21st Century* (Carnegie Forum on Education and the Economy, 1986). In this report, a call was put forth to create a national board modeled on those of the medical and legal professions. This new board, two-thirds of whom would be classroom teachers, was intended to serve as a beacon of leadership and high standards for the education profession.

The National Board has identified more than 30 areas of teacher specialization in generalist fields such as Early Childhood (students aged 3–8) or Early Adolescence (students aged 11–15), and in specialty areas such as Middle Childhood/English Language Arts (MC/ELA, students aged 11–15) or Adolescence and Young Adult/Mathematics (AYA/M, ages 15+).

The National Board's five core propositions for accomplished teachers relate to (i) commitment to students and learning, (ii) knowledge of content and how to teach it, (iii) responsibility for managing and monitoring student learning, (iv) thinking systematically about their practice and learning from experience, and (v) being members of learning communities. These core propositions have then been translated into specific standards for accomplished practice in each of the certificate areas by teams of teachers, subject matter experts, and scholars.

Teachers who applied for National Board certification completed a two-part assessment. The first part of the assessment required the teacher to compile a school-site portfolio reflecting various facets of teaching, including written commentaries describing teaching and learning in their classrooms, videotapes of interactions with students, and samples of student work. The second part required a teacher to participate in assessment center activities, such as viewing and responding to videotapes of classroom instruction and analyzing student work samples. These assessments, designed to evaluate the complex knowledge and teaching behaviors required by the standards, evaluated how the candidates analyzed and reflected on their practice and how effectively they acted on their insights.

An overview of the assessment for Middle Childhood/Generalist (MC/G) teachers of children of ages 7–12 is provided below.

Teacher Portfolio Entries. MC/Gs completed six portfolio entries (as did candidates in other certificate areas). The entries are described in Table 1.

For these six portfolio entries, candidates prepared and gathered a variety of artifacts, documents, and videotape segments as evidence of their excellence. In addition, candidates were asked to submit written commentaries for each of the entries. Teachers were given guidance in these commentaries through a series of prompts that directed them to specific features of the performance. These prompts directed teachers to not only describe the performance, but also to analyze and reflect on the performance. In the "Reflection" and "Evaluation" sections of the prompts, teachers were asked questions such as:

> If you were given the opportunity to use these writing assignments again with these students, what are the alternative strategies you might use? Why? (Entry 1, p. 7)

> How well do you feel the chosen theme and the selected big idea(s) from science worked together to help students grow in understanding of both? (Entry 2, p. 7)

> To what extent do you think your efforts to help students understand and consider perspectives other than their own have been successful? (Entry 3, p. 6)

> To what extent were the student learning goals for the learning experience met? (Entry 4, p. 8)

Table 1. Teacher Portfolio Entries.

Entry Number	Focus	Activity
Entry 1	Writing: thinking through the process	The teacher chooses two writing assignments associated with social studies and fictional narrative, and the responses from two students
Entry 2	Thematic exploration: connections to science	The teacher chooses three artifacts each from two students from an interdisciplinary unit
Entry 3	Building a classroom community	The teacher videotapes students in small learning groups
Entry 4	Building mathematical understanding	The teacher prepares a videotape of the whole class and collects responses from two students engaged in building understanding in a content area
Entry 5	Documented accomplishment I	The teacher provides evidence of contributions to the professional community
Entry 6	Documented accomplishment II	The teacher provides evidence of outreach to families or community

These prompts were often followed by hints such as:

Tell also how [the student work samples] reflect your approach to providing multiple paths for learning. (Entry 2, p. 7)

Bear in mind that candid discussions of perceived shortcomings are more likely to reveal accomplishments than are responses that gloss over problems. (Entry 3, p. 6)

The total number of pages that a candidate could submit to describe, analyze, and reflect on the contents of the portfolio was 66 pages. Written commentary page limits for the entries are given in Table 2.

Assessment Center. The assessment center exercises were given at a central location, and take one day to complete. MC/Gs were given four assessment tasks to complete:

Exercise 1: Analyzing student work. "This exercise focuses on the candidate's command of science content ability to analyze student work samples in science, and ability to plan instruction on a particular science topic to extend students' learning and address student misconceptions" (NBPTS, 1997, p. 23).

Exercise 2: Using assessment information. "This exercise focuses on the candidate's command of knowledge of reading pedagogy and ability to apply this knowledge appropriately to an individual student through assessment and teaching strategies" (NBPTS, 1997, p. 23).

Exercise 3: Using developmental inferences. "This exercise focuses on the candidate's knowledge of developmentally appropriate health

Table 2. Page Limits for Portfolio Written Commentaries.

Entry	Page Limit
Entry 1	12 pages
Entry 2	12 pages
Entry 3	13 pages
Entry 4	11 pages
Entry 5	9 pages
Entry 6	9 pages
Portfolio total	66 pages

issues and ability to integrate these subjects in age appropriate ways" (NBPTS, 1997, p. 24).

Exercise 4: Exploring curriculum resources. "The exercise focuses on the candidate's capacities to choose resources and to plan instruction using a range of instructional materials and encompassing multiple paths for learning" (NBPTS, 1997, p. 24).

Colorado Goals 2000 National Board Project

The teachers who participated in this study were members of a statewide project funded in part through a Goals 2000 grant to support teachers for certification with the National Board. Goals 2000 was a federally funded effort to increase student achievement through a focus on student standards, but it was broadly construed to include teacher professional development as well.

In this project, a partnership was formed among a university school of education, 10 school districts, the state department of education, and the NBPTS. This partnership provided both professional and financial support to approximately 100 teachers over the three-year life of the grant (1997–2000). The teachers were given a modest level of professional support in the form of statewide meetings, individual National Board Certified mentors, and electronic networking. The teachers were also given financial support through the grant. Of the $2,000 application fee, the grant paid $1,000, the school district 700, and the candidate the remaining 300.

LITERATURE REVIEW

This review discusses two key strands that underlie this study of the effects of the National Board certification process on teachers' thinking and practices – current directions in standards and assessment and the promise of new forms of professional development.

Current Directions in Standards and Assessments

Over the past decade and a half there had been a movement at the local, state, and national levels to set high standards for teachers (and their students as well). These standards were viewed as potentially powerful levers for improving teaching and learning. The National Commission on

Teaching and America's Future (NCTAF) described the role of standards for teachers in the following way:

> Standards for teaching are the linchpin for transforming current systems of preparation, licensing, certification, and ongoing development so that they better support student learning ... . Clearly, if students are to achieve high standards, we can expect no less from their teachers ... . (NCTAF, 1996, p. 67)

These new standards for professional practice, such as those put forth by the NBPTS (1996), called for a new vision of teachers' roles and responsibilities and higher expectations for teachers in a number of different ways.

These standards changed the nature of teaching work and knowledge, positing a more active, integrated, and intellectually challenging curriculum for all students, not just the most academically able. Thus, they also required more diagnostic teaching with multiple pathways to learning so that students who have difficulty get the help they need to succeed.

For teachers to reach the high levels of performance described by these new standards, however, they had to have frequent opportunities for professional growth at all stages of their career. One vehicle in which teachers can grow professionally is through assessment-driven professional development experiences such as those of the NBPTS.

Teacher assessment has undergone significant changes in the past 15 years as well (Darling-Hammond, Wise, & Klein, 1995; Haertel, 1991; Shulman, 1988). Traditional forms of assessment, either in the form of multiple-choice tests or in the form of school-based evaluations characterized by one or two classroom observations each year, have been criticized as being misleading and inadequate. Multiple-choice tests given to teachers entering a teacher education program or applying for a teaching license have been seen as invalid measures of a teacher's performance or potential because, among other reasons, they bear little resemblance to the actual tasks of teaching. At the same time, classroom observations by the school principal have been criticized as inadequate for gaining an accurate view of teacher performance because the number of observations is typically insufficient for obtaining a clear view of a teacher's competence and also because school principals often lack the necessary content knowledge to assess a teacher's subject matter expertise (Stodolsky, 1988). Moreover, both of these forms of assessment have been challenged because they do little to promote a teacher's effectiveness.

These criticisms sparked a search for teacher assessment approaches that more effectively capture and advance what teachers know and can do.

Shulman (1988) suggested that we create a "union of insufficiencies," in which various methods of assessment are combined in such a way that the strengths of one offset the limitations of the others. In this mix, he proposed performance assessments and teaching portfolios, along with more conventional written examination and classroom observations. The NBPTS (1989), as well as many educational organizations, university teacher education programs, and school districts began to move in this direction (Darling-Hammond et al., 1995).

The Promise of New Forms of Professional Development

Complaints about professional development experiences for teachers have abounded in recent years. Critics argue that the most common approaches to professional development provide few long-lasting benefits to teachers and their students. Conventional methods for professional development, which typically include school district in-service workshops or university courses, have been criticized for being too brief in intensity, too disconnected from the actual problems of practice, and too fragmented in approach. These approaches to professional development are based on a model in which experts provide one-shot presentations on various topics, with little or no follow up or support for incorporating new ideas into practice (Guskey, 1986). A number of research studies have shown that teachers rarely have sufficient skills or support to put what they have learned from these presentations into practice (Corcoran, 1995).

More recent approaches to professional development, however, take their lead from current research on learning, which points to the need for learners to take an active role in the construction and application of new knowledge and skills, and accepts the belief that learning is best facilitated when it occurs in authentic contexts in which learners work together over time to solve real world problems (Corcoran, 1995). This body of research suggests approaches to professional development such as action research (Hubbard & Power, 1993; Schmuck, 1997), in which teachers carry out extended investigations on their own teaching and their students' learning; cognitive coaching (Costa & Garmston, 1994), in which practicing teachers observe each other and provide feedback as "critical friends"; and teaching portfolios (Wolf, 1991, 1996), in which teachers systematically document and reflect on selected aspects of their practice, both individually and in concert with their colleagues, to advance their professional learning.

While these various approaches to professional development may take somewhat different routes, all of these approaches emphasize "reflective practice" as a central goal. "Reflection," in fact, is one of the Middle Childhood standards and is described in the following way:

> Accomplished teachers steadily reflect on their practice to extend their knowledge, perfect their teaching, and refine their evolving philosophy of education. The deliberate study of their own practice helps them determine their strengths and weaknesses and use that knowledge in their analysis and planning. These teachers stay abreast of developments in the profession, analyze the relative merits of teaching practices deemed exemplary and judge their appropriateness for their own particular circumstances. They strengthen their subject matter through research, reading, study and collaboration with colleagues. They display an openness to change and innovation. (NBPTS, 1996, p. 41)

The work of Dewey (1933/1988) and Schon (1983, 1987), in particular, have laid the foundation for the concept of reflective practice in teaching. Zeichner and colleagues have built on Dewey's ideas as well as the empirical literature in a number of publications (Zeichner, 1981; Zeichner & Liston, 1987; Zeichner & Tabachnick, 1991) to support the importance of reflective practice, but he has found that "teachers for the most part do not seem to be especially reflective or analytic about their work" (Zeichner, 1981, p. 9). LaBoskey, aiming to strengthen the reflective practices of the teachers with whom she worked, has drawn on the work of these scholars to identify the criteria of reflective thinking that she used in her teacher education courses:

- The teacher struggles with issues; she raises questions and expresses uncertainty;
- exhibits a propensity to consider alternatives and reconsider preconceptions;
- takes more of a long-term than a short-term view;
- shows primary concern for the needs of the student ...;
- seems to be open to learning about both practical and theoretical ideas ...;
- sees herself as a facilitator of learning rather than as a transmitter of knowledge;
- demonstrates an awareness of the need for tentative conclusions and multiple sources of feedback; and
- considers the moral and ethical implications of her ideas and actions ... (LaBoskey, 1997, pp. 153–154).

Reflection, according to these scholars and teacher educators, is a highly desirable professional development goal, and one they would argue is the necessary precursor to future growth for teachers.

RESEARCH QUESTION

This study addressed the following research question: "What are the effects of the National Board for Professional Teaching Standards certification process on teachers' professional perspectives and practices?"

METHOD

The findings reported in this study were based on two interviews conducted over a six-month period with six elementary school teachers who recently completed the National Board certification process.

Participants

The participants included six teachers (see Table 3). Given that the certification process is content-specific, we focused this investigation specifically on MC/Gs (teachers of students ages 7–12), who represented the largest group of National Board candidates. These six teachers taught in grades three through five (i.e., Middle Childhood years) in self-contained public (five teachers) and private (one teacher) school classrooms. They were all female, and ranged in years of full-time teaching experience from five to sixteen. All six teachers were members of the Colorado Goals 2000 project. These six teachers were randomly selected from an original group of eleven teachers who volunteered to participate in this study. The research was conducted in a large urban school district in Colorado and the surrounding suburban districts. The four suburban schools and the one private urban

Table 3.   Description of Respondents.

Names[a]	Experience	School Setting	Education
Beth	16 years	Suburban/Grade 4	BA/MA
Cathy	5 years	Suburban/Grade 5	BA/MA
Karen	5 years	Suburban/Grade 3/4	BA
Mary	13 years	Suburban/Grade 3	BA
Paula	10 years	Urban/Grade 5	BA/MA
Robin	10 years	Urban (private)/Grade 5	BA/MA

[a]Pseudonyms.

school were primarily middle-class and Anglo in student make-up, with the one urban school largely lower socioeconomic status and African-American and Latino in its student population.

Instrumentation

The data collection instrument used in this study was a semi-structured interview conducted by a single interviewer. Two separate interviews were carried out with each teacher. The first interview took place in June 1998, shortly after the teachers had submitted their portfolios to the NBPTS (a couple of months earlier in April), and the second interview took place approximately six months later in February 1999. While the questions in these interviews dealt with the NBPTS experience broadly, the interviews focused particularly on the Middle Childhood standards for teachers, and how the teachers' practices had changed in light of these standards (which are provided in Appendix M).

The first interview, conducted in June, consisted of 13 questions. In the first seven questions, the teachers were asked why they had decided to apply for Board certification and to describe the level of support they were receiving from the NBPTS and the Goals 2000 project. Questions eight and nine asked the teachers the degree to which the National Board standards *matched* their present views and practices, while questions 10 to 12 asked the teachers about *changes* in their views or practices. For question 10, the teachers were asked about changes in general, and then probed about changes that corresponded to the National Board standards. The final question of the interview invited the teachers to comment on anything else related to the impact of the certification process on their professional or personal lives.

In the second interview, which was conducted six months later in February (of the school year after completing the certification process), the teachers were asked to respond to nine questions about changes in their professional views or practices. The first question was customized for each teacher so that they were asked about the specific changes in the practices that they had described in the June interview six months earlier. They were then asked about additional changes that they would attribute to the certification process. In the following question, they were asked to what degree their present practices were consistent with the National Board standards. They were then asked for examples to illustrate the changes they described, as well as the degree to which these changes were now routine features of their practice. Finally, they were invited to report on anything else about the certification process that had impacted on their lives.

Procedures

The teachers in this study were interviewed in their classrooms and each of the interviews was transcribed. Each interview took between two and three hours. During these interviews, the teachers were invited to show artifacts or aspects of their classroom to illustrate their responses. A small set of open-ended interview questions were identified in advance, and then the interviewer flexibly followed-up on topics that directly pertained to changes in views and practices related to the National Board experience.

Data Analysis Process

This study employed a qualitative analytical framework for interpretation. The data analysis process used in this study is described by Marshall and Rossman (1989) as:

> mainstream qualitative research ... that values participants' perspectives on their worlds and seeks to discover those perspectives, that views inquiry as an interactive process between the researcher and the participants, and that is primarily descriptive and relies on people's words as the primary data. (p. 11)

Various schemes have been proposed for qualitative data analysis. Miles and Huberman (1984), for example, describe three concurrent activities that comprise qualitative data analysis: (1) data reduction, (2) data display, and (3) conclusion drawing. Marshall and Rossman (1989) describe five modes of qualitative analysis: (1) organizing the data, (2) generating themes, (3) testing the emergent hypothesis against the data, (4) searching for alternative explanations of the data, and (5) writing the report.

The data analysis process in the present study consisted of four overlapping phases: (1) coding, (2) grouping, (3) reduction, and (4) display. In phase one, the data were read and preliminarily coded. In the second phase, the data were tentatively grouped according to the preliminary codes, with a review of the data for additional examples and counter examples. This phase included multiple revisions of the codes and identification of significant themes. In the third phase of data reduction, the most representative data examples were selected to illustrate each theme, and the themes were framed with explanatory and interpretative comments. In the fourth and final phase, the data were woven together to create a coherent textual display.

FINDINGS

The six teachers interviewed for this study reported changes in their perspectives and practices for all of the eleven MC/G standards. While each of the standards was mentioned by one or more of the teachers, three standards stood out in particular – Reflection, Assessment, and Family Involvement. In addition, five of the six teachers reported "An increase in their confidence as a teacher," an area that is not specifically tied to the MC/G standards.

Reflection

All six of the teachers interviewed for this study reported significant changes in the quality and content of their reflections and understandings as a result of participating in the certification process. In most of their comments, the teachers discussed their reflections in the context of the 11 MC/G standards such as "Assessment," "Multiple Paths to Knowledge," and "Reflection."

Cathy, for example, asserted that although she had always considered herself a reflective practitioner, she became even more so through the certification process:

> *I always thought that I was a reflective teacher. ... I'd ask why I would do something. I would question what was the best for the kids. But this really like took me to a whole 'nother deeper level. I really, really had to dig deep. "What would you change? How would you change it? Would you change anything?"*

Mary echoed her sentiments and commented:

> *I think the changes that I would attribute to [the certification process] is that I am more regularly reflecting on what I am doing within the classroom. It has brought a greater awareness ... so that rather than having it in the back of my mind it is more in the forefront and ... I am doing it more on a regular basis.*

Beth as well commented on her growth as a reflective practitioner:

> *The reflective thinking. I did that a little bit [before National Board certification] but not as much as I do now. That was a really important piece, to stop and think about what we're doing and why we're doing it, and why it's important.*

Paula reported dramatic changes in her reflections:

> *It made me really look at why I do everything I do. Every assignment, every assessment now has 'Why are you doing that?' attached to it.*

Karen described herself as simply being more focused on the purpose of her classroom activities and their link to the National Board standards:

I'm trying to be more clear in what I do, and I always ask myself, 'What's the purpose, and what standard does this get at?' I guess it's just a whole thing of being more focused.

Robin highlighted how she was not only reflecting more often, but the nature of her reflection had changed so that did not just occur after the fact but in preparation for teaching. She remarked that:

There's reflection ahead of time. So that not only are you planning, but you're anticipating, I think. And I do that more now, and that's probably because in writing in the portfolio, the reflective portion was kind of dissecting. So now I'm dissecting ahead of time.

Many of the teachers also linked their reflections with the MC/G standards, asserting that the standards were often in the forefront of their minds as they planned and taught. Cathy, for example, reported how the National Board standards continually guided her thinking and helped her clarify the reasons for her instructional choices:

[Before the certification process] I would just do things just to do them. I'd do them because I thought they would work. I would do them because it was a good way to do it, or somebody else had shown me it was a good thing to do. It wasn't a very concrete reason. The standards are concrete and it's clear and concise and you know exactly what you are doing so you know why you are doing those things.

Mary commented as well that a change in her practice was that her reflections came to be guided by the National Board standards:

The standards are more in the forefront. And since they're more in the forefront of my mind, rather than the old way of planning where we would [say], 'OK, what do we want to teach?' And then, 'What resources do we have?' Now I'm thinking about, 'OK, what standards do I need to address, what do we want to accomplish at this time, and OK, we're going to be teaching about plate tectonics, OK, how will that fit the standards, and how will that address this, and what am I going to accomplish?' So I'm keeping the standards in mind.

Karen emphasized the importance of the standards as well in guiding her practice:

Every teacher should have to do [the National Board certification process]. Every teacher should get that book of standards …. The part that I felt was the most helpful was getting me to look at some very specific things in my classroom. Very specific standards. And saying, "How do you do this? How do you know you do it well? What evidence do you have that you do it well?"

Overall, the teachers unanimously reported significant changes in the quality and content of their reflections, often framing these reflections in the MC/G standards for professional practice. The most significant change that they reported was in the ways that they clarified the purposes of their instruction and viewed these practices through the lenses of the MC/G standards.

Assessment

All of the teachers described significant changes in their assessment practices as well. These reported changes included having a checklist of assessment questions that guide instruction, looking more carefully at student work, collecting a wider body of information about student learning, guiding students in assessing their own learning, gathering ongoing information about student learning, and developing assessment tools such as rubrics.

As an example of how this new awareness took form in her assessment practices, Beth described the checklist of questions that guided her practice:

> *Well I kind of just go through a checklist in my mind. ... Who is this kid? What kind of learner are they? ... Where are they at developmentally? ... What do they need and how can I help them? ... What resources can I provide for this kid? ... It's more overwhelming than it had been in the past when you really focus in on kids, on individuals, instead of [on the group].*

Beth also remarked that she had made adjustments in her practice in the area of promoting student self-reflection, and drew on these student self-assessments in her own assessments of students:

> *The big piece in this reflection was the kid reflection. [Before the National Board certification process] I didn't have my kids reflect. Well we did at the end of the day, but it was more like just real verbal. But through this process, I started to have them reflecting on lessons, certain lessons, you know, like how to just write a paragraph on how you felt this science experiment went. And it was really amazing and that part, reflecting can even be used as an assessment as well. And that was a whole new avenue that opened up to me.*

Mary reported that the current school year, as opposed to before the certification process, she carried out a closer inspection of student work. She commented:

> *I notice this year when I'm grading papers, I'm looking more for rather than just so they did this, why might they have done this? What is it that they're missing? So I'm trying to more closely analyze the work as I grade it.*

Cathy discussed a number of changes in her assessment practices as a result of participating in the certification process, including creating a larger body of evidence about each child's development. She described her expanded record-keeping in reading in the following way:

> *In reading I have done a lot more assessment with my kids and I have created a much bigger body of evidence. I've done a lot more running records than I did in the past; a lot more miscue analysis – so, that kind of assessment. I used to go with the gut and now I am really creating a body of evidence.*
>
> *[Moreover,] ... I used to do an informal reading assessment ... and if they were stumbling, I would probably give them a strategy to help them get through that word, but then I would keep that in my brain and not record it ... . But this year, I have running records and miscue analysis on every one of them, twenty-seven of them. So I think I am much better at it now.*

Robin mentioned how she was more willing to adjust her instruction based on what she learned about her students in an ongoing fashion. She remarked that she had a greater

> *... willingness to let the observational skills be the engine on this train ... I had planned to start out with a numeration unit and I looked at the kids and went 'Don't think so. Think we're going to do some measurements.' They seemed to be more active, they seemed to be more verbal and so we went that way.*

Karen described the ways that her assessment practices had changed from an end-of-activity process to one that framed her teaching both before and after:

> *I can't believe how much time I spend at the end of the day ... that I did not do before in just saying, "Where did they get today, where do they need to go tomorrow?" I just thought about it differently. About doing it more up front than after I'd given a lot of information.*

The changes in Karen's practice in assessment also included the ways in which she guided students in monitoring their own progress:

> *[I] ... also share some of that with students ... I think so many times ... they get papers back, and what do they do with the data? ... They don't really do that much with it ... . This is a small way to put it into your classroom, but even ... in math fact tests ... I started [asking my students questions]: "Now let's look at that and see, now look at your last week's test, and the week before, and look at that from analyzing data." Just like I was doing. "So what are you going to do differently this week? Do you want a higher score?" And getting kids to ... go through that same process of being responsible for learning and using data that I give to them.*

Paula described the ways in which she learned about rubrics and incorporated rubrics into one of her major assignments:

> *Part of what I did while I was going through the portfolio process was learn and teach myself everything I could find out about rubrics. So I think in that sense it made [the unit]*

assignment much richer and much more valuable to [the students]. They know exactly what to expect when I grade it.

In sum, the teachers reported changes in their assessment perspectives and practices across a number of dimensions, including creating a body of evidence that allowed them to more critically examine student work and more carefully assess the progress of individual student in an ongoing way.

Family Involvement

Four of the six teachers described changes in the ways in which they involved families in their classrooms and schools, and the teachers who report these changes described them as significant and provided numerous examples to illustrate the ways in which they had done so. Changes included increased consideration of ways to include families and inviting them to participate in after school events on topics such as the science curriculum or student learning standards.

Mary commented on how the "Family Involvement" standard and related portfolio entry prompted her to think more carefully about ways to connect with her students' families:

[The portfolio entry on family involvement] really forced me to look at how I relate to both the parents and the students in my classroom, and how I work in the school setting outside of the classroom. I think that is a piece that many teachers don't think about or consider as much. They just want to be left alone in their classroom … .

She went on to describe how she became more alert to involving families, but still struggled to make strong connections to some families:

I guess I'm a little bit frustrated this year because I don't necessarily feel like I have the tools to collaborate with some of my parents. And, in particular, I have one student who's completely monolingual himself, which means he only speaks his native language, which isn't English. And I have about eight other ESL students who've acquired some English, but they're better at speaking English than their parents. So how, how am I going to communicate with these parents and get these parents to feel comfortable communicating with me in regards to their child's education?

Cathy described how she had not previously involved parents, but the requirements of the certification process gave her the impetus for inviting parents to become more active participants in their children's school experiences:

I was never really one to really try to include the parents. If I had to have them in my classroom it would be OK. And with going through [the certification process], it really kind of gave me the spark to get them going. So I had like a parent meeting about standards and ... the kids would [show] the parents what a rubric would look like. And that was really interesting because, you know, there are some parents who ... have no clue about what a standard is ... I took the time to make the phone calls [and] invite parents in.

She also held a "science night" for parents to increase their knowledge of the science program and to involve them in at-home science projects as well as to strengthen their connection to the classroom. In addition, she had plans for a family "geography night."

For Paula, one of her most pronounced areas of change was also in the area of family involvement. She commented:

I teach in a school where family involvement is non-existent. So that was just something we struggled with at our school in general, but I always have felt that that's not my strength, dealing with parents. So [the National Board process] sort of made me say, "Well how can I get those parents? What do I need to do to make parents who are reluctant or you can't get a hold of?" So I had to kind of come up with some creative ideas as far as how I could do that.

To address the problem of not having parent participation in her classroom, as well as to have an activity to document in her portfolio, Paula decided to host an evening for parents to learn more about the math curriculum:

I had a math night for the parents. I promised [the students] I wouldn't talk about their behavior or their grades or anything like that. It was not about conferences. It was about you get your parents in here and we'll have some of the things we do in math here for you to do with your parents. Like some group problem solving, and like computers, and I have some math read-alouds. And so they just needed to get their parents to come in and do math together.

Beth reported that in the upcoming school year, she planned to involve families from the beginning. She commented that:

We're going to try a picnic this year with just my class ... I'm sending them a postcard inviting them to the picnic and getting to know the family before school starts. So that whole element I think I've missed [before the National Board certification process].

In sum, teachers reported that after completing the certification process, they paid more attention to strengthening communication with parents and inviting families to become more deeply involved in their children's school lives.

Remaining Standards

While Reflection, Assessment, and Family Involvement were the most frequently discussed areas of change, the teachers as a group mentioned each of the remaining eight standards in their comments. An example addressing each standard follows:

Knowledge of Students. Karen, for example, described how she came to spend the beginning of the school year trying to learn more about her students before she began her first unit of the year. It should be noted that while many of the MC/G standards build on and overlap with each other, "Knowledge of Students" and "Assessment" do so in particular, as evidenced in the following example:

> So for me, the whole thing of being very clear and [continuously] asking myself "What is the purpose?, What do my kids know?, Where do they need to go next?" And in these first few weeks, I know that I've been slower than other people, and you know, it's been really funny because people around me are already like way into these units and I've done much more assessing at the beginning of the year than I've done in the past.

Knowledge of Content and Curriculum. Paula described how her curricular focus changed to focus on the "big ideas," and how her planning changed as a result:

> I'm looking more at those big picture things. I told the parents the entire first semester science would focus on systems and what systems look like and through that we'll do solar, ecosystem, any kind of system that the kids can come up with so it's made ... my long term planning more focused but at the same time ... I've backed up and said here's the [whole] picture .... This is where ... these little pieces will fit in, whereas before I thought of long term planning as all these little pieces.

Learning Environment. A standard in which Karen's practices changed was in the ways she set up her classroom and created a classroom community. Again, in the overlap of certain standards, Karen's beginning-of-the-year assessments of her students as individuals and as a group informed her creation of her classroom environment:

> Well, I think this is the first year that I really paid attention to how I do set up a classroom. Because I felt like that's the part that I'm going to fail [in the portfolio] ... I was thinking to myself, 'How would I explain to someone how I set up a classroom community, because it's very involved.' But through each step of the way I've been thinking to myself, 'What is the purpose for doing that?' And it's been really clear to me that the purpose is the same. It's a risk-taking environment that needs to be safe. And that piece of clarification, everything

I do feeds into that. That everything that I put up on the board, everything that I share about myself, everything that I ask kids to share about them, is that whole.

She also explained that she shared this information with students as well and told them the reasons for setting up the classroom procedures and environment as she did.

Respect for Diversity. An area in which Mary described a heightened awareness as a result of the National Board process was in responding to the diverse needs of students and their families:

We're looking at what we can do differently [to meet the needs of our diverse students], ... and it's prompted ... our student council [in] considering making a video as far as new students coming into our school, and see if we can pull in some of these kids who speak other languages, [and have them] say, "Welcome to [our school]" in Russian, or have them say that in Bulgarian, or Hmong, or Vietnamese, or whatever. We're looking at ... how can we make our school look more inviting and more open to kids who have ... a different background. So it's brought ... greater awareness.

Instructional Resources. Paula cited the many ways in which she had broadened her resources and knowledge as a result of participating in the National Board certification process:

I think it made me more aware of how I picked my resources. It was [previously] more 'Here's my plan. What do I need?' It was not resource driven as much. So I think that was a pretty big change.

She went on to describe how her search for additional resources and knowledge in science and math led her to use the Internet to download national student standards in both content areas:

I was struggling with ["big ideas" in the content areas]. But getting some more information on the national science standards, and the big ideas and things like that gave me some ideas and thoughts about how I could structure my science instruction. And so I think that was really useful. I think it sort of helped me be able to focus in on those standards a little bit better, and teach in a more constructivist way.

I got [the national science standards] off the computer. I get everything off the Internet. If you go to the National ... Science Council, they have all of the science ones, and so do the math. Also if you go to the Eisenhower Clearing House web page, it tells you where you can find anything that has to do with science and math, from free to thousands of dollars.

Meaningful Applications of Knowledge. Karen demonstrated a strong awareness and application of "Meaningful Applications of Knowledge," or "connections," as she often called them. She described how her perspective had changed as a result of participating in the certification process and how she aimed to help students see and make connections across the contents areas and between their lives and their learning in school. She commented:

> It really made me think more carefully in every single unit that I taught, 'How can students connect to this? How are they going to use it in the next unit?'

She explained how her students, particularly the less academically advanced ones, had a fragmented view of the curriculum. With this insight in mind, she described how she created conditions for students, and how she made those connections visible to them:

> Some more able kids made connections very easily from subject to subject, [... but most] kids in my classroom saw things very fragmented ... so I began in every single lesson I taught, "Well so tell me, we're writing about this prairie dog, what do you need to know about ecosystems to be an effective writer when you sit down and write this letter to a [city] official so you can sound like someone who knows something about not only the prairie dog from an emotional standpoint, but from someone who knows something about science. And someone who knows something about math."

Multiple Paths to Knowledge. Cathy described how she paid greater attention to designing a variety of ways for her students to learn and demonstrate their learning:

> Now I have really created a place where my kids can show me that they are proficient in reading and writing in different ways. I have had them writing books, somebody is an illustrator and right now they are designing visual aids for their presentation for their castle and everybody is doing different things and so all of these different things ... different ways to show me that they know how to read and write.

Contributions to the Profession. Mary commented how her involvement with the NBPTS had led her to collaborate more with her colleagues:

> I have always enjoyed collaborating with others, but I think I am more pursuing opportunities to collaborate with others and get involved in different things with my colleagues .... This year we took ... a day to plan together at least with the other math/science teacher in my core. We came up with some fabulous units and it was worth it.

Increased Confidence as a Teacher

One reported change was not specifically linked to the MC/G standards. Five of the six teachers reported that they felt validated as teachers and more confident as professionals as a result of the certification process. They attributed this change in part to what they learned through the process and in part to their feeling of confirmation in finding that the standards for professional practice were consistent with their own views and practices. The teachers also reported that their colleagues viewed them with greater respect as well.

Beth reported that she felt more confident as a teacher as a result of having participated in the National Board certification process:

> *I feel more confident. I feel more confident in providing a good curriculum for my students. And just confidence as a teacher. I just feel more qualified.*

She reported that her colleagues and administrator treated her with more respect:

> *My principal is very proud that I'm in the program, and I think that she looks at me in a different way, and respects me for what I'm going through ... . And the immediate team that I'm working with, I think that they do listen to me and are really evaluating what I'm saying because I'm going through this process.*

Karen commented that going through the National Board process validated her as a teacher, and gave her the skills and confidence to explain and defend her practices:

> *A huge part of me feels validated also. I can be held accountable because I know what I'm doing, and I know why I do it, and I can tell somebody that.*

Robin saw the experience as not advancing her teaching as much as confirming the quality of it. She remarked that:

> *I think one of the things about this [is that] an awful lot of this was just confirming what you already did anyhow.*

Mary found that the National Board standards and practices were consonant with her beliefs and practices, and this realization made her feel more confident as a teacher:

> *I think what it did was reinforce that I am on the right track for the most part with what I am doing with students, and it made me feel good that I do address these components on a regular basis.*

Paula described how her own confidence as a teacher had increased, and how she became more willing to participate in professional discussions:

> *I notice I go to the faculty meetings now, and here I am this sort of new kid on the block, and I think before I would have been very hesitant to speak or say anything, but because I feel like I've been through this process and I've reflected and know what I know as a*

teacher I feel a lot more comfortable giving my input right off the bat at the very first teachers' meeting and volunteering what I can do and help with.

Thus, most of the teachers (five of the six) reported increased confidence as professionals in part due to the ways that the National Board standards and assessments confirmed their professional practices, and in part due to the way that colleagues treated them with more respect.

Change Overall

All six of the teachers contended that the National Board experience contributed to their learning. Four of the six teachers saw the changes as profound, with one of the six describing only modest changes and another stating that she made few changes as a result of participating in the process.

Karen, for example, in her interviews discussed many changes in her practice as a result of the National Board certification process, and how she had made these changes a routine part of her classroom. She commented that:

I'm a different teacher than I was when I started, and I'm a better teacher because of it. And I would never have come to some of the decisions that I made this year without that process.

Cathy found the National Board standards consistent with her regular practice, but she also attributed considerable changes in her practices as a result of participating in the certification process as well. In the interviews, she discussed specific changes in her practice for nearly every standard.

In describing the impact of the National Board process on her practice, Beth cited the overall experience as instrumental in raising her awareness of effective practice as highlighted in the National Board professional standards:

This whole experience. You can't walk away and not be changed at all. I really look at kids in a different way and it's more complex. I have to make sure I've got all those elements in, and so I just don't think that they would have impacted me as much if I didn't go through the process.

Paula asserted that the National Board certification process had a significant positive impact on her practice as well:

It was an incredible learning experience. [And] it was incredibly frustrating at times. It's been time consuming. I mean, it became sort of like my life for those four months I was

working on it. But the colleagues that I have met, and the learning community I'm a part of
now, made all that worth it. So it was mostly a really positive experience.

In describing its effects on her, she remarked that the best part of the
experience was the way it has shaped her thinking:

Really taking apart my teaching, piece by piece, and really looking at it. I don't think I'll
ever do anything in my classroom now without really asking myself "Why am I doing this?"
I think I've got a whole new kind of take on every little thing you do in class. It's not about
filling time. I mean, you know, I think I was a good teacher and that I was already
reflecting, but this most certainly made me really aware of what I do now.

Mary, on the other hand, did not attribute significant changes in her
practice to the National Board certification process. She believed that
her practice prior to the certification process was very consistent with the
NBPTS vision of accomplished practice, and that the certification process at
most gave her some additional ideas:

None of the standards are really something new to me that I hadn't really thought about
before. I think what it did was reinforced that I am on the right track for the most part with
what I am doing with students, and it made me feel good that I do address these components
on a regular basis … . [But] I think the [certification process] made me reflect on
[the standards] more, and made me make modifications on how I would approach some
things in the future, but not any big changes like, oh, man, I am way off base on this or
whatever. It gave me ideas … . And did it teach [me] some things? … Yes it did.

Robin reported few changes in practice in her initial comments during the
interviews, in part because she found it difficult to point to specific features
of the certification process that led her to change. She saw her practice as
consistent with the National Board standards prior to beginning the process,
and the certification experience mostly validated her teaching.

Summary

Overall, the six teachers described changes in their practices for each of the
eleven MC/G standards, with nearly all of the teachers describing changes
in three areas in particular – reflection, assessment, and family involvement.
In addition, most of them reported that the certification experience
increased their confidence as teachers in part because it validated their
current practice and in part because others treated them with more respect.
Overall, four of the six teachers described their experience as having had a
significant positive effect on their practice, with one teacher characterizing
the effect as modest while another reported little change. The teacher who

reported few changes did so because she believed that her practices were already consistent with the National Board vision.

DISCUSSION

Teachers who completed the National Board certification process reported a number of changes in their perspectives and practices. Specifically, they described changes in the amount and the quality of their reflections, and that these reflections focused on the National Board Standards for professional practice. They also reported changes in their practices for two standards in particular – student assessment and family involvement. In addition, the teachers reported an increase in their confidence as professionals.

Changes in Reflections

All six of the teachers interviewed reported significant changes in the frequency and content of their reflections. Mary, for example, commented that "*I am more regularly reflecting on what I am doing within the classroom,*" while Paula remarked, "*[The National Board experience] made me really look at why I do everything I do.*"

Moreover, they indicated that the content of their reflections had changed from "reflections in general" to "reflections on standards." Cathy, for example, noting how the content of her reflections had changed since beginning the certification process, remarked, "*I really have those standards going in my head,*" while Mary commented that she has gone from "*What [activities] do we want to teach?*" to "*What standards do I need to address?*"

These findings suggest that the National Board certification process does have a positive effect on teachers' perspectives, and likely on their future professional practices. We know that quality reflection is a necessary precursor to effective practice, and that teachers who more regularly engage in reflection become better at what they do, especially when these reflections are grounded in actual evidence and connected to professional standards (Freiberg & Waxman, 1988; Freiberg, Waxman, & Houston, 1987).

What about the National Board experience might account for these changes in the teachers' reflective practices? While teachers were not asked to identify specific causes for their changes other than the National Board experience itself, the changes in their reflective practices were likely due in large part to the tremendous amount of written reflection that teachers needed to provide in their portfolios. In terms of number of pages, teachers were required to provide up to 66 total pages in written reflections across the six portfolio entries in their portfolios (see Table 3). This amount of reflective writing represents much more reflection and writing than most teachers engage in on a regular basis. In fact, teachers reported that they spend on average of 100 hours preparing their portfolios, with much of this time devoted to drafting the written commentaries (Jaeger & Thompson, 1994). Moreover, many teachers work with colleagues on their portfolios, further increasing the amount of time they spend reflecting through professional conversations.

In terms of the content of their reflections, the teachers were guided in writing their commentaries by a series of prompts in the portfolio instructions. These prompts directed the teachers' attention to reflection (e.g., "If you were given the opportunity to use these writing assignments again with these students, what are the alternative strategies you might use? Why?"), and to the National Board standards (e.g., "Tell also how [the student work samples] reflect your approach to providing 'multiple paths for learning'.").

Thus, the changes in their reflective practices that teachers reported were likely due in part to the number and structure of the reflective commentaries that they were asked to prepare for the portfolio, and to the emphasis on a "reflection" standard itself in the Middle Childhood certificate area. The may also be due to the collaborative conversations that teachers hold as well. What form these reflections may take in the future when the teachers are not completing a high-stakes assessment, or simply as they move further from the certification experience, remains unknown for now. However, given what we know about the importance of reflection in informing practice (Schon, 1983; Zeichner & Liston, 1987), the teachers' increase in the frequency of their reflections, and their focus on important standards of practice, bodes well for the future.

Connections to Standards

In addition to changes in their reflections, the teachers reported specific changes in their practices as well. While the teachers as a group discussed changes in their understanding and practices for all eleven Middle Childhood Standards, all six teachers described changes in two areas in particular: student assessment practices and involvement with the families of their students.

In describing the changes in their assessment practices, the teachers reported that they now looked more carefully at student work, collecting a richer body of information about student learning, and developing assessment tools such as rubrics. Paula, for example, remarked how the certification process pushed her to *"learn and teach myself everything I could find out about rubrics."* Cathy expanded her data collection process by *"[creating] a much bigger body of evidence."* And Robin broadened her range of assessments by seeking out *"more diverse assessments."*

In terms of engagement with families, the teachers told the ways that they involved parents through a variety of gatherings, for example, such as those focused on math night or the district's new student learning standards. Mary, for example, described how the "Family Involvement" portfolio entry and related standard made her *"aware of how we sometimes do a disservice to families by not doing enough"* to involve them. Paula described how in her school family participation was virtually non-existent but changed that by having "a math night for parents." Along the same lines, Cathy held a "science night" for parents to increase their knowledge of the science program as well as to involve them in at-home science projects.

These specific changes in their practices represented a significant departure from past practices, and are ones that could be directly attributed to the National Board experience. The connection between the certification experience and the teachers' changes in their assessment practices is twofold. First, one of the Middle Childhood standards is "assessment," and the teachers reported that they paid close attention to the standards in their teaching and in preparing their portfolios. Secondly, a focus on student assessment is woven throughout the portfolio. Of the first four portfolio entries, the assessment standard is cited as one of the key focus areas for the entry. Specifically, in the portfolio handbook (NBPTS, n.d.) for Entry 1, for example, the teacher was asked in the written commentary to answer the following question: "How does this student's response to each of the two different genres demonstrate his or her abilities as a developing writer" (p. 7). In Entry 2, the teacher was asked to provide evidence and address the following question "What kind of feedback did this student receive about his or her response?" (p. 6).

The link between the certification experience and the teachers' increased attention to families was clear as well. One of the eleven standards for MC/Gs is "family involvement," and one of the portfolio entries focuses specifically on families. In "Documented Accomplishments II," teachers were directed to document "accomplishments that demonstrate how you have created ongoing interactive communication with families and other adults interested in students' progress and learning [in the current year]" (NBPTS, n.d., Entry 6, p. 4).

In addition to the National Board's explicit focus on student assessment and family involvement in the MC/G standards and portfolio entries, another reason for teachers' changes in these areas may have been that both of these areas were typically absent in even the best teachers' practices. Despite the fact that they can spend up to one-third of their professional time involved in assessment-related activities, for example, teachers' lack of assessment literacy is well-documented (Stiggins & Conklin, 1992).

Confidence as Teachers

One change not specifically connected to the National Board assessment architecture was the finding that teachers report feeling increased professional confidence in their interactions with their peers and administrators. This change, according to the teachers, came about because they believed that their knowledge was deepened and their practices confirmed, and because of the respectful way in which their colleagues interacted with them. Beth, for example, commented now that she felt "more confident" and "more qualified" as a result of completing the certification process. Karen stated that "*I can be held accountable because I know what I'm doing, and I know why I do it, and I can tell somebody that.*" While Mary, for example, observed that "*I think what it did was reinforce that I am on the right track for the most part with what I am doing with students.*" Paula recounted how her colleagues now came to her with questions more frequently than before.

This finding, however, is difficult to interpret in the short-run. On the surface, the increase in confidence was a good thing. We know that there is generally a positive connection between confidence and performance. However, based on what we know about human nature and on our experiences with other National Board candidates, this confidence may be short-lived for those who did not pass the assessment. Since this study was conducted before the teachers learned of their results, they may have been bathed in a glow of self-confidence that evaporated once they received their results. Given the potentially unstable and situation-specific nature of this feeling of confidence, this finding is one that deserves follow-up to determine the durability and direction of this confidence.

Overall

A number of features of the National Board certification process, therefore, appeared to contribute to the professional development of teachers. In particular, the *standards* themselves were a key ingredient. The standards served as a constant guide to the teachers in their teaching and in preparing their portfolios. The portfolio process also appeared to play a strong role in contributing to the teachers' growth. The specific *portfolio entries*, such as "Documented Accomplishments II," for example, directed the teachers to focus on the role of families in the education of their students. In addition, the task of *writing structured commentaries* about their practice appeared to help the teachers develop an informed reflective stance. Another feature of the certification process that may have contributed to the teachers' increased reflection may have been *professional conversations* with colleagues around the portfolio tasks. Since collaboration was encouraged but not required, it was difficult to determine the degree to which these interactions may have impacted the teachers' views or practices. The National Board assessment, it should be noted, had two components: the portfolio and the assessment center exercises. While these assessment exercises may have served a vital evaluation purpose in providing a view of a teacher's practice that is not as context-dependent as a portfolio, the teachers we interviewed for this study did not cite the assessment exercises as significantly affecting their views or practices. The assessment exercises were likely to have had little impact on the teachers because these were "on-demand" tasks that the teachers did not prepare for in advance as they did with the portfolio.

Researchers and professional organizations are now calling for professional development that is standards-based, content-driven, context-sensitive, job-embedded, inquiry-oriented, team-focused, and student-centered (Corcoran, 1995; Darling-Hammond, 2001; Feiman-Nemser, 2001). The National Board certification experience exemplifies many of the essential features of this new vision of professional development. The National Board assessment process is explicitly connected to sound national standards for teachers, and these standards permeate all aspects of the portfolio and assessment center processes. Each certificate area is organized around professional knowledge and skills in a specific content area. The portfolio process requires candidates to document their "on-the-job" practices with their actual students. By giving the teachers tasks and prompts (especially the written commentaries) that encourage reflection, the portfolio process takes teachers beyond describing their practices to reflecting on the principles that underlie those practices. On the issue of collaboration, the National Board does not require teachers to work together because it is an individual certification process, but many teachers do work closely with colleagues in their teaching and in preparing their portfolios. The portfolio process focuses teachers' attention on individual students through features such as the portfolio instructions (e.g., in Entry 1 the teacher is instructed to "select two students who represent different kinds of challenges to you") and through prompts for the written commentaries (e.g., in Entry 1, the teacher is asked "Describe the kind of challenge that [the student you have chosen] represents"). In sum, then, the National Board certification process provides teachers with learning opportunities that are consistent with this new vision of professional development.

CONCLUSIONS

The argument that one of the chief benefits of the National Board certification process is that teachers, even already accomplished ones, become better at what they did as a result of participating in the process was supported in this study. Overall, four of the six teachers interviewed for this study described their learning as significant, with one teacher reporting modest changes, and another reporting little change in her views and practices. The teacher who reported little change, however, described her pre-National Board practices as highly consistent with the National Board standards, and, as a consequence, felt she had less to learn from the experience than others might have. Across the six teachers each of the eleven standards was cited as an area of change by one or more of the teachers. All of the teachers reported changes in their reflective practices, and that their reflections became heavily grounded in the professional standards for teachers. The changes that teachers reported in their reflective practices were a very positive outcome of the certification process. While not a guarantee that these changes in reflective practices will lead to accomplished practices in the future, they provide strong support for its possibility.

REFERENCES

Athanases, S. (1994). Teachers' reports of the effects of preparing portfolios of literacy instruction. *The Elementary School Journal, 94,* 421–439.

Carnegie Forum on Education and the Economy. (1986). *A nation prepared: Teachers for the 21st century*. Washington, DC: Carnegie Forum on Education and the Economy, Task Force on Teaching as a Profession.

Corcoran, T. (1995). *Transforming professional development for teachers: A guide for state policymakers. Technical report*. Washington, DC: The National Governors Association.

Costa, A., & Garmston, R. (1994). *Cognitive coaching: A foundation for Renaissance schools*. Norwood, MA: Christopher-Gordon Publishers.

Darling-Hammond, L. (2001). Standard setting in teaching: Changes in licensing, certification, and assessment. In: V. Richardson (Ed.), *Handbook of research on teaching* (pp. 751–776). Washington, DC: American Educational Research Association.

Darling-Hammond, L., Wise, A., & Klein, S. (1995). *A license to teach: Building a profession for 21st century schools*. Boulder, CO: Westview Press.

Dewey, J. (1933/1998). *How we think: A restatement of the relation of reflective thinking to the educative process*. Boston: Houghton Mifflin.

Feiman-Nemser, S. (2001). From preparation to practice: Designing a continuum to strengthen and sustain teaching. *Teacher's College Record, 103*, 1013–1055.

Freiberg, H. J., & Waxman, H. C. (1988). Alternative feedback approaches for improving student teachers' classroom instruction. *Journal of Teacher Education, 39*(4), 8–14.

Freiberg, H. J., Waxman, H. C., & Houston, W. R. (1987). Enriching feedback to student teachers through small group discussion. *Teacher Education Quarterly, 14*(3), 71–82.

Guskey, T. (1986). Staff development and the process of teacher change. *Educational Researcher, 15*(5), 5–12.

Haertel, E. (1991). New forms of teacher assessment. In: G. Grant (Ed.), *Review of research in education* (pp. 3–29). Washington, DC: American Educational Research Association.

Hubbard, R. S., & Power, B. M. (1993). *The art of classroom inquiry: A handbook for teacher-researchers*. Portsmouth, NH: Heinemann.

Jaeger, R., & Thompson, M. (1994). *Evaluation of the National Board for Professional Teaching Standards 1993–94 field test of the Early Adolescence Generalist and Early Adolescence English/Language Arts assessments – a summary of responses of candidates for National Board certification to questions posed during face-to-face interviews, focus group discussions, and hour-long evaluative writing tasks*. Greensboro, NC: National Board for Professional Teaching Standards, Technical Analysis Group, Center for Educational Research and Evaluation, University of North Carolina-Greensboro.

LaBoskey, V. K. (1997). Teaching to teach with purpose and passion: Pedagogy for reflective practice. In: J. Loughran & T. Russell (Eds), *Teaching about teaching* (pp. 150–163). London: Falmer Press.

Marshall, C., & Rossman, G. (1989). *Designing qualitative research*. Newbury Park, CA: Sage.

Miles, M. B., & Huberman, A. M. (1984). *Qualitative data analysis: A sourcebook of new methods*. Newbury Park, CA: Sage.

National Board for Professional Teaching Standards. (n.d.). *Middle Childhood/ Generalist Portfolio*. Detroit, MI: NBPTS.

National Board for Professional Teaching Standards. (1989). *Toward high and rigorous standards for the teaching profession*. Washington, DC: Author.

National Board for Professional Teaching Standards. (1996). *Middle Childhood/Generalist Standards for National Board certification*. Detroit, MI: Author.

National Board for Professional Teaching Standards. (1997). *The National Board certification process in-depth*. Washington, DC: NBPTS. Retrieved 30 March 1998 from http://www.nbpts.org

(NCTAF) National Commission on Teaching and America's Future. (1996). *What matters most: Teaching for America's future*. New York: National Commission on Teaching and America's Future.

Schmuck, R. (1997). *Practical action research for change*. Arlington Heights, IL: IRI/Skylight.

Schon, D. (1983). *The reflective practitioner: How professionals think in action*. New York: Basic Books.

Schon, D. (1987). *Educating the reflective practitioner: Toward a new design for teaching and learning in the professions*. San Francisco: Jossey-Bass.

Shulman, L. (1988). A union of insufficiencies: Strategies for teacher assessment in a period of reform. *Educational Leadership, 46*, 36–41.

Stiggins, R., & Conklin, N. (1992). *In teachers' hands: Investigating the practice of classroom assessment*. Albany, NY: SUNY Press.

Stodolsky, S. (1988). *The subject matters*. Chicago, IL: University of Chicago Press.

Tracz, S. M., Sienty, S., & Mata, S. (1994). The self-reflection of teachers compiling portfolios for national certification: Work in progress. Paper presented at the Annual meeting of the American Association of Colleges for Teacher Education, Chicago, IL.

Tracz, S., Sienty, S., Todorov, K., Snyder, J., Takashima, B., Pensabene, R., Olsen, B., Pauls, L., & Sork, J. (1995). Improvement in teaching skills: Perspectives from National Board for Professional Teaching Standards field test network candidates. Paper presented at the Annual meeting of the American Educational Research Association, San Francisco, CA.

Wolf, K. (1991). The schoolteacher's portfolio: Issues in design, implementation, and evaluation. *Phi Delta Kappan, 73*, 129–136.

Wolf, K. (1996). Developing an effective teaching portfolio. *Educational Leadership, 53*, 34–37.

Zeichner, K. M. (1981). Reflective teaching and field-based experience in teacher education. *Interchange, 12*(4), 1–22.

Zeichner, K. M., & Liston, D. P. (1987). Teaching student teachers to reflect. *Harvard Educational Review, 57*(1), 23–48.

Zeichner, K. M., & Tabachnick, B. R. (1991). Reflections on reflective teaching. In: B. R. Tabachnick & K. M. Zeichner (Eds), *Issues and practices in inquiry-oriented teacher education* (pp. 1–21). New York: Falmer Press.

CHAPTER 14

PROVIDING FEEDBACK TO TEACHER CANDIDATES FOR NATIONAL BOARD CERTIFICATION: A STUDY OF TEACHER PREFERENCES AND LEARNING

Kenneth Wolf, Alan Davis and Hilda Borko

ABSTRACT

In this National Board-commissioned study, we examined types of feedback that teacher candidates for certification might receive along with their score reports after completing the Board's assessment process. We designed three standardized forms of feedback and interviewed 29 teachers from the 1993–1994 Early Adolescent/Generalist cohort about their preferences for each of the feedback options and about the inferences that they drew about their performance based on each type. The three feedback formats were (a) cases – extended descriptions of actual performances, annotated with scorer notes; (b) performance syntheses – brief descriptions of the scoring criteria accompanied by a variety of excerpts from candidate materials portraying performances at each level;

Assessing Teachers for Professional Certification:
The First Decade of the National Board for Professional Teaching Standards
Advances in Program Evaluation, Volume 11, 413–436
Copyright © 2008 by Elsevier Ltd.
All rights of reproduction in any form reserved
ISSN: 1474-7863/doi:10.1016/S1474-7863(07)11014-0

and (c) illustrative summaries – evaluative descriptions of various candidate responses. Teachers reported that, of the three standardized formats offered to them, they preferred the cases format with its extended descriptions of an actual performance accompanied by annotated scoring notes. In terms of learning effects, candidates drew reasonably accurate inferences about their performance based on both cases and performance syntheses. The central conclusion we reached based on these findings was that feedback needs to be clearly organized around the scoring criteria for the exercise, and that examples of actual performances illustrating the application of the scoring criteria are important. However, teachers also reported that they would have preferred individualized, customized feedback on their own performance, although this option was not offered by the Board. As well, teachers indicated they would have preferred receiving the standardized feedback as "feedfront" to use in guiding them in their teaching and in preparing their assessment materials.

STUDY FOCUS AND EVALUATION QUESTIONS

The National Board for Professional Teaching Standards (NBPTS) has established a system of voluntary professional certification as a means to upgrade the expertise and prestige of the teaching profession. In this certification process, teachers are assessed through a combination of exercises, some of which they complete at their school sites and others at assessment centers throughout the country. After the exercises have been scored and certification decisions made, teachers are notified whether they have received Board certification and given feedback about their performance. The purpose of the present study was to provide information to the NBPTS regarding the form that feedback to candidates should take.

We undertook this study with the understanding that feedback from the National Board should provide candidates with summative information to enable them to interpret how well they did on the assessment exercises, and formative information that could lead them to useful inferences regarding ways they could improve their practice. We also argued that feedback is an act of communicating information. If the information itself is accurate, the quality of this communication depends on its appropriateness for its intended audience – whether the information is perceived as comprehensible, clear, useful, and sufficient by those who receive it. The quality of feedback also depends on the match between the scorer judgments that underlie the feedback (the intended message) and the inferences that candidates make when feedback is received (the received message). These two evaluative criteria – appropriateness, as judged by the candidates themselves, and quality of inference, as judged by an examination of candidate learning – underlay our examination of candidates' preferences for feedback and the inferences they reached after receiving feedback.

In light of these considerations, three evaluation questions guide this study:

Question 1. What are teachers' preferences for the kind of feedback they receive after participating in the National Board certification process, and how do they perceive the usefulness of alternative types of feedback for interpreting their performance and learning about their practice?

We attended to teachers' preferences about the various feedback options by asking them to discuss each feedback alternative with respect to its usefulness for the two purposes of interpreting the scores (and the certification decision) and providing information to improve teaching practice; rate the feedback alternatives on a set of features including clarity, amount of information, respectfulness, and helpfulness in providing insights into teaching; and rank order the feedback options.

Question 2. What do the teachers learn from the feedback for (a) interpreting their scores and (b) improving their practice?

To obtain this information, we asked candidates to read the feedback materials, take notes about their own strengths and weaknesses as they read, and then answer a series of interview questions that focused on their learnings and insights about their practice and their exercise performance.

Question 3. How well do the teachers' reports of what they learned about their teaching based on various feedback types correspond to the scorers' assessments of the teachers' performance that were used as the basis for assigning scores?

To answer this question we compared what teachers reported they learned about their teaching from the feedback with the scorers' interpretations of the teachers' performance. This information allowed us to determine if teachers were drawing appropriate inferences from the feedback.

METHODS

To study what candidates learned from feedback and how useful they perceived it to be, we chose to provide realistic feedback to actual candidates at the exercise level under controlled conditions, and to conduct extensive interviews with them about their preferences for, and learnings from, these feedback options. The study was conducted with the first cohort of candidates participating in the Early Adolescent/Generalist (EA/G) certification process because it was the first fully operational assessment system, and the scoring procedures for the EA/G certification were best established at the time the study was undertaken.

Two very different exercises from that certification area, Teaching and Learning (T&L), and Exploring Curriculum Issues (ECI), were selected for the development of feedback. The extended, school-site T&L exercise, in which candidates documented their actual teaching in great detail over a period of several weeks, provided the best opportunity to determine what candidates might learn from feedback concerning their teaching. In contrast, ECI was a relatively brief Assessment Center exercise in which candidates described in an essay how they would structure a period of teaching and learning on a selected topic. This exercise provided an excellent opportunity to determine what candidates might learn from feedback concerning on-demand performance at the Assessment Centers. We chose these two exercises because they were representatives of the two assessment approaches taken by the NBPTS, and they differed substantially from each other in their focus and context. Candidates were selected for interviews to represent the full range of scores on these two exercises.

Feedback Options

Three types of feedback were presented to candidates: *Cases, Performance Syntheses, and Illustrative Summaries.* Cases and performance syntheses were developed for use in this study, while the illustrative summaries were developed by the Assessment Development Laboratory at the University of Georgia.

Cases
Cases featured edited examples of representative candidates' actual performances along with the corresponding comments of a scorer. Each "case" was three to four pages long, and consisted of (a) a one-paragraph overview of the performance; (b) edited excerpts from the portfolio or assessment center essay, with corresponding evaluator comments; and (c) evaluative comments organized by the scoring criteria for the exercise. The feedback packet for each exercise consisted of two cases representing

the highest level of performance, Level IV, and two cases at a candidate's own score level (see Appendix A for an example).

Performance Syntheses

Performance syntheses were intended to reveal, through examples from candidate materials, how specific scoring criteria were used to determine a candidate's score. Each candidate received feedback about the highest level of performance (Level IV) and the level of the candidate's own score. The Level-IV component of performance synthesis feedback consisted of a brief description of the general characteristics of Level-IV performance, followed by examples to illustrate exemplary performance on each of the four scoring criteria. The feedback component for each of the other three performance levels consisted of a brief statement of the general characteristics of performances at that level, followed by descriptions of patterns of responses at that level. Each description included an explanation of the pattern and two examples of candidate performances (see Appendix B for an example).

Illustrative Summaries

Illustrative summaries consisted of evaluative descriptions of actual candidates' responses to the exercise. For each of the four possible score levels, paragraph-length evaluative comments pertaining to three candidates' responses were provided on a single page, each formatted in a box (see Appendix C for an example).

Feedback prototypes developed for this study included examples and excerpts from candidate materials and evaluative comments from the scorer materials from the initial field-test materials (1993–1994) and the first operational year (1994–1995). Evaluative comments in the feedback materials were drawn, as much as possible, directly from scorers' written comments.

Sampling

Cluster sampling was used to draw an acceptably representative sample of EA/G candidates from the 1993–1994 cohort. Assessment Centers were sampled first. Centers with large numbers of candidates were identified and then stratified in respect to geographical location and urbanicity, attending to the percentage of non-white candidates. Five centers were drawn: San Diego, CA; Denver, CO; Detroit, MI; Columbia, SC; and Fort Lauderdale, FL. All candidates from these centers who participated in the 1993–1994

EA/G cohort were invited to participate in the study. A total of 33 candidates responded. Of these, 31 were interviewed, including all of the volunteers who were non-white and all who had not passed Board certification. Two interviews could not be transcribed and were dropped from the analysis. The final sample of 29 candidates consisted of 7 men and 22 women. Four candidates were African-American, one was Asian-American, and 24 were white. Fifteen candidates passed Board certification; 14 did not.

Data Collection Instruments

Data were collected through semi-structured, face-to-face interviews. Each interview lasted approximately four hours. The interview began with candidates reading a description of the T&L exercise and scoring criteria, and noting (in writing and orally) strengths and weaknesses in their teaching practices and exercise documentation. Candidates then read either case or performance synthesis feedback and identified additional strengths and weaknesses in their practice and documentation. This process was repeated with the second type of experimental feedback. Next, candidates were given the illustrative summaries to read. They rated each of the three feedback types on six characteristics (usefulness in interpreting score, clarity of content, amount of information, respectfulness, clarity of visual format, and insightfulness for teaching), using seven-point semantic differential scales, and they discussed each rating. Finally, candidates ranked the three forms of feedback in the order of preference and explained their ranking. The entire procedure was then repeated for the ECI exercise.

Analysis

Candidates' ratings of feedback preferences were analyzed as a three-factor (type of feedback × pass/fail certification decision × exercise) repeated-measures multivariate analysis of variance (MANOVA), in which type of feedback and exercise were within-subject variables. All six ratings were first analyzed together in an omnibus multivariate test. Univariate repeated-measures analyses of variance were then conducted if the omnibus test was significant ($a = .05$). To understand the perceptions that underlay candidates' preferences for feedback and to determine the amount and nature of candidate learning from feedback, the interviews were transcribed and coded. Coded candidate comments were then compared to scorers' comments for four representative participants to determine the match between the individual teachers' reports of what they learned and scorers' assessments of the teachers' performances.

RESULTS AND CONCLUSIONS

Candidate Preferences

Many of the teachers we interviewed believed that feedback from the Board ought to be individualized. They wanted feedback that explained the specific ways in which their own performance compared to the criteria used to evaluate it. As one candidate commented:

> The feedback from the Board was not personalized. They gave examples of what a four should be, what a three should be, two and one, but there was nothing written on comparing my performance against the standards, and that's what I would like to have. How does this match up to the standards that were put forth by our teaching? It would be helpful to me to say, "Well, in Standard One you demonstrated this and that; however, this was missing." That's what I would like to have.

This said, of the three feedback options, teachers clearly preferred cases with performance syntheses second and illustrative summaries third. Eighty-three percent of the candidates ranked cases first among types of feedback for the T&L exercise; 75% ranked them first for ECI.

Two factors emerged from the interviews as key in explaining this overall ranking of cases, performance syntheses, and illustrative summaries: the content and organization based on scoring criteria in the feedback, and the application of those criteria to direct examples of candidate materials. The teachers in our study criticized the illustrative summaries on both of these counts. Information in the illustrative summaries directly reflected the criteria used in scoring, but these criteria were not clearly labeled, and many candidates did not seem to recognize them. In contrast, the cases and performance syntheses were explicitly organized around scoring criteria. Illustrative summaries did not provide examples of what candidates had actually done. Our teachers pointed to the specific descriptions and excerpts of candidates' materials in the cases and performance syntheses as what they most valued about these types of feedback.

The majority of the candidates rated case feedback very favorably with respect to its format, the clarity of its content, the amount of information it provided, and its usefulness for interpreting their score and learning about their teaching. Several added that they would prefer receiving similar feedback regarding their own "case," but if this were not feasible, representative cases such as the ones we presented them were deemed useful and appropriate. A representative comment follows:

> This, on the other hand, is extremely detailed. This is the case study. What makes the case study so strong is, one, specific examples, boxed, of the student work, then an evaluator's comments that pinpoint, highlight, point out what it is that works or does not work, because then they go into where the weaknesses are too. So by seeing how the candidate did, specifics of what it is they did, and then the evaluator comments, then that gives me feedback, whether or not I'm using [my own materials]. I know now why maybe this wasn't a three. When I walked in here today I had no clue.

The majority of candidates also rated Performance syntheses favorably on all criteria. Several candidates commented that the variety of examples included in the performance syntheses was enlightening:

> Performance synthesis, I'm going to rate that one high on insights into teaching, too, because being that it is a synthesis over a lot of candidates, it's not as personal as the case study but once again getting more examples helps you to be even more insightful into your own teaching. You see what a lot of people do.

Some candidates, however, found the performance patterns confusing:

> I ranked the performance syntheses slightly lower because at the level four there is one feedback format used; at the second level there's a different feedback format used. The patterns ... were a little bit more diffuse.

A few candidates indicated that the illustrative summaries were useful, but many others found them unhelpful because they did not contain examples of candidate performance:

> The illustrative one, I did not like at all. It was just a dry narrative of what the evaluator thought of it and there was little evidence or very little backup from the work that the teacher did.

Candidate Learnings

Most candidates learned about their teaching practice and about their documentation from both cases and performance syntheses. We were not able to assess directly their learning from illustrative summaries, since they had received these before the study was conducted. The teachers' comments and ratings indicated, however, that they had not found Illustrative

Summaries very useful for understanding their performance on the exercise or for improving their practice. Although the teachers did learn from the set of experiences that we refer to as "the assessment experience," their learning appeared to be primarily due to the process of completing the exercises, rather than the illustrative summaries. After candidates read either performance syntheses or cases, in contrast, most were able to identify several additional ways in which their practice could be improved. For example, one candidate made the following comments after reading the cases feedback for the ECI exercise:

> OK, [I] did not address weaknesses and needs of ... strengths and needs of individual students [or] content knowledge. It showed up really strong after reading this under the weakness column. [Also,] assessing their prior knowledge coming into this activity so that wasn't addressed in the essay.

> I discuss the group needs or what they need to learn, but not in light of individual strengths and weaknesses. OK, I mentioned interests of young adolescents. No specific description of an activity, although a number of them [are] mentioned.

> This one tells me that I should have addressed misconceptions the students may bring with them and to tailor the activities more to their individual assessments. And those are ... things I would have done different in this piece.

A different candidate described what he learned from the performance synthesis feedback for the T&L exercise:

> As I was going through [the performance synthesis feedback] ... [these are] some of the things I wrote down ... .

> I did not include a complete description of each activity and show the integration and show the objectives and explain what the kids did ... . [Also,] I've gotten back into giving more ownership to the students. I realize that I had fallen back into teacher controlled classrooms.

> And something [else] I noted, it's very important, I think it's very important for the teacher to make a daily written log and these teachers that were rated number one, I think they took the time to make a daily log ... you know, I did not write this information down and the key thing with these teachers in terms of what they did was they described completely what they did, what the students did, how did it affect them, how did it affect the students, what was the objective, how did they make the changes ... .

Learning from both the cases and the performance syntheses closely matched the scoring criteria. When candidates listed the strengths and weaknesses they identified in their own performance after reading the feedback, their inferences corresponded to aspects of their performance that were attended to by the scorers. Candidates' learnings did not appear to be idiosyncratic to characteristics of the specific examples featured in the feedback alternatives. One reason for their more generalized learnings may be the way in which feedback alternatives were constructed. That is, we attended carefully to the Assessment Development Laboratory's scoring criteria in determining both the descriptive information (e.g., summaries of features of candidates' performances and excerpts from candidate materials) and evaluator comments (e.g., excerpts and summaries from the scorers' notes) that we included. We also designed the graphic format of both types of feedback in such a way that the specific examples of performance were linked visually to specific scoring criteria or to evaluator comments reflective of these specific scoring criteria.

In short, teachers made reasonably accurate inferences about their teaching and their exercise performance from the experimental feedback, and they were able to identify the characteristics of the feedback that best facilitated their learning. The central conclusion that we reached from this evidence was that there were two essential characteristics of effective feedback for teachers, which were present in both the cases and performance syntheses:

- Effective feedback identifies the scoring criteria clearly and the presentation of feedback includes information organized explicitly around these criteria.
- The feedback provides examples of actual performance to illustrate the application of the scoring criteria.

The identification of scoring criteria was associated with the visual formatting of feedback. Teachers responded to the use of bullets and bold fonts to highlight evaluation criteria. They particularly commented on the use of boxes located side by side in the cases to link scorer comments to specific elements of portfolio and assessment center exercise materials.

Candidates expressed a strong preference for the extended, contextualized examples of candidate performance contained in cases. They clearly learned about their own practice from these examples. However, they also learned from the shorter examples in the performance syntheses, which lacked any extended description of context.

In making a decision about feedback options, a difficult balance must be struck between the number and variety of examples presented in feedback, and the desire of teachers to sense the individual person and the context and unfolding of their performance over time. In a school-based exercise such as T&L, we favor the use of fewer, more contextualized and detailed examples. In center-based exercises such as ECI, where direct teaching practice is not reflected, a larger variety of shorter excerpts from candidate materials, selected to illustrate particular scoring criteria, may be equally effective.

Great care must be taken in the selection of exemplars; candidates tended to discount examples if these did not closely match their own topic or context. The best generalized feedback for school-based exercises should include a minimum of two cases at the highest level of performance along with two at the candidate's own level, and care should be taken to select cases representing diverse teaching contexts.

The improvement of teaching is at the heart of the Board's mission. Our study indicated that feedback that accurately conveyed scoring criteria based on NBPTS principles, and that illustrated these criteria through the use of carefully selected examples from candidate performances, could advance that mission.

FEEDBACK GUIDE CURRENTLY AVAILABLE TO CANDIDATES

In this section, as a postscript to our study, we will describe the National Board's approach to feedback at the time this research was conducted, and then comment on the differences between this approach and the one described in this chapter.

The National Board published a booklet entitled "Guide to Interpreting Your National Board Certification Scores" that candidates received – along with their scores – several months after completing the assessment process. This 150 page guide gave candidates background information about the National Board, a description of the assessment exercises for their certificate area, detailed information about the scoring materials and process, and information about policies such as appeals and retakes.

The "Guide to Interpreting Your National Board Certification Scores" for the 1996–1997 EA/G, for example, included the following sections:

- Background information
- Portfolio scoring materials
- Selected 1996–1997 assessment center prompts
- Assessment center scoring materials
- NBPTS score banking
- NBPTS appeals policy

Much of the information in the present feedback guide is essential. However, there were no samples and descriptions of actual performances, such as candidates' written commentaries or descriptions of their videotapes. And, based on our study, that is what candidates indicated that they were most interested in viewing.

In our study on feedback approaches, we presumed that background material on the National Board, descriptions of the assessment exercises, and policy information would be included in the feedback booklets given to candidates. Our focus was on the kinds of additional information that should be provided to candidates to help them interpret their scores and improve their practices.

The National Board feedback guide to candidates addressed this question by providing extensive information about the scoring process, including the training of scorers, the guides used by the scorers, and the scoring rubrics. Based on the findings of the study described in this chapter, however, candidates reported that examining samples of performances helped them both understand their score and improve their practice. In essence, teachers reported that they preferred actual examples and descriptions of performances in the form of excerpts and summaries from portfolios and assessment center performances (as illustrated in the "cases" and "illustrative summaries" formats). In the guide being used at the time, teachers were given detailed information about the scoring process and criteria, but no actual samples of performances.

A key question to consider, then, is: Should examples and descriptions of actual performances be included in the feedback booklet?

On the negative side, including examples of actual performances in the feedback booklet could add a further 50–100 pages to the booklet if all 10 exercises were addressed. Given the present decision about maintaining the security of the assessment center exercises, however, samples of performances for the assessment center exercises were not likely.

In addition, developing the examples and descriptions of candidate performances generates an additional expense. Based on our experience in developing similar materials, however, this expense (several hundred dollars per exercise) would not be substantial relative to the overall cost of developing the assessment package.

Moreover, there is always the concern that candidates could view the examples as prescriptive rather than as illustrative of a few of many ways that teachers can demonstrate their accomplished nature. However, including a variety of different examples would help to offset this potential problem.

Furthermore, the question remains as to whether candidates would actually read and study these materials. In our study, candidates found the examples and descriptions of candidate performances useful, but they read the materials as part of the study and were compensated for their time.

Nonetheless, given candidates' enthusiastic response to the examples and descriptions of performances in this study, and that these materials were useful to the teachers in gaining insights into their own practice, we recommend that the National Board strongly consider developing samples of actual performance as part of the feedback materials given to candidates. While further study is called for, evidence from our study indicated that candidates found examples and descriptions of performances quite useful, and the cost considerations and potential limitations did not appear substantial enough to rule out their development.

Interestingly, many of the candidates that we interviewed for our study said that the "feedback" would actually be more valuable as "feedfront." That is, instead of receiving the examples and descriptions of performances after they had completed the assessment, they would have benefited more by receiving the materials before they prepared their own performances. Given the National Board's commitment to improving teaching effectiveness, sending the feedback booklets with the portfolio instructions might actually facilitate professional development for the teacher candidates and their colleagues.

If the Board does decide that it is important to provide candidates with samples of candidate performances, however, they may find that others may have already begun to pave the way. National Board certification candidates have begun to share their portfolios with other National Board Certified Teachers and candidates through informal networks, and efforts are underway in projects around the country to develop casebooks of exemplary practice and other materials based on the National Board assessments.

APPENDIX A. CASES: TEACHING AND LEARNING

Performance Level III

Overview of the Unit
This T&L case documents a sixth grade middle school teacher's health unit on "communicable diseases." The candidate presented the students with a variety of reading materials on the topic and drew on several community resources. The unit focused, in particular, on two diseases: tuberculosis and

AIDS. The primary objective for the unit was for students to understand communicable diseases in terms of their own safety and well being. The candidate used a variety of teaching methods during the unit. She facilitated role-play, encouraged students to do research on their own and in groups using outside resources, developed artistic activities to increase student learning, and invited speakers from within the school and the community to address the class. Her own preparation for the unit included visiting and obtaining resources from a local AIDS project and the county hospital, and gathering articles from the national press.

Portfolio Exercise

The candidate's portfolio exercise in T&L is divided into four sections that correspond to the documentation instructions candidates were given for this exercise. The tables below include a *description of the candidate's work* with direct quotes from her/his portfolio *on the left* and *evaluator comments* on key features of the candidate's work *on the right*.

DESCRIPTION OF THE TEACHING SITUATION

Description of the Candidate's Work	Evaluator Comments
The 26 students in this sixth grade class come together in a "home room" for a rotating class in math and language arts as well as a core subject that "rotates approximately every six weeks." The candidate chose to focus on a curricular health unit on "communicable diseases."	The candidate places a strong emphasis on relevance in her topic selection. The topic is current as well as critical to her students' lives.
"I chose to feature this [subject] because the topic lends itself to integration and exploration of several related areas. Also, I believe that an understanding of communicable diseases is essential for all students in terms of their own safety and well being. It is a relevant topic encouraging close attention and participation on the part of the student at a personal level."	The candidate's focus on a close examination of highly debated issues helps her students to learn to explore multiple perspectives.

(Continued).

The three-week unit integrated "factual knowledge with current and highly debated events in this area, namely the resurgence of tuberculosis and the AIDS epidemic." The candidate also placed emphasis on news and trends because a number of her students were only "vaguely aware" of how to examine and analyze news documents.

Student Descriptions	Evaluator Comments
The candidate selected three students who were "representative of the learning characteristics and social-development range" in the class. The candidate reported that 'Eric' was an "inquisitive student who operates independently. He sort of 'makes up his own rules.' The work he turns in shows a high level of thinking and a strong ability to express himself through writing. He is advanced academically speaking. However, his social development has been slow, and he often draws attention to himself in inappropriate ways." The candidate described "Rico" as "opposite Eric in many respects" with a wide circle of friends and a strong focus on social interaction. Rico is "more or less attentive ... depending on his notion of a lesson's relevance in his life." Finally, "Ellen" is a student who had a "tremendously difficult time adjusting to the middle school." She is quite physically mature and "refused to come to school for weeks early in the fall." Working with the parents, counselor, and fellow teaching colleagues, the	The candidate's selection demonstrates her attention to academic as well as affective dimensions of her students. Relevance is emphasized in the selection of Rico and Ellen. While Rico's attention depends on the topic's relevance to him, Ellen's participation relies on opportunities for leadership, which the candidate provides within the development of her unit.

(Continued).

candidate found that putting Ellen in a
"leadership role that is positive, visible
and also safe" allowed her to feel more
comfortable in school. In the months
following the beginning of school "She
established a small group of friends and
has missed only a few days of school."

Account of Teaching and Learning	Evaluator Comments
The candidate described her unit as an opportunity to "educate students about their own role in leading a safe and healthy life. Since, in most cases, contracting a communicable disease can be avoided, awareness of the conditions in which particular diseases are passed is critical." Beginning with a discussion of students' background knowledge of communicable diseases and a chapter in the class textbook, the candidate designed the unit using varied resources such as current newspapers and community experts like the school nurse and a representative from the local AIDS project. The activities within the unit were also varied and included "lecture and note-taking, research, formal and informal discussion, student group presentation, artistic expression, family conversation, self-reflection, role-plays, guest speakers, video, and excursions."	The candidate did a thorough job of pulling in outside resources and stimulating students' thinking and reasoning. She took a short health textbook chapter and transformed it into an extensive multidisciplinary study. The candidate's use of parental support and community resources was exemplary.
Moving from a written review of their own health histories, which involved conversations with parents, the students were required to bring in "at least two current health-related articles [which] encouraged them to keep their focus on the study *outside of the classroom*." Building from student interest in	By allowing the students to examine their own background knowledge as well as maintaining the flexibility to follow student interest, the candidate provided a strong learner-centered environment where students had ownership and commitment to

(Continued).

---

tuberculosis, the candidate asked the students to prepare and conduct a Socratic Seminar on a current article on TB. The article was difficult and the candidate "asked that students read and discuss the article with their parents" a strategy that the candidate developed in collaboration with the parents of some of her "lowest readers." During the discussion students wove facts together with personal experience, including one student whose grandmother had come to their city for TB treatments. The candidate also suggested "Rico took a particularly compelling stance in support of the rights of TB patients." In reflecting on the resulting discussion, the candidate asked the students to "write a 'recommendation' to a fictitious board of directors about what should happen with these patients." The students then made presentations to the "board" which ended in a vote for the most effective "proposal."

their learning. In developing and voting on proposals, the students learned how decisions are made in the real world. Although the candidate was thoughtful about how her case-study students were progressing through the unit, her reflection on the unit as a whole was minimal.

The unit culminated with the students' study of AIDS. After reading current information including a book on the AIDS quilt, the students created their own "Identity Quilt" which was ultimately hung in the schools' main display case. The students also completed a comprehensive take-home test on AIDS and they were "encouraged to work with parents or family members, use their health notes, or even the county AIDS hotline, to complete their test."

The culminating activities illustrate the candidate's commendable use of community resources.

EXHIBITS: VIDEOTAPE VIGNETTES, STUDENT WORK SAMPLES, AND OPTIONAL EXHIBITS

The candidate's videotape described nine vignettes. Examples included:

- "I am starting a lesson on the 'anatomy of a textbook.' I ask students to complete this statement, 'A textbook is ....'"
- "I am setting the scene for a role-play, where students present proposals regarding plans for the confinement of TB patients."
- "A student presents her proposal and answers classmates' questions."
- "The strategy here is to give students an opportunity to teach other students."
- "I am addressing the myths and controversy that arise around a subject such as AIDS. This was an unplanned/unforeseen turn in the lesson. I work to validate the student's participation nonetheless."

The candidates' artifacts show wide diversity of approaches through writing, role-plays, and discussion. The candidate again demonstrates her flexibility as she accommodates her students' interests – pursuing topics that they initiate.

The candidate provided six work samples for the focus student called 'Eric' which included:

- "Eric's own definition of communicable diseases."
- "Coded text of New York Times article used in the Socratic Seminar."
- Eric underlined sections of the article in pen and wrote comments in the margins providing details of his response. He and his parents signed that he had read the article three times.

The requirement to 'code' difficult articles demonstrates the candidate's attention to comprehension strategies as well as parental involvement.

Eric's letter is an example of the unit's efficacy in establishing community connections. It also demonstrates Eric's commitment as he establishes his own philosophical stance regarding

(Continued).

- "Eric's proposal, in the form of a letter to the mayor, regarding confinement of TB patients." In this letter Eric argues for confinement, suggesting that "if we let [deadly diseases] get out of hand, the consequences would be great."
- "Health/Identify worksheet. The completion of this worksheet preceded a circle discussion about their views on this topic.
- "A copy of Eric's thank you [letter] to guest speakers. One is an AIDS activist and [the other] is a man with full-blown AIDS." In his letter Eric wrote, "I may come down to the AIDS center sometime to take a look at some books. Before you came, I never knew it existed. I am glad you feel children should know about AIDS. We should."

necessary information for children. The artifacts, however, are all final products with no evidence of process writing.

The candidate provided 19 optional exhibits which included:

- A variety of booklets on the unit topic
- The end-of-unit test
- The school's student health form
- A diagram of the immune system.
- A photograph of the "Identity Quilt" and students

The artifacts highlight the candidate's commitment to extensive and varied background research to prepare her unit.

CASE EVALUATION

Specific comments and examples follow for the four criteria on which the exercise was evaluated.

Learner-Centered Approach

The candidate did a thorough job of pulling in outside resources and stimulating students' thinking and reasoning. For example, the candidate drew on numerous resources in the community, such as visiting the local hospital and an AIDS project to collect information and identify guest speakers. She also invited the school nurse to speak on the topic. Moreover, she supplemented the short section on "communicable diseases" in the health textbook by collecting pamphlets from the hospital, and by having students search out newspaper articles on the topic. Throughout these activities the candidate helped her students make connections between what was being learned and their lives. This was particularly true of the articles the students analyzed, for they read for comprehension as well as enjoyment and their reading ultimately helped them develop their individual stance toward critical issues.

The candidate also designed learning activities that developed student commitment and ownership over tasks and goals. For example, after teaching about the "Names Project" the candidate created an opportunity for her class to do a similar artistic project. As a group, students decided to make an "Identity Quilt," and each student had responsibility for an individual piece. In these activities, the candidate helped to foster students' self-awareness, self-esteem, confidence, and independence.

The assessment in the classroom was largely formal in nature. Although there were hints about informal assessment, there was no reflective writing on the part of the candidate to show that her assessment strategies encouraged revision of the unit through review or further explanation. There was also no evidence of the candidate moving students to be evaluators of their own work. For example, there were no writing-process drafts that might indicate reflection and revision.

Integrated Approach to Curriculum and Learning

The candidate created opportunities for her students to think incisively about issues, raise their own questions, and be able to see issues from a variety of different perspectives. For example, the class held a mock board meeting where several students presented "plans" for the care of patients with tuberculosis, debating between the rights of the patient versus the rights of the community. The activities throughout the unit highlighted problem solving, effective communication, and active thinking.

Student Learning Community

The candidate created a non-threatening environment where students were motivated and encouraged to participate. She demonstrated that diversity was valued in her classroom by creating opportunities for students to share their diverse points of view on issues related to communicable diseases, and by developing learning activities that focused on the individual experiences of her students and their families. For example, she assigned each student to write a brief history about their own health, which also contributed to discussions at home. The candidate also developed learning activities that encouraged her students to work both independently and collaboratively with others. Students conducted research on their own and in groups and also worked individually and collaboratively on the "Identity Quilt."

The candidate worked with the families of her students to exchange ideas, communicate accomplishments, and share expectations to enhance student learning. For example, she worked out a strategy with the parents of her lowest readers to have the children read aloud any reading assignments to the parents at home. She also had students complete a "take-home" test on AIDS for which they needed to work with their parents and seek information from outside resources.

The candidate also sought out many outside resources to continue her own learning about the topic. She obtained information and pamphlets from the local AIDS project and county hospital, and found articles in journals and newspapers to enhance her students' and her own learning.

The Reflective Nature of Your Practice

While the candidate created and implemented a strong T&L experience, day-to-day reflective assessments were not evident. Occasionally, she drew upon her knowledge of her students to assess successful and unsuccessful learning activities in order to better understand what worked, what did not work, and why. For example, in her description of Eric during the group research project, she noted that he needed extra attention and guidance in working with others, even though individually he needed little assistance with the research. These examples, however, were not an integral part of her portfolio.

APPENDIX B. PERFORMANCE SYNTHESIS FEEDBACK

Level II Performance Synthesis Feedback for One Performance Pattern

DESCRIPTION AND EXAMPLES OF LEVEL II PERFORMANCE

General Characteristics

Candidate's response is limited despite evidence of having met some of the expectations for the exercise.

Two patterns characterize the majority of Level II performances. These patterns differ in the relationships among strengths and limitations on the four scoring criteria. Below, each pattern is described and concrete examples based on candidate portfolios are provided.

Specific pattern number 1.

Some candidates received a 2 for portfolios that displayed significant weakness related to one or more scoring criteria.

Example 1. One candidate described a unit on electricity that featured hands-on experiments with circuitry. The candidate's performance was strong with respect to some components of *Learner-Centered Approach* and *Student Learning Community*. The unit included several learner-centered experiences such as whole class discussions that considered the role of electricity in students' lives and circuitry experiments that required active student participation in cooperative working groups. The candidate also worked to establish a learning environment in which students felt comfortable taking risks, sharing their ideas:

I try to get my students to see that the correctness of the [scientific] predictions of little value. It is the thought process that is behind the prediction that is of vital importance.

The candidate met some of the expectations for the exercise; however, the portfolio was weak with respect to *Integrated Approach to Curriculum and Learning* and *Reflective Nature of Practice*. The unit on electricity appeared to be a stand-alone unit. The candidate did not draw connections to other scientific concepts or mention how activities might cross disciplinary boundaries. There was no evidence of informal assessment methods in either the narrative or the exhibits. Although formal assignments were given, the candidate did not appear to use them to analyze student learning or adapt instruction to changing student needs.

Example 2. One candidate featured a unit on fractions for a remedial math class. This candidate exhibited a number of strengths. *Learner-Centered Approach* was evident in a focus on affective as well as cognitive goals, attention to individual differences, and ongoing assessment and adjustment of instructional activities. For example, affective objectives for the unit included:

[to] develop confidence in their own ability, to develop an ability to take risks, to develop an ability to deal with frustration and failure in a positive manner, to learn from mistakes, to persevere at a task, and to be able to work with others in a cooperative situation.

The candidate also exhibited a number of strengths related to *Reflective Nature of Practice* such as using information about individual students' strengths and weaknesses to plan activities and lessons and making adjustments to plans on the basis of changing student needs:

The third week was when some of the students ran into some major difficulty. This was when we switched to subtraction, with and without renaming. I really didn't anticipate this as a problem area .... I dealt with this problem by regrouping my students in the fourth week.

The critical weakness in this candidate's portfolio was its lack of Integrated Approach to Curriculum and Learning. Content of the unit was almost exclusively skills and computation and did little to help students understand the role of mathematics in their daily lives. Activities described in the narrative and displayed in the exhibits were solely within the discipline of mathematics. Also, although the candidate created a safe learning environment for students, other elements of the Student Learning Community, particularly the extension to family and community, were missing.

APPENDIX C. ILLUSTRATIVE SUMMARIES

Level III

LEVEL III responses satisfy the expectations for this exercise

Example 1. During this period of instruction the candidate showed strengths in a variety of components of T&L. The candidate drew on his/ her knowledge of the needs, interests, and characteristics of young adolescents, as well as his/her knowledge of content, in planning a variety of active experiences designed to foster a lifelong commitment to learning. The candidate's use of assessment as a tool to improve instruction and give meaningful feedback to students to extend their understanding was a strong area of his/her practice. The candidate established a learner-centered classroom where s/he played an active role in guiding students to be more able to assume responsibility and independence. The candidate was sensitive to the needs of individual learners and to the needs of the group, and was able to monitor, assess, and adjust instruction as appropriate. The candidate's goals and themes were important, meaningful, and relevant. In an interdisciplinary way, the candidate skillfully and naturally integrated several subject areas in lessons, helping students understand the processes of thinking, the skills of mathematics, how to think for themselves, and how to communicate their ideas to others. The learning community was inviting, fostering a positive disposition to learning based on mutual respect. The candidate demonstrated insights from reflection, based on his/her account of classroom modifications to meet the needs of his/her students.

Example 2. The candidate's knowledge of mathematics and science concepts, his/her ability to integrate the two, and his/her awareness of the social and academic needs of students were apparent in his/her response. The culmination of the featured period of instruction was the collaborative design and creation of a high-interest student project, which served *as* a vehicle for students to apply their knowledge of content, raise their self-esteem, and increase self-awareness. The teacher provided academic preparation for the project, and the execution of the project was student-centered, involving the use of high-order thinking skills, such as problem solving. When the teacher provided the necessary academic instruction, the classroom was orderly and structured; during the student creation phase the environment *was* conducive to risk-taking and self-expression. The T&L during this period indicated a great deal of planning by the candidate, but with more of an organizational focus than a reflective focus. There was evidence of day-to-day reflection and modification of activities based on that reflection.

Example 3. This candidate used the newspaper as a tool to successfully integrate the teaching of reading skills and social studies, while also focusing on the development of social skills such as working cooperatively. Students actively participated in most activities and a high level of student interest was maintained throughout the featured period of instruction. Through group work students showed ownership and responsibility for their own learning. The candidate showed evidence of a great deal of reflection in planning for this unit, but did not reveal as much evidence of daily reflection having an impact on modifying instruction to meet individual student's needs. Assessment and feedback for this featured period of instruction centered around the group work.

SECTION 5:
THE NBPTS AND THE FUTURE

CHAPTER 15

THE NATIONAL BOARD FOR PROFESSIONAL TEACHING STANDARDS: AN INDISPENSABLE REFORM IN AMERICAN EDUCATION

Gary Sykes

ABSTRACT

Now nearly two decades into its existence, the National Board for Professional Teaching Standards (NBPTS) serves as an indispensable reform in American education, not only on its own merits but also in relation to other reform trends, including both standards-based, account-ability-oriented developments, and the unfolding of new parental choice and privatization movements. The NBPTS is a major strategy for recognizing and developing outstanding teachers, who are needed in all schools, whether organized around standards and assessments or mobilized via competitive market pressures. Drawing on an analogy with the medical field's National Board for Medical Examiners, this paper discusses the prospects for the NBPTS in the context of American educational reform, making the argument for its centrality, while also discussing the challenges that lie ahead for the Board.

Assessing Teachers for Professional Certification:
The First Decade of the National Board for Professional Teaching Standards
Advances in Program Evaluation, Volume 11, 439–460
Copyright © 2008 by Elsevier Ltd.
All rights of reproduction in any form reserved
ISSN: 1474-7863/doi:10.1016/S1474-7863(07)11015-2

Preceding chapters in this volume have explored many of the complex technical questions concerning the development of standards for teaching. Looking back over the first two decades of the National Board for Professional Teaching Standards (NBPTS, also referred to as the National Board, or simply, the Board), there is much evidence of remarkable progress, against long odds. At its inception, many skeptics predicted its early demise. Political wrangling among constituency groups would be its undoing; technical problems in assessment would prove impossible to resolve; efforts to set standards around contentious topics such as multiculturalism, the reading wars, history versus social studies, and others, would doom efforts at consensus; and the burden of raising sufficient funds would sink the enterprise. To nearly everyone's surprise, however, the Board has survived and prospered, due to extraordinary leadership from many quarters. The first generation problems are now nearly under control. Subsequent generations of problems remain, but the effort is well and truly launched. It exaggerates little to claim that the National Board is one of the most significant and promising reforms in American education in the post-war era. At the same time, its ultimate impact remains to be determined and many challenges lie ahead.

This chapter begins with an historical analogy to frame the significance of the National Board; places its work into an overview account of American educational reform; explores three broad strategies within which the Board might serve the twin goals of professional advancement and educational improvement; and concludes with final thoughts on the future of the teaching occupation in America.

AN HISTORICAL ANALOGY

In light of the enormous cultural power of American medicine, educators not surprisingly, turned to medicine as the professional exemplar. There are by now good reasons to avoid such analogies, for in an anti-professional age, American medicine has lost much of its luster, and is now in a state of enormous change, if not of crisis. Nevertheless, in the planning for the NBPTS, a certain analogy was powerful, and it is worth recounting both as part of the record and for its illuminating aspects.

In the early decades of the twentieth century, the American medical field was fractured. Each state had its own licensing boards and standards with little uniformity across states, little reciprocity. Modern, scientifically-based medicine had yet to emerge based on the discovery of the germ theory some years later. But the medical establishment was unhappy with the disarray of standards that regulated entry to the field. Medical quackery in various forms was prevalent, and the practice of medicine was neither well regarded nor particularly efficacious. At this historical juncture, Abraham Flexner made his famous visits to medical schools and his report stimulated a development that already had commenced, which was the elimination of weak, proprietary medical schools.

This certainly helped to form the American medical profession, but another development in this era has been less widely noted. Several of the medical associations, including the powerful American Medical Association, joined in creating a new entity, the National Board of Medical Examiners (NBME). The originating intent of the NBME was to create a standard for entry into the field, together with an assessment process, that would prove so convincing and compelling as to persuade all of the state medical boards to adopt the NBME standard. This strategy proved effective. In the years since its founding in 1915, the NBME has become a vital resource to the medical field. Its governance includes representatives from all the major organizations within the medical field, and it has provided consistently high quality R&D for licensure and certification assessments. The NBME was an explicit model for the NBPTS, but the point to note is the time frame. It took 40 years for the NBME standards and assessments to diffuse across all of the states.

Today, medicine offers more than one examination for licensure and also provides irregular routes into medicine (e.g., off-shore medical schools for those who cannot obtain admission to domestic schools); nevertheless, the field is essentially united around a core of knowledge established in a professional curriculum, together with an examination system that is rigorous, relatively uniform, and powerful. With any perspective, we should expect the NBPTS to exert influence over an arc of 40–50 years, nothing less. Lee Shulman, current president of the Carnegie Foundation for the Advancement of Teaching, has been arguing this point for some time. If the deep intent of the NBPTS is to work a gradual transformation of teaching, then that process must overcome an historical legacy, a tradition, a deeply institutionalized occupation that has been in the making for 150 years. The typical time frame of American reforms is ludicrously short; we expect "results" in 5 years or less, then cut off support if miracles have not occurred in that brief span. But the Board is in for the long haul, has negotiated the difficult issues of start up, and continues to advance at a brisk pace.

As other chapters document, the NBPTS already is beginning to exert impact on American education. The numbers must be updated annually, but in the first 5 cycles between 1993–1994 and 1997–1998, some 4,217 teachers undertook the rigorous certification process, among whom 1,837 (43.6%) successfully attained certification. By 2006, the total number of board certified teachers has reached over 55,000 (NBPTS, 2007). At the same time, as Darling-Hammond's chapter (Chapter 2, this volume) among others recounts, many districts and states are taking note of certification via new policies and procedures that encourage and support the process. And the standards developed by the National Board also are exerting influence on state licensure, program accreditation, teacher evaluation, and teacher education. These policy and programmatic developments are accelerating around the United States with every indication that the National Board and its work are well on their way to institutionalization within the densely woven fabric of American education. Judged against the precedent NBME, the NBPTS has achieved remarkable, even historic impact, in the short space of a decade and a half, with every indication that its influence will continue to grow.

EDUCATIONAL REFORM AS CONTEXT FOR THE NATIONAL BOARD

American education is a protean endeavor. Historical analogies may mislead not only because times have changed but because other developments may outweigh or overpower any particular initiative in the multifaceted, highly contentious arena of school reform. Any reckoning of the future significance of the National Board requires some assessment of complementary and competitive developments that are seeking to shape the countenance of American education. Where, then, might the National Board stand in relation to other developments seeking to shape American education? Are such developments likely to interfere or interact with the Board in the future? Crystal ball gazing of course is an exercise in speculation, but several observations may set the stage for a more pointed analysis of the Board's prospects.

One simplification of education's reform future depicts the coming struggle in terms of three classes of actor operating simultaneously at several levels of a federal system. The fictional or conceptual actors may be dubbed the "Government," the "Market," and the "Profession." The levels upon which these protagonists interact are the national, the state, the district, and the local school. One set of questions facing the American system of education – and many others around the world – concerns the extent to which government-run schools may be reformed to provide better education for all; the extent to which market or quasi-market forces together with new forms of private delivery should be introduced into public education; and the role that professional groups ought to play in shaping reform. A second set of questions concerns the level of the system around which to concert action by governments, markets, and professional forces. Here the classic tensions between centralized and decentralized solutions continue to play out, with both tendencies evident in some versions of reform. Within this conceptually simplified account, both the actors and the stage for reform are subject to dynamic developments.[1]

One prominent scenario locates reform at the state level via government-initiated efforts; standards, assessments, and related policy implements will drive so-called systemic reform of education. Protagonists in this version of reform include state governors, legislatures, boards and departments of education. While many nations around the world are in the process of decentering strongly centralized government school systems, the United States is anomalous in featuring a powerful tradition of local control. Consequently, one group of reformers looks to centralized government as the actor best able to bring focus, clarity, equity, and quality to school reform.

Such beliefs may seem odd in light of the international preoccupation with decentralization, but the examples of such countries as Japan, Germany, France, and Singapore suggest that strong government schools play a distinctive if not determinative part in producing high levels of academic achievement. Furthermore, at least some evidence from the U.S. points to growing influence of government-crafted solutions. States such as North Carolina, Texas, Kentucky, Connecticut, and others appear to be making educational progress based not only on increased expenditures but also on standards-based policies of various kinds. These developments recommend a strong role for state government in creating both pressures and supports for improved achievement. And, such state policy also can have a strong equity component. In Texas, for example, school scores on the state assessment now are disaggregated by ethnic group and trends by school are recorded at the state level and in the local newspapers, then linked to state-provided school rewards and sanctions. The aim is both to raise achievement overall and to close achievement gaps among white, African-American, and Hispanic students. Recent evidence indicates that both kinds of improvement are occurring.[2] More recently along these lines, the federal government has entered the "reform game" via the 2001

No Child Left Behind (NCLB) reauthorization of the Elementary and Secondary Education Act. With its requirements to produce "annual yearly progress" for defined subgroups of students who are tested in many subjects at many grade levels, its "highly qualified teacher" requirements, and its other provisions, NCLB is in process of exerting enormous influence (for good, evil, or perhaps both) on American schools. Hence, the turn to strongly centralized control by government is in full swing.

Other analysts though have argued for a decentralized variant of systemic, standards-based reform, calling for multiple varieties enacted within local communities united by some capacious state policies (for one account, see Clune, 1993). In practice, however, standards-based reforms tend to proceed from the federal and state levels, with local communities developing compatible versions. "Government" in this enactment refers to partnerships among federal, state, and district authorities to introduce more powerful (that is, high stakes) accountability policies to mandate student achievement in traditional public, zoned schools.

A challenge to strong government reform has emerged, however, in various efforts to decentralize education to the local level and to introduce market forces and privatized education into the public realm. Within this family of reforms united by a desire to cede more control over education to local communities and families there are a number of vanguard developments. One is administrative decentralization within the present public system. School- or site-based management seeks to devolve authority and resources to the school level so that school communities composed of teachers, parents, administrators, and others may form free of the bureaucratic entanglements of district offices and possibly collectively bargained contracts. The history of such efforts has not produced notable effects (see, for example, Malen, Ogawa, & Kranz, 1990; Mohrman & Wohlstetter, 1994), but the impulse toward local control remains strong, and tensions probably will persist between centralized and decentralized approaches to reform.

School choice advocates, however, argue that site-based management is too timid a reform, leading to reshuffling of chairs on the ship's deck rather than a strong course correction. What they propose instead is to introduce market-like mechanisms into the public school monopoly to give parents greater choice of schools. Choice policies also might encourage competitive dynamics to unfold among schools, thereby improving education overall. So, states and localities have been experimenting with charter schools, open enrollment plans, and vouchers funded both publicly and privately (for accounts of this trend in American education, see Cookson, 1994;

Henig, 1994; Wells, 1993). By 2000, over 30 states were experimenting with charter school and open enrollment options. Additionally, one state (Florida) passed a limited voucher law; while a variety of local voucher plans were also in operation. Indications are that school choice will continue to be a lively policy option in American education. While approximately 10 percent of American school children attend private schools and another 9 percent attend publicly funded schools of choice (e.g., magnet schools, alternative schools, etc.), there is no public support for private schools in the U.S., unlike most other countries; various calculations reckon some pent up demand for additional choices that include broader financial access to private and parochial schools.

A related yet distinct development seeks to alter the service delivery mechanism from direct public provision (e.g., publicly supported government-run schools) to "regulated competitive delivery" in Gintis' (1995) phrase. Rather than operating schools as part of a single, public system, communities or districts might be empowered to contract for services rendered by a mix of public and private "firms." Just as school districts currently contract for such services as transportation or meals, so they could contract with private vendors for educational products and services of various kinds, thereby introducing private firms into the public school monopoly (for accounts, see Murphy, 1996; Hill, Pierce, & Guthrie, 1997). Some districts and schools already have begun to explore this approach, although the number of such experiments remains small. Choice and contracting may be joined to produce a new schooling regime in which families as consumers are afforded access to a diverse set of schooling options supplied through a mix of public and private providers. In its most radical form, such a regime might disestablish the traditional public school system in favor of a schooling market-place only loosely regulated by the state.

A third set of reforms seeks to link educational research and development to school improvement. One stream champions improvements in the teaching and learning of school subjects, seeking to introduce new instructional methods and materials, including technology, into schools. This may be done on a subject specific basis or in terms of whole school models that have been validated through research. An example of the former approach is the mathematics standards developed by the National Council for the Teaching of Mathematics. An example of the latter is the spread of whole school or comprehensive school models such as 'Success for All' or 'America's Choice' that schools adopt. These reforms typically are championed by various organizations representing the educating professions.[3]

A second stream takes the teaching profession itself as the object of reform. A number of leading states, including Connecticut, North Carolina, and Ohio have developed policies that support the systematic upgrading of the teaching profession in terms of recruitment and selection, licensure and certification, teacher education and professional development, and innovative reward and incentive programs. These professionalizing reforms require a partnership between state government and representatives of the profession, including the teacher unions, which themselves are rethinking their strategies for advancement to better accommodate the professional theme. The National Board has been highly instrumental in supporting these developments and has become a central resource within this stream of policy.

So we might imagine educational reform in the United States as a vast plain upon which are camped three armies among whom combinations of conflict and alliance are possible. In one camp are those reformers who seek to develop strong government policy as a means of lifting educational performance. The primary instruments here are federal and state governments in combination with local school districts. In a second camp are market-based reformers who distrust government, whether local or central, and who seek to expand parental choice of schools as they introduce market-like elements into the public education monopoly. In the third camp are the professional reformers made up of members of the educational establishment. Their claim to influence is based neither on democratic politics nor on competitive markets that allow consumers to vote with their feet. Rather, they hope to persuade democratically elected governments and market advocates, on the basis of expertise and knowledge, to adopt reforms that embody the professional consensus (even acknowledging disagreements among experts, which mark all fields of practice). Both the professional camp and the market camp rely on the government camp as principal ally. Market advocates across the country are seeking to replace democratic/bureaucratic politics with market mechanisms encoded in state legislation, because at issue is the use of public funds to support market alternatives. Once enacted, however, school choice is likely to prove a one-way street, with no return to a pure system of government monopoly schools. Likewise, professional reformers seek the imprimatur of the state around such matters as teacher licensure and the accreditation of teacher education programs. To be sure the profession can promulgate and insist upon standards on its own, but they will require the force of law as well as professional custom if they are to exert long-term, widespread influence.

What can be said about the ensuing contest among these forces? First, because government is a key player in any of these reforms, an observation is in order. To a greater degree than in almost any other nation, the U.S. features a highly fragmented and decentralized system of governance. Reforms of any kind are difficult to pursue through government because American government was explicitly designed to frustrate concerted action. "In most nations," wrote Cohen and Spillane (1992, p. 7), "the relations between policy and practice are framed by systems of central power or by a small number of powerful state or provincial governments. The authority of the state is immense and, in many cases theoretically unlimited." The relationship between central power and public education, they went on to note, "is a world pattern to which the local mobilization of schooling in the United States is one of the few great exceptions" (p. 7). Yet in the present era, reformers have turned increasingly to government for solutions to education's problems, creating a deep and abiding contradiction:

> If government structure frames the formal relations between central policy and classroom practice, policy-making fills that frame with specific content. The two often are at odds. While the design of American government incarnates a deep mistrust of state power, the design of most education policy expresses an abiding hope for the power of government and a wish to harness it to social problem solving. (Cohen & Spillane, 1992, p. 7)

This "collision between cautious designs of government and hopeful designs for policy" (Cohen & Spillane, 1992, p. 10) means that many initiatives are likely to contend for influence from multiple points in the system, including federal, state, and district policy, together with sources of public, professional, and, increasingly, corporate power. The system of checks and balances cunningly constructed by the constitutional founders finds ready expression in culture, politics, and tradition as well as in institutions.

At the same time, I would venture two additional observations. First, it appears that while school choice policy is here to stay in some form, it will not replace the public school system as Americans have come to know that institution. Surveys continue to reveal that a majority of Americans are satisfied with their local, public schools. Dissatisfaction, however, is prevalent in pockets of the American commonwealth, most notably the cities and some of the surrounding middle class suburbs. Consequently, expanded opportunities for parental choice are likely to make headway and to engage a wider fraction of American families. Experiments with privatization, contracting, and expanded choice will exert influence on the margins of the public school system, and may play a very significant role in certain communities, but will not replace the public school system as an institution that has served American democracy remarkably well, all things considered. The defects of market solutions in education, alongside the advantages, will become apparent, thereby limiting their spread. Nevertheless, options and choices on both the supply and demand sides will continue to expand.

The second observation is that professionalizing policies are likely to be a necessary adjunct to other types of reform, for one very good reason. Schools of any kind – public, private, charter, or corporate – will require capable teachers in sufficient numbers if they are to be successful. A credible and growing body of research reveals what parents have long known, that the quality of the teachers a student is exposed to over time has the greatest impact on learning and development. Just as the curriculum reforms of the 1960s onward discovered that the curriculum could not be "teacher-proofed," so reformers are discovering that school improvement cannot be teacher-proofed. Consequently, state systemic reforms will necessarily require a corps of capable teachers to implement new standards and assessments. And, schools of choice will require a pool of talented teachers if they are to realize their learning goals. Systematic efforts to improve the quality and quantity of teachers and to add to the store of knowledge that informs teaching practice cannot be left to happenstance, because the teacher workforce and the cultural sum of knowledge undergirding the profession are the single most critical resource that schools deploy. This final observation points ineluctably to the National Board and related reforms as vital to the future of education, regardless of other reforms that also are underway.

In theory, then, the professional reforms are quite compatible with the other major thrusts. Comprehensive approaches to educational improvement require attention to teacher workforce issues not as the sole strategy but as an indispensable element in any overall strategy, whether government or market-based. And within the professional reforms, the National Board occupies a pivotal place. It serves as a unifying body for all of teaching's various constituencies – the teacher unions, subject matter associations, and related professional groups (e.g., school administrators, university teacher educators, etc.). It has developed the most complete, well-regarded set of standards for teaching that are available. It has created an assessment system that provides practical means for translating standards into operational instruments for the objective evaluation of teaching. And it has created a status – the National Board Certified Teacher (NBCT) – that both state and district policy may employ in various ways to structure, reward, and direct the work of teaching. Finally, the National Board's products and accomplishments may be used to rationalize other critical elements of the educating profession, including teacher compensation, preservice education, ongoing professional development, evaluation, selection, and indicator-based judgments about the quality of the teacher workforce. In short, I believe that no other development in American education holds so much promise for advancing the prospects of teacher professionalization, which in turn has a critical role to play in the overall improvement of American education.

What may seem evident in theory, however, is less clear as a matter of practical politics, for teaching is the most public of professions. Any moves to elevate the status of teaching may be regarded as a service in the public interest or as an act of special interest mobilization. Fiscal conservatives concerned with containing educational expenditures may not support policies that increase teacher compensation. Antigovernment critics seeking to deregulate education may argue to dispense with teaching standards in favor of allowing school communities to hire whomever they wish. Antiunion forces will regard the Board with suspicion as a front for organized labor in education. And, the equity implications of National Board certification may produce opposition within minority communities that regard the effort as one more stratagem for denying opportunity to otherwise well-qualified minority educators. So it would be naïve politically to regard professional standards, assessments, and certification as a universal good appreciated by all. Advocates for the National Board must expect to enter the rough and tumble of American school politics, making their case and building their coalition within the traditions of democratic practice that shape policy.

The National Board as Collective Advancement Strategy

Chapters in this volume for the most part take up topics related to the individual aspects of Board certification. Authors describe how to develop standards, validate assessments, and encourage teachers to undertake certification. They render the workings of the Board itself and consider how Board certification contributes to individual learning. From the outset, Board certification was intended to serve as a professional development experience for teachers, and early accounts by teachers who have submitted to the process bear out this expectation (see, for example, Darling-Hammond, Chapter 2, this volume; Ingvarson, 1998, 1999; Lustick & Sykes, 2006). If the National Board is to serve as a leader in the professionalization movement, it must establish its credibility on the basis of its standards and assessments, together with the experience of the vanguard teachers who first undertake certification. Word of mouth and the personal testimony of teachers about their experiences should not be underestimated as a persuasive force in spreading the Board's message. But there is another set of issues that will comprise the work of the Board in the future. These concern how to propagate the Board's work throughout the educational system to realize its deeper ideals. What can we say about the prospects for the Board as an educational improvement strategy and as a collective advancement initiative for the teaching profession?

One way to approach this question draws on distinctions supplied by Darling-Hammond and McLaughlin (1999). They parse policies supporting the improvement of practice into three bundles. They identify standards-based strategies with reference both to student learning and teaching standards. Creating a strong and unified set of such standards is the aim of this approach to reform. Teacher development strategies are those that concentrate on individual teacher's capacities via exchanges and experiences within and across schools. The third bundle, school-based improvement strategies, targets whole-school reform in various ways. All of these approaches are in play within the U.S. today.

The rough analog to these reform approaches includes (1) state and district policy in support of the standards; (2) networks that unite teachers across schools in joint pursuits related to the work of the National Board; and (3) school-based interventions. From a collective advancement perspective, each of these arenas makes necessary contributions to the ideals of the Board. Activity in each arena is already underway and may be sketched in greater detail.

Professional Advancement through Policy

Recall first the historical analogy with the NBME in medicine. The medical establishment was not in position simply to persuade state medical boards to adopt standards articulated by the profession. Rather, medicine had to establish the warrant for such standards together with their codification. Then, the hope was that such standards would prove evidently superior to existing alternatives so that state boards would voluntarily adopt them to protect the public interest. This is indeed what happened eventually. The NBME standards came to have the force of law, rather than simply the professional imprimatur. Put differently, government had to be invoked to propagate the NBME standards and to ensure their widespread influence in regulating entry to medicine.

State and district policy then is a critical resource for institutionalizing the work of the National Board. This accounts for the significance of the Interstate New Teacher Assessment and Support Consortium (INTASC) project, which seeks to influence mandatory state licensure standards as an adjunct to voluntary professional certification, which is likely to reach only a fraction of teachers over time. A parallel case is the National Council for the Accreditation of Teacher Education (NCATE), the organization that promulgates standards for judging the quality of teacher education programs. Like the National Board, NCATE is a voluntary professional group that is engaged in ongoing efforts to have their standards adopted by states which hold the formal authority to regulate programs of teacher education. The NCATE standard is gradually spreading across the states as NCATE has made significant improvements to both the accreditation process and the standards. Recent reform efforts focused on making its standards "performance based." The means for this have yet to emerge fully, but one version would link NCATE program and institutional standards to the National Board teaching standards, as an authoritative account of exemplary teaching. In this manner, the National Board's standards may enter the state policy stream directly via licensure and indirectly through teacher education program standards. At the same time, though, another accreditation strategy has emerged in the form of a new organization, the Teacher Education Accreditation Council (TEAC), that relies on self-reports from institutions around which evidence is gathered and presented. In consequence, the "three-legged stool" proposed by the National Commission on Teaching for America's Future (NCTAF) has not materialized (the legs being the NBC, state licensure, and professional accreditation harmonized around the similar standards). Further fragmenting the field have been the rise of many "alternative certification" programs that create entry paths into teaching that bypass traditional university-based education. In this sense, then, the professional vision predicated on the medical analogy has failed to emerge. Rather than unified and mutually reinforcing standards, the field remains fragmented. How the Board operates in this contentious environment is one of the strategic questions for future attention.

In addition to these strategic moves in state policy, other developments in support of the National Board also are needed. In particular, because the certification process is extremely demanding, states and districts can create a range of inducements to encourage teachers to undertake certification. State and district policies might include funds to help defray the costs of certification; salary increases for Board certification; and use of Board standards in teacher evaluation, promotion, and continuing professional development. Many states and localities already have begun to develop such policies; they are serving to increase the number of teachers who volunteer for certification.

A final issue for state and local policy concerns equity. As the number of NBCTs increases gradually in the coming years, the National Board will need to work with public and professional groups on two matters. First, proactive steps must be taken to ensure that a steady stream of minority applicants undertake and achieve certification in numbers roughly comparable to the general population. This means that the Board must monitor certification rates and set targets for improvement against the eventuality that gaps will appear between minority and majority populations. Then, the Board and its allies must mount targeted efforts to encourage urban and minority teachers to apply, together with assistance in preparing for and undergoing the process. Equally important, if NBCTs increasingly become a precious educational resource for schools, then policies must be developed to ensure that all schools have access to this resource. If it falls out that NBCTs gravitate to schools in wealthy communities serving privileged families, while schools serving poor children fail to attract a substantial share of highly accomplished teachers, then the National Board's – and more, the Nation's – deeper ideals will be lost. The distributional consequences of Board certification are critical to its success. Particularly in education, professionalism must embrace equity as a cardinal commitment. Policies will be needed to pursue this goal because local, voluntary efforts alone are likely to be insufficient. In fact, some research shows that poor and minority schools have not received their share of NBCTs so this issue has already surfaced as a problem (see Humphrey, Koppich, & Hough, 2005).

Teacher Networks for Professional Advancement

The second arena within which to advance the National Board's prospects are teacher networks that link teachers across schools around a range of professional activities. One underappreciated aspect of professionalism is the opportunity to consider one's daily work in larger contexts formed through interchanges with others doing the same work. Developing a cosmopolitan sense of the work, an understanding of how objective standards require not only their formal expression but also their interpretation in context, and an opportunity to add to the cultural store of knowledge about teaching is vitally important in establishing a profession-wide ethos. Traditions of this kind have taken root in Japan, for example, where teacher groups study common lessons and discuss alternative ways of presenting material to encourage conceptual understanding in children. Teacher journals and other publications communicate such teacher-produced knowledge so that expert teachers have vehicles for sharing their craft with others. In the United States, however, such traditions are quite weak and fail to reach many teachers. The National Board creates an exemplary opportunity for such teacher interchanges, which can become critical elements in profession building.

Specialization constitutes another reason for promoting teacher networks. In American medicine, specialization is now highly codified. Physicians organize their practice around advanced specialties that reflect the growth of technical knowledge as well as the organizing principle for practice. Medical specialty boards offer advanced certification, training, and assessment. They also organize continuing professional education for physicians in order that they keep up with the advance of modern medicine. What is the analog in teaching? Secondary teachers specialize in subject areas. Elementary teachers are generalists who may concentrate on particular grade levels. The specialization principle is not so well established as in medicine and is even contested. For example, some reforms seek to introduce interdisciplinary approaches to teaching, rather than perpetuating the subject organization of curriculum. Nevertheless, because much knowledge in teaching is subject and grade-specific, teachers require opportunities to engage with other specialists, identified both as fellow teachers and as other experts located in universities, intermediate agencies, and elsewhere. All professional development cannot be orchestrated at the school or individual level. A professional principle is membership in occupational communities defined in part by specialization. Because a strong component of teaching standards makes reference to teaching subjects and to the particular characteristics of learners, teachers can be engaged usefully around these commonplaces of their craft.

The National Board is admirably suited to encourage such teacher networks, in collaboration with other groups and agencies. Natural partners with the Board include teaching's many subject and professional associations together with state agencies that can form teacher networks as a capacity-building strategy of state policy. A few examples illustrate how this activity begins to unfold. Most obviously, the Board and partner organizations may facilitate teacher networks around preparation for and engagement with certification itself. The National Board's certificate

structure creates natural opportunities for networking teachers who prepare
for certification within common categories. Activities such as study groups,
sample exercise taking, sharing of portfolio entries, and others constitute
natural opportunities to engage with the Board's standards and assessments.
Sponsors for such activities that may be held during summer, on weekends,
and after school include subject matter associations, teacher unions, and
other professional groups such as the Council for Exceptional Children, an
advocacy organization for special needs students. States also may sponsor
such activity in the context of teacher networks organized around student
learning standards and other elements of systemic reform. Both California
and Vermont, for example, have sponsored such networks in relation to
state standards (for accounts, see Firestone & Pennell, 1995; Murnane &
Levy, 1996).

The National Board creates many other opportunities for professional
interchange among teachers as well. These include, for example, involvement in developing and scoring assessments, serving on standards
committees, engaging with university practitioners in designing teacher
education programs that reflect the Board standards, and refining state
licensure policies to reflect Board standards. As states and districts
increasingly move to induction and mentor programs for new teachers as
an indispensable component in learning to teach, veteran teachers associated
with the National Board can utilize the Board standards to provide
professional scaffolding for such programs.

These examples do not begin to exhaust the possibilities, and the National
Board itself has been active in building such networks. The point to stress is
the value of such interchanges around the work of the Board as an integral
aspect of profession-building, aimed at validating the teaching standards –
not as a technical, psychometric matter, but as a social process in reshaping
the ethos of teaching among its practitioners.

The School as Locus for Professional Advancement

The final arena within which to pursue the Board's agenda is the school as a
bounded professional community. Here the twin problems of scale and of
penetration come into play. "Going to scale" is a term now used in the
United States to refer to the prospect of spreading reform to an appreciable
number of schools, in light of reform's ephemeral impact (see, for example,
Coburn, 2003; Elmore, 1996). The parallel problem of penetration relates to
another historical tendency in schools, which has been dubbed "reform

without change." Even in those schools where reform may take hold, it often fails to penetrate very deeply into the regularities of schooling, so that teaching and learning often remain untouched by ostensible reforms. As historians Tyack and Cuban (1995) have described, the schools often domesticate reforms that are intended to alter the schools.

How will the introduction of NBCTs affect the schools? This is largely an unanswered question at present, because relatively few teachers are certified yet. And, it may be that the National Board's significance will unfold primarily at the state and district policy level rather than at the school or classroom practice level, shaping the profession gradually and indirectly. But the long-term prospects of the National Board will be damaged if it raises the consciousness of NBCTs around opportunities for leadership, and then frustrates those expectations because the schools constitute an unwilling host.

I foresee two approaches to this problem, which might be identified crudely as the "engineering" and the "cultural" strategies. Staffing arrangements for schools might be "re-engineered" to incorporate new roles and responsibilities for NBCTs as developed through state and district policy augmented by collective bargaining agreements. Board certification might form the new basis for advanced leadership positions in schools to which are attached extra pay, expanded responsibilities, altered work schedules, and such special duties as instructional supervision, curriculum and staff development, grant development, mentoring and induction of new teachers, district and school governance, and others. Such an approach would revisit prior experiments in American education with both merit pay and career ladders, but would utilize Board certification as an objective basis for allocating scarce leadership positions within a revised and expanded hierarchy jointly operated by the school administration and the teaching profession.

The second, culturally oriented approach would rely on creating a wide range of informal leadership opportunities for NBCTs depending on local circumstances in particular schools; and on orchestrating the process of Board certification as a school endeavor rather than as an individual accomplishment. In most schools today, teachers enjoy reputations that enhance or reduce their status with peers. This is simply an unavoidable aspect of school cultures. Good schools typically take advantage of well-regarded teachers by calling on them to perform such leadership tasks and functions as emerge in ongoing improvement efforts. Board certification could help to formally signal and demark such informal leaders among teachers within schools, particularly if school administrators chose to draw on such teachers. Rather than reifying leadership in special, hierarchically organized positions, the cultural approach would utilize NBCTs as informally recognized ambassadors for the profession, as experts with deep knowledge, and as exemplars of their craft.

School management alert to such possibilities, however, might also pursue certification as a school-wide endeavor. Just as teachers benefit from exchanges with other teachers outside their schools, particularly around elements of specialized practice, so teachers also benefit from professional exchanges with their fellow schoolteachers. The research literature on schools as professional communities now inscribes the critical importance of communal attributes that contribute alike to teacher and student learning (see, for example, Louis & Kruse, 1995; McLaughlin & Talbert, 2001, 2006; Newmann & Associates, 1996; Talbert & McLaughlin, 1994). The introduction of NBCTs into schools should enhance not simply the competence of the individual teacher but the creation of professional community among the school's faculty. Consequently, the National Board and its allies may experiment with various ways of engaging school faculties in Board certification processes, treated as a collective endeavor to improve the overall functioning of the school. Communal activity of this kind might include study groups to prepare for certification; faculty discussions about how best to utilize certified teachers in leadership roles; use of the Board standards in processes of individual and collective improvement; and others. It is not difficult to imagine in a dozen ways that the National Board's products and processes might be used by school faculties in local improvement efforts.

Restructuring school staffing arrangements through formally negotiated plans has the advantage of reaching many schools within a jurisdiction such as a district or state, so that the reform spreads. However, externally engineered interventions can become "contrivances" that fail to realize their deeper aims because such plans require supporting changes in school work cultures and in the occupational ethos of teaching itself. The cultural approach takes better advantage of this central truth about schools but can be difficult to spread to many schools, because of its locally contextualized, idiosyncratic nature. Careful combinations of engineering and cultural approaches may work best then in addressing the twin problems of scope and penetration.

Returning to the distinctions by Darling-Hammond and McLaughlin, they conclude their analysis with words that apply equally to the three approaches outlined here:

> It is easy to see how even in the best of circumstances, none of these strategies by itself can produce high-quality teaching. Without some system-wide agreements about what

constitutes useful teaching and teaching knowledge and some systematic supports for acquiring it, as well as school contexts for enacting it, the knowledge that teachers may gain from particular, independent development experiences may be at best partial and at worst unusable, leaving them feeling "all dressed up with no place to go". Thus, the three ... strategies ultimately rely on one another and serve as complements rather than as single solutions to the problems of improving teaching and schooling. (Darling-Hammond & McLaughlin, 1999, p. 391)

CONCLUSION

In their analysis of teaching in America at the century's turn, Grant and Murray (1999) asked whether the K-12 teaching occupation is likely to undergo the same kind of transformation that took place with teaching in higher education. They begin by reminding the reader that 100 years ago, college professors enjoyed approximately the same status as high school teachers. By the time of the Second World War, however, their circumstances had changed dramatically. Whereas university presidents had controlled universities, hiring and firing faculty at will, the academic profession successfully challenged the hegemony of university administration and gained substantial control over the work of scholarship and teaching. Today, university-based teachers (i.e., professors) enjoy not only tenure but academic freedom; largely determine the curriculum; evaluate their colleagues for promotion and merit increases; participate in institutional governance to varying but generally high degrees; strongly influence who will be hired to join the collegium; exert substantial control over their working lives and professional commitments; and sell their services in a competitive market where institutions bid for the most talented faculty. These circumstances all took shape over the last century, constituting what historians of the process proclaimed was an "academic revolution" (Jencks & Reisman, 1968).

Grant and Murray discern a "slow revolution" in progress, defined by K-12 teachers' struggle to take charge of their practice. However, they also admit that other scenarios are possible. For example, American universities may succumb to corporate controls that eventually erode if not replace the gains won by faculties of higher education. And, they reckon that market-based policies could cut two ways. On one hand, a more competitive labor market for teachers might enhance their status and income, if schools of choice begin to bid for teaching talent and if teachers themselves become active in founding and operating such schools, perhaps on a "managing partner" basis similar to American law firms. Imagine, for example, that

NBCTs become prized by schools, who actively seek to "grow them" internally or to attract them from other schools via salary and other inducements. Alternatively, however, market controls in education could follow the course of American medicine, where health maintenance organizations pit better care against profit margins, reducing the traditional influence of the physician in health care decision making.

As acknowledged at the outset, analogies to other professions are slippery at best. Teaching ought to consult its own traditions and circumstances in working out the best means for educational improvement and occupational advancement. Modesty in expectations is always wise, for American schools have proven remarkably hardy in the face of innumerable reform efforts. Given these caveats, however, the prospects for the National Board and its positive influence on American education look favorable despite the challenges ahead. The research base for the Board's work needs to be extended and strengthened; states and localities need to support Board certification more powerfully; the profession itself must embrace the claim of objective standards for teaching more fully; the numbers of NBCTs in American schools must grow gradually but surely; and schools must learn how to use NBCTs as a resource for community-building and educational improvement. These developments, however, are taking place, and they are a critical element in the slow revolution to professionalize teaching on behalf of America's children and youth. The indispensable reform is underway.

NOTES

1. A critical aspect of policy appraisal includes attention to what is *not* evident in problem formulation and policy development. In the U.S. at present, an element largely missing from – and ignored by – government, market, and professional reformers alike, is attention to underlying structural inequalities in society and economy that deeply influence the schooling and future prospects of poor children in urban and rural settings. To some extent each reform camp has an account of how its preferred policies will address inequalities, but American schooling continues to be grossly unequal in many respects at the same time that the political appetite for addressing such problems is relatively weak. Consequently, none of the three strategies makes a direct, frontal assault on what is arguably the most important condition underlying some children's school and life chances. A strong case can be made that the three reform families singly or in combination require stronger equity policies as part of serious amelioration.

2. Critics of Texas-style reform – and its extension to the federal NCLB law – argue that the tests in use fail to represent a rigorous standard of education. And, that such high stakes accountability is promoting both a dangerous narrowing of the

curriculum and a turn to more drill and test prep instead of solid instruction. Furthermore, they also argue that many schools have artificially improved their scores by manipulating the student test-taking population, e.g., by dropping out children categorized as bilingual or those who participate in special education. These criticisms likely are well taken, although the extent of manipulation is unknown. In defense, however, states are moving to close loopholes and to tighten up test taking procedures, even as they revise their standards frameworks and consider improvements in the state assessment instruments. These developments, then, might be regarded as typical of regulatory policy in any sphere of activity, rather than as an ultimate failure of a particular reform strategy.

3. Recently, the federal government has enacted a program that supports the adoption of whole-school reform models. The Comprehensive School Reform Demonstration Program, also known as "Obey-Porter" for its legislative sponsors in the Congress, identifies 17 programs that schools may adopt, whose effectiveness is judged to be supported by research evidence. The program makes modest grants to individual schools that volunteer to adopt one of the approved program models. This is one example of the complexity of federal relations, because the program encourages school-based responses yet is funded as a centrally targeted initiative.

REFERENCES

Clune, W. (1993). The best path to systemic and educational policy: Standard/centralized or differentiated/decentralized? *Educational Evaluation and Policy Analysis, 15*(3), 233–254.

Coburn, C. (2003). Rethinking scale: Moving beyond numbers to deep and lasting change. *Educational Researcher, 32*(6), 3–12.

Cohen, D., & Spillane, J. (1992). Policy and practice: The relations between governance and instruction. In: G. Grant (Ed.), *Review of research in education* (Vol. 18, pp. 3–49). Washington, DC: American Educational Research Association.

Cookson, P. (1994). *School choice. The struggle for the soul of American education.* New Haven, CT: Yale University Press.

Darling-Hammond, L., & McLaughlin, M. (1999). Investing in teaching as a learning profession: Policy problems and prospects. In: L. Darling-Hammond & G. Sykes (Eds), *Teaching as the learning profession. Handbook of policy and practice* (pp. 376–412). San Francisco, CA: Jossey Bass.

Elmore, R. (1996). Getting to scale with successful educational practices. In: S. Fuhrman & J. O'Day (Eds), *Rewards and reforms. Creating educational incentives that work* (pp. 294–329). San Francisco, CA: Jossey Bass.

Firestone, W., & Pennell, J. (1995). *State-run teacher networks: Capacity building and policy supporting approaches.* New Brunswick, NJ: Rutgers University, Eagleton Institute of Politics, Consortium for Policy Research in Education.

Gintis, H. (1995). The political economy of school choice. *Teachers College Record, 96*(3), 493–511.

Grant, G., & Murray, C. (1999). *Teaching in America. The slow revolution.* Cambridge, MA: Harvard University Press.

Henig, J. (1994). *Rethinking school choice. Limits of the market metaphor.* Princeton, NJ: Princeton University Press.

Hill, P., Pierce, L., & Guthrie, J. (1997). *Reinventing public education. How contracting can transform America's schools.* Chicago, IL: University of Chicago Press.

Humphrey, D. C., Koppich, J., & Hough, H. (2005). Sharing the wealth: National Board Certified Teachers and the students who need them most. *Educational Policy Analysis Archives, 13*(8). Retrieved 6 October 2006 from http://epaa.asu.edu/epaa/v13n8/

Ingvarson, L. C. (1998). Professional development as the pursuit of professional standards: The standards-based professional development system. *Teaching and Teacher Education, 14*(1), 127–140.

Ingvarson, L. C. (1999). The power of professional recognition. *Unicorn, 25*(2), 60–71.

Jencks, C., & Reisman, D. (1968). *The academic revolution.* New York: Doubleday.

Louis, K. S., & Kruse, K. D. (1995). *Professionalism and community: Perspectives on reforming urban schools.* Thousand Oaks, CA: Corwin Press.

Lustick, D., & Sykes, G. (2006). National Board Certification as professional development: What are teachers learning? *Educational Policy Analysis Archives, 14*(5). Retrieved 6 October 2006 from http://epaa.asu.edu/epaa/v14n5/

Malen, B., Ogawa, R., & Kranz, J. (1990). What do we know about school-based management? A case study of the literature – A call for research. In: W. Clune & J. Witte (Eds), *Choice and control in education* (Vol. 2, pp. 289–342). Philadelphia, PA: Falmer Press.

McLaughlin, M., & Talbert, J. (2001). *Professional communities and the work of high school teaching.* Chicago, IL: University of Chicago Press.

McLaughlin, M., & Talbert, J. (2006). *Building school-based teacher learning communities.* New York: Teachers College Press.

Mohrman, S., & Wohlstetter, P. (Eds). (1994). *School-based management. Organizing for high performance.* San Francisco, CA: Jossey Bass.

Murnane, R., & Levy, F. (1996). Teaching to new standards. In: S. Fuhrman & J. O'Day (Eds), *Rewards and reform. Creating educational incentives that work* (pp. 257–293). San Francisco, CA: Jossey Bass.

Murphy, J. (1996). *The privatization of schooling. Problems and possibilities.* Thousand Oaks, CA: Corwin Press.

National Board for Professional Teaching Standards (NBPTS). (2007). *Number of National Board Certified Teachers ® Tops 55,000.* Retrieved 22 March 2007 from http://www.nbpts.org/about_us/news_media/press_releases?ID = 90

Newmann, F. (1996). San Francisco, CA: Jossey Bass.

Talbert, J., & McLaughlin, M. (1994). Teacher professionalism in local school contexts. *American Journal of Education, 102,* 123–153.

Tyack, D., & Cuban, L. (1995). *Tinkering toward utopia. A century of public school reform.* Cambridge, MA: Harvard University Press.

Wells, A. S. (1993). *Time to choose. America at the crossroads of school choice policy.* New York: Hill and Wang.

CHAPTER 16

CAN PROFESSIONAL CERTIFICATION FOR TEACHERS RESHAPE TEACHING AS A CAREER? IMPLEMENTING CHANGE IN THE U.S.

Susan Moore Johnson

ABSTRACT

This chapter, originally written for a 1999 conference in Australia, considers the potential of National Board Certification to be a key lever in redesigning and differentiating the career structure for teachers in the U.S. It discusses the advantages of having a strong and well-regarded assessment system to identify prospective teacher leaders and increase the instructional capacity of schools. The author suggests what various parties must do in order for Board certification to achieve its potential. The National Board must increase the numbers and distribution of National Board certified teachers (NBCTs), keep access open for non-traditional candidates, and maintain high standards in assessment and re-certification. At the same time, states and local school districts must develop new roles and responsibilities for NBCTs, maintain or create new incentives for candidates, ensure that the credential is portable across

Assessing Teachers for Professional Certification:
The First Decade of the National Board for Professional Teaching Standards
Advances in Program Evaluation, Volume 11, 461–478
ISSN: 1474-7863/doi:10.1016/S1474-7863(07)11016-4

state and local boundaries, and see that NBCTs are encouraged to work in districts and schools that need them most. Meanwhile, NBCTs, themselves, must take the initiative to create and respond to new opportunities for professional growth and responsibility, drawing upon the Board's strong and growing network of accomplished teachers. The chapter closes with three alternative scenarios, suggesting how the future of U.S. public schools depends on making thoughtful decisions about Board certification today.

It was Dan Lortie (1975, p. 85), who first noted that teaching is an "unstaged" career. Yet teachers have long known, and often complained, that their responsibilities seldom change from the first to the last day of work. For most, the routines of planning, teaching, grading, and meeting, recur with little variation through the years. In the end, it is memorable students, rather than professional milestones, that highlight the phases of a typical career in teaching.

Analysts offer different explanations for the uniform character of teachers' careers. Teaching, widely regarded as "women's work" – a half step above child care – is seldom thought to require the promotions that signal progress in male-dominated careers. Because child rearing has shaped women's employment patterns, teaching also has been a field of high turnover and, thus, not one that could be staged easily (Biklen, 1995; Grant & Murray, 1999; Hoffman, 1981). Further, analysts explain that the "egg-crate" structure of schools (Feiman-Nemser & Floden, 1986; Lortie, 1975), in which teachers work alone, rather than as members of an integrated and tiered organization, reinforces the unstaged career notion. It is further fortified by the conservative culture of teaching, a culture that discourages efforts to distinguish individuals by competence, shuns those who proclaim their expertise, and protects educators from public judgment by their peers (Evans, 1996; Freedman, Jackson, & Boles, 1983; Johnson, 1990; Little, 1987). Finally, some analysts conclude that the "horizontal" teaching career results not so much from gender roles, organizational structures, or professional culture as it does from teachers' unique conception of their work, which leads them to discover variety, develop expertise, and define success within the classroom rather than outside it (McLaughlin & Yee, 1988). Over time, these factors, each of which likely plays a role in shaping the current career in teaching, interact, and reinforce one another.

As a result, not only are schools less effective than they might be, but also teaching does not attract all the candidates it could. Individuals drawn to teaching by a love of learning or delight in working with children often become disillusioned when they encounter the career's uniform responsibilities, roles, and rewards. Prospective teachers who are entrepreneurial, eager to lead, or ready to apprentice themselves to experienced colleagues often find little support for those interests in teaching (Metropolitan Life Insurance Company, 1991, 1992). Thus, professional knowledge remains privately protected, and expert practices are rarely transferred from one generation of teachers to the next. Meanwhile, the public persists in believing that anyone can teach.

In the mid-1980s, school reformers began to critique the unstaged career of teaching and the atomistic school structures that sustained it. Would teaching attract stronger candidates if their employment were treated by others as a long-term, rather than short-term, commitment? Would students be better served by a teaching staff who worked collaboratively, rather than as a "collection of individuals" (Lortie, 1975, p. 211)? The Carnegie Forum on Education and the Economy considered such questions, and in 1986 proposed a new professional structure for U.S. teachers' careers that would profoundly change their roles and relationships (Carnegie Forum on Education and the Economy, 1986). No longer would all teachers hold the same rank; some among them would become "lead" teachers and use their expertise to revitalize schooling.

In response to this proposal, some reforming districts introduced partial career ladders that included new titles for teachers, such as "novice" or "apprentice" (Kerchner & Koppich, 1993; Rosow & Zager, 1989). For the most part, though, these were minor alterations in teachers' otherwise flat careers, usually affecting only the earliest years of their work. These changes created a staged entry *into* teaching, but not a staged career *through* teaching. Some districts, such as Cincinnati and Toledo, Ohio, appointed experienced teachers to become peer evaluators or mentors, but these appointments were usually short-term, small in number, and dedicated to particular programs. The districts had little success establishing a set of advanced career steps open to all expert teachers. For even when local union and management officials agreed that such changes might improve schools and strengthen the profession, they lacked a means by which to accurately and fairly assess experienced teachers' work. Creating such a mechanism required more expertise, resources, and political will than any single school district or state could muster.

The National Board for Professional Teaching Standards (NBPTS), first proposed by the Carnegie Forum in 1986 and then established in 1987, now offers that much-needed assessment system. Over the past two decades, the

Board has steadily grown in political influence, financial strength, and professional respectability. It is poised to assume national responsibility for certifying "accomplished" teachers. In a country where local control has long ruled the day, creating inequities and perpetuating outmoded practice, this is a monumental achievement. For the first time since the Carnegie Forum issued its landmark report calling for a staged career in teaching, such a reform is possible. Yet there is no detailed plan for this complex venture. The Board deliberately focused its efforts on developing sound assessments, rather than specifying how certification should ultimately be used. Now it is up to analysts, policy makers, and practitioners to consider carefully where this reform might lead and how best to guide its progress.

THE CURRENT U.S. CONTEXT

During the next decade it will become clear whether Board certification will reshape the career of U.S. teachers. As research on policy implementation has repeatedly demonstrated, the context of new initiatives inevitably shapes what they become (Elmore & McLaughlin, 1988). Neither the Board's sophisticated assessment process, nor any calculated design for its use, will, in itself, produce change. Rather, progress will require the coordinated "steady work" of the Board, state and local officials, teacher union leaders, and individual teachers, each intent on doing its part to effect change.

Certain features of the U.S. context that will shape the possibilities for reform are worth considering here. For, although these circumstances are unique to the U.S. setting, they illustrate how complex and uncertain efforts to remake the teacher's career will be, wherever they are made. First, the U.S. will need over two million new teachers by 2010 (Olson, 2000a). Veteran teachers will retire in large numbers from U.S. schools, and there are not enough teachers being prepared to replace them. This demand is augmented by the fact that 20 percent of new teachers leave their jobs during the first four years because of dissatisfaction with their workplace (Fideler & Haselkorn, 1999; Olson, 2000a). Growing school enrollments, caused by higher birth and immigration rates, further increase the need for additional staff. Together, these forces will create severe teacher shortages in some areas of the country, especially in poor urban and rural districts. California, which in 1996 reduced class size to 20 in grades K-3, already is experiencing dramatic shortages of qualified teachers (Shields, Esch, Humphrey, Young, & Gaston, 1999).

In addition to this shortage, there is urgent and growing concern about the quality of U.S. public education, a concern initially fueled by students' unimpressive showing on international comparisons of standardized test scores, and in the past decade, by their poor performance on high-stakes tests aligned to new state curricula. At the same time, there is, among U.S. citizens and government officials, growing distrust and impatience with the conventional institutions and organization of public education. Many reformers promoted vouchers, charter schools, and other deregulation strategies intended to free schools from bureaucratic and union constraints, and to make them more nimble and responsive to the needs of students and the economy (Hill, Pierce, & Guthrie, 1997; Kanstoroom & Finn, 2000; Nathan, 1996).

All of this was occurring in the midst of an unusually strong economy. Governments at the state and federal level had large budget surpluses, and politicians were debating whether to cut taxes or invest further in social programs. Therefore, in the midst of this robust economy, there simultaneously existed intense concern about how to staff the nation's schools with high-quality teachers, unprecedented monitoring of student performance, and deep skepticism that schools, as they were currently organized, could meet the needs of the nation. If National Board certification is to change the career of teaching in the U.S., reformers must be attentive and responsive to each of these factors, demonstrating clearly to the profession and the public how a staged career would serve to attract and retain excellent teachers, revitalize pedagogy, strengthen instructional programs, and create more responsive schools.

What the Board Must Do

The NBPTS cannot be responsible for how the new certificates will be used, yet a staged career in teaching can only be achieved if Board certification becomes widely recognized as a selective award that represents high and legitimate standards, remains accessible to all experienced teachers, and maintains its currency over time. Therefore, as states and local districts decide how Board certification will change educational practice, there are important things that the Board must do.

Increase the Numbers and Distribution of Board-Certified Teachers

The 55,000 NBCTs in 2006 (NBPTS, 2007) represent approximately 0.015 of the nation's 3.1 million teachers. The number of NBCTs has grown steadily and there are optimistic projections for future growth. However, the board still faces the challenge of informing and convincing prospective candidates about the value and process of Board certification. Notably, distribution of NBCTs is uneven across states and districts. There are 9,800 NBCTs in North Carolina, a state that has collaborated with the Board since its inception and offers substantial incentives to applicants and successful candidates. By contrast, in Massachusetts, a state of roughly comparable size, there are only 427 NBCTs. Given teachers' general disregard for educational policy, it is likely that large numbers of teachers will seek Board certification only when they know respected colleagues who have achieved it. If Board certification is to define excellence in teaching nationwide, the Board must continue to widely inform teachers about the opportunities that certification provides, so that much larger numbers of expert teachers apply for, and attain this recognition (Rotberg, Futrell, & Lieberman, 1998).

Maintaining the Standard

At the same time, however, it is essential that the standard for awarding Board certification remain high and challenging. In moving to scale, the Board cannot afford to have the value or reputation of its certificate compromised. Initially, pass rates were low – 20 percent – and successful candidates had taught 10–12 years. They were not promising novices, but seasoned professionals. This has changed in recent years with far more candidates being early-career teachers and the pass rate increasing to 47 percent. Importantly, there are differences in pass rates by race, a fact that the Board is seeking to understand. Candidates now know more about how to prepare for the tests. Also, the Board now permits candidates to bank passing scores on sub-tests, while retaking sections they fail. It makes good sense to offer second chances to promising candidates, particularly when they have invested so much time and money in the process. However, Danielle Dunne Wilcox, who has written a critique of the Board, warns of the potential for cheating when candidates use the Board's web site to exchange information about the test (Wilcox, 1999). It is important that this assessment not become, or be perceived to become, a test to be "gamed."

Endorse Legitimate and Enduring Practices

In addition to increasing the number of NBCTs and ensuring that the award's high quality be maintained, it is important that the Board endorse instructional practices that are widely perceived to be legitimate and enduring. Currently, the Board explicitly promotes active, inquiry-based teaching, a pedagogy advanced by many prominent researchers and educators (Cohen, McLaughlin, & Talbert, 1994; Meier, 1995; Sizer, 1992; Stevenson & Stigler, 1992). However, inquiry-based approaches have their critics, often very vocal and influential ones. Wilcox summarizes opponents' views:

> The Board has clearly prioritized a particular teaching style – one that is inclusive and learner-centered – at the expense of a rigorous assessment of teachers' substantive expertise in their subject field. A teacher with little knowledge of her field might then have sufficient insight into children's psychology, sufficient classroom presence, and sufficient deference to multicultural ideology to score a high average grade and become certified as a superior teacher. This lack of emphasis on content knowledge among master teachers is alarming in an age when we cannot assume that teachers have studied their subjects in depth. (Wilcox, 1999, p. 12)

Proponents of the tests vigorously respond that the Board does assess subject-matter knowledge, a fact that must be well documented and widely conveyed, lest critics effectively depict the Board's work as trendy and irrelevant to serious reform.

The challenge from opponents will likely intensify in light of standardized assessments under the No Child Left Behind (NCLB) Act. There is certainly no obvious conflict between the best state assessments and the active, inquiry-based teaching required by the Board. However, some of the states' assessments focus more on facts than critical thinking, asking students only to choose the right answer rather than explain it. Such tests would seem to endorse lectures from the front of the room and passive, rote learning in the back, instead of the student-centered pedagogy espoused by the Board. It is important for the Board and those who promote its work to convince state officials of the value of inquiry-based teaching and active learning. Otherwise, these officials may conclude that attracting and rewarding NBCTs is inconsistent with achieving high standards for students.

Keep Access Open
The Board must also ensure that certification remains open to all experienced teachers, no matter what pathway they have taken to enter teaching. In a move to strengthen the teaching profession, the influential National Commission on Teaching and America's Future (NCTAF) recommended that all schools of education be accredited by the National Council for Accreditation of Teacher Education (NCATE), and that all state licensing of individual teachers conform to standards set by the Interstate New Teacher Assessment and Support Consortium (INTASC). These two reviews (NCATE and INTASC), plus Board certification, constitute the "three-legged stool of teacher quality" (NCTAF, 1996, p. 29).

Linking these programs might serve the Board well if there were uniformly strong support for these three organizations, but there is not. Only 500 of the 12,000 institutions that prepare U.S. teachers are NCATE-accredited, and many oppose the review process (Gitomer, Latham, & Ziomek 1999, p. 8). Moreover, 40 states have created new routes to teaching that diverge substantially from those endorsed by INTASC (Olson, 2000c), and there is evidence that such alternative routes are effective in attracting both more men and members of minority groups than traditional routes (Dill, 1996; Shen, 1998).

Many states and local districts are actively recruiting non-traditional teachers, both mid-career converts and beginning teachers who have not attended established teacher education programs (Johnson, Birkeland & Peske, 2005). For example, Teach for America, an independent organization, recruits strong liberal arts graduates and, after a seven-week training program, currently places 4,000 of them as full-time classroom teachers in "under-resourced" urban and rural schools. Local school districts in Boston and Chicago sponsor their own programs to prepare and certify teachers, subsidizing candidates and moving them quickly into the classroom. Applicant pools for these alternative ventures are large and growing. There may be inherent contradictions in trying to achieve high standards while also offering quick access to certification and jobs (Dill, 1996, p. 935). Yet, current enthusiasm for non-traditional candidates ensures that many new teachers will not follow the pathway charted by NCTAF.

It is important that the NBPTS maintain its independence. Aligned preparation programs and entry pathways should be available to prospective teachers but they will not be the routes that all teachers take to and through a teaching career. In maintaining its role and reputation as the primary assessor of expert teachers, the Board must simultaneously maintain strong links with traditional educational institutions, while ensuring access to Board certification for those non-traditional entrants who diverge from established paths of entry but, nonetheless, meet the Board's high standards.

Maintain the Currency of Certificates

Finally, the Board must maintain a re-certification process that sets high standards and provides regular and rigorous review of NBCTs. One of the most persistent, damaging caricatures in public education is that of the veteran who has "retired on the job." Such teachers are few in number, but those who do exist color many people's beliefs about all veteran teachers. If the Board is to maintain credibility over time, re-certification cannot be viewed as automatic or easy. In fact, standards should be heightened over the course of one's career, and re-certification should document teachers' continuous development as instructors, their sustained participation with colleagues, and their ongoing investment in school improvement.

Therefore, if Board certification is to effectively provide the foundation for a staged career in teaching, it must become widely known and respected as the badge of an outstanding educator; it must continue to be available to all experienced teachers; and the rigor of its assessment must not diminish over the course of an individual's career. However, even this is not enough. In order for the staged career in teaching to be realized, state and local officials, as well as teachers themselves, must think and act in new ways as they respond to the opportunities created by Board certification. They must redesign teachers' roles, create new financial incentives and rewards, make a teaching career more portable, ensure that the benefits of Board certification are available to all students in all communities, and transform the conservative professional culture, which now typifies teaching and reinforces the status quo. Each of these challenges is explored below.

What States and Districts Must Do

Central to the idea of Board certification for accomplished teachers is the expectation that these individuals will assume professional leadership in their schools and districts. The Carnegie Forum on Education and the Economy (1986) urged: "Restructure the teaching force, and introduce a new category of Lead Teachers with the proven ability to provide active leadership in the redesign of the schools and in helping their colleagues to uphold high standards of learning and teaching" (p. 3). Similarly, in its key document, "What Teachers Should Know and Be Able to Do" (NBPTS, 1994), the Board explains one of its core propositions – "Teachers are Members of Learning Communities":

> Board-certified teachers contribute to the effectiveness of the school by working collaboratively with other professionals on instructional policy, curriculum development and staff development. They can evaluate school progress and the allocation of school resources in light of their understanding of state and local educational objectives. (p. 8)

The Board's evaluative process not only assesses subject-matter knowledge and instructional practices, but also candidates' involvement with their colleagues and communities. In doing so, it signals that, no matter how good teachers are in the classroom, they do not deserve Board certification unless they engage with colleagues to improve their schools and profession.

Ultimately, however, it is states and districts that must devise the roles and responsibilities that Board certified teachers eventually assume.

Develop and Document New Roles and Responsibilities

Since 1986, schools and districts across the nation have experimented with expanded roles for teachers, and their experience provides important lessons for the work ahead. For example, Cincinnati and Toledo, Ohio now have well-established peer review programs that engage experienced teachers in two-year assignments to assist and judge both novice and veteran teachers (Kerchner & Koppich, 1993; Rosow & Zager, 1989). In District 2 of New York City, selected expert teachers have moved from teaching children to teaching teachers as they provide intensive professional development for colleagues within their classrooms (Elmore & Burney, 1997). In professional development schools throughout the country, individuals serve as master teachers for full-time teaching interns, thus enhancing the quality of teacher preparation and classroom instruction (Levine & Trachtman, 1997). In exemplary induction programs for new teachers, designated mentors offer guidance, not only about how to get books and paper, but also about how to teach clear and engaging lessons (Archer, 2000; Fideler & Haselkorn, 1999).

Research documents that able, mid-career teachers are attracted to such roles (Hart, 1994; Hart & Murphy, 1990), while both research and experience confirm that, in taking on new roles, expert teachers have little interest in ancillary duties, wanting instead to focus their expertise on teaching and learning (Hart & Murphy, 1990; Huberman, Thompson, & Weiland, 1997). The authors of *A Nation Prepared* envisioned the possibility of teacher-run schools, yet these have not materialized, and the need for full-time administrators has not diminished (Grant & Murray, 1999, p. 184). The successful, enduring programs engage expert teachers in roles that directly support and improve instruction (Fideler & Haselkorn, 1999). Often these are hybrid roles that combine classroom teaching with mentoring, professional development, peer review, or teacher preparation.

In the next five years, it will be important to document the most successful of these programs so that states and districts can make wise judgments about how to best utilize the talents and skills of NBCTs. School bureaucracies will not likely initiate or easily accommodate far-reaching changes in teachers' roles without convincing evidence about what works (Hargreaves & Goodson, 1996). Lacking explicit plans and programs to support new roles, NBCTs may receive personal recognition for their instructional accomplishments, yet make no progress in reforming either the profession or public education. In order to significantly affect schooling, a staged career in teaching must be more than a professional ladder for ambitious individuals. Rather, it must become a latticework of expertise, support, advancement, and leadership engaging more accomplished and experienced teachers in developing curriculum, mentoring junior colleagues, soliciting community support, and participating in important decisions about their schools.

Establish New Incentives

In order to make these new roles and responsibilities attractive, states, and districts will have to couple them with an effective system of incentives and rewards. Experts continue to dispute whether money matters to good teachers (Ballou & Podgursky, 1998; Johnson, 1990), but in the U.S., the link between income and professional status cannot be ignored. Public education must compete with other lines of work to attract strong candidates to teaching (Olson, 2000a, b). We know that those who have entered teaching in the past never anticipated high wages, but rather hoped that they could "afford to teach" while maintaining a decent life style (Johnson, 1990, p. 304). We have little information about the views of today's potential teachers, but findings from a 4-year longitudinal study of new teachers suggest that they are demoralized by the prospect of low, seniority-based salary scales that change little over time and offer no incentives for specialized expertise or entrepreneurial efforts (Johnson & The Project on the Next Generation of Teachers, 2004).

The Board has achieved remarkable success in convincing states and local districts to subsidize application costs and to award bonuses to successful candidates. For example, Mississippi grants NBCTs an annual bonus of $6,000 for the 10-year life of their certificate, while California awards a $20,000 bonus, paid over four years to NBCTs who work in high-need schools (Colvin, 1999; www.nbpts.org). These bonuses are attractive, yet Wilcox legitimately questions whether this level of financial support will continue when the number of NBCTs rises sharply. In the short run, intense competition for high-quality teachers, in the midst of a strong economy, may lead the states to continue offering substantial bonuses to successful candidates. Over time, however, rewards for Board certification must be built into teachers' salary scales if they are to signal advanced professional standing. In most of the U.S., this means that the awards must be negotiated, formally or informally, in each local district. Given the dismal history of merit pay in the U.S. (Johnson, 1986; Murnane & Cohen, 1986; Odden & Kelley, 1997), this will be a daunting task. However, teachers' major objection to merit pay has long been the absence of a fair and independent assessment process, something that the Board now provides. Currently, a small number of schools and districts are experimenting with pay scales that reward teachers for advanced knowledge and skills (Odden & Kelley, 1997), and Board certification is emerging as one accomplishment that can be fairly documented and compensated (Consortium for Policy Research in Education at the University of Wisconsin-Madison, 2007).

It will be politically challenging to redesign conventional salary scales, which have long rewarded teachers for their years of experience and advanced coursework. Senior teachers, who have been strong defenders of a uniform salary scale and now benefit most from it, can be expected to oppose committing special funds to reward NBCTs. However, as the demographic profile of the U.S. teaching force rapidly changes, the center of professional influence and power will shift from the senior cohort of teachers to the cohort of recent entrants, many of whom envision a system of roles, responsibilities, and rewards that differs markedly from that built by their predecessors.

Make Portability Real

It is also important for policymakers to see that Board certification functions as a portable credential. Currently, local policies, collective bargaining agreements, and state retirement systems make it difficult for teachers to accept new jobs across district or state lines without encountering additional licensing requirements or incurring substantial cuts in salary or retirement savings. To the extent that promotional opportunities for teachers already exist (for example, with subject department heads), U.S. schools historically have promoted from within, rarely seeking new talent elsewhere. Teaching remains a very stable career in a society that, otherwise, encourages and rewards mobility (Evans, 1996, p. 93). The Board designed its credential to be portable, but it will not function that way until local districts and states facilitate movement. In filling specialized roles at advanced steps on the salary scale, local districts must not only promote their own teachers, but also recruit Board certified teachers from other states and districts. Again, such change will require state and local school officials, as well as teachers, to act in fundamentally new ways.

Distribute the Talent

The prospect that NBCTs will be recognized and compensated for their expertise is far better in some districts and schools than others. Predictably, well-funded districts serving upper-middle class communities will encourage teachers to apply for certification, reward those who succeed with new roles and bonuses, and aggressively recruit NBCTs from other districts. Similarly, within large districts that include wide demographic and income differences, schools serving prosperous families will garner more than their share of NBCTs. Research demonstrates clearly that economically poor students more often are taught by weak, unqualified teachers than are wealthy students (Darling-Hammond, 2000; Haycock, 1998). If Board certification is to improve education for all students, states and districts must develop policies to encourage wide distribution of teaching expertise. Currently, a few districts and states are experimenting with various financial incentives – signing bonuses, educational loan forgiveness programs, rent subsidies, and salary supplements – in an effort to attract teachers to subjects that are hard to staff, as well as to schools in poor neighborhoods or remote geographical areas (Olson, 2000a). Similar approaches will be required to ensure that Board certified teaching talent is well distributed. Otherwise, affluent districts and schools will simply compete among themselves for those teachers who achieve Board certification, thus making the rich richer, and the poor poorer.

What Teachers Must Do

Ironically, the greatest challenge involved in building a staged career for teachers may well come from teachers, themselves, who have long been portrayed as cautious professionals. Many reformers of the mid-1980s were too optimistic when they devised new leadership roles for experienced teachers, only to discover that those very teachers had become "foes of school improvement" (Evans, 1996, p. xii). Few teachers were eager to assume roles that signaled different levels of expertise or implied the emergence of a new hierarchy. Perhaps more troubling, however, was the fact that teachers who did seek to exercise leadership frequently encountered contempt from their peers (Wasley, 1991). Over time, teachers' resistance to reforms hardened, the spirit to change waned, and many reform initiatives atrophied.

As the number of NBCTs rises, new roles develop, financial incentives increase, and public recognition grows, these old, conservative norms will surely be contested within the profession. The influence of a new cohort of teachers certainly will be felt, but a younger teaching force will not easily establish new ways of interacting in an organization that has forcefully discouraged and suppressed them.

NBCTs will likely rely on their own network for support and advice about how best to change the old system. Having an active Internet site where such issues are regularly discussed is important. Local groups of NBCTs from a number of districts may begin to meet and discuss strategies for using their status and skills to promote change. As NBCTs assume more responsibility for preparing and mentoring new teachers, they can influence younger professionals' views of what is possible. In the end, teachers, themselves, will be central in determining whether teaching becomes a staged, well-compensated career that commands public respect.

Possible Scenarios

Where, then, will Board certification lead? In part, the outcome will be shaped by the particular context of U.S. public education – its traditions of local control, current distress about student performance, the growing shortage of qualified teachers, and a very strong economy. In part, it will be determined by the Board's success in publicizing and maintaining the quality of its award. In part, it will be shaped by the actions, both deliberate and inadvertent, of policymakers, researchers, journalists, school officials, and teachers, themselves. Many alternative scenarios are possible, but three will illustrate the range of what might happen.

Scenario 1: Schools Staffed Like Summer Camp
Caught up in the immediate demands of the teacher shortage and political calls for tax cuts, schools and districts will discount the value of teachers' professional expertise and recruit the least qualified and most inexpensive teachers available. Covering all classes will take precedence over the careful selection of skilled staff. Demonstrated professional expertise will become less and less important as administrative attention shifts from the shrinking group of experienced teachers to the growing ranks of novices. Yet, because inexperienced recruits will not receive adequate guidance and support, they will falter, and school officials will use standardized test scores to make hasty judgments about their performance. Teacher-proof programs and top-down control of instructional practice will increase, quickly driving out the most able, and enterprising recruits. Teaching will once again be temporary work, marked by early exit and rapid turnover, and school staffs will come and go, like cohorts of summer camp counselors. To the extent that Board certification is known, it will be perceived as a quaint mark of status to be found only in the most prosperous communities and elite schools.

Scenario 2: Schools as Sorting Machines for the New Millennium
In this scenario, Board certification will indirectly increase the current inequities of U.S. public education. Elite suburban, independent, and

charter schools will aggressively compete to hire NBCTs by offering reduced teaching loads, impressive titles, and enticing bonuses. Because a school's reputation will be enhanced by the presence of NBCTs, real estate agents will routinely tout the excellence of local schools by citing not only standardized test scores, but also the number of local NBCTs employed there. Yet, the schools will remain essentially unchanged by these teachers' presence, for their expertise will be confined to individual classrooms. Meanwhile, schools in districts with few resources and ineffective leadership will be staffed largely by the leftover teachers who resent working with colleagues and resist helping new recruits. The small number of experienced, expert teachers among them who do want to improve ineffective schools will be less able than ever to mobilize the energy, support, or resources to make a difference outside their classrooms.

Scenario 3: Schools as Professional Organizations

In this scenario, the public and their politicians invest steadily and confidently in public education. States commit to long-term support for certification candidates, and award bonuses to those who succeed. Gradually, the financial incentives for Board certification become embedded in differentiated salary scales that reward accomplished teachers for their expertise and compensate them well for their work as curriculum coordinators, professional developers, mentors, and peer assessors. A professional latticework of expertise and responsibility supports new recruits with assistance and advice about teaching, offers them professional models to emulate, and provides career incentives that encourage continuous engagement and improvement. While schools compete to hire skilled and committed teachers, carefully designed policies ensure that all schools and regions benefit from the efforts and influence of NBCTs.

The outcome of this ambitious venture is yet undetermined. Never before have U.S. educators and the public had such an opportunity to improve schooling by developing a staged career for teachers. Whether and how they do that will depend on decisions they make and actions they take during the next decade.

REFERENCES

Archer, J. (2000). Earning their stripes. *Education Week (Quality Counts)*, *19*(January 13), 38–43.
Ballou, D., & Podgursky, M. (1998). Teacher recruitment and retention in public and private schools. *Journal of Policy Analysis and Management, 17*(3), 393–417.

Biklen, S. K. (1995). *School work: Gender and the cultural construction of teaching*. New York: Teachers College Press.

Carnegie Forum on Education and the Economy. (1986). *A nation prepared: Teachers for the 21st century*. New York: Carnegie Forum on Education and the Economy.

Cohen, D. K., McLaughlin, M., & Talbert, J. (1994). *Teaching for understanding*. San Francisco: Jossey-Bass.

Colvin, R. L. (1999, December 8). Opposing forces tug on teachers. *Los Angeles Times*.

Consortium for Policy Research in Education at the University of Wisconsin-Madison. (2007). *Seven reasons to change teacher compensation*. Madison, WI: CPRE. Retrieved 22 March 2007 from http://cpre.wceruw.org/tcomp/general/sevenreasons.php

Darling-Hammond, L. (2000). Teacher quality and student achievement: A review of state policy evidence. *Education Policy Analysis Archives, 8*(1), 1–51.

Dill, V. S. (1996). Alternative teacher certification. In: J. Sikula (Ed.), *Handbook of research on teacher education* (2nd ed., pp. 932–960). New York: MacMillan.

Elmore, R. F., & Burney, D. (1997). *School variation and systemic instructional improvement in Community School District #2*. Unpublished manuscript. New York.

Elmore, R. F., & McLaughlin, M. W. (1988). *Steady work: Policy, practice, and the reform of American education*. Santa Monica, CA: RAND.

Evans, R. (1996). *The human side of school change: Reform, resistance, and the real-life problems of innovation*. San Francisco: Jossey-Bass.

Feiman-Nemser, S., & Floden, R. E. (1986). The cultures of teaching. In: M. C. Witrock (Ed.), *Handbook of research on teaching* (3rd ed., pp. 505–526). New York: Macmillan.

Fideler, E. F., & Haselkorn, D. (1999). *Learning the ropes: Urban teacher induction programs and practices in the United States*. Belmont, MA: Recruiting New Teachers.

Freedman, S., Jackson, J., & Boles, K. C. (1983). Teaching: An imperiled "profession". In: L. Shulman & G. Sykes (Eds), *Handbook of teaching and policy* (pp. 261–299). New York: Longman.

Gitomer, D. H., Latham, A. S., & Ziomek, R. (1999). *The academic quality of prospective teachers: The impact of admissions and licensure testing*. Princeton, NJ: Educational Testing Service.

Grant, G., & Murray, C. (1999). *Teachers in America: The slow revolution*. Cambridge, MA: Harvard University Press.

Hargreaves, A., & Goodson, I. (1996). Teachers' professional lives: Aspirations and actualities. In: I. F. Goodson & A. Hargreaves (Eds), *Teachers' professional lives* (pp. 1–27). London: Falmer Press.

Hart, A. W. (1994). Work feature values of today's and tomorrow's teachers: Work redesign as an incentive and school improvement policy. *Educational Evaluation and Policy Analysis, 16*, 458–473.

Hart, A. W., & Murphy, M. J. (1990). New teachers react to redesigned work. *American Journal of Education, 98*, 224–250.

Haycock, K. (1998). Good teaching matters: How well-qualified teachers can close the gap. *Thinking K-16, 3*(2), 3–14.

Hill, P. T., Pierce, L. C., & Guthrie, J. W. (1997). *Reinventing public education: How contracting can transform America's schools*. Chicago: University of Chicago Press.

Hoffman, N. (1981). *Woman's "true" profession*. Old Westbury, NY: Feminist Press.

Huberman, M., Thompson, C. L., & Weiland, S. (1997). Perspectives on the teaching career. In: B. J. Biddle (Ed.), *International handbook of teachers and teaching* (pp. 11–78). Dordrecht, The Netherlands: Kluwer.

Johnson, S. M. (1986). Incentives for teachers: What motivates, what matters. *Educational Administration Quarterly, 22*(3), 54–79.

Johnson, S. M. (1990). *Teachers at work: Achieving success in our schools.* New York: Basic Books.

Johnson, S. M., Birkeland, S., & Peske, H. G. (2005). *A difficult balance: Incentives and quality control in alternative certification.* Cambridge, MA: Project on the Next Generation of Teachers, Harvard Graduate School of Education (www.gse.harvard.edu/~ngt).

Johnson, S. M.The Project on the Next Generation of Teachers. (2004). *Finders and keepers: Helping new teachers survive and thrive in our schools.* San Francisco: Jossey-Bass.

Kanstoroom, M., & Finn, C. E., Jr.. (2000). *Better teachers, better schools.* Washington, DC: Thomas B. Fordham Publications.

Kerchner, C. T., & Koppich, J. E. (1993). *A union of professionals: Labor relations and educational reform.* New York: Teachers College Press.

Levine, M., & Trachtman, R. (1997). *Making professional development schools work: Politics, practice, and policy.* New York: Teachers College Press.

Little, J. W. (1987). Teachers as colleagues. In: V. Koehler (Ed.), *Educator's handbook: A research perspective* (pp. 491–518). New York: Longman.

Lortie, D. C. (1975). *Schoolteacher: A sociological study.* Chicago: University of Chicago Press.

McLaughlin, M. W., & Yee, S. M.-L. (1988). School as a place to have a career. In: A. Lieberman (Ed.), *Building a professional culture in schools* (pp. 23–44). New York: Teachers College Press.

Meier, D. (1995). *The power of their ideas: Lessons from American and a small school in Harlem.* Boston: Beacon Press.

Metropolitan Life Insurance Company. (1991). *Survey of the American teacher: New teachers' expectations and ideals.* New York: Metropolitan Life Insurance Company.

Metropolitan Life Insurance Company. (1992). *Survey of the American teacher – the second year.* New York: Metropolitan Life Insurance Company.

Murnane, R., & Cohen, D. (1986). Merit pay and the evaluation problem: Why most merit pay plans fail and a few survive. *Harvard Educational Review, 56*(1), 1–17.

Nathan, J. (1996). *Charter schools: Creating hope and opportunity for American education.* San Francisco: Jossey-Bass.

National Board for Professional Teaching Standards (NBPTS). (1994). *What teachers should know and be able to do.* .

National Board for Professional Teaching Standards (NBPTS). (2007). *Number of National Board Certified Teachers® Tops 55,000.* Retrieved 22 March 2007 from http://www.nbpts.org/about_us/news_media/press_releases?ID = 90

National Commission on Teaching and America's Future (NCTAF). (1996). *What matters most: Teaching and America's future.* New York: Author.

Odden, A., & Kelley, C. (1997). *Paying teachers for what they know and do: New and smarter compensation strategies.* Thousand Oaks, CA: Corwin Press.

Olson, L. (2000a). Finding and keeping competent teachers. *Education Week, (Quality Counts)* (January 13), 12–18.

Olson, L. (2000b). Sweetening the pot. *Education Week (Quality Counts)* (January 13), 28–34.

Olson, L. (2000c). Taking a different road to teaching. *Education Week (Quality Counts)* (January 13), 35.

Rosow, J. M., & Zager, R. (Eds). (1989). *Allies in educational reform: How teachers, unions, and administrators can join forces for better schools.* San Francisco, CA: Jossey-Bass.

Rotberg, I. C., Futrell, M. H., & Lieberman, J. M. (1998). National Board certification: Increasing participation and assessing impacts. *Phi Delta Kappan, 72,* 462–466.

Shen, J. (1998). Alternative certification, minority teachers, and urban education. *Education and Urban Society, 31*(1), 30–41.

Shields, P. M., Esch, C. E., Humphrey, D. C., Young, V. M., & Gaston, M. (1999). *The status of the teaching profession: Research findings and policy recommendations. A report to the Teaching and California's Future Task Force.* Santa Cruz, CA: The Center for the Future of Teaching and Learning.

Sizer, T. R. (1992). *Horace's school: Redesigning the American high school.* Boston: Houghton Mifflin.

Stevenson, H. W., & Stigler, J. W. (1992). *The learning gap: Why our schools are failing and what we can learn from Japanese and Chinese education.* New York: Summit Books.

Wasley, P. (1991). *Teachers who lead: The rhetoric of reform and the realities of practice.* New York: Teachers College Press.

Wilcox, D. D. (1999). *The National Board for Professional Teaching Standards: Can it live up to its promise?* Washington, DC: The Thomas B. Fordham Foundation.

APPENDIX

APPENDIX A: FULL TEXT OF THE DIRECTIONS FOR THE EA/ELA PORTFOLIO TASK

Entry 1

Analysis of Student Response to Literature

Accomplished English language arts teachers understand their students and center their classrooms around students. They know that not all students learn in the same way and encourage self-directed learning on the part of each student. They set ambitious learning goals, organize, structure, and sequence learning activities that reflect these goals, and gauge student progress in terms of them. They expose students to a variety of texts, selected for their literary substance, diversity, and appeal to young adolescents. They engage all students as active participants in their own learning as they construct meaning from texts. They invite many interpretations of texts, at the same time insisting that interpretations be based on close examination of the text. They design and use a range of activities that permit students to demonstrate their comprehension, interpretation, and appreciation of texts.

Accomplished English language arts teachers have a command of a wide range of assessment methods and strategies aligned with their goals. They provide students with constructive feedback, highlighting successes and prompting student reflection about ways to improve. They use assessment findings to help shape instructional planning. They reflect on their practice, can talk persuasively about why they make the pedagogical decisions they do, and comment on ways to improve their practice.

Refer to the following *Standards* in the *NBPTS Early Adolescence/English Language Arts Standards* document when completing this entry:

  I. Knowledge of Students

  II. Curricular Choices

  V. Instructional Resources

  VI. Reading

  XI. Assessment

  XII. Self Reflection

1999–2000 Cycle

What Is The Nature Of This Entry?

In this entry you will demonstrate how you analyze students' responses to literature. The entry asks you to submit **three students' responses to literature** and for each student's response a **Written Commentary** about the goals for your teaching, the teaching context or assignment that led to the response, and your analysis of each student as a developing reader. It also asks you to explain how you assessed the response and presented feedback to the student, and to tell how you used this response to build further instruction. Finally, the entry asks you to submit a brief **Reflective Essay**, explaining how the entire entry, taken together, is indicative of your teaching of literature.

What Do I Need To Do?

Submit a **packet for each of three students** containing a **Student Work Caption Sheet** with answers to the three topics, the **student's response to literature,** and a **Written Commentary** about the response. You will also submit a brief **Reflective Essay** explaining how the students' responses, taken together, and the context that shaped them, are indicative of your practice as a teacher of literature. (See the "Making Good Choices" section for more details.)

Failure to submit any of these materials will make your response to this entry unscorable.

For this entry you will:

- Select three students who represent different kinds of challenges to you.
- Submit a packet for each student containing a **Student Work Caption Sheet,** the **Student's Response to Literature,** and **three pages of Written Commentary** for each of three students. (See the "Written Commentary" section for more details.)

- **Submit one two-page Reflective Essay** commenting on the work of the three students and how their work and the context are indicative of your practice. (See the "Written Commentary" section for more details.)

Making Good Choices

The suggestions in this section are designed to help you satisfy the scoring criteria for this entry, which appear in the section entitled "How Will My Response Be Scored."

To begin, you have two important choices to make for this entry: (1) selecting the students whose work you will feature; and (2) selecting two student responses.

1. Selecting the Students Whose Work You Will Feature

You must **select three students** whose work you will feature. These students might be members of the same class or might be drawn from several different classes that you teach. They must all be ages 11 through 15 and none of them should be among the students chosen for *Entry 2: Analysis of Student Writing.*

Choose three students who represent a range of kinds of students in terms of the ways in which they respond to literature and in terms of the challenges they present to you as a teacher. It is important to choose students whose responses give you an opportunity to discuss your practice. For this reason, the best-performing students in the class may not be the best choices for this entry. The focus is on your practice, not on the level of student performance.

2. Selecting Two Student Responses

You must select one **Student Response to Literature** from each of the students to analyze and use in your discussion of your practice. Choose responses that are indicative of your approach to teaching literature. These responses to literature can take many forms. Choose responses that illustrate different challenges, problems, or topics in the teaching and learning of literature, and of your approaches to teaching literature. Be certain to select responses that are substantial enough to support a discussion of the kind outlined in the "Written Commentary" section.

To prepare for this entry, you will want to select several (at least six) students as potential cases and collect or make copies of their work over the course of a few months of teaching. Collecting extra student work samples will give you more choices when deciding which students to feature, and will ensure that you have sufficient work samples in the event that a student permanently leaves your class prior to the completion of all assignments for your featured lesson for this entry.

As you collect the work, record or take notes on your reasons for selecting that particular student and his/her work, and details that might be helpful in completing your analysis (for example, your learning goals, what came before and after the assignment, how you responded, and how you built on your assessment of the student's response).

Also select any materials that explain what the assignment was or the conditions under which the assignment was done. Attach copies of these materials, if appropriate, to the **Student Work Caption Sheet**.

Written Commentary

Your **Written Commentary** must address the following questions and be organized into two sections with the headings that appear in boldface below:

   I. **Analysis of Individual Students**

   II. **Reflective Essay**

Consistent headings will help assessors locate the required information more easily. Be certain to address each of the *italicized* questions.

1999–2000 Cycle

The entire **Written Commentary** must be **no longer than 11 typed, double-spaced pages.** Suggested page lengths for each section of a **Written Commentary** are included for each entry to help you make decisions about how much to write for each section.

I. Analysis of Individual Students

For **each** of the three students, submit a packet (marked Student A, B, or C) containing the following:

1. A **Student Work Caption Sheet** that provides full responses to the three topics listed, with the materials described in your response to the third topic attached, if appropriate.

2. **The Student's Response to Literature**

If student work is (a):	Submit a:
piece of writing in any genre or form	clear copy or original
three-dimensional	photo
song	written copy
film or video	transcript and/or storyboard
oral discourse	transcript

3. A **Written Commentary** of **no more than three pages** that addresses each of the following. Please label each section with the heading that appears in boldface:

   A. **Context:** In this section, address the following questions:

   ■ *What was the teaching context of the assignment that led to this response?*

   ■ *What were your instructional goals for the teaching that went on at the time this response was created?*

B. The Student: In this section, address the following
questions:

- ■ *What about the student (background, skills, and
  interests) helps explain his/her response?*

- ■ *What do you see as the special, defining characteristics of
  the response? What does it suggest about the student's
  development and accomplishment as a reader?*

C. Assessment: In this section, address the following
question:

- ■ *How did you assess the response? How did you present
  feedback from that assessment to the student?*

D. Planning: In this section, address the following
question:

- ■ *Given this student response, what have you done or will
  you do as a teacher to build on what the student has
  already accomplished?*

[Maximum length for the **Written Commentary** for **each
student** is **3 pages.**]

II. Reflective Essay

Write **an essay of no more than two pages** that
addresses the following:

- ■ *How do these three students' responses, considered together, and
  the teaching context that shaped them demonstrate your goals and
  approaches to the teaching of literature and of the challenges
  you face as a teacher of literature?* Use the three students'
  work you have selected to illustrate your discussion.

Format Specifications: Written Commentary

In developing your **Written Commentary**, refer to "Part 3:
Writing About Teaching" and "Part 4: Analysis Practice" of
the *Getting Started* section. Your **Written Commentary** will
be scored based on the content of your analysis. However, it
is important to proofread your writing for spelling,
mechanics, and usage.

Your **Written Commentary** must:

- Be organized into the section headings used in the content specifications:

    I. Analysis of Individual Students

    II. Reflective Essay

- Be **typed in double-spaced text** on 8.5" x 11" paper, with one-inch margins on all sides, using a font no smaller than 10 point. Print only on one side of each page. Pages with pictures or text on two sides will count as two pages.
- Have all the pages sequentially numbered.
- Have your Candidate ID number in the upper right-hand corner on all pages. (Do **not** print your name.) If you are using a word processing program, you may find it saves time to create a "header" that will print your Candidate ID number in this position on each page.
- Be legible. (Be sure that your printer's ribbon or toner cartridge is in good condition. If you use a dot matrix printer, set it at the highest quality print option.)
- Be no longer than **11 pages total** (no longer than three pages per student). If you submit a longer document, only the first 11 pages will be read and scored. Your **Reflective Essay** must be no longer than two pages.

The Written Commentary you submit must meet all of the above requirements for the entry. If it fails to do so, your score may be reduced.

Student Work Caption Sheet/ Student Responses

The three **Student Work Caption Sheets** and three **Student Responses** in your **Written Commentary** will provide assessors with important information about how you implemented the assignment, the experiences of the three students, and your assessment of these students' learning.

The **Student Work Caption Sheets** must meet the following criteria:

- There is one sheet for each student (marked Student A, B, or C).
- Each sheet has responses to the three topics indicated.
- Materials described in the response to the third topic are attached, if applicable.

The **Student Responses to Literature** can take many forms. They can, of course, be any piece of writing occasioned by the reading of literature. They might include a formal or informal essay about literature, a reading log entry, a book report, an answer on an essay examination, a parody, an imitation, creative writing inspired by a text, a letter to an author or a character, or a reflective essay in which students analyze their own reading. They might also be transcriptions of students' oral language in a conference with a teacher, in a small group discussion with peers, or in more formal oral reports. And finally, they might be rendered in other media altogether (drawings, photographs, paintings, pieces of sculpture, songs, videos, films).

Format Specifications: Student Work Caption Sheets and Student Responses

In developing your responses to the questions on the **Student Work Caption Sheet,** refer to "Part 3: Writing About Teaching" of the *Getting Started* section. Send only two-dimensional responses that are not bigger than 8.5″ x 11″. Do not send videotapes or audiotapes as responses. Be sure to delete last names of students or any identifying information about their families. Do not send class sets. The **student responses** you submit must total no more than 12 pages.

Answers to the questions on the **Student Work Caption Sheet** may be typed, cut and pasted from a typed document, or you may recreate the form electronically and insert responses. If you recreate the form electronically it can be no larger than 8.5" x 11" and one page in length.

Put the **Student Work Caption Sheet**, the **Student Response** and your **Written Commentary** for that student together. Label each student response with the student's first name. Use this name when you refer to the student or the student's response in your **Written Commentary**. Be certain to respond to the topics on the **Student Work Caption Sheet**. When you have completed the entry, paperclip the **Student Work Caption Sheet**, the **Student Response** and your **Written Commentary** together, with the **Student Work Caption Sheet** on top.

The responses you submit must meet all of the requirements for the entry. If they fail to do so, your score may be reduced.

It is highly recommended that you review the **Candidate Final Inventory Sheet** and make certain that your submission is consistent with it.

The diagram below displays how your Entry 1 materials should be assembled.

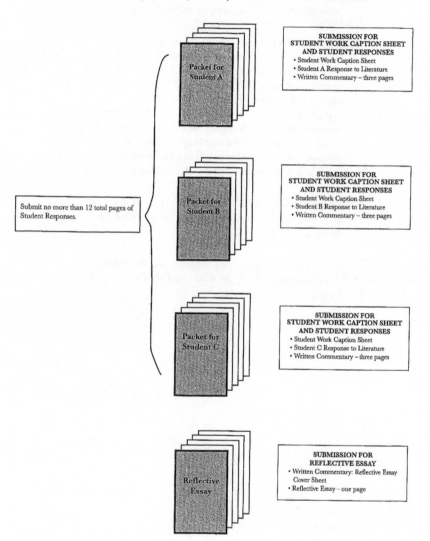

SUBMISSION FOR STUDENT WORK CAPTION SHEET AND STUDENT RESPONSES
- Student Work Caption Sheet
- Student A Response to Literature
- Written Commentary – three pages

SUBMISSION FOR STUDENT WORK CAPTION SHEET AND STUDENT RESPONSES
- Student Work Caption Sheet
- Student B Response to Literature
- Written Commentary – three pages

Submit no more than 12 total pages of Student Responses.

SUBMISSION FOR STUDENT WORK CAPTION SHEET AND STUDENT RESPONSES
- Student Work Caption Sheet
- Student C Response to Literature
- Written Commentary – three pages

SUBMISSION FOR REFLECTIVE ESSAY
- Written Commentary: Reflective Essay Cover Sheet
- Reflective Essay – one page

1999–2000 Cycle

How Will My Response Be Scored?

The following *Standards* for accomplished *Early Adolescence/English Language Arts* practice constitute the criteria that will be applied to score your response to this entry. It is strongly recommended that you review these *Standards* before beginning and periodically as you prepare your entry. This entry will be evaluated with respect to the following *Standards*:

I. Knowledge of Students	*VI. Reading*
II. Curricular Choices	*XI. Assessment*
V. Instructional Resources	*XII. Self Reflection*

Your response will be judged on the extent to which it **shows clear, consistent, and convincing evidence that the teacher is able to use thoughtful analysis of students' responses to literature to support students' growth as readers who are able to think and communicate effectively about literature** as reflected in the following criteria:

- The response shows **clear, consistent, and convincing** knowledge of each individual student's background and skills as a reader.

- The response shows **clear, consistent, and convincing** evidence of thoughtful analyses of what student responses to literature suggest about each student's growth and development as a reader.

- The response shows **clear, consistent, and convincing** evidence of ability to establish high, attainable, and worthwhile goals for student readers.

- The response shows **clear, consistent, and convincing** evidence of ability to establish an instructional context for literary response that encourages students' active exploration of literature and that encourages all students' active interpretation and critical, reflective reading of literary and non-literary texts.

- The response shows **clear, consistent, and convincing** evidence of respect for students' individual responses to texts and for the possibility of multiple interpretations, while insisting that students support interpretive claims with plausible textual or contextual evidence.

- The response shows **clear, consistent, and convincing** evidence of constructive responses to students' meaning-making efforts, directing the attention of students to the salient features of their language performance and prompting them to reflect more deeply on how they can be improved.

- The response shows **clear, consistent, and convincing** evidence of the teacher's ability to engage in insightful and well-informed analyses of classroom practices including a clear rationale for why those practices are appropriate for the students.

National Board for Professional Teaching Standards

early adolescence/ english language arts portfolio

Analysis of Student Response to Literature
Cover Sheet

PLACE BAR CODE LABEL HERE

1999–2000 Cycle

ANALYSIS OF STUDENT RESPONSE TO LITERATURE

Candidate Final Inventory

early
adolescence
ENGLISH
LANGUAGE
ARTS

You must complete, sign, and submit this form with your portfolio. Assemble the components of your entry in the Forms envelope in the sequence listed below. Please verify that each component is included in the appropriate entry envelope by checking the box next to the component. Be sure to sign at the bottom.

☐ **Contextual Information Sheet**

☐ **Three student packets, EACH containing**

  ☐ Student Response Cover Sheet – A, B, C

  ☐ Student responses labeled with student's first name

  ☐ Three separate commentaries for Students A, B, and C, three pages each

☐ One two-page Reflective Essay

☐ Attach a pre-printed Candidate ID label to the Entry Cover Sheet.

By my signature below, I affirm that all of the above checked materials are included in the materials I am submitting to the NBPTS and that all materials have been selected from my own classes and students I teach.

Signature: _____

Candidate ID #: _____

Date: _____

The Candidate Final Inventory Form will be submitted in the Forms envelope, not in the Entry 1 envelope.

Candidate ID # _____

NATIONAL BOARD FOR PROFESSIONAL
TEACHING STANDARDS

early adolescence/
english language arts portfolio

early
adolescence

ANALYSIS OF STUDENT RESPONSE TO LITERATURE

WRITTEN COMMENTARY: REFLECTIVE ESSAY
Cover Sheet

1999–2000 Cycle

Candidate ID # _____

ANALYSIS OF STUDENT RESPONSE TO LITERATURE
Student Work Caption Sheet: Student A

1. Describe the student makeup of the class in which this student is a member, including such features of the particular dynamics of the class that are important to understand the context of this work.

2. Briefly describe the student response you have attached.

3. Describe or list materials that explain what the assignment was or the conditions under which the assignment was done. Attach copies of these materials, if appropriate.

Candidate ID # _____

ANALYSIS OF STUDENT RESPONSE TO LITERATURE
Student Work Caption Sheet: Student B

early
adolescence

ENGLISH
LANGUAGE
ARTS

1. Describe the student makeup of the class in which this student is a member, including such features of the particular dynamics of the class that are important to understand the context of this work.

2. Briefly describe the student response you have attached.

3. Describe or list materials that explain what the assignment was or the conditions under which the assignment was done. Attach copies of these materials, if appropriate.

Candidate ID # _____

ANALYSIS OF STUDENT RESPONSE TO LITERATURE
Student Work Caption Sheet: Student C

1. Describe the student makeup of the class in which this student is a member, including such features of the particular dynamics of the class that are important to understand the context of this work.

2. Briefly describe the student response you have attached.

3. Describe or list materials that explain what the assignment was or the conditions under which the assignment was done. Attach copies of these materials, if appropriate.

Candidate ID # _____

Teacher Release Form
(to be completed by NBPTS candidates)

Re: Permission to Use Teacher Materials and Image in Videotape

As a participant in the certification assessment being conducted by the National Board for Professional Teaching Standards (NBPTS), I grant permission to NBPTS or any of its employees or authorized agents to assess videotape recordings of me and of my students as I teach a class. I understand and agree that NBPTS or its agents will use the videotape that contains my performance or image in assessing my practice for the purposes of the certification assessment.

As part of this project, I may submit classroom plans, assignments and comments. I hereby grant permission to NBPTS to use these teacher materials and understand that no student last names will appear on any materials that I submit. I understand that NBPTS, at its sole discretion, may use and distribute the videotape, my comments and classroom materials for assessment and research purposes and that the videotape, and all copies thereof, shall constitute the sole property of NBPTS. I understand that NBPTS will request additional permission for any other purposes.

_____
(Candidate Signature)

Candidate's Name: _____

Home Address: _____

_____

School/Institution: _____

_____

Date: _____

Name of Entry: _____

1999–2000 Cycle

National Board for Professional Teaching Standards

early adolescence/
english language arts portfolio

Analysis of Student Response to Literature

Student and Adult Release Forms
Cover Sheet

1999–2000 Cycle

Candidate ID # _____

STUDENT RELEASE FORM

(to be completed either by the parents/legal guardians of minor students involved in this project, or by students
who are more than 18 years of age that are involved in this project)

Dear Parent/Guardian:

I am a participant this school year in an assessment to certify experienced teachers as outstanding practitioners in teaching. My participation in this assessment, which is being conducted by the National Board for Professional Teaching Standards, is voluntary. One of the primary purposes of this assessment is to enhance student learning and encourage excellence in teaching.

This project requires that short videotapes of lessons taught in your child's class be submitted. Although the videotapes involve both the teacher and various students, the primary focus is on the teacher's instruction, not on the students in the class. In the course of taping, your child may appear on the videotape. Also, at times during the year, I may be asked to submit samples of student work as evidence of teaching practice, and that work may include some of your child's work.

No student's last name will appear on any materials that are submitted. All materials will be kept confidential. The form below will be used to document your permission for these activities.

Sincerely, _____
(Candidate Signature)

PERMISSION SLIP

Student Name: _____ School/Teacher: _____

Your Address: _____

I am the parent/legal guardian of the child named above. I have received and read your letter regarding a teacher assessment being conducted by the National Board for Professional Teaching Standards (NBPTS), and agree to the following:

(Please check the appropriate box below.)

❏   **I DO** give permission to you to include my child's image on videotape as he or she participates

in a class conducted at _____ by _____ and/or to
        (Name of School)   (Teacher's Name)
reproduce materials that my child may produce as part of classroom activities. No last names will appear on any materials submitted by the teacher.

❏   **I DO NOT** give permission to videotape my child or to reproduce materials that my child may produce as part of classroom activities.

Signature of Parent or Guardian: _____ **Date:** _____

I am the student named above and am more than 18 years of age. I have read and understand the project description given above. I understand that my performance is _not_ being evaluated by this project and that my last name will _not_ appear on any materials that may be submitted.

❏   **I DO** give permission to you to include my image on videotape as I participate in this class and/or to reproduce materials that I may produce as part of classroom activities.

❏   **I DO NOT** give permission to videotape me or to reproduce materials that I may produce as part of classroom activities.

Signature of Student: _____ **Date:** _____

Date of Birth: ____ / ____ / ____
              MM   DD   YY

1999–2000 Cycle

Candidate ID # _____

PERMISO DE AUTORIZACIÓN
(para los padres o encargados de los estudiantes involucrados)

Estimado padre o madre de familia, encargado o tutor legal:

Este año soy uno de los participantes en un examen voluntario para certificar a maestros con experiencia como educadores sobresalientes, llevado a cabo por el "National Board for Professional Teaching Standards" (Comité de Normas Profesionales para la Enseñanza). Uno de los propósitos principales del examen es mejorar el aprendizaje de los alumnos y fomentar la excelencia en la enseñanza.

Este proyecto requiere que yo exhiba videos de las lecciones que doy en el grupo de su hijo(a). Aunque en los videos aparecen el maestro y sus estudiantes, la atención se centra en el maestro y su manera de dar clase, no en los estudiantes. Al videograbar mi clase, su hijo(a) podría aparecer en el video. También se le pide al maestro que exhiba muestras del trabajo de sus estudiantes en varias ocasiones durante el año como evidencia de su práctica docente. El trabajo de su hijo(a) podría ser incluido en esas muestras.

Los apellidos de los estudiantes no aparecerán en los materiales que se exhiban. Todos los materiales serán tratados de manera confidencial. El formulario que aparece abajo será utilizado como prueba de su autorización para que su hijo(a) pueda ser incluido(a) en estas actividades.

Atentamente, _____

Firma del (de la) maestro(a)

AUTORIZACIÓN

Nombre del (de la) Estudiante: _____

Domicilio: _____

Escuela y Maestro(a): _____

Yo, padre, madre, encargado o tutor legal del (de la) estudiante que se menciona arriba. He recibido y leído su carta sobre el examen para maestros que lleva a cabo el "National Board for Professional Teaching Standards" (NBPTS, Comité de Normas Profesionales para la Enseñanza), y expreso lo siguiente:

(Por favor marque abajo en el cuadro correspondiente)

❑   **DOY mi autorización para que la imagen de mi hijo(a) aparezca** en el video al participar en la clase impartida en _____ por _____ y para que se haga copia de los materiales que él (ella) pueda llegar a producir como parte de sus actividades en el salón de clases. Los apellidos de los estudiantes no aparecerán en los materiales que el maestro exhiba.

❑   **NO DOY mi autorización para videograbar a mi hijo(a)** ni para que se haga copia de los materiales que él (ella) llegue a producir como parte de sus actividades en el salón de clases.

Firma del padre o madre, encargado o tutor: _____ Fecha: _____

Yo soy el (la) estudiante que se menciona arriba y tengo más de 18 años. He leído la descripción del proyecto y entiendo que mi trabajo <u>no</u> será evaluado y que mi nombre completo <u>no</u> aparecerá en los materiales que serán entregados:

(Por favor marque abajo en el cuadro correspondiente)

❑   **DOY mi autorización para que mi imagen aparezca** en el video al participar en la clase impartida en _____ por _____ y para que se haga copia de los materiales que yo produzca como parte de mis actividades en el salón de clases. Mi apellido no aparecerá en los materiales que el maestro exhiba.

❑   **NO DOY mi autorización para videograbarme** ni para que se haga copia de los materiales que yo produzca como parte de mis actividades en el salón de clases.

Firma del (de la) estudiante: _____ Fecha: _____

Fecha de nacimiento: _____ / _____ / _____
                  Mes   Día   Año

ADULT RELEASE FORM

(to be completed by non-students involved in project)

Dear Sir or Madam:

I am a participant this school year in an assessment to certify experienced teachers as outstanding practitioners in teaching. My participation in this assessment, which is being conducted by the National Board for Professional Teaching Standards, is voluntary. One of the primary purposes of this assessment is to enhance student learning and encourage excellence in teaching.

This project requires that short videotapes of lessons taught in the class be submitted. Although the videotapes involve both the teacher and various students, the primary focus is on the teacher's instruction, not on the students in the class. In the course of taping, your image may appear on the videotape.

No last names will appear on any materials that are submitted. All materials will be kept confidential. The form below will be used to document your permission for these activities.

Sincerely, _____

(Candidate Signature)

PERMISSION SLIP

Name: _____

Address: _____

School/Teacher: _____

I am the person named above. I have received and read your letter regarding a teacher assessment being conducted by the National Board for Professional Teaching Standards (NBPTS), and agree to the following:

(Please check the appropriate box.)

❑ **I DO** give permission to you to include my image on videotape as a participant in a class
conducted at _____ by _____
(Name of school)   (Teacher's Name)
as part of classroom activities. No last names will appear on any materials submitted by the teacher.

❑ **I DO NOT** give permission to videotape my image as a part of classroom activities.

Signature: _____ **Date:** _____

Entry 2

Analysis of Student Writing

Accomplished English language arts teachers understand their students and center their classrooms around students. They know that not all students learn in the same way and encourage self-directed learning on th part of each student. They set ambitious learning goals, organize, structure, and sequence learning activities that reflect these goals, and gauge student progress in terms of them. They understand that writing is a complex, recursive thinking process, and that each writer discovers and uses individual writing processes. They engage all students as active participants in their own learning and nurture their students' enthusiasm for writing by motivating them to write about issues that matter in their lives. They respect the integrity and value of their students' home languages, while modeling and teaching the conventions of English.

Accomplished English language arts teachers have a command of a wide range of assessment methods and strategies aligned with their goals. They provide students with constructive feedback, highlighting successes and prompting student reflection about ways to improve. They use assessment findings to help shape instructional planning. They reflect on their practice, can talk persuasively about why they make the pedagogical decisions they do, and comment on ways to improve their practice.

Refer to the following *Standards* in the *NBPTS Early Adolescence/English Language Arts Standards* document when completing this entry:

    I. *Knowledge of Students*

    II. *Curricular Choices*

    V. *Instructional Resources*

   VII. *Writing*

   XI. *Assessment*

   XII. *Self Reflection*

1999–2000 Cycle

What Is The Nature Of This Entry?

In this entry you will demonstrate how you teach and analyze student writing. The entry asks you to submit student writing for three students and, for each piece of student writing, a **Written Commentary** about the goals for your teaching, the teaching context or assignment that led to the writing, and an analysis of each student as a developing writer. It also asks you to explain how you assessed the writing and presented feedback to the student, and to tell how you used this writing to build further instruction. Finally, the entry asks you to reflect on how the three entries, taken together, are indicative of your teaching of writing.

What Do I Need To Do?

Submit a packet for each of three students containing a **Student Work Caption Sheet** with answers to the three topics, a **Student Writing Sample** with work that shows the student's writing process and any written feedback the student received, and a **Written Commentary** about the writing. You will also submit a brief **Reflective Essay** explaining how the three students' writing and related work and the context that shaped them are indicative of your practice as a teacher. (See the "Making Good Choices" section for more details.)

Failure to submit any of these materials will make your response to this entry unscorable.

For this entry you will:

- **Select three students** who represent different kinds of challenges to you.

- **Submit a packet for each student** containing a **Student Work Caption Sheet,** a **Student Writing Sample** and other related work by the student that shows the writing process that the student used and feedback the student received, and **three pages of Written Commentary** for each of three students. (See the "Written Commentary" section for more details.)

■ **Submit one two-page Reflective Essay** commenting on the work of the three students and how their work and the context are indicative of your practice. (See the "Written Commentary" section for more details.)

Making Good Choices

The suggestions in this section are designed to help you satisfy the scoring criteria for this entry, which appear in the section entitled "How Will My Response Be Scored."

To begin, you have two important choices to make for this entry: (1) selecting the students whose work you will feature; and (2) selecting the student writing samples.

1. Selecting the Students Whose Work You Will Feature

You must select three students whose work you will feature. These students might be members of the same class or might be drawn from several different classes that you teach. They must all be ages 11 through 15 and none of them should be among the students chosen for *Entry 1: Analysis of Student Response to Literature*.

Choose three students who represent a range of kinds of writers and challenges to you as a teacher. It is important to choose students whose writing gives you an opportunity to discuss your practice. For this reason, the best-performing students in the class may not be the best choices for this entry. The focus is on your practice, not on the level of student performance.

2. Selecting Student Writing Samples

You must select three pieces of student writing – one for each student – that, taken together, are indicative of your approach to teaching writing. For each of the three students, select one piece of writing, with the drafts and other student work, that shows the writing process that the student used. The student writing you select can take many forms. Choose pieces of writing that illustrate different challenges, problems, or topics in the teaching of writing, and that illustrate your approaches to teaching writing. Be certain to select pieces of writing that are substantial enough to support a discussion of the kind outlined in the "Written Commentary" section.

To prepare for this entry, over a period of time you will want to select several (at least six) students as potential cases and collect or make copies of written work for each of them, including all drafts and other work showing the writing process that they used. Collecting extra student work samples will give you more choices when deciding which students to feature, and will ensure that you have sufficient work samples in the event that a student permanently leaves your class prior to the completion of all assignments for your featured lesson for this entry.

As you collect the work, record or take notes on your reasons for selecting that particular student and his/her work, and details that might be helpful in completing your analysis – for examples, your learning goals, what came before and after the assignment, steps in the student's writing process, how you responded, how you built on your assessment of the student's writing.

Also select any materials that explain what the assignment was or the conditions under which the assignment was done. Attach copies of these materials, if appropriate, to the **Student Work Caption Sheet**. (See the "Student Work Caption Sheet/Student Response" section for more details.)

Written Commentary

Your **Written Commentary** must address the following
questions and be organized into two sections with the
headings that appear in boldface below:

   I. Analysis of Individual Students

   II. Reflective Essay

Consistent headings will help assessors locate the required
information more easily. Be certain to address each of the
italicized questions.

The entire **Written Commentary** must be **no longer than
11 typed double-spaced pages**. Suggested page lengths
for each section of a **Written Commentary** are included
for each entry to help you make decisions about how much to
write for each section.

I. Analysis of Individual Students

For each of the three students, submit a packet (marked
Student A, B, or C) containing the following:

1. A **Student Work Caption Sheet** that provides full
   responses to the three topics listed, with the materials
   described in your response to the third topic attached, if
   appropriate.

2. The piece of student writing.

3. A **Written Commentary** of no more than **three
   pages** that addresses each of the following. Please label
   each section with the heading that appears in boldface:

   A. Instructional Context: In this section, address the
   following questions:

   - *What was the instructional sequence that led to the piece of
     student writing?*
   - *What prompted this piece of writing?*
   - *What were your instructional goals?*

B. **The Student:** In this section, address the following
question:

> ■ *What about the student (background, skills, and
> interests) helps explain this piece of writing?*

C. **The Student's Writing:** In this section, address
the following questions:

> ■ *What do you see as the special, defining
> characteristics of the writing?*
>
> ■ *What does it suggest about the student's development
> and accomplishment as a writer?*
>
> ■ *How did you assess this writing?*
>
> ■ *How did you present assessment feedback to the
> student?*

D. **Planning:**

> ■ *In light of this student writing, what did you do
> next to build on what the student accomplished?*

[Maximum length for the **Written Commentary** for each
student is **3 pages.**]

II. Reflective Essay

Write **an essay of no more than two pages** that
addresses the following question:

> ■ *How do these three students' writings, considered together, and
> the teaching context that shaped them demonstrate your goals and
> approaches to the teaching of writing and the challenges you face
> as a teacher of writing?* Use the three students' work you
> have submitted to illustrate your discussion.

Format Specifications: Written Commentary

In developing your **Written Commentary**, refer to "Part 3:
Writing About Teaching" and "Part 4: Analysis Practice" of
the *Getting Started* section. Your **Written Commentary** will
be scored based on the content of your analysis. However, it
is important to proofread your writing for spelling, mechanics,
and usage.

Your **Written Commentary** must:

- Be organized into the section headings used in the content specifications:

    I. Analysis of Individual Students

    II. Reflective Essay

- Be typed in **double-spaced text** on 8.5″ x 11″ paper, with one-inch margins on all sides, using a font no smaller than 10 point. Print only on one side of each page. Pages with pictures or text on two sides will count as two pages.

- Have all the pages sequentially numbered.

- Have your Candidate ID number in the upper right-hand corner on all pages. (Do **not** print your name.) If you are using a word processing program, you may find it saves time to create a "header" that will print your Candidate ID number in this position on each page.

- Be legible. (Be sure that your printer's ribbon or toner cartridge is in good condition. If you use a dot matrix printer, set it at the highest quality print option.)

- Be no longer than **11 pages total** (no longer than three pages per student). If you submit a longer document, only the first 11 pages will be read and scored. Your **Reflective Essay** must be no longer than two pages.

The Written Commentary you submit must meet all of the requirements for the entry. If it fails to do so, your score may be reduced.

Student Work Caption Sheet/ Student Writing Sample

The three **Student Work Caption Sheets** and three **Student Writing Sample** in your **Written Commentary** will provide assessors with important information about how you implemented the assignment, the experiences of the three students, and your assessment of these students' learning.

The **Student Work Caption Sheets** must meet the following criteria:

- There is one sheet for each student (marked Student A, B, or C).
- Each sheet has responses to the three topics indicated.
- Materials described in the response to the third topic are attached, if applicable.

The student writing you select can take many forms. These might include a formal or informal essay, a reading log entry, a book report, a narrative, an answer on an essay examination, a parody, an imitation, an example of creative writing, a letter to an author or a character, or a reflective essay in which a student analyzes his/her own writing. For the purposes of this assessment, you must include the prompt or assignment that occasioned the writing, all drafts and other student work that shows the writing process that the student used, peer or teacher conference notes, and any written feedback you provided.

Format Specifications: Student Work Caption Sheets and Student Writing Samples

In developing your responses to the questions on the **Student Work Caption Sheet**, refer to "Part 3: Writing About Teaching" of the *Getting Started* section. Send only two-dimensional responses that are not bigger than 8.5" x 11". Do not send videotapes or audiotapes as responses. Be sure to delete last names of students or any identifying information about their families. Do not send class sets.

The **Student Writing Samples** you submit **must total no more than 45 pages**. The quantity of student work produced in response to the assignment will depend on many factors, including the age of your students, the nature of the topics, and the assignments. Thus, 45 pages is intended as an upper limit. **You are not *required* to submit a full 45 pages of student responses**.

Answers to the questions on the **Student Work Caption Sheets** may be typed, cut, and pasted from a typed document, or you may recreate the form electronically and insert responses. If you recreate the form electronically it can be no larger than 8.5″ x 11″ and one page in length.

Put the **Student Work Caption Sheet,** the **Student Writing Sample** and your **Written Commentary** for that student together. Label each student response with the student's first name. Use this name when you refer to the student or the student's response in your **Written Commentary**. Be certain to respond to the topics on the **Student Work Caption Sheet**. When you have completed the entry, paperclip the **Student Work Caption Sheet,** the **Writing Sample,** and your **Written Commentary** together, with the **Student Work Caption Sheet** on top.

The responses you submit must meet all of the requirements for the entry. If they fail to do so, your score may be reduced.

It is highly recommended that you review the **Candidate Final Inventory Sheet** and make certain that your submission is consistent with it.

The diagram below displays how your Entry 2 materials should be assembled.

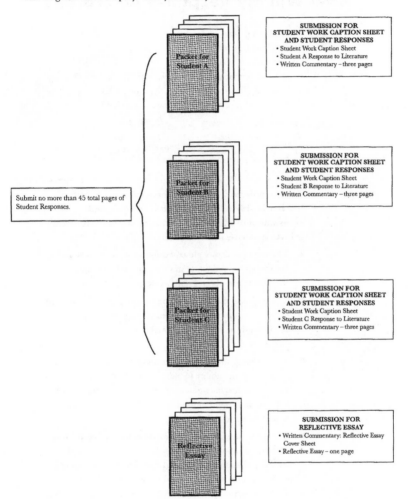

How Will My Response Be Scored?

The following *Standards* for accomplished early adolescence
English language arts constitute the criteria that will be
applied to score your response to this entry. It is strongly
recommended that you review these *Standards* before beginning
and periodically as you prepare your entry. This entry will be
evaluated with respect to the following *Standards*:

I. *Knowledge of Students*	II. *Writing*
II. *Curricular Choices*	XI. *Assessment*
V. *Instructional Resources*	XII. *Self Reflection*

AQ :1

Your response will be judged on the extent to which it **shows
clear, consistent, and convincing evidence that the
teacher is able to use thoughtful analysis and
assessment of students' writing to support students'
growth as writers** as reflected in the following criteria:

- The response shows **clear, consistent, and convincing**
  knowledge of individual students through descriptions of
  their backgrounds and skills as writers.

- The response shows **clear, consistent, and convincing**
  evidence of thoughtful analyses of student texts to
  understand the individual growth and development of
  student writers.

- The response shows **clear, consistent, and convincing**
  evidence of the ability to establish attainable and
  worthwhile learning goals and to make curricular choices
  and instructional resources designed to enable student
  writers to achieve those goals.

- The response shows **clear, consistent, and convincing**
  evidence of an understanding that writing is a complex,
  recursive thinking process and that writers vary widely in
  how they orchestrate the creative process, and of the
  ability to establish an instructional context for writing that
  encourages students' active exploration of individual
  writing processes.

- The response shows **clear, consistent, and convincin** evidence of the use of formal and/or informal assessment methods to monitor student progress, to encourage student self-assessment, and to plan instruction.

- The response shows **clear, consistent, and convincin** evidence of insightful and well-informed analyses of the teacher's classroom practices including a clear rationale for why those practices are appropriate for the students

National Board for Professional Teaching Standards

early adolescence/
english language arts portfolio

Analysis of Student Writing
Cover Sheet

PLACE BAR CODE LABEL HERE

1999–2000 Cycle

ANALYSIS OF STUDENT WRITING
Candidate Final Inventory

You must complete, sign, and submit this form with your portfolio. Assemble the components of your entry in the Forms envelope in the sequence listed below. Please verify that each component is included in the appropriate entry envelope by checking the box next to the component. Be sure to sign at the bottom.

☐ **Contextual Information Sheet**

☐ **Three student packets, EACH containing**

    ☐ **Student Work Caption Sheet – A, B, C**

    ☐ **Student responses labeled with student's first name**

    ☐ **Three separate commentaries for Students A, B, and C, three pages each**

☐ **One two-page Reflective Essay**

☐ **Attach a pre-printed Candidate ID label to the Entry Cover Sheet.**

By my signature below, I affirm that all of the above checked materials are included in the materials I am submitting to the NBPTS and that all materials have been selected from my own classes and students I teach.

Signature: _____

Candidate ID #: _____

Date: _____

The Candidate Final Inventory Form will be submitted in the Forms envelope, not in the Entry 2 envelope.

Candidate ID # _____

National Board for Professional Teaching Standards

early adolescence/
english language arts portfolio

Analysis of Student Writing

Written Commentary: Reflective Essay
Cover Sheet

1999–2000 Cycle

Candidate ID # _____

ANALYSIS OF STUDENT WRITING
Student Work Caption Sheet: Student A

early
adolescence

ENGLISH
LANGUAGE
ARTS

1. Describe the student makeup of the class of which this student is a member, including such features of the particular dynamics of the class that are important to understand the context of this work.

2. Briefly describe the student writing you have attached.

3. Describe or list materials that explain what the assignment was or the conditions under which the assignment was done. Attach copies of these materials, if appropriate.

Candidate ID # _____

ANALYSIS OF STUDENT WRITING
Student Work Caption Sheet: Student B

1. Describe the student makeup of the class of which this student is a member, including such features of the particular dynamics of the class that are important to understand the context of this work.

2. Briefly describe the student writing you have attached.

3. Describe or list materials that explain what the assignment was or the conditions under which the assignment was done. Attach copies of these materials, if appropriate.

1999–2000 Cycle

Candidate ID # _____

ANALYSIS OF STUDENT WRITING
Student Work Caption Sheet: Student C

1. Describe the student makeup of the class of which this student is a member, including such features of the particular dynamics of the class that are important to understand the context of this work.

2. Briefly describe the student writing you have attached.

3. Describe or list materials that explain what the assignment was or the conditions under which the assignment was done. Attach copies of these materials, if appropriate.

1999–2000 Cycle

National Board for Professional Teaching Standards

**early adolescence/
english language arts portfolio**

early
adolescence

ENGLISH
LANGUAGE
ARTS

Analysis of Student Writing

Student and Adult Release Forms
Cover Sheet

1999–2000 Cycle

Candidate ID # _____

STUDENT RELEASE FORM

(to be completed either by the parents/legal guardians of minor students involved in this project, or by students who are more than 18 years of age that are involved in this project)

Dear Parent/Guardian:

I am a participant this school year in an assessment to certify experienced teachers as outstanding practitioners in teaching. My participation in this assessment, which is being conducted by the National Board for Professional Teaching Standards, is voluntary. One of the primary purposes of this assessment is to enhance student learning and encourage excellence in teaching.

This project requires that short videotapes of lessons taught in your child's class be submitted. Although the videotapes involve both the teacher and various students, the primary focus is on the teacher's instruction, not on the students in the class. In the course of taping, your child may appear on the videotape. Also, at times during the year, I may be asked to submit samples of student work as evidence of teaching practice, and that work may include some of your child's work.

No student's last name will appear on any materials that are submitted. All materials will be kept confidential. The form below will be used to document your permission for these activities.

Sincerely, _____

(Candidate Signature)

PERMISSION SLIP

Student Name: _____ School/Teacher: _____

Your Address: _____

I am the parent/legal guardian of the child named above. I have received and read your letter regarding a teacher assessment being conducted by the National Board for Professional Teaching Standards (NBPTS), and agree to the following:

(Please check the appropriate box below.)

❑   **I DO** give permission to you to include my child's image on videotape as he or she participates

in a class conducted at _____ by _____ and/or to

                        (Name of School)   (Teacher's Name)

reproduce materials that my child may produce as part of classroom activities. No last names will appear on any materials submitted by the teacher.

❑   **I DO NOT** give permission to videotape my child or to reproduce materials that my child may produce as part of classroom activities.

Signature of Parent or Guardian: _____ **Date:** _____

I am the student named above and am more than 18 years of age. I have read and understand the project description given above. I understand that my performance is _not_ being evaluated by this project and that my last name will _not_ appear on any materials that may be submitted.

❑   **I DO** give permission to you to include my image on videotape as I participate in this class and/or to reproduce materials that I may produce as part of classroom activities.

❑   **I DO NOT** give permission to videotape me or to reproduce materials that I may produce as part of classroom activities.

Signature of Student: _____ **Date:** _____

Date of Birth: ____ / ____ / ____
          MM   DD   YY

1999–2000 Cycle

Candidate ID # _____

ADULT RELEASE FORM
(to be completed by non-students involved in project)

Dear Sir or Madam:

I am a participant this school year in an assessment to certify experienced teachers as outstanding practitioners in teaching. My participation in this assessment, which is being conducted by the National Board for Professional Teaching Standards, is voluntary. One of the primary purposes of this assessment is to enhance student learning and encourage excellence in teaching.

This project requires that short videotapes of lessons taught in the class be submitted. Although the videotapes involve both the teacher and various students, the primary focus is on the teacher's instruction, not on the students in the class. In the course of taping, your image may appear on the videotape.

No last names will appear on any materials that are submitted. All materials will be kept confidential. The form below will be used to document your permission for these activities.

Sincerely, _____
(Candidate Signature)

PERMISSION SLIP

Name: _____

Address: _____

School/Teacher: _____

I am the person named above. I have received and read your letter regarding a teacher assessment being conducted by the National Board for Professional Teaching Standards (NBPTS), and agree to the following:

(Please check the appropriate box.)

❑   **I DO** give permission to you to include my image on videotape as a participant in a class
conducted at _____ by _____
(Name of school)   (Teacher's Name)
as part of classroom activities. No last names will appear on any materials submitted by the teacher.

❑   **I DO NOT** give permission to videotape my image as a part of classroom activities.

Signature: _____ Date: _____

1999–2000 Cycle

Entry 4 ▮ Instructional Analysis: Whole Class Discussion

*Accomplished English language arts teachers understand their students
and center their classrooms around students. They know that not all
students learn in the same way and encourage self-directed learning on
the part of each student. They set ambitious learning goals, organize,
structure, and sequence learning activities that reflect these goals, and
gauge student progress in terms of them. They adjust their practice, as
appropriate, based on student feedback.*

*They provide opportunities for students to engage actively for meaningful
expression about issues and texts that matter to them. They provide
opportunities for students to be constructively and actively engaged in
discussions about literature and other topics. They create open-ended
questions that require students to pay attention to the dynamics of the
interactions and contributions to discourse. They provide opportunities for
students to take creative risks, offer conjectures, question the assertions
proposed by others, or find their own ideas challenged or validated in a
classroom culture of trust and mutual respect. They adapt and create
curricular resources that support active student exploration of literature
and language processes. They integrate reading, writing, speaking, and
listening opportunities.*

*They reflect on their practice, can talk persuasively about why they make
the pedagogical decisions they do, and comment on ways to improve their
practice.*

Refer to the following *Standards* in the *NBPTS Early
Adolescence/English Language Arts Standards* document when
completing this entry:

I. Knowledge of Students	*V. Instructional Resources*
II. Curricular Choices	*VIII. Discourse*
III. Engagement	*X. Integrated Instruction*
IV. Learning Environment	*XII. Self Reflection*

1999–2000 Cycle

What Is The Nature Of This Entry?

In this entry you will demonstrate the teaching strategies you use for whole class discussion and present a picture of the characteristics of the students you teach. The entry asks you to submit **one 20-minute Videotape** of whole class instruction and a **Written Commentary** about the teaching on that tape. The focus of the scoring is on the development of students' ability to engage with you and with each other in meaningful discourse and on your integration of instruction. Thus, this **Videotape** should show you and your students involved in a discussion about a topic, concept, or text important to your instruction. You will also provide evidence of your ability to reflect on your own work.

What Do I Need To Do?

Submit a **Videotape** of a lesson that involves a substantial discussion among you and all the students in the class and a **Written Commentary** about that lesson. The lesson should show a whole class actively engaged in a discussion; the entry should allow you to show how you integrate the language arts, although this integration may be evidenced in your analysis and not just in the videotape.

Failure to submit either a 20-minute Videotape or a Written Commentary will make your response to this entry unscorable.

In addition, you may submit **Instructional Artifacts** (copy of overhead transparency, blackboard notes, etc.) of no more than three pages that will help an assessor understand the content of the **Videotape.**

For this entry you will:

- **Submit a 20-minute, unedited and uninterrupted Videotape** of whole-class discussion. (See the "Videotape" section for more details.)

- **Submit a Written Commentary** of the lesson that is no longer than 10-page maximum – two pages about students, four pages about the lesson itself, and four pages of reflection. (See the "Written Commentary" section for more details.)

- **Submit any Instructional Artifacts** related to the lesson on the **Videotape**. (See the "Instructional Artifacts" section for more details.)

Making Good Choices

The suggestions in this section are designed to help you satisfy the scoring criteria for this entry, which appear in the section entitled "How Will My Response Be Scored."

To begin, you have one important choice to make for this entry: selecting the 20-minute, uninterrupted and unedited **Videotape** to submit.

1. Selecting the 20-minute Videotape

You must submit a 20-minute **Videotape** of whole class discussion. **Remember that your Whole Class Discussion Video clip must come from a different lesson and different unit of instruction than those featured in any other entry.** If you teach in a self-contained classroom, be certain that you choose units of instruction that are separated in time for each of your entries. Also, remember that at least 51% of the students in each class must be ages 11 through 15.

Videotape a number of different class periods of whole class instruction with at least two of your classes (if you have different classes), and during different units and at different times of the day (if you teach in a self-contained classroom).

Remember that you will need one 20-minute, uninterrupted and unedited **Videotape** of whole class instruction to complete this entry; having several from which to select will allow you to make a careful choice. Remember that the lesson is to show clearly how you lead a whole class discussion to engage students in active learning by asking open-ended questions and listening attentively to student responses in ways that enable you to foster active student participation in the discussion. Be certain to have student's parents or legal guardians complete the **Student Release Forms** for participation in the videos before you videotape.

Arrange for someone (another teacher or a student) to do the videotaping. If possible, arrange for that person to be available for several class sessions. Review procedures with that individual and encourage him or her to read "Tips for Videotaping" in the *Getting Started* section.

Before you videotape, review the **Written Commentary** directions. As you videotape classes that may serve as the basis of your entry submission, jot down notes that will allow you to recall the details necessary to assist you in writing the analysis of the videotape you eventually select. Be sure to include in your notes a clear way of identifying which notes go with which videotape.

Review your videotapes to choose the 20-minute continuous segment that you will submit for *Entry 4: Instructional Analysis: Whole Class Discussion.* Choose your clip carefully – evidence of active student engagement, as well as of your integration of language arts strands, is important in this entry. Review the section "How Will My Response Be Scored" with particular attention to the section pertaining to the videotape, to help you make your selection carefully. Also, be sure that all voices are audible. Assessors will view only the first 20 minutes of any **Videotape**. The 20-minute continuous segment that you select can come from any point in the whole class discussion; select the uninterrupted, unedited segment that provides the best evidence of the *Standards* being assessed.

To prepare to do the **Written Commentary**, carefully watch the **Videotape** you have selected. You may want to watch it several times, taking notes as you watch. Note the monitor counter at the beginning and end of the segment you have chosen to analyze. After you have completed your analysis of the segment, copy onto a blank videotape the 20-minute, unedited and uninterrupted portion of the **Videotape** to submit with this entry.

Written Commentary

Your **Written Commentary** must address the following questions and be organized into three sections with the headings that appear in boldface below:

I. **Students**

II. **Planning and Teaching**

III. **Reflection**

Consistent headings will help assessors locate the required information more easily. Be certain to address each of the *italicized* questions.

The entire **Written Commentary** must be **no longer than 10 typed double-spaced pages**. Suggested page lengths for each section of a **Written Commentary** are included for each entry to help you make decisions about how much to write for each section.

I. Students

In this section, address the following questions:

- *What are the relevant features of the class?*
  Include such features as special needs students and the particular dynamics of the class that are important to understand the context of the videotape and the lesson.

- *What are the instructional challenges represented by this particular group of students?*

- *What other information will help an assessor "see" this class?*

[Suggested total page length for **Students: 2 pages**]

1999–2000 Cycle

II. Planning and Teaching

In this section, address the following questions:

■ *What was the instructional purpose for the lesson on the video and your rationale for choosing the whole-class discussion format for this lesson?*

■ *In what ways does the lesson fit into your long-term goals – that is, your goals for the unit of study and your goals for the whole school year? Why are these goals appropriate for these students?*

■ *What materials did you use in the lesson? What were your reasons for choosing these materials?* If you used a student handout, attach it and complete an **Instructional Artifacts Cover Sheet**.

■ *What specific procedures and teaching strategies did you use in this lesson and what were your reasons for those choices?*

■ *What activities came before and after this video clip? What was your rationale for selecting that sequence? How did you provide for integrated instruction?*

[Suggested total page length for **Planning and Teaching: 4 pages**]

III. Reflection

In this section, address the following questions:

■ *How well was the purpose(s) of the lesson met?* Provide evidence for your answer.

■ *What was the influence of the lesson's outcome on future instruction of this class or members of this class?*

■ *What was a successful moment/aspect of this lesson from which the videotape is taken?* Explain why it was successful.

■ *What would you do differently, if anything, if you were to reteach this particular lesson? If you would not change anything, explain why.*

[Suggested total page length for **Reflection: 4 pages**]

Format Specifications

In developing your **Written Commentary,** refer to "Part 3: Writing About Teaching" and "Part 4: Analysis Practice" of the *Getting Started* section. Your **Written Commentary** will be scored based on the content of your analysis, however, it is important to proofread your writing for spelling, mechanics, and usage.

Your **Written Commentary** must:

- Be organized into the section headings used in the content specifications:
    - **I. Students**
    - **II. Planning and Teaching**
    - **III. Reflection**
- Be **typed in double-spaced text** on 8.5″ x 11″ paper, with one-inch margins on all sides, using a font no smaller than 10 point. Print only on one side of each page. Pages with pictures or text on two sides will count as two pages.
- Have all the pages sequentially numbered.
- Have your Candidate ID number in the upper right-hand corner on all pages. (Do **not** print your name.) If you are using a word processing program, you may find it saves time to create a "header" that will print your Candidate ID number in this position on each page.
- Be legible. (Be sure that your printer's ribbon or toner cartridge is in good condition. If you use a dot matrix printer, set it at the highest quality print option.)
- Be no longer than **10 pages total.** If you submit a longer document, only the first 10 pages will be read and scored.

The Written Commentary you submit must meet all of the requirements for the entry. If they fail to do so, your score may be reduced.

Videotape

Submit a 20-minute **Videotape** that reveals how you facilitated students' engagement with you and with each other in meaningful discourse about a topic, concept, or text important to your instruction.

Your **Videotape** must:

■ show your facilitation of a substantial discussion among you and all the students in the class;

■ be taken from an angle that includes you and as many of the students' faces as possible; and

■ have sound quality that enables assessors to understand what you say and most of what students say.

Format Specifications: Videotape

Your **Videotape** must:

■ Have voices that are audible.

■ Be no longer than 20 minutes. If you submit a longer **Videotape**, only the first 20 minutes will be viewed and scored.

■ Be continuous and unedited. Stopping and restarting the camera during taping will be regarded as editing. The tape must contain no graphics (e.g., titles) or special effects (e.g., fade in/fade out). It must be in VHS format. Read "Part 5: Tips for Videotaping" in the *Getting Started* section for more information.

The Videotape you submit must meet all of the requirements for the entry. If they fail to do so, your score may be reduced.

Instructional Artifacts

If students were using a piece of literature, a writing prompt and/or other materials during the time period shown in the videotape, please include a copy or complete description of that material. Use the **Optional Instructional Artifacts Cover Sheet** for this purpose. Paperclip copies of your instructional materials to this form. If the material being used is larger than 8.5" x 11", if it is software, or if it is three-dimensional, attach a description, drawing, or a photograph to the **Optional Instructional Artifacts Cover Sheet.** If overhead transparencies or writing on the chalkboard are important for assessors to see, but do not show up clearly on the **Videotape**, attach a copy of the material. A maximum of 3 pages of **Optional Instructional Artifacts** may be submitted. The artifacts themselves will not be assessed. **Instructional Artifacts** are optional; they are not required in order for this entry to be scored. **Do not send originals.** No materials will be returned.

It is highly recommended that you review the **Candidate Final Inventory Sheet** and make certain that your submission is consistent with it.

The diagram below displays how your Entry 4 materials should be assembled.

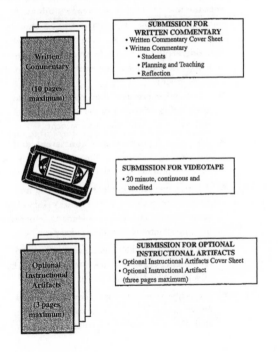

Written Commentary (10 pages maximum)

SUBMISSION FOR WRITTEN COMMENTARY
• Written Commentary Cover Sheet
• Written Commentary
  • Students
  • Planning and Teaching
  • Reflection

SUBMISSION FOR VIDEOTAPE
• 20 minute, continuous and unedited

Optional Instructional Artifacts (3 pages maximum)

SUBMISSION FOR OPTIONAL INSTRUCTIONAL ARTIFACTS
• Optional Instructional Artifacts Cover Sheet
• Optional Instructional Artifact (three pages maximum)

How Will My Response Be Scored?

The following *Standards* for accomplished early adolescence English language arts practice constitute the criteria that will be applied to score your response to this entry. It is strongly recommended that you review these *Standards* before beginning and periodically as you prepare your entry. This entry will be evaluated with respect to the following *Standards*:

I. *Knowledge of Students*	V. *Instructional Resources*
II. *Curricular Choices*	VIII. *Discourse*
III. *Engagement*	X. *Integrated Instruction*
IV. *Learning Environment*	XII. *Self Reflection*

Your response will be judged on the extent to which it **provides clear, consistent, and convincing evidence that the teacher is able to engage students in a substantial whole class discussion on an important English language arts topic in the context of a learning sequence that effectively integrates reading, writing, speaking, and listening** as reflected in the following criteria:

■ The response provides **clear, consistent, and convincing** evidence that the teacher provides a safe, inclusive, and challenging environment.

■ The response provides **clear, consistent, and convincing** evidence that the teacher actively engages the students in the activities and substance of the lesson.

■ The response provides **clear, consistent, and convincing** evidence of the teacher's skill in supporting active learning by asking open-ended questions and listening attentively to student responses.

■ The response provides **clear, consistent, and convincing** evidence of the teacher's detailed knowledge of students' backgrounds and interests.

■ The response provides **clear, consistent, and convincing** evidence that the teacher establishes high, attainable, and worthwhile goals for student learning.

- The response provides **clear, consistent, and convincing** evidence that the teacher integrates reading, writing, listening, and speaking activities that are connected to the goals, and plans and uses organized, sequenced, and structured learning activities that afford students significant learning experiences that enable them to achieve the goals.

- The response provides **clear, consistent, and convincing** evidence that the teacher uses varied, appropriate, and thought-provoking instructional resources to engage students.

- The response provides **clear, consistent, and convincing** evidence of the teacher's ability to engage in insightful and well-informed analysis of the effectiveness and quality of the teaching.

National Board for Professional Teaching Standards

early adolescence/
english language arts portfolio

Instructional Analysis: Whole Class Discussion
Cover Sheet

PLACE BAR CODE LABEL HERE

1999–2000 Cycle

INSTRUCTIONAL ANALYSIS: WHOLE CLASS DISCUSSION

Candidate Final Inventory

You must complete, sign, and submit this form with your portfolio. Assemble the components of your entry in the Forms envelope in the sequence listed below. Please verify that each component is included in the appropriate entry envelope by checking the box next to the component. Be sure to sign at the bottom.

☐ **Contextual Information Sheet**

☐ **A 20-minute, unedited and uninterrupted VHS videotape**
    ☐ **Voice of students and teacher are audible**
    ☐ **Videotape image is viewable**

☐ **A 10-page Written Commentary**

☐ **Optional Instructional Artifacts Cover Sheet (3 pages maximum)**

☐ **Photocopy of government-issued photo ID**

☐ **Attach a pre-printed Candidate ID label to the Entry Cover Sheet**

By my signature below, I affirm that all of the above checked materials are included in the materials I am submitting to the NBPTS and that all materials have been selected from my own classes and students I teach.

Signature: _____

Candidate ID #: _____

Date: _____

The Candidate Final Inventory Form will be submitted in the Forms envelope, not in the Entry 4 envelope.

Candidate ID # _____

NATIONAL BOARD FOR PROFESSIONAL TEACHING STANDARDS

early adolescence/
english language arts portfolio

early
adolescence
ENGLISH
LANGUAGE
ARTS

INSTRUCTIONAL ANALYSIS: WHOLE CLASS DISCUSSION

WRITTEN COMMENTARY
COVER SHEET

1999–2000 Cycle

Candidate ID # _____

INSTRUCTIONAL ANALYSIS: WHOLE CLASS DISCUSSION
Optional Instructional Artifacts Cover Sheet

Briefly describe the attached materials and explain their connection to your **Videotape** and **Written Commentary**.

Reproduce this form as necessary. No more than 3 pages of Instructional Artifacts may be submitted.

Candidate ID # _____

INSTRUCTIONAL ANALYSIS: WHOLE CLASS DISCUSSIONS

CLASSROOM LAYOUT
(For Informational Purposes Only)

Please make a sketch of the physical layout of the classroom as it appears in the **Videotape**. This sketch will provide assessors with a context for the **Videotape** since the camera cannot capture the whole classroom.

It is helpful to assessors for you to identify where particular students are located in the room by using the same student identifiers that you refer to in your **Written Commentary** (e.g., "the girl in the green sweater"). The sketch will **not** be scored.

1999–2000 Cycle

INSTRUCTIONAL ANALYSIS: WHOLE CLASS DISCUSSION
NOTES FOR VIDEOCAMERA OPERATION

(To be given to the person who is assisting you by operating the videocamera.)

In order to assist you when you are filming the lesson, you should also refer to "Tips for Videotaping" in the *Getting Started* section.

The **Videotape** you are making must:

- show the teacher's facilitation of a substantial discussion among the teacher and all the students in the class.

- show clearly how you lead a whole class discussion to engage students in active learning by asking open-ended questions and listening attentively to student responses in ways that enable the teacher to foster active student participation in the discussion.

- show evidence of active student engagement as well as the teacher's integration of language arts strands.

- be taken from an angle that includes as many of the students' faces as possible.

- have sound quality that enables assessors to understand all of what the teacher says and most of what students say.

- be no longer than 20 minutes.

Stopping and restarting the camera or the sound during taping will be regarded as editing and will be **unscorable**. The tape must contain no graphics (e.g., titles) or special effects (e.g., fade in/fade out). It must be in VHS format.

Candidate ID # _____

TEACHER RELEASE FORM
(to be completed by NBPTS candidates)

Re: Permission to Use Teacher Materials and Image in Videotape

As a participant in the certification assessment being conducted by the National Board for Professional Teaching Standards (NBPTS), I grant permission to NBPTS or any of its employees or authorized agents to assess videotape recordings of me and of my students as I teach a class. I understand and agree that NBPTS or its agents will use the videotape that contains my performance or image in assessing my practice for the purposes of the certification assessment.

As part of this project, I may submit classroom plans, assignments, and comments. I hereby grant permission to NBPTS to use these teacher materials and understand that no student last names will appear on any materials that I submit. I understand that NBPTS, at its sole discretion, may use and distribute the videotape, my comments and classroom materials for assessment and research purposes and that the videotape, and all copies thereof, shall constitute the sole property of NBPTS. I understand that NBPTS will request additional permission for any other purposes.

_____
(Candidate Signature)

Candidate's Name: _____

Home Address: _____

_____

School/Institution: _____

_____

Date: _____

Name of Entry: _____

1999–2000 Cycle

NATIONAL BOARD FOR PROFESSIONAL TEACHING STANDARDS

early adolescence/ english language arts portfolio

early adolescence

ENGLISH LANGUAGE ARTS

INSTRUCTIONAL ANALYSIS: WHOLE CLASS DISCUSSION

STUDENT AND ADULT RELEASE FORMS
COVER SHEET

1999–2000 Cycle

Candidate ID # _____

STUDENT RELEASE FORM

(to be completed either by the parents/legal guardians of minor students involved in this project, or by students
who are more than 18 years of age that are involved in this project)

Dear Parent/Guardian:

I am a participant this school year in an assessment to certify experienced teachers as outstanding
practitioners in teaching. My participation in this assessment, which is being conducted by the National
Board for Professional Teaching Standards, is voluntary. One of the primary purposes of this assessment is
to enhance student learning and encourage excellence in teaching.

This project requires that short videotapes of lessons taught in your child's class be submitted. Although the
videotapes involve both the teacher and various students, the primary focus is on the teacher's instruction,
not on the students in the class. In the course of taping, your child may appear on the videotape. Also, at
times during the year, I may be asked to submit samples of student work as evidence of teaching practice,
and that work may include some of your child's work.

No student's last name will appear on any materials that are submitted. All materials will be kept
confidential. The form below will be used to document your permission for these activities.

Sincerely, _____
(Candidate Signature)

PERMISSION SLIP

Student Name: _____ School/Teacher: _____

Your Address: _____

**I am the parent/legal guardian of the child named above. I have received and read your letter
regarding a teacher assessment being conducted by the National Board for Professional
Teaching Standards (NBPTS), and agree to the following:**

(Please check the appropriate box below.)

❑   **I DO** give permission to you to include my child's image on videotape as he or she participates

in a class conducted at _____ by _____ and/or to
(Name of School)   (Teacher's Name)
reproduce materials that my child may produce as part of classroom activities. No last names
will appear on any materials submitted by the teacher.

❑   **I DO NOT** give permission to videotape my child or to reproduce materials that
my child may produce as part of classroom activities.

Signature of Parent or Guardian: _____ Date: _____

**I am the student named above and am more than 18 years of age. I have read and understand
the project description given above. I understand that my performance is not being evaluated by
this project and that my last name will not appear on any materials that may be submitted.**

❑   **I DO** give permission to you to include my image on videotape as I participate in this class and/or
to reproduce materials that I may produce as part of classroom activities.

❑   **I DO NOT** give permission to videotape me or to reproduce materials that I may produce as part
of classroom activities.

Signature of Student: _____ Date: _____

Date of Birth: _____ / _____ / _____
                MM   DD   YY

1999–2000 Cycle

Candidate ID # _____

PERMISO DE AUTORIZACIÓN
(para los padres o encargados de los estudiantes involucrados)

Estimado padre o madre de familia, encargado o tutor legal:

Este año soy uno de los participantes en un examen voluntario para certificar a maestros con experiencia como educadores sobresalientes, llevado a cabo por el "National Board for Professional Teaching Standards" (Comité de Normas Profesionales para la Enseñanza). Uno de los propósitos principales del examen es mejorar el aprendizaje de los alumnos y fomentar la excelencia en la enseñanza.

Este proyecto requiere que yo exhiba videos de las lecciones que doy en el grupo de su hijo(a). Aunque en los videos aparecen el maestro y sus estudiantes, la atención se centra en el maestro y su manera de dar clase, no en los estudiantes. Al videograbar mi clase, su hijo(a) podría aparecer en el video. También se le pide al maestro que exhiba muestras del trabajo de sus estudiantes en varias ocasiones durante el año como evidencia de su práctica docente. El trabajo de su hijo(a) podría ser incluido en esas muestras.

Los apellidos de los estudiantes no aparecerán en los materiales que se exhiban. Todos los materiales serán tratados de manera confidencial. El formulario que aparece abajo será utilizado como prueba de su autorización para que su hijo(a) pueda ser incluido(a) en estas actividades.

Atentamente, _____
Firma del (de la) maestro(a)

AUTORIZACIÓN

Nombre del (de la) Estudiante: _____

Domicilio: _____

Escuela y Maestro(a): _____

Yo, padre, madre, encargado o tutor legal del (de la) estudiante que se menciona arriba. He recibido y leído su carta sobre el examen para maestros que lleva a cabo el "National Board for Professional Teaching Standards" (NBPTS, Comité de Normas Profesionales para la Enseñanza), y expreso lo siguiente:
(Por favor marque abajo en el cuadro correspondiente)

❏ **DOY mi autorización para que la imagen de mi hijo(a) aparezca** en el video al participar en la clase impartida en _____ por _____ y para que se haga copia de los materiales que él (ella) pueda llegar a producir como parte de sus actividades en el salón de clases. Los apellidos de los estudiantes no aparecerán en los materiales que el maestro exhiba.

❏ **NO DOY mi autorización para videograbar a mi hijo(a)** ni para que se haga copia de los materiales que él (ella) llegue a producir como parte de sus actividades en el salón de clases.

Firma del padre o madre, encargado o tutor: _____ Fecha: _____

Yo soy el (la) estudiante que se menciona arriba y tengo más de 18 años. He leído la descripción del proyecto y entiendo que mi trabajo no será evaluado y que mi nombre completo no aparecerá en los materiales que serán entregados:
(Por favor marque abajo en el cuadro correspondiente)

❏ **DOY mi autorización para que mi imagen aparezca** en el video al participar en la clase impartida en _____ por _____ y para que se haga copia de los materiales que yo produzca como parte de mis actividades en el salón de clases. Mi apellido no aparecerá en los materiales que el maestro exhiba.

❏ **NO DOY mi autorización para videograbarme** ni para que se haga copia de los materiales que yo produzca como parte de mis actividades en el salón de clases.

Firma del (de la) estudiante: _____ Fecha: _____

Fecha de nacimiento: _____ / _____ / _____
          Mes   Día   Año

Candidate ID # _____

ADULT RELEASE FORM

(to be completed by non-students involved in project)

Dear Sir or Madam:

I am a participant this school year in an assessment to certify experienced teachers as outstanding practitioners in teaching. My participation in this assessment, which is being conducted by the National Board for Professional Teaching Standards, is voluntary. One of the primary purposes of this assessment is to enhance student learning and encourage excellence in teaching.

This project requires that short videotapes of lessons taught in the class be submitted. Although the videotapes involve both the teacher and various students, the primary focus is on the teacher's instruction, not on the students in the class. In the course of taping, your image may appear on the videotape.

No last names will appear on any materials that are submitted. All materials will be kept confidential. The form below will be used to document your permission for these activities.

Sincerely, _____

(Candidate Signature)

PERMISSION SLIP

Name: _____

Address: _____

School/Teacher: _____

I am the person named above. I have received and read your letter regarding a teacher assessment being conducted by the National Board for Professional Teaching Standards (NBPTS), and agree to the following:

(Please check the appropriate box.)

❏ **I DO** give permission to you to include my image on videotape as a participant in a class conducted at _____ by _____
　　　　　　　　　　(Name of school)　　　　　　　　　　　　(Teacher's Name)
as part of classroom activities. No last names will appear on any materials submitted by the teacher.

❏ **I DO NOT** give permission to videotape my image as a part of classroom activities.

Signature: _____ Date: _____

1999–2000 Cycle

APPENDIX B:
FULL SPECIFICATIONS OF THE EA/ELA ASSESSMENT CENTRE ☆

Early Adolescence/English Language Arts Assessment Center Descriptions (Retake Only) (Age Range:Students 11–15)

Exercise 1: Teaching Literature

Content Focus: Literature **Assessment Focus:** **Standards I, II, VI, VII, X, and XI** This exercise focuses on your knowledge of literature and the ability to choose a group ofreading materials to teach to early adolescents, to plan instruction based on these materials, and to explain the reasoning behind the choices made.	**Stimulus Materials: Advance** The stimulus consists of a reading list (i.e., novels, plays, short stories, poems, essays) and copies of many of the poems, essays, and short stories on that reading list. The reading list is mailed to you prior to your arrival at the assessment center. **Prompts:** You are asked to establish goals and design instruction for early adolescent students based on three to five works from the reading list.

Exercise 2: Teaching Writing

Content Focus: Writing **Assessment Focus:** **Standards I, II, and VII** This exercise focuses on your knowledge of writing instruction,ability to construct an argument regarding an issue related to writing instruction presented in a written scenario,and ability to use information from professional articles to support that argument. **Stimulus Materials: Advance** The stimulus consists of articles about writing instruction from professional publications and a written scenario presenting a topic on which an argument will be constructed. The articles are mailed to you prior to your arrival at the assessment center.	**Stimulus Materials: On-Screen** A written scenario is presented. **Prompts:** You are sent articles about writing instruction from professional publications in preparation for an exercise in which you will be asked to use information from the articles as a basis for discussing writing instruction. You are asked to construct an argument on a topic presented by the scenario presented on-screen, using the stimulus articles as support.

2001-2002 Assessment Center Orientation Booklet
Copyright © National Board for Professional Teaching Standards

Exercise 3: Language Study

Content Focus: Language Instruction **Assessment Focus:** **Standards I,II,IX,and XI** This exercise focuses on your knowledge of issues related to second-language learning and bilingualism,ability to use student work to design instruction,and ability to use stimulus articles as support.	**Stimulus Materials: Advance** The stimulus consists of articles on second language learning sent to you prior to your arrival at the assessment center. **Stimulus Materials: On-Screen** You are presented with samples of both oral and written language from an English language learner. **Prompts:** You are asked to analyze the student's language, identify additional information needed to plan instruction, and discuss strategies for instruction and assessment.

Exercise 4: Selecting Texts

Content Focus: Criteria and materials for student reading program **Assessment Focus:** **Standards I, V, and VI** This exercise focuses on your knowledge of a range of literature and on your ability to establish and apply criteria to judge the quality oftexts and to select texts that both appeal to early adolescents' interests and represent cultural diversity among authors, characters, settings, plots, and topics.	**Stimulus Materials: On-Screen** The stimulus consists of a scenario in which the teachers have been asked for help in choosing books for students, and a list of possible (but not required) titles of books for teachers to consider in framing a response. **Prompts:** In this exercise, you are asked to assume that the English language arts teachers have been asked for assistance in thinking about reading selections they might recommend for students at this age.You write a response providing guidelines and recommendations for texts.

APPENDIX C: OVERALL ASSESSMENT DESIGN FOR EA/ELA ☆

EARLY ADOLESCENCE/ENGLISH LANGUAGE ARTS SUMMARY OF REQUIREMENTS (1999–2000)

EA/English Language Arts Portfolio Entry Requirements			
Analysis of Student Response to Literature	Analysis of Student Writing	Instructional Analysis: Small Groups	Instructional Analysis: Whole-Class Discussion
Through three students' responses to literature and a Written Commentary for each student's response, candidates discuss the goals for their teaching, the teaching context or assignment that led to the response, and analyze each student as a developing reader. Candidates also explain how they assessed the response and presented feedback to the student and tell how they used this response to build further instruction. Finally, candidates submit a brief Reflective Essay, explaining how the entire exercise, taken as a whole, is indicative of their teaching of literature.	Through three pieces of student writing and a Written Commentary, candidates discuss the goals for their teaching, the teaching context or assignment that led to the writing, and analyze the students as developing writers. Candidates also explain how they assessed the writing and presented feedback to the student and tell how they used this writing to build further instruction. Finally, candidates reflect on how the three analyses, taken together, are indicative of their teaching of writing.	Through a 20-minute Videotape in which students work in small groups and a Written Commentary about the teaching on that tape, candidates discuss teacher-student and student-student discourse as students work in small groups. Thus, this videotape should show the teacher's facilitation of and interaction with small groups of students who are working together. This interaction is necessarily intermittent as the teacher circulates among the small groups in the class. Candidates also provide evidence of their ability to reflect on their own work.	Through a Videotape of whole-class instruction and a Written Commentary about the teaching practice depicted on that tape, candidates discuss their development of students' ability to engage with the teacher and with each other in meaningful discourse and on the teacher's integration of instruction. The videotape should show the teacher and the students involved in a discussion about a topic, concept or text important to their instruction. Candidates also provide evidence of their ability to reflect on their own work.

(*Continued.*)

Documented Accomplishments I – Collaboration in the Professional Community

---

This exercise asks candidates to demonstrate evidence of sustained or significant contributions to the development and/or substantive review of instructional resources and/or practices, to educational policy and practices, and/or to collaborative work with colleagues in developing pedagogy. Through written description together with work products and/or letters of verification from others, candidates provide support for each accomplishment. Finally, candidates write an Interpretive Summary that synthesizes the accomplishments and evidence presented.

Documented Accomplishments II – Outreach to Families and the Community

---

This exercise asks all candidates to demonstrate evidence of how they create ongoing interactive communication with families and other adults interested in students' progress and learning. In addition, candidates may demonstrate evidence of efforts to understand parents' concerns about student learning, subject matter, and curriculum and/or contributions to connecting the school program to community needs, resources, and interests. Through written description together with work products of the teacher and/or letters of verification from others, candidates provide support for each accomplishment. Finally, candidates write an Interpretive Summary that synthesizes the accomplishments and evidence presented.

EA/English Language Arts Assessment Center Exercise Requirements

---

Teaching Literature	Teaching Writing	Language Study	Selecting Texts
Candidates are sent a reading list prior to attending the assessment center and are asked to plan some instruction for early adolescent students based on three to five works from the list. At the assessment center, they are asked to address specific questions about the works they have chosen and the instruction they have planned around those works.	Candidates are sent three professional articles about writing instruction prior to attending the assessment center. They are told to read the articles in preparation for an exercise in which they will be asked to use information from the articles as a basis for discussing writing instruction.	Candidates are sent four professional articles on second-language learning and bilingualism prior to attending the assessment center. They are told to read the articles in preparation for an exercise in which they will be asked to use information from the articles as a basis for discussing language instruction.	Candidates are asked to assume that the school in which they teach has appealed to parents for help in engaging students in reading. To this end, the parents have asked the English language arts teachers for assistance in thinking about reading selections in various genres they might recommend for students at this age. Candidates write a letter to parents providing guidelines and recommendations for texts.

APPENDIX D: OVERVIEW OF PORTFOLIO REQUIREMENTS AND ASSESSMENT CENTRE SPECIFICATIONS FOR ONE OF THE NEWLY DEVELOPED EA/ELA NEXT GENERATION ASSESSMENTS

EA-ENGLISH LANGUAGE ARTS

	Original Configuration			Next Generation Configuration		
	Evidence Sources	Standards Assessed	What's Measured	Evidence Sources	Standards Assessed	What's Measured
Entry 1 Analysis of Student Response to Literature	Literature selected Student responses to text Written commentary Instructional materials	I. Knowledge of Students II. Curricular Choices V. Instructional Resources VI. Reading XI. Assessment XII. Self Reflection	Knowledge of literature Understanding of varying levels of student reading Connection of S to literature Awareness, acceptance, encouragement of multiple interpretations. Adjustment of teaching strategies	**Entry 1 Analysis of Student Growth in Reading and Writing** Student responses to text Choices of texts Student writing in response to print and non-print text Written commentary Instructional materials	I. Knowledge of Students II. Knowledge of the Field VI. Instructional Resources VIII. Reading IX. Writing XIII. Assessment XIV. Self Reflection	Knowledge of literature and writing process Understanding of the varying levels of student understanding Acceptance, awareness, encouraging of multiple interpretations Ability to respond appropriately to student work Ability to establish reading and writing goals based on assessment of student work

Appendix D. (Continued)

	Original Configuration			Next Generation Configuration		
	Evidence Sources	Standards Assessed	What's Measured	Evidence Sources	Standards Assessed	What's Measured
Entry 2 Analysis of Student Writing	Students Writing Stimulus material Written commentary Instructional materials	I. Knowledge of Students II. Curricular Choices V. Instructional Resources VII. Writing XI. Assessment XII. Self Reflection	Understanding writing as a recursive process Adjust instruction Repertoire of material Creation of appropriate assignments Assignments that engender S interest	**Entry 2 Instructional Analysis: Whole-Class Discussion** 15-minute video Written commentary Instructional materials	I. Knowledge of Students II. Knowledge of the Field III. Engagement IV. Learning Environment V. Equity, Fairness, Diversity VI. Instructional Resources VII. Instructional Decision Making X. Speaking, Listening, Viewing XI. Integrated Instruction XII. Self-Reflection	Understanding of whole class discussion Ability to facilitate discussion Knowledge of English language arts Ability to adjust to student needs and context Ability to integrate instruction Ability to deal equally with all students Ability to articulate teacher behavior
Entry 3 Instructional Analysis: Small Group	20-minute video Written commentary Instructional materials	I. Knowledge of Students II. Curricular choices III. Engagement IV. Learning Environment V. Instructional Resources VIII. Discourse	Understanding of small-group dynamics Ability to facilitate discussion Knowledge of English language arts Ability to adjust to student needs and context	**Entry 3 Instructional Analysis: Small-Group Discussion** 15-minute video Written commentary Instructional materials	I. Knowledge of Students II. Knowledge of the Field III. Engagement IV. Learning Environment V. Equity, Fairness, Diversity	Understanding of small-group discussion Ability to facilitate discussion Knowledge of English language arts Ability to adjust to student needs and context

		X. Integrated Instruction XII. Self Reflection	Ability to integrate instruction Ability to articulate teacher behavior
		VI. Instructional Resources VII. Instructional Decision Making X. Speaking, Listening, Viewing XI. Integrated Instruction XII. Self-Reflection	Ability to integrate instruction Ability to deal equally with all students Ability to articulate teacher behavior
Entry 4 Instructional Analysis: Whole Class Discussion	20-minute video Written commentary Instructional materials	I. Knowledge of Students II. Curricular Choices III. Engagement IV. Learning Environment V. Instructional Resources VII. Discourse XII. Integrated Instruction XII. Self Reflection	Understanding of whole class discussion Ability to facilitate discussion Knowledge of English language arts Ability to adjust to student needs and context Ability to integrate instruction

RATIONALE FOR CHANGES FROM 4-ENTRY TO 3-ENTRY SPECIFICATIONS

Critical Competencies Covered in 4-Entry Portfolio	Critical Competencies Covered in 3-Entry Portfolio
• Knowledge of reading and writing processes	• Knowledge of reading and writing processes
• Knowledge of students as readers and writers	• Knowledge of students as readers and writers
• Awareness, acceptance, encouragement of multiple levels of interpretation	• Link between reading, writing, speaking
• Ability to adjust instruction	• Ability to foster one skill to enhance the other
• Ability to create assignments that challenge	• Ability to adjust tasks to individual needs of learners
• Ability to respond appropriately to student work	• Focus on print and non-print texts
	• Knowledge of reading and writing
	• Knowledge of students as readers and writers
	• Awareness, acceptance, encouragement of multiple levels of interpretation
	• Ability to adjust instruction
	• Ability to create assignments that challenge
	• Ability to respond appropriately to student work

APPENDIX E: EXAMPLE OF PORTFOLIO TASK FOR NEXT GENERATION EA/ELA ASSESSMENT ☆

Entry 1

Analysis of Student Growth in Reading and Writing

Accomplished Early Adolescence/English Language Arts teachers understand their students and center their classrooms around students to help develop student literacy. They know that not all students learn in the same way and encourage self-directed learning on the part of each student. They see reading as a process and use appropriate strategies to address student strengths as well as weaknesses. They set ambitious learning goals, organize, structure, and sequence learning activities that reflect these goals, and gauge student progress in terms of them. They expose students to a variety of texts selected for their literary substance, diversity, and appeal to young adolescents.

Accomplished Early Adolescence/English Language Arts teachers engage all students as active participants in their own learning as students construct meaning from texts. They invite many interpretations of texts, at the same time insisting that interpretations be based on close examination of the text. They design and use a range of activities that permit students to demonstrate their comprehension, interpretation, and appreciation of texts in a variety of media.

Accomplished Early Adolescence/English Language Arts teachers understand that writing is a diverse, complex, and recursive thinking process, and that there are forms, approaches, tools, styles, and conventions used in writing in different genres that can assist authors in communicating their ideas for a wide variety of purposes and audiences. They nurture their students' enthusiasm for writing by motivating them to write about issues that matter in their lives.

Accomplished Early Adolescence/English Language Arts teachers have a command of a wide range of assessment methods and strategies aligned with their goals. They provide students with constructive feedback, highlighting successes and prompting student reflection about ways to improve. They use assessment findings to help shape instructional planning. They reflect on their practice, can talk persuasively about why they make the pedagogical decisions they do, and comment on ways to improve their practice.

☆ Reprinted with permission from the National Board for Professional Teaching Standards. www.nbpts.org. All rights reserved.

The following *Standards* represent the focus of this entry:

   I.   *Knowledge of Students*
  II.   *Knowledge of the Field*

  VI.   *Instructional Resources*
 VII.   *Instructional Decision Making*
VIII.   *Reading*
  IX.   *Writing*

XIII.   *Assessment*
XIV.   *Self-Reflection*

Entry 1 directions include the following sections:

        What Do I Need To Do?
        How Will My Response Be Scored?
        Composing My Written Commentary
        Making Good Choices
        Format Specifications
        Cover Sheets and Forms

Entry 1

What Do I Need To Do?

In this entry, you will demonstrate how you teach your students to read, to respond to various kinds of texts, and to write. Although accomplished English language arts teachers integrate reading and writing, this entry is divided into half (reading, then writing) for the purpose of discussion and analysis in order to give assessors a clear picture of your approach to both reading and writing. You will describe the goals for your teaching, the teaching context or assignment (prompt) that led to the students' responses, and your analysis of the students' growth and development as individuals who can interact with texts and effectively communicate in writing. You must also explain how the entire entry, taken together, is indicative of your instruction of reading and writing.

For this entry you must submit the following:

- **Written Commentary (13 pages maximum)**
  that analyzes four responses from two students. These students might be members of the same class or might be drawn from two different classes that you teach.
- **One packet for each student**
  containing the student's responses to four assignments/prompts (two reading assignments and two writing assignments), the assignments/prompts themselves, and the rubrics or scoring criteria you used to score the student's responses.
- **All forms required for this entry can be found in Forms & Specs.**

See Making Good Choices and Format Specifications for more detail regarding each of the above.

It may be helpful to have a colleague help you record video, watch and analyze the video recordings, read and comment on your analyses and on the student work you have chosen. **However**, all the work you submit as part of your response to **any entry must be yours and yours alone**. This means that your written analyses, the student work you submit, and your video recordings must all feature teaching that **you** did and work that **you** oversaw. For more detailed information, see Ethics and Collaboration in the *Intro* and the National Board's Ethics Policy.

Entry 1

How Will My Response Be Scored?

Your response to this entry will be scored based on the following *NBPTS Early Adolescence/English Language Arts Standards*:

   I.   *Knowledge of Students*
   II.   *Knowledge of the Field*

   VI.   *Instructional Resources*
   VII. *Instructional Decision Making*
  VIII. *Reading*
   IX.   *Writing*

  XIII. *Assessment*
  XIV. *Self-Reflection*

It is strongly recommended that you review these standards before you begin and periodically as you prepare your response to this entry.

Your response will be judged on the extent to which it **provides clear, consistent, and convincing evidence of your ability to develop students' interpretive and critical reading and reasoning skills and students' writing skills.**

The Level-4 rubric, the highest level of the rubric, specifically requires **clear, consistent, and convincing evidence** in your response that you:

- acquire knowledge of each individual student's background and skills as a reader and interpreter of text in both print and nonprint media (e.g., a film, a recording, a staged production, a computer-generated product, or other appropriate technology);
- thoughtfully analyze student responses to texts to discover what the responses suggest about each student's growth and development as a reader/interpreter of text;
- establish high, attainable, and worthwhile reading/interpretation goals with each of your students and make curricular choices and use instructional resources designed to enable these students to achieve those goals;
- establish an instructional context that encourages students' active exploration, interpretation, and critical, reflective reading of literary and nonliterary texts;
- respect the possibility of multiple interpretations, while insisting that students support interpretive claims with plausible textual or contextual evidence;
- constructively respond to students' meaning-making efforts, directing the attention of students to the salient features of their reading/interpretation development, prompting them to reflect more deeply on how they can improve, and encouraging revision in their thinking;
- acquire knowledge of each student's background and skills as a writer and effective communicator;
- thoughtfully analyze student writing samples to discover what the writing suggests about each student's growth and development as a writer;

- establish high, attainable, and worthwhile writing goals with each of your students and make curricular choices and use instructional resources designed to enable these students to achieve those goals;
- establish an instructional context that encourages student development in the process of writing for multiple purposes and audiences;
- constructively respond to students' communication skills, directing their attention to the salient features of the writing and communication process, prompting them to reflect more deeply on how they can be improved, and encouraging revision in thinking and writing;
- use formal and/or informal assessment methods to monitor student progress, to encourage student selfassessment, and to plan instruction; and
- engage in insightful reflection and well-informed analyses of classroom practices, including a clear rationale for why those practices are appropriate for the students.

Entry 1

Composing My Written Commentary

The Written Commentary has been divided into sections with specific questions to help organize and direct your response. Your Written Commentary must address the following italicized questions and be organized into three sections using the headings that appear in boldface below.

1. Instructional Context
2. Analysis of Student Work
3. Reflection

Consistent headings will help assessors locate the required information more easily. Statements in plain text that immediately follow an italicized question will assist you in interpreting the question. It is not necessary to include the italicized questions within the body of your response.

The entire Written Commentary must be **no longer than 13 typed pages**. Suggested page lengths for each section are included to help you make decisions about how much to write for each of the three sections. (See Format Specifications for more detail.)

1. Instructional Context

This information is in addition to the information provided on the Contextual Information Sheet, which focuses on the school/district at large. In this section, address the following questions about your selected class:

- *What are the number, ages, and grades of the students in the class featured in this entry and subject matter of the class?* (Example: 21 students in grades 8 and 9, ages 13 through 15, American literature)
- *What are the relevant characteristics of this class that influenced your instructional strategies for this lesson: ethnic, cultural, and linguistic diversity; the range of abilities of the students; the personality of the class? What are the instructional challenges represented by these particular students?*
- *What are the relevant characteristics of the students with exceptional needs and abilities that influenced your planning for this sequence of instruction (for example, the range of abilities and the cognitive, social/behavioral, attentional, sensory, and/or physical challenges of your students)?* Give any other information that might help the assessor "see" this class.
- *What are the relevant features of your teaching context that influenced the selection of this instruction?* This might include other realities of the social and physical teaching context (e.g., available resources such as technology, scheduling of classes, room allocation–own classroom or shared space) that are relevant to your response.

(Suggested total page length for **Instructional Context: 1 page**)

---

2. Analysis of Student Work

Answer the following questions in separate sections labeled **The Student as Reader** and **The Student as Writer.** Within each of these sections, be sure to identify the students as Student A or Student B as you write about them. Cite specific examples from the students responses to illustrate points in your analysis.

The Student as Reader. In this section, address the following questions as they relate to the student responses to your reading assignments. Be sure to address the questions for each student.

- *What about the student as an individual (experiences, skills, interests) provides insight into his/her work samples and your analysis of them?*
- *What are your instructional goals to promote growth for this student as a reader and interpreter of text? What texts, assignments, and strategies did you use to accomplish this?*
- *What characteristics of the selected work samples demonstrate the student's ability to understand and interpret text?*
- *How did your assessment and feedback to the student promote growth as a reader and interpreter of text?* Explain how your assessment approach(es) and any related feedback connect with your instructional goals.
- *Given this student's responses, what will you do as a teacher to build on what the student has already accomplished as a reader/interpreter of text?*

The Student as Writer. In this section, address the following questions as they relate to the student responses to your writing assignments. Be sure to address the questions for each student.

- *What about the student as an individual (experiences, skills, interests) provides insight into his/her writing samples and your analysis of them?*
- *What are your instructional goals to promote growth for this student as a writer? What assignments and strategies did you use to accomplish this?*
- *What characteristics of these writing samples demonstrate the student's growth and development as a writer?*
- *How did your assessment and feedback to the student promote growth as a writer?* Explain how your assessment approach(es) and any related feedback connect with your instructional goals.
- *Given this student's responses, what will you do as a teacher to build on what the student has already accomplished as a writer?*

(Suggested total page length for **Analysis of Student Work: 10 pages** (5 pages for each student))

3. Reflection

Using the four student responses that you have submitted to illustrate your discussion, address the following questions:

- *To what extent did you achieve the goals you set?*
- *Taken in total, what do all of these student responses say about your strengths and weaknesses as a teacher of reading and writing?* Consider the four student responses together with the teaching context that shaped them.

(Suggested total page length for **Reflection: 2 pages**)

Entry 1

Making Good Choices

Selecting two students

You will need to select two students whom you will feature. These students should represent different instructional challenges to you as a teacher. It is important to choose students whose responses give you an opportunity to discuss your practice. Remember, the focus of this entry is on your ability to provide students with instruction that supports their growth and development as readers/interpreters of texts and as writers. For this reason, the best-performing students in the class may not be the best choices for this entry. The focus is on your practice, not on the level of student performance.

To prepare for this entry, you may want to select several students as potential cases and collect or make copies of their work over a period of time. As you collect the work, you might want to record your reasons for selecting that particular student and his or her work, and the details that might be helpful in completing your analysis. For example, you may want to take notes on your learning goals, what came before and after the assignment, and how you assessed the assignment and responded to the student.

Selecting the texts and the writing prompts

For the **Reading Component,** you will need to select a print and a nonprint text that will prompt the student responses you choose to feature in this entry. One text must be a printed literary text such as a book, short story, or poem. The other text must be presented to students through a nonprint medium such as a film, a work of art, a recording, or a staged production. However, **the two texts must be different from each other**, regardless of the medium in which they are presented. For example, submitting a student's response to the film version of a text along with a response to the print version of the same text would not meet this requirement.

It is important to select texts that provide students with opportunities to demonstrate their abilities to read, think critically about, and interpret text. As such, the selected text should be appropriately engaging and challenging for your students. The texts that you select may be related to each other in an instructional sequence.

You may submit responses to the same two texts for both students, or you may submit responses to up to four different texts for both students. Remember, one response to text from each student must be in a nonprint mode (e.g., a drawing, film, speech, presentations, newscasts, newspaper/magazines, collage, graph, computer-generated product, or other appropriate technology). The nonprint response can be to either the print-based or nonprint-based text.

You will be scored on your strategies for teaching students to read and respond to a variety of texts. Selecting two different texts for each student may give you a good opportunity to show your range of teaching strategies to foster students' development as readers and interpreters of text. However, one or more of the texts may be used for both students, if doing so allows you to demonstrate how you deal differently with the same texts with different students. Either approach meets the requirements of this entry.

For the **Writing Component,** select responses that show your understanding of the writing process. You do not need to include multiple drafts for each response. Carefully selected pages from each draft or from writer-response forms such as peer conference and self-editing forms can provide effective evidence. Writing prompts should provide students with opportunities to communicate their ideas effectively for multiple purposes and audiences.

You may submit responses to the same two writing prompts for both students, or you may submit responses to up to four different writing prompts for both students. You will be scored on your strategies for teaching students to communicate their ideas effectively in writing. Selecting two different kinds of prompts for each student may give you a good opportunity to show your range of teaching strategies to foster students' development as writers. However, one or more of the prompts may be used for both students, if doing so allows you to demonstrate how you deal differently with the same kinds of writing with different students. Either approach meets the requirements of this entry.

Note: For both the **Reading** and **Writing Components,** each student response must be accompanied by its assignment/prompt. Each assignment/prompt must be no longer than one page.

Selecting four responses for each student

You must choose **two responses to texts** and **two writing samples for each student**. Each student response must be **no longer than 3 pages**.

For the **Reading Component,** one of the two texts must be a print-based literary text, and one text must be of any genre in a nonprint medium. One response must be written and the other nonwritten (e.g., a drawing, film, speech, collage, graph, computer-generated product, or other appropriate technology). Remember, the focus for the reading component is on the student's analysis and interpretation of text, **not** on the quality of the work sample.

For the **Writing Component,** choose samples that will allow you to show the range of writing instruction in your classroom. Remember, the focus for the writing component is on the decisions you make regarding the student's growth as an effective writer and communicator.

The samples you choose should illustrate different challenges, problems, or topics in the teaching and learning of writing. Be certain to select samples that are substantial enough to support the level of analysis required in the Written Commentary.

Note: For both the **Reading** and **Writing Components,** each student response must be accompanied by the rubric or scoring criteria you used to evaluate it. Each rubric/scoring criteria must be **no longer than one page**.

Entry 1

Format Specifications

This section presents detailed guidelines for preparing your entry materials. Please follow these guidelines carefully. As a further aid to your preparation of these entry materials, refer to the Entry 1 Assembly Final Inventory Form and *Pack & Ship*.

Written Commentary

Writing About Teaching in *Get Started* provides useful advice for developing your Written Commentary. Your response will be scored based on the content of your analysis. However, it is important to proofread your writing for spelling, mechanics, and usage. Your response must meet the requirements listed below:

- Be organized into the section headings given in Composing My Written Commentary:
    1. Instructional Context
    2. Analysis of Student Work
    3. Reflection
- Be typed in double-spaced text on 8.5″ × 11″ paper with one-inch margins on all sides using Times New Roman 12 point font. Print on only one side of each page. Pages with pictures or text on two sides will count as two pages. Consult Formatting Written Materials in *Forms & Specs* for more specific instructions.
- Be written in English.
- Have all pages sequentially numbered.
- Have your Candidate ID number in the upper right corner on all pages. Do **not** include your name. If you are using a word-processing program, you may find that it saves time to create a "header" that will print your Candidate ID number on each page.
- Be legible. Be sure that your printer's ribbon or toner cartridge is in good condition.
- Preserve the anonymity of the students. Do not use students' last names.
- Be no longer than **13 typed pages in total**. If you submit a longer Written Commentary, only the **first 13 pages** will be read and scored.

The Written Commentary you submit for this entry must meet all of the requirements above. Failure to meet the requirements may make it difficult for assessors to locate evidence, which could impact your score.

Student Work Samples, Assignments/Prompts, Rubrics

The student work samples that you submit must satisfy the following criteria:

- Represent each student's original work. The original student work or clear copies of student work are acceptable.
- Come from the students who are the basis for your Written Commentary.
- Be from two different students, responding to the four activities that you are featuring in this entry.

Reading Component

- Assignment/Prompt for *print-based text* (**one page maximum**)
- Student Response to assignment/prompt (**three pages maximum**)
- Rubric for assignment/prompt (**one page maximum**)
- Assignment/Prompt for *nonprint-based text* (**one page maximum**)
- Student Response to assignment/prompt (**three pages maximum**)
- Rubric for assignment/prompt (**one page maximum**)

Writing Component

- Assignment/Prompt for writing assignment #1 (**one page maximum**)
- Student Writing Sample in response to assignment/ prompt (**three pages maximum**)
- Rubric for assignment/prompt (**one page maximum**)
- Assignment/Prompt for writing assignment #2 (**one page maximum**)
- Student Writing Sample in response to assignment/ prompt (**three pages maximum**)
- Rubric for assignment/prompt (**one page maximum**)

Note: The writing assignment numbers are not meant to prescribe the order in which you need to present the assignments. They are only meant to provide a means of organizing and labeling your materials.

The student work samples, assignments/prompts, and rubrics must be prepared as follows:

- Be clearly labeled (Student A or Student B) on all pages and show the student's first name only. Delete students' last names, teachers' names, or any identifying information about the students' families.
- Be 8.5″ × 11″ A smaller item (e.g., a photograph) must be affixed to an 8.5″ × 1 1″ sheet of paper.
  - o **Note:** If a student work sample, assignment/prompt, or rubric was created in PowerPoint, HyperStudio, or other similar media, you may format up to 6 slides on one 8.5″ × 11″ sheet. Each sheet will count as one page toward your page total.
  - o **Note:** If an assignment/prompt contains Web pages, each Web page printout (one 8.5″ × 11″ sheet) will count as one page toward your page total.
  - o **Note:** Do not photocopy full-size pages of assignments/ prompts in a reduced format in order to fit more than one assignment/prompt onto a single sheet of paper.
  - o **Note:** Do **not** send video recordings, audiotapes, models, etc. If a student creates such a product, have **the student** write a one-page description of the assignment and what the student made. You may include photograph(s) or student made drawings to accompany the description, if appropriate. The one-page description counts toward your page total.
- Be legible.
- Have all pages sequentially numbered.
- Have your Candidate ID number in the upper right corner on all pages. Do **not** include your name.
- Be no more than **20 pages** of student work samples, assignments/prompts, and rubrics for each student. Cover sheets do not count toward this total. No materials will be returned.

The student work samples, assignments/prompts, and rubrics you submit for this entry must meet all of the requirements above. Failure to meet the requirements may make it difficult for assessors to locate evidence, which could impact your score.

Failure to submit a Written Commentary, student work samples, assignments/prompts, and rubrics will make your response to this entry unscoreable.

Entry 1

Cover Sheets and Forms

All cover sheets and forms required for this entry are listed below and can be found in Forms & Specs. To read and print these documents, you must install Adobe Acrobat Reader® software on your computer. You may download Adobe Reader for free by following the instructions provided by Adobe Systems. Responses can be entered electronically and printed in Adobe Reader. However, Adobe Reader will not allow you to save the forms. You will need to print your completed forms or obtain a full version of Adobe Acrobat in order to save your work.

As you prepare your portfolio, keep in mind the following:

- Print as many copies of the Student Release Form and Adult Release Form as needed.
- The Entry 1 Assembly Final Inventory Form and Candidte Release Form, when complete, are submitted in the Forms envelope, not the envelope for this entry.
- Some cover sheets may contain directions. Adhere as closely as possible to the directions on such cover sheets. Information that you are asked to supply on cover sheets may be electronically entered directly into the space provided, single-spaced using 12 point Times New Roman type, or handwritten.

Packing and Returning Your Portfolio Entries

Please refer to the Entry 1 Assembly Final Inventory Form and *Pack & Ship* for detailed instructions and diagrams that show you how to arrange your materials before placing them in the envelopes provided.

We provide detailed instructions for assembling and packaging your entries to ensure your entries are easily inventoried. Staff at the NBPTS Processing Center and scoring sites need to follow a detailed, ordered list when they check-in your portfolio and entries. Therefore, it is important to make sure that no materials are left out of an entry envelope and that no materials are placed in the wrong entry envelope. **Incorrectly packaged entries may not be scoreable.**

Cover Sheets and Forms for Entry 1

Listed below are all the cover sheets and forms you need to complete this entry.

For Your Entry 1 Envelope

- Entry 1 Cover Sheet
- Contextual Information Sheet
- Written Commentary Cover Sheet
- **Student Packet-Student A**
  - Student A Response to Print-based Text – Cover Sheet
  - Student A Response to Nonprint-based Text – Cover Sheet
  - Student A Writing Sample #1 – Cover Sheet
  - Student A Writing Sample #2 – Cover Sheet

- **Student Packet-Student B**
  - o   Student B Response to Print-based Text – Cover Sheet
  - o   Student B Response to Nonprint-based Text – Cover Sheet
  - o   Student B Writing Sample #1 – Cover Sheet
  - o   Student B Writing Sample #2 – Cover Sheet

For Your Forms Envelope

- Entry 1 Assembly Final Inventory Form
- Candidate Release Form
- Attestation Form

For Your Records

- Student and Adult Release Form Cover Sheet
- Student Release Form (English)*
- Student Release Form (Spanish)*
- Adult Release Form*

*Print as needed.

APPENDIX F:
PORTFOLIO ASSESSOR TRAINING MATERIALS LIST ☆

NBPTS PORTFOLIO TRAINING MATERIALS TABLE OF CONTENTS					
Order	Title	Print for	Handout	Overhead	Poster
1	Bias Exercise 1A Competence	All: one per assessor	X		
2	Bias Exe rcise 1B Accomplished Teaching	All: one per assessor	X		
3	Ground rules for Explori ng Bias	Trainer's Use			X
4	What is Bias	Trainer's Use		X	
5	Goal: Open, Honest, Self Examination	Trainer's Use		X	
6	Vignettes Cover Sheet	All: one per assessor	X		
7	Vignettes: Classroom Based	Entries 1 – 3 – one per assessor	X		
7 SC	Vignettes: 1 – 3 SC Based				
8	Vignettes: DAE (Entry 4)	Entry 4 – one per assessor	X		
8 SC	Vignettes: DAE SC Based				
9	Vignettes: Exceptional Needs	Entries 1 – 4 ENS – trainer's use	X		
10	Trainers Guide to Vignettes: Classroom	Entries 1 – 3 – trainer's use	X		
10 SC	Trainers Guide to Vignettes: 1 – 3 SC				
11	Trainers Guide to Vignettes: DAE (Entry 4)	Entry #4 – trainer's use	X		
11 SC	Trainers Guide to Vignettes: DAE SC				
12	Personal Trigger List ***	All: one per assessor	X	X	
13	Architecture of Teaching	Trainer's Use		X	
14	Five Core Propositions	All: one per assessor	X		
15	Architecture & Five Core Proposition	Trainer's Use			X
16	Standards Homework	All: one per assessor	X		
17	Abbreviated Standards	Entry Specific – one per assessor	X		
18	Entry Directions	Entry Specific – one per assessor	X		
19	Rubric ***	Entry Specific – one per assessor	X		
20	Note -Taking Guide ***	Entry Specific – one per assessor	X		

		NBPTS PORTFOLIO TRAINING MATERIALS TABLE OF CONTENTS				
21	Maintaining the Proper Attitude Toward Performance	Trainer's Use			X	
22	Societal Bias Flash Cards	Trainer's Use	X			
23	Societal Bias: First Reaction Sheet	All: one per assessor	X			
24	Societal Bias: Thoughtful Reaction Sheet	All: one per assessor	X			
25	How Does Society Shape/Reactions	Trainer's Use			X	
26	Trainer's Guide to "Ism s"	Trainer's Use	X			
27	How might your Views/Ability	Trainer's Use			X	
28	Societal Bias Reflections	All: one per assessor	X			
29	Assessor Pacing Sheet	All: one per assessor	X			
30	Score Scale & Architectural Helix	Trainer's Use				X
31	Evaluation Words ***	All: one per assessor	X			X
32	Taking Good Notes	All: one per assessor	X			
33	Blank ESR	Trainer's Use			X	X
34	ESR Template Entries 1–3	Trainer's Use	X			
35	ESR Template Entry (Entry 4)	Trainer's Use	X			
36	More than one Path to Accomplishment: Writing Exercise	All: one per assessor	X			
37	More than one Path to Accomplishment: Writing Exercise Trainer's Guide	Trainer's Use	X			
38	Writing Quotations from Standards	Trainer's Use	X			
39	NBPTS Camera Lens	Trainer's Use			X	
40	Qualifying Round	Trainer's Use			X	
41	ESR Rules for the Assessors	Data Manager use: one per assessor	X			
42	Training Material Table of Contents	Trainer's Use	X			
43	Portfolio Entry Checklist	All	X			

***   Blue designates materials that are entry specific

APPENDIX G: SAMPLE RUBRIC FOR THE NEXT GENERATION EA/ELA ASSESSMENT *

EARLY ADOLESCENCE/ENGLISH LANGUAGE ARTS

Entry 1 Analysis of Student Growth in Reading and Writing Scoring Rubric

Level 4. The Level 4 performance provides clear, consistent, and convincing evidence that the teacher is able to use analysis and assessment of student responses to literature and student writing to support growth as both interpreters of text and as writers.

The Level 4 performance provides clear, consistent, and convincing evidence that the teacher has a thorough knowledge of students as individual learners and sets high, worthwhile, and attainable goals for growth in student learning. The Level 4 performance offers clear, consistent, and convincing evidence that the teacher encourages active exploration and critical interpretation of print and nonprint text and recognizes multiple interpretations while requiring them to be grounded in the text. The Level 4 performance provides clear, consistent, and convincing evidence that the teacher understands the complex, recursive, individual nature of the writing process and provides a context that encourages students' active exploration of their own writing processes. There is clear, consistent, and convincing evidence that students engage in writing for multiple purposes and audiences. There is clear, consistent, and convincing evidence that the teacher employs varied, rich, and appropriate instructional resources, including print and nonprint media formats, to support students' growth as interpreters of text and as writers. The Level 4 performance offers clear, consistent, and convincing evidence that the teacher is able to accurately and thoughtfully describe and analyze student work in ways that recognize students' progress and offers means for students to build on their accomplishments. There is clear, consistent, and convincing evidence that the teacher uses appropriate assessment methods (formal or informal) on an ongoing basis to monitor student progress, encourage student self-assessment, and plan future instruction. There is clear, consistent, and convincing evidence of detailed and effective communication with students that directs their attention to the salient features of their work and encourages them to reflect upon how their work can be improved. The Level 4 performance offers clear, consistent, and convincing evidence that the teacher is able to describe his/her practice fully and accurately and reflect insightfully on its effectiveness in meeting the challenges of teaching texts and writing. Overall, there is clear, consistent, and convincing evidence that the teacher is able to use analysis and assessment of student responses to literature and student writing to support growth as both interpreters of text and as writers.

Level 3. The Level 3 performance provides clear evidence that the teacher is able to use analysis and assessment of student responses to literature and student writing to support growth as both interpreters of text and as writers.

The Level 3 performance provides clear evidence that the teacher has a knowledge of students as individual learners and sets appropriate goals for growth in student learning. There is clear evidence that the teacher encourages active exploration and critical interpretation of print and nonprint text and recognizes multiple interpretations while requiring them to be grounded in text, though the text may not be as stimulating nor the range of student responses as broad as in a Level 4 performance. The Level 3 performance provides clear evidence that the teacher understands the complex, recursive, individual nature of the writing process, and provides a context that encourages students' exploration of their own writing processes though the evidence may not be as well developed as in a Level 4 performance. There is clear evidence that students engage in writing for multiple purposes and audiences, and that the teacher employs appropriate instructional resources, including print and nonprint media formats, to support students' growth as interpreters of text and as writers. The Level 3 performance offers clear evidence that the teacher is able to accurately describe and analyze student work in ways that recognize students' progress and offers means for students to build on their accomplishments. There is clear evidence that the teacher uses appropriate assessment methods (formal or informal) on an ongoing basis to monitor student progress, encourage student self-assessment, and plan future instruction. However, the assessment and/or feedback may not be as detailed or insightful as in a Level 4 performance, or the area of student self-assessment may not be fully addressed. There is clear evidence of effective communication with students that directs their attention to the salient features of their work and encourages them to reflect upon how their work can be improved. The Level 3 performance offers clear evidence that the teacher is able to describe his/her practice and reflect on its effectiveness in meeting the challenges of teaching texts and writing. However, the reflection may not be as detailed or insightful as in the Level 4 performance. One part of the response may be more indicative of accomplished practice than another, but overall, there is clear evidence that the teacher is able to use analysis and assessment of student responses to literature and student writing to support growth as both interpreters of text and as writers.

Level 2. The Level 2 performance provides limited evidence that the teacher is able to use analysis and assessment of student responses to literature and student writing to support growth as both interpreters of text and as writers.

The Level 2 performance offers limited evidence of the teacher's knowledge of students as individual learners and sets appropriate goals for growth in student learning. The goals may be general, of limited significance, or only loosely related to the instruction. The Level 2 performance offers limited evidence that the teacher encourages active and critical interpretation of texts, which may be only loosely grounded in the text with little or no comment on this by the teacher. The Level 2 performance provides limited evidence that the teacher understands the complex, recursive, individual nature of the writing process. There is limited evidence that students engage in writing for multiple purposes and audiences and the teacher employs appropriate instructional resources, including print and nonprint media formats, to support student's growth as interpreters of text and as writers. Instructional resources and activities may be formulaic, lacking a convincing rationale, or restricted to a single media format. The Level 2 performance offers limited evidence that the teacher is able to describe and analyze student work. The analysis may recognize students' progress but may not offer students ways to build on their accomplishment. There is limited evidence that the teacher uses appropriate assessment methods to monitor student progress. Assessment may not be ongoing or may not be used by the teacher to plan future instruction. There is limited evidence of communication with students about their work, or the feedback may be too general to offer students ways to improve their work or may not promote student self-reflection. The Level 2 performance may offer evidence that the teacher is able to describe and analyze his/her practice, but the reflection may be vague, general, or focused solely on the procedural aspects of teaching. The Level 2 performance may be characterized by evidence that hints at accomplished practice, but is too fragmented or uneven to support a classification as a Level 3 performance. Overall, there is limited evidence that the teacher is able to use analysis and assessment of student responses to literature and student writing to support growth as both interpreters of text and as writers.

Level 1. The Level 1 performance provides little or no evidence that the teacher is able to use analysis and assessment of student responses to literature and student writing to support growth as both interpreters of text and as writers.

The Level 1 performance provides little or no evidence that the teacher has a knowledge of students as individual learners and sets appropriate goals for growth in student learning. The goals for student learning may not be goals at all, but rather activities. When stated, the goals may be confused, trivial, inappropriate, or not connected to the instruction. The Level 1 performance offers little or no evidence that the teacher encourages active and critical interpretation of texts in different media; instead, students may be expected to simply recall elements of the text. The Level 1 performance provides little or no evidence that the teacher understands the complex, recursive, individual nature of the writing process and may even contain misconceptions about the writing process. There is little or no evidence that students engage in writing for multiple purposes and audiences. Instructional resources, including print and nonprint media format, may be inappropriate and/or completely unengaging to these students. Questions and/or prompts may be entirely close-ended with "right" and "wrong" answers. There may be no recognition of nonprint media as text. The Level 1 performance offers little or no evidence that the teacher is able to describe and analyze student work. The analysis may fail to recognize students' progress and instead focus on students' mistakes, or it may be so superficial that it misses important elements of the work that merit attention. There may be an exclusive emphasis on the grammar and mechanics of students' writing, as opposed to addressing students' thinking. There is little or no evidence that the teacher uses appropriate assessment methods to monitor student progress or communicates effectively with students about their work. Assessment and feedback may be superficial, infrequent, and may actually discourage students from reflecting upon their work. The Level 1 performance offers little or no evidence that the teacher is able to describe and analyze his/her practice. The reflection may be missing or disconnected from the instructional evidence. Overall, there is little or no evidence that the teacher is able to use analysis and assessment of student responses to literature and student writing to support growth as both interpreters of text and as writers.

EARLY ADOLESCENCE/ENGLISH LANGUAGE ARTS

Entry 1: Analysis of Student Growth in Reading and Writing

Note-Taking Guide

1. **Aspects of Teaching. As you read through the performance, note evidence pertaining to EACH of the aspects listed below. Evidence may come from one or more data sources.**
   a. KNOWLEDGE OF STUDENTS (KOS): Knowledge of students both as individuals and as readers and writers.
   b. GOALS/CONNECTIONS (G/C): Goals and connections among the goals, student needs, and instruction.
   c. ANALYSIS OF STUDENT RESPONSES (ANA): Accuracy, completeness, awareness of understandings and misunderstandings, recognition of student progress as seen in the student work.
   d. READING PROCESS (RP): The context for reading and interpretation of texts established by the teacher; ways students are or are not encouraged and supported to take an active, critical stance towards texts; support for multiple interpretations that are grounded in text; support for nonprint based media as legitimate textual sources; types and range of genres represented.
   e. WRITING PROCESS (WP): The teacher's understanding and teaching of the writing process as a complex, recursive, individual process, including support for individual approaches, writing for multiple purposes and audiences, multiple stages of development, review, and editing.
   f. ASSESSMENT (ASMT): How student work is assessed and feedback is given.
   g. PLANNING (P): What will be done to address student strengths and weaknesses?
   h. INSTRUCTIONAL RESOURCES (IR): The texts, resources, and activities the teacher used to engage students in reading and writing.

    i. REFLECTION (R): Evidence the teacher is thinking critically about his or her own practice in relation to individual students and their general approach to reading and writing.

2. **Does the instruction promote the student's growth as a reader and as a writer? (Answer for each student.) Think about the quality of and the links among the different parts of the evidence. Are the parts and links logical, accurate, and complete? The links to think about are:**
   - Information about the student ↔ the goals ↔ the instruction.
   - The instruction, including next steps and feedback ↔ the teacher's analysis of the student work.
   - The teacher's analysis ↔ the student work (i.e., quality of "fit:" Do the two sources support and enhance each other, or do they conflict and undermine each other?)

3. **Does the teacher's general approach to reading and writing support student growth? Consider:**
   - Is there support for students to be active, critical readers?
   - Does the instruction support multiple interpretations of literature that are grounded in text?
   - Does the teacher recognize that the writing process is a complex, recursive, individual process, teaching and allowing for multiple approaches, multiple stages of development, multiple drafts, review (by student, peers, and/or teacher), and revision?
   - Does the instruction support students in active exploration of their own ideas and the writing process?
   - Does the teacher's use of instructional texts, resources, assessment, and feedback support continued growth in reading and writing?

4. **Think about the performance as a whole. Overall, what is the nature of the evidence that the teacher is able to use analysis and assessment of students' responses to literature and student writing to support student growth? Think about:**
   - The evidence in the analysis of the responses by both students.
   - Your judgment of the effectiveness of the instruction for each of the students.
   - The evidence pertaining to the teacher's general approach to teaching reading, interpretation of texts, and writing.
   - The links among the different aspects of the performance.

APPENDIX H: EA/ELA LANGUAGE STUDY SAMPLE ASSESSMENT CENTRE TASK, ESSENTIAL FEATURES, AND SCORING RUBRIC [☆]

LANGUAGE STUDY

In order to activate the prompt screen, you must scroll completely through this screen.

Introduction

In this exercise, you will use your knowledge of English language arts to build a profile of a student as a second-language learner and to plan ways to facilitate this student's language development. You will be asked to respond to two prompts.

Criteria for Scoring

To satisfy the highest level of the scoring rubric, your response must provide clear, consistent, and convincing evidence of the following:

- an in-depth analysis of discourse; and
- a thorough description of teaching strategies used to facilitate the acquisition of English by second-language learners.

Directions

You may preview all of the prompts by clicking on the "Next" button. The "Previous" button will enable you to return to any of the prompts in order to compose or revise your response in the space provided. Your response will automatically be linked to the prompt that is displayed.

Stimulus
Carefully read the following Scenario, prompt, and student responses.

Your seventh-grade class has been asked to respond to the topic, "A Special Adventure." Both the transcript of the oral discourse and the written response are from the same seventh-grade student for whom English is a second language. Please refer to the student's response when answering the questions. Do not assess the student's reading comprehension.

The Student's Oral Transcript:
One time … (3-second pause) my special adventure is … (2-second pause) my family we come to America. Umh … I was very scared. I think I can no never … live (4-second pause) in this place. My father … (2-second pause) he tell me not never to be scared … (3-second pause) he help me. It very … (3-second pause) different here … but I like it now … (3-second pause). I do good here and I have friend.

The Student's Written Response (unedited first draft):
My special adventure is my family come to America. I did not want to leve my frends at home. I like to be with them and I did not want to go to new place. My brother he tell me I like new place. I am scared to go. We move here and I did not like it. Bit I mak fren and I am happy now here.

Prompts

After reading the Scenario, prompt, and student responses, respond to the following prompts:

1. What is one significant feature of the student's oral discourse? What is one significant feature of the student's written discourse? What do these features tell you about the student's second-language development?
2. What are two instructional strategies that you would use to address the significant features of this student's second-language development? Provide a rationale for each strategy.

EA/ENGLISH LANGUAGE ARTS
EXERCISE #4 LANGUAGE STUDY
ESSENTIAL FEATURES
VARIATION A

Prompt #1

BOTH THE ORAL AND WRITTEN FEATURES THAT THE CANDIDATE DISCUSSES MUST BE SIGNIFICANT. (Spelling is not significant, nor is punctuation)

A response may differ from the list below.

Possible oral features:

- verb omission/tense
- fluency problems
- lack of developing details

Possible written features:

- word omissions
- word order
- lack of developing detail

Possible features of second-language development (Must reflect what the candidate stated in oral and written features).

- problem with development of ideas
- overall limited English fluency
- word omission

Prompt #2

BOTH STRATEGIES MUST ADDRESS THE SIGNIFICANT FEATURES STATED IN PROMPT #1. A RATIONALE MUST BE PROVIDED. ONE RESPONSE MUST REFLECT THE NEED FOR COMFORT OF THE STUDENT. Specific ideas may differ from the list below; they may reflect the positive and/or negative features.

- graphic organizer to develop number of details
- small group activities to encourage more conversation about a chosen topic
- choose topics for development that are familiar to the speaker

- develop a series of questions related to the history of the student's arrival in the US. Try to get answers in sentences, then turn sentences into paragraphs
- create a small group story that parallels the idea of coming to the US. Each person adds more detail to what is already written. The sharing and working with someone give the student comfort

EA/ENGLISH LANGUAGE ARTS

Assessment Center Exercise 4 – Language Study Scoring Rubric

Level 4. The response shows clear, consistent, and convincing evidence that the candidate is able to provide an in-depth analysis of discourse and a thorough description of teaching strategies used to facilitate the acquisition of English by second-language learners.

Characteristics:

- Identification of a significant feature of the student's oral discourse is accurate.
- Identification of a significant feature of the student's written discourse is accurate.
- Explanation of the student's second-language development is insightful.
- The two instructional strategies are informed and closely linked to the features of the student's second-language development.
- The rationales are tightly connected to each strategy.

Level 3. The response shows clear evidence that the candidate is able to provide an in-depth analysis of discourse and a thorough description of teaching strategies used to facilitate the acquisition of English by second-language learners.

Characteristics:

- Identification of a significant feature of the student's oral discourse is accurate.
- Identification of a significant feature of the student's written discourse is accurate.
- Explanation of the student's second-language development is appropriate.

- The two instructional strategies are appropriate and targeted to the features of the student's second-language development.
- The rationales are connected to each strategy.

Level 2. The response shows limited evidence that the candidate is able to provide an in-depth analysis of discourse and a thorough description of teaching strategies used to facilitate the acquisition of English by second-language learners.

Characteristics:

- Identification of a significant feature of the student's oral discourse is over-broad or unclear.
- Identification of a significant feature of the student's written discourse is over-broad or unclear
- Explanation of the student's second-language development is minimal.
- The two instructional strategies are vague and loosely linked to the features of the student's second-language development.
- The rationales are weak or loosely connected to each strategy.

Level 1. The response shows little or no evidence that the candidate is able to provide an in-depth analysis of discourse and a thorough description of teaching strategies used to facilitate the acquisition of English by second-language learners.

Characteristics:

- Identification of a significant feature of the student's oral discourse is inaccurate or misinformed.
- Identification of a significant feature of the student's written discourse is inaccurate or misinformed.
- Explanation of the student's second-language development is weak or confused.
- The two instructional strategies are simplistic or inappropriate to the features of the student's second-language development.
- The rationales are missing or disconnected from each strategy.

APPENDIX I : PROCEDURES AND INSTRUCTIONS FOR WEIGHTING ENTRIES AND EXERCISES

INSTRUCTIONS

From research on previous National Board assessments, we know that teachers who participate in the development of exercises and entries do not consider those components of an assessment to be equally important and valuable in identifying candidates who should receive National Board Certification. Some entries or exercises are judged by teachers to reflect more effectively the content standards that define what accomplished teachers in the field should know and be able to do. Similarly, some entries or exercises are judged by teachers to elicit performances that are more important indicators of candidates' levels of accomplishment in the field. For these reasons, expert teachers in a field for which National Board Certification is to be granted have indicated that some entries and exercises should be given greater weight in determining which candidates receive National Board Certification.

The weighting procedure in which you will engage is designed to elicit your judgments concerning the weight that should be assigned to each entry and exercise that is a part of the EA/AYA/Art assessment when overall performance scores are computed for candidates seeking National Board Certification in this field. As a member of the EA/AYA/Art Assessment Development Team, you are an expert in EA/AYA/Art teaching and you are intimately familiar with the entries and exercises that compose the assessment. You are therefore highly qualified to provide recommendations on the weights that should be assigned to entries and exercises.

The procedure you will follow is composed of a number of sequential steps. These steps are described below.

Step 1

In the first step, of the weighting procedure, you will be asked to think about the content standards that are assessed by each entry and exercise in the EA/AYA/Art assessment, as well as the nature of the evidence of teaching accomplishment that is elicited by each entry and exercise. Based on your knowledge and your judgment concerning these factors, please place each of the 12 entries and exercises into one of the three categories:

Category 1: The four entries and/or exercises that should *receive the LOWEST weights. Write the names (or mnemonics)* of these entries and/or exercises in the "Category 1" section of the table that is on the sheet headed **"Exercise Categorization."**

Category 3: The four entries and/or exercises that should *receive the HIGHEST weights. Write the names (or mnemonics)* of these entries and/or exercises in the "Category 3" section of the table that is on the sheet headed **"Exercise Categorization."**

Category 2: The remaining four entries and/or exercises. (These will be entries or exercises that you judge to be neither among the four that should receive the highest weights nor among the four that should receive the lowest weights; they should, therefore, receive weights that are in the middle of your allocation among all entries and/or exercises that compose the EA/AYA/Art assessment. Write the names (or mnemonics) of these entries and/or exercises in the "Category 2" section of the table that is on the sheet headed **"Exercise Categorization."**

Step 2

In the second step of the weighting procedure, you will be asked to rank order the entries and/or exercises that you have placed within each of the three categories, in terms of the weight each should receive. Begin with the entries and/or exercises in Category 1: The four entries and/or exercises that you believe should receive the lowest weights.

1. Assign a *Rank of 1* to the entry or exercise that, in your judgment, should receive the *lowest weight* among the four entries or exercises in Category 1. Write the rank of this entry or exercise (1) beside its name in the "Rank" column on the sheet headed **"Exercise Categorization."**
2. Assign a *Rank of 2* to the entry or exercise that, in your judgment, should receive the *second-lowest weight* among the four entries or exercises in

Category 1. Write the rank of this entry or exercise (2) beside its name in the "Rank" column on the sheet headed **"Exercise Categorization."**

3. Assign a *Rank of 3* to the entry or exercise that, in your judgment, should receive the *third-lowest weight* among the four entries or exercises in Category 1. Write the rank of this entry or exercise (3) beside its name in the "Rank" column on the sheet headed **"Exercise Categorization."**
4. Assign a *Rank of 4* to the entry or exercise that, in your judgment, should receive the *highest weight* among the four entries or exercises in Category 1. Write the rank of this entry or exercise (4) beside its name in the "Rank" column on the sheet headed **"Exercise Categorization."**

Next move to the entries and exercises in Category 2 (Middle Weights):

5. Assign a *Rank of 5* to the entry or exercise that, in your judgment, should receive the *lowest weight* among the four entries or exercises in Category 2. Write the rank of this entry or exercise (5) beside its name in the "Rank" column on the sheet headed **"Exercise Categorization."**
6. Assign a *Rank of 6* to the entry or exercise that, in your judgment, should receive the *second-lowest weight* among the four entries or exercises in Category 2. Write the rank of this entry or exercise (6) beside its name in the "Rank" column on the sheet headed **"Exercise Categorization."**
7. Assign a *Rank of 7* to the entry or exercise that, in your judgment, should receive the *third-lowest weight* among the four entries or exercises in Category 2. Write the rank of this entry or exercise (7) beside its name in the "Rank" column on the sheet headed **"Exercise Categorization."**
8. Assign a *Rank of 8* to the entry or exercise that, in your judgment, should receive the *highest weight* among the four entries or exercises in Category 2. Write the rank of this entry or exercise (8) beside its name in the "Rank" column on the sheet headed **"Exercise Categorization."**

Finally, move to the entries and exercises in Category 3 (Highest Weights):

9. Assign a *Rank of 9* to the entry or exercise that, in your judgment, should receive the *lowest weight* among the four entries or exercises in Category 3. Write the rank of this entry or exercise (9) beside its name in the "Rank" column on the sheet headed **"Exercise Categorization."**
10. Assign a *Rank of 10* to the entry or exercise that, in your judgment, should receive the *second-lowest weight* among the four entries or exercises in Category 3. Write the rank of this entry or exercise (10) beside its name in the "Rank" column on the sheet headed **"Exercise Categorization."**

11. Assign a *Rank of 11* to the entry or exercise that, in your judgment, should receive the *third-lowest weight* among the four entries or exercises in Category 3. Write the rank of this entry or exercise (11) beside its name in the "Rank" column on the sheet headed **"Exercise Categorization."**

12. Finally, assign a *Rank of 12* to the entry or exercise that, in your judgment, should receive the *highest weight* among the four entries or exercises in Category 3. Write the rank of this entry or exercise (12) beside its name in the "Rank" column on the sheet headed **"Exercise Categorization."**

At this point, you should have assigned a rank to each of the 12 entries and exercises that compose the EA/AYA/Art assessment, with the entry or exercise you judge to be the *least important* among the 12 assigned *Rank 1*, and the entry or exercise you judge to be the *most important* assigned *Rank 12*.

Step 3

In the third step of the weighting procedure, you will assign an importance weight to each of the 12 entries and exercises that compose the EA/AYA/Art assessment. Do so by following the procedure described below:

1. Write the names or mnemonics of all 12 entries or exercises in the column headed "Entry or Exercise Name (Mnemonic)" on the sheet headed **"Initial Entry and Exercise Weights"** *in rank order*, with the name of the entry or exercise assigned Rank 1 on the first line, the name of the entry or exercise assigned Rank 2 on the second line, and so on. Write the Rank of each exercise beside its name, in the column headed "Rank."

2. Assign a weight of 100 points to the entry or exercise you have ranked 1; that is, the entry or exercise you judge to be *least important* among the 12 that compose the EA/AYA/Art assessment. Write the value 100 beside the name of this entry or exercise in the column headed "First Weight" on the sheet headed **"Initial Entry and Exercise Weights."**

3. Consider the entry or exercise that you have ranked 2; that is, the entry or exercise you judge to be *second-least important* among the 12 that compose the EA/AYA/Art assessment. Ask yourself: "How much more important is this entry or exercise than the one I judged to be least important; that is, the entry or exercise that I ranked 1?" The weight you assign this entry or exercise will depend on your answer to this question. If, for example, you considered this entry or exercise to be 10 percent more important than the

least-important entry or exercise, you would assign it a weight of 110. If you considered it to be 50 percent more important, you would assign it a weight of 150. If you considered it to be twice as important, you would assign it a weight of 200. Write the weight you want to assign beside the name of this entry or exercise in the column headed "First Weight" on the sheet headed **"Initial Entry and Exercise Weights."**

4. Consider the entry or exercise that you have ranked 3; that is, the entry or exercise you judge to be *third-least important* among the 12 that compose the EA/AYA/Art assessment. Ask yourself: "How much more important is this entry or exercise than the one I judged to be least important; that is, the entry or exercise that I ranked 1?" The weight you assign this entry or exercise will depend on your answer to this question. If, for example, you considered this entry or exercise to be 20 percent more important than the least-important entry or exercise, you would assign it a weight of 120. If you considered it to be 50 percent more important, you would assign it a weight of 150. If you considered it to be twice as important, you would assign it a weight of 200. Write the weight you want to assign beside the name of this entry or exercise in the column headed "First Weight" on the sheet headed **"Initial Entry and Exercise Weights."** Note that the weight you assign to this entry or exercise should not be smaller than the weight you assigned to the entry or exercise you ranked 2.

5. Consider the entry or exercise that you have ranked 4; that is, the entry or exercise you judge to be *fourth-least important* among the 12 that compose the EA/AYA/Art assessment. Ask yourself: "How much more important is this entry or exercise than the one I judged to be least important; that is, the entry or exercise that I ranked 1?" The weight you assign this entry or exercise will depend on your answer to this question. If, for example, you considered this entry or exercise to be 30 percent more important than the least-important entry or exercise, you would assign it a weight of 130. If you considered it to be 60 percent more important, you would assign it a weight of 160. If you considered it to be three times as important, you would assign it a weight of 300. Write the weight you want to assign beside the name of this entry or exercise in the column headed "First Weight" on the sheet headed **"Initial Entry and Exercise Weights."** Note that the weight you assign to this entry or exercise should not be smaller than the weight you assigned to the entry or exercise you ranked 3.

Continue this process with the entries or exercises that you ranked 5 through 12. For each of these entries or exercises, ask yourself: "How much more important is this entry or exercise than the one I judged to be least important that is, the entry or exercise that I ranked 1?" Write down the resulting weight you assign beside the name of each of these entries or exercises in the column headed "First Weight" on the sheet headed **"Initial Entry and Exercise Weights."** Note that there is no limit to the values of the weights you can assign to the entries and exercises that compose the EA/AYA/Art assessment. The values you choose are strictly a matter of your judgment concerning how much more important each entry or exercise is, compared to the one you judged to be least important.

Step 4

In the fourth step of the weighting procedure, you will again assign importance weights. This time you will be working with the entries or exercises that you ranked 2 through 12. The reference point for your weighting will be the entry or exercise that you judged to be second-least important. You will assign this entry or exercise a weight of 100, and then consider the importance of each of the entries or exercises you assigned ranks of 3 or higher, compared to the entry or exercise you judged to be second-least important. It is important that you *do not* consider the weights that you assigned in the "First Weight" column of the **"Initial Entry and Exercise Weights"** sheet when you complete this step. To help you avoid this temptation, you have been given a bookmark. Please use the bookmark to cover the "First Weight" column when you complete this step. Please follow the procedure described below:

1. Assign a weight of 100 points to the entry or exercise you have ranked 2; that is, the entry or exercise you judged to be *second-least important* among the 12 that compose the EA/AYA/Art assessment. Write the value 100 beside the name of this entry or exercise in the column headed "Second Weight" on the sheet headed **"Initial Entry and Exercise Weights."**

2. Consider the entry or exercise that you have ranked 3; that is, the entry or exercise you judged to be *third-least important* among the 12 that compose the EA/AYA/Art assessment. Ask yourself: "How much more important is this entry or exercise than the one I judged to be second-least important; that is, the entry or exercise that I ranked 2?" The weight you assign this entry or exercise will depend on your answer to this question. If, for example, you considered this entry or exercise to be 10 percent more important than the second-least important entry or exercise, you

would assign it a weight of 110. If you considered it to be 50 percent more important, you would assign it a weight of 150. If you considered it to be twice as important, you would assign it a weight of 200. Write the weight you want to assign beside the name of this entry or exercise in the column headed "Second Weight" on the sheet headed **"Initial Entry and Exercise Weights."**

3. Consider the entry or exercise that you have ranked 4; that is, the entry or exercise you judged to be *fourth-least important* among the 12 that compose the EA/AYA/Art assessment. Ask yourself: "How much more important is this entry or exercise than the one I judged to be second-least important; that is, the entry or exercise that I ranked 2?" The weight you assign this entry or exercise will depend on your answer to this question. If, for example, you considered this entry or exercise to be 20 percent more important than the second-least-important entry or exercise, you would assign it a weight of 120. If you considered it to be 50 percent more important, you would assign it a weight of 150. If you considered it to be twice as important, you would assign it a weight of 200. Write the weight you want to assign beside the name of this entry or exercise in the column headed "Second Weight" on the sheet headed **"Initial Entry and Exercise Weights."** Note that the weight you assign to this entry or exercise should not be smaller than the weight you assigned to the entry or exercise you ranked 3.

4. Consider the entry or exercise that you have ranked 5; that is, the entry or exercise you judged to be *fifth-least important* among the 12 that compose the EA/AYA/Art assessment. Ask yourself: "How much more important is this entry or exercise than the one I judged to be second-least important; that is, the entry or exercise that I ranked 2?" The weight you assign this entry or exercise will depend on your answer to this question. If, for example, you considered this entry or exercise to be 30 percent more important than the second-least important entry or exercise, you would assign it a weight of 130. If you considered it to be 60 percent more important, you would assign it a weight of 160. If you considered it to be three times as important, you would assign it a weight of 300. Write the weight you want to assign beside the name of this entry or exercise in the column headed "Second Weight" on the sheet headed **"Initial Entry and Exercise Weights."** Note that the weight you assign to this entry or exercise should not be smaller than the weight you assigned to the entry or exercise you ranked 4.

5. – 11. Continue the process with the entries or exercises that you ranked 6 through 12. For each of these entries or exercises, ask yourself: "How

much more important is this entry or exercise than the one that I judged to be second-least important; that is, the entry or exercise that I ranked 2?" Write down the resulting weight you assign beside the name of each of these entries or exercises in the column headed "Second Weight" on the sheet headed **"Initial Entry and Exercise Weights."** Note that there is no limit to the values of the weights you can assign to the entries and exercises that compose the EA/AYA/Art assessment. The values you choose are strictly a matter of your judgment concerning how much more important each entry or exercise is, compared to the one you judged to be second-least important.

This is the last major step of the weighting process. It is identical to Steps 3 and 4, except that in this step, the entry or exercise that you ranked 3 will become the reference point for weighting each of the entries and exercises that you assigned higher ranks. You will first assign the entry or exercise that you ranked 3 a weight of 100. Then you will begin with the entry or exercise that you ranked 4 and assign it a weight, depending on your judgment of its importance, compared to the entry or exercise that you ranked 3. You will continue assigning relative weights to the entries and exercises that you ranked 5 through 12, again, considering their importance, compared to the entry or exercise that you assigned a rank of 3. It is important that you *do not* consider the weights that you assigned in the "First Weight" column or the "Second Weight" column of the **"Initial Entry and Exercise Weights"** sheet when you complete this step. To help you avoid this temptation, please use your bookmark to cover the "First Weight and "Second Weight" columns when you complete this step.

1. Assign a weight of 100 points to the entry or exercise you have ranked 3; that is, the entry or exercise you judged to be *third-least important* among the 12 that compose the EA/AYA/Art assessment. Write the value 100 beside the name of this entry or exercise in the column headed "Third Weight" on the sheet headed **"Initial Entry and Exercise Weights."**
2. Consider the entry or exercise that you have ranked 4; that is, the entry or exercise you judged to be *fourth-least important* among the 12 that compose the EA/AYA/Art assessment. Ask yourself: "How much more important is this entry or exercise than the one I judged to be third-least important; that is, the entry or exercise that I ranked 3?" The weight you assign this entry or exercise will depend on your answer to this question. If, for example, you considered this entry or exercise to be 10 percent more important than the third-least important entry or exercise, you would assign it a weight of 110. If you considered it to be 50 percent more

important, you would assign it a weight of 150. If you considered it to be twice as important, you would assign it a weight of 200. Write the weight you want to assign beside the name of this entry or exercise in the column headed "Third Weight" on the sheet headed **"Initial Entry and Exercise Weights."**

3. Consider the entry or exercise that you have ranked 5; that is, the entry or exercise you judged to be *fifth-least important* among the 12 that compose the EA/AYA/Art assessment. Ask yourself: "How much more important is this entry' or exercise than the one I judged to be third-least important; that is, the entry or exercise that I ranked 3?" The weight you assign this entry or exercise will depend on your answer to this question. If, for example, you considered this entry or exercise to be 20 percent more important than the third-least important entry or exercise, you would assign it a weight of 120. If you considered it to be 50 percent more important, you would assign it a weight of 150. If you considered it to be twice as important, you would assign it a weight of 200. Write the weight you want to assign beside the name of this entry or exercise in the column headed "Third Weight" on the sheet headed **"Initial Entry and Exercise Weights."** Note that the weight you assign to this entry or exercise should not be smaller than the weight you assigned to the entry or exercise you ranked 4.

Continue the process with the entries or exercises that you ranked 6 through 12. For each of these entries or exercises, ask yourself: "How much more important is this entry or exercise than the one I judged to be third-least important; that is, the entry or exercise that I ranked 3?" Write down the resulting weight you assign beside the name of each of these entries or exercises in the column headed "Third Weight" on the sheet headed "**Initial Entry and Exercise Weights.**" Note that there is no limit to the values of the weights you can assign to the entries and exercises that compose the EA/AYA/Art assessment. The values you choose are strictly a matter of your judgment concerning how much more important each entry or exercise is, compared to the one you judged to be third-least important.

Step 5

At this point, you will have completed all but three entries in the columns headed "First Weight," "Second Weight," and "Third Weight" on the sheet headed "**Initial Entry and Exercise Weights**." In this step, you will assign weights in the three remaining spaces.

1. The first empty cell of the table on the sheet headed "**Initial Entry and Exercise Weights**" is in the row for the entry or exercise you assigned Rank 1, in the column headed "Second Weight." To assign a weight to this entry or exercise, ask yourself the following question: "How much less important is the entry or exercise that I assigned Rank 1 than the entry or exercise that I assigned Rank 2?" If the answer to this question were "Half as important," you would assign a weight of 50 in the "Second Weight" column to the entry or exercise you assigned a Rank of 1. If the answer were "Three-fourths as important," you would assign a weight of 75. If the answer were "80 percent as important," you would assign a weight of 80. And if the answer were "Just as important," you would assign the entry or exercise a weight of 100. You can assign any weight you desire, depending on your judgment of how much less important is the entry or exercise you assigned Rank 1, than the entry or exercise you assigned Rank 2. However, the weight you assign to the entry or exercise you assigned Rank 1 should not be larger than 100.

2. There are two empty cells in the column headed "Third Weight." The first is in the row for the entry or exercise you assigned Rank 1. To assign a weight to this entry or exercise, ask yourself the following question: "How much *less important* than the entry or exercise that I assigned Rank 3 is the entry or exercise that I assigned Rank 1?" Again, if the answer to this question were "a fourth as important," you would assign a weight of 25 in the "Third Weight" column to the entry or exercise you assigned a Rank of 1. If the answer were "half as important," you would assign a weight of 50. If the answer were "60 percent as important," you would assign a weight of 60. You can assign any weight you desire, depending on your judgment of how much less important the entry or exercise you assigned Rank 1 is, compared to the entry or exercise you assigned Rank 3. However, the weight you assign to the entry or exercise you assigned Rank 1 should not be larger than the weight you will assign to the entry or exercise you assigned Rank 2; which is the next judgment you will make.

3. Now fill in the last empty cell of the table on the sheet headed "**Initial Entry and Exercise Weights.**" This cell is in the column headed "Third Weight," and in the row for the entry or exercise you assigned Rank 2. To assign a "Third Weight" to this entry or exercise, you must ask yourself, "How much *less important* is the entry or exercise that I assigned Rank 2 than the entry or exercise that I assigned Rank 3?" Your answer to this question can lead to a weight that is anywhere between the "Third Weight" you assigned to the entry or exercise you assigned Rank 1 and the "Third Weight" of 100 that you assigned to the entry or

exercise you assigned a Rank of 3. Again, if you judged the Rank 2 entry or exercise to be only 60 percent as important as the Rank 3 entry or exercise, you would assign a weight of 60; three-fourths as important would lead to a weight of 75; equally important would lead to a weight of 100. The weight you assign depends only on your professional judgment.

Step 6

Please check the sheets headed "**Exercise Categorization**" and "**Initial Entry and Exercise Weights**" carefully. *Be certain that*:

1. You have printed your name and your Panelist Number on each sheet.
2. You have printed the name of a different entry or exercise in each blank row of the table on the "**Exercise Categorization**" sheet, and that you have assigned a different rank (from 1 to 12, inclusive) to each entry or exercise.
3. You have listed the entries and exercises, *in rank order*, beginning with the entry or exercise you have ranked 1, and ending with the entry or exercise you have ranked 12, on the sheet headed "**Initial Entry and Exercise Weights**."
4. You have assigned a weight to all 12 entries and exercises, in each of the three columns headed "First Weight," "Second Weight," and "Third Weight."
5. When you have finished checking your work, please bring your completed "**Exercise Categorization**" and "**Initial Entry and Exercise Weights**" sheets to the proctor at the front of the room. You are free to take a break until our next session begins.

APPENDIX J: RELIABILITY ESTIMATION ATTRIBUTABLE TO ASSESSORS

Let x_{ik} represent the rating assigned on the kth scoring of an examinee's response to the ith exercise.

Let w_i represent the scoring weight for the ith exercise.

Then the examinee's score is:

$$x = \sum_i w_i(x_{i1} + x_{i2})$$

First, compute the variances and covariances of all the variables x_{ik}. One way to do this would be to define a vector:

$(x_{11}, x_{12}, x_{21}, x_{22}, x_{31}, \ldots)$

and compute the variance-covariance matrix of this vector. Then let:

$$\begin{aligned} \text{ESTVAR}(i) &= \text{Var}(x_{i1} + x_{i2}) \\ &= \text{Var}(x_{i1}) + \text{Var}(x_{i2}) + 2\text{Cov}(x_{i1}, x_{i2}). \end{aligned}$$

ESTVAR(i) is simply the variance of scores (sum of two ratings) on exercise i. Let:

$$\text{ESTCOV}(ii) = 4\text{Cov}(x_{i1}, x_{i2}).$$

ESTCOV(ii) is the estimated covariance of the score (sum of the two ratings) on exercise i with the score on exercise i that would result if the assessment were scored by a different group of assessors. And let:

$$\begin{aligned} \text{ESTCOV}(ij) &= \text{Cov}(x_{i1} + x_{i2}, x_{j1}, x_{j2}) \\ &= \text{Cov}(x_{i1}, x_{j1}) + \text{Cov}(x_{i1}, x_{j2}) + \text{Cov}(x_{i2}, x_{j1}) \\ &\quad + \text{Cov}(x_{i2}, x_{j2}). \end{aligned}$$

ESTCOV(ij) is the covariance of scores (sum of two ratings) on exercises i and j. Since different exercises are scored by different assessors, it is also the estimated covariance of the score on exercise i with the score on exercise j that would result if the assessment were scored by a different group of assessors. Now let:

$$\text{ESTCOV}(XX) = \sum_i w_i^2 \text{ESTCOV}(ii) + \sum_i \sum_j w_i w_j \text{ESTCOV}(ij);$$

$$\text{ESTVAR}(X) = \sum_i w_i^2 \text{ESTVAR}(i) + \sum_i \sum_j w_i w_j \text{ESTCOV}(ij).$$

Finally, estimate the scoring reliability of the total scores by

$$\text{ESTREL}(X) = \frac{\text{ESTCOV}(XX)}{\text{ESTVAR}(X)}$$

APPENDIX K: RELIABILITY ESTIMATION ATTRIBUTABLE TO EXERCISES

In order to calculate the alternate forms reliability, a standard error estimate is required. An estimate of the standard error for each exercise is computed using a jackknife-regression: the scores from the dependent measure are regressed on each of the nine independent measures. This regression approach estimates how well the scores of the other nine exercises predict performance on a tenth exercise. The standard error of prediction is then used as an estimate of the standard error of measurement for the exercise that was held as the dependent measure. The error variance is the square of the standard error. The process is repeated for each of the other nine exercises in turn. Reliability for each exercise, R_i, is then computed from the error variance of each exercise, using the following formula, where σ is the variance of candidates' observed total scores for exercise i:

$$R_i = 1 - \frac{(SE_i)^2}{\sigma_i}$$

Reliability of a section, R_s, within a certificate (that is, classroom-based portfolio entries, documented accomplishment portfolio entries, or assessment center exercises) is calculated by applying weights to the exercise scores within that section. For example, to obtain a reliability estimate for the classroom-based portfolio entries, each exercise is in turn regressed against the other three exercises in the portfolio section to obtain an estimate of the standard error of measurement. To obtain an estimate of the error variance of candidate scores for the section, the square of the exercise weight multiplied by the error variance for each exercise in the section is summed across the section exercises. The square root of this value provides an estimate of the standard error of measurement for the section. With σ_s as the variance of candidates' observed total weighted-scores for the section, reliability is then calculated as:

$$R_s = 1 - \frac{\sum_i w_i^2 \times SE_i^2}{\sigma_s}.$$

To obtain a reliability estimate for the entire assessment, R_a, the exercise weights are applied to the standard error of each exercise, to obtain the total error variance for the whole certificate. With σ_a as the variance of candidates' total weighted-scores over the entire assessment, reliability is then calculated as:

$$R_a = 1 - \frac{\sum_i w_s^2 \times SE_i^2}{\sigma_a}.$$

APPENDIX L: ESTIMATION OF DECISION CONSISTENCY AND ACCURACY

First, estimate the scoring reliability coefficient on the basis of the covariances, with each covariance computed from all the data that is available (i.e., pair-wise present). Call it r_{xx}.

Then find the failure rate on the full test, using the scores that are actually used to make pass/fail decisions (i.e., the average of the first and second scores). Call it p_f.

Find $z_f = \Phi^{-1}(p_f)$, where Φ is the unit normal cdf.

In a bivariate normal distribution of X_1 and X_2 with $\mu_1 = \mu_2 = 0$, $\sigma_1 = \sqrt{r_{xx}}$, $\sigma_2 = 1$, and $\rho = \sqrt{r_{xx}}$, find the probabilities:

$$\pi_{11} = \text{Prob}\{X_1 < z_f, \ X_2 < z_f\};$$
$$\pi_{12} = \text{Prob}\{X_1 < z_f, \ X_2 \geq z_f\};$$
$$\pi_{21} = \text{Prob}\{X_1 \geq z_f, \ X_2 < z_f\};$$
$$\pi_{22} = \text{Prob}\{X_1 \geq z_f, \ X_2 \geq z_f\};$$

Print the decision accuracy table:

	Fail	Pass
True Fail	π_{11}	π_{12}
True Pass	π_{21}	π_{22}

599

APPENDIX M: MC/G STANDARDS OVERVIEW [☆]

MIDDLE CHILDHOOD
GENERALIST STANDARDS OVERVIEW 1999

National Board: Middle Childhood Generalist Standards

The requirements for certification as a Middle Childhood/Generalist by the National Board for Professional Teaching Standards are organized into the following eleven standards. The standards have been ordered as they have to facilitate understanding, not to assign priorities. They are each important facets of the art and science of teaching, which often occur concurrently given the seamless quality of highly accomplished practice.

I. Knowledge of Students
  Accomplished teachers draw on their knowledge of child development and their relationships with students to understand their students' abilities, interests, aspirations and values.

II. Knowledge of Content and Curriculum
  Accomplished teachers draw on their knowledge of subject matter and curriculum to make sound decisions about what is important for students to learn within and across the subject areas that comprise the middle childhood curriculum.

III. Learning Environment
  Accomplished teachers establish a caring inclusive, stimulating and safe school community where students can take intellect risks, practice democracy, and work collaboratively and independently.

IV. Respect for Diversity
  Accomplished teachers help students learn to respect individual and group differences.

V. Instructional Resources

Accomplished teachers create, assess, select and adapt a rich and varied collection of materials and draw on other resources such as staff, community members and students to support learning.

VI. Meaningful Applications of Knowledge

Accomplished teachers engage students in learning within and across the disciplines, and help students understand how the subjects they study can be used to explore important issues in their lives and the world around them.

VII. Multiple Paths to Knowledge

Accomplished teachers provide students with multiple paths needed to learn the central concepts in each school subject, explore important themes and topics that cut across subject areas, and build knowledge and understanding.

VIII. Assessment

Accomplished teachers understand the strengths and weaknesses of different assessment methods, base their instruction on ongoing assessment, and encourage students to monitor their own learning.

IX. Family Involvement

Accomplished teachers work to create positive relationships with families as they participate in the education of their children.

X. Reflection

Accomplished teachers regularly analyze and strengthen the effectiveness and quality of their practice.

XI. Contributions to the Profession

Accomplished teachers work with colleagues to improve schools and to advance knowledge and practice in their field.

Source: From NBPTS (1996, p. 13–14).

ABOUT THE AUTHORS

VOLUME EDITORS

Lawrence Ingvarson is a principal research fellow at the Australian Council for Educational Research. Prior to taking up his present part-time position, he was the research director of the Teaching and Leadership Program at ACER. He began his career as a science and mathematics teacher, teaching in West Australia, Scotland, and England before undertaking further studies at the University of London. He has held academic positions at the University of Stirling in Scotland and Monash University in Melbourne.

John Hattie is a professor in the faculty of education at The University of Auckland, New Zealand, and the director of project asTTle (Assessment Tools for Teaching and Learning). His areas of research include measurement models and their application to educational problems, meta-analysis, and models of teaching and learning. Over the past six years, he has headed a team introducing a model of assessment for teachers in schools in New Zealand, and thus providing schools with evidence-based information about teaching and learning. When at the University of North Carolina in Greensboro, he worked with Dick Jaeger and Lloyd Bond in the NBPTS Technical Analysis Group to consider issues of the reliability and validity of the NBPTS assessments. He subsequently also undertook investigations to attempt to distinguish the qualities of National Board-Certified Teachers from their non-certified colleagues. He holds a Ph.D. in measurement from the University of Toronto.

CHAPTER AUTHORS

Wanda K. Baker is a senior research analyst in the Office of University Evaluation at Arizona State University. She specializes in institutional effectiveness, assessment, and accreditation in higher education. She has served as the director of assessment for Rogers State University, and the Frank Lloyd Wright School of Architecture. As the project manager at the Center for Educational Research and Evaluation at the University of North

Carolina, Greensboro, she served on a research team that examined effective teaching practices. This work included numerous studies for the National Board for Professional Teaching Standards. She has an M.Ed. from the University of North Carolina, Greensboro.

Lloyd Bond works in the area of assessment with the Carnegie Foundation. Prior to that he held professorships in the Department of Educational Research Methodology at the University of North Carolina, Greensboro, and in the Psychology Department at the University of Pittsburgh. A measurement and assessment specialist known for his research on test bias, cognitive processes underlying test performance, the assessment of teaching performance, and, most recently, assessment in higher education, he has been an associate editor and member of the editorial boards of the leading journals in educational and psychological measurement, and consults with school districts, state departments of education, testing organizations, research and development centers, and other organizations. A Fellow of the American Psychological Association, he served on both the 1985 and 1999 national education research committees to revise the standards for educational and psychological testing. From 1997 to 2002, he was senior advisor to the National Board for Professional Teaching Standards. He holds a Ph.D. in psychology from The Johns Hopkins University.

Hilda Borko is a professor of education at Stanford University. Her research explores teacher cognition and the process of learning to teach, with an emphasis on changes in novice and experienced teachers' knowledge and beliefs about teaching, learning, and subject matter, and their classroom practices as they participate in reform-based teacher education and professional development programs. Her teaching interests are in the related areas of classroom processes, teaching for understanding, and teacher learning. Her contribution to the development of the NBPTS assessments centered on designing a model of feedback to maximize candidate learning was completed while on the faculty at the University of Colorado, Boulder. Her Ph.D. in educational psychology is from the University of California, Los Angeles.

Kristin Hershbell has been the associate dean of Grants and Resource Development at City College of San Francisco since 2002, where she oversees proposal development, and grants administration college wide. Prior to working at CCSF, She was a Senior Research Associate at WestEd, where she coordinated the team development of the Adolescence and Young Adulthood/Science Assessment on behalf of the National Board for Professional Teaching Standards. She also served as an evaluator for science and math education projects funded by NSF, NASA, and the U.S. Department of Education and co-developed a series of NSF-sponsored biotechnology case studies for training community college students. She has an M.A. in public affairs and policy analysis with an emphasis in science education from the University of Wisconsin-Madison.

Janet Clinton is a senior lecturer in evaluation in the School of Population Health at The University of Auckland, New Zealand. She has extensive national and international experience as an evaluator, psychologist, and educator. Janet has worked in Australia, New Zealand, and the USA as a program evaluator and researcher and has collaborated both nationally and internationally on large-scale research projects. She has also directed projects such as Smart Start and the Paideia Project in North Carolina, USA, and the Flaxmere Project in New Zealand. When in North Carolina, Greensboro, she collaborated with colleagues at the University of North Carolina in a number of studies, in particular looking to identify accomplished teachers for the NBPTS. Her Ph.D. is from the University of Western Australia.

Kirsten R. Daehler is a senior research associate in the Science and Mathematics Program at WestEd, where her work focuses on K-12 science education reform. She is the co-principal investigator of the Understanding Science Initiative, a practice-based professional development project. She has extensive experience working in K-12 science education and understands related issues from multiple perspectives. She began her work in education as a high school chemistry and physics teacher and department chair. More recently, she provides technical assistance to states, districts, schools, and teachers in the areas of assessment, professional development and program evaluation. She served as the lead developer and content expert with the National Board for Professional Teaching Standards project. Kirsten holds an M.A. in secondary education from San Francisco State University.

Linda Darling-Hammond is Charles E. Ducommun Professor of education at Stanford University School of Education. She served as an executive director of the National Commission on Teaching and America's Future which produced the 1996 widely cited blueprint for reform: *What Matters Most: Teaching for America's Future*. She has been active in the development of standards for teaching, having served as a two-term member of the National Board for Professional Teaching Standards, and as chair of the Interstate New Teacher Assessment and Support Consortium (INTASC) committee that drafted model standards for licensing beginning teachers. Her Ed.D. in urban education is from Temple University.

Alan Davis is an associate professor of research and evaluation methodology in the School of Education and Human Development at the University of Colorado Denver. He conducts research on formative assessment and on the social dynamics of teaching and learning in secondary schools. His Ph.D. in research and evaluation methodology is from the University of Colorado at Boulder.

Drew Gitomer is an ETS Distinguished Researcher. His research interests include policy and evaluation issues related to teacher education, licensure, induction, and professional development. His studies have focused on enhancing the validity base for teacher licensure assessments (*Praxis*™) and advanced certification of teacher assessments (National Board for Professional Teaching Standards). He was senior vice president for research and development at ETS from 1999 to 2004, and is co-editor of *Educational Evaluation and Policy Analysis*. His research has also focused on the design of assessments, particularly those that support improvement of instruction. He is currently co-directing the Cognitively Based Assessments for Learning Project (CBAL), an effort designed to transform current K-12 assessment practices. From 1991 to 1995, Gitomer was the project co-director for the Science Education through Portfolio Instruction and Assessment (SEPIA), which was funded by the National Science Foundation and the University of Pittsburgh. He was the project co-director of Arts PROPEL, a portfolio assessment effort involving middle and high school teachers and students in music, visual arts, and writing. In addition, he led an effort to develop an interactive, video-based intelligent tutoring system to help users develop skills in technical troubleshooting of aircraft hydraulic systems. He earned a Ph.D. in cognitive psychology from the University of Pittsburgh.

Richard M. Jaeger[†] (1938–2000) died on 22 October 2000. The chapter he wrote for this book was written during the final year of his life. Dick was a prolific and immensely significant contributor to the fields of educational measurement, statistics, research design, and policy research. Arguably, his biggest impact was in the field of educational standard-setting. He contributed broad philosophical ideas about the process of standard-setting, introduced many new methods, and carried on a research program over 25 years that touched on every aspect of the standard-setting process (Hambleton, Plake, & Engelhard, 2001). From 1991 to 1995, he was the Co-Director of the Technical Analysis Group, and worked for the National Board for Professional Teaching Standards, carrying out research on several new standard-setting methods for use with performance assessments. From 1996 until his death in October 2000, his research shifted to standard-setting on state and national assessments. Again, he developed new methods and addressed their validity (Hambleton et al., 2001). His contributions to education, though, were not only academic – although his writing and editing skills were legendary. Many also remember him for his kindness, hospitality, and generosity. He was a great believer in mentoring others, a wonderful colleague to work with, and a fantastic teacher. Even now, a number of years after his death, he is remembered fondly by many, and he is ever present in the long-lasting impact of his work.

Susan Moore Johnson studies and teaches about teacher policy, organizational change, and administrative practice at Harvard University. A former high-school teacher and administrator, she has a continuing research interest in the work of teachers and the reform of schools. She has studied the leadership of superintendents, the effects of collective bargaining on schools, the use of incentive pay plans for teachers, and the school as a context for adult work. Her involvement with the NBPTS focused on how professional certification could reshape teaching as a career. Currently, she and a group of advanced doctoral students at Harvard are engaged in a multiyear research study, The Project on the Next Generation of Teachers, which examines how best to recruit, support, and retain a strong teaching force. The project, which is funded by several foundations includes studies of hiring practices, alternative certification programs, new teachers' attitudes toward careers, and new teachers' experiences with colleagues. Her Ed.D. is from Harvard University.

Jody McCarthy was education programs consultant in the Professional Development Unit of the California Department of Education, specializing in Science education. She worked with a team at WestEd in the development of the Science assessments.

Pamela A. Moss is a professor of education at the University of Michigan School of Education. Her research agenda focuses on validity theory in educational assessment, assessment as a social practice, and the assessment of teaching. Her approach to the study of assessment engages the critical potential of dialogue across research discourses – educational measurement, hermeneutics and critical theory, and sociocultural studies – sometimes to complement, sometimes to challenge established theory and practice in assessment. Her research has been funded by the Spencer Foundation, the Institute for Education Sciences, and the National Science Foundation. She was a member of the joint committee revising the 1999 AERA, APA, NCME Standards for Educational and Psychological Testing, of the National Research Council's Committee on Assessment and Teacher Quality, and chair of AERA's Task Force on Standards for Reporting on Empirical Social Science Research in AERA Publications. She has served as a member of the technical advisory committee for the NBPTS since 1997. She received her Ph.D. in educational measurement from the University of Pittsburgh.

Mari Pearlman was the senior vice president and general manager of the Higher Education Division at Educational Testing Service until May 2007. The Division's programs and services include College Board Programs (SAT, PSAT, AP); English Language Programs (TOEFL, TOEIC); Graduate and Professional Programs (GRE, GMAT); and Teacher Programs (formative and summative assessment and professional development for educators across the continuum of their careers). She began her career at ETS in 1981 as a test developer, and was the director of ETS's work with the National Board for Professional Teaching Standards from 1992 through 1998, when she became the vice president of ETS's Teaching and Learning Division, which included the NBPTS program. Her Ph.D. in English Literature is from Rutgers University.

Steven A. Schneider is the program director of mathematics, science, and technology at WestEd. He served as the project director overseeing the development of the National Board for Professional Teaching Standard's Adolescent and Young Adult Science Assessment. He has led numerous, large science education initiatives in the US including the $12.2 million NSF Center for Assessment and Evaluation of Student Learning (CAESL) and the National Assessment Governing Board's development of the 2009–2021 National Assessment of Educational Progress Science Framework and Test Specification (NAEP). He has over 30 years of science, mathematics, and technology education experience, including K-12 pre-service teacher education, professional development, and teaching biology, physics, and oceanography at the high school level. His Ph.D. is from Stanford University in the Design and Evaluation of Educational Programs with an emphasis in science, mathematics, and technology education.

Jerome Shaw is an assistant professor of education at the University of California, Santa Cruz, where his research addresses science teaching and learning for culturally and linguistically diverse students. His current work focuses on the assessment of science inquiry skills, teacher use of student assessment data to improve instruction, and equity issues in science assessment, especially with English learners. He teaches courses on the assessment of K-12 student learning and science instruction methods for pre-service elementary teachers. Prior to joining the UCSC faculty, he provided technical assistance to several K-12 science education reform initiatives across the US in the areas of curriculum, instruction, and assessment and his involvement in developing the Adolescence and Young Adulthood assessment for science teachers (AYA/S) for the National Board for Professional teaching Standards (NBPTS) is a case in point. He has over 10 years experience as a classroom teacher, both mainstream and bilingual (Spanish–English), in QJ;K-12 California public schools. His Ph.D., on Science Performance Assessment and Language Minority Students, is from Stanford University.

Tracy W. Smith is an associate professor in the Department of Curriculum and Instruction at Appalachian State University in Boone, North Carolina, where she also serves as assistant middle grades education program coordinator. She has participated in two major research studies examining the depth of student learning in the classrooms of teachers who have attempted and/or earned National Board Certification. She is a former middle and high school English language arts teacher. Her publications and research focus on middle-level teacher preparation, teacher expertise, depth of student learning, and responsive teaching practices for young adolescents. She earned her Ph.D. in curriculum and teaching from the University of North Carolina at Greensboro.

Guillermo Solano-Flores is an associate professor of bilingual education and English as a second language at the School of Education of the University of Colorado, Boulder. A psychometrician by formal training, he specializes in educational measurement, assessment development, and the linguistic and cultural issues that are relevant to both international test comparisons and the testing of linguistic minorities. His work focuses on the development of alternative multidisciplinary approaches that address linguistic and cultural diversity in the development of tests and instructional materials in science and mathematics. He has conducted research on test translation, test localization, test review, the development of science and mathematics assessments for elementary schools, the construction of tools for generating science and mathematics tasks, the design of software for computer-assisted scoring, and has worked on the development of assessments for the certification of arts and science teachers for the NBPTS. He has been principal investigator in several NSF-funded projects that have investigated the intersection of psychometrics and linguistics in the testing of linguistically diverse populations. He has provided advice to Latin American countries in their efforts to develop national assessment systems. His Ph.D., in education with a specialty in Methodology and Measurement, is from the University of California, Santa Barbara.

Gary Sykes is a professor in the Department of Teacher Education, Michigan State University, where his interests concentrate on education policy directed to teachers, teaching, and teacher education. He contributed several analyses that served to found and launch the National Board for Professional Teaching Standards. His Ph.D. from Stanford University is about excellence and equity in educational standard-setting.

Grace Taylor graduated with her doctorate in education from the University of Colorado at Boulder. The article in which she was a co-author was based on her Ph.D. dissertation research, entitled "Teacher Change and the National Board for Professional Teaching Standards: A Case Study of Eleven Colorado Teachers."

Sam Wineburg is the chair, dept. of curriculum and teacher education, school of education, and professor of history (by courtesy) at Stanford University. His book, *Historical Thinking and Other Unnatural Acts: Charting the Future of Teaching the Past* was the 2001 recipient of the Frederick W. Ness Award from the Association of American Colleges and Universities for the work that makes the "most important contribution to understanding and advancing the Liberal Arts." He was a member of the Technical Analysis Group of the National Board for five years, working on issues of assessment in history. His Ph.D. on psychological studies in education is from Stanford University.

Kenneth Wolf is the interim director of assessment for the University of Colorado Denver and an associate professor in the School of Education and Human Development. As a graduate student at Stanford University, he was a member of the Teacher Assessment Project, the research group that designed and pilot tested the initial assessment architecture that was later adopted by the National Board. He has worked on a variety of projects related to the National Board, including administering the initial field test of the assessment center in Colorado and securing state funding to support teachers for advanced certification. He has also published a number of articles on various features of the National Board assessment process. His Ph.D. is from Stanford University.

REFERENCES

Hambleton, R. K., Plake, B. S., & Engelhard, G., Jr. (2001). Richard M. Jaeger's contributions to the field of standard-setting. *The Newsletter of Division D, Measurement and Research Methodology, The American Educational Research Association, 11*(1), 5–6.

SET UP A CONTINUATION ORDER TODAY!

Did you know that you can set up a continuation order on all Elsevier-JAI series and have each new volume sent directly to you upon publication? For details on how to set up a **continuation order**, contact your nearest regional sales office listed below.

To view related series in Sociology,
please visit:

www.elsevier.com/sociology

30% Discount for Authors on All Books!

A 30% discount is available to Elsevier book and journal contributors on all books *(except multi-volume reference works)*.

To claim your discount, full payment is required with your order, which must be sent directly to the publisher at the nearest regional sales office above.